DIALECTIC AND DIALOGUE

SPEP Studies
in Historical Philosophy

General Editors John McCumber
               David Kolb

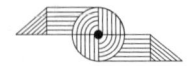

DIALECTIC AND DIALOGUE

Plato's Practice of Philosophical Inquiry

Francisco J. Gonzalez

Northwestern University Press
Evanston, Illinois

Northwestern University Press
Evanston, Illinois 60208-4210
Copyright © 1998 by Northwestern University Press.
Published 1998. All rights reserved.

Printed in the United States of America

ISBN 0-8101-1529-8 (cloth)
ISBN 0-8101-1530-1 (paper)

Library of Congress Cataloging-in-Publication Data

González, Francisco J.
  Dialectic and dialogue : Plato's practice of philosophical inquiry / Francisco J. González.
    p. cm.—(SPEP studies in historical philosophy)
  Includes bibliographical references and index.
  ISBN 0-8101-1529-8 (alk. paper).—ISBN 0-8101-1530-1 (pbk. : alk. paper)
  1. Plato. 2. Dialectic—History. I. Title. II. Series.
B398.D5G66 1998
184-dc21   98-27564
                                                         CIP

The paper used in this publication meets the minimum requirements of the American National Standard for Information Sciences—Permanence of Paper for Printed Library Materials, ANSI Z39.48-1984.

For Sabra

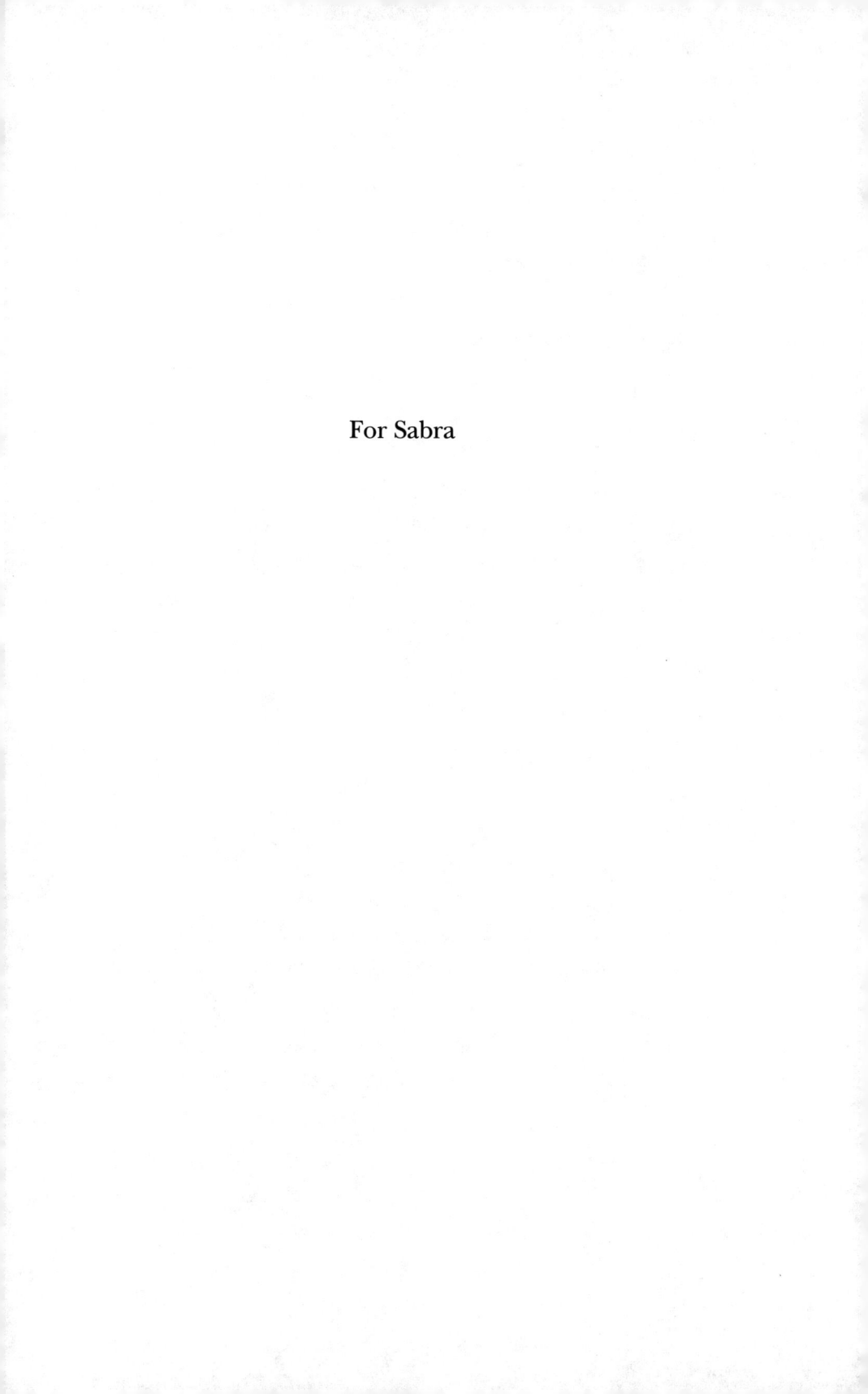

Contents

	Preface	ix
1.	Introduction: The Need for a Reexamination of Plato's Dialectic	1

Part I: Dialectic in Between Ordinary and Sophistic Discourse

2.	Dialectic at Work in the *Laches* and the *Charmides*	19
3.	The *Cratylus* on the Use of Words	62
4.	Dialectic and Eristic in the *Euthydemus*	94
5.	Philosophical Imitation	129

Part II: The Method of Hypothesis

6.	Failed Virtue and Failed Knowledge in the *Meno*	153
7.	A Second Sailing in the *Phaedo*	188
8.	Idealization and the Destruction of Hypotheses in the *Republic*	209
9.	Conclusion: Dialectic in the *Seventh Letter*	245
	Notes	275
	Works Cited	389
	Index	405

Preface

> I think that Homer said it all in the line, "Going in tandem, one perceives before the other." Human beings are simply more resourceful this way in action, speech and thought. If someone has a private perception, he immediately starts going around and looking until he finds somebody he can show it to and have it corroborated. (*Protagoras* 348c7–d5; trans. Lombardo and Bell)

The study of the Platonic dialogues should ideally be itself a dialogue, primarily with the dialogues themselves, but also with others who have seriously studied them. Although the present study is devoted mainly to a conversation with the texts, it is my hope that the reader will also benefit from the conversations with other scholars in the extensive notes. Given the number of unorthodox positions I defend, as well as the extremely controversial character of the texts I discuss, much of what I have to say about the work of others is critical. This should not, however, hide, but rather confirm, my debt to them: in many cases they have seen something before I have; in other cases, they have helped me corroborate, either positively or negatively, what I have seen for myself. It has also been my aim to make the dialogue as inclusive as possible, in reaction to what I sadly perceive to be a growing insularity in Platonic studies, especially among English-speaking scholars: extremely helpful and worthy work is ignored simply because it is not in the right language or school.

Then there is my debt to those who have read and commented on this manuscript in its many mutations during the past few years. Its first form was a dissertation written for the University of Toronto. The keen and critical eye of my supervisor, John Rist, saved me from many an error and exuberant exaggeration. He was the Hans Sachs to my Walter von Stolzing. Paul Gooch, my sympathetic advisor, gave me the benefit of his stimulating and enjoyable conversation, both in and out of class, and Drew Hyland, my external reader, kindly provided me with valuable and

PREFACE

encouraging written comments. My oral exam, in which the examiners included Brad Inwood and Thomas Pangle in addition to the above, was uncommonly helpful. Among readers of this book in its later incarnations, my greatest debt is to Walter Watson, who commented on both the general project and important details: specifically, he spotted and enabled me to correct some errors in the *Meno* chapter. Gerald A. Press read the manuscript, made some helpful comments, drew my attention to the work of Stefanini and, most important, provided moral support for the way of reading Plato pursued here. I have greatly profited not only from Rafael Ferber's published work (as the numerous references in the notes demonstrate) but also from extensive correspondence with him on the issue of nonpropositional knowledge. I have a very special debt to my friend and undergraduate mentor Michael Gelven: he first sparked in me a love for Plato's dialogues in certainly one of the best Plato seminars anywhere; our many conversations throughout the years have been the closest I have come to the ideal of philosophical *sunousia* described in the *Seventh Letter*. Needless to say, genuine dialogue is not the same as agreement, and therefore none of those acknowledged here should be seen as endorsing any of the positions I defend in what follows.

Last, but by no means least, I must thank my wife, Sabra Sanwal, to whom the book is dedicated. My debt to her is immeasurable and ranges from the tangible to the intangible: from her extraordinary feats of weight lifting in delivering to my advisor several corrected copies of the dissertation to her ability to cope with the infidelity of a husband who often spends more time with Plato than with her. Finally, I must express the hope that my daughter Shivani, born at the same time this book was accepted for publication, will one day understand why her father so often prefers staring at funny lights on a screen high up in the air to joining her in playing with more tangible objects on the floor.

F.J.G.
Saratoga Springs
July 1997

1

Introduction: The Need for a Reexamination of Plato's Dialectic

> [W]e find the seeds of all philosophical systems in Plato's thought, without it itself being one of these systems; it is the idea of philosophy, the crucible in which the different forms of philosophy are born, the unchanging sun in the middle of philosophy's planetary movements and formations.... Plato philosophizes where others indoctrinate, he lifts one's spirit to the pure essence of the Idea where others degrade and confine it to the letter of a system. This is why Platonism is the very spirit of philosophy or Philosophy Itself (F. Ast; trans. F.J.G.)

There are many specific questions which Plato's dialogues, to the great chagrin of interpreters, have so far refused to answer conclusively. The result is the cacophony that still characterizes much Platonic scholarship. Yet while specific issues within Plato's philosophy have been hotly debated, there has been much too little explicit debate and discussion concerning what is perhaps the greatest source of discord: Plato's conception of philosophy. What, in Plato's view, are we doing when we philosophize? Exactly what kind of knowledge are we seeking to acquire, and what are the means by which we can acquire it? Since the dialogues normally identify philosophy with "dialectic," these questions also concern the nature of dialectic. What kind of a process, what form of argumentation, is dialectic? And what exactly can this process achieve? What is the nature of the knowledge possessed by the dialectician?

Even if it does not explicitly raise these questions, every study of Plato presupposes some kind of answer to them. What happens, therefore, when little or no effort is made to arrive at *Plato's*[1] answer is that each scholar assumes his or her own conception of philosophy as the model for formulating and discussing specific questions in Plato's philosophy. We may have an example of such an assumption in the very attempt to compartmentalize Plato's thought by discussing dialectic under the heading of "methodology" or "logic," thus sharply distinguishing it from his "physics," "ethics," or "ontology." In this case Plato's thought is interpreted according to a model of philosophical knowledge not necessarily his own. Since the specific model assumed can be anything from modern natural science, mathematics, or formal logic to Hegelian dialectic, existentialism, or deconstructionism, the variance between the ways in which different scholars *approach* Plato's works is great indeed.

The present study seeks to get at the root of this variance by addressing precisely Plato's conception of philosophy or dialectic. Because a thorough examination of how dialectic is found and understood in *all* of Plato's dialogues is hardly manageable in one book-length study and because the "late" dialogues are a very distinct group presenting problems of their own, the scope of the present work is confined to what are normally considered the "early" and "middle" dialogues.[2]

I do not believe that a detailed study of this length on Plato's "earlier dialectic" requires any apology. In the first place, as just noted, an understanding of Plato's conception of philosophy must provide the foundation for any interpretation of his specific views. Before we can know how to read the dialogues, before we can interpret any of the claims made in the dialogues, we must have some general idea of what Plato sees himself doing as a philosopher. Second, to this day the most thorough and influential treatment of Plato's "earlier dialectic" is to be found in Richard Robinson's book of that name, first published in 1941 and then revised in 1953.[3] Apart from the fact that Robinson's book could not benefit from the more than forty years of Platonic scholarship appearing since its publication, its basic approach to the examination of dialectic is fundamentally flawed. Robinson's book is a book on *logic*. He thus treats dialectic as a purely formal method of constructing arguments and accordingly believes that he can define dialectic in total abstraction from the *content* of Plato's philosophy.[4] The result is that dialectic, understood as the exchange of questions and answers, is rendered accidental to this content and thus without real point or purpose.[5] A related problem is that Robinson focuses on the more technical descriptions of dialectic in the dialogues without making any attempt to relate these descriptions to dialectic as actually *practiced*, to a greater or lesser degree, in the dialogues (in fact, he sees little relation here).[6] Thus one finds in Robinson's book no interpretations of whole dialogues, but only detailed analyses of passages taken out of context. But can one truly understand Plato's dialectic if one refuses to examine in detail how he depicts dramatically, throughout the course of a whole dialogue, the methods and results of a philosophical conversation? Is not a Platonic dialogue simply a dramatic portrayal of dialectic at work? In not even considering this possibility,

INTRODUCTION: THE NEED FOR A
REEXAMINATION OF PLATO'S DIALECTIC

Robinson has provided us with at best the bleached skeleton of dialectic. However, Robinson has not simply failed to say all that can be said. As I show throughout the course of the present study, in abstracting from the content and dramatic life of dialectic, Robinson distorts its nature and answers incorrectly the important questions: *what* kind of knowledge does dialectic provide and *how* does it do so?

A detailed reexamination of Plato's earlier dialectic is therefore long overdue. However, it is made *especially* timely by the present state of Platonic scholarship. Since the publication of Robinson's book, two new and antagonistic movements have emerged in Platonic scholarship and are gaining increasing acceptance. I will call one the "nondoctrinal" interpretation of Plato and the other the "esotericist" interpretation ("unwritten doctrines"). In showing the origin of these two movements as well as what is at issue in their opposition, I hope to make clear just how great the need is for a new interpretation of Plato's dialectic. The account of Platonic scholarship that follows is schematic and therefore suffers from the defects of any "schema." Nevertheless, I think it is important, even at the risk of oversimplification, to have in view the main outlines of this otherwise complex spectacle.

The modern era of Platonic scholarship can be said to have begun with the publication in 1804 of Friedrich Schleiermacher's general introduction to his new German translation of Plato's dialogues. Such has been Schleiermacher's influence that his interpretation of Plato's philosophy has provided the foundation for both sides of the debate mentioned above.[7] The two main principles of this interpretation are the following: first, the content of Plato's philosophy is inseparable from the artistic form of the written dialogue;[8] this principle has as a corollary the view that Plato's philosophy is completely contained in the written dialogues. Second, the content of Plato's philosophy is systematic.[9] These two claims are the guiding principles of much Platonic scholarship to this day.

It is true that Schleiermacher's view that the dialogues are a gradual presentation of a philosophical system that remained constant throughout Plato's career has been widely rejected. This view has been thought to be incompatible with the obvious existence of contradictions and gaps in the dialogues taken as a whole. However, the view that has come to take its place, namely, that the dialogues are records of an evolution in Plato's philosophical system (or of failed attempts to build such a system), shares the same presuppositions. First, the unity of form and content is maintained in the view that the differences between one dialogue and another reflect actual changes in Plato's thought occurring between the dates at which the two dialogues were written. Thus the great importance which stylometry has come to have in Platonic scholarship is a consequence of this Schleiermacherian conviction that Plato's philosophy, whether unchanging or evolving, is completely contained in the written word of the dialogues. Second, the "developmentalist" interpretation also preserves Schleiermacher's characterization of Plato as a "systematic philosopher." Even if the system is now understood as having been subject to revision throughout Plato's life, it is still a system which is considered to have been the aim of Plato's philosophical activity.[10]

Yet despite this influence that the two principles of Schleiermacher's interpretation have had on subsequent scholarship, it is not hard to see that there is a tension, if not a contradiction, between them. Can one really maintain the unity of form and content in Plato's philosophy and at the same time see this philosophy as "systematic"? Can there be any form of writing *less* suited to presenting a systematic philosophy than Plato's dramatic dialogues? Schleiermacher's own work on Plato was unable to reconcile his two principles, and thus he bequeathed to modern scholarship a dilemma that ultimately led scholars to formulate the "developmentalist" interpretation as a possible solution. When, however, we look at recent work done within this "developmentalist" orthodoxy we note the same flaw: scholars can assert the unity of form and content *and* the systematic nature of Plato's philosophy only at the cost of failing to do justice to the dialogue form of Plato's works.[11] In other words, in accepting Schleiermacher's two principles, scholars are eventually forced to interpret the dialogues as if they were treatises, because the "treatise" is the only form of writing completely suited to a systematic philosophy. This distortion of the dialogue form represents the breakdown of this line of interpretation.

Accordingly, an opposition movement has recently formed. This opposing camp insists that the dialogues be read *as dialogues*. An interpretation must do justice to the dramatic, ironic, suggestive character of Plato's written works. Individual arguments are to be understood in their dramatic context and not in abstraction. The significance of what is said in a dialogue depends on who says it and why. This approach is still itself an offshoot of Schleiermacher's interpretation: after all, it was Schleiermacher who said that "no proposition is to be rightly understood, except in its own place, and with the combinations and limitations which Plato has assigned to it."[12] However, this line of interpretation, in accepting the first of Schleiermacher's principles, rejects the second, that is, that Plato was a systematic philosopher. The emphasis is thus placed on the "aporetic" character of the dialogues, and Plato is portrayed as remaining for the most part faithful to Socrates' avowal of ignorance. This is therefore what

INTRODUCTION: THE NEED FOR A
REEXAMINATION OF PLATO'S DIALECTIC

I call above the "nondoctrinal" interpretation.[13] By denying that Plato's thought is "systematic," it is able to show, much more adequately than Schleiermacher, the unity of form and content in Plato's writings. It has therefore given rise to many sensitive and insightful interpretations of individual dialogues. However, there is a flaw in this approach as well: namely, that in rejecting Schleiermacher's second principle it tends to put nothing in its place. In other words, many interpreters have vehemently denied that Plato's philosophy is systematic and doctrinal without giving us an alternative model by which to understand this philosophy. How did Plato understand philosophy if he did not see it as systematic? What evidence is there for attributing to Plato a conception of philosophy radically different from that of the subsequent philosophical tradition? What allows us to call Plato a "philosopher" if his thinking is not systematic?[14] Without answers to these questions, this line of approach cannot help but deprive Plato's philosophy of any content and thus "turn Platonism into empty 'philosophizing.' "[15]

This takes us, then, to another movement in Platonic scholarship which can be called the "esotericist" interpretation and which has its origin in the "Tübingen School" of H. J. Krämer and K. Gaiser.[16] The esotericists have criticized the "Schleiermacherianism" in both of the approaches (the "developmentalist" and the "nondoctrinal") described above. They criticize the developmentalist approach for its conviction that Plato's philosophy is completely contained in the dialogues. They rightly point out that we are not told in the *Republic* what the Good is and that the dialogues leave other crucial gaps in the presentation of Plato's metaphysical principles.[17] (One could add that we are not told in the dialogues what the nature of the relation is between Form and particular, another cornerstone of Plato's philosophy.) This objection is related to the one made above: the dialogues are completely inadequate as treatises expounding Plato's philosophical system.[18]

The esotericists, however, also reject the "nondoctrinal" interpretation because they see it as both denying the evident fact that Plato was a "metaphysician" and anachronistically attributing to him the skepticism with regard to the existence of "ultimate answers" which characterizes modern "existentialism."[19] Yet their rejection is clearly also motivated by a value judgment concerning what counts as "real philosophy."[20] They do not see how any seriousness could remain in Plato's "philosophy" once it is denied its systematic character. Plato in this case could be called an artist or a poet, but what would it mean to call him a "philosopher"? This criticism has been best expressed by J. N. Findlay, the major exponent of the "esotericist" interpretation in the English-speaking world:

> Many are satisified with this tentative, suggestive thought-fragmentation which is certainly worth a pack of low-grade systematization, but the *nisus* of Plato's thought is none the less towards systematic completion, and if we lose the willingness to run along with this *nisus*, the fragments lose all their meaning, become even trivial and ridiculous. A Plato who merely played around with notions and arguments is a Plato corrupted, a Plato unworthy of serious study. (1974, 6)

We have already seen that there is a point in this criticism. In rejecting the "doctrinal" or "systematic" characterization of Plato's philosophy, we run the risk of depriving the dialogues of philosophical content altogether.

The esotericists, in rejecting the approaches they identify with Schleiermacher, are in fact rejecting only one of his principles: the inseparability of the content of Plato's philosophy from the form of the written dialogues. They claim instead that there are "unwritten doctrines" which are even more important than what is said in the dialogues for an understanding of Plato's philosophy. These doctrines were communicated by Plato only orally within the Academy and are known to us only through the reports of other philosophers (especially Aristotle) within the Academic tradition. However, the esotericists completely accept Schleiermacher's second principle, that is, that Plato's philosophy is systematic.[21] All they have done is to locate the system outside of the dialogues and thus to sever the form and content which Schleiermacher and others have tried so hard to join. The Tübingen School is thus a natural outgrowth of the tensions which Schleiermacher bequeathed to Platonic scholarship. The natural consequence of the failure to reconcile Schleiermacher's two principles was their separation into two opposed camps: one that affirms the unity of form and content in seeking a nondoctrinal, nonsystematic interpretation of the dialogues, and one that rejects this unity in affirming the existence of a system outside the dialogues.[22]

In the present study I align myself primarily with the "nondoctrinal" camp in emphasizing the inseparability of the philosophical content of the dialogues from their dramatic form, in rejecting the presupposition that Plato understood philosophy to be systematic, and in maintaining that Plato was much closer to Socrates than he was to the dogmatic metaphysics that succeeded him. However, a "nondoctrinal" approach to the dialogues cannot be fruitful if it simply dismisses the claim made by both esotericists and developmentalists that Plato's philosophy is a "system." It must show what conception of philosophy is to be put in the place of this Schleiermacherian principle. More specifically, it must show that there is a viable conception of philosophy that renders it fundamentally opposed to systematization, and that this conception of philosophy is

INTRODUCTION: THE NEED FOR A REEXAMINATION OF PLATO'S DIALECTIC

Plato's own. Once the "doctrinal" interpretation is refuted in this way, we are in a position to ground philosophically the "nondoctrinal" approach to Plato's dialogues in such a way as to rid it of the appearance of arbitrariness.

This is precisely the aim of the present study. This aim cannot be met unless two assumptions of the "dogmatic" or "systematic"[23] interpretation are refuted. I will briefly describe these assumptions and indicate how they will be brought into question.

The first assumption is that the knowledge which philosophy strives to obtain is a knowledge of propositions. The characterization of knowledge as propositional means not simply that we can speak about the objects of philosophy, but rather that we can do so without profound distortion. In other words, in order for philosophical knowledge to be propositional, it must be the case not only that we can form propositions about the fundamental principles of reality, but also that these propositions can express these principles *as they truly are*. If philosophical propositions are so far from doing this that they distort as much as reveal these principles, then philosophical knowledge can be neither propositional nor systematic. Indeed, even in this case one could construct a deductive system, but such a system would be empty and next to worthless. It would be foreign to the essence and content of philosophy, which in this case would have to reside in some sort of nonpropositional insight. Furthermore, such a system, due to its appearance of completeness, would be dangerously deceptive; it would suggest that we have finally grasped in our definitions and deductions a truth that can never be thus grasped. It is therefore important to keep the question of whether we can through our language formulate a philosophical system (something always possible) distinct from the question of whether we *should* do so. The answer to this latter question will depend on what we take the nature of philosophical knowledge to be.

Since reference will be made to nonpropositional knowledge throughout the present study and since this notion is often misunderstood, a few introductory comments should be made here concerning its nature. To have *propositional* knowledge of something is to know *that* certain predicates are true of it. For example, I can "know a triangle" by knowing *that* it has three sides, *that* it has angles totaling 180 degrees, and so on. This kind of knowledge can have propositions as its content because it is precisely by means of them that we predicate x of y. Knowledge that a triangle has three sides can be seen as knowledge of the *proposition* that a triangle has three sides. However, knowledge is nonpropositional when it *cannot* be identified with knowing what can truly be asserted *of* its object.

In knowing a proposition about something, I can only know *that* certain things are true *of* it; therefore, any form of knowledge that does not have this character cannot have propositions as its content. But what would be some examples of this? One clear example is knowledge of a certain skill: knowing *how* to do something. There are many propositions that truly assert something about skiing, but *knowing how* to ski is not equivalent to knowing any or all of these propositions.[24] A different example, however, is knowledge of something whose nature or essence cannot be reduced to a set of properties; its unity cannot be resolved into any multiplicity through analysis. Because such a nature or essence does not have the complexity of a "fact" or "state of affairs" it cannot be *articulated* in any proposition.[25] Again, even in this case we can talk around this "object," we can express in propositions states of affairs in which it is involved, we can predicate certain properties of it, but the nature of the object in its unity cannot be thus expressed. "Knowing x" is in this case *not* reducible to "knowing that x is y" and for this reason is nonpropositional.[26] As argued in chapter 6, this is what Socrates has in mind when he distinguishes between knowing what a thing *is* (*ti esti*) and knowing how it *is qualified* (*poion ti esti*).[27] I will also suggest another possible candidate for nonpropositional knowledge: *self*-knowledge. What is peculiar about self-knowledge is that it does not seem to be equivalent to knowing *that* certain facts are true about yourself. After all, this knowledge of facts about yourself is knowledge that *someone else* could theoretically (even if not in fact, at present) have; yet it seems utterly nonsensical to say that someone else could have *your* self-knowledge. Perhaps, then, self-knowledge itself cannot be assimilated to knowledge *that* something is the case.[28]

The distinction between nonpropositional and propositional knowledge parallels a distinction I will develop further in what follows (especially in chapter 3) between the "manifest" and the "describable." Nonpropositional knowledge is of what is manifest *without* being describable.[29] This means that the manifestness is not reducible to any description, not that it is completely ineffable. In each of the three cases cited above, all our descriptions will necessarily fail to do justice to how what we are describing manifests itself. Here truth, as this "manifestness," is more than a fact or state of affairs which can be described.

To determine, therefore, whether or not the knowledge achieved by dialectic is nonpropositional, one must determine what kind of knowledge this is ("knowledge that" or "knowledge how") as well as what kind of "objects" it has. (Can their natures, that is, *what* they are, be identified with a complex set of properties? Are they distinct from the knowing subject or inseparable from this subject?) I will argue below *ambulando* that the knowledge provided by dialectic bears a resemblance to all the forms of nonpropositional knowledge mentioned above.[30] All that is being claimed here, however, is that if philosophical knowledge has this character, it clearly cannot be said to be in any meaningful sense "systematic."

The second assumption is that philosophical *method* is subordinate to, and terminates in, some final result. Apart from the method of inquiry, a system exists which is thought to be the end (in both senses of the word) of the method. The process of questioning and investigating has a terminus that ultimately renders this process no longer necessary. An "open-ended system"[31] is an oxymoron if by that one means a system that leaves fundamental questions without final answers.

Both assumptions can be seen at work in the "developmentalist" interpretation. One current dispute within this approach concerns the nature of Socrates' elenchus in the so-called "early" dialogues: the "constructivist" thesis, most forcefully and thoroughly defended by Gregory Vlastos,[32] maintains that the elenchus is actually capable of establishing philosophical propositions (though without absolute certainty), while the "nonconstructivist" thesis denies this, maintaining that the elenchus has only the negative aim of purging the interlocutors of the conceit of wisdom.[33] Another dispute concerns the relation between this elenctic method of the "early" dialogues and the "dialectic" of the "middle" dialogues: most of these scholars believe that the "middle period" dialectic is more positive than the "early period" dialectic, because it approaches more the axiomatic-deductive method of mathematics, thus arriving at propositional results which the earlier elenctic method was not capable of establishing either at all or with as much certainty.[34] There are, however, some dissenters who do not see the "hypothetical method" of the middle dialogues as in any significant way overcoming the skeptical results of the elenctic method.[35] What I wish to draw attention to, however, is that on all sides of this dispute dialectic is judged to be "constructive" only to the extent that it is capable of establishing propositions. Whatever lip service might be paid to visual metaphors and "insight" by these interpreters, the possibility of nonpropositional knowledge plays no role in their conception of Plato's dialectic. The second, related assumption is to be found here as well: dialectic is viewed as simply a logical "tool" for the establishment of philosophical propositions, a tool that presumably can be dispensed with once it has done its work.[36] The disagreements are simply over how exactly this tool works and how productive it is. In short, the model that appears to guide scholars working within the "developmentalist" interpretation is the kind of deductive system of propositions that characterizes mathematics: all that is open to debate is the extent to which Plato's dialectic, at different points in his "development," approximates this model.

In this study I challenge both of these general assumptions by arguing that the dialectic practiced in the "aporetic" dialogues is positive and constructive despite the lack of propositional results, that this dialectic is itself in some sense the "solution," rather than a mere tool for arriving at a solution, and that the method of hypothesis, which is so admired by modern interpreters for its modest ability to deduce propositions, is in the dialogues consistently considered inferior to this dialectic or "second-best." Thus this study at different points challenges all sides of the current disputes within the "developmentalist" interpretation.

Since the main thesis of the esotericist interpretation cannot be addressed as such in the course of a study focused on the dialogues (though interpretations of specific texts by which the esotericists seek to defend their thesis will receive much critical scrutiny), I wish to provide here some general criticisms aimed at the problematic commitment of this interpretation to the two assumptions mentioned above.

Despite the centrality of the *Seventh Letter* in their interpretation, a text in which the author claims that the subject matter of philosophy "cannot be expressed at all in words as other studies can" (341c5–6), the esotericists insist on the propositional character of philosophical thought for Plato. They attempt to explain away the above claim by interpreting it as denying only expression in writing.[37] But as the final chapter of the present study will show, the argument the letter proceeds to make rules out *oral* as well as *written* discourse. This is not to deny that we can talk about the ultimate principles of philosophy. The point is instead that the propositions we speak or write cannot express, without profound distortion, the principles *as they truly are*.

Gaiser (1968), apparently more than Krämer,[38] is aware of this aspect of Plato's thought, and this leads him to make admissions that threaten to undermine the "esotericist" position. He recognizes that the ultimate principles are for Plato "inexpressible" and that therefore any attempt to express their natures falls into contradictions and paradoxes.[39] On account of this ineffable, aporetic character of Plato's philosophy,[40] Gaiser must confess that the systematic reconstruction of Plato's thought carried out by the Tübingen School is of little value *in itself*.[41] But if this is the case, is not the indirect, suggestive, aporetic approach to the principles found in the dialogues a much better expression of Plato's philosophy than a reconstructed system whose words, due to the ineffability of these principles, in themselves say nothing?

INTRODUCTION: THE NEED FOR A REEXAMINATION OF PLATO'S DIALECTIC

The second assumption, however, betrays the fundamental weakness in the "esotericist" approach. This assumption is clearly enunciated by Krämer when he says of the dialectic depicted in the dialogues: "What is at issue here is the method, not the essence itself of Platonic philosophy."[42] Here the method of Plato's philosophy is seen as being completely distinct from its content. The method is merely a matter of inquiry, the content is the system that finally results from this inquiry. It is this view which, as I have already suggested and show in this study, is most foreign to Plato's thought. Rather than seeing dialectic as a mere tool used in system building, Plato clearly understands the very content of philosophy to be dialectical. In claiming that the content of Plato's philosophy is a deductive system, on the other hand, the esotericists render dialectic completely accidental to this content. As a result, their interpretation of Plato's philosophy almost completely ignores Socrates and the method he represents. Plato the systematic philosopher and Socrates the dialectician have, in their eyes, nothing to do with each other.[43]

However, they themselves do not consistently hold this view, but sometimes allow that the dialectical process depicted in the dialogues is essential to philosophy as Plato understands it. Thus Krämer speaks of the "hermeneutic superiority of the written work, which is founded on a movement of thought developed in detail, while the indirect tradition is hardened into a block, and offers, so to say, petrified results. And these results have need of being loosened by means of the reconstruction of their argumentative origin, on the model of the dialectical method developed in the dialogues" (1990a, 69; see also 1994, 7). But then is the essence of Plato's philosophy to be found in the "petrified results" or in the argumentative process without which these results are meaningless?[44] It turns out that the dialogues are the primary source for Plato's philosophy and that what is known through the indirect tradition can be evaluated and understood only in light of the dialectic practiced in the dialogues.

A related problem is the apparent contradiction between the emphasis placed by the esotericists on the essentially oral character of Plato's philosophy and their characterization of this philosophy as systematic. Nothing stands in the way of expressing a system in writing: Leibniz, Kant, and Hegel were able to do so without the slightest difficulty or reservation. If Plato himself had a philosophical system, why was he so hesitant to write it down? According to what the esotericists sometimes say, Plato's philosophy was systematic and yet essentially oral. What could this possibly mean? On the other hand, when they retreat from saying that Plato's philosophy was *essentially* oral and simply claim that he refrained from communicating his system in writing for fear of being misunderstood by those without sufficient philosophical training,[45] then their explanation renders incomprehensible the existence of what philosophical content there is in the dialogues. If this is the reason why Plato decided to leave unwritten his doctrines concerning the One and the Dyad, then he for the same reason should have left unwritten *any* substantial philosophical doctrines. As the history of Platonic scholarship demonstrates, many philosophical claims made in the dialogues, such as that the Good is beyond being, that sensible objects are what they are through participation in eternal, immaterial forms, that learning is recollection, and so on, have caused as much confusion and misunderstanding as anything Plato might have written about the One and the Dyad. This weaker, "pedagogical" explanation of the oral character of Plato's philosophy is therefore completely inadequate.[46]

However, if the dialectical process is essential to the very content of Plato's philosophy, then it makes perfect sense to say that this content cannot be written down. The esotericists have not come to terms with Plato's dialectic. Sometimes they see it as accidental (when it is thought to be a mere method of inquiry distinct from the systematic content of philosophy), while at other times they see it as essential (when they recognize the emptiness of the system they have reconstructed).

The main problem, in short, is that the esotericists mistake the doctrines reported in the secondary sources for the *spirit* of Plato's philosophy. And this is what is really at issue. No one can reasonably deny that Plato said something like what he is reported by Aristotle to have said. What remains an open question is the context and way in which Plato spoke of the ultimate principles.[47] Did he believe that the principles could be fully known and expressed without distortion? Did he think that the relation between the One and Ideas, on the one hand, and between Ideas and sensible objects, on the other, could be explained in precise and unambiguous terms?[48] (Aristotle at *Metaphysics* 991a20 criticizes Plato for *not* doing this and for instead resorting to poetical metaphors.) Did Plato believe that the first principles could be used as axioms from which to deduce all existing things, and did he himself attempt this? In other words, did he think it was possible to go beyond the view that the Ideas have unity and multiplicity as their principles, to the actual construction of a detailed system based on these principles? Are the claims reported as the unwritten doctrines a *program* for the development of a detailed, rigorous system of propositions? Or did Plato understand these claims as truths into which dialectic can provide some insight, but which, due to the limitations of language and the nonpropositional character of knowledge, do not lend themselves to systematization? These questions, I maintain, are left *unanswered* by the indirect tradition. It is precisely the failure to recognize this that leads the esotericists astray. For

INTRODUCTION: THE NEED FOR A
REEXAMINATION OF PLATO'S DIALECTIC

understanding Plato's philosophy, even more important than what is said, whether in writing or orally, are the meanings, functions, and limitations assigned to what is said. The dialogues give us this essential context; the indirect tradition does not. This fact does not make the indirect tradition superfluous, but it does make it subordinate to the dialogues.

The reason why Krämer, for example, resists this subordination is his unjustified belief that the indirect tradition not only preserves for us some of Plato's teachings but also reveals the context and way in which Plato understood them, that is, in Krämer's view, as parts of a propositional, deductive system that could fully and unambiguously explicate the whole of reality: "Plato . . . allowed for the introduction of starting points of a philosophy *more geometrico demonstrata* [as axioms] and connected to this *a conception of reality as totally knowable and available*" (1990a, 153). But the indirect tradition does not show us that Plato understood the principles in this way and therefore accepting the evidence of this tradition need not commit one to Krämer's interpretation of it.[49] Krämer is therefore deceived in thinking that his *Platonbild* is the historically objective one, that it simply follows from accepting and doing justice to all the available evidence (1990a, 183; 1988, 610–21). In fact, the esotericist interpretation depends on a number of philosophical and methodological presuppositions, one of which being that any "philosophy" worthy of the name must be *wissenschaft-exakt* and *systematisch*.[50]

These criticisms of the esotericists show that the real alternative to seeing Plato's philosophy as "systematic" is an adequate understanding of the dialectic with which Plato explicitly identifies philosophy. If we can show the real opposition between philosophy understood as systematic and philosophy understood as dialectic and show further that Plato sides with the latter conception of philosophy, then we will be in a position to avoid both "developmentalism" and "esotericism." We will also be in a position finally to do justice to the valid presupposition of Schleiermacher's interpretation, that is, the unity of form and content in Plato's philosophy, since dialectic is clearly in a sense both the form *and* the content of the dialogues.

Something needs to be said here about the general plan of this study. As already indicated, I examine the nature of dialectic by means of interpreting whole dialogues, wherever possible. Yet the choice of dialogues as well as the order in which they are presented is determined by the general framework within which I have chosen to examine dialectic. The three basic principles of this framework are as follows. (1) There are three major means employed by dialectic in its search for truth: verbal analysis, arguments, and images. (2) This study portrays dialectic as existing between everyday discourse and sophistic discourse (my reasons for approaching dialectic in this way will be explained in the introduction to the second chapter). (3) This study seeks to understand the relation between dialectic in the "early" dialogues and the hypothetical method in the "middle" dialogues.

The plan of the study is therefore as follows. The first part is an examination of dialectic in terms of its position between the extremes of ordinary discourse and sophistic discourse. The second chapter is an interpretation of the *Laches* and the *Charmides* that aims to show that the understanding sought and attained in dialectic differs both from the intuition characteristic of ordinary experience and from the "technical" knowledge of the sophists. Chapters 3, 4, and 5 distinguish the dialectician from the sophist in terms of each of the three means of inquiry enumerated above: chapter 3 shows, by means of an interpretation of the *Cratylus*, how the dialectician's understanding and use of words differs from that of his sophistic rivals; chapter 4, by means of an interpretation of the *Euthydemus*, shows how the dialectician's use of argumentation differs from that of the eristics; chapter 5, by means of an interpretation of the tenth book of the *Republic* and related texts, shows how the dialectician's use of images differs from that of the poets. What emerges from these chapters is that dialectic is a "knowledge of how to use" language, argumentation, and images in such a way as to awaken an insight that transcends them (i.e., cannot be directly expressed by any of these means). It therefore becomes necessary to determine the exact relation between dialectic and strictly propositional knowledge. Part 2 (chapters 6, 7, and 8) shows that the *Meno*, the *Phaedo*, and the *Republic* introduce, discuss, and use a method that is clearly restricted to knowledge of propositions: *the method of hypothesis*. In each of these dialogues, however, dialectic is *distinguished from* this method and given priority over it. The ninth and final chapter is a discussion of the *Seventh Letter:* even though the authenticity of this letter is debated and even though, if genuine, it is apparently much later than the dialogues discussed in previous chapters, it will be seen to bring together with great conciseness and insight the different characteristics of dialectic that the interpretation of these dialogues will have uncovered.

There are, of course, disadvantages to pursuing the study in this somewhat schematic way. In order to devote a chapter to dialectic's use of images and to keep the chapters on the hypothetical method in the *Phaedo* and the *Republic* to a manageable length, I have had to depart to some extent from my general principle of interpreting whole dialogues (though even in these cases I am careful to relate the passages I discuss to the context of the whole dialogue, even if only briefly and tentatively). My inclusion of the *Seventh Letter* (a work which is not even a dialogue), with the purpose of bringing together the conclusions of the preceding chapters, must also cause some initial unease. Yet it is my hope that the described framework will enable the present study to achieve clarity and order without sacrificing richness or depth.

Although the subject of this study is dialectic as discussed and practiced in the "early" and "middle" dialogues, I of course cannot deal with all of the dialogues that fall within this group. The most important works that have not been included are the *Gorgias* and the *Protagoras*. Apart, however, from the obvious problem of space, there are two reasons for their omission: first, most of what we learn from these dialogues about the opposition between Socrates and the sophists can also, I believe, be learned from the dialogues with which I do deal and which are more central to the topic of dialectic. Second, this inquiry into the nature of dialectic is mainly concerned with what I see as its positive function, namely, the discovery of truth, and with the corresponding What-is-x? question.[51] What distinguishes the *Gorgias* and the *Protagoras*, however, is that in them this positive, "zetetic" function of dialectic recedes into the background, if not disappears altogether: the What-is-x? question is not even pursued (even though its central importance is explicitly noted by Socrates at the end of the *Protagoras*), and Socrates at the start has already reached conclusions which he then simply defends against adversaries, in full confidence that they will be proven wrong and he will be proven right. And yet Gregory Vlastos has based his account of the Socratic elenchus,[52] which he himself sees as essentially a method of *searching* for the truth,[53] almost exclusively on the *Gorgias* and the *Protagoras* and has virtually ignored those "aporetic" dialogues in which Socrates engages in a genuine search for the answer to what he clearly considered the most important question: What is x? In fact, the method pursued in these two dialogues bears a greater resemblance to the hypothetical method introduced in the *Meno*, that is, a method that bypasses the What-is-x? question, than to the method pursued in other so-called "early" dialogues. The *Gorgias* and the *Protagoras* are very important dialogues with their own special aims. Other dialogues, however, are more revealing of the way in which Socrates searches for the essential truth.

This, then, is the plan and scope of the present study. The understanding of dialectic resulting from this study will, I hope, prove to be more than a historical curiosity. Today when, after a long tradition of systematic metaphysics, the very possibility of such a thing as "philosophy" is being seriously questioned in all quarters, it seems imperative that we consider alternative ways of doing philosophy. Of course, the archenemy which the logical positivists and the pragmatists, the deconstructionists and the existentialists, all have in common is "Platonism." As will be made clear, however, Plato shares very little with this "Platonism." It is unfortunate that this myth of an "-ism" shared by Plato and the whole tradition which succeeded him has stood in the way of a real confrontation with philosophy as Plato understood and depicted it in his singularly elusive dialogues. The reward of such a confrontation is a viable philosophical method that avoids the pitfalls of both the pragmatist and the "absolutist" while reconciling their virtues.

PART   I

DIALECTIC IN BETWEEN ORDINARY AND SOPHISTIC DISCOURSE

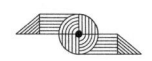

2

Dialectic at Work in the *Laches* and the *Charmides*

Introduction

The question addressed in this chapter is the following: What exactly does Socrates' dialectic accomplish in two paradigm "aporetic dialogues," the *Laches* and the *Charmides*?[1] In each of these dialogues Socrates searches for an answer to a question of the form "What is x?" and fails to find it. Nevertheless, Socrates never doubts the validity or importance of his question. He is unwilling to accept definitions focused on examples from ordinary experience,[2] even though his attempt to go beyond such definitions ends in failure. These dialogues therefore present us with a paradox: Socrates is not satisfied with whatever intuitive awareness of the virtues is involved in our everyday experience (i.e., in our ability to recognize examples of virtue and even in our practice of virtue), and yet, by his own admission, his method fails in each dialogue to provide any higher form of knowledge. At the end of the discussion he *claims* to be as ignorant about courage as the generals with whom he converses.

Of course, we must ask whether or not this claim is true. The challenge in interpreting the aporetic dialogues is to show how (if at all) Socrates' peculiar way of talking about virtue distinguishes itself from everyday talk. Socrates' interlocutors, and we ourselves, frequently converse about courage, friendship, temperance, and virtue in general. We do so, however, in specific contexts and in response to specific situations. When betrayed by someone dear to us, we complain that he or she was not a true friend. When confronted with someone who complains incessantly about the slightest illness or discomfort, we accuse this person of acting cowardly. What we do not normally do, however, is ask context-free questions such as "What is courage?" or "What is friendship?" Such questions, precisely because they are so general, seem pointless.[3] How can they teach us more than, or even as much as, what we know on the level of ordinary experience?[4] Socrates' dialectic was often dismissed as "idle talk" by his contemporaries,[5] the suggestion being that it tells us no more than what we already know. His failure to answer his own questions seems only to prove that he was wrong to abstract from the concrete context of ordinary experience in the first place.[6]

A consideration of Plato's intentions in writing the aporetic dialogues renders the problem even more acute. Even if the historical Socrates failed to answer his What-is-x? question, why would Plato muster all his talent to depict this? Why would he care to stress the failure of Socrates' method to yield positive results? Are not these dialogues more successful condemnations of Socrates' procedure than anything Socrates' actual accusers could write? Do they not show that Socrates' dialectic is in fact nothing but idle talk?

Thus we see again the important question in interpreting the aporetic dialogues: how does Socrates' dialectic distinguish itself from everyday discourse? Socrates' inquiry *begins* at the level of ordinary experience (thus his penchant for frequenting the agora). He discusses courage with two generals, friendship with friends, and temperance with a boy reputed to be temperate. In asking "What is virtue?" however, he is not seeking some knowledge possessed by generals, friends, or temperate people, but rather a distinctly *philosophical* knowledge. In beginning with ordinary experience he clearly intends to transcend it.

But the question is whether or not Socrates succeeds in leading his interlocutors and us the readers beyond ordinary experience. If the search for definitions ends in failure, are we not left with that vague understanding of the virtues with which we came to the inquiry?[7] We can imagine that after their discussion with Socrates Laches and Nicias will return to their duties and will continue to display courage themselves and to demand courage from their soldiers. After reading the *Laches*, we ourselves will fall back on whatever intuitive understanding of courage our experience provides. The failure of the inquiry will indeed caution us against presuming that we can give an irrefutable definition of courage. But why should this bother us? Why should this bother Nicias and Laches? Socrates' failure can even be seen as proving the futility of his question.[8] We and his interlocutors can therefore feel justified in sticking to ordinary experience and refusing to "philosophize." Socrates' inability to answer his own questions, it might be thought, is the best proof that philosophy is useless. Any attempt to go beyond "common sense" and everyday know-how cannot succeed. Socrates' What-is-x? question simply should not be asked.[9]

Chapter 1 referred to the debate between "constructivist" and "nonconstructivist" interpretations of the elenchus. Given what has been said, an obvious problem with the "nonconstructivist" interpretation is the difficulty it faces in defending the value of the elenchus vis-à-vis ordinary experience. If the elenchus provides no positive results, if it has nothing to put in the place of the opinions it refutes, then why should we not dismiss it as mere eristic in favor of our everyday, mostly reliable intuitions?[10] The "constructivist" interpretation might appear in this respect more attractive. However, as already noted in chapter 1, the main proponent of this interpretation, Gregory Vlastos, bases it mainly on the *Gorgias* because he does not see the elenchus as generating answers to the What-is-x? question of other dialogues. Of course, some have argued that the aporetic dialogues, despite their apparent inconclusiveness, in each case make clear what the right definition is.[11] This interpretation, however, has a hard time explaining why Plato would choose to play hide-and-seek: if there is a correct definition, why is it not explicitly defended as the conclusion of an argument? What could be his motive in cultivating the appearance of *aporia* where there is none?[12]

The interpretation which I defend differs from both of these. Unlike one, it maintains that in each dialogue the inquiry actually attains knowledge of the virtue in question. Unlike the other, however, it maintains that this knowledge is not knowledge of a definition. My explanation of the nature of this knowledge will distinguish it both from the naive awareness implicit in everyday experience and from the "sophistic" understanding that attempts to substitute definitions for this experience. In other words, the knowledge of virtue attained in the "aporetic" dialogues will be seen to be neither unreflective intuition (which characterizes everyday experience) nor a knowledge of propositions (which is what the sophist claims to have). It differs from the former, I will argue, in requiring the process of examining and refuting proposed definitions for its attainment and differs from the latter in being nonpropositional.

In both the *Laches* and the *Charmides*, Socrates' inquiry seeks to go beyond the level of ordinary discourse with which it begins, while at the same time avoiding the trap of thinking that any formulas can adequately convey a knowledge of the virtue in question. The title characters of both dialogues represent the naive understanding of virtue involved in simply acting virtuously. Laches has not thought much about courage, but he can usually be courageous when the situation demands it, and he can recognize courage in his soldiers. Charmides has not thought much about temperance, but when put to the test, he shows himself to possess it to some degree. In contrast, there is in each dialogue a "more sophisticated" character who thinks that ordinary experience tells us nothing and that a knowledge of virtue is to be had by possessing a definition or proposition (Nicias in the *Laches* and Critias in the *Charmides*). Socrates, however, steers a course between the overly naive and the overly "sophisticated" understandings of virtue and thus in his ignorance displays a knowledge that is nonpropositional and yet can be acquired only through philosophical inquiry conducted by means of propositions.

The *Laches* on Courage

It is often pointed out that while the *Laches* is said to be about courage, the actual inquiry into the essence of courage does not begin until halfway through the dialogue.[13] The first half consists of a "prologue" in which education is the main theme. This "prologue," however, is essential to understanding what transpires in the discussion on courage. It reveals what is truly at stake in this discussion. It also makes us aware of the characters of the interlocutors, and this will prove crucial in understanding why each one says what he says about courage. Therefore, I will not skip the "prologue," as is too often done,[14] but will instead endeavor to show how it provides us with the context in which the "What is courage?" question is to be understood.

Lysimachus and Melisias will spare no pains to ensure that their sons are properly educated and therefore seek to determine if the art of fighting in armor should form part of their education. With this purpose they invite the generals Laches and Nicias[15] to an exhibition of the art and ask their opinion. The two generals surprisingly refer them to Socrates. Lysimachus asks in astonishment whether Socrates concerns himself with such matters (i.e., fighting in armor and education in general). Nicias attests to Socrates' knowledge in this field, telling of how Socrates provided his sons with an excellent music teacher. Now Socrates' further credentials are presented. He is loved and admired by the boys of Lysimachus and Melisias. He proved himself an excellent soldier in the retreat from Delium (where he was Laches' companion). Yet when asked whether or not he thinks that fighting in armor is an advantageous art for boys to learn, he defers the question to Laches and Nicias because he is less experienced than they are (ἀπειρότερον τούτων, 181d4). Already we are made to wonder about the relation between the generals, whose knowledge is based on their greater experience in the art of fighting, and Socrates the philosopher, whose knowledge, though not altogether separated from practice (witness his deeds at Delium), seems of a different nature.

The two generals disagree. Nicias maintains (181d8–182d5) that the art of fighting in armor is one worth learning. Besides its other advantages this art can make one braver and more confident in battle (182c6). Thus Nicias is presupposing that a certain skill or knowledge (*mathēma*) can in fact make one braver. Laches, on the other hand, first questions whether this art is a *mathēma* at all, since even the Spartans, who give such importance to prowess in war, do not concern themselves with it. Laches' final conclusion, however, is that even if it were a *mathēma* it would be of little or no use. Knowledge of this art has not proven to increase the bravery of its teachers or students. Laches thus shows himself to be very skeptical that an acquired art or skill can make one braver (182d6–184c5).

What is at issue in the dispute between Nicias and Laches is made especially clear in the story Laches tells of the fighter Stesilaus, whose exhibition they have just seen (183c8–184a7). This Stesilaus, during his service as a marine, was armed with an unusual weapon (half spear, half scythe) of his own invention (significantly referred to as a *sophisma*, 183d7). Once in the midst of fighting, this weapon got caught in the rigging of the enemy ship. Stesilaus, refusing to let it go, struggled to pull it free. As a result, he was pulled along with it as the other ship began to pass his own, thereby provoking the laughter of his own fellow crewmen as well as of the enemy. He finally had to let go of his precious scythe-spear, and the sight of him standing there while his weapon waved in the air provided the spectators with another occasion for mirth. The moral of Laches' story is the foolishness of depending too much on an acquired skill or art. Stesilaus refuses to let go of his weapon because he has placed all his confidence in it; he has invented it in order to give himself the edge over his opponents, and now he simply cannot do without it. By relying too much on his *sophisma*, he proves himself a coward when threatened with its loss. Stesilaus is clearly someone who attempts to win battles through intelligence; he therefore invents an unusual weapon which he feels will respond to the peculiar needs of sea fighting. In thus attempting to anticipate the contingencies of battle, however, he proves incapable of dealing with the unforeseen (his weapon getting stuck). Being a good soldier clearly involves for Laches openness to the contingencies of the moment, and such openness is incompatible with excessive reliance on a special skill or art.

The importance of this apparently minor dispute between Laches and Nicias will become particularly evident toward the end of the dialogue where the role played by knowledge in courage becomes the central issue. For now Lysimachus attempts to settle the dispute by asking for Socrates' judgment. If the two generals were in agreement, Lysimachus explains, Socrates' advice would be less needed. Since they disagree, however, Socrates must cast his vote. It is important to note that the reason why Socrates must enter the discussion is that experience has proven unreliable. Both Laches and Nicias are experienced generals, and yet they are completely at odds on a question which is right in their field. Just as in the *Republic* we are told that reason is awakened by contradictions in sense experience (523a–524d), so here Socrates' inquiry begins only when the two people with experience give contradictory verdicts.

Socrates objects, however, to merely adding his opinion to the opinions of the two generals. The question cannot be decided by majority vote. Like questions in other fields, it can be conclusively answered only by an expert, that is, someone who has *knowledge*. Socrates specifies that one must have *a knowledge of what is good for the soul* in order to determine whether or not the art of fighting in armor will benefit the sons of Lysimachus and Melisias (185e1–6). In this way he raises the discussion to a different plane. From now on the discussion cannot remain on the level of experience or everyday discourse (what the many say). Socrates does not assume that because the generals are experienced they have the knowledge in question. If either they or Socrates himself are to claim to have this knowledge, they must either state from whom they learned it or give proof that they have it (186a3–b8).

Yet the nature of this knowledge which is to take us beyond ordinary experience is immediately rendered problematic when Socrates goes on to confess that he does not have it, due to his lack of the means with which to pay the sophists who teach it. Is this knowledge, then, of the kind that could be taught by the sophists? Socrates appeals to the sophists because they are the only ones who profess to be able to "treat one's soul" in the same way that doctors treat one's body. But then is the knowledge Socrates seeks really analogous to a knowledge of medicine? Is it something in which there can be "experts" in the ordinary sense of the term? Is it something that can be communicated through positive instruction?[16] In that case, Socrates is clearly right in claiming that he does not have it. By the end of the dialogue he will prove as unable as Laches and Nicias to answer Lysimachus's question. But if this knowledge is really not like what the sophists profess to teach, might not Socrates prove to have it after all?

After confessing his ignorance and his inability to pass judgment on the opinions of Laches and Nicias, Socrates suggests that the two generals be tested to see whether they possess the requisite knowledge. In responding to this suggestion, Laches and Nicias once again display their different characters. Nicias is accustomed to Socrates' discourse and enjoys it because he feels that he can learn much from it. He is aware that Socrates has a peculiar way of turning the discussion upon his interlocutors so that they are forced to give an account of themselves, but he thinks that this can be profitable (187e6–188c3). Laches, on the other hand, has no knowledge of Socrates' discourse but has witnessed his deeds. He admits that he could even be mistaken for a hater of discourse (*misologos,* 188c6), since he will listen to a man's words only if they harmonize with his deeds (188c4–189b7). The opposition here between the characters of Nicias and Laches is therefore an opposition between an emphasis on self-reflective discourse (giving an account of oneself and one's life in words) and an emphasis on almost instinctual action.[17] Just as Laches feels that knowledge of a particular art is of little or no use in the heat of battle, so does he subscribe to the view that "talk is cheap." Nicias, on the other hand, clearly feels that learning anything is valuable.

Already we begin to see the limitations of the opposed and one-sided positions of Nicias and Laches. Though Nicias recognizes that his own character and actions are under scrutiny in a conversation with Socrates, his description of this conversation as *not unpleasant* (188b5) seems incredibly superficial, especially when compared to Alcibiades' description in the *Symposium* of the agony and despair which Socrates' words made him suffer.[18] Despite Nicias's eloquent words, one has the suspicion that there is in him a divide between words and deeds that prevents the former from more than superficially affecting the latter. Laches, on the other hand, gives eloquent testimony to the importance of achieving a "Doric" harmony between words and deeds. However, the general impression given by his speech is that while talk is cheap without action, there is nothing wrong with action without talk.[19] One must therefore wonder if Nicias's and Laches' own words in these two speeches are in harmony with their characters and deeds. Indeed, while their limitations can only be suspected here, they will become clear by the end of the dialogue. Also significant for the rest of the dialogue is that *both* generals find something to admire in Socrates. Nicias admires his words and Laches his deeds. This suggests that the tension between the opposed, one-sided views of both characters, a tension that will reach a critical level toward the end of the dialogue, may ultimately be resolved in Socrates as the one who truly achieves a Doric harmony between words and deeds.

In commencing his discussion with the two generals, Socrates suggests that they try to determine who their teachers were or whom they have made better. But Socrates then suggests another approach to the problem that seems more fundamental and prior (189e1–3). When we know the nature of something which will improve that in which it is present, we can then and only then advise someone on how this thing is to be acquired. In the present case, Socrates and the generals want to know how virtue might be implanted in the souls of the sons of Lysimachus and Melisias (more specifically, whether learning the art of fighting in armor will contribute to this). But to know this they must first know *what virtue itself is:* "For if we do not at all know what virtue is (τὸ παράπαν ὅτι ποτε τυγχάνει ὄν), how could we possibly advise someone on the best way in which it is to be acquired?" (190b8–c2).[20] Socrates, however, fears that it might be too big a task to try to understand the whole of virtue, and so he decides to focus on that "part" of virtue most relevant to the present discussion, namely, *courage*. And so finally at 190e3 we have the question *ti estin andreia?* Only once we answer this question, according to Socrates, will we be able to determine to what extent courage might be implanted in the boys through practice and learning (καθ' ὅσον οἷόν τε ἐξ ἐπιτηδευμάτων τε καὶ μαθημάτων παραγενέσθαι, 190e1–2). This is, as has been seen, the major point of contention between Laches and Nicias.

What Socrates says here appears initially quite plausible. It makes sense to say that until we know *what* virtue is we cannot possibly know *how* it is acquired. The problem, however, is determining just what kind of knowledge is required. What exactly is prior to what here? What lends Socrates' claim its initial plausibility is our apparent inability to recognize a thing's properties unless we first have some awareness of what this thing is. However, Socrates has been seen by some to make the stronger claim that one cannot know that a particular act is courageous nor how courage is acquired unless one has a definition of courage.[21] If this means that without such a definition we have *no* ability to recognize instances and properties of courage with *any* reliability, then Socrates' acceptance of this view would render his very inquiry impossible.[22] It would be impossible to determine whether a suggested definition was to be rejected or accepted if Socrates and his interlocutors were not able to recognize some instances and properties of the thing being defined. Socrates clearly assumes that his interlocutors can recognize courage and distinguish it from its opposite. Yet the disagreement between Laches and Nicias also shows that their understanding of courage is unclear and indistinct. What is needed, therefore, is that Socrates and his interlocutors clarify and render distinct what they already confusedly know. There is no suggestion that a "definition" of courage is to be found independently of experience in order that experience may then be judged by it. Socrates' What-is-x? question seems to seek only a clarification and deepening of experience. We already recognize virtue in practice, but perhaps through questioning we may become even better able to recognize it and thus better able to answer the question as to how it is acquired. Socrates in asking his question therefore seems to remain very close to ordinary experience.

Yet a weaker version of the "priority of knowing-what principle" has also been attributed to Socrates: while one may at the level of ordinary experience have *true beliefs* concerning instances and properties of courage, a definition of courage is needed to turn these beliefs into knowledge.[23] While it seems reasonable to characterize what the interlocutors have at the beginning of the inquiry as "belief," this formulation, like the previous one, begs the question of whether or not the knowledge Socrates seeks is definitional knowledge. But is this even a question?

According to a surprisingly universal assumption among scholars, Socrates' What-is-x? question commits him to the identification of the knowledge of what virtue is with knowledge of a definition.[24] They see this commitment as necessarily implied by Socrates' insistence on definitions and his apparent assumption that if his interlocutor knows x, he must also be able to define x. In fact, however, what Socrates says and does commits him to no more than the following: *if one knows x in the way in which Socrates' interlocutors claim to know it, that is, in a way that is final, dogmatic, and in no need of philosophical inquiry, then one should be able to define exactly what x is.* Socrates does not force the definition requirement on his interlocutors: they themselves believe that it is easy to say what the virtue in question is. Socrates therefore could be demanding a definition from his interlocutors for the purpose of undermining *their* confidence that they have the kind of knowledge of x that enables them to say exactly what x is. But this itself might seem to imply the above commitment: if Socrates did not equate knowledge of virtue with definitional knowledge, then in showing that his interlocutors do not have the latter, he could not conclude, as he apparently does, that they also do not have the former.[25] But an explanation is readily available: perhaps what betrays the interlocutor's ignorance is precisely his *presumption* to be able to say exactly what virtue is, his own claim to possess definitional knowledge. The goal of Socrates' elenchus could then be to demonstrate the impossibility of such knowledge *and in this way* demonstrate the ignorance of the interlocutor who claimed to have such knowledge.[26] The pursuit of this goal, which is perfectly compatible with the What-is-x? question, obviously would not commit Socrates to the view that virtue can be defined and must be defined in order to be known. We can even avoid such a commitment while giving Socrates a more positive goal: even if Socrates does not think that definitions can provide a knowledge of virtue, he could still consider *the very process* of examining and refuting different definitions an indispensable part of pursuing such knowledge. Whether or not Socrates has these goals can be decided only by a careful examination of what actually takes place in the dialogues, both dramatically and argumentatively. What is unjustifiable is attributing to Socrates a priori the pursuit of definitional knowledge, without considering at all the context that alone reveals Socrates' aims.

In summation, the following can be said at this point concerning Socrates' "priority principle": First, it need not contradict the necessary presupposition of Socratic inquiry, that is, that our minds are not blank slates with regard to the virtue under discussion. That we have some ability to recognize instances and properties of the virtue is due to our possession of some awareness, however obscure, of what the virtue is (even if this is no more than having some sense of what the word means). Second, this everyday awareness can nevertheless be terribly confused and unreliable (as it is in Laches and Nicias). A knowledge of what the virtue is, a knowledge that transcends this unreflective intuition, is needed before we can reliably determine how the virtue is to be acquired. Whether or not this knowledge is knowledge of a definition is yet undetermined.

Equally undetermined is whether or not this knowledge is comparable to "technical" knowledge. But the above observations have revealed one possible difference. Knowledge of a *technē* such as medicine can be handed over through positive instruction and therefore does not presuppose in the student any prior awareness of the nature of medicine. Initially, the student need not even understand the terminology of medicine, since definitions can be provided as part of the instruction. Since, on the other hand, Socrates seeks to lead his interlocutors to a knowledge of virtue solely through questioning, rather than through positive instruction, he necessarily presupposes some prior awareness of virtue without which the questioning not only would lead nowhere but also could never get started.[27] This is why Socrates' elenctic method would be absurdly ineffectual in learning or teaching medicine, carpentry, or any of the other *technai*. We might therefore see in Socrates' very method a disanalogy between the knowledge he seeks and a *technē*. Yet even in this case Socrates could have a good reason for making the analogy: he might want to show that the knowledge which he seeks is not simply the knowledge of ordinary experience. Here we see the first signs of a tension that will become increasingly evident as the dialogue proceeds: the knowledge of courage Socrates seeks approximates a *technē* by transcending ordinary experience (as is shown by what he says), but differs from a *technē* by being in some way already implicit in ordinary experience (as is shown by what he does).

Laches considers Socrates' question "What is courage?" easy to answer (οὐ χαλεπὸν εἰπεῖν, 190e4). This confirms the suggestion made above that the interlocutor is the one who, complacent in his unreflective intuition, believes that courage can be easily defined. Courage, Laches replies, is to remain at one's post and not run away. Laches is here describing courage as it reveals itself to his own experience (though he perhaps is also giving expression to the traditional Greek conception of courage).[28] He recognizes as courageous only those of his men who remain at their post in battle. Socrates admits that what Laches says is true: such a soldier would indeed be courageous. Yet Socrates objects that this true statement does not answer his question. There are many different kinds of courage of which Laches has isolated only one. The courage of cavalrymen, for example, requires them to *flee* rather than remain at their post. Furthermore, courage is not found only in war. One can exhibit courage in fighting disease and poverty, in pursuing politics, and even in resisting certain harmful or shameful desires. In this way Socrates widens the scope of the question.[29] Nevertheless, Socrates still believes that the question "What is courage?" asks for only *one* thing. In applying the word "courage" to the many different activities just mentioned, we are referring to something which all these activities have in common. In sickness, in poverty, and in war courage remains one thing. What Socrates seeks to know, therefore, is what courage itself is in all these different cases (τί ὂν ἐν πᾶσι τούτοις ταὐτὸν ἐστιν, 191e10–11). To make his point clearer, Socrates uses the example of "quickness."[30] There are many different kinds of quickness: quickness in running, quickness in playing the lyre, quickness in learning, and so on. But if one were asked what quickness *is* in all these cases, one could reply that it is "accomplishing much in little time." What Socrates seems to be seeking is an analogous definition of courage that would apply to all the varied kinds of courage. It must be noted again, however, that there could be a variety of motives behind Socrates' request and that the belief that the nature of courage can be adequately expressed in a definition need not be one of them.

Even though it is now clear that Socrates' question seeks more than specific examples from experience, Laches still considers it easy to answer. What courage is in all of the different cases mentioned above is a kind of *endurance of the soul* (καρτερία τις τῆς ψυχῆς, 192b9–c1). Laches' definition is obviously a good one. Whether in fighting a disease or in fighting a battle, courage appears always to involve *enduring* something. Laches has therefore understood and followed Socrates' directives: he has pointed out something that is common to all the different kinds of courage. Socrates, however, is looking for not only what is *common* to courageous actions, but also what is *unique* to them. Therefore, he points out that Laches himself does not recognize every case of endurance to be a case of courage. Endurance unaccompanied by knowledge is sheer foolishness and therefore a bad thing. Yet Laches himself recognizes that courage is always a good thing. Courage, therefore, cannot be endurance if this endurance is unaccompanied by knowledge. It is important to note that in this argument Socrates is not introducing any principles extraneous to Laches' experience. Every step of the argument is based on what Laches himself already recognizes to be true. Therefore here too Socrates is asking of Laches no more than that he clarify what he already knows.

On the basis of the preceding argument, the definition of courage is now revised to "wise endurance" (φρόνιμος καρτερία, 192d10–11). Finally we appear to have an adequate definition. "Endurance" picks out something common to all cases of courage, while "knowledge" distinguishes courage from bad kinds of endurance. But now something startling happens: this definition by which we thought to isolate courageous acts turns out to mean the very opposite of courage! Endurance when accompanied by knowledge is not courage at all, but only prudence (which is, after all, a meaning of *phronimos*). For example, someone who goes into battle knowing that the odds are greatly in his favor (on account, for example, of a larger army or a better position) is definitely wise, but is he courageous? On the other hand, someone going into battle with the odds greatly against him is definitely not wise, but is he not thereby more courageous? The calculation and foresight involved in avoiding great danger are signs of wisdom, but hardly signs of courage. The person who runs into battle at great risk to himself may be called foolish, but such foolishness is indispensable to courage. Courage, rather than being wise endurance, turns out to be the opposite: *foolish endurance.*

What is put into question here, of course, is the kind of knowledge involved in courage. We all recognize a distinction between courage and rashness and explain it as due to the involvement in courage of a certain knowledge or even prudence. On the other hand, we recognize that certain kinds of knowledge exclude courage. Besides the case discussed above, Socrates uses as his examples expertise in the different *technai*. Someone very skilled in horsemanship will not be as courageous in a cavalry charge as someone less skilled. A doctor who knows medicine will not be as courageous in fighting disease as someone who lacks this knowledge. A skilled archer who endures in battle will not be as courageous as someone who endures without this skill. Why is this so? In each of these cases, the *technē* gives the person control over the situation. The doctor, for example, has more control over disease than does the layman. It is indeed the very purpose of a *technē* to predict, to give one some control over what is going to happen.[31] This kind of knowledge is therefore the best armor against danger. By eliminating contingency as much as possible, it reduces vulnerability. What Socrates is trying to get us to see, however, is that courage is *incompatible* with having complete control over a situation. Courage involves taking a risk, hurling oneself into the unknown (like the divers κολυμβῶντες, 193c3), enduring in a situation where one is exposed to the unpredictable. Courage is therefore a virtue only of the ignorant. Insofar as one has attained "technical" knowledge, insofar as one no longer has a fear of the unknown, one has lost the possibility of being courageous. We have nevertheless seen that courage must involve some kind of knowledge to distinguish itself from rashness. But given what has just been shown, what kind of knowledge could this be (η εἰς τί φρόνιμος; 192e1)? In order for courage to be distinct from rashness and yet remain *courage,* the knowledge it involves can be neither a *technē* as described above nor something incompatible with ignorance. The above reflections make this conclusion inevitable. This "conclusion," however, does not solve the present *aporia* for the simple reason that it seems hardly intelligible. Knowledge just seems to be what enables one to predict, control, and even master a certain state of affairs. As such it is necessarily incompatible with ignorance and risk. What could be meant by "knowledge" that does not have these characteristics?[32]

The purpose of these remarks is simply to locate the *aporia* in which Socrates and his interlocutor are trapped. They already begin to reveal, however, a peculiar circularity in the *Laches.* Socrates in this dialogue is seeking a knowledge of courage. He distinguishes this knowledge from the opinions of the many and suggests that its possession will make one an expert in courage, just as there are experts in medicine and horsemanship. But, as was already asked above, does the analogy really hold? Is a knowledge of courage truly analogous to a knowledge of medicine? We have seen that the knowledge Socrates is looking for is already in some sense and to some degree possessed by his interlocutors, so that he can constantly appeal to their perceptions in conducting the inquiry; in other words, the interlocutors are not blank slates (though what exactly they have, whether it be "belief" or something else, is not made clear in this dialogue). We have also seen that this in itself appears to distinguish this knowledge from a *technē,* which need not be in any way known prior to positive instruction. Thus the question that demands our constant attention throughout the inquiry is: just what kind of a knowledge is Socrates seeking to attain? What qualifies as a "knowledge of courage"? On the other hand, the question Socrates and Laches have encountered at this stage of the dialogue is: what kind of knowledge is involved in courage? Here is the circularity. Can we know what kind of a knowledge of courage the present inquiry can expect to attain without knowing what kind of knowledge is involved in courage? One could argue that there is no circularity here because knowing what courage is and having the knowledge involved in being courageous are not the same thing. Yet we know that elsewhere in the dialogues Socrates does not think that there is any distinction here: to be virtuous and to know what virtue is are the same thing.[33] In all likelihood, then, he does not make the distinction here either. We have seen that there are reasons for thinking that both the knowledge involved in courage and the knowledge of what courage is are unlike the kind of knowledge that defines a *technē*. Perhaps, then, we are dealing in both cases with the same question. The problem involved in understanding the nature of Socrates' inquiry is the same as the problem involved in understanding the nature of courage.

This circularity is reinforced by what Socrates says after he and Laches have reached their apparent impasse: "If you agree, we too must persevere and endure in the inquiry [ἐπιμείνωμέν τε καὶ καρτερήσωμεν]), and then courage will not laugh at us *for failing to inquire courageously into the nature of courage* [ὅτι οὐκ ἀνδρείως αὐτὴν ζητοῦμεν], which after all may frequently be endurance" (194a1–5).[34] In inquiring into the nature of courage, Socrates and his interlocutor must themselves exhibit courage. This passage is often taken to be nothing but a casual, playful remark. Given, however, the circularity noted above, its significance is evident. The knowledge involved in courage is also the knowledge which Socrates is seeking to attain in the inquiry. Yet according to what Socrates says in this passage, the inquiry has so far been characterized by endurance, just as courage has so far only been understood as endurance. But is the inquiry wise endurance or foolish endurance? If we answer that it is wise endurance and understand what we mean by the word "wise," then we have also understood courage. In other words, because of the peculiar circularity noted above, the answer to the question "What is courage?" may be found in the very nature of the search for this answer. In understanding the wisdom involved in the inquiry we also understand the wisdom involved in courage.[35]

Throughout the rest of the discussion, the difference between Laches and Nicias concerning the nature of courage shows itself not only in *what* they say, but also in *how* they say it. After Socrates and Laches have reached their impasse, the latter expresses a willingness to continue the search; however, he confesses to not being accustomed to this kind of inquiry (194a7). Here we see the limitations of Laches' experiential, intuitive courage. This courage allows him to *endure* in the inquiry, but it does not provide him with the skills necessary to *make progress* in the inquiry. This is why Nicias, with his sophistic education, must be called into the discussion. We immediately see the gulf that separates the two generals. Nicias claims that courage is nothing but knowledge of what inspires fear and confidence in war or in anything else (τὴν τῶν δεινῶν καὶ θαρραλέων ἐπιστήμην, 194e11–195a1). Laches vehemently objects: in his view, knowledge has nothing to do with courage (χωρὶς δήπου σοφία ἐστὶν ἀνδρείας, 195a4). Here we have the return, at a more general level, of the earlier debate between the two generals concerning the value of learning the art of fighting in armor. Laches, as was seen, was skeptical about the ability of any art or knowledge to make one braver. Nicias, on the other hand, was seen to value learning generally and to think that an acquired skill could in fact make one braver. This difference between the two generals now becomes critical. They show themselves to be in total disagreement about the role that knowledge plays in being courageous.

Laches first criticizes Nicias's definition by citing counterexamples. Do not the doctor and the farmer know what is and is not to be feared in sickness and in farming, respectively? We would not, however, say that they are thereby courageous. In short, every craftsman (*dēmiourgos*) knows what is and is not to be feared in his appropriate craft (*technē*), but no one would say that this knowledge provides the craftsman with courage. Thus Laches confirms Socrates' suggestion that courage cannot be the result of a *technē*. Nicias's response is to dismiss the examples by saying that the doctor and the farmer really do not know what is and is not to be feared. The doctor, for example, knows how to cure his patient but does not know whether it is really best for his patient to be cured. Some people are so miserable and their souls so corrupt that they are better off dead than alive. Yet the doctor knows only how to promote health and, *qua* doctor, knows no higher good. Even the seer who predicts the future does not know whether or not what will happen is for the best.[36] Thus the knowledge that Nicias identifies with courage is clearly more than that involved in any particular art or craft. Laches for this reason accuses Nicias of "empty talk." It seems that on Nicias's view only a god could be courageous; in denying that the doctor and the seer are courageous, he has not told us what human being, if any, *is* courageous.

The next objection against Nicias's position (suggested by Socrates) is that it excludes the possibility of animals being courageous, unless they are admitted to have a wisdom few human beings possess. Yet it is common opinion that certain animals (lions, for instance) exhibit courage. Nicias responds by again rejecting the counterexample. He agrees that animals can be "daring" (*thrasea*), but denies that they can be courageous (*andreia*). This verbal "play" further angers Laches, who claims that Nicias's talk more befits a sophist than a leader of the city (197d).[37]

In this last point about the sophist we begin to see how what Laches and Nicias say about courage is paralleled by the very way in which they argue. Laches admits to not being accustomed to the kind of argumentation practiced by Socrates (194a7). However, he displays a good intuitive understanding of courage based on examples from his experience. He therefore can recognize specific instances of courage but is not gifted with the power of abstraction. Though he can vaguely intuit (νοεῖν) what courage is in each of its instances, he proves incapable of expressing this intuition in words (συλλαβεῖν τῷ λόγῳ αὐτὴν καὶ εἰπεῖν ὅτι ἔστιν, 194b3–4). Despite these shortcomings, however, Laches trusts his practical sense and persists stolidly in the inquiry with Socrates. The kind of courage which Laches displays in the discussion is clearly not "knowledge"; it is instead an endurance made possible by his reliance on experience.

Nicias, on the other hand, prides himself on "knowledge" he has acquired from others and has little more than contempt for what ordinary experience can tell us. His suggested definition is therefore much more general and removed from experience than any of those proposed by Laches. This definition is not his own invention, but he claims to get it from Socrates (the significance of this will be discussed below). Socrates observes that Nicias's reply to the second objection (the distinction between "daring" and "courage") is taken from the sophist Damon, who in turn learned it from that master of words Prodicus (197d1–5). Nicias's wisdom is thus shown to be a borrowed one. It is also a conceited wisdom: Nicias clearly believes that the definitions he has picked up from others place him far above ordinary experience and opinion. He therefore has no respect for examples drawn from experience and is perfectly willing to contradict common sense; after all, if his identification of courage with knowledge is correct, then not only animals and children, but Laches himself and all of the great, but unreflective, Greek heroes lack courage (though Nicias denies this implication, 197c5–7). The courage Nicias displays in the discussion is therefore a confidence based on the presumption of knowledge. His own courage in this sense corresponds to his definition of courage: it is nothing but "knowledge."

In another sense, however, Nicias's identification of courage with knowledge is belied by the "knowledge" he himself exhibits in the inquiry. There hardly seems to be anything courageous about Nicias's arrogant assimilation of borrowed opinions. He is another Stesilaus, except that his weapon is not a clever scythe-spear, but rather a clever definition. He places all his confidence in the definition and hangs onto it as much as he can, only to appear a fool when the definition finally slips through his hands. Laches then laughs at him, just as Stesilaus was mocked by his fellow crewmen. This important parallel links the first and second halves of the dialogue. While fighting in armor was the ostensible concern of the first half, at issue in the second half is fighting in words. Thus, when Laches accuses Nicias of speaking in a way more befitting the courts, he is making an important objection (196b4–7). The method of Nicias is the same as that which Laches criticizes in Stesilaus.

These observations about Nicias's character are needed to explain Socrates' attitude toward him. As already noted, Nicias claims to have derived his definition from something he heard Socrates say, that is, that a person is good with respect to those things of which he has knowledge and bad with respect to those things of which he is ignorant (194d1–2). Nicias expresses his surprise that Socrates has not made use of this claim and so proceeds to make use of it himself. If the courageous man is good insofar as he is courageous, then he must also be wise insofar as he is good. Courage, therefore, must be a kind of wisdom. When asked to be more specific, Nicias provides a definition adovcated by Socrates himself elsewhere in the dialogues.[38] He then defends this definition by means of another "Socratic" view, namely, that the specific arts do not know what is really good.[39] In all these respects, then, Nicias seems to be arguing for a distinctly Socratic position. Nevertheless, rather than acknowledging and embracing such a faithful pupil, Socrates proceeds to refute him. This results in the strange spectacle of Socrates examining and refuting views which in the dialogue itself are said to originate with him.

Socrates' behavior is explained by Nicias's character. Nicias clearly remembers what he has heard Socrates say, but the way in which he deals with what he has heard is clearly "unsocratic." He believes that in having learned a definition of courage, he has acquired *knowledge* of courage. His contempt for experience and common opinion is the result of his confidence that with his definition he has come into the possession of something invulnerable. Socrates proceeds in the rest of the dialogue to destroy this confidence by showing that Nicias's presumed knowledge is empty. His definition proves inadequate for exactly the opposite reason that Laches' definitions proved inadequate. Rather than being too limited to particular examples, it is so general and abstract as to have no specific content: it covers *all* of virtue, rather than just courage (199c–e). Even if Socrates himself believed that all the virtues are ultimately one, this unity for Nicias clearly remains an abstraction which has not been carefully thought through.[40] Nicias's definition is a mere formula that has provided him with no genuine insight. He therefore can maintain it only at the cost of abstracting from experience and thus from "endurance" which, as Laches rightly points out, is an important characteristic of courageous acts. In the character of Nicias we have one reason why the *Laches* does not end with a definition: a definition would create in the interlocutors and in the reader that conceit of wisdom which is inimical to the exercise of the virtue in question. In presuming to know what courage is, Nicias shows himself to be no more courageous than Stesilaus. Their cleverness prevents that openness to the contingent and unknown that has been shown to be essential to courage.[41]

The dialogue therefore shows that the opposed positions of Laches and Nicias are both deficient. Their respective understandings of courage, as described by their definitions and displayed by their comportment in the discussion, do not succeed in capturing all there is to courage.[42] Laches' understanding of courage is purely intuitive and does not rise above ordinary experience. He therefore displays nothing but the endurance of the foot soldier. Nicias, on the other hand, places himself above ordinary experience only by possessing an abstract and superficial wisdom (consisting of definitions borrowed from others). His courage is therefore one based entirely on skill and cleverness. These deficiencies explain the one thing Laches and Nicias have in common: both of them are motivated in the present discussion by contentiousness (*philonikia*).[43] For neither is *truth* at issue. Both Laches' slight regard for arguments and Nicias's "speaking for the sake of speaking"[44] cut off any access to the truth. We are still talking about *courage* here. Because courage has been found neither in ignorant endurance nor in a sophistical conceit of wisdom, it must have something to do with the search for truth. To see this, however, we must look beyond the "combative" interpretations of courage represented by Laches and Nicias.

Socrates' involvement in the discussion clearly differs from the *philonikia* of the two generals. He is willing to listen to arguments in a way that Laches is not, and he is willing to let go of presumed knowledge in a way that Nicias is not. Yet what exactly distinguishes Socrates' method? If what has been said above is correct, we can expect that the answer to this question will also answer the question What is courage? Just as the generals were seen to display their defective understandings of courage in the very way in which they comport themselves in the discussion, so Socrates can be expected to display a true understanding of courage in the peculiar manner of his comportment.

At the end of the dialogue Socrates claims to be as ignorant as his interlocutors. In one very important sense this is true: Socrates, like Laches and Nicias, has failed to find an irrefutable definition of courage. Throughout the course of the discussion, however, Socrates' ignorance somehow shows itself to be more "knowing" than the ignorance of his interlocutors. This is what explains the very strange closing scene of the dialogue. While earlier in the discussion Socrates kept silent in deference to the greater experience of the two generals, in the closing scene the two generals are unanimous in their opinion that Socrates is the best teacher one could find. They even desire to place their sons under Socrates' tutelage (though Laches regrets that his boys are too young). Why do Laches and Nicias respond in this way to the discussion's outcome? Socrates has proven no more able than they to find the right definition; one would therefore think that they would fall back on their experience and dismiss Socrates as an idle babbler. Yet, despite Socrates' apparent failure to provide a knowledge of courage that goes beyond what ordinary experience tells us, the generals recognize him as their superior. Even odder is the behavior of Lysimachus. Instead of being disappointed with Socrates' failure to define courage, he decides that Socrates is the person to whom he must commit his sons if they are to be as good as possible. But this is not all. Earlier Lysimachus excused himself from participating in the discussion by complaining of his old age and faulty memory (189c6–d1). Now he desires to join his sons in becoming a pupil of Socrates and asserts that as he is the oldest, so is he the most eager to learn (προθυμότατα μανθάνειν, 201b6–8)! He is indeed so eager that he begs Socrates to come to his home *at dawn* the next day.

Anyone who believes that Socrates' "elenchus" is exclusively or even primarily negative in outcome has not looked carefully at this closing scene.[45] Socrates' ignorance is clearly seen to differ from the ignorance of his interlocutors, and Socrates has succeeded in somehow exhibiting a knowledge of the virtue in question. But what exactly is the nature of the courage which Socrates exhibits in the inquiry? The answer is to be found in Socrates' avoidance of the two extremes (and thus the two one-sided accounts of courage) represented by Laches and Nicias. In contrast to Nicias and Stesilaus, Socrates does not place all his trust in any presumed expertise but is ready to abandon what he has achieved if the truth reveals itself to be elsewhere. His method is one exposed to risk and danger, aware that the truth is as elusive as the contingencies of battle and can never be mastered through rules or definitions. Socrates therefore has the courage of recognizing the fallibility of his argumentative expertise and therefore his own vulnerability before the truth. His courage is inseparable from his confession of ignorance. In contrast to Laches, on the other hand, Socrates is not a misologist who questions what argumentation and learning can achieve and passively endures the onslaught of the unknown. He has the courage to risk inquiring beyond experience, to seek knowledge actively, despite the recognition that this knowledge will never provide the victory of complete mastery nor dispel ignorance once and for all.[46] Neither technical expertise nor ignorance require courage: courage is instead to be found in the kind of wisdom that is always threatened by ignorance, that must be reconquered again and again without ever being fully possessed or mastered. It was earlier suggested that the *aporia* encountered in determining whether courage does or does not involve knowledge could be solved, or rather *explained,* by the possibility of a knowledge which is compatible with ignorance and is not a *technē* (i.e., is not a particular skill for controlling and predicting experience). It can now be seen that the possibility of such knowledge is proven by the very way in which Socrates inquires and that Socrates thereby succeeds in *showing* us what courage is despite his failure to define it.

In this way a reading of the *Laches* proves indispensable to understanding Socrates' method, especially in its relation, raised above as a problem, to technical knowledge and knowledge of definitions. Socrates is sometimes thought to be seeking "technical" knowledge.[47] In the present dialogue, however, such knowledge is shown to be not only unnecessary, but even inimical to the exercise of courage (and, apparently, of virtue in general).[48] The knowledge sought by Socrates is the same as that involved in *being* courageous: an open-ended knowledge that does not presume to have eliminated ignorance. Knowledge of a *technē* does not make one courageous; on the contrary, it engenders cowardice by encouraging excessive confidence in one's limited skill. The doctor and the archer are not as such courageous *precisely because they have technical knowledge.* To think, then, that this kind of knowledge is precisely what Socrates seeks is to go against everything the *Laches* shows us.[49] Courage does not involve the anticipation and control of contingencies, and therefore Socrates in seeking to know and have courage cannot be seen as seeking this control. Of course, even the *technai* must fear accidents and chance. However, in this case the *technē* itself is not risky or frightening, since the truth of its principles is assured: the fear and the risk are centered on events completely external to it. In the case of Socratic inquiry, however, it is the inquiry itself that is risky and frightening and that therefore demands great endurance.[50] The knowledge that characterizes both Socrates' own method and his own courage consists of questions, not answers. It is *knowledge* nevertheless, but not of the sort involved in the *technai.*

Some interpreters, however, have attempted to avoid this conclusion. They have argued that the objections made against Laches' definition of courage as "wise endurance," as well as against Nicias's definition of courage as a kind of knowledge, are not meant to apply to *moral knowledge.* In short, the argument is that while courage is incompatible with complete mastery of physical, psychological, or social contingencies and thus with the elimination of any risk or danger in these areas, it is not incompatible with moral certainty, understood as the mastery of moral contingencies and the elimination of all moral risk. In this view, for example, if I go into a battle without expert fighting skill, but with the *absolute certainty* that dying in battle is a greater good for me than running away, I would still be called by Socrates "courageous." This interpretation, if correct, would refute my claim that the only knowledge of good and evil compatible with courage is one that is "open-ended" and has not fully eliminated ignorance.

What reason is there for exempting moral knowledge from the objections in the *Laches* to the identification of courage with "technical" knowledge? Santas has argued that the objections apply only to "knowledge of fact" and not to "knowledge of values" (1969, 446 ff.). This distinction, however, is anachronistic, as Vlastos has noted (1994d, 111). The distinction introduced in its stead by Vlastos himself (1994d, 111–2) and by Carol Gould (1987)[51] is a distinction between the knowledge of lesser goods, which is "technical knowledge," and the knowledge of the greatest good, which is moral knowledge. However, it is hard to see how the simple identification of moral knowledge with knowledge of a good greater than the goods known by the *technai* makes it proof against the arguments of the *Laches*. This interpretation sees the dialogue as allowing us to identify courage with a knowledge of good and evil that is strictly analogous to the *technai*, but is to be found at a higher level, that is, the level of the greatest goods and evils, which are moral goods and evils. But if moral knowledge is *technical* knowledge in the sense that it, like the *technai*, makes possible mastery and the elimination of risk in its own subject matter, then no matter what its subject matter may be, whether the greatest good or lesser goods, it cannot escape the arguments made against identifying courage with technical knowledge per se. Neither Vlastos nor Gould even attempt to show how having as its subject matter the greatest good makes moral knowledge an entirely *different kind of knowledge* from the knowledge that characterizes the *technai:* but this is exactly what they must show if, despite the arguments in the dialogue, they wish to identify courage with knowledge. Santas is therefore closer to the mark in realizing that he must distinguish between two entirely different kinds of knowledge: knowledge of fact and knowledge of value. Unfortunately, he simply appeals to the most readily available modern distinction, rather than letting the dialogue itself reveal the relevant distinction. What the dialogue shows us, in my interpretation, is that the knowledge to be identified with courage must be entirely unlike "technical knowledge," that is, that whatever awareness of the good it provides cannot be such as to enable us fully to master moral contingencies and eliminate moral risk. Santas himself provides a good description of the difference between moral certainty and moral risk but, misled by his fact-value distinction, he does not find any awareness of this difference in the dialogue: "If such general, scientific-like knowledge of good and evil can be had, with its comforting assurance, courage may indeed by dared with confidence—and the other virtues as well. For no matter what the risks, we would at least know that we were doing the better thing. But if not, we are left with the agony of existential decision" (1969, 459). The point of the dialogue is that such "scientific-like knowledge of good and evil" is as incompatible with courage, and for the same reasons, as the "scientific-like knowledge" of the other *technai*.[52] To dare courage with complete confidence is a contradiction, whether this confidence be in one's moral expertise or in one's medical expertise. The dialogue has shown that courage cannot be completely ignorant, that someone ignorant of good and evil could not be courageous. The knowledge of good and evil involved in courage, however, cannot be such as to spare us "the agony of existential decision." This paradoxical "ignorant knowledge" or "knowing ignorance" is not defined in the dialogue; it can't be. However, it is clearly displayed in what Socrates himself does.

This critique of attempts to escape the "agony" with which the dialogue leaves us can conclude with one of Socrates' own examples. Socrates describes a doctor who refuses a patient's entreaty for food and drink and suggests that this doctor is not courageous (192e6–3a2). This claim might seem unproblematic until we recognize a detail that Socrates casually throws in: the patient is the doctor's *son*. Clearly in this case the doctor would suffer greatly at hearing his son's desparate entreaties and would require a good deal of courage to resist them! Why does Socrates refuse to call the doctor's action courageous? There is one simple reason: the doctor *knows* that it is *better* for his son not to drink and eat. It is this completely confident knowledge of what is good that is incompatible with genuine courage. Despite the claims of Vlastos and Gould, I do not see how the point would be any different if the good known were moral rather than physical. If the same man were to refuse his son's entreaties for money to be spent in debauchery, aware that in doing so he runs the terrible risk of losing his rebellious son, but knowing with full confidence that to refuse is morally better, the logic would be the same: he would not be acting courageously. The conclusion is inescapable: courage involves moral risk as much as physical risk, uncertainty concerning the highest good as much as uncertainty concerning the accidents and contingencies of life. Indeed, if the present interpretation of the dialogue is correct, the most dreadful and agonzing, and therefore the greatest, courage is the courage Socrates exhibits in the face of ignorance concerning the ultimate good. This ignorance is not totally blind, since then Socrates' inquiry would be rash and foolish. It is instead that paradoxical "knowing ignorance" encountered above.

For the same reason that the knowledge involved in courage, as well as our knowledge *of* courage, is not a "technical" or "scientific-like" knowledge that could be formulated in any theory, whether as a set of practical rules or as a set of theoretical propositions, it is also not a knowledge of defintions. Not only is there no basis for the common assumption that Socrates sees the knowledge of courage as *definitional*, but this assumption runs counter to the whole thrust of the dialogue. The person who equates the knowledge of courage, and courage itself, with a knowledge of definitions or propositions is *Nicias,* and this belief results in nothing but conceited wisdom and cowardice.[53]

The *Laches* must fail to define courage in order to show us what courage is. The present interpretation of course attempts to express its characteristics in words, and this is to some extent legitimate. Courage is "effable" to the extent that the present dialogue is itself a *discussion* of courage in which everything that is said has its own truth and therefore importance. The knowledge, however, in which all of these elements are unified and grounded cannot itself be adequately expressed in any propositions but is communicated solely by the *way* in which Socrates *inquires* (and more generally by what takes place in the dialogue as a whole). The present remarks are intended only to distinguish this knowledge from what it is not and point the reader in its direction.

The dialogue ends with an image that captures perfectly what we have been *shown* in the discussion on courage: the old Lysimachus surrendering the security and complacency to which his old age entitles him in order to place himself on a level with boys in the quest for truth.

The *Charmides* on Temperance

In the *Charmides* we find some of the same themes encountered in the *Laches*. Though these two dialogues focus on different virtues, they prove upon examination to be very similar in both structure and content. If there is any significant sense in which the virtues are "one," it is to be found in this similarity.

The dialogue is narrated by Socrates, who begins by recounting his return from the battle of Potidaea. Socrates has been away for some time and so is eager to hear about the present state of philosophy in Athens. More specifically, he wants to know if there are now any young men in the city who distinguish themselves through either wisdom or beauty or both. Critias informs him that there is in fact a youth who excels in both respects and that he is Critias's own cousin Charmides. At that moment the boy enters the palaestra where Socrates and Critias are conversing. Socrates is struck by his beauty and noble mien. When Charmides approaches and sits down beside him Socrates happens to see inside the boy's cloak and almost loses control of himself (ἐφλεγόμην καὶ οὐκέτ' ἐν ἐμαυτοῦ ἦν, 155d4). However, Socrates wants to know whether or not the beauty of the boy's body is matched by the beauty of his soul. Therefore, having heard that Charmides suffers from bad headaches, he lures the boy into a discussion on the pretext that the head can be cured only if the soul is cured and the soul can be treated only through "beautiful discourse" (καλοὶ λόγοι, 157a3–5). Such discourse can implant in the soul *sōphrosunē* (temperance), and, once this is present, it is easy to procure health for the head as well as for the rest of the body.

Especially noteworthy in this opening scene is the way in which Socrates almost loses control of himself in perceiving Charmides' beauty but then tries to regain self-control by *talking* to the boy. The discussion therefore begins as an act of temperance on Socrates' part.[54] But does the opening scene tell us anything about the presence or absence of temperance in the young Charmides? Drew Hyland has suggested that Charmides' "morning headaches" are nothing more mysterious than the common hangover.[55] Charmides is therefore to be seen as "something of a young carouser" who can be cured only by the temperance which Socrates' discourse can instill. This is an interesting suggestion, though I do not find it entirely convincing.[56] However, even if we accept the existence of this serious flaw in Charmides' character, it is important to recognize that the dialogue also portrays him as a youth of great promise who possesses at least an incipient, naive form of temperance. This is made clear in a crucial episode that immediately follows Socrates' description of his cure, an episode that Hyland unfortunately ignores (158c–d). Critias has asserted that Charmides excels all others not only in appearance but also in temperance (157c–d). Socrates responds by first praising at much length Charmides' ancestors in what is obviously an effort to tempt the boy to indulge in pride. After this temptation Socrates directly asks the boy whether or not he in fact possesses temperance. As the poor Charmides recognizes, he cannot answer this question without self-contradiction. If he asserts that he has temperance, this assertion will exhibit a pride that contradicts the possession of what he claims to have. If, on the other hand, he denies that he has temperance, this denial will wrong both himself and his cousin and thus show him to be lacking in virtue. What then is Charmides to do? *He blushes.* This failure to answer the question is the best answer he could have given. His blush *shows* that he possesses the temperance which he only would have concealed in *claiming* to have it.

The rest of the dialogue, I suggest, can be regarded as a reenactment of this scene on a higher plane. At the dialogue's end we have, instead of a blush, an avowal of ignorance. After having shown the inadequacy of several proposed definitions of temperance, Socrates confesses to not knowing what it is. In this very confession, however, Socrates succeeds in *showing* us what temperance is. To demonstrate this is the aim of the following discussion of the dialogue. The parallel between Charmides' blush and Socrates' avowal of ignorance is drawn here at the outset in order to raise as a problem their difference: if Socrates fails to define temperance, does he yet succeed in going beyond the ordinary understanding of temperance represented by Charmides' blush? In the *Laches* we were presented with a parallel problem: how does the "ignorant" courage Socrates exhibits differ from the purely intuitive and "experiential" courage displayed by Laches? The general question is again how Socrates' dialectic, in failing to attain "results," might yet attain a knowledge that is not already present at the level of ordinary experience and discourse. Is Socrates' failure to answer the question "What is temperance?" really any advance over Charmides' inability to answer the same question?

What must be avoided is the mistake of thinking that Charmides really does not have any temperance.[57] What Socrates proceeds to say might encourage this mistake. In explaining his demand that Charmides say what temperance is, Socrates makes the following suggestion: "If temperance is in you it must necessarily provide some perception of itself [αἴσθησίν τινα παρέχειν] on which you might base an opinion as to just what kind of a thing it is" (ὅτι ἐστὶν καὶ ὁποῖον τι, 159a1–3). Since Charmides ultimately does not succeed in saying what temperance is, this might be seen as proof that he does not have temperance. It must be noted, however, that Charmides *will* proceed to say something about temperance. Though his definitions will prove inadequate, they clearly are not altogether false.[58] He does not provide an *irrefutable* definition of temperance, but then neither does Socrates. Furthermore, Socrates' claim in the above passage is only that the possession of temperance must provide us with *some perception* of it. What exactly this perception is or can be, we are not told.[59] The question is precisely whether or not Socrates' dialectic succeeds in providing us with a kind of "perception" that differs from that vague intuition present at the level of ordinary experience.

After having "looked within himself," Charmides offers a definition that remains very close to the ordinary understanding of temperance: it is a kind of "quietness" or "stillness" (ἡσυχιότης τις, 159b5). Charmides' perception certainly does not deceive him here. He knows that people who are boisterous, obnoxious, highly excitable, and overly eager are thereby found wanting in temperance. Charmides recognizes that he is temperate precisely in lacking such qualities and that therefore temperance must in contrast be a form of quietness. Charmides has thus done exactly what Socrates asked him to do.

Socrates, however, shows this definition to be inadequate. Temperance cannot be defined as quietness because there are some cases in which quietness is not temperance. Socrates makes this point by having Charmides agree that temperance is *good* and then showing that there are some actions in which quietness is *not* good. For example, in reading, writing, playing the lyre, or wrestling, quickness or eagerness (ταχυτής, ὀξύτης)[60] is clearly better than quietness. If temperance, then, were nothing but quietness, in the case of these activities it would be something bad: this, however, contradicts the supposition that temperance is always good. So far Socrates' argument is perfectly cogent. What has troubled some commentators is Socrates' further claim that in the mentioned activities temperance is actually quickness.[61] In reaching this conclusion Socrates' reasoning appears to be as follows:

1. Temperance is good.
2. In actions x, y, and z, quietness is not good.
3. Therefore, in actions x, y, and z, temperance is not quietness.
4. In actions x, y, and z, quickness is good.
5. Therefore, in actions x, y, and z, temperance is quickness.

This argument would be valid if (1) were turned into an identity statement: temperance is *the same as* goodness. Then in showing that quickness is good, we would also be showing that it is temperate. As Socrates introduces (1), however, it is *not* an identity statement: temperance is said only to belong to the class of goods. The argument therefore appears fallacious. Socrates, however, can make assumptions which he does not explicitly state, and the one he clearly makes here is: (6) in the case of activities x, y, and z, there is a temperate way of engaging in x, y, and z. Since temperance is good, the temperate way of engaging in these activities must correspond to the *good* way. Since in these activities the quick way is the best way, Socrates concludes that it must also be the temperate way. The final conclusion is that temperance is to be found as much in quick as in quiet actions. (This is surely confirmed by experience: temperance is not sloth.) It may still be objected that Socrates fails to distinguish between temperate actions and other kinds of good actions. But how could he make this distinction? He does not claim to know yet what temperance is. Furthermore, his intention is not to prove Charmides' definition completely wrong, but to show that it does not do justice to temperance as a good.

After thinking further and making a brave effort to examine himself, Charmides suggests a second definition: temperance is shame or modesty (αἰδώς, 160e3–5). This definition suffers from the same defect as the previous one: temperance has been agreed to be always good, while shame is often bad. This definition, in other words, does not tell us what makes temperance *good*. However, it represents an advance over the first one in at least one very important respect. We know from other dialogues, especially the *Gorgias* and the *Symposium*, that shame can be a distinctively philosophical feeling. Alcibiades describes how Socrates' discourse has the effect of making him feel ashamed of himself (216b–c). Gorgias and Polus (and perhaps even Callicles in his silence) succumb to shame as a result of Socrates' arguments (461b, 482c–e). Socrates' ability to make his interlocutors feel shame, however, coincides with his ability *to make them know themselves*. Shame is the beginning of self-knowledge. When we consider, therefore, that temperance will later in the dialogue be explicitly identified with self-knowledge, the importance of Charmides' definition becomes clear. The self-knowledge whose nature Socrates will attempt to determine in the remainder of the dialogue is already partly manifest in the shame which Charmides sees as essential to being temperate. In this sense, then, Charmides' definition anticipates what Socrates will say later: the difference is that what Charmides says does not rise above the level of naive, ordinary experience.

Charmides' definition also reveals a circularity in the inquiry like that noted in the *Laches*. In defining temperance as shame Charmides is only describing temperance as he himself exhibited it earlier when he blushed at Socrates' "indiscreet" question. But this is of course what Socrates is asking him to do: to examine and look within himself and then report on what he perceives. If, however, temperance is in some sense self-knowledge, as is suggested later, Socrates is asking the boy not only to *define* temperance, but also to *exhibit* it in the process. Thus the circularity that will be seen to characterize temperance as self-knowledge also characterizes the very inquiry into temperance. In seeking to understand temperance, Charmides seeks only to understand himself, but then temperance appears to be precisely this self-understanding. We might then expect to find a parallel process in Socrates. In seeking to define self-knowledge Socrates is only seeking to understand himself and is therefore in this very search already exhibiting self-knowledge. These circles cannot be ignored by any attempt to understand the dialogue.

The first two definitions of temperance proposed by Charmides have been seen to reflect our ordinary experience and on this level they are clearly *true*. With the third definition, however, the dialogue arrives at a major turning point. Charmides now stops looking within himself, stops relying on his own experience, and instead merely reports a definition which he has heard suggested by someone else. Temperance, he has heard said, is "doing your own business" (τὸ τὰ ἑαυτοῦ πράττειν, 161b5–6). Socrates immediately suspects that Critias himself or some other "wise" person (τῶν σοφῶν, 161c1) is the source of the definition. Despite his initial denial, Critias is indeed the source and therefore takes Charmides' place as Socrates' interlocutor in the second half of the dialogue. The transition is a very important one. While Charmides has been seen to rely on his own experience in answering Socrates' questions, Critias will be seen to rely on what he has learned from the sophists. As a result, Critias's definitions will indeed be more "sophisticated," but they will lack the immediacy and concreteness of those suggested by his cousin. If Charmides' definitions proved *too concrete*, too narrowly limited to his own experience, those of Critias will prove to be empty formulas. The discussion of the dialogue as a whole therefore occurs in the tension between these two extremes.

The transition is also important in demonstrating the inability of ordinary experience to provide a real understanding of virtue and thus the need for the analytical skills perfected by the sophists. Charmides does not persist in the arduous task of self-inquiry but instead offers a definition picked up from someone else. Given what has been said above concerning the self-referential character of the discussion, it is not hard to see that Charmides in failing at this point to look within himself is *failing to be temperate*. Though his blush in reply to Socrates' earlier question exhibited temperance, we now see that this temperance does not go very deep. When seriously challenged, Charmides contradicts the promise he had initially shown. This is why Socrates at this point calls him "wicked" (μιαρέ, 161b8), partly in jest, but clearly with some seriousness. This is the general problem with ordinary experience: it clearly exhibits some awareness of the nature of virtue, but this awareness is easily clouded and abandoned. This defect then creates an opening for the positive instruction offered by the sophists. This sophistic knowledge will in turn prove to be divorced from experience and concrete self-awareness and thus equally capable of degenerating into the opposite of virtue.

The parallel here between the *Charmides* and the *Laches* is striking. There the first part of the discussion takes place between Laches and Socrates. Laches, like Charmides, provides definitions that are based on ordinary experience, but that for this very reason prove too limited. When this discussion reaches an impasse, Laches is unable to persist in the inquiry and thereby betrays a lack of courage. Nicias then takes Laches' place as Socrates' interlocutor. Nicias, like Critias, cares little for experience and has acquired his knowledge from the sophists. For this reason his definition, like those of Critias, proves to lack determinate content. Socrates' own ignorance was seen to mediate between the extremes represented by his naive and sophisticated interlocutors. This will prove to be the case in the *Charmides* as well. This similarity of structure in the two dialogues is grounded in the tension within dialectic itself between the understanding of virtue found within our ordinary experience and the "purely rational" account of virtue on which the sophists pride themselves.

Socrates first brings into question the definition of temperance as "doing one's own business" by interpreting it so narrowly that it is taken to exclude even writing another person's name. In the *Republic* we find the same definition, but there it is a definition of justice and "doing one's own business" is given a very different interpretation: doing that particular task for which one has a natural aptitude. Here "doing one's own business" is instead interpreted as doing everything that concerns one (such as making one's own shoes or weaving one's own coat). Socrates can therefore claim here that a state in which everyone did his own business would *not* be a temperate state, since it would not be *well ordered* (σωφρόνως γε οἰκοῦσα εὖ ἂν οἰκοῖτο 162a; note how here again temperance is assumed to be good).

The element of self-knowledge in this definition of temperance should not be overlooked. One cannot do one's own business if one does not know oneself. In Socrates' interpretation of the definition, however, the self-knowledge required is a superficial one: to know oneself is here simply to know what belongs to one (such as one's name, one's shoes, or one's coat). But why does Socrates give such a superficial interpretation of the definition, when he could have interpreted it in the way he does in the *Republic*? One reason is surely his desire to lure the suspected author of the definition, Critias, into the discussion. But Socrates also wants to show that the definition, unless qualified and given specific content, is just an empty formula vulnerable to the most ludicrous interpretations.

Seeing that Charmides is allowing what is in fact his own definition to be refuted, Critias can no longer control himself (162c) but joins the argument, angry and quarrelsome. Thus Critias's very entrance into the discussion, not to mention the highly aggressive manner in which he proceeds to defend his definition, betrays his intemperance. The obvious reply to Socrates' criticism would be to suggest an interpretation of "doing one's own business" like that given in the *Republic*. This is not, however, Critias's reply. What he objects to in Socrates' criticism is its suggestion that temperance should involve such base activities as making shoes. He therefore makes a distinction between "making" (ποιεῖν) and "doing" (πράττειν), supporting it through a ludicrous interpretation of Hesiod (163b–c). Nicias, it will be recalled, answered an objection to his definition of courage by making a similar verbal distinction. The source in both cases is said to be the sophist Prodicus. Critias's distinction is that "making" can often be something bad or base, whereas "doing" is by definition always "doing what is good." In defining temperance as *doing one's own business*," therefore, he was *really* defining it as nothing but "doing what is good" (ἡ τῶν ἀγαθῶν πρᾶξις, 163e10–11).

Critias thus saves his definition only at the cost of leaving out any element of self-knowledge. While "doing one's own business" necessarily involves knowing oneself, it is not immediately evident that this is also true of "doing what is good." We can suspect that Critias has also omitted self-knowledge in another important sense: he has clearly not introspected or employed self-reflection in discovering his new definition. Instead he has used a verbal distinction learned from the sophists simply to avoid refutation. Here we encounter the peculiar circularity once again. Not only does Critias fail to take account of self-knowledge in what he says, but he also thereby reveals a lack of self-knowledge.

Socrates therefore concentrates on exposing this deficiency in the definition. He points out that in many cases one does not know whether one's actions will result in good or evil. If, then, temperance is equated with doing good, one will often not know whether or not one is being temperate. As Critias himself admits, however, this is impossible. One cannot be temperate without knowing it. This impossibility brings out the element of self-knowledge that has more than once already proven to be essential to temperance.

Critias's response is revealing. Instead of qualifying his definition in such a way as to include self-knowledge, he abandons it altogether. He claims not to be ashamed (αἰσχύνεσθαι) to admit that he made a mistake and offers to retract everything he said previously (165a8–b1). This lack of shame itself betrays, if there is any truth in Charmides' second definition, a lack of temperance. The position Critias now wants to defend, and in support of which he cites the authority of the oracle at Delphi, is that temperance is identical with knowing oneself (τὸ γιγνώσκειν αὐτὸν ἑαυτόν, 165b4). Note that while the previous definition left out any element of self-knowledge, the present one ignores any relation that temperance might have to the good. Yet this relation has asserted itself throughout the whole of the preceding discussion. The definitions of Charmides were shown to be inadequate precisely by an appeal to this relation. Now Critias wants in effect to leave behind all that has gone before, as if the preceding discussion has been of no value whatsoever. In this respect Critias is like many interpreters of the dialogues who think that, if a definition is proven inadequate, it has not succeeded in showing us anything. Therefore, what did come through in the previous discussion, namely, the relation between temperance and the good, is completely left out of account by Critias's new definition.

Yet the definition of temperance as "knowing oneself" is clearly a good one and is perhaps the most promising of the definitions advanced so far. As has been suggested, Charmides' definition of temperance as shame already foreshadowed this identification of temperance with self-knowledge. However, though promising, this identification remains a bare assertion unless it is given some definite content. Charmides' definitions were given content by his own experience: he not only claimed that temperance is shame, but this is how temperance actually showed itself in him. In the case of Critias, however, we do not find this correspondence: in asserting that temperance is self-knowledge, he himself displays very little self-knowledge. When one of his definitions proves inadequate, he simply latches on to another and challenges Socrates to refute him if he disagrees (165b3–4).[62] He therefore clearly believes that the truth is to be found in a definition, rather than in himself or in what is revealed gradually through the process of inquiry. In thus thinking that the "wisdom" he has borrowed from the sophists assures him of a firm hold on the truth, he deceives himself. This self-deception is what Socrates will uncover in showing that Critias can in fact give no content to his definition. The self-knowledge with which he identifies temperance will prove to be as empty as his own self-knowledge.

Because Critias's new definition divorces temperance from the good, Socrates begins his refutation by questioning the *value* of self-knowledge. If temperance is knowing oneself, then it clearly must be a kind of "knowledge" (*epistēmē*, 165c4–6). Other kinds of knowledge, however, such as medicine and the art of building, bring about some good (health in the one case and shelter in the other). What good, then, does the "knowledge of the self" bring about (ἀπεργάζεσθαι, 165c8–e2)? Critias's response is that not every kind of knowledge *produces* something: geometry and arithmetic, for example, have no product (165e3–166a2). Socrates points out, however, that even these types of knowledge have objects that are distinct from themselves. In other words, each one is a knowledge *of* something (τινος; 166a3–b6). Of what, then, is temperance the knowledge? Critias responds again that the analogy does not hold: other types of knowledge are indeed of something other than themselves; temperance, however, is the only kind of knowledge that is *a knowledge of itself and of other kinds of knowledge* (166b9–e6). Temperance is therefore a kind of "metaknowledge." It is not knowledge of a specific object distinct from itself, but rather knowledge of all types of knowledge as such, including itself. It is, in short, *a knowledge of knowledge*.

Many scholars have considered illegitimate the move from self-knowledge to the knowledge of knowledge.[63] Clearly, they argue, self-knowledge is knowledge of an object distinct from itself, namely the self, and therefore is not rightly defined as an empty knowledge of knowledge. Yet this objection ignores the following problem: if in self-knowledge the self is made distinct from the activity of knowing as its *object*, it ceases to be *the self*. In this case, the self is what is doing the knowing, not what is known. If knowledge, therefore, is necessarily always directed toward an object distinct from itself, there can be no genuine *self*-knowledge. Conversely, if there is to be any genuine self-knowledge, knowledge must be capable of turning back upon itself; self-knowledge, in other words, can take place only as the knowledge of knowledge. Therefore, the problems that will be encountered in attempting to show the possibility and usefulness of a knowledge of knowledge are also problems encountered in any attempt to understand self-knowledge. The paradox of self-knowledge is that by definition it undermines the distinction between the subject knowing and the object known. Once this is seen, the transition from self-knowledge to the knowledge of knowledge appears not only legitimate but profound: it enables us to see just what kind of a knowledge we are dealing with in knowing ourselves.[64]

When Critias ends his reply by accusing Socrates of picking a fight, Socrates responds that he is acting only out of fear that he might deceive himself into thinking that he knows what he in fact does not know (166d1–2). Plato's dramatic skill is here most apparent. While Critias is merely asserting that temperance is a knowledge of knowledge, Plato has Socrates *display* this knowledge of knowledge. The juxtaposition is revealing: Critias, who confidently asserts that he knows what temperance is, shows little sign of having it, whereas Socrates, who does not presume to know what it is, clearly does have it.[65] Here we begin to see the possibility of a more positive reading of the *Charmides* than has been offered by other interpreters. Critias is incapable of giving content to his definition of temperance as a knowledge of knowledge: he himself does not display this knowledge, and he is incapable of defining it. Therefore his definition will prove empty by the end of the dialogue: the knowledge of which he speaks will appear neither beneficial nor even possible. What the present passage suggests, however, is that what Critias says about a knowledge of knowledge may be given content by the temperance which Socrates himself displays in the course of the inquiry. What we must ask ourselves, then, is whether the knowledge Socrates himself exhibits is a knowledge with no object other than itself. And if this is the case, is Socrates' self-knowledge empty, as the ostensive results of the inquiry would suggest? Or do we find reconciled in Socrates the two poles between which temperance oscillates in the dialogue, that is, the good and self-knowledge?

Not surprisingly, Critias has overlooked the fact that self-knowledge involves more than knowing what one knows: it also, and perhaps most important, involves knowing what one *does not know*. (This is not surprising because Critias has so far shown little awareness of his own ignorance.) Socrates therefore points out that the knowledge of knowledge must also be knowledge of the lack of knowledge (166e7–9). His subsequent description of the man who has this knowledge perfectly parallels his self-description in the *Apology:* such a man would go around testing others to determine what they know and what they only think they know (167a1–7). This is one more indication that Socrates has the knowledge which he and Critias are seeking to define.[66] Yet Socrates proceeds to ask if this knowledge is possible and if it is of any use (ὠφελία). The first obstacle to a demonstration of its possibility is its uniqueness. Nothing can be found that is related to itself in the way in which temperance appears to be. There is no such thing as a seeing of seeing or a hearing of hearing or a desire of desire or a will of will. It would therefore require a great man, Socrates says, to show that there is a class of self-related things and that temperance is among them (169a1–7).

This is a serious problem. How do you demonstrate the existence of a type of knowledge that is unique and prior to all other types? In what terms could you explain this knowledge? Its existence clearly does not admit of direct proof but must be shown, if at all, *indirectly*. Specifically, it can be shown to be presupposed by something else that clearly *is* possible. But then is not the existence of a knowledge of knowledge demonstrated by the mere *possibility* of the present inquiry, regardless of its success or failure? Indeed, does not the negative result of the inquiry itself exhibit this knowledge of knowledge?

This will prove to be the case, but for now Socrates allows the possibility of a knowledge of knowledge to be assumed; he is more concerned with the other question of what *benefit* it might provide. For even if a knowledge of knowledge is possible, it cannot be identified with temperance unless it can do us some good. In this way Socrates brings the discussion back to the relation between temperance and the good. If the knowledge of knowledge does not prove beneficial, it can no more be identified with temperance than could quietness and shame.

The knowledge of knowledge would clearly be of great benefit if it could help us determine whether or not we know something in particular. Socrates objects, however, that only a particular science can determine whether or not one knows the object of that science. For example, only a knowledge of medicine will enable one to distinguish between a quack and a true physician. In the absence of this knowledge, no "knowledge of knowledge" will enable one to determine, by testing others, whether or not *they* know medicine (170a6–c11).[67] Here, then, we encounter an important problem: the priority and uniqueness of the knowledge of knowledge has apparently been bought only at the cost of depriving it of content. Because it is distinct from and higher than the other forms of knowledge, it cannot know their objects. Socrates therefore concludes that if temperance is a knowledge of knowledge, it cannot involve knowing *what* one does or does not know (ἅ τε οἶδεν καὶ ἃ μὴ οἶδεν), but only *that* one does or does not know (ὅτι οἶδεν καὶ ὅτι οὐκ οἶδεν μόνον, 170d1–3). The temperate man could therefore determine whether or not a person has knowledge, but not whether or not this person has knowledge of something in particular. In this case, however, temperance would be totally useless. The knowledge of knowledge, precisely on account of its self-relatedness, has proven empty and therefore incapable of benefiting us.

Socrates does suggest that this knowledge may have some small advantage. For example, one may be quicker at learning if one knows what knowledge is, and one may also be better able to determine whether or not someone else knows something which one knows oneself (172b1–c3). However, this paltry benefit seems unworthy of temperance. A parallel is the recommendation of philosophy as a means of improving one's reasoning skills. While this may indeed be a benefit provided by philosophy, it is only incidental. Likewise, temperance must be much more than a technique for greater facility in learning.

Now the discussion takes a startling turn. Socrates claims that *even if* temperance could provide us with a knowledge of *what* we do and do not know, *it is still not clear that it would really benefit us* (172c4–173a6)! Socrates then tells of a "dream" in which he has seen that a state characterized by temperance in this sense would indeed be one in which no error or falsehood exists. Each person would do only what he or she knows how to do. Only those who really know medicine would claim to be doctors, and only those who really know how to steer a ship would claim to be pilots. Because no one in this state would believe that he knows those things of which he is in fact ignorant, no one would either deceive or be deceived. Even prophecy would not mislead, but would accurately describe the future. The state would thus be perfectly ordered: all citizens would live in comfort and safety, enjoying the fruits of true human knowledge without succumbing to the dangers of feigned knowledge. But how can Socrates doubt that temperance would in this case be of the greatest benefit to us? What Socrates doubts is that the state just described would be a *good* and *happy* state. In this state there is knowledge of all the arts and sciences and no falsehood: but can this knowledge ensure happiness and goodness? This is exactly what Socrates questions: "that in acting with knowledge we will act well and be happy [ὅτι δ' ἐπιστημόνως ἂν πράττοντες εὖ ἂν πράττοιμεν καὶ εὐδαιμονοῖμεν], this we have yet to learn, my dear Critias" (173d3–5). Knowledge of any or all objects of the arts and sciences does not seem to guarantee goodness or happiness—a state, therefore, in which everyone does what he or she knows how to do is not necessarily a good or happy state.[68]

When Critias objects that, if knowledge does not provide one with happiness and goodness, nothing else can, Socrates asks him to specify what kind of knowledge he is talking about (173d6–174b9). Is it a knowledge of making shoes that will make us happy? Or a knowledge of working bronze? When Critias rejects these and other suggestions, Socrates asks him to specify what kind of knowledge he considers the happy man to have, since he clearly believes that one is happy by having knowledge *of something*. Finally, Critias is led to identify the knowledge that will make one happy with the knowledge of good and evil. Here Socrates vehemently protests that Critias has been leading him around in circles (κύκλῳ, 174b11). The circle is of course the movement away from, and the present return to, the association of temperance with the good. Critias has spoken as if *knowledge as such* is what makes one happy, when in fact he has been thinking all along of a very specific knowledge, that is, the knowledge of good and evil. This latter knowledge, however, is completely distinct from all other kinds of knowledge. If it were not to exist, all arts and sciences would still exist. The art of shoemaking would still cover our feet, medicine would still cure us, and strategy would still win battles. Without the knowledge of good and evil, however, none of these things would be well and beneficially done (174c3–d2).

One might expect Socrates simply to identify temperance with a knowledge of good and evil. Yet he does not do so. Instead the dialogue ends in *aporia*. What is to be made of this outcome? What is it supposed to show us about the nature of temperance? There are four possible interpretations: (I1) there really is no solution; Plato in writing the dialogue simply did not know what temperance is;[69] (I2) temperance is the knowledge of knowledge; the arguments against this view are not decisive;[70] (I3) temperance is the knowledge of good and evil; the refutation of the view that temperance is the knowledge of knowledge is conclusive and therefore justifies the inference that the rival suggestion is the true one;[71] (I4) temperance is *both* the knowledge of knowledge *and* the knowledge of good and evil.[72] I1 should be considered last, since we cannot reasonably accept it without first looking to see if the dialogue offers a positive solution.

The arguments presented against the knowledge of knowledge appear too thorough and strong to allow for I2. The difficulties in understanding the possibility and benefit of knowledge *which has solely itself as its content and subject matter* seem genuine.[73] More importantly, the connection between temperance and the good receives too much emphasis in this dialogue (not only at the end, but in Critias's second definition and in the refutations of all the other definitions) to allow us to disassociate temperance from knowledge of the good.

I3 does not appear any more desirable. In Charmides' definition of temperance as "shame," in Socrates' objection that Critias's definition, "doing what is good," excludes self-knowledge, in Critias's reference to the famous command "Know thyself!" in the allusions to Socrates' own self-knowledge, the association of temperance with self-knowledge is too persistent to be simply dismissed. Furthermore, since Socrates never claims to know more than his own lack of knowledge, a consequence of I3 is that Socrates lacks temperance.[74] This consequence is very hard to reconcile with how Socrates is portrayed in the dialogue: his calm return from battle, his self-control before the allure of Charmides' radiant nakedness, his ability to spot immediately what is wrong in the different accounts of temperance and to steer the discussion toward increased understanding of at least the requirements and conditions of temperance, and the assumption on the part of all the interlocutors at the end of the dialogue that Socrates is the person from whom to learn temperance: all of these facets of Socrates' portrayal make it highly unlikely that we are meant to see him as lacking temperance.

Given the defects of I2 and I3, I4, which can combine their strengths, cannot help but appear ideal. However, the reason why hardly any scholars have jumped at this solution is the extraordinary difficulty of explaining it. This difficulty becomes apparent when we recognize what the solution *cannot* mean: it cannot mean that temperance is simply the "adding together" of a knowledge of knowledge and a knowledge of good and evil that otherwise are completely distinct and have nothing to do with each other. Such a solution would lack the unity Socrates always seeks in asking what a virtue is: in form it would not differ from Meno's definition of virtue as this *and* that *and* that. Also, this solution, by allowing the knowledge of knowledge to remain completely external and accidental to the knowledge of good and evil, would not save it from the objections against its possibility and benefit. Therefore, in order to work, I4 would need to make a much stronger claim: that temperance can be both the knowledge of knowledge and the knowledge of good and evil because these two kinds of knowledge *are essentially the same and inseparable.*

The difficulty with this suggestion is obvious. How can these two kinds of knowledge possibly be the same? The most striking and apparently insurmountable difference between the knowledge of knowledge and the knowledge of good and evil is that, while the former was seen to have no object distinct from itself, the latter clearly does. There is a difference between knowledge of the good and the good itself. But what exactly is the nature of this difference? And is it the same as the difference that is *not* supposed to exist between subject and "object" in the case of knowledge of knowledge? As Socrates' questions suggest, there are two ways in which the *technai*[75] can differ from their objects: the object either is *produced* by the *technē* (as in the case of the art of building) or is its preexistent subject matter (as the odd and the even are distinct from calculation). The knowledge of knowledge was shown not to have an object in either of these two senses. Therefore, the knowledge of the good can also be a knowledge of knowledge *only if it is not a technē*, that is, only if the good of which it is the knowledge is neither a "product" like a house nor an "object" like the "odd and the even."[76]

But now this solution, despite its remaining obscurity, begins to look more promising. The interpretation of the *Laches* offered above revealed that the knowledge of the good does not there, any more than the knowledge of knowledge here, fit the *technē* model. In the knowledge of the good that characterizes courage, the good cannot be some "product"[77] over which we have complete control and for the attainment of which we can prescribe infallible rules, nor can it be an "object" which we can fully analyze and explicate in a theory. Therefore, such a knowledge of the good, not being *of* some product or object, could perhaps be characterized by the reflexivity that characterizes the knowledge of knowledge.

But what is the nature of this reflexivity? It should be recalled that Socrates himself in the *Charmides* makes clear that he does not consider the knowledge of good and evil to be on a level with the *technai*. With his "dream" he shows that a scientific and technical life, by which apparently is meant a life in which any of the objects which can be known *are* known, is possible without a knowledge of good and evil. The reason is that this knowledge, rather than being *of* a particular domain of objects, concerns the *manner* in which the *technai* produce and examine *their* objects. In this sense, the knowledge of good and evil *is* a knowledge of knowledge. "Good" and "evil" are not objects among other objects that as such comprise the subject matter of a particular science. Good and evil are not known in the way that the stars are known by astronomy. Good and evil are instead to be found in the *way* in which we deal with objects or, more specifically, in the *way* in which we live. The knowledge of good and evil is of a higher order than the other sciences because, not being restricted to a certain kind of objects, it knows whether or not the *way* in which any of the arts and sciences go about their business is good. This of course does not mean that a person with this knowledge can tell a carpenter how to make a chair, but this person could tell the carpenter whether or not the chair he makes is fitting or suitable within the context of its intended use or even within the wider context of well-being and happiness. In short, the knowledge of good and evil is not a *technē*, that is, it is not an art that enables one to master a particular domain of objects. This knowledge is directed more toward the "how" of knowing and living than the "what."[78] Knowledge *of* the good means here knowing *how to be good* or *how to do things well.*[79] This knowledge thus does not appear distinct from its "object" in the way that the *technai* are distinct from their objects. In an important sense, the knowledge of good and evil *does not have* an "object."[80]

As a result, the knowledge of good and evil has a second peculiar characteristic: it is assumed throughout the present inquiry that in *knowing* the good one *is* good. Here the distinction between this knowledge and the *technai* becomes especially clear. In knowing the odd and the even one does not become odd and even. In calculation, the object is completely external to the knowledge. This externality, however, is not present in the knowledge of good and evil. My knowledge of the good is itself good; in knowing the good I become good. This means that in some sense the good *is the same as* the knowledge of the good. Yet the good cannot be the same as knowledge *simpliciter*, since then Socrates' distinction between the scientific life and the good life would no longer hold. The good must therefore be found in a *particular kind of knowing*. For the reasons given above, however, one cannot define what kind of knowledge this is by simply pointing to its "object."

But if the good is not just any kind of knowledge and also does not differ from other kinds of knowledge by being restricted to a particular subject matter, then what kind of knowledge is it? The answer seems to be that it is knowledge of knowledge. But if it is true that the good is to be located in this kind of knowledge, it is not true that it is to be *reduced* to it. The knowledge of knowledge has been shown to be empty when given no further content. The good, then, must be made manifest in the knowledge of knowledge without being reducible to it. But how can the knowledge of knowledge as such be the knowledge of something distinct from itself (the good)? The answer is that the good is not a particular object *of* knowledge but is rather something revealed in the very knowledge of knowledge. I know the good in the very process of examining myself and what I know. Though I can know a mathematical theorem in abstraction from any self-knowledge, I cannot know the good in this way. But now we see what makes the knowledge of knowledge beneficial: in this knowledge alone do we know the good. The converse holds as well: only in knowing the good do we know ourselves.

Yet the stated result of the inquiry is that the knowledge of knowledge is empty and therefore incapable of benefiting anyone. What explains this result if I4 is the intended solution and the knowledge of knowledge in fact *does* have content as knowledge of the good? Part of the explanation is to be found in the very way in which the inquiry began. As has been seen, Critias went from defining temperance as "doing what is good" to defining it as "self-knowledge," without any awareness of a connection between the two. When his first definition failed, he simply abandoned it in favor of an altogether different one by which he thought to have more success in the argument. This procedure was seen to be a sign of Critias's own lack of real temperance. In his case knowledge is truly disassociated from the good in such a way as to become empty. This means that the conclusion according to which temperance as the knowledge of knowledge is empty and useless is a result of Critias's own lack of temperance and of the consequent flaw in his own method of inquiry.[81]

All the "blame," however, cannot be put on Critias. The major cause of the *aporia* as well as its solution are revealed in a sentence by which Socrates summarizes what has taken place throughout the course of the dialogue: "For certainly that which is agreed to be the best of all things [temperance] would not have appeared of no benefit if I had been of any benefit in searching well" (οὐ γὰρ ἄν που . . . τοῦτο ἡμῖν ἀνωφελὲς ἐφάνη, εἴ τι ἐμοῦ ὄφελος ἦν πρὸς τὸ καλῶς ζητεῖν, 175a11–b2). Read superficially, this sentence is simply another expression of Socrates' humility; looked at more carefully, however, it neatly ties together the questions "Is temperance beneficial?" and "Is Socrates' method of inquiry beneficial?" Here a recognition of the previously mentioned reflexivity of the dialogue proves most fruitful. Temperance would prove beneficial if Socrates' method of inquiry were beneficial. Temperance would show itself to be good if Socrates' search for it were itself good. At first glance, however, Socrates' method does not seem at all beneficial. It is essential to recognize that the negative description of temperance with which the dialogue concludes is a description of what Socrates' own method at first appears to be. What Socrates himself practices is not this art or that science, but only "the knowledge of knowledge." This is brought out in the allusion to the *Apology* mentioned above but is also evident in what Socrates *does* throughout the dialogue. When he expresses his fear of thinking that he knows what he does not know, he shows himself to be striving for "knowledge of knowledge." When throughout the course of the dialogue he refutes definitions proposed by his interlocutors, he shows himself to have more "knowledge of knowledge" than they do. When at the end of the dialogue he confesses his own ignorance, he once again shows himself to be in possession of this "knowledge of knowledge." Is, then, Socrates' own knowledge of knowledge beneficial? At first this does not seem to be the case: unlike the carpenter, Socrates does not produce anything useful and, unlike the mathematician, he does not provide us with useful knowledge concerning a certain domain of objects. Even if Socrates succeeds in showing us what we do and do not know, he has himself claimed that such knowledge in itself will not make us any better or any happier. Here is the circle once again: the *aporia* faced in trying to understand temperance is the same as the *aporia* faced in trying to understand Socrates' method.

But in this circle also lies the "answer." A careful reading of this dialogue should provoke the following question: how does Socrates' knowledge of knowledge differ from Critias's knowledge of knowledge, on the one hand, and Charmides' blush, on the other? Socrates differs from Charmides in his dissatisfaction with the contingent, limited awareness that ordinary experience can provide and in his search for a knowledge that goes beyond such experience. But how, then, does Socrates differ from Critias and his empty, sophistic knowledge of knowledge? The difference is clearly not to be found in the products or conclusions of Socrates' method, since it has none. The difference is rather that Socrates in practicing the knowledge of knowledge *shows us what it means to be good*. We see no good in Critias's contentious employment of definitions, but the good is revealed in the way in which Socrates examines and refutes definitions. As has been seen, Socrates' refutations depend on an appeal to the good; the good thus lays claim on him throughout the inquiry. In making clear the limitations of the proposed definitions, he shows an understanding of the good. In Socrates the knowledge of knowledge *is* the knowledge of the good.[82]

However, though the dialogue succeeds in *showing* us this knowledge at work and in distinguishing it from the perceptions of Charmides and the definitions of Critias, it must end in *aporia* because this knowledge is nonpropositional. In the knowledge of knowledge the good is not revealed as something that could be made the object of any kind of description or definition. Unlike a knowledge *of* numbers or *of* the heavens, the knowledge of knowledge is not directed toward some object external to itself. Instead, *the good is revealed indirectly in the very process of self-examination*. But this means that knowledge of the good is not of the kind that could be expressed in any set of propositions,[83] no matter how comprehensive; rather it is a knowledge that can be shown only *at work*. Elsewhere this knowledge is compared to a knowledge of how to *use* something.[84] The comparison is illuminating. We may receive instructions on how to use a hammer, but we do not really *know* how to use it until we actually try it out. No knowledge of propositions can take the place of that knowledge gained by actually *using* a thing. More important, it is precisely in a thing's use that its *good* is revealed. No *description* of a thing will provide us with *knowledge* of its good; only in the thing's actual use will this good be known.

The knowledge involved in Socrates' own method has this character. It is in the very process of self-inquiry (here called "knowledge of knowledge") that a knowledge of the good is had and not in some final result, product, or theory. What the dialogue leads us to conclude on a conceptual level, namely, that the knowledge of knowledge is a knowledge of the good and as such is unlike any other kind of knowledge, is made concrete in what Socrates does.[85] Socrates' knowledge of knowledge is clearly a knowledge of the good. The very way in which he goes about attempting to define temperance shows us what temperance is. The *aporia* at the end of the dialogue shows us not that no knowledge of temperance has been gained, but rather that this knowledge is not of the sort that could bring the dialogue to a *conclusion*. I1, therefore, misunderstands the *aporia* in seeing it as simply the lack of any solution whatsoever. Temperance by its very nature involves an openness to further self-examination, to the ever renewed quest of a knowledge of knowledge. The knowledge involved in temperance never ceases to be a question in such a way as to become an "answer."

The nature of Socrates' method, which has just been described conceptually, is depicted dramatically in a closing scene very similar to that of the *Laches*. One might expect Critias and Charmides to be disappointed at Socrates' failure to define temperance. They themselves are indeed guilty of a similar failure, but should they not be upset that Socrates has proven no more successful? Should they not be suspicious of a man who claims to value temperance so highly and yet cannot say what it is? Should they not agree with Socrates' own description of himself as a foolish babbler (λῆρος, 176a3)? Instead, Charmides decides with irresistible resolution never to leave Socrates' side and to submit himself daily to Socrates' discourse. Even more surprising is Critias's comment: he describes Charmides' decision always to follow Socrates as *proof of the boy's temperance* (176b5–8)! Both Critias and Charmides have clearly decided that Socrates' "knowledge of knowledge," though not capable, like the *technai*, of providing them with particular goods or "scientific" knowledge, is nevertheless beneficial.

This dialogue, however, ends on a somewhat more sinister note than did the *Laches*. Charmides does not ask Socrates whether or not he is willing to be his teacher; he instead intends to get the knowledge he wants by force. Charmides is of course teasing Socrates. Yet there is something malicious in this play. Both Charmides and his cousin Critias seem to have failed to understand that the temperance they seek can be acquired only through *self*-knowledge and *self*-control; they think that they can acquire it by exerting power (βιάζειν, 176c7–d5) over someone else who has it. It is no accident that the traditional definition of temperance as "self-control" is conspicuously missing from this dialogue.[86] Genuine self-control would require some kind of reconciliation between the naive, concrete self-awareness of Charmides and the sophistry of Critias. It would require both of the two aspects of temperance which have been kept separate throughout the dialogue: goodness and self-knowledge. Because both Charmides and Critias understand and exhibit temperance in one-sided and superficial, though opposed, ways, they both turn out to lack self-control. The end of the dialogue reminds us that both men would later become members of the government of the Thirty Tyrants. We have seen throughout the dialogue the weaknesses that might propel both into their violent careers: Charmides is overly naive, and his cousin is overly "sophisticated." Is Socrates at fault for not teaching them? Because Socrates' knowledge is not of the kind that can be communicated through any kind of "positive instruction," he cannot be blamed for being often misunderstood.

Conclusion

In both the *Laches* and the *Charmides* we see the same "dialectical" movement: Socrates rises above the perception of virtue found on the level of ordinary experience without negating or abandoning this experience in favor of an empty, formal "wisdom." Socrates' dialectic takes place as a mediation of the extremes represented by Charmides and Laches, on the one hand, and Critias and Nicias, on the other. Yet the insight at which Socrates' method aims is in a sense more akin to the naive intuition of Charmides and Laches than it is to the sophisticated cleverness of Nicias and Critias. This, I believe, is the reason why the dialogues are named after the former and not the latter. For all their simplicity, Laches and Charmides have some faint perception of the truth, a truth from which the other interlocutors have distanced themselves.[87] Yet it has been seen that Socrates is not satisfied with the perception presupposed by everyday discourse and uses the means of the sophists to transcend it. Unlike Critias and Nicias, however, he does so while remaining true to this perception. He does not pretend to substitute a definition or formula for a concrete experience of the virtues.[88] The insight at which his method aims, an insight gained through the *process* of inquiry, does not negate or abandon ordinary experience but rather makes explicit the truth that is confusedly and partially revealed by it. For example, our ordinary intuitions show us that courage can be neither foolish nor free of ignorance and risk: the aim of Socratic inquiry is to exhibit the truth hidden in these apparently contradictory intuitions. The insight thus attained is not a final answer that would render further discussion superfluous. It rather motivates and nourishes renewed questioning.

The *Laches* and the *Charmides* thus demonstrate Socrates' ability to rise above ordinary experience without falling into the empty intellectualism of his sophistic counterparts. They thereby also display three important characteristics of the knowledge Socrates seeks through the dialectical method: (1) it is "knowledge how" in the sense that it is instantiated by the very way in which Socrates conducts the inquiry (as the understanding of virtue possessed by Laches and Charmides shows itself in *their* actions); (2) it is "self-knowledge" in the sense that its "object" is not completely external to the knower (this is the "circle" encountered in both dialogues);[89] (3) it is "nonpropositional knowledge" in the sense that its theoretical "content" cannot be expressed in propositions/definitions (thus the inevitable *aporia*).[90] These three characteristics of dialectical knowledge will be encountered again in the dialogues discussed in following chapters. Most immediately, the next three chapters will further articulate what is involved in the "knowledge how" that enables Socrates to use correctly the same means that are abused by the sophists, namely, language, argumentation, and imitation.

3

The *Cratylus* on the Use of Words

In the previous chapter we have seen Socrates' dialectic at work in the *Laches* and the *Charmides*. Dialectic there showed itself to be steering a middle course between the intuitions of ordinary experience and the intellectualism represented by Critias and Nicias. Now in seeking to distinguish Socrates from those sophists who bear the greatest resemblance to him, we must consider certain presuppositions of the dialectic which he practices. Two of these presuppositions concern the role of arguments and images in philosophy and will be dealt with in chapters 4 and 5. The third presupposition, however, concerns the nature of language and is the focus of the present chapter. As has been seen, the knowledge gained through dialectic is "beyond words" in the sense that it cannot be adequately communicated or expressed in any definitions or propositions. Yet it is also clear that dialectic's only means of arriving at this knowledge are words. Socrates, after all, is asking for the meaning of a specific word when he asks a question such as "What is courage?" The problem, then, can be succinctly stated as follows: in pursuing an analysis that is confined to words Socrates is seeking knowledge that is beyond words.[1] But what must be presupposed about the nature of language, and what *denied*, in order for this to be possible? This question receives its answer in the *Cratylus*. The account of language in this dialogue enables us to understand how Socrates can ask his What-is-x? question with the intention of doing more than carrying out a verbal analysis and with the goal of attaining knowledge which as such cannot be given verbal expression. The dialogue will thereby also reveal an important difference between Socrates and the sophists, since the latter (at least as represented here) are characterized by a peculiar confinement to words which is inimical to dialectic. Because the *Cratylus* communicates its message as a dramatic and argumentative whole, rather than in a specific passage or argument, the following interpretation must be fairly detailed. Besides addressing the specific problem raised above, this chapter also aims to provide a convincing overall interpretation of a dialogue that is among Plato's most puzzling works.

The discussion gets under way when Socrates is asked to participate in a debate between Hermogenes and Cratylus about whether names[2] are conventional or natural. Hermogenes is maintaining that they are conventional, and he accuses Cratylus of not clearly explaining his own view that they are natural. Socrates as usual claims ignorance but is willing to inquire. Hermogenes' view is that names are simply given and agreed upon by human beings. If we use the word "tree" to refer to a certain object, this is only because we have agreed to allow this word to signify this object. The word does not naturally belong to the object.[3]

Socrates, however, immediately senses the danger that Hermogenes' assertion of the conventionality of names might slip imperceptibly into an assertion of the conventionality *of truth*. He therefore asks whether or not it is right to call a man a "horse" and a horse a "man." This is of course an ambiguous question. It may simply ask if it is possible for us to agree to use the letters *h-o-r-s-e* to signify a man and the letters *m-a-n* to signify a horse. It may also ask, however, if we could rightly maintain that a horse is *in truth* a man and a man is *in truth* a horse.[4] In this case the question is ludicrous; it could, however, become much more serious if words such as "justice" and "injustice" were involved. Socrates initially asks his question in the first sense, which concerns only a conventionality of names. However, Socrates suspects that Hermogenes might be tempted to answer the question affirmatively even in the second sense. This suspicion is encouraged by the example to which Hermogenes appeals in first defending his view: we change the names of our slaves, and the new name is as good as the old one (384d3–5). This example suggests that according to Hermogenes things are our slaves in the sense that we in naming them determine what they *are*.[5] Therefore, after Hermogenes has pointed out that names for the same thing differ from one country to another (thus affirming only a conventionality of names), Socrates asks whether or not this relativism can also be affirmed with respect to *ta onta:* "But let us see, Hermogenes, whether things themselves appear to you to be disposed in such a way that the being of each differs from individual to individual, just as Protagoras says that man is the measure of all things: as they appear to me so *are* they to me and as they appear to you so *are* they to you. Or does it seem to you that things possess some stable nature of their own?" (βεβαιότητα τῆς οὐσίας, 385e4–386a4). We thus see how Socrates leads the question of the conventionality of names into a much deeper issue. He suspects that Hermogenes is tempted to take his relativism beyond names to the things themselves.[6]

His suspicion is justified: Hermogenes admits to having found Protagoras's position tempting, though he does not at present accept it (386a5–7). Socrates now casts suspicion on Protagoras's thesis by showing that it undermines any distinction between the wise and the ignorant. Hermogenes agrees that such a distinction is and can be made and that therefore Protagoras's relativism is to be rejected. In the words of Socrates, "things do not follow us up and down in accordance with our fancy, but each thing has its own being in itself in accordance with its own nature" (386e2–4); in other words, things are *not* our slaves. Socrates then proceeds to claim that not only things but also activities (πράξεις) have their own proper natures. "Activities are done in accordance with their own nature, not in accordance with our opinion" (387a1–2). Socrates next points out that speaking (τὸ λέγειν) is itself an activity. Consequently, someone who speaks as he pleases will not thereby speak correctly. One must speak according to the way in which things are naturally to be spoken of (ἧ πέφυκε τὰ πράγματα λέγειν τε καὶ λέγεσθαι καὶ ᾧ, 387c1–2). Here it is clear that to say that the activity of speech has its own nature is not to say that it is autonomous and self-contained. The correctness of speech is determined by the way in which it addresses the things themselves. Yet we are not told here what it means to speak of things in the way in which they are naturally to be spoken of.

This problem is further specified when Socrates claims that the activity of naming (ὀνομάζειν) is part of the activity of speaking. Since naming is itself an activity, it too must have its own proper nature. In other words, one cannot name things in whatever way one pleases, but one must name them just as they are by nature to be named: "Οὐκοῦν καὶ ὀνομαστέον [ἐστὶν] ᾗ πέφυκε τὰ πράγματα ὀνομάζειν τε καὶ ὀνομάζεσθαι καὶ ᾧ" (387d4–5). A great deal depends on the meaning of this ambiguous sentence. Clearly, some kind of "naturalness of names" is being asserted here. But in exactly what way is a name natural? What does it mean to say that a thing is to be named in the way that is natural to it?

There are two possible interpretations. According to one, the "naturalness of names" need mean no more than the following: the name "horse" cannot be used to refer to a man, not because the letters *h-o-r-s-e* are distinct from the letters *m-a-n*, but because the former letters have been given the function of referring to a nature distinct from human nature. That these particular letters were chosen to refer to a horse is a matter of convention, but that whichever letters are chosen must refer to the nature of a horse and *no other* is not a matter of convention. Whether we use "ανήρ" or "homo" or "*Mensch*" to refer to a man depends on the particular language into whose conventions we are born; convention, however, has nothing to do with the fact that there is one specific nature here to which all of these names exclusively refer. This, then, is one sense in which names are natural.

According to the second possible interpetation, what is natural is precisely the choice of these specific letters to represent this specific nature. In this case, the nature of a thing determines not only that certain letters, once chosen, will refer exclusively to itself, but also which specific letters are to be chosen in the first place. For example, not only is the use of the word "horse" to refer to one specific thing in accordance with nature, but the very choice of the letters *h-o-r-s-e* to serve this use is in accordance with nature. Interpreted in this way, the naturalness of names denies the view that it is solely a matter of convention which letters are chosen to refer to which things. Interpreted in the other way discussed above, however, the naturalness of names is perfectly compatible with this view and denies only that truth is conventional (Protagoras's doctrine).

If one fails to recognize this fundamental ambiguity in the "natural names" position (an ambiguity which Socrates does his best to make us see), one will be at a loss in attempting to follow the rest of the dialogue.[7] The question which must be asked is whether Socrates in arguing for a naturalness of names understands this in one sense or in the other. What Socrates immediately proceeds to say makes clear that he understands names to be natural only in the first sense described above. He draws an analogy between naming and other skills or crafts such as weaving. A name is an instrument (ὄργανον) and therefore, like a shuttle, must be properly suited to its work (388a). Just as the carpenter is the one who makes the shuttle used in weaving, so is the "legislator" the one who makes the names used in naming. Furthermore, in the same way that in making a shuttle the carpenter must have the form of a shuttle in mind, so in making names the legislator must use as his pattern the "true natural name" of each thing. "Is it not necessary, my noble friend, for this legislator to know how to put into sounds and syllables the natural name of each thing [τὸ ἑκάστῳ φύσει πεφυκὸς ὄνομα], making and establishing all names by looking to what a name itself is [αὐτὸ ἐκεῖνο ὃ ἔστιν ὄνομα], if he is to be a genuine maker of names?"(389d4–8).

What is unusual about this natural name is that it is not identical with the collection of syllables and sounds that make up a name; it is rather that which is *put into* syllables and sounds. Later in the same passage Socrates claims that a thing, though referred to by different sounds in different languages, nevertheless has one and the same natural name in all cases. He calls this common element "the form of the name" (τὸ τοῦ ὀνόματος εἶδος) and contrasts it with the syllables as the matter, in the way that the form of a shuttle differs from the wood of which the shuttle is made

(389d8–390a10). The important thing to note is that the "natural name" of which Socrates speaks is not the same as the syllables and sounds that make up a word in a particular language. Therefore, the natural fitness of names which Socrates describes here is not the view that the actual constituents of a name are natural. Instead, what is considered natural is the form (εἶδος), which can be expressed by using different syllables, where the choice of the exact syllables used is apparently a matter of convention. In anticipation it can be said that the natural fitness of names understood in this way contrasts sharply with the attempt to discover the truth of things in the sounds and syllables of particular Greek words.

Yet how exactly is one to define this "natural name"? It seems, to say the least, a rather mysterious notion. Normally we understand by "name" something that consists of specific letters or syllables and belongs to a particular language. How, then, are we to understand a name that transcends any given language and does not have any particular sound?[8] How exactly is this natural name known and how is it put into syllables? One might think that a thing's natural name is identical with its form or nature. After all, it is this nature which is expressed by means of certain sounds whenever we name something. Yet when Socrates speaks of the "form of name" or "what a name itself is," he is attributing to a name as such its own specific nature, a nature distinct from that of a man or a horse.[9]

In order to determine what Socrates means by the "form of name," we must consider how he would answer the question: what *is* a name? A name is described by Socrates as having the function of selecting one nature from among others (διακριτικὸν τῆς οὐσίας, 388c1). This function that defines a name can be said to be its form, just as the form of a shuttle, as opposed to its matter, is defined in terms of its function. Consequently, what Socrates means by the "form of name" is the function that a name as such has of referring to one specific stable nature.[10] Of course, there will be as many of these functions or relations of referring as there are distinct natures. For any given nature there is a way of referring exclusively to this nature. This "way of referring" is the thing's specific "natural name."[11] The "natural name" is not itself a collection of specific syllables or sounds but is rather this relation to a specific nature, a relation that can be "embodied" in particular sounds. The important point to remember is the following: what is claimed to be natural here are not the physical constituents of a name, but the name's function. Different letters can of course be used to serve one and the same function. Protagoras, who is the opponent throughout this section, would deny that even the function of a name is natural since he would deny the existence of a stable nature to which a name could exclusively refer.[12]

This interpretation of a natural name is confirmed by what Socrates now proceeds to ask: who will be able to judge concerning the proper form of a thing, he who makes this thing or he who uses it? In the case of a shuttle, for example, it is the weaver instead of the carpenter who can best judge whether or not the shuttle has the proper form. The reason is that the thing's form is defined in terms of its use. We have already seen that the ability to make names is attributed to some mysterious "legislator." Yet, as in the case of the shuttle, it seems that he who can best judge whether or not a name serves its proper function, that is, has the right form, will be not he who makes names, but he who *uses names*. But if the legislator makes names, what are we to call the person who uses names? According to Socrates, the user of names will be that person who knows how to ask and answer questions. The person with this knowledge is none other than the dialectician (390c). Therefore, the dialectician is the one who will know a thing's natural name by using a name (in whatever language) in such a way that it serves its proper function of referring to this thing.

This description of the dialectician is brief and leaves some crucial questions unanswered. One question is why the dialectician has a special claim to knowing how to use names. The use of names does not seem to be a special art like weaving. Anyone who speaks a language will know how to use names to refer to things. Such knowledge does not seem to be the possession of a select few. Socrates clearly claims, however, that the dialectician is the one who really knows how to use names and who can therefore determine whether or not a given name is serving its proper function. But what exactly does this mean? What does the dialectican know concerning the use of names that the average person does not know?[13]

This question is not explicitly raised in the dialogue, but we can here begin to reflect on the possible answer. In dialectic the actual constituents of a name, the letters of which it is made, are a matter of indifference. What is of importance is the function of a name or its form. This function is clearly brought out in a question such as "What is virtue?" This question shows that the specific function of a name is to distinguish and make manifest a determinate nature.[14] Even if the question for some reason cannot be definitively answered, the very fact that it is meaningful shows what the proper use of a name is. Yet to the average person the question "What is virtue?" sounds strange. The reason is that in everyday talk a word is used without an explicit awareness of its proper function.

Yet there is a problem here: surely the average person can use a name in such a way as to refer to, and call to one's attention, a particular thing. The name "virtue" is used to refer to a specific instance of virtue, and the name "tree" is used to refer to a particular tree. It is true that in everyday discourse one does not focus on the referential relation itself, but what is to be gained by doing so? It is enough for the name to be used in order for it to "call up" that particular thing to which it refers. In focusing on the referential relation itself, what does the dialectician make manifest except the particular thing referred to? In asking the question "What is virtue?" what is he bringing to our attention except those particular instances of virtue to which we refer in everyday discourse by using the name "virtue"? These questions must be answered if the dialectician's use of names is to be adequately distinguished from their ordinary use. However, they cannot be answered at this point in the dialogue. Socrates up to now has simply described names as referring to *ta onta* or to a thing's *phusis*. What is not yet clear is if, in using a name to refer to a particular thing, something can be made manifest besides the particular thing itself. For example, the use of the name "tree" to refer to a particular tree might also, and perhaps even *primarily*, make reference to "treeness" or the nature common to all trees.[15] Though Socrates has not yet made a distinction between these two kinds of objects, by the end of the dialogue he will do so, and it will then become clear just what is revealed in the dialectician's focus on the use or function of words that is not revealed in their unreflective use.

What demands immediate attention, however, is the lack of clarity concerning the relation between the function of referring to and distinguishing the nature of a thing, or that thing's natural name, and the actual letters and sounds in which this name is supposedly embodied. A name is obviously more than the letters that make it up: it is also essentially a relation to some objective nature (this relation is its form). A name can thus be said always to point beyond itself, to transcend itself. But this transcendence is precisely what is hard to explain. How can we get from the actual sound of a name to some objective reality? How can we get beyond names in our use of them? Yet in dialectic as described above and even in everyday discourse, we see this transcendence taking place.

That this characteristic of names does not receive an adequate explanation at this point of the dialogue is in part due to a failure to place sufficient emphasis on the ability of names to make things *manifest* (δηλοῖ). Names are not self-contained and self-enclosed for precisely the reason that they make manifest a reality that lies outside and beyond them. It is this aspect of naming that the shuttle analogy fails to take into account. Though this analogy is of extreme importance in showing that the nature of a name is to be found in its *use* (how important this insight is will become all too apparent when it is forgotten in the following etymologies), the analogy does not capture the fact that names are not only practical tools, but are also the medium through which reality becomes manifest to us. A shuttle can be used to weave a garment, but it cannot in any meaningful sense be said to reveal or make manifest this garment. The analogy therefore conceals this aspect of a name and thus its transcendence, its ability to point beyond itself.

The failure to take this transcendence into account is what ultimately leads to the comic attempts in the dialogue to discover the truth of a thing's nature in the actual sounds that make up its corresponding name. Such attempts clearly go against everything that we are told here about "natural names." Yet, because what constitutes a "natural name" is precisely a transcendence to the thing itself and this transcendence remains unexplained, the phrase "natural name" can be mistakenly thought to mean that what is natural is just the name as a collection of specific sounds or letters. There is a temptation here to abstract a name from its use in dialectic (where its function is to make manifest an objective nature) and to treat it as something self-contained, self-sufficient. That is, the name is made to contain its truth entirely within its physical constituents (its syllables) rather than in a relation to something beyond itself.[16] In this way words are believed to provide knowledge only as objects of etymology. This temptation to go from a meaningful sense of the "naturalness of names" to a ridiculous sense is not resisted in the dialogue. After 390c the dialectician will not be mentioned again nor will there be any discussion of the *use* of words. Because Socrates is himself a dialectician, however, we can expect that the genuine naturalness of names will not be entirely lost.

At 390d Socrates asserts that Cratylus is right in claiming that names are natural (φύσει τὰ ὀνόματα εἶναι τοῖς πράγμασι). Yet, as we might suspect, Cratylus will prove to understand this "naturalness" in the reductive way described above. Before Cratylus can enter the discussion, however, Hermogenes asks Socrates what he means by the "natural fitness of names." Socrates replies by claiming ignorance, saying that he is merely sharing the inquiry. He is willing to examine the question but advises Hermogenes to go to the sophists for an answer (391a–c). Indeed, Socrates seems to have some contempt for the whole question. After Hermogenes objects that he is not in agreement with Protagoras, Socrates advises him to seek an answer in Homer. In this way Socrates seems to want to leave the question to those who are more "clever" than himself.

It is important to understand Socrates' behavior here. Why does he refuse to answer what seems to be a relevant and important question? Why does he distance himself from this question by means of irony? There is a good reason. As has been seen, the natural fitness of a name is revealed only through its *use*. The dialectician as a user of names is the one who can show what makes a name in accordance with nature. Yet the dialectician does not do this by pointing to some constituent of a name that makes it natural. There is nothing in the physical makeup of a name that makes it correspond to nature. Instead, the dialectician reveals the nature of a name, its *form, by showing it at work*. Only in the use of names is the natural name (that aspect of a name which is more than a mere collection of letters) revealed. Therefore, Hermogenes' question, in looking for some trait that makes a name naturally fit, is misguided.[17] By referring Hermogenes to the sophists and Homer, Socrates is disassociating himself from the subsequent etymologies that will attempt to answer this question.

When Hermogenes expresses his distaste for the sophists, Socrates tells him that he must learn from Homer, whose supposed views on the correctness (ὀρθότης) of names Socrates then proceeds to expound (391d). There are passages in which Homer tells us that a thing is called one name by the gods and another name by mortals. According to Socrates, Homer intends us to understand that the name used by the gods is more correct than the name used by mortals (391d). What is left unclear, however, is what makes this name more correct besides the fact that the gods use it. What is also left unclear is in what way the two names differ. According to what Socrates has said so far, if the two names are used in the same way, if they have the same function, then as far as natural fitness is concerned they are the same name.

This point is explicitly made in the case of the different words that signify "king." Socrates gives the following example: the fact that two medicines look different and smell different may fool the layman into thinking that they actually are different, but the doctor who knows that the two have *the same power* (δύναμις) will not be thus fooled. He knows that if the two medicines have the same power, then, despite any differences in smell or color, they are one and the same medicine (394a–b). Likewise, someone who understands the power of synonymous names will not be fooled by the fact that they are made up of different letters. Even though "Archepolis," "Astuanax," and "Hector" share few or no letters, they yet have the same meaning, the same power of referring to one determinate nature (kingship), and therefore can be said to be *one name*. To use an English example, the words "below" and "under" have basically the same meaning. If by a "word" one means only a collection of letters, then they are different words; if, however, one means the power of referring to, and bringing to one's attention, a specific nature, then they can be said to be the same word. So far Socrates has understood *onoma* in the latter sense. Though by the end of the upcoming etymologies specific letters will become essential to a word's meaning, here they are not important (οὐδὲν πρᾶγμα): "And we might find many other words which in their syllables and letters sound different, but in their *power* express the same thing" (394c6–9). Names made up of different letters can be equally fit to make manifest the one nature to which they refer. The natural correctness of a name does not depend on the specific letters or syllables of which it is composed.

On what, then, does this natural correctness depend? In the first set of etymologies Socrates examines proper names. He shows their correctness by analyzing them into words that correctly describe the person to whom the name refers. For example, the name "Agamemnon" is shown to be a compound of the words for "admirable" (ἀγαστός) and "staying" (μονή). It so happens that the man Agamemnon was indeed admirable for staying, since he persevered with his army in front of Troy for so many years. Thus the name actually fits him and is "correct."

This attempt to demonstrate the correctness of names is odd for several reasons. In the first place, it does not seem to be the case that the proper function of a proper name is to *describe* the person to whom it refers. If we want to describe Agamemnon as being admirable for staying, we can use the words "ἀγαστός" and "μονή." These are words that could also be used of other individuals who share these characteristics. When we ask for "Agamemnon," however, we are not just asking for anyone who happens to be admirable for staying. We use the name "Agamemnon" to refer to a specific individual. Yet a fundamental presupposition of the present etymologies is that every name is some sort of description. This view can be maintained only at the cost of ignoring what a name is *used* for.

The second point to be made against this analysis is that it is irrelevant to the question at hand. All that the analysis shows is that certain proper names can be broken down into words which describe that to which the name refers. The question concerning the natural fitness of names, however, does not ask whether or not words can be used to describe specific things. Even the conventionalist would allow that once we agree on what a given word is going to mean, we can then use this word to describe things in the world. The question is whether there is any natural correspondence between the word and the nature to which it refers. For example, the question is whether the word "ἀγαστός" itself is naturally fit to refer to and make manifest the actual state of being admirable. Of this natural fitness Socrates has so far said nothing. The question is whether or not he will deal with it in the following series of etymologies where the words considered are not all proper names.

With this in mind we can outline the series of etymologies while focusing on the important turning points.[18] First, however, it is necessary to look at the context. This context is provided by Socrates' words at 396d–397a and is indispensable for determining the extent to which he is aware of the inadequacy of his etymologies and intends to draw our attention to their absurdity. Socrates here claims to be inspired by the "Great Euthyphro," with whom he was conversing early that morning,[19] and it is under this inspiration that he decides to finish the investigation of names. He tells us, however, that he will afterward try to purge himself of Euthyphro's influence through the help of someone skilled in purifications, this being, one can assume, none other than the person who knows the *proper* use of names, namely, the dialectician.[20] Socrates could hardly say more to dissociate himself from the etymological comedy about to ensue. He is even careful in places explicitly to attribute to Euthyphro what is being said. At one point Socrates even advises Hermogenes to guard against being deceived by him (393c8–9). It is therefore hard to see how the following etymologies could be taken as a straightforward presentation of Plato's or Socrates' philosophy of language. Plato could hardly do more to discredit this investigation of names without actually stating in his own person that it is not to be taken seriously.[21]

In the series of etymologies starting at 397a Socrates sometimes gives both a fairly straightforward etymology and a more subtle one to satisfy the pupils of Euthyphro. For example, the word for hero (ἥρως) is first associated with "love" (ἔρως), but then later with the verbs for questioning (ἐρωτᾶν) and speaking (εἴρειν), so that the ancient heroes look like "a tribe of sophists and rhetors" (398c–e). The word for soul (ψυχή) is first associated with breath and life; then it is derived from the phrase "which moves and sustains reality" (ἡ φύσιν ὀχεῖ καὶ ἔχει) in order to support the view of Anaxagoras (399d–400b).[22] Socrates confesses to finding this last interpretation laughable (400b6–7). Already these etymologies reveal that Socrates' procedure in explaining ordinary nouns does not essentially differ from his procedure in explaining proper names. In each case the explanation involves reducing a word to other words that *describe* the thing referred to. The question that is not even addressed, however, is how these other words themselves are related by nature to what they signify.

The next series of etymologies (400d–408d) concerns the names of gods. For each name Socrates gives several etymologies, thus indicating how arbitrary the whole procedure is. With the discussion of the name of "Hestia" (401b–e) the contest begins between those who believe in the stability of being (οὐσία) and those who believe that all things are in motion (ὠσία, ὠθοῦν). An etymology can be used to support either view. Here we begin to see that though a word can be *used* to make manifest the nature of a thing, one cannot get at this nature by abstracting from the word's use and providing its etymology. The dialectician might be able through the use of words to see whether things have stable natures or everything is in constant flux. The etymologist, however, in simply deriving one word from other words, will not be able to see the true nature of things. He remains confined within language rather than allowing language to serve its natural function of referring beyond itself. Socrates' investigation of names is comical precisely because it conceals the proper use of names. It is a game of finding words in other words that ignores what is to be taken seriously in language: the use of words to refer beyond them to the nature of things.

The investigation of the names of the gods builds up to a climax of absurdity. One etymology of "Pluto" makes the god "a perfect and accomplished Sophist" who through the power of his words charms people into *wanting* to stay in Hades (403a–404b). In the case of the names of Aphrodite and Dionysus, Socrates openly confesses that his derivations are only a joke (406b–c; yet one would think that Socrates would be particularly concerned with understanding the natures of these two gods!).

The next series of etymologies concerns natural objects such as the sun, the moon, air, earth, and fire (408d-410e). Socrates here proves incapable of providing etymologies of the words for "fire" (πῦρ) and "water" (ὕδωρ). He deals with this *aporia*, however, by means of the contrivance (μηχανή) of assigning these words a foreign (βαρβαρικός) origin (409d–410b). Here we see just how far from his initial position Socrates' inspiration has led him. The "naturally fit name" of which Socrates spoke earlier is one remaining the same in all languages, regardless of the sounds in which it is clothed. Now Socrates claims to be concerned only with the natural fitness of *Greek* words.

The next set of words to be investigated are mostly ethical terms (411a–420e). Here the contrast with what the dialectician does is most striking. An attempt is made to discover the meaning of the different virtues, not by inquiring into their natures through the use of their names, but by simply providing etymologies of these names. The result is that the names are all shown, when analyzed, to support the view that everything is in constant flux and that therefore there are no stable natures. The contrast between this and the way in which Socrates investigates the nature of virtue in other dialogues (particularly the *Laches* and the *Charmides* as discussed in chapter 2) is obvious. He there does not give an etymology of the word "virtue" but instead uses this word in an attempt to make manifest the unique, unchanging nature of virtue. Likewise, in the present dialogue, the dialectician is described as using words in such a way that their proper function is seen to involve a relation to determinate, stable natures. Thus the dialectician, though not providing etymologies, shows what is presupposed by the very nature of words. The paradox of the present etymologies, on the other hand, can be stated as follows:

the result of these etymologies contradicts what is presupposed by the very use of words, that is, the existence of stable natures.[23] We thus see just how far astray Euthyphro's inspiration has led the investigation.

The inadequacy of etymologies, as opposed to dialectic, in getting at the nature of things is now actually commented on by Socrates (413a–c). He describes how people waste their time arguing about the etymology of justice and how he himself comes away from these disputes as perplexed as ever concerning the nature of justice. This is precisely the point: an etymology of the word "justice" provides one with no knowledge of the nature of justice and consequently tells one nothing about the "natural fitness" of this word.

Of particular interest among the other etymologies Socrates proceeds to provide is that of the word for "yoke" (ζυγόν). Socrates claims that it has no meaning in its present form (οὐδὲν δηλοῖ), but that in its ancient form, "δυογὸν," it means the binding of two (δυοῖν) together for the purpose of drawing (ἀγωγή, 418d7–e3). The meaning of the word is thus seen to depend entirely upon other words into which it can be analyzed. When a word through change in spelling loses its connection to the other words that are its elements, it loses its meaning. A word's meaning no longer depends on its relation in use to the nature of the thing it signifies; its meaning now depends on its relation *to other words*. Language becomes progressively more self-contained and more disassociated from the reality it signifies. This tendency is now about to reach its climax.

The etymologies continue with the derivation of the word "ὄν" (being) from "ἰόν" (flowing; 421b7–c2). (But why not the other way around?) This derivation is meant to show once again that the meaning of a word ultimately comes down to the fact that everything is in a constant state of flux. Here the word "being" itself is shown to have this meaning. The paradox is that the word "being" is thereby shown to mean that *there is no being*, since what the "flux theory" will later be seen to maintain is precisely that nothing *is*, that there is no "ὄν."

The discussion now reaches a major turning point (421c3–8) when Hermogenes asks Socrates to show the natural fitness or correctness of the word "ἰόν" itself. Up to now words have only been taken back to other words, but how are we to explain the natural fitness of these primary words themselves? If he is to continue in the same direction Socrates has only one alternative: to break words up into even simpler elements, that is, individual letters. Socrates states that in order to understand the correctness of primary names a method is needed distinct from that used to account for the correctness of secondary names: "For is it not the case that the names you are asking about now are primary elements (στοιχεῖα) and that therefore their correctness must be examined in another way?" (422b6–8). Yet the method Socrates ends up using with primary names does not essentially differ from the one used with secondary names.[24] In the latter case a name is shown to have meaning by being analyzed into other names that have meaning. In the former case the primary names themselves are shown to have meaning by being analyzed into letters that individually have meaning. In both cases, then, the meaning of the whole is thought to be reducible to the meaning of its parts. This reductionist view of language presupposes that, if the simplest elements taken in themselves do not have meaning, the language as a whole will be without meaning. In other words, if individual letters such as *l*, *r*, and *t* do not signify anything, then the names they compose will themselves not signify anything.

It is important to see how far the discussion has strayed from the original position presented at the beginning of the dialogue. Socrates had claimed that the actual letters of which a name is composed are irrelevant to an understanding of its meaning and natural fitness. Now individual letters are taken to be all-important.[25] The meaning of a word can depend entirely on the presence or absence of a certain letter. More important, only letters seem to stand in a direct relation to the nature of things. Both primary and secondary names have their meaning, not through a direct relation to the things themselves, but through a relation to their own elements. Letters, as the simplest elements of language, seem to be the only point of contact between language and reality. The fact that letters do not seem to mean anything when abstracted from the words in which they are used cannot stand in the way of Socrates' "inspiration."

One should expect that Socrates' discussion of the correctness of letters will finally force him to step outside of language and explain the nature of its relation to reality. He indeed does so, characterizing this relation as one of imitation (*mimēsis*, 423b). As has already been explained, the proper function of a word is to make manifest the nature of a thing (δηλῶσαι τὴν φύσιν). A word is now said to carry out this function by *imitating* the thing's nature. The analogy drawn is between naming and painting (423d–425a). Just as the painter employs different colors in imitating a given object, so a name imitates things through the use of different letters. What a name imitates, however, is not the way a thing sounds or how it appears to sight but rather what it in essence *is* (its οὐσία, 423b–424a). Thus it would be incorrect to use the word "moo" to refer to a cow since this word, though imitating the sound a cow makes, reveals nothing about the cow's nature. A name is a peculiar kind of image which imitates in sound something that is not itself a sound, that is, a thing's very essence.

The difference between this theory of language and the one presented toward the beginning of the dialogue can be seen in the choice of comparisons. In the one case, a name is compared to an instrument like a shuttle, the similarity being that the proper form or function of either is revealed in its use. Accordingly, the person who best understands the nature of a name is he who knows how to use names: the dialectician. In the other case, a name is compared to a painting that reveals the nature of things *not by being used, but by simply being contemplated.* Here it seems that the person who best understands the nature of a name is the one who *makes* names: the legislator (and thus the dialectician is not mentioned). This latter theory of language is the culmination of a tendency that has already been noted in the preceding investigation: names are abstracted from their use and are thought to posses their meaning entirely within themselves. The result is the view that the nature of things is made manifest in the very sounds that are a name's basic elements.

The *mimēsis* model of language is appealing, however, because it takes into account the ability of language to make manifest that which it is about. As pointed out above, the shuttle analogy goes only so far because it cannot explain the fact that a name, besides being used like the shuttle to do something, can also, unlike the shuttle, *reveal* something. In simply forgetting the shuttle analogy, however, the present inquiry tries to show how a name *in abstraction from its use* can show us the nature of a thing. The *mimēsis* model of names will fail precisely because it does not take into account what the shuttle analogy has shown, that is, that the natural name of a thing is found only in the use of a name and that, if a name is to make manifest anything about the nature of the thing to which it refers, it must do so precisely in this use. In separating the use of a name from a name's ability to make something manifest, both opposed models prove inadequate.[26]

Since he has just suggested that language derives all its meaning from letters as its most basic elements and that the relation between language and reality is one of imitation, Socrates must conclude that letters are capable of imitating all kinds of objects. He acknowledges that this conclusion appears ridiculous but argues that it is inescapable: "I recognize, Hermogenes, how ridiculous [γελοῖα] it seems that objects should be imitated in letters and syllables and thereby become manifest [κατάδηλα], but this is nevertheless necessary (ἀνάγκη)" (425d1–3). But in what sense is this view necessary? It is certainly a necessary result of the present investigation, but this investigation, as we have seen, is in need of purification.

Socrates himself describes the theory concerning first names that he now presents as completely wild and ridiculous (πάνυ ὑβριστικὰ καὶ γελοῖα, 426b6). His description of the way in which individual letters themselves express or imitate different things (426c1–427d3) is indeed as absurd as can be. The letter *r*, Socrates tells us, is used to express motion (*kinēsis*). The reason is that the tongue is most agitated or most in motion in the pronunciation of this letter. The letters *d* and *t* are expressive of binding and rest in place, since there is a certain pressure and closing of the tongue when they are uttered. The letter *l* expresses smoothness, since in uttering it the tongue slips or slides (ὀλισθάνει). Thus the meaning of a name has been reduced to a certain motion of the tongue. Such a view represents a complete distortion of the nature of names as understood at the beginning of the dialogue. Socrates must himself be aware of this, since the absurdity of his theory is too blatant to be unintentional. For example, though the letter *r* is supposed to express motion, it is not present in the word for motion itself (*kinēsis*).[27] More important, however, the examples provided explain the meaning of a word in terms of only one of its letters; *kermatizein* ("crumble") signifies a kind of motion due to the presence in it of the letter *r*. But what about the other ten letters? Does each of them have its own distinct meaning? And how in this case are these different meanings combined to form the one meaning of the word? These questions must be answered if the present theory is to be at all coherent. Socrates, however, does not even suggest how they might be answered.

This section of the *Cratylus* has misled many scholars into believing that Plato aspired to an ideal language in which there would be a one-to-one correspondence between the components of language and the elements of reality.[28] It seems to be almost universally agreed that the specific results of Socrates' theory of letters are indeed ridiculous. However, it is nevertheless believed that the general *project* is one that Plato considered worthwhile and that he intended us to take seriously.[29] The principal textual evidence for this view is to be found at 424c6–425b4. Socrates, in comparing the way in which language imitates an object to the way in which a painting imitates its object, says the following:

> we will apply the elements [letters] to things [τὰ στοιχεῖα ἐπὶ τὰ πράγματα ἐποίσομεν], one in correspondence to one [ἓν ἐπὶ ἕν], when this seems necessary, or several at a time by making [συντιθέντες] what are called syllables and by combining them [συντίθενται] in turn to make names and predicates [ὀνόματα καὶ τὰ ῥήματα]. Then from the names and predicates we will compose [συστήσομεν] a large and beautiful whole by using the art of words or rhetoric or whatever the art [τέχνη] may be,

just as we use the art of painting to compose an image. Not that I am really talking about ourselves,[30] since the ancients were the ones who put together language in this way, but I got carried away by my speech. *Our* task, if we are to attain technical expertise in our examination of these matters, is to take language apart in the way in which it was assembled and see whether or not the primary and secondary names are rightly given. (424e4–425b3)

This passage has been called "a vision of a perfect language."[31] It seems to support the view of some scholars that Plato in this dialogue is searching for a "technical nomenclature" (Grote 1888, 3:290) and an "artificial language" (Kretzmann 1971, 137). Because the actual conclusions of Socrates' theory of letters are recognized by these same scholars to be so odd that Plato could not have taken them seriously,[32] and because Socrates himself later in the dialogue dismisses these conclusions in favor of a convention theory, the view that Plato is aspiring here to an ideal language depends on a distinction between the project outlined in the above passage and the way in which Socrates actually carries out the project, or between a general theory of names and a special theory. According to Schleiermacher (1857, 2:8), for instance, we are to take seriously the view that "in den Buchstaben die ursprüngliche Bedeutsamkeit müsse gesucht werden." The way in which Socrates actually carries out this search for meaning in letters, however, can hardly be taken seriously: "Wie nun aber dieses beispielweise an einzelnen Buchstaben erläutert and ihre Bedeutung aufgesucht wird, das kann man wieder kaum für Ernst erkennen." For whatever reason Plato, though perfectly serious about the general theory, decided to make the specific application of the theory comical. Similarly, Norman Kretzmann admits that the etymological account of the correctness of names, or what he calls the "special theory," is a failure in Plato's eyes, but he maintains that the approach or direction of this account, the "general theory," is one of which Plato approves. He claims that in the passage quoted above "there is a transition from the problem of the analysis of actual primary names to the project of a precise perfectly systematic conceptual notation, an artificial language consciously designed on the pattern of proteronyms, primary names, and secondary names, as the embodiment of the results of Platonic dialectic and possibly also as a device by means of which to extend the process of division."[33] Even Weingartner, who argues that Socrates' subsequent criticism of the theory of letters shows that "a completely natural language without any element of convention is logically impossible" (1970, 13), thinks that Plato is looking for a technical language in which "it would be possible to compose names by choosing syllables to designate different

THE *CRATYLUS* ON THE USE OF WORDS

aspects of the nature of the thing named so that the name in effect constitutes an abbreviation of the definition" (1970, 20). Thus the view is once again that though the specific theory of names Socrates presents is a failure, Plato yet believed that this theory was on the right track and that something like it must be the truth.

There are presuppositions of this interpretation that can be dealt with only after a discussion of the remainder of the dialogue, namely, the identification of the "ideal name" with a concept and the associated view that letters can be used for a kind of conceptual notation that would make a name an abbreviated definition. The criticism that *can* be made here, however, is that the "general theory" of names cannot be distinguished from the specific theory in such a way as to make the interpretation work. The project of an ideal language cannot be separated from Socrates' ridiculous theory that letters imitate the nature of things. This is shown by the context in which the latter theory is presented and criticized. After confessing that his theory of letters appears ridiculous, Socrates asserts that it is nevertheless *necessary* (425d3). What does he mean by this? He apparently can mean only that this theory provides the sole means of carrying out the project which he has just outlined, that it provides the only means of constructing an "ideal language." If it fails, the project fails. What is "ridiculous" about Socrates' theory is the view that a letter can have meaning in and of itself and that the name as a whole derives its meaning from this letter which it contains. The letter *r* in the word "*trechein*" (to run) must in and of itself signify something if the word is to signify something. But this is exactly what the project of an ideal language calls for: "ἓν ἐπὶ ἕν"—the primary elements of language must correspond to and signify the primary elements of reality. The whole of language is to be constructed from these, its meaningful elements. If this is the character of the "ideal language," then an attempt to construct it has no choice but to show how a letter or a syllable taken by itself can reveal the nature of a thing. The proponents of the "ideal language" interpretation themselves appear to recognize that this is the form the language must take. They apparently think, however, that this can be done in a way other than the way in which Socrates attempts it. Yet what this other specific theory could be, we are not told. What is clear is that Plato himself presents us with no theory other than the ridiculous one.

The "ideal language" interpretation also appears to render Plato's intentions in writing the dialogue incoherent. If Plato was in earnest about the general theory that there could be a one-to-one correspondence between the constituents of a name and the constituents of reality, why would he exemplify it in a specific theory that is held up to ridicule and exposed as a failure? Since a plausible answer to this question is apparently lacking, Plato's rejection of the specific theory cannot be separated from a rejection of the general theory. It is not the case that Plato was looking for an ideal language and simply failed to find it. He presents us with a characterization of such a language and then rejects it.

Socrates after conceding convention will indeed say: "I myself would be pleased if names were as like [ὅμοια] as possible to the things they name . . . since perhaps the best way to speak, to the extent possible, would be with words all or most of which are like the things named, that is, *appropriate* to them [προσήκουσιν], while the worst way would be the opposite" (435c2–d1). Yet this passage is perfectly compatible with the view that language in fact is not what it is here hoped to be. It would be a wonderful thing if we could see reality reflected in the actual constituents of a word, but if this is not the case, then we must try to understand language differently. Socrates himself suggests in this very passage that the dragging in of imitation to explain the correctness of names has been a "sticky haul"[34] and that we must resort to "vulgar" convention (435c4–7). It may well be that in this respect language is a very imperfect thing and that therefore the search for an "ideal language" is an act of self-delusion. If we place this and the above passage in the context of the dialogue as a whole, we see that the problem with the series of etymologies and the investigation of letters lies not so much in their specific results as in the general project of seeking to discover a name's meaning and natural fitness by reducing it to its simplest components, as if language could be something this self-contained, this complete, this perfect.

Some of the mentioned interpreters would indeed reply that though language is not naturally this perfect, it can be "fixed" through artificial (conventional) means. Yet again such a "correction" of language would have to take the form of Socrates' ridiculous theory of letters. What is ridiculous about the theory is not just that it does not correspond to language as we actually possess it, but that it attempts to derive a word's meaning from the correspondence of each of its letters to some distinct component of reality. Imitation here just does not work, whether to explain langauge as it already exists or to construct a new language. Furthermore, Socrates nowhere so much as *suggests* the possibility of a conventional (artificial) language being ideal or perfect. When he must finally resort to convention, he characterizes it as something rough and crude. There is no indication that we could make language perfect by simply agreeing on a "technical nomenclature."

But there is another objection that is sufficient by itself to undermine this common interpretation. The reason why the dialogue shows no interest in an ideal artificial language is that such a language would not serve the function which is maintained throughout the dialogue to be essential to language, that is, to discover or make manifest reality. Instead, the construction of an ideal language would *presuppose* a *full* elucidation of reality. The ideal language would therefore play no role in such an elucidation but would at best help us to *communicate* what has already been disclosed.[35] Yet throughout the dialogue discovery, not communication, is seen as the primary function of naming.[36] A further and related point is that such a language could not serve as an instrument of dialectic since, in reflecting clearly and unambiguously an already manifest reality, it would instead render dialectic superfluous.[37] An ideal artificial language, in short, would have none of the uses which language is consistently asserted to have in the *Cratylus*. The talk among interpreters about an ideal artifical language clearly derives mainly from contemporary discussions in analytical philosophy and not from anything in the dialogue itself. The question addressed by the dialogue is whether language *as it actually exists and is spoken* is natural or conventional.[38]

After Socrates' account of the meaning of letters, Cratylus is finally brought into the discussion by being asked whether or not he agrees with this account (427d–428c). Socrates confesses that he is not at all certain about what he has said and is therefore willing to learn from Cratylus. Cratylus, however, expresses his delight at the fact that the inspired Socrates has spoken entirely in accord with his own mind. He does not know whether Socrates is inspired by Euthyphro or by some other Muse, but he entirely agrees with what Socrates has said (428c6–8). Socrates, however, replies that he distrusts his own wisdom (428d1–4). The following discussion reveals the reason for this distrust.

Despite their initial agreement, a dispute soon arises between Socrates and Cratylus (429a–430a). The former claims that it is possible for a name to be incorrect, while the latter holds that a name is either correct or no name at all.[39] This latter position involves the rejection of the possibility of falsehood. Neither a name nor a statement consisting of names can be false.[40] If a sentence is meaningful, it must be true. One now begins to see why Cratylus accepts so enthusiastically Socrates' account of natural names. According to this account, only letters acquire their meaning through a direct relation to reality, while names and statements derive their meaning from their letters. If this is the case, it is hard to see how one could account for the possibility of falsehood. If the letters refer to and imitate something, then the name they compose will be meaningful. If the letters do not refer to or imitate anything, then the collection of them will not be a name (since a name is understood precisely in terms of its ability to make something manifest). It is therefore impossible for there to be a name that is meaningful in the sense that its component letters refer to something and that yet is false, that is, in some way does not refer to something. The investigation into what makes a name correct has thus resulted in the view that no name is incorrect. The reason is the investigation's tendency to confine itself to the analyses of names while abstracting from their use. The distinction between correct and incorrect application cannot be made simply by looking at the constituents of a word.

Socrates now argues for the possibility of falsehood by claiming that though a name is an imitation, it can be either a good or a bad one (430a–431e). A bad name will preserve some of the characteristics of its object and thus still be a *name,* but it will distort and mistake other characteristics. Just as with two paintings of the same object one can be a more accurate depiction than the other, so can one name be more correct than another. Cratylus's response is to deny the analogy (431e–432a). Unlike a painting a name is either a correct imitation or no imitation (and therefore no name) at all. Socrates' reply is of special importance. He objects that Cratylus's standard for what counts as a name is so high that it results in the collapse of the distinction between language and reality. For Cratylus a name, in order to be a name, must reproduce perfectly and exhaustively all of the characteristics of the object that it is supposed to make manifest; if the name falls in any way short of being a perfect imitation, it is not a name. Yet, as Socrates points out, a *perfect imitation* would be no imitation at all, but a duplicate of the object imitated (432a–d). If, for example, we could imagine a sculptor capable of perfectly reproducing all of Cratylus's parts, including his internal organs, the result would be another Cratylus, alive and breathing just like the first. Similarly, if a name were perfectly to reproduce its object, it would itself become this object. There would cease to be a difference between the language that makes reality manifest and this reality itself: "A funny thing [γελοῖα], Cratylus, would happen to those things of which names are names if names were in every way like them [ει πάντα πανταχῇ αὐτοῖς ὁμοιωθείη]: they would all be doubled and no one would be able to say in each case which is the thing itself and which is the name" (432d5–9). The etymologies sought the nature of reality in language; now we have the culmination of this tendency: *language has simply become reality.*

What needs to be recognized is that Cratylus is more consistent here than Socrates. He is claiming that if a name is to be properly assigned to an object, it must be like that object in every way. If the name in any way differs from the object, if it contains certain features which do not correspond to anything in the object, then it seems that it would have to be assigned to *another object* which *does* have these features. *But the consequence of this theory of names is that a name can be rightly assigned only to itself; it can be the natural name of an object only if it is identical with this object.*[41]

For example, consider a name with characteristics "abcd." Consider in turn two objects, one with only characteristics "abcd" and one with only characteristics "abce" (the "d" which the latter object is lacking could just be the characteristic of "being a sound"). According to the theory of names which the "inspired" Socrates has proposed and which Cratylus accepts, the name "abcd" would be the name of the object "abcd," rather than of the object "abce" (even if we agreed to apply the name to the latter object). But this means that the name would be identical with that which it names. The consequence is inevitable: if "likeness" is the only basis for the assignment of names, then a name will be a name of that which is in every way like it, rather than of that which in any way differs from it. In claiming that a name either is a perfect imitation of its referent or does not refer to it at all, Cratylus is drawing a conclusion that is perfectly consistent with the principles of the general theory of names under investigation. In making a distinction between correct and incorrect names, Socrates is bringing into question not only Cratylus's denial of the possibility of falsehood, but the very imitation theory of names from which this denial follows.

At 433e Socrates therefore suggests convention to Cratylus as an alternative to imitation. When Cratylus persists in preferring imitation, Socrates points out that the imitation theory of names depends on the possiblity of individual letters resembling the things which names signify: "If a name is to be like [ὅμοιον] the thing named, is it not necessary for the individual elements [τὰ στοιχεῖα] out of which the first names are composed also to be like things?" (434a3–6). Socrates then proceeds to bring into question the letter/thing correspondence and thus, by implication, the general theory that depends on the existence of such a correspondence. Socrates earlier claimed that the letter *l* signifies smoothness. Now he points out that the word "sklērotēs," though containing an *l*, means (δηλοῖ) harshness (434c4–5, d7–8). But how can the meaning of this word be the opposite of what its letters signify? How can it make manifest (δηλοῖ) something *unlike* one of its constituent letters? The answer is: through convention. It has been agreed that this word will refer to the quality of being harsh, regardless of the letters that make it up. Which specific letters are to be used to refer to harshness is decided by convention.[42] Thus Socrates exposes the gulf between what a word is supposed to mean according to a reduction to its simplest elements and what it means in actual use. This represents not so much a return to Hermogenes' position[43] as a return to Socrates' own original position concerning the naturalness of names, that is, that the natural correctness of a name does not depend on the specific letters of which it is composed.

Following this turning point in the discussion, Socrates asks Cratylus to give an account of the function of names (435d1–3). Cratylus replies that it is to teach (διδάσκειν). His meaning is clear: if one knows the name of a thing, one will know the thing itself, not because the name is used in such a way as to refer to the thing (this possibility is not even considered here), but because the name is *like* the thing; as Cratylus explicitly maintains, "whoever knows the names will know also the things" (435d5–6). Cratylus asserts that names are not just the best way, but even the *only* way, of providing knowledge. Socrates now asks whether or not they are also the only way of *discovering* things, that is, whether or not someone who discovers the name for something thereby also discovers the thing itself (436a3–6). Cratylus replies that the method of teaching and the method of discovery are the same. It is not the case that we can know things themselves independently of language and then use language simply to teach them to others. All we know of reality are the names that imitate it. This is comparable to having no more knowledge of the world than what we see in paintings. Etymologies enable us to relate words to other words, but we can never get beyond words. Yet this does not represent for Cratylus a *limit* to our knowledge. If a name is a perfect imitation of the thing named, then though we cannot know anything prior to, or independently of, knowing its name, knowledge of its name enables us to know it exactly as it is. Thus we see again why Cratylus denies the possibility of falsehood.

It should be noted that what Cratylus says here is similar to Socrates' own claim in the context of the tool analogy that names have the two functions of teaching and "distinguishing natures" (388b7–c1). Despite this similarity, however, the two views are profoundly different. While Socrates claimed that we *use* a name to teach and distinguish a specific nature, Cratylus maintains that we know this nature only *in* the name as reflected in its constituents.[44] Socrates' view allowed for the possibility of not remaining confined within language in using it as a tool to disclose reality, but Cratylus's substitution of language for reality excludes this possibility. This difference also explains another striking difference: whereas in Socrates' earlier account the dialectician, as the person who knows how to *use* names, was described as instructing and directing the "legislator" who only makes names, the dialectician receives no mention in Cratylus's account, his place being usurped by the "legislator."[45]

Socrates therefore proceeds to point out that if we are as confined within language as Cratylus believes, the truth of our discoveries depends entirely upon the wisdom of the legislator who first created names (436b5–11). Only this legislator could have stood in a relation between names and the things they signify; all subsequent speakers are confined entirely within language and thus depend for the truth of what they say on the meanings initially given to names by the legislator. What Cratylus's view comes down to is the claim that all knowledge is some form of etymology (understanding "etymology" here in the broad sense of "any knowledge obtained solely through an analysis of words," since Cratylus's principle, "if you know or discover the names you will know or discover the things themselves," is clearly not to be restricted to "etymology" in the narrow sense). In "discovery" all we are doing is basing the meaning of some names on the meaning of other names in the hope that the legislator made these names in such a way that their meanings correspond to reality.

Socrates now proceeds to show just how inaccurate etymologies are in discovering the truth (437a–c). In the earlier etymologies many names were shown to signify that reality is in a state of perpetual flux and that there are consequently no stable, unchanging natures. Motion is the basic characteristic of reality. However, Socrates now provides different etymologies to show that reality is "at rest." The word "epistēmē" (knowledge), earlier said to mean "following things around" and thus to indicate that things are in constant motion (412a1–4), is now shown to mean "stopping the soul at things" and thus to signify that the nature of things is stable (437a2–8). In this way etymologies of the same word lead to contradictory conclusions concerning the nature of reality. The unreliability of etymologies is further demonstrated when Socrates shows that words such as "hamartia" (error) and "amathia" (ignorance), which in actual use have a bad sense, are given a good sense and thus made desirable states by their etymologies (437b4–c4).

The problem is that an etymology tells us nothing about the way in which a word is actually used and about the nature that becomes manifest in this use. In short, an etymology tells us nothing about the *truth*. It is a play with words that can lead to now one result and now another. If our knowledge is really confined to words in the way suggested by Cratylus, then we can in fact do no more than play such games. We can only derive one word from other words or letters, incapable of transcending words in a knowledge of those natures which they signify (438d). In this way all genuine search for truth is rendered impossible. Dialectic degenerates into wordplay.

Cratylus, however, might still want to maintain that the truth of language is guaranteed by the knowledge of the original legislator. Socrates now asks the important question: if all of our knowledge comes through names, then how did the legislator, prior to his invention of names, come to know the nature of things to which he subsequently made names correspond (437e6–438b7)? And if the legislator could know the nature of things directly without the use of names, then why are we denied this direct knowledge? Why are we confined within language? Cratylus suggests that the legislator was not a mortal like us, but a god (438b8–c3). Yet, as Socrates points out, this answer leaves unexplained the inconsistencies seen in the meaning of names, some signifying that all is in motion and others signifying that all is at rest. If the maker of names was a god, names should display more consistency than they in fact do (438c4–5). Therefore, we can know whether reality is in flux or whether there are stable natures only by going beyond words in a direct knowledge of the nature of things themselves. The hypothesis of an original legislator of names that has guided the discussion from the very beginning is thus proven, if not false, at least superfluous.

Socrates consequently concludes that the best way of knowing things is through themselves rather than through names. Since a name is some kind of image of the thing it signifies (in the sense that it makes this thing manifest), it is clearly better to know about the original through acquaintance with the original itself than through its image. One cannot know whether a word is a correct image of the thing it signifies unless one has some kind of direct knowledge of the thing itself. Socrates, however, confesses ignorance of how such direct knowledge is to be had: "The method by which beings are to be learned or discovered is probably more than you or I can know. We must, however, content ourselves with the agreement that they are not to be investigated in and learned from names [ἐξ ὀνομάτων], but much more in and from themselves [ἐξ αὐτῶν] than in and from the names" (439b4–8).[46] In this way Socrates repudiates his earlier attempt to discover the true nature of things through etymologies. Knowledge of beings is not to be had from names. Socrates does not say that names are to play no role at all in the search for truth,[47] but only that the true nature of things is not to be found within names taken as objects of analysis.[48] A name can perhaps be used as some kind of instrument in getting at the truth, but only if, besides knowing the name, we also have some knowledge of that to which the name refers.

After suggesting that the original name-givers wrongly believed that all things are constantly changing, Socrates describes a "dream"[49] he has often had in which he has seen beauty itself, the good itself, and other such beings (439c–d). Something like beauty itself never changes but always remains what it is. If beauty were constantly changing into its opposite, we could never even rightly call it "beauty." Of course, something that is now beautiful can cease to be beautiful at a future time. The word "beauty," however, does not thereby change its meaning; it continues to refer to one determinate, unchanging nature. It is this nature by reference to which the word "beauty" has stable meaning that Socrates calls "beauty itself."

Without the existence of such stable natures, the very activity of naming (if this activity is to be anything more than the utterance of sounds) would be rendered impossible. One cannot correctly name something the nature of which is constantly changing. The very activity of naming presupposes a stability in nature; it presupposes the existence of unchanging natures[50] by reference to which names are meaningful and correct: "If beauty were always passing away, would you be able to address it correctly [προσειπεῖν αὐτὸ ὀρθῶς], first by saying that it is *this* thing and then by saying that it is *such* [πρῶτον μὲν ὅτι ἐκεῖνό ἐστιν, ἔπειτα ὅτι τοιοῦτον], or would it not necessarily immediately change, fade away, and no longer be the same while we were still speaking of it?" (439d8–11). This question reveals just how misguided the "inspired" etymologies were. A result of many of Socrates' derivations was the conclusion that there is no stability in reality, that everything is constantly in motion. Therefore, *not only were these etymologies incapable of demonstrating the correctness of names, but their results contradicted the fundamental presupposition of all correct naming*. This is what happens when one attempts to determine the correctness of names entirely from within names and in abstraction from their actual use. Now, however, Socrates is explaining this correctness by showing us what is involved in any correct naming, that is, a reference to unchanging natures. Even though Socrates has just claimed that we should not look for the true nature of things *in names*, he is now arguing for the existence of stable natures by showing us what is presupposed by the *activity* of naming.

The dialectician was described earlier as the one who reveals the natural correctness of names by properly using them. The investigation of names that Socrates carried out under the inspiration of Euthyphro proved inadequate precisely because it abstracted from this use. A word's correctness cannot be found within its isolated constituents. Socrates now proves himself to be the kind of dialectican described earlier by showing us, not what is contained within a name, but what is presupposed by the *use* of names. In this way the actual activity of naming is seen to transcend names in making manifest their ultimate ground. In the *use* of the word "virtue," that unchanging nature by reference to which this word is meaningful is somehow made manifest. This nature, however, is not made manifest through an analysis of the word into either its letters or other words.[51]

Nowhere in the dialogue is it claimed that we can in fact know the nature of a thing directly without making any use of names. What Socrates' "dream" makes clear, however, is that we do not need such direct knowledge in order for a method of discovery to consist of more than etymologies or analyses of words. Because the very activity of naming presupposes a reference to determinate, unchanging natures, we are not restricted to a choice between discovering the truth *in* names (etymology) and discovering the truth directly *without* names. The alternative exists of discovering the truth *through* names by using them in such a way as to make manifest those stable natures presupposed by their very use. The nature of reality is to be known neither in names nor in itself, but in the very function of names as revealed in use.[52] This is why the dialectician, as one who more than anyone else should have knowledge of *ta onta*, is described neither as an "etymologist" nor as an "intuitionist," but as one who knows *how to use words* (390c).[53]

As already noted above, however, one does not have to be a dialectician in order to know how to use words. In everyday discourse we use words and clearly mean something by them. We speak of "virtue" and "happiness" and "trees" and clearly are aware of the contexts in which these words are to be used.[54] What distinguishes dialectic from this everyday discourse, however, is that it uses words precisely with the intention of making manifest those natures which the proper function of words presupposes. In introducing the good itself and beauty itself, Socrates has shown us what is made manifest in a word's function of referring besides the particular thing referred to. In using the word "virtue" to refer to a particular instance of virtue, we make manifest that unchanging nature (virtue itself) presupposed by this naming.[55] If, on the other hand, we use the word "virtue" to refer to a vicious act, we are using it incorrectly by contradicting its natural function of distinguishing the nature of virtue from the nature of vice.

Dialectic focuses on the function of a word precisely in order to reveal the nature presupposed by this function. It abstracts from ends external to words and focuses on these words themselves. It is not concerned with using words to obtain something desired or to communicate ideas or even to point to sensible particulars. Words are not subordinated to some function accidental to them, but are allowed to serve and reveal their own function. In this way dialectic counters a danger of everyday discourse, that is, that in it a word such as "virtue" can cease to serve its natural function. The word is uttered but is no longer used to make manifest a specific nature. It is simply tossed back and forth between people who have a vague feeling that it means something positive. A possible consequence is that the word will even cease to serve the function of referring to genuine cases of virtue.

This difference between dialectic and everyday discourse brings the former closer than the latter to etymology. However, dialectic differentiates itself in turn from etymology in that it is not concerned with words as particular sounds in a particular language. Its focus is instead what

Socrates calls the "natural name" or a word's "form," that is, the word as a relation to a specific stable nature (389d). Everyday discourse uses words to refer; however, its attention is not directed at this referential relation itself and what is revealed by it. To use again the above example, in everyday discourse we use the word "virtue" to refer to virtuous actions or people, but we do not focus our attention on this reference or use itself and thus on the nature of virtue as revealed in this use. In short, *dialectic and everyday discourse differ in that the latter uses up words for certain extrinsic ends, whereas the former focuses on these words themselves; etymology and dialectic differ in that the former is concerned with the sensible constituents of words (the material, conventional word), whereas the latter is concerned with the word's "form" (the natural word), that is, the word's function in which is made manifest the nature of things.*

This interpretation of Plato's understanding of language differs markedly from that defended by many scholars.[56] It is often said that a name according to Plato is an abbreviated description, a *concept* embodied in sounds, and that naming can occur only by means of such a concept or description: "Concepts set the identity conditions for any entity which may be called by a particular name, and only when the entity in question satisfies the identity conditions specified by the concept will reference be secured."[57] Our ability to describe a thing precedes our ability to name it: "names refer through their descriptive content" (Fine 1977, 301). According to the interpretation presented above, this account of naming, by making the concept or description *prior* to the activity of naming (as its ground), has everything upside-down. What the etymological comedy has demonstrated is the absurdity of trying to explain the correctness of names by turning names (and even letters) into descriptions: such descriptions, rather than explaining the relation between name and thing, *themselves already presuppose such a relation.* In looking *within* names for descriptions of the nature of things one ignores the fundamental relation between name and thing through which a thing's nature is first made manifest and on the basis of which a description of that thing first becomes possible. This confinement within names at the cost of a name's natural function of referring beyond itself is the comic action of the dialogue. The solution is not to bridge over (by means of a concept) the gap thereby created between name and thing, but to go back to that original activity of naming in which there is no such gap. Only because the inquiry has distanced itself from the actual use of names has it had to look within names for more names in an effort to get back to the things themselves. What the *Cratylus* shows us, however, is that the activity of naming is a *brute fact*;[58] because in any inquiry we already exist in the relation between name and thing, we cannot explain how this relation comes about. The positive conclusion of the dialogue, however, is that because the activity of naming presupposes the stable natures of those things to which the names refer, these natures are made manifest by this very activity. Though language is a brute fact, it is a transparent one.

I believe that the view that names for Plato are abbreviated descriptions has already been refuted by my account of Socrates' tool analogy, my criticism of the "ideal language" interpretation, and my account of Socrates' critique of Cratylus's mimetic theory. However, because this view is so widespread,[59] it must be addressed here more directly. Apparently, a basis for attributing this view to Plato has been found in the statement made throughout the dialogue that a name makes manifest (δηλοῖ) the thing to which it refers.[60] This statement is assumed to mean that names *describe* things. After all, what else could it mean? Palmer clearly makes this assumption when he writes: "A name is correct, then, not only if it successfully (and directly) refers to a real unit or kind or object, but if it also discloses the *ousia* of a thing, or *correctly describes it*" (1989, 127; my italics). Thus for Palmer, a name does not disclose a thing's nature by simply referring to it as a distinct kind or unit: for this disclosure to take place, the name must also *describe* the thing. What the failure of the etymological investigation demonstrates, however, is that a description *presupposes* the disclosure of the nature of a thing. Already in its use to refer to one kind of thing, the name is disclosing the nature of this thing; any subsequent description will depend for its truth on this disclosure. It is this activity of referring to a specific nature and showing it forth in its distinctness ("I am referring to this, not that") that is the proper function of a name and that makes it a means of manifesting (δήλωμα). In the very use of the word "virtue," the nature of virtue is disclosed to me, and only because this is the case can I then proceed to try to describe or define virtue. This of course means that in the disclosure brought about through the use of a name, we have not once and for all grasped the nature of the thing named. This nature is manifest to us in its distinctness, but we then need to make explicit what is only implicit in this disclosure. It is only here, subsequent to the activity of naming and what it discloses, that description and conceptualization come in. It may then turn out to be the case that no description and no concept can entirely do justice to the nature of the thing as revealed by the very activity of naming. In other words, more may be disclosed in the use of a name than can be adequately expressed in a description or concept. This possibility makes especially clear how backward it is to think that our ability to describe a thing is prior to our ability to name it. It is not the case that we can name a thing only if we can describe it; on the contrary, we can describe it only if we can name it.

A major presupposition of the inquiries taking place in the so-called Socratic dialogues is that the very ability to use a word such as "virtue" guarantees that the nature of virtue is somehow disclosed. Without this disclosure provided by the name's use, the search for a definition of the thing named could never get underway. In other words, the very question "What is virtue?" presupposes that there is a difference between the manifestation of a thing's nature and a description of this nature, since the question presupposes *both* that the nature of virtue is manifest (otherwise the question would make no sense, and we could not even begin to answer it) *and* that we are not yet in possession of a description or definition of virtue. This difference is only reinforced by what the last chapter's reading of the *Laches* and the *Charmides* discovered, that is, that the *aporia* in which these two dialogues end results from the fact that no definition can do justice to the nature of temperance or courage as revealed in the course of the inquiry.

The etymologies carried out in the *Cratylus* indeed presuppose that a name can disclose a thing only by describing it, but that is precisely why they fail to account for the correctness of names and why the inquiry finds itself trapped within language with no access to the true natures of things. In the dialectical use of names described in connection with the shuttle analogy, and in Socrates' claim that the activity of naming as such presupposes the existence of stable natures, we see exactly what is missing in the reduction of a name's function of manifesting to its descriptive content. The etymologies fail because to use a name in disclosing a thing is *not* to describe that thing.[61] This is why the attempt to locate a name's function in its descriptive content must finally cede to the convention view, that is, the view that a name can pick out and disclose a thing *simply because that is how it is used* and not because it is an abbreviated description. Even if the letters of a name are unlike the thing named, the name still succeeds in making this thing manifest (δηλοῖ καὶ τὰ ὅμοια καὶ τὰ ἀνόμοια γράμματα, ἔθους τε καὶ συνθήκης τυχόντα) (435a9–10). Since the only way in which a name could *describe* a thing is through its constituent letters (if it is a secondary name that describes by being composed of primary names, these primary names themselves can describe only by being composed of letters that individually describe), the cited sentence in essence says: by means of custom and convention, letters that do not describe a thing make this thing manifest no less than letters that do describe it. Can it be made any clearer that Socrates in his critique of the mimetic theory is disassociating a word's ability to make manifest or disclose from its ability to describe? To attribute to Plato the view that a name can disclose a thing only by describing it, one must ignore everything that comes before and after the etymological section, as well as the irony of the etymological section itself.[62]

At the end of the dialogue, we are not given an answer to the question that began the whole discussion: are names conventional or natural? The reason is that something has been shown to be wrong with the very question. In the course of the dialogue, Socrates has refuted the positions of *both* Hermogenes and Cratylus. He could do so because these apparently opposed positions are really not opposed at all.[63] Hermogenes' position, by asserting that the meaning of a name is conventional, easily degenerates into the view that all truth is conventional and relative. Cratylus's position, by abstracting language from the things themselves and confining truth within language, ends up denying the possibility of falsehood (which is just the other side of the Protagorean view that whatever appears to one is true).

Therefore, the dialectician, in seeing that the very possibility of language presupposes the existence of unchanging natures of which we can have some kind of knowledge, must deny both positions.[64] He must claim that names are neither natural nor conventional in the way in which Hermogenes and Cratylus understand them to be. The dialectician's use of names, however, reveals them to be in a different sense *both* natural *and* conventional. A name is conventional insofar as its meaning is not to be found in other names or in the sounds and letters that are its elements, but rather in the way in which we use it.[65] Yet a name is natural insofar as its use reveals the true nature of the thing signified; what the name *means*, what it makes manifest in discussion, is neither conventional nor relative. Hermogenes is right in thinking that a name as a set of letters and syllables does not possess any inherent meaning; he is wrong, however, in thinking that a name's function of manifesting the true nature of a thing (what Socrates calls the "natural name") is conventional. Cratylus is right in thinking that the meaning of a name is in accord with nature; yet he is wrong in thinking that this meaning is contained in a name's elements (those words or letters into which it can be analyzed).[66]

By refuting the positions of Hermogenes and Cratylus insofar as they are false, Socrates reveals the ways in which both are true. The problem the dialogue raises, however, does not thereby receive a final solution. The essence of language, though saved from misrepresentation, is left a mystery. How can a word in its use make manifest the true nature of a thing? How can this word, though not containing the truth in its component parts, nevertheless *express* this truth that transcends it? How are we to explain the fact that, though confined to words in our discourse and argumentation, our knowledge of the true nature of a thing is not *derived* from words? *How can an inquiry into the nature of virtue be anything more than an etymology or analysis of the word?* The dialectician, in contrast to the etymologist, clearly knows how to use words in such a way that they point beyond themselves in making manifest those unchanging natures to which they are essentially related (i.e., they would not be meaningful words without such a relation). However, this relation between word and thing is not *created* by the dialectician, and how it could ever come about is a mystery.

The dialogue, then, does not explain the exact nature of the relation between name and thing. The shuttle analogy goes only so far, since a shuttle, unlike a name, is not used to make anything manifest. The painting analogy, on the other hand, is inadequate because it abstracts from the actual *use* of words and replaces this use with a static mirroring. The absence of a final solution, however, is not to be explained by temporary uncertainty on Plato's part. What the negative results of this dialogue show is that there is no "answer." *One can inquire into the nature of language only by means of language.* Thus any model or theory of language, as presupposing and formulated within language, will not be able to get outside language in such a way as to explain the nature of its relation to reality.[67] This is what the etymological comedy makes clear. In looking for the reality to which names correspond Socrates finds only more names. The myth of an original legislator of names in immediate contact with the things themselves, a myth that enables us to distinguish between an original positing of names and our present use of them, was appealing because it provided a way out of this circle of language referring to language.[68] However, Socrates' critique of Cratylus undermined this myth. In the process, we have seen how the legislator's rival, the dialectician, can remain within the circle without being confined to words: that is, by using names in such a way that the stable natures presupposed by the very activity of naming become manifest in this use. In this way the two opposed models of language are reconciled in what the dialectician *does,* rather than in any answer or theory. Instead of attempting in vain to get outside of language to see how it "matches up" with reality, one should situate oneself within this relation. This does not mean that one should simply revert to the everyday use of names; one must make this use transparent to its ultimate grounds. Instead of simply using the word "virtue" to refer to virtuous acts, one must pay attention to the nature that is made manifest by the very way in which the word "virtue" is used. One thereby avoids the mistake of trying to step outside the everyday use of language, but one also does not simply acquiesce in this use. The *Cratylus* does not provide us with a "theory of language." It instead provides us with the insight that language, as presupposing in its function the existence of stable natures, can be used in such a way as to make these natures manifest. Though incapable of getting outside language, our search for truth is not confined to verbal analyses.

4

Dialectic and Eristic in the *Euthydemus*

I

The examination of the *Cratylus* in the preceding chapter has uncovered the understanding of language presupposed by the practice of dialectic. The goal of the present chapter is to make clear how the dialectician understands and uses *arguments*. Here the main task will be to distinguish dialectic from its very close neighbor, eristic. Passages distinguishing dialectic from eristic in one way or another are found throughout Plato's dialogues. Only the *Euthydemus,* however, is devoted to carrying out this distinction. This dialogue shows how eristic abuses the argumentative skill which the dialectician knows how to use properly. Yet what allows dialectic and eristic to be so easily confounded is the difficulty of understanding this distinction between the use and abuse of argumentation. This is why the *Euthydemus* has as one of its major themes the notion of use (χρῆσις) in its relation to the good. The dialogue therefore shows us the difference between dialectic and eristic by alternating between scenes in which Socrates discusses this notion and scenes in which eristic is allowed to run wild.[1]

The dialogue begins when a friend of Socrates, Crito, asks him with whom he was conversing the day before in the Lyceum. There was such a large crowd that Crito could not get close enough to hear anything clearly. By looking over the heads of others, however, he was able to see Socrates conversing with someone who appeared to be a foreigner. Socrates corrects Crito by observing that he was in fact conversing with *two* men: the brothers Euthydemus and Dionysodorus. In reply to Crito's questions, Socrates now reveals the origin of the two brothers, as well as the nature of the wisdom (σοφία) on which they pride themselves. The brothers are apparently from Chios originally (though Socrates does not seem to be sure about this), but they later joined a colony at Thurii from which they in turn fled (271c3–4). For many years since they have lived in Greece. We are not told why the brothers had to flee from the colony, though this silence is enough to place them in an unfavorable light.[2] What is to be gathered from Socrates' remarks, however, is that the brothers are essentially homeless. Far from being insignificant, this homelessness will later be made an object of reproach. Angered by one of the brothers' arguments, Ctesippus addresses them as "Men of Thurii or men of Chios or men from whatever place and in whatever way it pleases you to derive your names"(288a8-b1). This form of address is extremely insulting. Ctesippus is implying that because the two brothers do not really belong anywhere, they may as well pick a place from which they would like to be said to be.

The significance of the brothers' "homelessness" is revealed by Socrates' response to Crito's question concerning the nature of their *sophia*. Socrates asserts that the brothers are in possession of a wisdom incredible (θαυμασία) for its universality. The brothers are wise concerning practically every subject matter (271c6) and can defeat any opinion. The scope of their skill is not even limited by the distinction between truth and falsehood. They are as capable of refuting a true opinion as a false one. Socrates also characterizes this art as combative. The brothers were at one time known for their skill at fighting in armor (ἐν ὅπλοις μάχεσθαι); now they have also mastered the art of fighting with words (ἐν τοῖς λόγοις μάχεσθαι).[3] Whatever the subject of an opinion, whatever its truth value, this art enables one to refute it. Thus is seen the way in which the method of the two brothers is a homeless or rootless one: neither is it confined to a particular subject matter nor is it even bound by the truth. It is a method of complete freedom, or rather, license.[4]

Having learned this about the two brothers, one cannot help being surprised when Socrates confesses his intention of becoming their pupil. Socrates is of course being ironic, but as usual with Socratic irony, there is an element of seriousness here. Socrates must recognize the resemblance between what the brothers are doing and what he himself does. He, like they, practices an art of refutation and seems capable of defeating any opinion he encounters. Socrates does indeed claim to be concerned with the truth, but he also admits to being ignorant. Furthermore, as far as anyone can tell, his method does not make any progress toward acquiring knowledge. After the whole process of questioning and answering, he claims to be as ignorant as before. As was already seen in chapter 2, Socrates is easily confused with his sophistic counterparts (Nicias and Critias). Socrates' wish to learn the brothers' "wonderful wisdom" is humorous insofar as there will prove to be a major difference between what he is doing and what they are doing: it is serious insofar as this difference is easily concealed by the similarity.

II

When Socrates narrates to Crito his discussion with Euthydemus and Dionysodorus, one of the first things we learn is that the two brothers claim to be in possession of a knowledge of virtue that they can impart "quickly" to anyone (273d8–9). However, when the brothers agree to demonstrate their incredible wisdom, Socrates demands something else of them. He asks whether, besides teaching virtue to someone who is already persuaded that virtue must be learned from them, the brothers can also use their art to persuade the unconverted who thinks either that virtue cannot be learned at all or that the brothers are not teachers of it. The brothers reply that their art can indeed justify itself in this way, from which Socrates infers that it can turn one toward (*protrepein*, 275a1) philosophy and the pursuit of virtue. When the brothers agree, Socrates asks them to save the demonstration of their other skills for another day and to demonstrate for now nothing but this: that their art can persuade the boy Cleinias that it is necessary for him to philosophize and to concern himself with virtue (ὡς χρὴ φιλοσοφεῖν καὶ ἀρετῆς ἐπιμελεῖσθαι, 275a6).

Why does Socrates make precisely this request? Three answers can be given. First, the brothers have a questionable understanding of what it means to teach virtue, since they believe that it is simply a matter of handing virtue over to the student (παραδοῦναι, 273d8). Therefore, Socrates wants them to make clear in just what way they think virtue can be taught. Second, and more important, Socrates must at this point suspect that the last thing a "homeless," purely combative art of disputation could do is instill in one a love of virtue and wisdom. When it comes to "teaching" virtue in the sense of providing positive instruction on it, Socrates may prove no more successful than the two brothers. On the other hand, when it comes to persuading one that virtue is teachable and should be pursued, there is a chance that dialectic will succeed where eristic fails.[5]

There may be, however, a third and even more important reason for the way in which Socrates sets up the discussion. Perhaps the "protreptic" question "Why philosophize and why concern oneself with virtue?" cannot be sharply distinguished from the substantive questions "What is virtue? What is the good?" A knowledge of why it is necessary to pursue virtue seems hardly separable from a knowledge of what virtue is. A knowledge of why it is necessary to pursue philosophy, that is, of why it is *good* to pursue philosophy, is hardly separable from knowledge of the good.[6] Furthermore, it will become clear in Socrates' protreptic discussions with Cleinias that philosophy, rather than being simply a tool for attaining the good, is itself comprised in the good. Philosophy will thus prove to be characterized by a "reflexivity" that ultimately makes the protreptic and substantive questions indistinguishable. Therefore, rather than dismissing here as irrelevant to the discussion his own or the brothers' ability to provide a knowledge of virtue and the good, Socrates is instead hinting at the nature of this knowledge: it is not knowledge that can be simply handed over as a theory or teaching but is instead gained only in the process of learning to philosophize. To learn why and how to pursue the good, that is, why and how to *philosophize*, is to learn what the good is. That is why the brothers' ignorance of the former will prove their ignorance of the latter.

Having agreed to test their skill on Cleinias, the brothers begin their display (275d). The first question they ask the boy is whether those who learn are the ignorant or the wise. As Cleinias is thinking of what to say, Dionysodorus whispers into Socrates' ear that the boy will be refuted no matter what he answers (275e3–6). Before Socrates can warn him, however, Cleinias answers that those who learn are the wise. Euthydemus refutes this answer by showing that one learns only what one does not yet know and that therefore the ignorant are the ones who learn. Before the boy has a chance to catch his breath, Dionysodorus shows him that he was wrong to agree with Euthydemus, since the pupils who learn a grammarian's dictation are the wise ones, not the ignorant. Therefore, it is the wise who learn.

This part of the discussion already makes clear certain essential features of the eristic method. One concerns the kind of questions asked. These questions almost always present the respondent with a choice between two mutually exclusive alternatives: either the wise are the learners or the ignorant.[7] The respondent is given no third choice nor is allowed to explain his answer. The brothers never ask open-ended questions such as "What is virtue?" A response to such a question would require careful examination of the subject matter. In forcing one to choose between preformulated answers, the brothers preclude such examination.

What proves the respondent's downfall is that each suggested answer, due to its inherent ambiguity, can be interpreted in such a way as to be false. The brothers first interpret the proposition "The ignorant are the ones who learn" as meaning "One learns what one does not yet know." In this case the proposition is clearly true and its negation is false. When the brothers want to arrive at the opposite conclusion, however, they interpret the proposition as meaning "Those who lack all knowledge and insight are the ones who learn." In this case the proposition is clearly false, and its negation is true. Thus the questioner knows beforehand that either alternative the respondent chooses can be refuted. What makes this possible, that is, that the same proposition is given different meanings, is not allowed to become an issue in the discussion itself. All that is allowed to matter is the "letter" of what is said, not its "spirit."

This last observation explains another characteristic of the method: its *speed*. Socrates remarks that the brothers' arguments follow upon one another so quickly that the boy cannot even catch his breath. Speed here prevents the interlocutor from noticing the shift in meaning. *No pauses or digressions are allowed* because the attention of the interlocutor must at all times be kept focused on the precise formulation of the proposition in question (rather than on its meaning). Examples are kept to a minimum and are not carefully explained or developed. Propositions must be used adroitly and quickly, like the foil of a fencing master.

Encouraged by the cheers of his admirers, Euthydemus proceeds to ask what is basically the same question, but in slightly different terms: Do those who learn learn what they know or what they do not know? The boy answers that they learn what they do not know. Euthydemus's refutation uses, according to Socrates, the same means as before (277a1). Only a student who knows all the letters can learn a teacher's dictation. What a teacher dictates are precisely letters. Therefore, the learner is learning what he knows.

Now Dionysodorus joins the fray to refute the boy's acceptance of Euthydemus's conclusion. To learn is to acquire knowledge of something. Not yet to have this knowledge is not yet to know. Someone who is in the process of acquiring something does not yet have this thing. Someone who is learning does not yet know that which he is learning. Cleinias is wrong again.

That the two brothers can repeat the same arguments couched in slightly different terms shows that their method is indeed concerned only with the exact form of a question and not with its content. Even if the point is the same, the use of different wording allows the brothers to score another point.

Just as Euthydemus is getting ready to throw Cleinias down to the mat a third time, Socrates comes to the boy's rescue. He tells him not to be amazed if the brothers' arguments seem a bit unusual (ἀηθεῖς οἱ λόγοι, 277d5). Cleinias does not realize that their purpose is to initiate him into the sophistic mysteries (τῶν ἱερῶν σοφιστικῶν). They believe that before proceeding any further he must learn the correctness of names (περὶ ὀνομάτων ὀρθότητος, 277e4). They want the boy to recognize that the word "learn" is used in two different senses: in one case, it means obtaining knowledge of what one does not yet know, and, in the other case, it means using the knowledge one has of a thing to examine and understand this thing further (277e–278a; Socrates observes that in this case the word "understand" [συνιέναι] is more appropriate, but that the word "learn" is nevertheless sometimes used in this sense, 278a4–5).

Though Socrates' point is surely correct, it seems rather simplistic.[8] There are clearly other ambiguities at play in the brothers' arguments. "Wisdom" is identified in one case with a capacity for learning quickly and easily and in the other with the actual possession of knowledge. Furthermore, whole is confused with part when learning a teacher's dictation is confused with learning the individual letters that are dictated (cf. Hawtrey 1981, 67). Socrates also misrepresents the purpose of the eristic method (knowingly, we might presume) by claiming that the two brothers wish Cleinias to recognize the ambiguity of the word "learn." As has been seen, nothing could be further from their purpose. It is indeed likely that the brothers themselves have not pursued the difficult task of sorting out all of these ambiguities. Even Socrates' attempt to clarify one of them is not entirely successful, since it leaves unexplained the distinction between knowing something and understanding it.[9] All the brothers need to know is that words such as "learn," "know," and "wisdom" can lead the respondent into a quagmire where, finding no sure footing, he can easily be made to fall.

Socrates now accuses the brothers of merely *playing a game* with Cleinias (παιδιά, 278c1–2). The harshness of this accusation is alleviated by the suggestion that the brothers will of course soon display something serious (τὰ σπουδαῖα, 278c3).[10] It is left for us to see that this promise is never fulfilled. Socrates now explains his meaning: if one were to learn most or even all of what the brothers teach, one would not thereby become any more knowledgeable about *the way things actually are* (278b2–5).[11] Yet the criticism can be taken even further (and is by Socrates later in the dialogue): not only has their game not really taught Cleinias anything, but in arguing that Cleinias can learn neither what he knows nor what he does not know, the brothers have denied the very possibility that they will ever teach Cleinias anything. Their game not only happens to lack seriousness but negates the very possibility of seriousness.

It is important to note that Socrates does not criticize the brothers for failing to clarify their terms. It may be that what these terms denote is too complex to be fully susceptible to such clarification. In this case, confining the word to one meaning would not necessarily provide one with greater insight into the nature of the referent.[12] Socrates' implied criticism is rather that the purely verbal or "formal" character of the brothers' arguments prevents reflection on the ambiguities and thus insight into the truth. Even if notions such as "learning" and "wisdom" are inherently ambiguous, there may still be a serious way of dealing with the ambiguities that illuminates these notions. The eristic method, however, is not characterized by such seriousness. It is incapable of taking seriously the only thing which the Socratic method seems to think is worth taking seriously, namely, truth.

III

Now Socrates assures Cleinias that the brothers will certainly stop fooling around and get serious. They said, after all, that they would display a "protreptic wisdom" (τὴν προτρεπτικὴν σοφίαν, 278c5–6). Socrates now addresses the two brothers and tells them that they have played enough. They should now fulfill their promise. Socrates will himself give them a demonstration of what he understands by a protreptic discourse. In this way Socrates' ensuing discussion with Cleinias is itself meant to be a display and as such should be contrasted with the display of the two brothers.

First we should focus on Socrates' actual argument and its conclusion (278e–282d) and ask how it contrasts with the wisdom claimed by the two brothers. Then we should look at how Socrates leads Cleinias to this conclusion and contrast this with the way in which the brothers deal with the boy.

The argument is basically as follows: we all desire to "fare well" (εὖ πράττειν). This depends, however, on our possession of certain goods. Numbered among things good are wealth, health, beauty, good birth, honor, temperance, justice, courage, and wisdom. It may seem that one very important good has been excluded from the list, namely, good fortune (εὐτυχία). Yet it has in fact been included with wisdom, since the two are the same. One has good fortune concerning those things of which one has knowledge. The flute-player has good fortune or success in playing the flute. The grammarian has good fortune in reading and writing. The wise pilot has good fortune in confronting the dangers of the sea. In each case wisdom is what brings good fortune.

The mention of wisdom here leads to the reconsideration of the main point above: the possession of goods will not make us happy unless these goods benefit us. Furthermore, we will not benefit from them unless we make use of them (χρῆσθαι). Having food will not benefit us unless we eat it; having something to drink will not benefit us unless we drink it. Yet our happiness depends not only on the use of these goods, but also on their *correct use* (ὀρθῶς χρῆσθαι). If we use them incorrectly, they can be much more harmful than their opposites. It is clear, for example, that if one overeats, the possession of food becomes more harmful than its lack. However, the goods spoken of here include even the virtues. If courage is not used correctly, it can be worse than cowardice. It can place us in a situation where we will lose our lives pointlessly and unnecessarily. What this means is that so-called goods such as wealth, health, and the virtues are, taken in themselves, neither good nor bad. What makes them good is their proper use. What guides and determines this proper use, on the other hand, is wisdom or knowledge. The result is that wisdom is the only thing that is good without qualification. If wisdom, then, can be taught and if we want to be happy, it is necessary that we pursue wisdom, that is, that we "philosophize."

Socrates' emphasis in this argument on the importance of correct use in becoming happy should be contrasted with an earlier comment concerning the value of the skill possessed by the two brothers. When first informed of the nature of the brothers' wisdom, Socrates congratulated them for being more happy in the possession of such a skill (τοῦ κτήματος) than a king in the possession of power (274a6–7). Compare with this passage the following, in which Socrates emphasizes the inability of mere possession to provide happiness: "It is necessary, it seems, that he who is to be happy not only possess [κεκτῆσθαι] these goods but also use [χρῆσθαι] them; otherwise the possession of them will not at all benefit him" (280d4–7). The contrast between these two passages provides us with the terms in which the eristic method is to be criticized. The brothers are clearly in possession of a skill that is by no means contemptible: a sense of the ambiguities of words as well as extraordinary dexterity in formulating arguments are presupposed by their ability to refute any position whatsoever. Yet what characterizes the eristic is his *misuse* of this skill, a skill that could conceivably be put to good use in philosophy. It is therefore this misuse, and not the skill per se, that requires us to dismiss eristic's pretension to the good and happy life.[13]

It is clear, then, how important the notion of correct use (ὀρθὴ χρῆσις) is in the context of the dialogue as a whole. At this stage of the discussion, however, two important questions remain unanswered: First, what exactly distinguishes the proper use of arguments from their misuse? How exactly does the way in which Socrates argues differ from the way in which the brothers argue? Second, Socrates' discussion with Cleinias concludes that what guides and determines correct use is knowledge (ἐπιστήμη). Yet the art which the brothers claim to possess is itself a kind of knowledge. Is it not mistaken, then, to judge this knowledge in terms of correct use rather than vice versa? Or is the brothers' skill of argumentation not included in what Socrates means when he speaks of "knowledge" as guaranteeing one's happiness? The nature of the knowledge that Socrates describes as determining the goodness of all subordinate "goods" must be specified if the brothers are to be disqualified from possessing it.

The second question will be answered in Socrates' second discussion with Cleinias (starting 288d). We can begin to answer the first question, however, by looking at the *form* of Socrates' first example of protreptic discourse.

We should first focus on the similarity between Socrates' arguments and those of the two brothers in order then to try to bring out the most important difference. Despite a prevalent misconception, both the eristic and dialectical methods employ what is, strictly speaking, fallacious reasoning. A major characteristic of eristic arguments noted above is the play on ambiguities. Socrates himself, however, cannot avoid this charge. His argument begins with the claim that wisdom is good fortune (*eutuchia*). His examples, however, only show a close connection between wisdom and "acting well" (*eupragia*, 279e1) in the sense of succeeding (εὐτυχὴς εἶναι) at that particular endeavor of which one has knowledge. Someone who knows how to play the flute will have the most success in playing the flute well. Someone who knows how to pilot a ship will have the most success in piloting the ship well. All that these examples show is that being good at something (*eupragia*) depends on having knowledge and that success in doing something well is itself an instance of good fortune (*eutuchia*). What the examples do not show, however, is that every case of good fortune (*eutuchia*) is also a case of acting well (*eupragia*) and that therefore every case of the former, like every case of the latter, depends on wisdom.[14] Conversely, the examples also fail to show that every case of misfortune is a case of acting badly and that therefore the former, like the latter, results from ignorance. Socrates seems to be confusing the notions of *eupragia* and *eutuchia*, even though later on in the discussion (281b2–3) and in a different context he himself distinguishes between them (cf. Canto 1987, 130).

The problems do not end here. Even if wisdom is a necessary condition of *eupragia*, it is not a sufficient condition. Knowledge of how to play the flute does not ensure that one will play it well, since one might, for example, have arthritis. Knowledge of how to pilot a ship does not ensure a safe voyage, since the ship might be destroyed by a powerful storm. There are, then, other factors involved in acting well besides knowledge. It is not even clear that Socrates' examples show knowledge to be a necessary condition. Could one not act well through habit or imitation, without real knowledge of what one is doing? Socrates' claim that the person who acts with wisdom will be *more* successful (*eutuchesterous*, 280a4–5) appears to allow that someone without wisdom may succeed too, though to a lesser degree. However, not only does this qualified claim conflict with Socrates' unqualified conclusion that wisdom simply *is* good fortune, but it also seems inherently questionable. An expert flute player with broken fingers will not succeed as well in playing the flute as will someone with little or no knowledge but good fingers.

Another problem concerns the ambiguity of the word "wisdom." Even if it is admitted that knowledge of a certain art will grant one good fortune *in that art,* it is hard to see how knowledge could grant one good fortune *simpliciter*. Socrates concludes: "he who has wisdom (*sophia*) is in no way lacking in good fortune" (280b2–3). What is meant by *sophia* here? It cannot mean knowledge of a particular art, since such knowledge would not guarantee one every kind of good fortune. Does it then refer to the possession of all kinds of knowledge? Then it seems simply unattainable. Whatever *sophia* might mean here, Socrates seems to be committing the following fallacy: he shifts from speaking of particular forms of knowledge to speaking simply of "knowledge," or from speaking of good fortune in particular activities to speaking of good fortune in general.

Were the above objections to be answered, Socrates' conclusion would still be untenable. Even if one grants that wisdom is both a necessary and sufficient condition of *eupragia,* and even if one shows further that it is a necessary and sufficient condition of *eutuchia,* one still cannot conclude that wisdom simply *is eupragia* or *eutuchia*. The existence of a necessary relation between two ideas does not allow one to identify them.

The fallacies, in conclusion, are the following:

1. The term used in the premises (*eupragia*) is not the same as the term used in the conclusion (*eutuchia*).
2. Arguments that at most show wisdom to be a *necessary* condition of happiness are taken to show that it is a *sufficient* condition.
3. There is an unexplained shift in Socrates' argument from good fortune and knowledge *secundum quid* to good fortune and knowledge *simpliciter.*
4. The conclusion that wisdom is a necessary condition of good fortune is wrongly taken to be equivalent to the conclusion that it is identical with good fortune.

The distinction between eristic and dialectic cannot be made by asserting that the former employs fallacies while the latter does not.[15] This does not mean, however, that both methods of argumentation should be judged solely in terms of the fallacious/valid distinction and therefore equally condemned. The charge of fallacy is a devastating one only when the sole intent of an argument is to *prove* something, that is, *to force the universal acceptance of a conclusion which otherwise need not be accepted*. This intent is usually accompanied by the assumption that there is no way of *knowing* this conclusion to be true except through such a proof. In this case, the presence of a fallacy would destroy the argument's claim to provide knowledge and would allow one to refrain from accepting the conclusion. However, the charge of fallacy touches neither the eristic nor Socrates, since neither argues with this intent. The eristic's goal is the refutation *of a particular respondent;* therefore, the use of fallacy, rather than being an objection to what he is doing, is simply a sign of his skill. The best way to win an argument is to commit fallacies not spotted as such by the respondent.

Socrates' goal, on the other hand, is equally removed from wanting to force universal acceptance of a conclusion. Socrates' method is protreptic precisely in that it aims to convert the interlocutor to a certain course of action. In getting Cleinias to see the importance of wisdom in determining the goodness of things such as health, wealth, and even the virtues, Socrates' goal is *to encourage the boy to pursue wisdom.* Therefore, the premises of a Socratic argument, rather than being understood as means of logically necessitating a certain conclusion, are meant to be *aids* in turning a particular individual in a certain direction.[16] The argument serves the goal of conversion rather than proof. But then it is pointless to object that it commits a logical fallacy.[17] The question is not whether the argument succeeds in universally proving the conclusion, since this was never the intention; the question is instead whether or not the argument points us in the right direction, inspires us with the right goal. The measure of success is practical and not purely theoretical. By this measure, the present argument is extraordinarily successful, as Cleinias's performance in his second discussion with Socrates will show.

Yet these observations raise some important questions. Does Socrates' dialectic have only the purely practical purpose of exhortation (a purpose compatible with the existence of fallacies)? Does it only exhort us to pursue virtue and wisdom without providing us with any knowledge of what they are? In short, is the only purpose of dialectic to convince others to practice dialectic? As will be seen, a similar question presents itself in Socrates' second protreptic discussion. What needs to be noted here is the possibility, already suggested above, that the dichotomy operative in these questions is a false one. Perhaps knowing why one should pursue virtue and wisdom is inseparable from knowing what virtue and wisdom are. Perhaps the practical, protreptic function of dialectic most in evidence in Socrates' first discussion with Cleinias is inseparable from a theoretical function. Most important, it is possible that both functions in their unity have nothing to do with arguments that aim through their validity to necessitate the universal acceptance of certain conclusions. Perhaps we acquire a knowledge of virtue through the practical decision to pursue it and not through the conclusion of any theoretical argument. These possibilities must await a discussion of the exact nature of that wisdom which the philosopher pursues.

The similarity between eristic and dialectic is therefore that neither method has as its goal necessitating the universal acceptance of a given thesis and that both methods are immune to the charge of fallacy. The dissimilarity, on the other hand, is this: while eristic aims to force a conclusion on the respondent with the purpose of defeating him, dialectic aims to convert the respondent to the pursuit of wisdom and virtue, a conversion that is not forced but is freely undergone (through *agreement*).[18] As the reading of the *Laches* and the *Charmides* in chapter 2 has already suggested, it is wrong to see the goal of a Socratic argument as being the introduction of entirely new knowledge into the mind of the respondent. Its purpose is rather *to suggest*, to occasion the *recognition* of, what is in some way already known. Cleinias himself sees that things such as wealth and virtue are in some sense good; he himself sees that they are good only if used wisely.[19] These are not conclusions which Socrates through the brilliance and coherence of his arguments forces the boy to accept; the boy himself, with Socrates' guidance, comes to see the importance of wisdom and the necessity of its pursuit. The remainder of the dialogue will show even more clearly that eristic has the opposite practical effect, that it is a "protreptic" failure. What is common to dialectic and eristic, however, is their compatibility with fallacious reasoning.[20]

IV

At this stage of the dialogue we see important dissimilarities as well as similarities between eristic and dialectic. The first discussion with Cleinias ends with the conclusion that since wisdom determines the proper use and therefore goodness of all that is normally called "good," it is to be pursued above all else. Socrates describes this as his layman's (ἰδιωτικόν) attempt at the kind of protreptic discourse which he desires to hear (282d4–7). He wants the brothers to demonstrate what such discourse is like when skillfully carried out. This request gives them the opportunity for another display. Dionysodorus begins by asking whether Socrates and the others are serious (σπουδάζετε) or only joking (παίζετε) when they say that they want the boy Cleinias to become wise. Until now Socrates is the one who has accused the brothers of not being serious; now this accusation is hurled back at him.[21] Furthermore, each is accused of lacking seriousness precisely in what each asserts to be his peculiar art: Socrates denies the seriousness of the brothers' skill of refutation, and Dionysodorus denies the seriousness of Socrates' protreptic skill of turning one toward the pursuit of wisdom. It is therefore left for the reader to decide, on the basis of what Plato shows us in this dialogue, which method is in fact to be taken seriously.

When Socrates replies that he is incredibly (θαυμαστῶς) serious in his wish, Dionysodorus argues that in wanting the boy to become wise Socrates wants him *not to be* what he at present is, that is, wants him *destroyed*. This argument well exemplifies a general procedure of the two brothers: to present as unambiguous and unqualified a statement that is ambiguous and requires qualification. The statement "Socrates wants Cleinias not to be" is in some sense certainly true. He wants Cleinias *not to be ignorant,* but he clearly does not want Cleinias *not to be* in the sense of ceasing to exist. The brothers, however, do not care to distinguish between these two senses of "not-being." Socrates either does or does not want Cleinias not to be: there is no other alternative.

Involved in the brothers' play, then, is a serious principle: it is not possible for a thing to be simultaneously F and not-F. This has been called the principle of "noncontradiction" and since Aristotle has been regarded as a principle so fundamental that without it we would not be able to reason at all. What is peculiar to the eristic method, however, is the way in which it interprets this principle. According to Aristotle, statements such as "Socrates wants Cleinias to be and not to be" and "Those who learn are wise and not wise" are not contradictions if the term affirmed and denied in each case *has a different sense.* For Euthydemus and Dionysodorus, however, these statements are contradictory because the term affirmed and denied *is the same word.* In other words, they recognize only *verbal* contradiction. For a statement of the form "F and not-F" to be a contradiction it is not necessary that F have the same meaning; all that is required is that F be the same set of sounds or syllables. This principle is behind all of the brothers' arguments.[22]

The connection between the *Euthydemus* and the *Cratylus* begins to emerge here: in the latter dialogue we see the etymologist searching for the truth of words by abstracting them from their function of referring in actual use to something beyond themselves, while in the present dialogue we see the eristic abstracting a word from the varied meanings it has in specific contexts and basing his arguments on its superficial identity. In both cases words as such are given a certain autonomy. Words are used for the sake of words. No attention is paid to what should be taken seriously: the truth that lies beyond words. Both eristic and etymology are forms of *wordplay* (cf. *Republic* 454a4–9).

We begin to see some of the important consequences of eristic's guiding principle when Cleinias's lover, Ctesippus, joins the discussion, infuriated by Dionysodorus's suggestion that he wants to see his beloved destroyed. He accuses Dionysodorus of speaking falsely concerning such an important matter. At this point Euthydemus joins in by asking Ctesippus if he in fact believes that it is possible to speak falsely (283e7–8). When Ctesippus replies that he does, Euthydemus proceeds to show how this is impossible (283e–284c). A statement (λόγος) is always about something. The person who utters the statement is addressing a specific being in distinction from other beings. For example, in saying that "The sun is blue," one is talking specifically about the sun and not about a tree or a dog. But if even a false statement is always about something in particular, then in uttering this statement one is speaking of *something that is.* "Saying what is," however, is the accepted definition of truth. In *saying what is* one is *speaking truly.* If, therefore, every statement is about *something that is,* no statement can be false. Counter to Ctesippus's opinion, Dionysodorus cannot have spoken falsely.

This argument, like previous ones, rests on an opposition between two exclusive alternatives: one says either what is or what is not. In this opposition there is no room for falsehood. If one says what is, one is speaking truly; if one says what is not, one is saying nothing and therefore not speaking at all. A defense of the possibility of falsehood would require a distinction between different senses of "what is" and "what is not." As has been seen, however, this is exactly what the brothers will not allow.

When Ctesippus attempts to make such a distinction by suggesting that a false statement is one that speaks of things that are, but not *as they are,* Dionysodorus reduces the suggestion to absurdity (284d–e). Ctesippus now becomes so annoyed at what he must recognize to be verbal tricks that Socrates must intervene. He tries to calm the young man by jesting with him (προσέπαιζον, 285a3; note how Socrates is himself capable of play), suggesting that they should accept what the brothers say and not dispute about mere words. If the brothers use the word "destruction" to refer to what happens to a man when he is led from being ignorant and bad to being wise and good, then this usage should be accepted and not allowed to stand in the way of what is really at issue. Socrates here distances his own procedure as much as possible from that of the two brothers. As has been noted, the eristic arguments are concerned with only *verbal differences.* In the present passage, on the other hand, Socrates refuses to dispute about words: "μὴ ὀνόματι διαφέρεσθαι"

(285a5–6). The brothers can call making a man virtuous "destroying" him if they so please. In this way Socrates dismisses their whole argument as nothing but a peculiar use of the word "destruction." An eristic argument does no more than shuffle words around. Beneath this shuffle all remains as before.

Moreover, the extent to which eristic undermines its own pretensions now becomes fully evident. The brothers claimed that their art could show Cleinias the necessity of pursuing philosophy and concerning himself with virtue. Now not only have they failed to fulfill this promise, but they have even made its fulfillment impossible: they have argued that it is not only not necessary, but *impossible*, for Cleinias to become wiser and better (since such a change would be equivalent to his destruction). In this way the brothers' "wisdom" exposes itself for what it is. Not only is it incapable of having any "protreptic" effect on Cleinias, but by maintaining, with its principle of noncontradiction, that one learns *either* what one does not know *or* what one knows, and that one *either* is what one is *or* is not at all, this "wisdom" ironically renders impossible any learning, any philosophy, any moral improvement whatsoever.

In the next round of argumentation, we see that eristic not only cannot improve anyone through conversion or teaching, but it cannot even remain true to its own minimum presupposition as a negative method of refutation. When Ctesippus assures Dionysodorus that he is not angry with him, but is only contradicting (ἀντιλέγειν) what he has found ill said, Dionysodorus asks whether it is really possible to "contradict" anyone (285d). Ctesippus replies that he certainly thinks so and even has *evidence*, namely, the fact that he is now contradicting what Dionysodorus says. Apparently unimpressed by this evidence, Dionysodorus proceeds to "demonstrate" the impossibility of contradiction (285e–286b).

The rejection of the possibility of falsehood has the consequence that there will be only one kind of *logos*, that is, a true one, corresponding to each thing (πρᾶγμα, which can simply mean a particular state of affairs). Therefore, two people speaking of the same thing necessarily *say the same thing* and thus cannot contradict each other. If, on the other hand, they are speaking about different things, it is equally impossible for them to contradict each other. They are in this case speaking *past*, rather than against, each other. Likewise, someone who is speaking of something cannot contradict someone who is speaking of nothing. There seems, then, to be no situation in which two people could speak against each other.

Ctesippus is silenced. Socrates, however, expresses his amazement. He has often heard this argument and has always found it rather strange, since in overthrowing others it manages to overthrow itself (286c3–4).

In this way Socrates introduces his next major objection to the eristic method: it *undermines itself.* Though the brothers' arguments have shown themselves to be no more than wordplay, they must at least give the appearance of refuting the respondent's opinion. Yet, in just denying the possibility of "contradiction," the brothers have in effect denied the possibility of refutation. The conclusions of their arguments contradict the very purpose which these arguments are supposed to serve. They have argued against the very possibility of arguing against.

Because the brothers only dispute about words and are not concerned with the thing itself under discussion, it is in fact impossible for them genuinely to contradict or refute anyone. To contradict another's opinion is to have a different understanding of the thing at issue and not simply to use different words in talking about it. Socrates therefore claimed earlier that Dionysodorus's argument that the lovers of Cleinias want the boy destroyed did not really contradict their opinion, but only used words in a funny way (the word "destroyed" for "becoming good"). The brothers' conclusion that it is impossible to refute or speak against another is in this sense consistent with the nature of their own arguments. However, in order for their arguments to serve their purpose of defeating the respondent, *they must appear* to refute him. The brothers have now come close to destroying this illusion and thereby exposing themselves.

Yet they are not defeated. They escape all of Socrates' subsequent attempts to catch them in their own self-contradiction (i.e., the contradiction between what they are doing and what they appear to be doing). They maintain their illusion by arguing in such a way as to render impossible any reflection on their own procedure. They do not even allow what they say at one time to be related to what they say at another time.[23] In this way they avoid being pinned down. Socrates realizes, however, that if he can expose their illusion for what it is, he will, if not defeat them, at least render them innocuous.

V

The barrenness of the brothers' second display necessitates Socrates' second discussion with Cleinias (288d–293a). This discussion begins where the previous one ended, that is, at the conclusion that it is necessary to philosophize (φιλοσοφητέον). Philosophy is defined as the possession of knowledge (288d8). There are, however, many different kinds of knowledge. Which one, then, is it necessary for us to possess? Clearly the one that will benefit us. As the earlier discussion showed, in order to be benefited by a good we must not only *possess* it but also know how to *use* it. Consequently, the beneficial knowledge we seek must not only produce some good but also instruct us in its proper use. Medicine, for example, does not meet this qualification because it does not know how to use the health it produces. The sole possession of health does not guarantee happiness. Happiness depends on knowing how to use this health to live the best life possible. Any science or art that teaches us how to use health would therefore be a better candidate for the knowledge we seek than medicine itself. If this higher science or art itself produces a good which it does not know how to use, then we would need to find an even higher science or art that does know how to use it. Only when the regress terminates at a type of knowledge that itself knows how to use the good which it itself produces and is therefore subordinate to no other knowledge will we find the guarantee of our happiness. What is unclear at this point, however, is whether or not the knowledge of how to use the good and the knowledge of how to produce it are distinct or the same in the case of this highest science.[24] How can they be the same, given the obvious difference between using and producing? On the other hand, how can they be distinct and yet form *one* science?

Throughout the discussion Socrates and Cleinias (and later even Crito) consider different candidates for this highest science. One is the art of making speeches (ἡ λογοποιικὴ τέχνη, 289c7). Cleinias, however, objects that those who make speeches are often not the same as those who know how to use speeches (i.e., the orator and the statesman). In the case of speeches, then, the art of producing and the art of using are separate (289d5–7).[25]

Socrates next suggests the general's art (στρατηγική).[26] Cleinias objects that this art belongs to the class of *hunting arts* (θηρευτικὴ τέχνη, 290b5), that is, arts of *discovery* as opposed to *production*. What geometry, astronomy, and calculation have in common with the art of hunting animals is that the proper work of each is *to find and obtain* a certain object. Having obtained their object, however, these arts do not know how to use it but must hand it over to another art. When the hunter has caught his prey, he must hand it over to the cook. Geometry, astronomy, and calculation do not know how to use the realities they discover (τὰ ὄντα ἀνευρίσκουσιν, 290c) and must therefore hand over their discoveries to the *dialectician*.[27] Likewise, a general is trained only to "hunt" cities or armies and therefore does not know what to do with them once captured, but must hand them over to the politicians. The general's art, then, along with the other "hunting" arts, cannot be the kind of knowledge which will make us happy since it does not know how to *use* that which it discovers and captures.

In rejecting the general's art as a candidate for the highest knowledge, this passage clearly suggests two other possible candidates: the political art, which knows how to make use of what the generals capture, and dialectic, which knows how to make use of the discoveries of important sciences such as geometry, astronomy, and calculation. The next logical step would be to decide between these two. It is therefore surprising that the following discussion does not even consider dialectic as a possible candidate.[28] It proceeds as if dialectic had never even been mentioned. How is this strange forgetfulness to be explained? How could Socrates and Cleinias have missed such an important clue as to the nature of the knowledge which they are seeking?

It is significant that Socrates attributes the account of dialectic to a "higher power" (τις τῶν κρειττόνων, 291a4) when Crito questions its attribution to the boy Cleinias.[29] The suggestion, then, is that neither Socrates nor Cleinias nor Crito is the source of this account. It is in this case understandable that, despite its great importance to the discussion, they should overlook it. This is especially true if they have certain preconceptions which prevent them from granting this description of dialectic its proper due. It remains, however, in the background as the words of a higher power with which we must reckon in understanding and judging the present discussion and its results.

What immediately follows reveals the preconception that prevents dialectic from being considered a candidate for that knowledge which will make us happy. Socrates narrates that it appeared to him and Cleinias that the political art must be capable of producing something (τὶ ἡμῖν ἀπεργάζεται ἔργον, 291d7–e1). How, after all, could it make us happy if it does not provide us with some good? Given this requirement, an unproductive type of knowledge such as dialectic cannot be a serious candidate. Yet it will turn out that not even the political art can meet this requirement.

There is an important development at this point in the discussion. Socrates has so far been simply narrating to Crito his earlier discussion with Cleinias. When the discussion turns to the political art as a productive art, however, Crito becomes increasingly involved in what Socrates is saying. The result is that Socrates from this point on, rather than simply reporting the questions he asked Cleinias, will address these questions to Crito himself. In this way Socrates' narration to Crito of the previous day's discussion becomes a present discussion between the two of them. This change emphasizes the discussion's importance.[30] Up to now Crito has simply listened to Socrates' words. Now his concern with the truth at issue causes him actually to become involved.[31]

The discussion thus proceeds when Socrates asks Crito to identify the product (*ergon*) which, as agreed, the political art must have. Medicine, for example, can bring about health, which is a good thing. In ruling all the other arts, then, what does the political art *itself produce* (291d–292a)? Crito confesses perplexity. Socrates, however, continues by insisting that this art must provide us with some good in order to be beneficial. Socrates and Cleinias earlier agreed that the only unqualified good is knowledge (292b). Therefore, the product of the political art, since it cannot be something in itself neither good nor bad, such as wealth, must be *nothing but knowledge* (292b–c). But what kind of knowledge? Knowledge of making shoes or building houses? The political art must not produce qualified goods such as shoes and houses; it must provide only knowledge, and this knowledge is apparently identical with itself (since it could not be any subordinate form of knowledge). The political art, therefore, appears to be its own product: *it provides us with nothing but itself* (292d3–4). Yet Socrates insists that to make us happy this knowledge must be good for something. Perhaps, he suggests, we could use it to make others good. But good *at what*? Since the political art hands over only itself, we must reply that it is good at making others good at making others good, ad infinitum. This, then, is the *aporia* with which the discussion between Socrates and Cleinias (and now Socrates and Crito) ends (292e). The political art has shown itself to be a type of knowledge that is its own product and its own object; yet, in order to be beneficial, it must be good for something other than itself. An empty knowledge of knowledge is good for nothing. What was thought to be the highest knowledge, in that it knows how to use correctly the discoveries and products of the other sciences or arts, has turned out to be itself empty. *It is higher than all the other forms of knowledge only at the cost of being without content.* This is the *aporia*.[32]

This *aporia* cannot be solved by finding a type of knowledge which, though producing nothing but itself, is good for something other than itself. This is simply an impossibility. If the knowledge is good for something other than itself, then it provides something other than itself. If it provides something other than itself, then the ultimate good will be not this knowledge itself, but what it provides. The *aporia* does not represent a failure to find the highest knowledge, but rather a difficulty inherent in its very nature.

An important outcome of the discussion is that the political art has proven no more capable than dialectic of producing a good distinct from itself, so that the basis for distinguishing the two and preferring the former to the latter as a candidate for the highest knowledge disappears. In the *Republic* dialectic and the political art seem to be closely associated or even identified (i.e., in the well-known paradox of the "philosopher-king," 473c).[33] Likewise here the political art, as a self-producing, self-contained knowledge, seems in no way to differ from dialectic. Dialectic in using the discoveries of the other sciences itself appears to produce no good other than itself. But if there has ceased to be a distinction between dialectic and the political art, then what keeps us from identifying dialectic with the highest knowledge for which we are searching? The words of the "higher power" impose themselves here. Perhaps the political art has proven empty in producing nothing but itself because it is identical with dialectic.[34]

This suggestion of course does not solve the *aporia*, but simply transfers it to dialectic. If dialectic knows how to use the discoveries and products of other arts and sciences, then what does it itself produce or discover? What is it good for? If for nothing but itself, then how can it benefit us and make us happy?

The difficulty of showing the use of dialectic as the highest knowledge is precisely the *aporia* which here confronts us. We have seen, however, that the *Euthydemus* as a whole is concerned with nothing but the problematic nature of dialectic or, more specifically, the difficulty of distinguishing dialectic from eristic. The *aporia* encountered in Socrates' discussion with Cleinias is therefore the *aporia* which the whole dialogue (or Socrates' narration of it) is meant to address. This is why the present discussion transcends being a display for the brothers and, as a dialogue between Socrates and Crito, becomes a means of reflecting on what has been taking place in the dialogue as a whole. The *aporia* of the highest knowledge, as an *aporia* concerning the nature of dialectic, is the very problem that gives rise to and necessitates Socrates' narration of the previous day's discussion. As we learn at the end of the dialogue (304d–305b), Crito's interest in Socrates' conversation with the two brothers was provoked by the comments of a witness who saw this conversation as confirming the worthlessness of philosophy. Crito becomes involved in the discussion concerning the highest knowledge because this was his concern from the very beginning. What is at stake in Socrates' protreptic discourse is what is at stake in the dialogue as a whole: the worth of dialectic.

As Socrates suggests at one point, eristic is nothing but a "speaking for the sake of speaking" (λόγου ἕνεκα λέγειν τὸν λόγον).[35] As a purely verbal dispute concerned with nothing but words and the forms of arguments, it is devoid of content. The brothers do not aim to benefit others or make them good. They argue simply for the sake of arguing. In this sense eristic is its own end and can hand over to others nothing but itself. (Later on we will see Ctesippus learning the brothers' skill.) If, however, Socrates' own dialectic does not provide solutions (as even the present discussion with Cleinias shows) and if it does not produce any good besides itself, can it be said to be any better than eristic?[36] Is it any less empty than eristic? Does it have any more content? These are the questions that the dialogue renders inescapable.

The *aporia* at the heart of that highest knowledge which will make us happy arises from the assumption that it analogous to the *technai*. Medicine is defined in terms of the health it brings about. Shipbuilding is defined in terms of the ships produced. Geometry is defined in terms of the figures whose properties it discovers. Analogously, the highest knowledge must be defined in terms of something else it discovers or produces.

But are we perhaps meant to see that this analogy does not hold? It should be recalled that the *Laches* and the *Charmides* made a similar analogy between "technical knowledge" and the knowledge of virtue. Yet the very nature of Socrates' inquiry in both dialogues was seen to undermine this analogy. Socrates reveals the nature of the virtue in question through the very way in which he conducts the inquiry, rather than in some final conclusion or definition. The *Charmides* in particular shows that this characteristic of dialectic has the paradoxical consequence of making it a "knowledge of knowledge." Yet this dialogue also explains the paradox by suggesting that the knowledge of knowledge is itself also a knowledge of the good. This is possible because the good, rather than being an object external to the inquiry, is a characteristic of it.

In denying, then, the analogy between dialectic and "technical" knowledge, the conclusions of chapter 2 can explain the *aporia* encountered here in the *Euthydemus*. The highest knowledge is not to be understood as discovering or producing a good external to itself. *In properly using and thus rendering good the products and discoveries of the arts and sciences it is itself a manifestation*[37] *of the good.* As was seen in the *Charmides* and as is seen again in the present dialogue, the good is revealed not in the objects dialectic deals with, but in *how* it deals with them.[38] Dialectic is in this sense a *user's art*. However, because in this very use it instantiates or brings about the good, dialectic is also *an art of production*. Furthermore, because the good is not something it invents, but rather something it manifests, dialectic is also an *art of discovery* or "hunter's art."[39] The ability of dialectic to unite all three kinds of art or knowledge depends on its peculiar unity with its object ("peculiar" because not found in the arts or sciences). If the good were to appear as an object completely distinct from, and external to, dialectic, then it would have to be *either* simply *produced or* simply *discovered* by it. The fact that the good manifests itself and is instantiated in the very process of dialectic blurs the distinction between production and discovery. Furthermore, the distinction between use and production/discovery is blurred if the good is discovered/produced in the very use which dialectic makes of the products and discoveries of the arts and sciences. Thus dialectic can transcend the distinctions applicable to the *technai* and reconcile the characteristics which the discussion has shown it must have; it can do this because it is not distinct from its object in the way that the *technai* are. This unity of the highest knowledge and the good is evident in Socrates' earlier claim that this knowledge is itself an unqualified good. Rather than being referred to some good extrinsic to itself, this knowledge, as a knowledge of determining the proper use and goodness of other goods, makes manifest and instantiates within itself the nature of the good. In this case the highest knowledge is still a "knowledge of knowledge" that produces nothing completely external to, or completely other than, itself.[40]

This response to the *aporia* of Socrates' second discussion with Cleinias is also a response to the *aporia* confronted by the dialogue as a whole in its attempt to distinguish between dialectic and eristic. It is true that dialectic is no more capable than eristic of finding final answers or of producing something other than itself.[41] Like eristic, it gives the appearance of "arguing for the sake of arguing." Perhaps, however, in its endless, apparently blind, and unproductive arguing, dialectic reveals and produces something eristic cannot. The following has become apparent: the truth under discussion somehow participates in, and makes claims upon, Socrates' dialectic, whereas the eristic method seems entirely indifferent to truth; dialectic differs from eristic in making proper use of arguments. Finally, Socrates' dialectic is capable of making Cleinias a *better* person and thus of producing good, not by proving conclusions for Cleinias's acceptance, but by getting him to philosophize, while the eristic of the two brothers not only cannot do this but even denies its possibility (to improve Cleinias, they argue, is to destroy him). In accordance with the conclusions reached about the highest knowledge, it seems that dialectic, as a knowledge of properly using arguments, makes manifest and instantiates the truth *precisely in this use,* rather than in some conclusion or result.[42]

It also becomes clear here why Socrates chooses a "protreptic" discussion as the basis upon which to distinguish dialectic from eristic. As was already suspected above, the peculiar unity of dialectic with its object, the good, makes the protreptic question of why and how to pursue philosophy not *preliminary,* but rather *central* to knowledge of the good. It is not the case that a person is first converted to the pursuit of philosophy and only afterward comes to know, perhaps, the nature of its object. We come to know the nature of the good not *after,* but rather *at the same time as,* learning why and how to philosophize. This learning is not a preliminary step that can be completed once and for all, but rather a process that coincides with learning the good, and is as incapable as the latter of coming to an end. Philosophy is in this way always, and in its very essence, "protreptic." Yet this characteristic is sufficient in itself to distinguish philosophy from eristic.

The process of learning the good is unending because even what has been said above cannot "resolve" the *aporia* concerning the highest knowledge. The exact nature of the relation between this knowledge and the good it manifests remains mysterious.[43] What the above reflections are meant to show, however, is that the *aporia* inherent in the very nature of the highest knowledge, though making it difficult for us to describe this knowledge or provide instructions for its attainment, should not force us to dismiss its possibility. The *aporia* itself, after all, sheds light on just what kind of a knowledge this is.[44]

It is important to note the reflexivity of the dialogue at this point: in coming to the recognition that the highest knowledge is "good *for* nothing," the discussion itself proves to be "good *for* nothing." It goes nowhere and in the end is as far from any conclusion as it was at the beginning (this is Socrates' own observation at 291b–c). It has proven empty just like the knowledge under discussion. The reason has already been seen: the type of knowledge under discussion is the same as that actually employed by Socrates in the discussion, dialectic. In the *aporia* the object sought and the method by which it is sought become one.[45]

The above response to the *aporia* sheds light simultaneously on the nature of that highest knowledge that will ensure our happiness and on the nature of Socrates' dialectic, the two appearing to be one and the same. The important result is this: *what distinguishes Socrates' dialectic from eristic is to be sought not in its results nor in the formal validity of its reasoning, but in what it manifests through the very method of its argumentation.* Dialectic is full of content, whereas eristic is empty, and this difference can hold even though both are equally, in the normal sense of the word, "unproductive."[46]

VI

This insight having been sparked by his discussion with Crito, Socrates can now return to his narrative. The remainder of the discussion between Socrates and the two brothers (292e–304c) seems at first sight little more than a compendium of sophistical arguments (which is indeed how Aristotle uses it). The verbal tricks of the two brothers become increasingly extravagant and the fallacies increasingly perspicuous. The important result, however, is that the illusion with which the brothers veil their method becomes transparent. Though they remain undefeated at the end, the terrain which they manage to hold onto is small and barren.

The objective of the following is not to examine the details of every eristic argument, but rather to outline the points of the discussion that most clearly reveal the difference between dialectic and eristic. After ending his conversation with Cleinias, Socrates begs the two brothers to save the boy and himself from the *aporia* into which they have fallen. In reply to this cry of distress Euthydemus offers even more help than is asked of him. He allows Socrates to choose between being taught this knowledge which he seeks *or being shown to be already in possession of it* (293b). This is a clear allusion to Socrates' claim elsewhere in the dialogues (see *Meno* 81e–82a and *Theaetetus* 150c–d) that he does not *teach* anything, but only reveals to the student what the student already knows.[47] This characteristic of Socrates' dialectic was made apparent by his first conversation with Cleinias: as already noted, the goal of his protreptic there is not to introduce new knowledge into the boy's head by means of the logical rigor of his arguments, but rather to lead the boy to the recognition of what he in some sense already knows. Now in the present passage Euthydemus claims this characteristic for his own method, thus introducing the major action of this part of the dialogue: the attempt of eristic to usurp the place of dialectic.[48]

This attempt, however, only further illuminates the gulf between the two methods. Euthydemus does not elicit from Socrates in maieutic fashion the knowledge which Socrates seeks. Instead he uses the principle of non- (verbal) contradiction to "prove" that Socrates has this knowledge (293b–d): because Socrates cannot be knowing and unknowing at the same time, it is impossible for him to *know* x and at the same time *not know* y; therefore, he must know everything, if he knows anything at all. Socrates attempts to refute this argument by emphasizing its implication that the brothers themselves must be all-knowing and as such must know, among other things, how many stars there are in the sky. This attempt fails, since the brothers are willing to accept whatever absurd consequences logic requires. Euthydemus then uses another argument to show that Socrates must have *always* known everything, even before birth (295b–296d; the argument is drawn out because Socrates is uncooperative). The argument is simple: because we *always* know everything through the same means (the soul), we *always* know everything. The conclusion that Socrates knew everything before birth clearly employs the words of the doctrine of recollection as presented in the *Meno* and the *Phaedo* but, we might suspect, *the words only*. Most important, while the doctrine of recollection is for Socrates a stimulus to persistent and courageous inquiry (see *Meno* 86b–c), it is for the brothers an excuse for abandoning all inquiry.[49] If Socrates presently knows everything and has always known everything, then why should he engage in the kind of inquiry he was just pursuing with Cleinias? He should let philosophy be and rest content with his omniscience. Thus the brothers again, rather than showing the neccessity of philosophizing, use their pinciple of noncontradiction to demonstrate the pointlessness of philosophy and of the perplexity it engenders.

What is of particular interest in the passage where this argument occurs is Socrates' attempt to qualify (and thus restrict the sense of) the premises. If his qualifications were allowed the argument would be "because we always *when we know* know *what we know* by means of *the soul*, we have always known everything." In this case the argument clearly does not work. However, *we mistake the true nature of eristic if we fail to see that Socrates' qualifications are ineffectual against it.* When, in response to Euthydemus's protests, Socrates offers to remove his qualification "what we know," the latter responds: "But do not take back a single word. . . . I do not need your favors. Just answer this question: can you possibly know all things if you do not know everything?" (296b9–c2). Whether Socrates says simply that he "knows all" or adds some words to say that he "knows all that which he knows," he is in either case claiming to know *all.* The argument is concerned only with this one word "all" in drawing its conclusion, and the addition of more words irrelevant to the argument changes nothing. Euthydemus is not asking Socrates whether he knows all that he knows, but whether he knows all. He therefore has reason to be annoyed when Socrates insists on changing the question.[50]

Socrates' attempt to defeat Euthydemus's argument thus fails. This argument is invulnerable precisely because it is not concerned with what its conclusions or premises *mean*.[51] The argument is not meant to *show* anything (if the respondent takes it to show something, that is another matter). The strategy for defeating an eristic is not to change his question (something impermissible in any dispute), but to get him to mean or make something manifest by it, that is, to lure him into a genuine dialectical discussion. Eristic cannot be defeated directly or, as it were, head on. By "sticking to words" the brothers are immune to any such attack. One can defeat them only indirectly by bringing their words back into a context where they mean something, where they are more than chesspieces to be moved around at will. *Yet one cannot provide this context by simply adding more words.* The opposite of eristic and its antidote is dialectic, not logic.[52]

Thus when Socrates at one point (296d–297a) lures Dionysodorus into dialectic by getting him to concern himself momentarily with the meaning and truth of what is said, he finally wins a major victory. Socrates is attempting to refute the brothers' position by showing them that in knowing *everything* one must also know what is false, a consequence so absurd as to appear unacceptable even to them. Socrates thus asks if he can know that *the good are unjust,* to which Dionysodorus replies that he cannot. Euthydemus then upbraids his brother, telling him that from this concession Socrates will appear both knowing and unknowing. Dionysodorus blushes.

This passage shows that what threatens to destroy the eristic's word-play is a momentary recognition, on the part of Dionysodorus, of the true nature of the good (i.e., that it is not possible for someone who is good to be unjust).[53] That Dionysodorus should answer counter to his own purpose shows the influence that some awareness of the good already has on his judgment. Even the brothers' sham "wisdom" cannot escape a determinate understanding of the good, a fact that emphasizes the close and indivisible union of wisdom and the good which Socrates' second discussion with Cleinias revealed.

Nevertheless, the brothers recover from this setback and continue parodying Socrates' dialectic by eventually aiming their arguments at the very thing that got them in trouble: our relation to *goods* (299a–e). There are two arguments here: by referring in their premises only to goods relative to a certain need (such as medicine), they prove to Ctesippus (who is now the respondent) that it is not the case that we are in need of as much good as possible, and they likewise give a reductio ad absurdum of the claim that "goods should be had at all times and everywhere" (299d3–4), by arguing that though gold is a good we would not care to have it everywhere (in our stomachs, for example). These arguments confirm Socrates' claim that the goodness of such things depends on their proper use rather than on their possession. This, however, is clearly not the intention. Not only are the brothers simply playing with the word "good" and are therefore unconcerned with using these arguments in such a way as to make manifest the true nature of the good, but their goal is the exact opposite of Socrates': they seek to *diminish* the importance of the good. This shows that while the eristic can use Socratic arguments, he uses them in such a way as to subvert completely their protreptic aim. What is becoming clear, however, is that the brothers *must* imitate dialectic in order to preserve any illusion of seriousness in their arguments. Eristic is parasitic upon the very dialectic it seeks to undermine because, without the semblance of dialectic, it is exposed for what it is: wordplay not at all to be taken seriously.

The present discussion therefore reaches its climax when the brothers virtually destroy their illusion by undermining the only serious principle to which their method has been seen to commit them. Ctesippus, having by now mastered through imitation the skill of eristic, has forced the two brothers into a corner by asking them a question that demands a choice between two equally impossible alternatives: are all things silent or do all things speak? Euthydemus then makes the fatal mistake of declining both alternatives (300c), apparently because *he feels that neither one is true*. In attempting to save his brother, Dionysodorus makes an even more fatal mistake: he answers "both and neither" (300d1), thereby undermining the one principle presupposed by all of the eristic arguments: the prohibition of verbal contradiction and the corresponding demand that in reply to a question only one alternative be chosen. Ctesippus exclaims in triumph: "Look Euthydemus! Your brother has rendered your account contradictory [ἐξημφοτέρικεν τὸν λόγον] and so it is dead and beaten!" (300d4–5).

It is important, however, to recognize that the eristic method thus self-destructs only when brought into the context of a dialectical discussion where it itself has to answer questions. On its own terms it remains unconquerable. Yet what has so far allowed eristic to be absorbed into dialectic and thus defeated is the illusion it gives of making meaningful utterances. Therefore, eristic can escape defeat only at the cost of giving up this illusion. This is why the brothers' arguments become increasingly absurd and "silly" toward the end of the dialogue.[54] They have been forced to give up any appearance of seriousness, and as a result their game is rendered harmless.

Dionysodorus, however, attempts to make one more excursion into the serious territory of dialectic. He asks if beautiful things (τὰ καλά) are distinct from, or the same as, beauty itself (τὸ καλόν, 300e3–301a1). Here again the brothers are imitating Socrates' language while depriving it of its content. When Socrates replies with hesitation that, while beautiful things are distinct from beauty itself, some beauty (κάλλος τι) is present (πάρεστιν) in each (301a3–4), he is asked whether the presence of an ox next to him would make him an ox. Socrates finds this suggestion blasphemous (Εὐφήμει τοῦτό γε, 301a), thus betraying the importance to him of what Dionysodorus is ridiculing. Dionysodorus then asks more generally *how, when one thing comes to be next to another thing, the other can be the other* (we would say, "the one can be the other").[55] He is thus in essence asking how two different things can become the same through mere presence, the two things here being beauty itself and a beautiful thing.

It is wrong to accuse Dionysodorus of mere equivocation in his "ox example."[56] The reason why Socrates is embarrassed by the objection is that he himself cannot explain the nature of the relation between beauty itself and beautiful things.[57] Therefore, he cannot accuse Dionysodorus of mistaking his meaning. The charge of equivocation presupposes that a word has two meanings that can be clearly defined and distinguished. In the present case, however, we have a common sense meaning of "presence" opposed to an arcane and unexplained philosophical meaning. Dionysodorus cannot be blamed for taking the word in its ordinary sense.[58] What he *is* guilty of, however, is a failure to recognize that the relation between universal and particular, whether or not it can be adequately explained, lies at the basis of all meaningful discourse. The dialectician, on the other hand, recognizes this and therefore, as was seen in the *Laches*, the *Charmides*, and the *Cratylus*, talks about particulars in such a way that the common nature such talk presupposes is made manifest. In arguing about beautiful things the dialectician brings beauty itself into view. The purely verbal arguments of the eristic, however, undermine this relation to truth presupposed by dialectic.

Dionysodorus's question therefore represents the brothers' most serious attack on dialectic. But Socrates' defence is masterful: he simply turns Dionysodorus's eristic against him by simplifying his question to mean "how can the other be other?" and then asking rhetorically how the other could *not* be other (301b–c).[59] Dionysodorus cannot protest that this is a misconstruction of his meaning without getting involved in a dialectical discussion with Socrates in which he would be sure to lose. He has no choice, then, but to retreat. By turning eristic upon itself Socrates forces it out of the territory of dialectic to where it can do no harm.

Being thus forced to play out their game with no pretension of seriousness, the brothers' arguments become increasingly absurd until they reach a climax with an absolutely inane play on two words Ctesippus uses in an exclamation (303a). This leads the latter to observe that the brothers are unbeatable (ἀμάχω, 303a9). The brothers have indeed proven unbeatable in the sense that they refuse to remain upon ground where one could defeat them. The display of Euthydemus and his brother thus ends amid universal applause and praise. We, however, have seen the cost at which their victory is bought.[60]

VII

Socrates' narration ends with a description of the eulogy he addressed to the two brothers subsequent to their wonderful display. Socrates praised the following characteristics:

1. The brothers are not concerned with the opinions of those unlike themselves.
2. Their method is democratic (i.e., egalitarian). They stitch up not only the mouths of others, but their own mouths as well.
3. Their skill can be learned very quickly, as Ctesippus demonstrated. Socrates therefore advises them to avoid speaking in public, since the auditors could easily learn their art without paying them for it.

What is striking about Socrates' eulogy is that it focuses on those characteristics bearing a superficial resemblance to his own method. In the first case, Socrates credits the brothers with a contempt for the opinions of "the many" which he himself clearly shares. When Crito, in the dialogue named after him, expresses concern with what the many will think of him and Socrates' other friends if they do not help Socrates escape prison, Socrates asks: "But, my dear Crito, what does the opinion of the many matter to us? Those who are best, and who are therefore more deserving of our consideration, believe that these things should have been done in the way in which they have been done" (44c6–9). He goes on to say that the many act *at random* and are capable of neither great good nor great evil (44d6–10). It is therefore no wonder that Socrates should praise the two brothers for sharing this slight regard for what the many think and do. He recognizes in them fellow elitists.

However, Socrates is also characterized by an egalitarianism in apparent conflict with his elitism: he insists that he knows no more than those whom he refutes. Thus when Meno, in the dialogue named after him, accuses Socrates of numbing with perplexity his mind and lips, just like a stingray (80a–b), Socrates replies: "If the stingray paralyzes others by paralyzing itself first, then your comparison holds; if not, then it does not. For it is not the case that I go and perplex people while I myself am successful in discovering the truth. It is much more the case that, being myself perplexed, I simply pass on this perplexity to others" (80c6–d1). In this way Socrates places himself on a level with the interlocutor; both suffer the negative effects of the argument. This is precisely what Socrates finds praiseworthy in the brothers' method (303d5–6): "[T]ruly and without a doubt you sew up people's mouths, as you claim. That in addition, however, you also appear to sew up your own mouths is most considerate and removes the offensiveness of your arguments" (303e1–4). Socrates is again eulogizing in the brothers one of his own traits. Both the dialectician and the eristic do not spare themselves the numbing effects of their own arguments.

However, the greatest thing about the brothers' method, according to Socrates, is that it is so skillfully crafted that anyone can learn it in a short time. At the beginning of the discussion the brothers claimed to teach virtue not only more effectively, but also more *quickly*, than anyone else (273d8–9). The "virtue" they teach has turned out to be the art of refutation. The brother's claim is borne out by the speed with which Ctesippus masters this art and learns to use it against the brothers themselves. This speed also appears to characterize Socrates' dialectic. In the present dialogue Socrates leads the young Cleinias in a very short time to the recognition of important truths. If we are to believe Socrates' testimony, in the second protreptic discussion the boy even usurps Socrates' role. In other dialogues we see Socrates engaged in fairly subtle discussions with interlocutors possessing no prior philosophical training.

In his eulogy, then, Socrates appears to praise in the eristics his own characteristics.[61] His desire to become their student comes from his recognition in what they are doing of something akin to his own method. In the brothers he greets fellow dialecticians. However, what has been revealed throughout the course of the dialogue prevents us from any longer being taken in by this semblance. Behind the apparent similarities lie irreconcilable differences. Socrates' eulogy is both playful and in earnest: it is in earnest insofar as it praises characteristics Socrates truly values, but it is playful insofar as the semblance of these characteristics in the brothers has proven very far from the real thing.

Socrates' description of the brothers' contempt for the opinions of the multitude paradoxically follows directly upon his description of the praise and laughter that followed their display. The brothers are real crowd pleasers. Socrates' advice that they practice their eristic in private among themselves and their pupils is comical in its absurdity. Like any other competitive sport, eristic needs spectators. If the brothers have contempt for the multitude, it is only the contempt that a demagogue or a "star" has for the ignorant masses on whose opinion his or her success depends. The crowd makes them what they are, and yet they in turn like to think themselves above the crowd. Socrates' dialectic, on the other hand, is clearly not a spectator sport. It is true that in this dialogue Socrates' discussion with Cleinias, due to the circumstances, takes the form of a display before a large group of listeners. However, Socrates narrates it in an apparently private discussion with Crito. To engage in a dialectical discussion Socrates clearly needs no more than one other person, as a number of dialogues show (*Meno, Euthyphro, Crito, Hippias Minor* and *Major, Ion*). He has contempt for majority opinion because it does not guarantee truth. The elitism of the eristics, however, is an arrogance having nothing to do with truth.

Both Socrates and the eristic silence themselves in silencing others. However, apart from the fact that this is intentional in the one case only (the brothers clearly do not intend to have their eristic backfire), this self-refutation has completely opposed causes in both cases. Socrates states the cause of the eristic's silence in the following passage: "When you assert that nothing beautiful or good or white or possessing any other such quality exists, and nothing at all that is other than other things, then you truly and without a doubt sew up people's mouths, as you claim" (303d7–e2). The view Socrates attributes to the brothers, though nowhere explicitly stated in the dialogue,[62] is clearly the import of the passage in which Dionysodorus asks Socrates if he has ever seen a beautiful thing. In refuting Socrates' view that beauty itself both differs from beautiful things and is present in each of them, Dionysodorus is rejecting a description of the only way in which beautiful things can exist. The strategy of his original question was clearly to have Socrates reply either that beautiful things and beauty itself are the same or that they are simply different. He could then refute the first reply by showing that it allows beautiful things to be absorbed into beauty itself so that they cease to be distinct particulars. He could also refute the second reply by pointing out that in simply distinguishing beauty from particular beautiful things it cannot explain how these particulars can all have beauty in common.[63] In short, either reply could be shown to render impossible the existence of *a beautiful thing*. If beautiful things are the same as beauty itself, they cease to be *particular* beautiful *things* (they are identified with their attribute); if they are simply distinguished from beauty itself, they cease to be *beautiful,* that is, they become simply other than beauty. In order to avoid both undesirable consequences, Socrates states his view that, while beautiful things and beauty itself are different, the one is "present" in the other. In rejecting this suggestion, Dionysodorus is denying that different things can have a quality in common or that things which share such a quality can yet be different ("other" than each other). He in this way eliminates a fundamental presupposition of meaningful discourse. We simply could not speak if it were the case either that different things can have absolutely no nature in common or that things having a nature in common can in no way differ from each other. Language clearly requires that there be *both* universals *and* particulars instantiating these universals. In refuting this possibility, Dionysodorus is indeed "stitching up his own mouth."

In contrast, Socrates numbs himself and others in the recognition that, for example, virtue or beauty has an objective nature that cannot be reduced to the particulars that nevertheless instantiate it. Socrates' attempts to define such a nature, such as in the *Laches* and the *Charmides*, fail and, as chapter 2 suggested and chapter 6 will further confirm, *necessarily so*. On the other hand, in the *Cratylus* Socrates recognizes that meaningful discourse would be impossible without the assumption that there exist stable, unchanging natures beyond the flux of particulars. Therefore, the *aporia* with which Socrates numbs himself, unlike the intricate logical needlework with which the eristics stitch up their own mouths, is a result of *faithfulness* to the fundamental presupposition of meaningful discourse.

As for the speed with which the eristic skill is learned, it is made possible by a lack of content. The art of Euthydemus and his brother is a wordplay almost completely disassociated from what the words signify. Precisely this formality is what enables it to be easily learned. Dialectic, however, is accessible for the opposite reason: because it *has* a concrete content. Socrates' discussions concern truths of which everyone in daily life has some awareness. In asking questions about the different virtues, Socrates is addressing something that matters to everyone and not just to fellow philosophers. This accessibility is of course somewhat deceiving: the everyday subjects with which dialectic deals prove at a deeper level incredibly difficult and obscure. Despite this hidden depth, however, it is still no harder to *enter into* a dialectical discussion than it is to learn eristic. The difference is simply this: while dialectic is accessible because it deals with truths that matter to everyone, eristic is easily learned because it is a game that matters to no one.

In conclusion, the appearance of Socrates in the characteristics he attributes to the brothers is only a semblance. Despite surface similarities that might tempt one to identify the eristic with the dialectician, the differences are profound. With the eulogy, Socrates' narration comes to an end. The remainder of the dialogue is a discussion between Socrates and Crito. This discussion provides the context in which to evaluate the preceding narration.

Prior to Socrates' own account of his conversation with the two brothers, Crito had already heard about it from someone else. This person, identified only as someone clever at writing speeches for the courts, had a very negative opinion of what he had just come from witnessing. His criticisms were directed against Socrates in particular and philosophy in general. On the one hand, he found Socrates' behavior shameful. Is it not strange, he asked, that Socrates should willingly associate with men who care not what they say (οἷς οὐδὲν μέλει ὅτι ἂν λέγωσιν) and who cling to every word[64] (παντὸς δὲ ῥήματος ἀντέχονται, 305a3–4)? On the other hand, he found in their discussion only further proof that philosophy itself (τὸ πρᾶγμα αὐτό) is contemptible and laughable (305a6–8). Though Crito claims not to share the speechwriter's condemnation of philosophy, he does agree that it was wrong for Socrates to associate with people like Euthydemus and Dionysodorus.

Socrates responds to this criticism by pointing out that the speechwriter,[65] as someone dabbling in both politics and philosophy and thus situated between them, is to be esteemed less, not more, than either the true politician or the true philosopher (305c-306d). The claim of Socrates' critic to partake moderately of both philosophy and politics (see 305d8) should remind us of the implicit identification of these two sciences in the discussion between Socrates and Cleinias (and Crito).[66] This critic, however, has only a superfical knowledge of both politics and philosophy and therefore cannot reconcile them, that is, cannot see the *benefit* of philosophy for the *polis*. Indeed, he has contempt for philosophy because he believes himself to be in possession of wisdom: a wisdom that need not subject itself to dialectical examination and that therefore is immune to the danger posed by that negative image of dialectic called "eristic" (305c–e). Socrates' suggestion, however, is that this wisdom which does not risk itself in debate, which enables its possessor to condemn anonymously a discussion in which he was not even willing to take part, is a sham. The speechwriter is really no better than the two brothers, though he represents the opposite danger: whereas the brothers undermine everything and commit themselves to nothing, the speechwriter is a dogmatist who claims a wisdom so determinate and unshakable that it renders philosophy, with its ever-present risk of *aporia* and absurdity, irrelevant and contemptible.[67]

Caught in the middle of these two extremes, Socrates concludes that Crito must let be the practitioners of philosophy while attending to and testing the thing itself (307b6–8). If philosophy turns out to be a bad thing, he must turn everyone away from it. If, on the other hand, philosophy proves a good thing, Crito and his sons must take heart and pursue and practice it (θαρρῶν δίωκε καὶ ἄσκει, 307c3). In form eristic and dialectic may be the same, but Socrates is telling us that we must transcend this similarity in giving our attention to the thing itself.

This concluding section of the dialogue raises two important issues. One is the surprising weakness of Socrates' defense of philosophy. Instead of arguing that philosophy is a good thing, he simply tells Crito to try it out and see for himself whether it is good or bad. Yet what this dialogue has revealed about the nature of philosophy explains why Socrates has no more to say. Given the "reflexivity" of philosophy, its peculiar unity with its object, it is not possible to define or evaluate it before actually engaging in it.[68] Socrates "protreptic" "introduction" to philosophy is already philosophy itself. Because the speechwriter is unwilling to enter a philosophical discussion, Socrates could never convince him that philosophy is a good thing.

Readers of this dialogue often share the speechwriter's and Crito's bewilderment that Socrates should deign to engage in a discussion with such shallow verbal tricksters as the two brothers and should moreover praise them and beg to be accepted as their student. This strange behavior is usually explained away as "irony." If, however, one sees Socrates' irony as dissembling, one is faced with the formidable problem of explaining why he should find it necessary to dissemble before his own friend Crito. Socrates does not, after all, praise the brothers to their faces only to criticize them behind their backs. Before Crito, who is genuinely interested in having his sons pursue philosophy, Socrates never stops praising Euthydemus and his brother. If there is no seriousness in these praises, how can Socrates' deception of a friend be anything less than malicious?[69]

The dialogue does suggest an explanation of Socrates' apparently strange behavior. There are two ways of dealing effectively with the eristic: one either engages him in a dialectical discussion where he must refute himself in making meaningful utterances, or one confines eristic to eristic, that is, destroys its illusion of seriousness, so that it is rendered a harmless game. In short, if the eristic is caught being serious, he is doomed; if he refrains from being serious, he is harmless. Neither way of dealing with eristic, however, involves direct opposition to it. Such opposition, in fact, would be a serious mistake. It would give eristic a seriousness to which it is not entitled while at the same time allowing it to remain on its own ground. This is of course exactly what sophists such as Euthydemus and Dionysodorus want. They want both to be taken seriously and to be allowed to play a mere wordgame by which they can defeat all their opponents. Yet by declining to oppose them directly and even joining them, Socrates places the eristics in a situation where they must either become involved in a serious discussion and thus give up their eristic or retreat to a harmless puerility.

Socrates' defense of the brothers, however, is also a defense of philosophy. People like the speechwriter are led by their vehement opposition to the eristic abuse of arguments into a general misology.[70] In Socrates' view, however, the same means abused by eristic can be used in the pursuit of truth, and eristic is harmless against someone engaged in such a pursuit. If we are true dialecticians, the skill of argumentation worked to perfection by the eristics will either benefit us or do us no harm; we therefore have no reason to reject philosophy on their account but can even go so far as to welcome them into it. Precisely because dialectic and eristic are so close in form, the speechwriter in rejecting one rejects the other.[71] Socrates, on the other hand, values dialectic so highly that he cannot completely reject the eristic that is its shadow. Instead, he surrenders to it, assimilates it, and finally conquers it by making proper use of those same arguments it abuses.

5

Philosophical Imitation

The last two chapters have sought to elucidate the way in which the dialectician speaks as well as the way in which he argues. The present chapter concerns the dialectician's role as *imitator*. Whether in drawing an analogy or telling a story, there are times when the dialectician finds it necessary to appeal to the imaginations of his interlocutors through the use of images (εἴδωλα, εἰκόνες). Reason in this case requires such images as aids in the attainment of a certain insight. If dialectic is to serve its function of awakening insight into the truth, it must know how to employ correctly not only language and argumentation, but also images.

Yet the role played by images in dialectic extends beyond the use of comparisons and analogies. In seeking to grasp the nature of virtue the dialectician cannot escape confronting and dealing with the reflections of this nature in sensible particulars. In formulating, examining, and refuting distinct definitions of virtue reference must constantly be made, at least implicitly, to persons or actions that exhibit virtue. Thus in the early dialogues Socrates often brings a definition into question by citing a specific case it fails to cover; to Laches' definition of courage as "Standing at one's post," for example, Socrates objects by referring to cavalrymen who are courageous in flight. It would be unacceptable for Laches to respond that he is not concerned with specific examples, but only with the general nature. In seeking to understand a universal or common "form," dialectic cannot ignore its instantiations. A Socratic inquiry never proceeds a priori, if this means that it turns its back to appearances. In seeking to understand a nature that transcends its sensible images, Socrates' dialectic must always start with these images and return to them. It is grounded in the concrete world of experience even if its vision is directed elsewhere.[1]

But there is another level at which images play a role. Not only does dialectic employ images (in comparisons) and proceed from images (the concrete situation that instantiates the truth sought), but what we know of it through the Platonic dialogues is itself an image. Plato chose to communicate the truths of philosophy by imitating the process of philosophizing. Therefore, this process (dialectic) not only employs imitation, but is itself an object of imitation. An examination of the use of images in dialectic is further complicated by the need to explain the relation between this dialectic and its instantiation in the written dialogue.

To understand the role that imitation (*mimēsis*) plays at all three levels distinguished above, an account is needed both of its nature and of its correct and incorrect uses. Just as Plato's views on the correct use of language and argumentation had to be largely inferred from his critique, in the *Cratylus* and the *Euthydemus*, of their misuse by the sophists, so his views on the proper or philosophical use of imitation must be largely inferred from his critique of its misuse by the poets (whom he tends to classify as a type of sophist). However, the latter task is made especially difficult by the fact that there is no one dialogue devoted solely to the use and abuse of imitation. The most thorough account of imitation, as well as the most thorough critique of its poetic use, are to be found in passages of the *Republic*, especially book 10. However, the *Ion*, which focuses on poetic *inspiration* rather than imitation, and the *Phaedrus*, which discusses *philosophical* inspiration, supplement in important ways, without contradicting, what is said in the *Republic*. Therefore, the present chapter must depart from the principle followed by preceding chapters of reading a specific dialogue in its entirety. This means that the following discussion cannot pretend to do justice to the overall context of the selected passages examined and consequently must always run the risk of being one-sided. Furthermore, this discussion cannot aspire to more than cursory and schematic treatment of the very large issues it explores. However, its success or failure should be measured against its very specific and limited goal: to show that imitation does indeed play a central role in dialectic and to gain some insight into how exactly the dialectician's use of images differs from the poet's.

Socrates' criticism of poetry in book 10 of the *Republic* is concerned with determining two things: the nature of imitation and its effect on the soul. The latter concern has priority. If poetry were simply an idle amusement, then, no matter how shallow and how remote from the truth it might be, Socrates would feel no need to discuss it here at the end of his account of the just republic and the just soul. Accordingly, he justifies his turn, or rather return, to poetry by characterizing it as a "destruction of the mind" (λώβη τῆς ἀκουόντων διανοίας, 595b5–6). Yet Socrates adds a very important qualification: poetic imitation is dangerous only to those who do not possess as an antidote (φάρμακον) a knowledge of its real nature (595b6–7). What this claim suggests is that imitation is dangerous only when mistaken for something other than what it truly is. The drug that can cure one of whatever ill effects poetic imitation may have is simply *knowledge.*

It is this knowledge which Socrates proceeds to request from Glaucon (595c). According to his own confession, Socrates is possessed by a love for poetry (especially Homer) and therefore needs the antidote as much as anyone. Glaucon, however, is shocked by the request. If Socrates does not know what *mimēsis* is, how can Glaucon be expected to know! When Socrates observes that those with dimmer vision sometimes see things in advance of those with keener vision, Glaucon replies that in Socrates' presence he cannot even muster the courage to say what appears to him to be the case. This excessive timidity on Glaucon's part is unusual. While he normally recognizes Socrates as his superior in the discussion, he is nevertheless always willing to express his mind. Glaucon is the one, after all, who tells Socrates that his defense of justice in book 1 was not persuasive and who thus forces Socrates to draw it out to its length of ten books (357a-b). In the present passage, however, Glaucon acts as if he could not possibly dare to say anything about the nature of *mimēsis* in the presence of Socrates. Why?

Elsewhere in the *Republic* we learn that Socrates is notorious for *his use of images.*[2] In book 6 Adeimantus opposes to Socrates' claim that rulers must be philosophers the view of the majority that philosophers are at best useless and at worst pernicious (487b–d). Socrates surprisingly agrees (487d10). How then, Adeimantus asks, can it be that cities will not be free of evil until philosophers become their rulers? Socrates replies that this question needs to be answered with an image (δι' εἰκόνος, 487e4–5). Adeimantus's sarcastic response is very revealing: "And you, Socrates, are surely not used to speaking in images!" (οὐκ εἴωθας δι' εἰκόνων λέγειν, 487e6). The implication is that responding to a question with an image is common practice with Socrates, perhaps even to the point of being tiresome. And indeed it is. Instead of denying Adeimantus's implied charge, Socrates not only proceeds to use the image that compares the philosopher's fate in contemporary cities to that of a pilot in a ship taken over by inexperienced sailors, but describes this as confirming his "greediness for images."[3] Yet confirmation is hardly necessary, given the extensive use of images throughout the rest of the *Republic.* Later in book 6 Socrates discusses the nature of the good by means of an image (εἰκών, 509a9): the sun. Then to clarify this image he introduces another: that of a line proportionally divided into four sections. At the beginning of book 7 Socrates asks us to compare (ἀπείκασον, 514a1) our state of education to men dwelling in a cave, incapable of seeing anything but the shadows cast on the wall in front of them by implements situated behind their backs (this image is also called an εἰκών at 515a4, 517a8, 517d1). In book 9 Socrates responds to the claim that injustice is profitable to the unjust man who is reputed just, by fashioning in his discourse an image of the soul (588b10). On a larger scale, the Myth of Er with which the dialogue ends is an imitation of the rewards of justice. Finally, there is a sense in which the just city that forms the topic of the greater part of the dialogue is itself an image of justice in the individual soul (see 369a1–3). Add to this wealth of imagery images on a smaller scale, such as that of the dog used to describe the nature of the philosopher (εἰκών, 375d5), and Adeimantus's ironic exclamation will appear by no means unwarranted.[4]

We thus see why Glaucon in book 10 hints that Socrates more than anyone knows what imitation is.[5] Denying this knowledge, however, Socrates proposes that the two of them inquire into the nature of imitation. The first crucial step in the discussion is the introduction of the craftsman (δημιουργός). Socrates defines the craftsman in terms of the distinction, which he and his interlocutors are in the habit of making, between a single intelligible form and its many sensible instantiations (596a–b). The craftsman makes a particular bed or table by looking to its form (ἰδέα). He does not, however, make this form itself, that is, table as such or bed as such, but only *a* table or *a* bed. He can fashion certain materials into a table, but he does not thereby make *what a table is*. Throughout the following discussion, this description of the craftsman's relation to sensible particulars and their forms serves as the paradigm for judging the imitative artist.

Accordingly, Socrates first introduces the artist as a strange type of craftsman. He asks Glaucon what he would call someone who can himself make not only all the things that other craftsmen make, but also all natural objects, including plants, animals, and even the gods themselves. When Glaucon exclaims that this would be an incredibly clever person (σοφίστης, 596d1), Socrates counters that the kind of production at issue here is nothing difficult (οὐ χάλεπος, d8). The only tool it requires is a mirror which, when carried before the sun, the earth, plants, and animals, will produce all of these things. The difference between this production and the production of the craftsman, however, becomes evident when Glaucon replies that such a mirror would produce not these things themselves, but only their appearances (596e4). Socrates agrees and adds that this production of appearances is precisely the art of the painter. In this way, artistic imitation is judged solely in terms of its relation to "technical" production.

The language of this passage, especially Glaucon's exclamation that the person Socrates is describing must be an incredible *"sophistēs,"* suggests another, closely parallel discussion of imitation. In the *Sophist* (233d–235a), the Stranger describes how the imitator in a sense can make all things. With nothing more than a pencil he can create plants and animals, earth and sky, even the gods themselves. This incredible skill, however, is nothing but the art of imitation. This art, because it does not in reality create anything, is only a form of play (παιδιά, 234a7–b2). It reproduces solely the appearance of things, without the corresponding reality. This art is not confined to drawing or painting. Things can be imitated not only with a brush, but also with words (234c). It is precisely in this form of verbal imitation that the Stranger locates the sophist. The sophist is an "imitator of beings" (μίμητης τῶν ὄντων, 235a1–2). He can argue about anything, as opposed to the craftsmen who have a special field of expertise, only because his discourse can imitate things without knowledge of their true natures.[6] If this is the nature of the sophist, then Socrates in book 10 of the *Republic* is criticizing the poet precisely as such a sophist.

To clarify further the difference between imitative artist and craftsman, Socrates makes his well-known distinction between three beds. The first bed, the "form" that truly is (τὸ ὄν), is produced by god and copied by the carpenter in the particular material bed, which is in turn copied by the imitator in, for example, a painting. In thus being a copy of a copy, the bed produced by the imitator is three times removed from what truly exists in nature (597e3–4).[7] This is the model that will provide the framework for most of Socrates' discussion. What should be noted is that it makes both the craftsman and the painter imitators. The difference is that while the craftsman produces concrete things in imitating the forms, the painter produces only phantasms in imitating concrete things. When Socrates proceeds to describe how the painter will attempt to fool the ignorant into believing that his imitations are the real thing (598b–c), we see again that sophistic imitation is the target here, since such deception is exactly what the sophist is described as practicing in the *Sophist* (234c).

Up to now Socrates has directed his specific criticisms against painting.[8] Now (598d) he turns to poetry or, more specifically, *tragedy* (which here includes Homer). Tragedy is the focus because it is the art form with the most pretensions. The tragedian is known for speaking of serious and lofty things. The aim of his works is not to provide idle entertainment, but to communicate important truths. The seriousness of tragedy therefore seems a counterexample to any theory that considers art to be mere "play." If any artist can make a claim to knowledge, it is the tragedian.

Socrates nevertheless argues that the tragedians do not know what they are talking about. His first point (599a–b) is that someone who can produce both the original and its imitation will not put forward the imitation as the best thing he has to offer. He will seriously concern himself with bringing forth great and noble deeds rather than with producing imitations of these deeds (πολὺ πρότερον ἐν τοῖς ἔργοις ἂν σπουδάσειεν ἢ ἐπὶ τοῖς μιμήμασι, 599b4–5). He will prefer to be a man whose deeds are praised over a man who praises the deeds of others. The implication is that a poet who prides himself on his ability to imitate virtue and presents his imitations to the city as the best he has to offer does not really know the true nature of virtue. Inferior to the soldier or the statesman who exhibit virtue in action, he is three times removed from true being.

Socrates' second point (599c–600e) is that Homer, despite his reputation for knowing all the arts, is not known to have restored anyone to health or led an army or governed a city. Furthermore, if Homer was truly capable of educating men and making them better, is it likely that instead of having many disciples and companions he should have been neglected as, according to tradition, he was? If Homer had known how to govern a city and make his fellow citizens virtuous, he surely would not have wasted his time on simply imitating these things. Socrates' conclusion is that tragic poetry, despite its apparent gravity, is nothing to be taken seriously (602b8).

This conclusion should trouble us. What is disconcerting is not simply the dismissal of poetry as a shallow copyist's art, though this is indeed hard to accept and hard to reconcile with the fact that the work advocating this dismissal is itself an imitative masterpiece.[9] Even more troubling is that Socrates' dismissal of the poets seems to dismiss much more. As noted above, Socrates' critique judges artistic production solely in comparison with technical production. Accordingly, the crucial premise in the argument against the poet is that the deed (*ergon*) is prior to the word (*logos*). The poet is criticized for talking about the cobbler instead of himself practicing the art of cobbling. He is criticized for talking about virtue instead of performing virtuous acts. In each case, the poet as an imitator is shown to be inferior to the real world of making shoes, constructing beds, and winning battles. The implication is that only activities producing tangible results are to be taken seriously. Anything else is idle play.

Yet if concrete action and technical production are the paradigms, there is another activity as vulnerable to criticism as poetry: *philosophy*. Socrates' critics, from Aristophanes to Callicles, saw in his dialectic nothing but idle talk, a mere excuse for not taking on a role of responsibility in the affairs of the city. The whole of the present dialogue, it must be remembered, is nothing but talk about a city that does not exist now and probably never will. And yet Socrates, in the process of imitating in language this nonexistent city (see 369c9), thinks that he can criticize the poets for merely imitating what others do in reality! What city, Homer could retort, has *Socrates* governed? What qualifies *him* to speak about how a city is ideally to be ordered? Does not Socrates' criticism of the poets turn against his own philosophical activity?[10]

Earlier in the dialogue Socrates can justify his account of the ideal, and perhaps impossible, republic only by maintaining the opposite of what he asserts against the poets in book 10, namely, that there *is less truth in the deed than in the word:* "But can a thing be in practice what it is in words, or is it not the nature of action to be less in contact with the truth than speech, even if there are those who do not think so" (473a1–3). This can be as much a defense of the poet as of Socrates. There is more truth, one might say, in Homer's account of Achilles' courage than could be found in any particular courageous act. What, then, makes Socrates think that he can defend his discourse by asserting the priority of speech over action and then turn around and criticize the poet for not actually doing any of those things of which he speaks? If Socrates can talk like a ruler without ever having actually ruled, then why should the poet be denied this privilege? Judged by the hierarchy set up in book 10, Socrates' speech seems no nearer the truth than the poet's.[11]

That Socrates would not want his critique of poetry to be turned against his own dialectic is shown by a passage in the *Phaedo* (99d–100a). Socrates there describes how, fearful of blinding his soul, he abandoned the attempt to examine things directly and decided instead to search for the truth of things in *logoi,* just as those who wish to preserve their eyesight do not gaze directly at the eclipsed sun but instead observe its reflection (εἰκών) in water. This comparison suggests that a *logos* is inferior to, and less real than, the thing itself (*to ergon*). In this case, by taking refuge in *logoi,* Socrates would be distancing himself from truth and reality. Yet to the extent that the comparison suggests this, Socrates claims that it is inadequate, since he denies that a *logos* is any more of an image than an *ergon* (99e6–100a3). He does not agree that those who examine reality in discourse are dealing with images any more than those who examine reality in concrete actions and things. But how can Socrates say this? Certainly a *logos* refers to real things and therefore is at least in this sense an image of these things. It is true that real things are themselves images of that form from which they derive their names. But as Socrates points out in *Republic* 10, talk about real things is the image of an image. In this sense, *logoi* must be images to a greater degree than are *erga:* the former are thrice removed from the truth whereas the latter are twice removed. Yet this priority of *ergon* over *logos*, which in *Republic* 10 seems to necessitate the dismissal of philosophy as well as poetry, is denied by Socrates in the passage of the *Phaedo* in which he describes his own method. Is Socrates contradicting himself? Or is there a sense in which Socrates' discourse is less of an image and nearer to the truth than that of the poets?

To answer this question, we must return to the *Republic* and the next stage of Socrates' critique. Having explained the nature of *mimēsis*, he can now proceed to his next question: on what part of us does imitation exert its power? (602c4–5)? Socrates distinguishes between rational and irrational parts of the soul. When a straight stick is placed in water, one part of us sees the stick as bent while another recognizes this to be an illusion. The part of us that is not deceived is "rational" and as such can weigh, count, and measure things (602e). It can determine the length and shape that the stick has in reality. The part of us that is deceived, on the other hand, is irrational. This distinction shows that painting, in simply reproducing the appearance of the "bent" stick in water, appeals to the irrational part of us capable of being fooled by appearances.

Socrates next proceeds to show that the lack of true "measurement" is as characteristic of poetry as it is of painting. He begins with the general statement that mimetic poetry imitates human beings acting voluntarily or involuntarily and having the opinions or emotions attendant upon these actions (603c). Can this kind of action, Socrates now asks, cause strife and division in a person? In the case of the stick appearing bent in water, part of the soul believes it to be bent and another part believes it to be straight. Is there a similar conflict in the soul with regard to human action and suffering? To show that there is, Socrates gives the example of a good man who experiences the loss of a son whom he holds dear (603e–604d). A part of this man will want to give way to grief, while another part will resist and fight it. What resists the grief is reason and law (λόγος καὶ νόμος), while what gives in to it is just feeling (τὸ πάθος, 604a10–b1). Reason will tell the lamenting father that we cannot know what is really good or evil in such a case (604b10–11) and that mortal life is not worthy of great concern. Presumably, the deceptive appearance here, analogous to the bent stick in water, is that what has happened is a great evil, since it may in reality be a great good (especially if, as Socrates will soon argue, the soul is immortal). A part of the father can see nothing but the loss of his son, which appears greater than it is precisely because it is so close. Another part of him, however, rises above the appearance to see the real good or evil in what has happened. To which part, then, does the mimetic poet appeal? Precisely the emotional part, the part prone to lamentation

(605b–c). By depicting calamities that make us weep and dangers that make us afraid, the poet achieves his renown. That concerning which the poet cannot distinguish between greater and less is therefore the good itself.

To see the extent to which Socrates in this critique aims to distance himself from the poet, we must briefly bring into view the wider context of the dialogue. While the poet imitates only the appearance of the good, Socrates' task in the *Republic* as a whole is to separate the reality from this appearance. The question posed by Glaucon and Adeimantus at the beginning of book 2 is in essence the following: is not the *semblance* of justice more beneficial than the reality? Imagine two men, one thoroughly wicked but reputed just, the other truly just but reputed wicked. Will not the former be the happier of the two? He will enjoy both the benefits of crime and the benefits of apparent virtue, while the other man will enjoy neither. What Socrates fails to show in book 1, according to Glaucon and Adeimantus, is that the *reality* of justice is always to be preferred over vice. Though the benefits of *seeming* virtuous are universally recognized, it is hard to see beyond this semblance the benefits of *being* virtuous. In words of the wise cited by Adeimantus, "seeming overpowers the truth" (365c1–2).

Socrates first tries to get beyond the mere semblance of the different virtues by defining them. The reason, however, for the long "digression" comprising books 5–7 is that these definitions, while providing a sketch of the real being of virtue, still do not succeed in showing that this reality is better than the semblance.[12] For this to be shown, justice and the different virtues must be grounded in that one thing concerning which no one prefers the semblance over the reality—the good: "Isn't it clear that while many would choose what appears [τὰ δοκοῦντα] just and noble and would be content to believe, possess, and do what appears so, even if it isn't really so, in the case of what is good no one is satisfied with possessing the mere appearance, but everyone seeks to know the reality [τὰ ὄντα ζητοῦσι] and therefore disdains mere belief?" (505d5–9). Socrates here states as clearly as possible the dilemma with which he wrestles in the present dialogue. Some people (apparently the majority) prefer the semblance of justice over the reality, and yet these same people would never knowingly choose what merely appears good over what is really good. If, then, the reality of justice is to be preferred to the mere appearance, justice must be shown to be itself good. Thus the need for the "greatest study." If the goal of the *Republic* as a whole is to free being from its enslavement to seeming, the purpose of Socrates' critique of the poets becomes clear. What makes the poet dangerous is that he imitates only the appearance of the different virtues and in so doing conceals the reality. It is in large part due to the enchantments of poetry that "seeming overpowers the truth."

These general observations on the direction of the dialogue as a whole make clear that Socrates does not see his discourse as confined to appearance in the way that that of the poets is. The philosopher is capable of "measuring" what is truly good and thus can avoid being deceived by what merely appears good. However, it is one thing to affirm this distinction between the philosopher and the poet and another to justify it. We have seen that by making the *craftsman's technē* the paradigm of knowledge in his critique of poetry, Socrates at the beginning of book 10 fails to demonstrate the *philosopher's* superiority over the poet. In comparison with the craftsman and the man of action, the philosopher seems as much an imitator as the poet.

This problematic proximity between the philosopher and the poet becomes particularly evident when we turn to the point in book 10 at which Socrates performs an unexpected about-face (612a ff.). So far he has complied with the wish of Glaucon and Adeimantus that he extricate the true being of justice from its appearance. He has resisted following Homer and Hesiod in talking of the rewards and honors attending justice and has instead shown that justice in itself (αὐτὸ δικαιοσύνη) is best (612b). With this accomplished, however, Socrates asks Glaucon and Adeimantus *to return to him the appearance of justice* (612c–d). He now wants to describe the just man as receiving the rewards he deserves and as recognized by both gods and men for his virtue. We are to imagine the just man not as dying in poverty, despised by all, but rather as achieving honor in his old age and holding the most important offices. In short, even though Socrates has resisted Homer throughout the course of the *Republic* and has just subjected the great poet to very harsh criticism, he himself now wants to do what Homer and other poets do so well, that is, imitate the appearance of justice. Thus, the dialogue that like no other has fought for philosophy in the struggle against poetry ends with a poetic myth recounting the rewards alotted to the just after death. In combating the poets Socrates has himself become a poet.[13] This outcome, of course, is not entirely unexpected, given that Socrates throughout the dialogue produces images with a fecundity rivaling that of any poet.

How can Socrates turn to poetry and the appearance of virtue after the harsh criticism to which he has subjected both?[14] He explains that there can no longer be any reproach (ἀνεπίφθονος) to considering the external rewards of virtue (612b–c). He has succeeded in distinguishing the reality of justice from the appearance; with this done, what harm can there be in returning to the appearance? It must be remembered that Socrates earlier prescribed an understanding of the nature of imitation as the antidote to its charms (595b). Now that poetry has been put in its proper place, now that it is recognized to be three times removed from the truth, there can be nothing wrong with indulging in it a little.

By far the more difficult question, however, is *why* Socrates chooses to end his discussion of justice with a poetic account of its appearance. Why not end with the claim that justice is inherently better than injustice even if the just man must suffer the greatest hardships and be hated by all? Would this not be a more striking and forceful conclusion? Would it not more effectively prevent any misunderstanding of what Socrates has said? In returning to the multifarious and ambivalent world of seeming, Socrates appears to endanger the conclusions that have been reached with such great difficulty.

So far we have seen how philosophy clashes with poetry, but we have yet to see how philosophy can use poetry and why it must do so. In returning to appearance, is Socrates simply amusing himself with the form of idle play which is poetry or is there in his play a seriousness lacking in the works of the poets? In other words, is Socrates simply lowering himself to the level of the poets (a level thrice removed from the truth), or is he using their means to achieve a much higher purpose? *Does the insight that being is better than seeming require that we abandon appearance altogether or does it instead make possible a form of imitation to rival that of the poets?*

Anyone wishing to affirm the latter alternative faces the problem that the model used by Socrates' critique of imitation seems to rule out the possibility of a form of imitation capable of assisting the philosopher in his search for truth. According to this model there are only two forms of imitation: the concrete imitation (the particular table or bed), which is the product and concern of the craftsman, and the imitation of this imitation, which is the product and concern of the poet. Neither form of imitation appears to have anything to do with philosophy. The dialectician is not versed in any handicraft, and therefore his knowledge of the forms is not gained through an ability to produce beds or tables. Poetic imitation, on the other hand, in reproducing only a thing's appearance, contradicts the dialectician's very goal of getting beyond appearance by grasping a thing's true being. In Socrates' hierarchical model, only god, the craftsman, and the poet have a place. The dialectician is left out altogether.

With the problem defined in this way, it is now finally possible to appreciate the full significance of the fact that Socrates in book 10 *revises this model.* In a digression which the above account of the main argument (601c–602b) passed over, he introduces *someone who uses* what the craftsman only makes.[15] But what motivates this addition to the original model? Socrates earlier claimed that the craftsman looks directly at the form in producing its concrete copy, but he now maintains that an intermediary is needed to bring the craftsman into contact with the form. This intermediary is the person who, by knowing the *use* of the thing to be produced, *knows* its true nature and can guide the craftsman's production accordingly. Even though the user and the craftsman are concerned with the same object (the concrete particular), the difference is that the former *in using this thing* has *knowledge* of its form, whereas the craftsman *in making this thing* has only *true belief* (πίστις ὀρθή 601e7, δόξα ὀρθή 602a4–5).[16] For example, the flute-maker does not himself know whether his flutes are well made, that is, whether they approximate the true form of a flute. The *flute-player* is the one who can tell the maker that a flute is either well or badly made. The flute-player is therefore the one who knows the form, while the flute-maker makes the flutes, not by looking directly at the form himself, but by following the flute-player's instructions.[17] Socrates' new model, then, distinguishes between three arts: the user's art, the productive art, and the imitative art (601d1–2). As in the *Cratylus* (390b–d) and the *Euthydemus* (290b–d), the user's art is ranked higher than the productive art.[18]

But why is the user's art introduced here? The hierarchy established in the first model is all that Socrates needs for his critique of poetry *qua* imitation. The new model, however, does add something to our understanding of this critique. As noted above, the craftsman's product is itself a kind of image. Particular beds and particular tables are themselves images of their corresponding forms. What the introduction of the user's art now shows, however, is that *the original is revealed more clearly in the use of the image than in the image itself.* In other words, a thing's form is revealed in the use made of it, rather than in its concrete, sensible qualities. We know what a flute should be by playing one, not by making one.

In Socrates' original model, that is, before the introduction of the user's art, there are only originals and their images. The image reveals the original only by means of its sensible qualities. A painting of a table, for example, reveals only so much of the table as can be reproduced on the canvas, that is, only one side of it seen from one perspective (see 598a–b). The table itself reveals only so much of the form as its particular, physical constituents can instantiate. The user's art, however, makes possible a knowledge that reveals more of the original than is actually expressed in the image itself and that yet has as its immediate object nothing but this image. The original is revealed in the *use* of the image. What a table is does not receive its clearest manifestation in the concrete table itself as produced by the craftsman. What a table is receives its clearest manifestation in the use made of the concrete table. This, then, is the dimension which the user's art adds to the image/original relation. The extent to which the image reveals the original depends on the use made of this image. An unused table shows us next to nothing about what a table is.

But cannot this insight apply equally to the kind of imitation produced by the poet? Even though this imitation taken in itself and as the mere product of the poet does not reveal a thing's true nature, might it not be used in such a way as to do so? Granted that imitation by its very nature reproduces only the appearance of a thing, might it not be used in such a way as to suggest what lies beyond this appearance? When poetic imitation is taken out of the hands of the poet and used by the philosopher, might it not become much more than what the poet intended it to be?

These questions are answered not by what Socrates says, but rather by what he does. Since Socrates turns to imitation at the end of the dialogue, having indeed used it throughout, and clearly intends such imitation to reveal more than is contained in the appearances it reproduces, he must recognize a philosophical use of imitation. Insofar as Socrates' dialectic, like poetry and sophistry, turns from *erga* to *logoi* and is not restricted to any special field of objects, what characterizes it is not the use of the concrete images produced by the craftsman, but the use of "poetic" images. In Socrates' revised hierarchical model there is a place for dialectic: it is a user's art related to poetry in the way that horsemanship is related to saddlery.[19]

The main concern of dialectic, however, is clearly not to talk about saddles and beds (though, notoriously, Socrates does talk about such things all the time: see *Symposium* 221e). Socrates' choice of artifacts as his examples has clearly made it easier for him to rank the poet beneath the craftsman in the first model and to introduce now the user's art in the revised model. Yet has not this choice also restricted the scope of the discussion? How are we to extend the two models to cover natural objects or human beings and their actions which, after all, are the primary subject of the poet? Who, for example, makes virtue and who uses it? Socrates clearly does not see what he says as limited to artifacts: the priority of use over production is meant to apply to *everything that is*. The excellence or correctness of a thing, whether natural or artificial, is defined by its use: "Is it not the case that the excellence, beauty, and correctness [ἀρετὴ καὶ κάλλος καὶ ὀρθότης] of each artifact *or living thing or activity* concerns nothing other than the use [χρεία] for which it was made or came to be?" (601d4–6). The word "chreia" in this passage clearly is not to be understood in some crude utilitarian sense. A thing's use is not some good external to it. It is not that to which a thing is forcefully and accidentally subordinated. The *chreia* of a thing is the thing's own good. But it is precisely in a thing's proper good that its true being is found. What a thing *is* is defined in terms of its good. Therefore, what becomes manifest in a thing's *chreia* is the form in relation to which its excellence and correctness are defined. The priority of the user's art is only a consequence of the priority of the good asserted in book 6.

Now that Socrates' scope is seen to include all existing things, we should try to apply his models to something that is not an artifact. The appropriate example in the present context is virtuous action, which is the subject of both poets and philosophers. Virtuous action is brought about by one who practices virtue. The just or courageous man is here the analogue to the craftsman. The poet imitates this man's actions without knowing how to be virtuous himself. He reproduces only the external appearance of virtuous actions, showing us no more than the reputation and rewards that accompany them.[20] Socrates' first model would have us believe that this is all there is: the man who practices virtue and the poet who imitates it. Socrates' revised model, however, introduces an art that knows how to *use* the virtuous actions which the virtuous man only produces. What does this mean? The mere "producer" of virtuous action is the person who has only what Socrates elsewhere in the *Republic* calls "civic virtue" (430c, 500d, 619c–d): this person does what is good without reflecting on the reason for, or point of, doing good (an example is Cephalus).[21] The practitioner of the user's art, however, is here someone who recognizes the importance of going beyond simply conditioned or habitual virtue and examining what virtue *is for*. This person, like Socrates, knows that the virtues are in themselves as capable of corrupting the soul as of improving it and that therefore they are essentially subordinated to some higher good (491b7–10). In the republic sketched out by Socrates, this user would be the statesman who determines the proper role of the different virtues (and thus of the classes exhibiting these virtues) within the state.[22] Within the individual, the user is that highest part of the soul which knows that the different virtues are to be used only as approximations to the good and are not to be allowed to usurp its place. In either case, the true nature of the virtues is known only in their proper use.[23]

To the extent, however, that the philosopher is neither king nor wiseman,[24] to the extent that he is not in direct contact with reality but must take refuge in *logoi*, he needs a user's art that does not deal with the *erga* themselves, but with their images. Whether in employing analogies, narrating a myth, or simply describing particular instantiations of the form under discussion, this user's art would be able to reveal a thing's nature through its mere appearance. The use of an image of virtue would reveal more about the nature of virtue than is actually expressed in this image. If this is possible, as Socrates' revised hierarchical model suggests, then we have finally found a distinctly philosophical form of imitation, that is, an imitating that is not confined to appearance.[25]

Now that philosophical imitation has been identified with a specific use of images, the exact character of this use must be more exactly determined. Of primary importance is a recognition of the image's inadequacy.[26] Anyone who believes that in simply reproducing the appearance imitation has expressed *the thing itself* will be more blinded than enlightened by it. This is precisely the danger of poetry. If, however, the imitation makes no pretence to accuracy and does not hide its inferiority to the original, then it can be an effective tool in making the original manifest. A passage from the *Phaedo* best describes the way in which an image can express what transcends it. Socrates there claims that our very ability to describe two things as being equal (e.g., two equal sticks) while recognizing that they fall short of true equality shows that we must already have some knowledge of what true equality is: "When a person sees something and thinks, 'what I now see, while striving [βούλεται] to be like [οἷον] something else, falls short [ἐνδεῖ] and cannot be like that thing, but is inferior,' do we not agree that the person who thinks this must already know [προειδότα] the thing to which he compares what he sees in saying that the latter resembles [προσεοικέναι] it, but only deficiently [ἐνδεεστέρως δὲ ἔχειν]?" (74d9–e4).

According to Socrates, even though the image (in this case the equal sticks) is unlike the original, it can still serve to reveal the original. The recognition that the two approximately equal sticks fall short of true equality causes us to *recollect* the knowledge of equality we already possess. Yet this section of the *Phaedo* shows not only that the original can be known through its image, but also that this is the *only way* in which it can be known. Thus Socrates insists that we acquire our understanding of equality only by means of perceiving equal sensible objects (75a5–7). It is important to note the tension here: on the one hand, our idea of equality is not *derived* from sensible images insofar as it transcends anything contained in these images (thus the need for presupposing that we already have this idea and need only "recollect it"); on the other hand, we come into explicit possession of this idea only through the perception of its images. What enables us to acquire knowledge that transcends the sensible images with which we start is a recognition of their defects, a recognition that is itself made possible by our prior possession of an implicit knowledge of the original. In general, philosophy's use of imitation is characterized by this tension between the necessity of starting with appearance and the goal of transcending appearance. Essential to this use is a recognition of deficiency. Only someone who recognizes that imitation copies nothing but an appearance quite unlike the original nature can use it to intimate what lies beyond this appearance. *This is why Socrates' critique of poetic imitation must precede his use of it.*[27]

Now it is possible to explain the fact that Socrates in book 10 *does not* banish all of the poets from the city but admits a certain kind of poetry, namely, hymns to gods and the praises of good men (607a3–5).[28] There is therefore no contradiction between Socrates' discussion of poetry here and his earlier discussion in books 2–3. Earlier, as again here, Socrates recognizes the value of an imitation of the good (τὴν τοῦ ἀγαθοῦ εἰκόνα ἤθους, 401b2). Accordingly, he recognizes a type of poetry that is worth making use of: "But we ourselves, for our benefit, should use [χρώμεθα] the more austere and less pleasant poet and storyteller, who would imitate the words of the good man [ὃς ἡμῖν τὴν τοῦ ἐπιεικοῦς λέξιν μιμοῖτο] and tell his story according to the patterns which we legislated at the beginning, when we undertook to educate our guardians" (398a8–b4). Note the language: we *use* the austere poet with the goal of *benefiting* from him. It is the user's art that determines the goodness and acceptability of poetry.

In the context of book 10, however, the passing mention of an acceptable form of poetry is very odd, since Socrates in the rest of this book criticizes not a specific, degenerate form of poetry, but *all* poetry *qua* imitation (ὅση μιμητική, 595a5). Are not hymns to the gods and praises of good men forms of imitation? If they are, how can Socrates allow them to escape the general ban without explanation? The most plausible answer is that Socrates does not consider this admissible poetry to be imitation in the strictest sense of the word. Socrates tells us (604d–605a) that the type of nature which most lends itself to imitation is the irritable, variable, inconstant type. Only appearances rich in detail and variety can provide sufficient material for the poet's virtuosity. Only here does imitation fulfill its nature, which is to be "varied" (ποικίλη, 604e1). The more complex the appearance, the better the imitation.[29] For precisely this reason, hymns to the gods and praises of good men are not "good" imitations. The "intelligent and temperate disposition," by "always remaining similar to itself" (παραπλήσιον ὂν ἀεὶ αὐτὸ αὑτῷ), is neither easy to imitate nor, once imitated, easy to understand (604e2–4). To the imitator, it must appear without content. Imitation thrives on multiplicity, but the good man is characterized by simplicity and unity. Furthermore, because the good man is defined by his resistance to appearance and to the desires aroused by it, "imitations of good men" are almost an impossibility. The good disposition, and one might say the good generally, evades imitation. The poetry Socrates admits into the city is *qua* imitation "bad" because it forces imitation to express something which it is not its nature to express.

These observations explain how Plato's own dialogues can be imitations while escaping condemnation.[30] According to some scholars, one thing that distinguishes a Platonic dialogue from a Homeric poem or a Sophoclean play is that it fails to be completely satisfying as a work of art.[31] Despite attempts to characterize Plato's dialogues as dramas (e.g., in Arieti 1991), the fact is that they would be a boring evening in the theater. Through their carefully crafted plots and vivid characterization, Sophocles' plays can engage and entertain even an audience not inclined to reflect on the deeper mysteries of human life. In comparison, the characters of Plato's dialogues appear pale and one-dimensional,[32] and "action" is either nonexistent or disjointed and aimless. There can be no doubt that in a dramatic contest Plato's dialogues would place last. The reason is not that the dialogue is lacking in form or unity, but rather that the form or unity it has is not a distinctly aesthetic one. What unifies the dialogue is neither the setting nor the characters nor the plot nor the myths nor even the arguments, but rather the subject under discussion whose nature all these other elements simply reflect. Indeed, these different elements often contradict each other: a contradiction that forces us to look beyond them for the truth.[33] Even as dramatically vivid a work as the *Lysis* will be unappealing and even incoherent to someone simply seeking a convincing portrayal of specific friendships; it will interest only someone willing to go beyond such a portrayal in the search for an understanding of friendship itself. The dialogue, unlike a poetic imitation, does not try to hide its flaws, that is, its occasional monotony, its digressions, the thinness of its plot, and the incompleteness of its scene and character sketches. It does not hide these flaws because, rather than attempting to take the place of the original, it wants to draw our vision beyond itself; it is a work of art we can see through.[34] The dialogue is an imitation that transcends imitation.[35]

In conclusion, the philosopher in using imitation works against it rather than with it. He recognizes that it is not a proper medium for the expression of the truth he seeks. Yet as long as this recognition exists, as long as the imitation does not hide its flaws, a philosophical use of imitation remains possible. Subordinated to a higher truth, imitation must be made transparent to this truth. Such transparency, however, is not found in the varied imitation (ποικίλη μίμησις) of which the best poets are masters. The philosopher is a bad poet, but for precisely this reason he makes better use of poetry than does any poet.[36]

A problem, however, remains. Though the philosopher may recognize the inferiority of the image, it is not thereby rendered any less inferior. How, then, can this image awaken insight into an original so unlike it? The artistic imitation which Socrates criticizes confounds image with original. Philosophical imitation, on the other hand, recognizes the gulf between the two. None of the characteristics of the image can be taken to be a simple "copy" of some characteristic of the original. There is therefore no way of inferring or deducing the nature of the thing imitated from its imitation. Reason alone seems incapable of bridging the gap between them. This is precisely why a knowledge based on images appears to be no knowledge at all, but only the kind of "conjecture" (εἰκασία) described in the simile of the Divided Line (509e–510a, 511e2). If philosophical imitation is to be more than such "conjecture," one must explain just how the philosopher can arrive at the original through its mere image.[37]

There is an explanation: what allows the philosopher to transcend the image in a knowledge of its original is not deductive reasoning, but rather *inspiration* (ἐνθουσιασμός). There are a few passages in the *Republic* that associate philosophy with at least the language of inspiration.[38] The most important is 499b6–c2 where Socrates mentions the possibility that the love of philosophy might one day take possession of the leaders of the city through some sort of divine inspiration (θεία ἐπιπνοία). Despite such hints in the *Republic,* however, the clearest account of philosophical inspiration is found in the *Phaedrus.* In his great speech in praise of love, Socrates characterizes sensible objects as images that serve to remind us of those intelligible forms which the soul has seen prior to its embodiment. Just acts recall to mind the nature of justice itself, which we in some way already know and which enables us to recognize these particular acts as being just acts in the first place. The movement, however, from images of justice to a recollection of justice itself is by no means an easy or unimpeded one. Only in the case of beauty does the image preserve some of the luster of the original. In the case of the other intelligible forms, the road from image to original is a difficult one traversed only by a select few. "Justice, temperance, and all the other things valued by the soul do not shine forth in their sensible images, but very few people, approaching the images [τὰς εἰκόνας] with dull organs, can see just barely [μόγις] that which is imitated" (250b1–5). Socrates describes this difficulty in the context of characterizing philosophy as one of the forms of inspired madness. The philosopher's inspiration consists precisely in his ability to use the sensible image as a reminder of an intelligible reality. This use of images must be characterized as inspiration because it transcends the deductive reasoning characteristic of the sane and sober mind.

In a way that he himself cannot explain, the philosopher just barely sees the original in the image that is in many ways so unlike it. Not considering sensible objects the ultimate reality, he does not take seriously any action that has only such objects as its ends but rather sees in these objects mere images to be used in the recollection of a reality that transcends them. This "use" is what raises the philosopher above everyday commerce and lends him the ecstatic look of someone either mad or inspired.

> It is therefore fitting that only the philosopher's understanding [διάνοια] should acquire wings, for he is always as near in memory [μνήμη] as possible to those things a nearness to which makes him truly divine. By making *proper use* [ὀρθῶς χρώμενος] of these means of remembrance [ὑπομνήμασιν] and by being initiated into the highest mysteries, he alone reaches true perfection. Remaining aloof from purely human concerns and drawing near to the divine, he is rebuked by the multitude as being out of his mind when in fact, unknown to them, he is inspired [ἐνθουσιάζων]. (249c4-d3)

This passage confirms the view defended above that in relation to images the philosopher's art is a *user's art*. What characterizes the philosopher is an ability to use sensible images *correctly*, that is, as means of recollecting that knowledge of intelligible forms which is the soul's birthright. As we have seen, the *Phaedo* also assigns recollection a central role in the correct use of images. The above passage, however, describes in addition the *inspired* character of this way of using images. The philosopher's understanding is "winged" because, through the use of images as remembrances of their originals, it attains knowledge that cannot be had through mere inference or deduction. "Flights of understanding" here lead to the recognition of truth and cannot be replaced by the step-by-step workings of a purely rational mind. Sensible images taken by themselves and subjected to analysis reveal little or nothing about the nature of the reality they imitate. The philosopher must therefore use these images in such a way that he is transported beyond them. Herein lies the ecstatic character of philosophy.

This admission of an apparently "irrational" element into philosophy, however, seems once again to confound the philosopher with the poet. In the *Phaedrus* itself we are told that a poet's works are worth nothing if he is not inspired in writing them (245a). In the *Ion* Socrates claims that the poet, as the mouthpiece of a god, speaks not with understanding, but under inspiration. "The poet is a delicate, flighty and holy thing and is unable to create before he becomes inspired [ἔνθεός] and out of his senses [ἔκφρων], so that understanding [νοῦς] no longer remains in him" (534b3-6). As in book 10 of the *Republic*, Socrates in the

Ion contrasts the poet with the craftsman, claiming that the former lacks the knowledge possessed by the latter: in the *Ion*, however, this difference is attributed to the poet's inspiration.[39] The *Ion* says nothing about the philosopher, and we might assume that, like the craftsman, he bases what he says on reasoned judgment rather than on inspiration. This assumption is contradicted by the *Phaedrus*. The philosopher turns out to be as "flighty" as the poet and thus equally unlike the worldly craftsman. Our expectation that the philosopher might distinguish himself from the poet through sobriety of judgment and clarity of reasoning is disappointed. Instead, the philosopher claims to glimpse just barely in the sensible image a form whose nature and relation to this image he cannot clearly explain. He speaks of "illumination," "vision," "ascent," "love," and looks down with contempt on what the "wingless" mind can achieve through its own meager resources. The philosopher then seems no better than the "enthusiastic" and pretentious Ion.

Yet a better understanding of the nature of inspiration and the danger it involves can preserve the distinction between philosopher and poet. Because inspiration transports us from the image to the original without the intermediary steps of a deduction or inference, it tends to conceal the distance between the two. Not having had to traverse any ground in flying from the appearance to the reality, we can overlook the abyss that exists between the two and that renders such a land journey impossible. Inspiration is dangerous because in surmounting the gap between sensible appearance and intelligible reality it can conceal the existence of such a gap. The inspired poet takes his imitations too seriously; he fails to see that they fall far short of reality and are therefore mere play.[40] He is thus led to mistake the appearance for the reality and this is Socrates' chief complaint against him.[41] The philosopher's inspiration, on the other hand, is controlled by the awareness that the image is greatly inferior to the original and cannot adequately express it. The philosopher does not simply allow himself to be transported to the original but is critical of this movement. He is aware that it is not the image itself which renders this movement possible, but rather a prior knowledge which this image can only be used to suggest. In using the image to reveal the original, the philosopher is also intent on destroying the image's pretensions. His inspiration is thus tempered by critical thought.[42] This is why, while the poet's inspiration excludes knowledge, the philosopher's inspiration presupposes it. The philosopher's understanding is indeed "winged," but it is still *understanding*.[43]

In summation, a distinctly philosophical or dialectical form of imitation requires the recognition of the following points: (1) an image (εἴδωλον, εἰκών), though merely duplicating an appearance, can be used in such a way as to point beyond appearance; (2) the intelligible original is revealed in the use of the image, rather than in the image itself; (3) the deficiency of the image must be recognized in order for the original to appear through it; (4) the "perception" of the original through the image is the result of neither deductive reasoning nor "conjecture," but rather of some form of inspiration; (5) this inspiration, unlike that of the poets, does not blind the philosopher to the immeasurable gulf between image and original.

The denial of any one of these claims renders impossible a distinctly philosophical imitation that does not succumb to the criticisms leveled at the poets. This, of course, would not be a problem if the philosopher could dispense with imitation altogether. If it were possible in this life to escape completely the world of appearance and attain a direct, unmediated apprehension of the forms, imitation would become superfluous.[44] Yet the passages from the *Phaedo* and the *Phaedrus* discussed above show that vision of the forms cannot be attained except through the mediation of their images. In the *Republic* itself, Socrates' constant use of images and his return to appearance in the concluding myth show that the philosopher cannot entirely escape the power of seeming: though seeking a knowledge of eternal and intelligible forms, he must always start with, and return to, the shadows in the Cave.

The need for a distinctly philosophical form of imitation arises from this tension within philosophy itself between a subjection to appearance and a persistent drive to transcend appearance. What has been seen to distinguish such imitation from the artistic variety is simply a knowledge of how to use images in such a way as to overcome them. This knowledge has in turn shown itself to be distinct from any propositional knowledge that would infer or deduce the original from the image: instead, it is characterized by "inspiration." It is precisely in the philosospher's inspired use of images that the world of seeming and the world of being are reconciled.

PART II

THE METHOD OF HYPOTHESIS

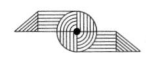

6

Failed Virtue and Failed Knowledge in the *Meno*

In the preceding chapters dialectic has been contrasted with the opposite poles of everyday discourse and sophistic discourse. It is now necessary to turn to a method introduced in the *Meno* and prominent in the *Phaedo* and the *Republic:* the method of hypothesis. I have argued that the insight provided by Socrates' dialectic cannot be adequately expressed in propositions. The method of hypothesis, on the other hand, *does* yield propositional results. Some scholars have therefore concluded that the questions Socrates asks fruitlessly in the aporetic dialogues are or can be answered by this method. This conclusion clearly contradicts the account of dialectic presented in the preceding chapters. It makes dialectic (in its elenctic form), rather than a source of insight, nothing but a propaedeutic, a "clearing the ground" for the positive work to be accomplished by means of another method.[1] This is why some account is needed here of the goal and limits of the hypothetical method. Such an account may also serve to dispel the fears normally aroused by any talk of "nonpropositional insight." An explanation of the relation between the elenchus and the hypothetical method may show that the insight yielded by the former is hardly "mystical" or "irrational."

The guiding questions of this and the next two chapters are accordingly the following: Is the hypothetical method intended to *replace* dialectic as understood in dialogues such as the *Laches* and the *Charmides*? In other words, are the answers it yields the same as those Socrates seeks in the aporetic dialogues? Does this method come nearer to the attainment of philosophical knowledge?

With regard to these questions, the *Meno* is of special importance since it explicitly introduces the method of hypothesis as a supplement to the What-is-x? question characteristic of the aporetic dialogues. Just when the attempts to answer the question "What is virtue?" reach an impasse,

Socrates introduces this method as a means of attaining positive results. The *Meno* thereby becomes more than just another dialogue ending in *aporia*. It shows us how we might proceed to say something *about* virtue despite the failure to say just what it *is*. More generally, it shows how we can proceed to draw philosophically interesting conclusions even when we fail to answer Socrates' What-is-x? question. However, in reading the *Meno* we must ask ourselves if this question thereby becomes irrelevant and if the conclusions attained through its sacrifice are really as "positive" and as illuminating as they might at first appear.

The dialogue begins abruptly with Meno's question: "Can you tell me, Socrates, if virtue is teachable [διδακτόν]?" Meno then lists the other alternatives: virtue could be acquired through practice (ἀσκητόν) or by nature (φύσει) or in some other way. This abrupt beginning is telling. Unlike other dialogues concerned with similar themes, the *Meno* does not provide the central question under discussion with any context. In the *Protagoras* the question concerning the teachability of virtue arises from a concrete situation, that is, Hippocrates' desire to learn virtue from Protagoras. Similarly, Socrates' questions in other dialogues always respond to particular circumstances, for example, Charmides' reputation for temperance, the concern of Lysimachus and Melisias for the education of their sons, and Hippothales' love for Lysis. Meno's question, however, is asked in the abstract, with no indication of his motives. Yet this very lack of context is revealing, since it suggests that Meno's question is not inspired by any practical dilemma but is "academic," that is, "sophistic." Furthermore, since Meno later in the discussion (80b) reveals that he has lectured on virtue many times and before large audiences, there is clearly no real thirst for knowledge behind his question.[2] We must therefore suspect that its purpose is either to let Meno show off the wisdom he thinks he has or to enable him to ensnare the renowned Socrates in an eristic trap (or both). The latter is a real possiblity, since it is likely that Meno has learned in advance arguments for refuting all three possible answers.[3]

Socrates immediately confirms our initial impressions about Meno by associating him with Gorgias and by praising the proverbially boorish Thessalians, of whom Meno is one, for their great cleverness. In contrast to the store of wisdom in Thessaly, Socrates complains, there is a dearth of wisdom in Athens, and for this reason he cannot answer Meno's question. Indeed, not only does he not know if virtue can be taught, he does not even know altogether *what it is* (οὐδὲ αὐτὸ ὅτι ποτ' ἐστὶ τὸ παράπαν[4] ἀρετὴ τυγχάνω εἰδώς, 71a6–7). Socrates then asserts the priority of the question concerning *what* something *is* (τί ἐστιν) over the question concerning *what kind* of a thing (ὁποῖόν τι) it is. This means that in the present case we must first know what virtue is before we can know whether or not it is the kind of thing that can be taught. "For how can I know what *kind* of a thing it is if I do not even know *what* it is?" (71b3–4). In this way Socrates succeeds in avoiding Meno's trap and in taking the discussion back to the kind of question that interests him: "What *is* virtue?"

It is important to reflect here on the problematic character of this priority which Socrates assigns to his What-is-x? question. What is the meaning of the sharp distinction he makes between *what* (*ti*) a thing is and *what kind* of a thing (*poion*) it is? He explains that one cannot know whether Meno is handsome, rich, and well born or the opposite if one does not know altogether *who* Meno is (μὴ γιγνώσκει τὸ παράπαν ὅστις ἐστίν, 71b5–6). The point seems to be that before one can know Meno's properties, one must know Meno himself. Yet this is an odd claim. Do we not come to know who Meno is by knowing his properties? We do not simply know "Meno," but rather we know him *as* such and such a *kind* of person. Thus, if we had to "define" Meno, we would say that he is a wealthy Thessalian aristocrat, a student of Gorgias, and so on. For this reason, answering the *poion*-question seems here to be the condition for answering the *ti*-question, and not vice versa, as Socrates claims. The same problem presents itself in the case of virtue. It seems that we come to know *what* virtue is by means of knowing what *kind* of a thing it is, for instance, if it is teachable, if it is good, and if it is knowledge. Indeed, it is hard to imagine a definition of virtue that would not simply state certain properties of it and thus simply tell us what *kind* of a thing it is. Again, the *poion*-question seems to take priority over Socrates' ambiguous and seemingly vacuous *ti*-question.

These difficulties could of course be solved by reading into what Socrates says a distinction between "essential" and "accidental" properties.[5] Socrates' point would then be that one must know a thing's essential properties before its accidental ones. Yet there are serious problems with this interpretation. First, though the view it attributes to Socrates is perhaps philosophically defensible,[6] it certainly is not self-evident. Yet both Socrates and Meno appear to see the priority principle as requiring no defense. Second, this interpretation does not make any sense of Socrates' example. How could it be true to say that we cannot know whether or not Meno is rich until we know his essential properties (whatever those might be)? Can we accept an interpretation of Socrates' distinction which renders nonsensical his own illustration of it? Even if "knowing Meno" is only an analogy, it for that very reason should not be utterly disanalogous. Third, there is the evidence of *Republic* 1 (354b–c), where Socrates asserts that he cannot possibly know whether or not justice is a virtue if he does not first know *what* it is. To know that justice is a virtue is to know only something *about it,* not *what* it is. Yet if anything deserves to be called an "essential property" of justice, it is "being a virtue." In excluding whatever is known only *about* a thing, Socrates appears to be distinguishing *all* of a thing's properties from what the thing *itself is*. Likewise, Socrates' claim in the present dialogue appears to be, not that we cannot know some of Meno's properties before knowing others, but rather that we cannot know *any* of his properties before knowing Meno himself. In conclusion, Socrates' problematic distinction between the *ti-* question and the *poion-* question cannot be explained in terms of a distinction between different kinds of properties.

How, then, is it to be explained? Is there any sense in which we must first know Meno before knowing any of his properties? This claim is plausible only if we take "knowledge" in the first case to mean some form of "acquaintance": I must become acquainted with Meno, I must meet Meno, before knowing any of his properties. An obvious objection has been voiced by Fine: "I know who he [Meno] is from having read Plato's dialogues."[7] But the question is precisely whether or not *Socrates* would call reading about Meno a case of "knowing" Meno. And he clearly *could not:* how in this case would knowing who Meno is differ from knowing what *kind* of a person he is? In claiming to know who Meno is by reading about him, Fine presumably means that she knows he is a student of Gorgias, a Thessalian aristocrat, arrogant, and so on. Yet this knowledge does not appear in any way to differ from, nor therefore to be prior to, what Socrates would call knowing what *kind* of a person Meno is. We do not run into this problem if we take Socrates to mean that while we may read, or hear through second hand reports, that Meno is noble or rich, we cannot *know* that Meno is this kind of a person until we actually meet him and "see for ourselves." This acquaintance with Meno serves as the ground for knowing his properties and is clearly distinct from knowing his properties. This seems, therefore, to be the only interpretation that makes sense of what Socrates *says*. The example of "knowing Meno" also in this case parallels the later example of knowing the road to Larissa: we do not "know" the road until we have actually traveled on it and seen it for ourselves.

But can this interpretation be extended to the analogue: knowing virtue? Many scholars take the answer to be negative.[8] In their view, the point of Socrates' distinction and priority principle is that we must first define the essential properties of virtue before we can know any of its nonessential properties. If this view is correct, Socrates' analogy would be largely disanalogous: the only similarity would be that in both cases some kind of knowledge precedes another, but the nature of this priority would be completely different in each case. It is not, of course, impossible that the analogy is this weak, but it is at least surprising that Socrates would not have used a more appropriate example. Add to this surprise the first and third reasons stated above for finding implausible this interpretation of Socrates' distinction, and it becomes clear that an alternative should at least be *considered*.

What alternative is there? In order for Socrates' analogy to be a strict one, the following must be the case: *to know what is true about virtue (i.e., its properties) is not the same as to know virtue itself.* Knowledge of virtue as a whole is not reducible to knowledge of its different aspects or of the different ways in which it is "qualified." As a result, *what* virtue is would strictly speaking not be definable, since any definition would provide merely a list of properties and to know such properties is not the same as to know the thing itself. The definition may state something true *of* virtue, but it will still leave unexpressed *what* virtue is in its unity and wholeness. Knowledge of what virtue is will therefore be, like our knowledge of who Meno is, a kind of knowledge by acquaintance.[9]

However, the word "acquaintance" should be understood here in its rich, everyday meaning, rather than in the extremely narrow sense it tends to have in contemporary philosophy, according to which "acquaintance" is simply a direct cognitive relation to sense data or simple objects.[10] Being "acquainted" with Meno in the ordinary sense of the word involves more than perceiving sense data and even more than perceiving an "object": to be acquainted with Meno is to have some intercourse with him, to enter into some relation with him (however superficial). This sense of knowledge by acquaintance differs from the narrow philosophical sense in admitting variation in degree:[11] from barely being acquainted with Meno to knowing him very well. It is not the case, however, that this possibility of degrees makes "knowing Meno" propositional. The claim that I am better acquainted with a person than you are need not be (and I doubt that it even *can* be) translated into the claim that I know more true propositions about this person. Am I better acquainted with my wife than with my dentist only in the sense that I know more true propositions about her? Likewise, if I claim to be better acquainted with Paris than you are, I do not mean that I know more true propositions about Paris. In fact, you could have the greater store of propositional knowledge derived from extensive research, and yet I could still meaningfully insist that I am better acquainted with the city. There is in short a kind of knowledge by acquaintance which, unlike the immediate perception of sense data, admits degrees and is complex, but is not reducible to knowledge of propositions. This third kind of knowledge has already been described in previous chapters and seen at work in the dialogues. It may also prove to be central to this dialogue. The point that needs emphasis now is that we should not impose upon the dialogue a simplistic dichotomy between immediate intuition and knowledge of propositions, as if nothing else were imaginable.

But what exactly would "acquaintance with virtue" involve if not a direct, immediate intuition of the essence of virtue? According to a strict analogy with "knowing Meno," it would involve knowing virtue firsthand, that is, presumably, *having* virtue. In other words, knowing what virtue is "by acquaintance" would be indistinguishable from *becoming virtuous*.[12] This would explain Meno's surprise (71b9-c2) when Socrates claims not to "know" what virtue is: such a claim would, under this interpretation, be equivalent to confessing not to *have* virtue. The point of Socrates' priority principle thus may be that to know propositions about virtue, even if these propositions constitute an elaborate moral theory, is not equivalent to knowing virtue itself, that is, being acquainted with it firsthand, and that indeed the first kind of knowledge is worth nothing if not based on the second. But then is Socrates saying that knowing virtue is just a practical matter? Are we to believe that he is dismissing the possibility of a *theoretical knowledge* of virtue? Whether virtue is acquired through practice or theoretically (by being taught) is in fact a principal question addressed by the dialogue. What needs to be noted here, however, is that this interpretation of "knowing what virtue is" as "being acquainted with virtue" need not commit Socrates to the "practice" view. It may be the case that for Socrates philosophical inquiry is essential to having virtue, not because it produces definitions and theories which then constitute virtue, but because virtue is found in the very willingness to inquire persistently in the face of *aporia*. This should sound familiar: the interpretations offered in previous chapters have already defended this thesis that the knowledge of virtue which Socrates seeks is found instantiated in the inquiry itself. If this turns out to be the case in the present dialogue, then we have a sense in which for Socrates knowledge of virtue is "acquaintance with virtue," as opposed to knowledge of propositions about virtue.

On the suggested interpretation, there is no absurdity in Socrates' ranking of the *ti*-question higher than the *poion*-question. If "acquaintance" with virtue is not exhausted by knowledge of any of the properties that may be asserted of it, and if this "acquaintance" provides the sole ground for genuinely knowing the truth of any such assertions, then it is true that we must know what virtue is before we can know anything about it. In this case, however, the priority of the *ti*-question is bought only at the cost of allowing that in a certain sense it cannot be answered. The challenge to say *what* virtue is will remain, while we will be able to say only what *kind* of a thing it is.

Whether or not this characterization of the knowledge of virtue is really behind what Socrates says at the beginning of the dialogue cannot yet be determined. Several points, however, can be made. First, this interpretation *is* an alternative to the essential/accidental properties interpretation. Second, we have seen reasons why this latter interpretation is implausible. Third, we have also seen that the suggested interpretation makes Socrates' example of "knowing Meno" a much better example than it would otherwise be. Finally, this interpretation agrees with how, according to the conclusions of chapters 2 and 4, philosophical knowledge is characterized in the *Laches*, the *Charmides*, and the *Euthydemus*.

Another advantage of the suggested interpretation is that it saves Socrates from the so-called Socratic Fallacy, that is, the view that we cannot know anything about virtue until we know the definition of virtue. The reason why so many scholars have attributed the "fallacy" to Socrates in this dialogue is their assumption that the knowledge to which Socrates gives priority here can be nothing other than knowledge of a definition stating the essential properties of virtue.[13] Since the suggested interpretation rejects this assumption, the "fallacy" does not exist for it. This is not to say, however, that it renders Socrates' priority principle completely unproblematic. There remains the fundamental problem that will make Socrates vulnerable to Meno's eristic paradox: if we cannot know anything *about* virtue (any of virtue's "qualities") before becoming "acquainted" with virtue as a whole, how can we possibly acquire this acquaintance in the first place? How do we know where to look or what to do? We cannot simply walk up to virtue as we might walk up to Meno.

Despite the above observations, how the knowledge of virtue and the *ti*-question are to be interpreted in the *Meno* cannot be decided without a careful reading of the rest of the dialogue. Meno does not at first understand Socrates' question, and indeed a good portion of the dialogue is taken up by Socrates' efforts to explain it to him. It is also important to note that Socrates asks Meno simply to recall *Gorgias'* definition of virtue (71c–d, 73c). It is thus made clear that Meno throughout the discussion is not giving original answers based on his own self-reflection and inquiry but is instead simply recalling what he has heard the sophists say. This will prove to be the only kind of "recollection" of which Meno is capable.[14] Meno's first definition of virtue is nothing but a list of the different kinds of actions recognized to be virtuous according to a person's class and sex (71e–72a). It is virtuous for a man to manage well the city's affairs, it is virtuous for a woman to obey her husband, and other actions are virtuous for slaves and children. Socrates objects that his question seeks *one thing*, not a swarm (σμῆνος) of different virtues. In other words, he is looking for that one *form* of virtue (ἕν γέ τι εἶδος) which different kinds of behavior must possess in order to be *virtuous* and to which one can look (ἀποβλέψαντα) in attempting to clarify to another what virtue is (72c–d). Thus Socrates rejects Meno's next definition ("virtue is the capacity to govern men," 73c9) because, though displaying greater unity, it does not cover specific instances (the virtues of children and slaves). A definition of virtue, then, must be of one thing or nature, but it must also cover the most diverse instances. In other words, it must point to a unity in the multiplicity *without reducing this unity to the multiplicity*. This principle applies not only to the relation between virtue and its different instances, but also to the relation between virtue and its different parts (see 73d–74a). Thus Socrates' objection to Meno's next definition ("virtue is desiring fine things and being able to acquire them," 77b4–5) is that it really amounts to the definition of virtue as "*just* acquisition of the goods we all desire" and thus defines virtue in terms of one of its parts: justice, the other parts being piety, courage, and temperance (79a–c). Though these are in fact the different kinds of virtue and though virtue never occurs except as one of these kinds, it is nevertheless the case that virtue is not simply this multiplicity but is rather the unity that causes each kind to be referred to by the same word "virtue." An answer to the question "What is virtue?" must therefore meet the following criterion: it must state what virtue itself is as a whole without breaking it up into parts (μὴ καταγνύναι μηδὲ κερματίζειν τὴν ἀρετήν, 79a9–10); it must avoid reducing the unity of virtue to a multiplicity (παῦσαι πολλὰ ποιῶν ἐκ τοῦ ἑνός, 77a7).[15] Socrates relates this criterion to his distinction between the *ti* question and the *poion* question. To know only something *about* a thing is to break it up into parts and thus to fail to grasp it in its unity. Thus Socrates summarizes his challenge to Meno in the following words: "While we are still inquiring into what virtue is as a whole, do not think, best of men, that you can make its nature manifest [δηλώσειν] by stating its parts [διὰ τῶν ταύτης μορίων] or that you can make anything else manifest by speaking in this way. Instead, understand that the same question must be put to you again: what do you take virtue *itself* to be in saying what you say [about it] [τίνος ὄντος ἀρετῆς λέγεις ἃ λέγεις]?" (79d6-e3). It is no wonder that Meno is left completely perplexed by this challenge. How is one supposed to define something without breaking it up into parts or without merely saying something about it? It seems that every definition, by presenting one with a multiplicity where what one seeks is a unity, is necessarily reductionistic. It can be protested against any definition of x as "y and z" that x is *one thing* and therefore cannot be reduced to y and z. What, then, does Socrates want? Is not his demand totally unreasonable?

Earlier in the discussion, Socrates does give Meno an example of the kind of definition he is looking for, but this example is at first glance more perplexing than illuminating. We apply the word "shape" to both the straight and the round. But an answer to the question "What is shape itself?" cannot simply list the different kinds of shape but must state what is common to all of them and allows them all to be called "shapes." Socrates then says that he would be satisfied if Meno gave a definition of virtue analogous to the following definition of shape: shape is the only thing that always accompanies color (75b10–11). This example is surprising. Despite his earlier insistence on the priority of the *ti*-question, Socrates here recommends a definition that does not tell us what shape itself is but states only that it always accompanies something else, that is, color.[16] This definition seems to answer only the *poion*-question: "What *kind* of a thing is shape?" Socrates is therefore vulnerable here to same kind of objection he makes against Meno: how can we know whether or not shape accompanies color if we do not know what shape itself is?

Meno himself objects that Socrates' definition is "naive" (εὔηθες, 75c2), but only because it defines shape by means of another undefined term. Socrates in response offers another definition that employs terms Meno claims to understand: "shape is the limit of a solid" (στερεοῦ πέρας, 76a7). It is surprising that while Meno pretends not to understand something as empirically obvious as color, he claims to understand the much more abstract technical terms: "limit" and "solid." It is quite likely that he does not really understand the latter terms more than the former, but prefers them simply because he is in the *habit* of using them. This betrays once again his sophistic training. He will not recognize the obvious, but he will respond positively to any statement that triggers his memory of what he has learned from the "wise."[17] Yet we ourselves might find Socrates' second definition more satisfying than the first precisely because it is more "technical" and defines shape in terms of concepts that seem less extrinsic to its nature than color.[18] Socrates himself, however, shows no preference for the second definition. He considers the first one true (75c8) and is satisfied with it; he offers the second only for Meno's sake. Again Socrates makes no distinction between essential and accidental properties. The definitions of shape as "what always accompanies color" and as "what limits a solid" are equally good. But then perhaps they are both open to the same kind of objection: how can we know if shape limits a solid or always accompanies color if we do not first know what shape itself is?

To understand Socrates' satisfaction with these two definitions of shape, we must understand why he is *not* satisfied with the definition *à la Gorgias* which, at Meno's request, he gives of color: color is "an effluence [ἀπορροή] of shapes commensurate with sight and perceptible by it" (76d4–5). Meno considers this to be the best definition (because it is of the sort he is used to, as Socrates explains at 76d), while Socrates himself is convinced that the definitions[19] of shape are better (76e). There is good reason for siding with Meno here. Whether or not the definition of color is in fact correct (which does not seem to be the issue), it is at least informative: it says something about what color *is*, namely, that it is an effluence, and also about the *kind* of effluence it is, namely, one of shapes commensurate with sight. What, then, does Socrates find wrong with it? And why does he think that the definitions of shape are better definitions? Those definitions define shape in terms of its relation to something else (i.e., color or a solid). The definition of color, on the other hand, does not define it in terms of its relation to something else but attempts to say what it itself is. This definition, then, rather than either of the ones of which Socrates approves, seems in form to answer best Socrates' What-is-x? question.

What, then, is Socrates up to? On the one hand, he asserts the priority of his *ti* question. On the other hand, he puts forward, as an example of what he seeks, a definition that does not at all answer a question of this form, while he disapproves of a definition that apparently would answer such a question. And there is an even more serious problem. While Socrates' definition of color is meant to clarify the term left undefined in his first definition of shape, the result is instead a vicious *circle:* shape is defined in terms of color, but color is itself defined as an "effluence of shapes"! A similar circularity may afflict even the second definition of shape: a peculiar characteristic of this definition is that it defines the more simple (shape) in terms of the more complex (solid), while it is surely the latter that should be defined in terms of the former.[20] But in this case Socrates' model definitions exhibit the same flaw he criticized in Meno's definitions: they *presuppose* an understanding of what they are supposed to define. Meno defined virtue in terms of "parts" (either specific examples of virtue or different kinds of virtue) that presuppose an understanding of "virtue as a whole" in order to be recognized as such. Socrates defines "shape" in terms of "color" and "solid," though we apparently cannot know what the latter are unless we already know what shape is. To repeat, what *is* Socrates up to?

If Socrates' intention is to show Meno that virtue can be adequately defined and that knowing a definition of virtue is equivalent to knowing what virtue is, then he is unbelievably careless in his choice of examples, so careless that he offers as models definitions just as bad as Meno's. If we assume, however, that Socrates is not obtuse and that his examples are carefully and deliberately chosen (not a terribly controversial assumption), his intention must be the exact opposite: to show that virtue cannot be adequately defined because any definition, rather than itself *providing* a knowledge of virtue, *presupposes* such knowledge. In other words, the circularity encountered above is unavoidable. A complex moral theory is as vulnerable here as a solitary definition: the elements of such a theory could not be properly understood without prior knowledge of what virtue is "as a whole."[21] Meno's demand that a definition contain no undefined terms, implied by his objection to the first definition of shape, shows what the alternative is to circularity: an infinite regress.[22]

Yet if Socrates' intention is to show that no definition of virtue can provide us with knowledge of its nature, is he not being extremely unfair with Meno? Why should he object to the inadequacy of Meno's definitions if an adequate definition is not to be found? More important, why should he in this case insist that Meno keep trying to define virtue? This difficulty disappears with a little reflection. It is important to remember that the person who thinks he can say exactly what virtue is, the person who has lectured many times on virtue in front of large audiences, is *Meno*. Socrates' intention, therefore, could be to undermine Meno's pretense of wisdom by showing him that virtue cannot be known in the way he thinks it can, that is, in formulas and definitions analogous to the definition of color which Socrates ridicules. Yet Socrates can also have a more positive, complementary goal: to get Meno genuinely to *inquire* for the first time in his life, *not because inquiry is the means to an adequate definition of virtue, but because inquiry is itself an essential part of being virtuous.* A reading of the rest of the dialogue will reveal that these are in fact Socrates' goals.

In assuming as self-evident and indisputable that for Socrates knowledge of virtue is knowledge of a definition, many scholars apparently reason as follows ("apparently" because they usually give no reason at all): Socrates demands that interlocutors who claim to know what x is *define* x; furthermore, he sees their inability to do so as evidence that they lack the knowledge they claim to have; therefore, Socrates believes that one can know what x is only by defining x.[23] Chapter 2 already exposed how faulty this reasoning is. The mere possibility that Socrates has the two goals described above shows that he need not believe either that x *can* be defined or that a definition is necessary for knowledge of x. Socrates' method may assume only that the ability to define x is presupposed *by the kind of knowledge the interlocutor believes himself to have:* a knowledge that is final, dogmatic, and in no need of further inquiry. This assumption does not commit Socrates to the view that the knowledge of virtue available to us is in fact like this; his aim could instead be to *destroy* this pretension. But then how can Socrates conclude that the interlocutor does not have whatever kind of knowledge *is* available to us, if this knowledge does not depend on a definition? Might not Meno in this case know what virtue is despite his inability to define it and thus despite his lack of the kind of knowledge he wrongly claims to have? The answer is that Meno's arrogance and confidence themselves show that he has no true knowledge of virtue, just as someone who claims that philosophy is easy thereby betrays profound ignorance of its nature. The above reasoning must therefore be recognized for what it is: a non sequitur, even if this non sequitur is the starting point of much Platonic scholarship.

The proposed interpretation leaves an important question unanswered: why does Socrates *prefer* his two definitions of shape to the definition of color? An answer is available if we take seriously Socrates' demand that a thing not be "broken up" in being defined, that it be left "whole" and "intact" (77a8–9). The definition of shape as that which always accompanies color leaves it "whole" and "intact," because, by defining it in terms of its *relation* to something else, it does not *reduce* it to any multiplicity. In other words, the virtue of the definition is precisely that it does not pretend to state what shape is but simply provides a means of recognizing shape in its relation to something else. The second definition, by defining shape in terms of its relation to a solid, likewise appears to leave shape intact and avoid reducing it to something other than itself (though it may come closer to doing so than the first one and therefore may be less appealing to Socrates). The definition of color, on the other hand, is clearly reductive in its identification of the two things which the first definition of shape keeps distinct: shape and color.[24]

What Socrates may be trying to show is that definitions can help us identify things as long as they are not mistakenly taken to express what the thing being identified *itself is*. Just as secondhand reports about Meno can provide us with information that might help us to identify or locate him without themselves providing a knowledge of (i.e., acquaintance with) Meno, so certain descriptions of virtue might help us to locate or identify it without themselves providing a knowledge of what virtue itself is. This function that propositions might have *even if* knowledge of virtue itself is nonpropositional will be illustrated by the slave episode and, especially, by the description and use of the method of hypothesis.

This interpretation, which has the virtue of making sense of Socrates' peculiar preference, has a consequence already encountered above: Socrates' What-is-x? question cannot be answered. Any attempt to answer it must, like the definition of color, and even like the definitions of shape if misunderstood as essential definitions, be dismissed as reductionistic and circular. In this way, the excursus on definition seems to confirm the tentative conclusions drawn above on the basis of the analogy between "knowing Meno" and "knowing virtue." If it is the case, however, that we can say only what *kind* of a thing something is and not *what* it is, can the priority of the What-is-x? question be maintained? This problem is at the heart of Meno's attempt to stop Socrates' inquiry dead in its tracks.

Meno is understandably perplexed. Every attempt to define virtue has failed, and no end to the inquiry appears in sight. Meno characteristically blames his helplessness on Socrates, protesting that Socrates like a stingray has so numbed his mind and lips (ναρκᾶν, which Meno equates with ἀπορεῖν) that, even though he has spoken about virtue a hundred times in front of large audiences, he now cannot even say what it is (80a–b). Socrates accepts the comparison only with the qualification that he puts others in *aporia* by being himself in *aporia*. When Socrates suggests that he and Meno pursue the inquiry together in an effort to find out what virtue is, Meno attempts to avoid further humiliation by introducing an argument against the very possibility of inquiry (one he has clearly picked up from sophists of the Euthydemus and Dionysodorus variety): how can we even *look* for something when we do not in the least know what it is? And even if we find it, how will we recognize it to be the thing we were looking for? The paradox, in Socrates' restatement, is that we can search neither for what we already know nor for what we do not know. If both Socrates and Meno are in *aporia*, if both do not know what virtue is, the inquiry Socrates proposes is not even possible. If, on the other hand, they already know what virtue is, the inquiry is unnecessary. In either case, Meno escapes any obligation to continue answering Socrates' questions.

Though nothing but a sophistic trick in Meno's hands, this argument presents a very serious problem for Socrates' peculiar method of inquiry. We ourselves might reply that it is not the case that we must *either* know a thing completely *or* not know it at all. We can, for example, know one property of a thing and then with the help of this knowledge discover its other properties. For example, if we know that virtue is good, we have a basis upon which to inquire into the nature of virtue. However, this is exactly what Socrates' priority principle will not allow: we must first know a thing *as a whole* before we can know anything *about* it. It is precisely Socrates' insistence on this point that led the inquiry to its present *aporia*.[25] Socrates therefore appears truly vulnerable to Meno's objection. The priority principle implies that before knowing virtue as a whole we know *absolutely nothing about it*. But then how can we even look for it? Again Socrates' What-is-x? question proves unanswerable. Because we cannot know what *kind* of a thing virtue is before we know *what* it is, there is no way of *coming to know* what virtue is. We either know it or we don't.[26]

Socrates responds to Meno's argument in the only way he can: by claiming that *we already in fact know what virtue as a whole is*. Socrates quotes the view of priests and priestesses, as well as of the inspired poets, that the soul is immortal and has been born many times (81a–e). We should therefore expect that the soul has already seen all things. Thus what the soul learns in the present life it already knows and is therefore simply *recalling*. Learning, in short, is recollection (ἀνάμνησις).[27] If this is the case, then the priority Socrates grants his What-is-x? question can no longer be said to render inquiry impossible: this question seeks only to elicit knowledge that we already implicitly have. If we must know what virtue is as a whole *before* we can know anything *about* it, then the knowledge of virtue cannot be acquired a posteriori and piecemeal through some form of induction: it must already be "in" us in its entirety.

Meno now asks Socrates to "teach him" how learning can be the same as recollection (81e). Socrates pretends to think that Meno's innocent and unthinking use of an ordinary word is a calculated trick: Meno, he claims, is trying to catch him in a contradiction by asking him to "teach" when he has in effect just denied that there is such a thing as "teaching" (81e-82a). Although Meno apparently did not really have this intention and therefore is not *in this sense* wicked (πανοῦργος, 81e6), Socrates' accusation brings to our attention a serious flaw in Meno's character. The kind of "teaching" that is ruled out by the identification of learning with recollection is the kind that seeks to "put into" the mind of the student an understanding that is not already there: in the words of a poem by Theognis cited later in the discussion (95e), the assumption this "teaching" makes is that "understanding can be produced and instilled in men" (ποιητὸν καὶ ἔνθετον ἀνδρὶ νόημα). A flaw in Meno's character evident throughout the present discussion is his view that to *learn* is no more than to *be taught* in this way. This is the way in which he has been "taught" by Gorgias and the other sophists. This is the way in which he sought to be "taught" by Socrates how virtue is to be acquired. Now he simply wants to be "taught" that learning is recollection so that he can add this bit of information to his warehouse of "wisdom." What Socrates wants us to see is that Meno's very character stands in the way of his being able to understand the claim that "learning is recollection." Learning as Meno knows and experiences it is *not* recollection, and it would be a self-refuting endeavor for Socrates to try to change this by *telling* and *teaching* Meno that this is what learning is.[28]

Socrates therefore instead tries to *show* that learning is recollection by conversing with one of Meno's slaves. He proposes to awaken knowledge in the slave *without teaching him anything*. If he succeeds, he will have shown that the slave in some sense already had this knowledge and only needed help in recollecting it. This demonstration of recollection at work will then perhaps also help Meno recollect that this, and not simple memorization, is what learning really is.

Socrates proposes to deal with a geometrical problem and makes certain that the slave both speaks Greek and has never been taught geometry. Socrates first asks the slave to consider a square, each of whose sides has a length of two feet. When asked for the area of this square, the slave himself figures out that it must be two times two or four. Socrates now asks him to imagine a square twice as large as the first, that is, having an area of eight feet. The question Socrates then poses, and whose answer he will try to make the slave recollect, asks for the length of each of the sides of this square. The boy at first thinks that because the square is twice as large as the first, the length of its sides must be twice as long. His first answer is therefore four feet. Socrates easily shows that this answer is incorrect by pointing out that a square with sides of this length would have an area of sixteen feet. Recognizing his error and realizing that the length Socrates seeks must be between four feet (which is too long) and two feet (which is too short), the boy next suggests that it is three feet. This answer is again easily shown to be wrong, since a square with sides three feet long would have an area of nine feet, not eight.

At this point the boy is completely perplexed. It is easy to see why. He obviously thought that if the right answer is between two and four it must be three. What other alternative is there?[29] Socrates remarks that the boy's perplexity is similar to Meno's and that this is a good state to be in, since it makes one aware of one's own ignorance, and such awareness is the first step toward knowledge.[30]

Yet what is especially significant about the present episode is that Socrates does not leave the boy in perplexity, but instead leads him toward the recollection of some kind of knowledge. Socrates in this way will finally show us just what kind of an answer he expects his What-is-x? question to receive. Uncertainty on this point has been the source of all of the difficulty encountered above in trying to understand the nature of Socrates' inquiry. Now there is a chance to see what this inquiry is really aiming at.

Through further questioning, and with the help of a diagram, Socrates gets the slave to see that the side of a square with an area of eight feet is equal to the diagonal of the square with an area of four feet. Though Socrates clearly helps the slave toward this recognition, it is nevertheless the slave who points to the diagonal and recognizes it to be the side he is looking for. In this way the slave is led out of his state of ignorance and made to see the truth. Therefore, if Socrates' discussion with the slave is really analogous to his inquiry into the natures of the different virtues, he apparently can not think that this inquiry must always end in *aporia*. Just as the question he asks the slave admits a definite answer, so should the question "What is virtue?"

Yet the above account has glossed over a most important fact, though one overlooked by many commentators: *the question Socrates asks the slave is never directly answered and cannot be answered*. The reason is simple: in asking for the length of the side of a square with an area of eight feet, Socrates is asking for an *irrational number* (the square root of eight).[31] The slave must of course fail to provide this number, though he tries every whole, rational number that approximates it. Socrates has thus presented him with an impossible task.[32] No matter how long and hard the slave might think, he will never be able to work out the square root of eight. In this respect what happens here turns out to be no different from what happens in aporetic dialogues such as the *Laches* and the *Charmides*. Just as in the one case no final definition of courage or temperance is found, so in the other the irrational number Socrates seeks cannot be articulated. Strictly speaking, Socrates' discussion with the slave also ends in *aporia*.

Yet it cannot be denied that in the present episode we do get an answer of sorts: in the end the slave can point to the right side; he can recognize it.[33] His knowledge thus has the character of "acquaintance," though not in the narrow sense of direct cognition of some sensible object:[34] the boy now has genuine insight into the nature of the side he points to, something he could not have gained by simply seeing a drawing of it.[35] Thus we receive further confirmation and explanation of the suggestion made above, that is, that as we know through acquaintance who Meno is, so do we know in an analogous way what virtue itself is. That the boy is led by Socrates to this kind of "answer," however, does not destroy the parallel with the aporetic dialogues.[36] As was argued in chapter 2, we get the same kind of "answer" in the *Laches* and the *Charmides*: though courage and temperance are not *defined* in these dialogues, we are nevertheless *shown* throughout the course of the inquiry what each one is. Thus even though both dialogues end in *aporia*, Socrates' interlocutors would not agree with Meno that therefore the inquiry was futile. In this way the slave episode and Socrates' method of inquiry in the aporetic dialogues can shed light on each other. The slave cannot state the length of the side Socrates is looking for since this length is an irrational number, but the very process of question and answer can lead him to recognize this length. Likewise, one cannot say *what* virtue is because virtue, like an irrational number, cannot be comprehended in any proposition. Yet the very process of inquiring into virtue can show one what it is.

The slave episode also sheds light on the difficult distinction between knowing what something is and knowing what kind of a thing it is. By getting the slave to see the relation between the side in question and the square with an area of four feet (the former is the diagonal of the latter), Socrates helps him see what this side is. The parallel with Socrates' first definition of shape is obvious. Just as Socrates defines shape by describing its relation to something else, color, so does he identify the side of a square with an area of eight feet by relating it to something else, a square with an area of four feet. In either case Socrates avoids the danger of pretending to express in a proposition the nature of the thing itself: shape is not reduced to something other than shape, and the square root of eight is not reduced to a whole number.[37]

But if Socrates' choice of an irrational number is meant to show, as I have suggested, that his What-is-x? question in both this and other dialogues is itself unanswerable, then how are we to explain the priority Socrates grants this question? Does the present episode help us at all with *this* problem? We must ask what would be lacking if the slave had simply been told at the beginning that the side in question is the diagonal of a square with an area of four feet. What does the slave learn through the process of refutation that he could not know if he had simply been taught this definition? In the latter case, he would have no awareness of the side's length, and therefore his knowledge of something *about* the side would be empty. Likewise, if one knew no more about shape than that it always accompanies color, one would have only an empty opinion of how shape is *qualified* without any knowledge of what shape itself *is*. However, this defect of the two definitions, namely, that they both state only *poion ti* and not *ti esti*, can be remedied by the actual process of inquiry. In having his answers refuted, the boy comes to see that the side he is looking for is neither two nor three nor four feet long. His ensuing perplexity is the right attitude to have toward a side whose length is an irrational number, and it therefore brings him nearer to knowing this side. As will become clearer later, this attitude is the truly positive gain of the inquiry. The reading of the *Laches* in chapter 2 showed that the knowledge of virtue, rather than having the character of mastery or certainty, contains an irreducible component of ignorance and perplexity. In other words, to know courage, and therefore to be courageous, is necessarily to be ignorant. In leading his interlocutors into perplexity, Socrates is not leading them away from an understanding of the virtue in question, but is in fact beginning to awaken this understanding in them. Analogously, Socrates' questions here, precisely in perplexing the slave, awaken in him an insight into the nature of the side of a square with an area of eight feet, which he would not have obtained by simply being taught its relation to a square with an area of four feet.[38] These reflections show how Socrates' priority principle is maintained. As long as the slave continued to think that the side in question was four or three feet long, he could not be said to know that it is the diagonal of a square with an area of four feet. He can now at the end of the inquiry know this *about* the side only because the failure of the attempt to express directly its length has enabled him to *recognize* it for what it is.[39] This recognition or understanding may be expressed only negatively, but, like that gained in the aporetic dialogues, it is understanding nevertheless.

Therefore, it is true that we cannot know how a thing is qualified (*poion ti*) before we know what it is (*ti*) and that accordingly the What-is-x? question has priority. This does not mean, however, that we must first *define* what a thing is before we can know anything about it. Instead, what comes first is gaining *insight* into what a thing is through the very process of question and answer. On the basis of this insight we can then talk meaningfully about this thing. In short, a proposition stating how a thing is *qualified* (what properties it has) is given content and meaning by nonpropositional insight into what the thing *is*.

Yet the inquiry through which this insight is gained clearly requires that we talk *about* a thing, that is, relate it to other things and discuss its properties. Are we not, then, led into the same circle: we cannot inquire into a thing unless we know it, and we cannot know it unless we inquire into it? It is precisely to explain this circle that Socrates introduces his view that learning is recollection. In inquiring into the nature of virtue we already know what virtue is as a whole: the different aspects of virtue that are examined and the definitions that are considered and refuted serve only to bring out this knowledge. The process of examining definitions and showing their limitations *both* presupposes *and* helps recollect knowledge of what virtue is. This means that virtue does not have to be defined in order to be known. The goal of the inquiry is not to find a final definition of virtue (which the dialogue has so far suggested to be impossible), but to recover that nonpropositional knowledge of virtue as a whole which we already have. The definitions considered, the descriptions of how virtue is qualified, are only means toward this end.

Thus Socrates claims that nothing but the same process of questioning which he demonstrates in the slave episode is needed to attain knowledge. Because the slave's latent beliefs have only just been aroused, he is in a dreamlike state at the end of the discussion. However, to awaken from this state and acquire knowledge comparable to that of anyone else, the slave does not need to be "taught" anything new but only needs to be asked "the same questions ... on many occasions and in different ways" (πολλάκις τὰ αὐτα ταῦτα καὶ πολλαχῇ, 85c9–d1).[40]

Socrates clearly cannot believe that through further questioning the boy will finally be able to work out the square root of eight. Instead, the result Socrates expects must be that the slave will further recognize the irrational number for what it is and thus will come to understand the impossibility of expressing it directly and completely. But then what exactly is the distinction here between true belief and knowledge? The process by which both are attained is the same: the boy's true beliefs have been "awakened" through questioning; these beliefs will become knowledge by being further "awakened" through frequent repetition of this questioning. In addition, the origin of the two is the same: the knowledge the boy will attain is as much already "inside" him as were his true beliefs (see 85d3–4, 86a7–8). A *sharp* distinction, then, between belief and knowledge cannot be made here. They are simply different degrees of an awareness that emerges gradually from being implicit to being explicit.[41]

But what does it mean to speak of "degrees" here? Either you believe something or you don't. Either you know something or you don't. It apparently makes no sense to talk about "clearer or dimmer" belief, "clearer or dimmer" knowledge. This is true if we are speaking of "propositional belief" or "propositional knowledge." This is why the account of recollection in the slave episode requires us to understand belief and knowledge according to the model of the kind of "acquaintance" discussed above, an acquaintance that admits degrees. What the slave has at the beginning of the inquiry is not "belief that" concerning the side in question[42] nor, obviously, "knowledge that," but rather a certain awareness of space and its properties. This awareness is only implicit because, though in some sense presupposed by the slave's ability to recognize spatial relations in daily life, it has not been brought to the focus of his attention and is in fact *prevented* from emerging by a tendency to think in easily graspable quantities (i.e., whole numbers).[43] What the slave gains from the inquiry is an ability to recognize and point to a side that cannot be defined numerically and therefore a greater degree of explicitness in the awareness he already had of the whole and irreducible nature of space (space is not "broken up" into something else by being reduced to number). Yet the boy is still in a daze concerning this incommensurable side, and only further questioning can bring him to a clearer recognition of it (which does not correspond to an ability to *define* its length).

These observations also show why Socrates' demonstration that learning is recollection succeeds: what the slave learns is not something that can be *taught*. What he acquires through the discussion is the ability to recognize and talk *about* a side whose length neither he nor anyone else can define. This recognition ultimately depends on him and cannot possibly be *given* to him by Socrates. Socrates could indeed tell the slave that the side of a square with an area of eight feet is the diagonal of a square with an area of four feet; this definition, however, would only be so many words if the slave lacked the recognition of what this side is that only the inquiry could awaken in him and if he still thought that the side could be three or four feet long. Socrates' point is that the slave already knew the side could have neither length and that only questioning was needed to bring out this knowledge. This is not to say that the slave already knew *that,* or even believed *that,* the side could have neither length, but that he already had the implicit intuition of space which would by itself, with the help only of questions, enable him to recognize this. In general terms, the solution to Meno's paradox is that we are always in contact with the truth, a contact not mediated by propositions because *presupposed* by our ability to recognize the truth or falsity of propositions, a contact that lies hidden and needs to be recovered through persistent inquiry.

The lesson to be gained from this demonstration that learning is recollection is expressed by Socrates in the following words: "I will not insist on the other points of my account, but what I will fight with all my might in both word and deed to defend, as far as I am able, is that we shall be better, braver, and less lazy men [cf. 81d3–4] if we believe that we should search for what we don't know than if we believe there is no point in searching because what we don't know we can never discover" (86b6–c2). This passage is of crucial importance because it reveals once again the reflexivity of dialectic encountered in reading the *Laches* and the *Charmides.* Here, as there, virtue is found in the inquiry itself. We become more virtuous in the very process of seeking to know what virtue is. Virtue is not some theory or result attained at the end of inquiry but is rather exhibited in the very process of inquiry. One thing (perhaps the only thing?) Socrates knows is that we will be *better* people if we believe that we should constantly inquire into that which we do not know (as the *Euthydemus* has shown, the goal of philosophy as *protreptic* is precisely to convince us of this). Thus Socrates' willingness to fight for this belief both in word and in deed exhibits his own virtue and how he has acquired it.[44] This passage is therefore important for the further reason that it answers Meno's question. Virtue is acquired through the recognition of one's ignorance and the attentent desire constantly and persistently to examine both oneself and the world. Again, knowledge of virtue is not some definition held out as a reward at the end of the path of inquiry; this knowledge *is* the inquiry, and virtue is therefore something we become "acquainted" with *only by engaging in the inquiry.* Something like this knowledge is what the slave has begun to acquire with Socrates' help. He has not learned an "answer" and thus has not been "taught";

what he has learned is to recognize his own ignorance and to be willing to inquire into something (the irrational number) which he does not, and never will, fully comprehend. This recognition and this willingness have in themselves made him a better person.

These are the two traits that Meno, on the other hand, utterly lacks. As has already been noted, his point-blank question is not motivated by any recognition of his own ignorance nor therefore by the attendant thirst to inquire.[45] It is at best idle and at worst malicious. *The very way in which Meno asks whether or not virtue can be taught shows his lack of virtue.* Now we can better understand why Socrates earlier called Meno "wicked" for seeking to be "taught": the realization that learning is recollection and the willingness to inquire that follows upon this realization are essential to virtue. Therefore, the nature of the virtue which Meno lacks is not such that it could be *given* to him. Because the knowledge of virtue is not a knowledge of definitions, because it consists in the very willingness and ability to inquire into what is not definable, it is not something that Socrates could "teach" Meno. All he can do is use the demonstration with the slave *to show* Meno what virtue is and how it is to be acquired.[46] And this demonstration is hardly obscure or ambivalent. For example, Socrates suggests quite clearly that the knowledge of virtue is acquired in *all* of the ways Meno considers exclusive alternatives. It is *possessed by nature* insofar as it already exists "in" us. It is *learned* insofar as it needs to be recollected. It is acquired *through practice* insofar as it depends on repeated questioning.[47] This last characteristic in particular recalls something that has been noted again and again in previous chapters: knowledge of virtue is a *practical* knowledge.

Despite these clear indications, however, it soon becomes clear that Meno has not learned the lesson of Socrates' demonstration.[48] The reason for this blindness is that he is looking for simple, straightforward answers and is not willing to endure in the kind of perplexity in which the slave finds himself even at the end of his discussion with Socrates. *Aporia* only *numbs* Meno, while Socrates has been at great pains to show that it should have the opposite effect: *aporia* is a *stimulus* to inquiry and as such is an essential component of virtue.[49] Meno therefore only shows his lack of virtue thus understood when he insists on passing over the question of what virtue is in order to go back to his original question concerning whether or not it can be taught.[50] Socrates protests but recognizes that he cannot force Meno to inquire. He must deal with Meno's question of whether virtue can be taught before dealing with the question of what virtue is, though he still insists that this is a mistake: "so it seems that we must examine what kind of a thing virtue is even though we do not yet know what it is" (86d8–e1). What Socrates finds objectionable is that

Meno wants to talk about the teachability of virtue before submitting to an inquiry through which he might gain some insight into (though not a definition of) the nature of virtue. He wants to draw a conclusion about something that remains for him an empty word. Argument without insight (and without perplexity): that is Meno's desire.

It is in this context that Socrates' introduction of a new method must be understood. Socrates asks Meno to grant him one concession, namely, that they examine *from hypotheses* (ἐξ ὑποθέσεως) whether or not virtue is teachable (86e). Socrates then proceeds to explain that he is referring to a method like that often used by geometers. Ironically, the geometrical problem that Socrates cites as an illustration has proven more baffling than what it was meant to illustrate. However, the gist is clear. The problem apparently concerns inscribing a certain figure within a circle.[51] In dealing with this problem *from hypotheses*, the geometer says that if the figure is such and such (*toiouton hoion*), then it will be such as to be inscribable within a circle; if, however, it is not such and such, then it will not be thus inscribable. Given what Socrates has already said, this example immediately brings out the general character of the hypothetical method: it assumes a relation between different properties of a thing so that, if the thing is agreed to have one, it can be concluded to have the other. The method can thus reach conclusions about a thing while restricting itself to the level of how the thing is *qualified* (*poion ti*): the What-is-x? question (*ti esti*) is not even raised.

Socrates now applies the hypothetical method to the question at hand. In default of insight into what virtue is, what is needed to get the inquiry started is the perception of a relation between a property that virtue is agreed to have and the property that it is not yet known to have. Thus Socrates' hypothetical procedure is as follows: he maintains (and Meno agrees) that if virtue is the kind of thing that is knowledge (ποῖόν τί ἐστιν is the question [87b5], οἷον ἐπιστήμη the answer [87b7]), then it is also the kind of thing that can be taught. Socrates then attempts to prove that virtue is knowledge (87d–89a). This argument itself depends on what Socrates calls a "hypothesis" (87d2–3), namely, that virtue is good. Those actions thought virtuous are not good if they are ignorant (performed without knowledge). Therefore, since virtue is necessarily good, virtue must be inseparable from knowledge (i.e., for Socrates' purposes here, virtue "is" knowledge). Now the conclusion can be drawn: because virtue is the kind of thing that is knowledge, we can conclude, given the relation asserted above, that virtue is the kind of thing that can be taught.

What makes this argument "hypothetical"? It clearly is not less "certain" than any other Socratic argument.[52] After all, the premise on which the whole argument rests, that is, "virtue is knowledge," is *proven* by means of what is thought to be a self-evident truth, or, "virtue is good." What, then, is "hypothetical" in that? Even the conditional, "If virtue is knowledge, it is teachable," is described by Socrates as "evident" (δῆλον, 87c2,5) and is never questioned, either here or elsewhere in the dialogues. Clearly, therefore, what makes the argument "hypothetical" has nothing to do with a lack of certainty. Instead, as Socrates' own explanation reveals, what makes the method he is currently employing "hypothetical" is simply its failure to address the question whose priority he has never stopped asserting: "What is virtue?" The distinctive characteristic of the method is that it draws logical connections between different properties of a thing without any attempt to transcend these properties in an understanding of what the thing itself is.[53] A hypothetical argument can even be said to be almost (though not quite, as I argue below) a purely verbal argument: connections are drawn between different words while little effort is made to clarify their meanings. If virtue is good, then virtue is knowledge, and if virtue is knowledge, then virtue can be taught: to follow this reasoning we need no more than a very confused and limited understanding of what these words mean. The reason, for example, why Socrates calls the claim that "virtue is good" a "hypothesis" (87d) is not that its truth is in doubt or should be questioned (Socrates never questions it), but that its meaning is not really known. Can we have any real insight into what we are saying when we say that "virtue is good" if we refuse to inquire into what virtue or the good *is?* The lack of such insight, and not a need to be verified or proven, is what makes this claim a "hypothesis." Even if we had an argument to prove that virtue is good, it would not guarantee an understanding of what this means. In this respect the claim would still remain a hypothesis. The same is true of the conditional, "If virtue is knowledge, it is teachable." Socrates has no *doubts* about the truth of this claim. What makes the claim a "hypothesis" is the opaqueness of the terms "knowledge" and "teachable." As I hope the present study shows, to say that virtue is knowledge is not to say much, because the important question is: what *kind* of knowledge? As for the term "teachable," Socrates makes the extremely surprising claim at 87b7–c1 that whether this word or the word "recollectable" is used should make no difference to us. During the slave episode, this made all the difference in the world! But for the purposes of the hypothetical method, debates about the true nature of teaching and learning are irrelevant. To perform its role in the argument, the word "teachable" does not need to be given any specific or concrete meaning but can be left vague.

The point of these observations is to show the *limitations* of the hypothetical method, not its worthlessness. The method has a positive role to play once it is recognized for what it is. It is first important to note that the method is not completely blind. Even though it does not address the question "What is virtue?" it certainly presupposes some understanding, however vague, of what virtue is. If Socrates and his interlocutors are to recognize the connections they make between suggested properties of virtue as anything more than arbitrary, they must have some vague awareness of what the word "virtue" means. This awareness is possible because they already in some sense know what virtue is, even if this knowledge has not yet been made explicit or "awakened" through questioning. The method of hypothesis is thus inseparable (at least here) from the theory of recollection.[54] Socrates never in the dialogue abandons his view that we cannot know how a thing is *qualified* unless we first know what it *is*. If this claim, however, is not joined with the view that learning is recollection, the method of hypothesis is rendered arbitrary and incoherent. For if we cannot know how a thing is qualified before we know what it is, and if the method of hypothesis considers only how a thing is qualified without *any* knowledge of what it is, then the method is groping in total darkness. It would indeed be nothing but wordplay in which terms are simply thrown around without any understanding of what they mean. The theory of recollection, however, saves the method of hypothesis from this fate. Even before we inquire into the nature of virtue, we are in possession of a knowledge of what virtue is. Before this knowledge is recollected to the point of becoming explicit, it remains implicit in our ordinary use of the word "virtue." This knowledge implicit in our everyday discourse can be likened to a kind of inspiration. We have a sense of what we are talking about when we claim that virtue is good, and we also have a sense that this claim is true; we cannot, however, explain where this "sense" comes from.[55] We thus normally rely on this kind of inspiration to guide our words and actions. The method of hypothesis too, as a method that avoids raising the What-is-x? question, needs to be grounded on nothing more than this kind of inspiration. As the slave episode has already suggested and as will be made fully clear later in the dialogue, this inspiration which has yet to be transformed into explicit knowledge is "true belief." This is all the method needs to have content and thus avoid being empty wordplay.[56]

We can expect, then, that the method of hypothesis will suffer from defects similar to those suffered by ordinary experience. Though its conclusions will be true in a sense, as well as clearer and more coherent than ordinary perceptions, they nevertheless will, like these perceptions, be somewhat one-sided. As already noted above, the claims that "virtue is knowledge" and "virtue is teachable," while in some sense true, are so ambiguous that it would not be surprising if they were equally false. A hypothetical argument has content and can tell us something, but it does not seem to rise much above the confused and vague half-truths of ordinary experience.[57]

Having noted these limitations, however, we are now in a position to see the importance of the hypothetical method. First, it is important to recognize that if we could define all our terms in such a way as to eliminate all ambiguity and if accordingly our propositions could contain the whole truth (and not just a half-truth), then the method of hypothesis would become unnecessary. As I have argued above, however, Socrates does not think it possible to express in a proposition without reductionism (and thus one-sidedness) what a thing is as a whole. On this view, if one were to refute every proposition that failed unambiguously to express the whole truth, none would survive. This process of refutation could provide insight into the whole truth, but this insight would not be another proposition. The *Laches* and the *Charmides* were seen to have precisely this outcome: every definition put forward is refuted for its limitations (not because it is simply false), but this very process reveals to the interlocutors the truth that all of the definitions are trying, but failing, to express. What lends the hypothetical method its importance, however, is that, despite this priority of dialectic and the insight it awakens, there is still some value in propositional results, no matter how limited and open to misinterpretation. We want to be able to *say something* in response to certain problems, even though we realize that what we say cannot do justice to the insight we have gained through dialectic. We want to be able to analyze a thing and discuss its properties, even though we recognize that what the thing *is* remains beyond such analysis. We want to organize our knowledge and render our claims consistent, even though we recognize that such consistency in itself does not bring us any closer to the truth. All this we can do through the hypothetical method. If we simply want "truth," then dialectic as interpreted in previous chapters is the method to pursue; if we want propositional results that are within limits true and informative, then we should proceed "from hypotheses."[58]

This is the point at which to address an increasingly popular interpretation of Plato's methodology that, in my view, sees Plato as pursuing nothing more than the method of hypothesis as described above. In reaction to interpretations (such as Richard Robinson's) that attribute to Plato a Cartesian conception of knowledge as "certainty," a number of scholars have argued that the word *epistēmē* as used in Plato's dialogues should be translated not as "knowledge" but as "understanding."[59] In other words, Platonic *epistēmē* is not "justified true belief"; instead, its meaning is closer to that of our word "understanding." I agree with this translation. The kind of "acquaintance with virtue" described above is not any justified true belief about virtue nor any form of certainty. On the other hand, it differs from "acquaintance" in the narrow sense ("unmediated intuition of some object") by involving an *understanding* of what virtue is, an understanding that can be more or less explicit. However, some of the scholars who advocate the translation of *epistēmē* as "understanding" see this as an *alternative* to interpreting *epistēmē* as any form of "acquaintance" or nonpropositional knowledge.[60] What they identify with an "understanding" of virtue is not any kind of nonpropositional insight into the nature of virtue, but rather the *organization and systematization* of one's beliefs about virtue.[61] We know, that is, "understand," a proposition about virtue, not by deducing it from some ultimate principle, but by *explaining* it, where this explanation involves situating the proposition in a coherent system of other propositions about virtue. Alexander Nehamas (1989, 276–85), in developing his own interpretation of this view, defends an "interrelational model of *epistēmē*" as opposed to an "additive model." What transforms beliefs into *epistēmē* = understanding is not the *addition* of some "justification" or "account," but rather the interconnection of these beliefs in a comprehensive system: "What counts as *epistēmē* is the large set of beliefs that is expressed through the totality of statements about the interrelations of the members of that domain" (1989, 281). The beliefs that can be connected in a system are beliefs which themselves express relations between things, such as between virtue itself and things related to virtue.[62]

This "interrelational model of knowledge" appears to be simply an extension of the hypothetical method and therefore subject to the same criticisms. The function of the hypothetical method is precisely to connect beliefs about virtue, beliefs that, as stating only relations between virtue and other things, do no more than state what *kind* of thing virtue is.[63] Socrates insists that such a method can never provide us with *epistēmē* or "understanding" of what virtue is. Socrates gives no indication that the organization of our different beliefs about virtue could provide such "understanding" if only it were more systematic and comprehensive.[64] The indication is instead that an "understanding" of virtue would require an approach altogether different from that of the hypothetical method. *Epistēmē* of virtue requires not simply greater systematization of our propositional knowledge, but rather something of an altogether different order: the kind of "understanding" that is not expressible in propositions, however much systematized, and involves the kind of "acquaintance" described above;[65] an understanding, moreover, that is *presupposed* by, rather than the *result* of, any attempt to relate and organize our beliefs.[66] This "understanding"[67] can be supplied only by the kind of dialectic Socrates practices in the first half of this dialogue and in the slave episode but is forced to give up in the second half. By turning to the hypothetical method, "positive" propositional results are achieved, but these results will never yield *epistēmē*, even if they are related to many other such results.

Therefore, though the method of hypothesis has its positive function, this does not justify Meno's refusal to address the What-is-x? question. Though the method needs no more than the "inspiration" that guides ordinary experience, it should be based on the kind of insight that can be gained only by addressing this question. That this is so is shown most clearly by what happens next.

Immediately after he concludes that virtue is teachable Socrates begins to express doubts (89c). He does not, however, do what we might expect him to do: he does not return to the beginning of the argument and question either the premise that virtue is good or the premise that virtue is knowledge. Instead he introduces a new "hypothesis": if virtue is the kind of thing that can be taught, then it must also be the kind of thing of which there actually are teachers and learners. At this point Anytus enters the scene (89e). Anytus is an Athenian politician with the ambition to become a great statesman. For him virtue is a matter of being born into the right family and having, as it were, nobility in one's blood. He therefore has utter contempt for the sophists and believes that they can only corrupt one's noble instincts. How dare the sophists claim to have an expertise in virtue that the "gentlemen" of Athens do not have! How dare the sophists charge money for teaching virtue when Anytus, his friends, and other "gentlemen" know perfectly well what it is and can serve as role models! What emerges from Socrates' discussion with Anytus, however, is that there are no teachers of virtue. What requires us to conclude that the great statesmen of Athens, as well as gentlemen of the Anytus variety, cannot teach virtue is that they appear incapable of passing on the virtue they possess to their own sons (93c–94e) and cannot even agree among themselves whether or not virtue can be taught (95b). We must also conclude that the sophists cannot teach it, since others neither recognize them as teachers nor believe them to have any understanding of virtue (96a–b). Here we should recall the distinction between sophistic discourse and everyday discourse and the deficiencies that dialectic has been seen to uncover in both. Neither of the two candidates for teacher of virtue, neither the sophist nor the man of practical experience, proves to be able to teach it. But according to the hypothesis, if there are no teachers of virtue, virtue is simply not teachable.

We have at this point two contradictory conclusions drawn from two different arguments: that virtue is teachable and that it is not teachable. The key to this "antinomy" is clearly the ambiguity of the word "teachable" (not to mention the ambiguity of the word "virtue"). It is not clear, for example, that in the first argument the word "teachable" means "teachable by sophists and/or statesmen," but then it is not clear what it *does* mean.[68] As we have seen, while Socrates in the slave episode sharply distinguishes between "being taught" and "recollecting," in the argument that virtue is teachable he ignores this distinction as irrelevant (87b–c). But surely this distinction is highly relevant to an *understanding* of the issue at hand: if virtue can only be "recollected," there is nothing surprising about the inability of statesmen and sophists to "teach" it in the sense of introducing knowledge of it into someone's head (see 95e5). The method of hypothesis, however, does not inquire into the meanings of the terms used but simply goes on whatever meaning is implied by a given context; it is context-bound.[69] It thus presents us with only two ambiguous half-truths: virtue is teachable, and virtue is not teachable.[70]

However, Socrates shows a flaw in his first argument in the course of dealing with the following problem: if virtue is not taught, then no one learns virtue. But if no one learns virtue, then how can anyone become good? It is only in response to this question that Socrates reconsiders the premise that virtue is knowledge (96e). This premise, as has been seen, was itself deduced from the premises that virtue is good and that an action cannot be good or beneficial unless accompanied by knowledge. It is the second claim that Socrates now retracts: in order to be beneficial, one's actions need not be guided by more than *true belief* (*doxa*). Socrates explains his point with an example (97a–b). Someone who *knows* the road to Larissa, in the sense of being acquainted with it through having taken it before, will clearly be able to guide others to the town.[71] Just as good a guide, however, will be the person who has not taken the road before, but has true belief about it (acquired by means of a map or through information gathered from others who have been to Larissa). The point is that as far as right actions are concerned, true belief can be as good a guide as knowledge.[72]

What Socrates says here explains the hypothetical method itself. As has been seen, this method—though not addressing the question "What is virtue?"—nevertheless presupposes that we have some vague awareness of what virtue is. Now we can give this vague awareness a name: it is "true belief."[73] When Socrates asks his interlocutors whether or not virtue is good, he is appealing to their ability to recognize the truth in this claim. This ability does not presuppose *knowledge,* since the interlocutors do not really see what the claim means; it does, however, presuppose true belief. This true belief is precisely what the hypothetical method relies on: one must be able to recognize the truth of the claims asserting properties of certain things, even when this truth is very limited and only confusedly understood. Just as true belief is capable of guiding us along the road to Larissa, so can it guide us through the hypothetical method.

A few words need to be said at this point about just what Plato means by *doxa*. The above identification of *doxa* with a vague, implicit understanding that guides our everyday practice and discourse and that also serves as the starting point for the hypothetical method probably sounds strange. This strangeness, however, is appropriate, given the difference between Platonic *doxa* and "belief" as commonly understood today. The thorough analysis of "belief" in Price (1969) betrays this difference. After having distinguished between different types of knowledge (knowledge by acquaintance; knowledge that, which includes knowledge by description; and knowledge how), Price argues that only "knowledge that" can be contrasted with belief: in other words, the distinction between knowledge and belief is always a distinction between "knowledge that" and "belief that" (79). Yet the claim that belief can guide practice, as well as the identification that will be made at the end of the *Meno* between belief and some form of inspiration, show that *doxa* in Plato does not mean "belief that";[74] it means instead a correct but unarticulated intuition that guides our everyday actions and that enables us to recognize the truth of certain propositions which we do not fully understand.[75] It is *doxa*, for example, that enables people such Charmides and Laches to act virtuously, to recognize virtue in others, and to acknowledge the truth expressed in a proposition such as "virtue is good." Yet this *doxa* is clearly not "belief that": it is an intuition that need not be, and usually is not, articulated in propositions. *Doxa* can guide the actions and assent of Charmides and Laches even though they have never even attempted to state *that* virtue is such and such or *that* all actions having a certain characteristic are virtuous.[76] Even in the case where *doxa* is given propositional content (as in the belief that virtue is good), what Plato would call *doxa* is apparently not the act itself of assenting to the proposition, but rather the intuition that guides this assent. *Doxa* is here primarily a state of awareness.[77]

Precisely this kind of belief, however, and not "belief that," is what Plato distinguishes from knowledge in the *Meno* and, as we shall see, in the *Republic*. One way in which the distinction is made is revealing. As noted above, Socrates compares the slave's belief to a "dream" (85c); this same comparison occurs in the *Republic* with regard to belief as such (476c–d). The point of the comparison seems to be that while true belief brings us into contact with the truth, it leaves the truth "fuzzy" and strange. Nothing is clearly distinguished, articulated, or recognized. Because true belief conveys only a vague impression of the truth, it allows the truth to appear now one way and now another: there is thus as little stability in such belief as there is in a dream (Socrates will later describe knowledge as "tying down" belief). For example, we recognize that virtue is good, but the words "virtue" and "good" convey little more than a vague impression of positiveness and desirability. The slave recognizes the side of a square with an area of eight feet, but because this side's length is none of the whole numbers with which he is familiar, he finds it strange and indistinct, like a dream. Even in the Larissa example, what seems to characterize true belief is not only the dependence on secondhand reports, but also the inability of these reports to provide more than a vague impression of what the road to Larissa is really like. The knowledge contrasted with belief is therefore that clear and stable insight into a thing's nature which renders this nature familiar and distinct. Just as the dialectical knowledge Socrates seeks has been seen not to be reducible to knowledge of propositions, so must the belief contrasted to this knowledge not be reduced to "belief that."[78]

To return to the text, the introduction of true belief has led Socrates to reject one step of his first argument, that is, the step from "virtue is good" to "virtue is knowledge." However, Socrates does not thereby refute the conclusion that virtue is teachable: he only shows that it does not follow. Likewise, he does not prove false the premise that virtue is knowledge but only shows that it does not follow from the hypothesis that virtue is good. However, Socrates now proceeds to *refute* this premise by means of the conclusion of the *second* argument. His reasoning is as follows: the second argument has shown that virtue is not teachable, therefore the conclusion of the first argument is false, and therefore one of its premises must be false. Since Socrates does not question the hypothesis that "if virtue is knowledge, virtue can be taught," he must reject the premise that "virtue is knowledge" (99b). The refutation of this premise thus depends entirely on the second argument. Socrates' distinction between true belief and knowledge in good actions does not of itself show that virtue is not knowledge. But then why is the second argument being given so much weight? Is it not as "hypothetical" as the first? Specifically, it fails, as we have seen, to clarify or even address the meaning of the word "teachable." Does it not therefore leave open the possibility that virtue is "teachable" in a sense (that of being "recollected"?) distinct from the sense in which sophists and statesmen claim to teach it? And might not virtue in that case be knowledge after all, though in a sense not yet specified (but perhaps already exhibited by the inquiry itself)? It is important to keep in mind how many questions are left unexplored in the rush to reach a conclusion.

Having argued that virtue is not knowledge, Socrates can conclude that it is merely true belief. But how does this answer the original question? If the true belief involved in virtue cannot be taught, how is it acquired? Socrates does not even consider the possibility that it comes by nature, since he apparently assumes that belief no less than knowledge cannot be "natural" (though this is again a highly ambiguous word; according to the doctrine of recollection, there is a sense in which virtue *is* natural). He also does not consider the possibility that it is acquired through practice (apparently because even practice would *presuppose* true belief), though we did see above a sense in which virtue *does* come through practice. What Socrates concludes instead is that this true belief without knowledge is acquired through *divine dispensation* (θείᾳ μοίρᾳ, 99e6). The comparison here is with prophets, priests, and poets who can be inspired to say many wonderful things without knowing what they are talking about (ἴσασι δὲ οὐδὲν ὧν λέγουσιν, 99c4–5).[79]

This conclusion is not as unexpected as it might seem, since *it only makes explicit what the method of hypothesis has presupposed all along*. The method's discussion of a thing's properties has been seen to depend on a vague awareness of what this thing is: an awareness that could be likened to a kind of inspiration. When inquiring hypothetically about virtue, for example, we must rely on "inspiration" for an awareness of what virtue is. Now Socrates, in proceeding "from hypotheses," concludes at the dialogue's end that virtue is divinely inspired. In this way the conclusion reflects the method used to attain it. Not only do statesmen depend on inspiration for their virtuous deeds, but we ourselves rely on such inspiration when we reason hypothetically.

Given the reflexivity just described, we can suspect that the conclusion of the dialogue is as limited and "superficial" as the method used to attain it.[80] The argument was indeed seen to abandon too easily the view that virtue is knowledge. Similarly, the method of hypothesis itself was seen to be defined by an abandonment of the search for a knowledge of virtue. Note again the circularity: *in leaving behind the search for a knowledge of virtue we conclude that virtue is not knowledge*. Therefore, as the dialogue comes to a close, Socrates reiterates the limitations of both the method and the conclusion: "But we will have clear knowledge about this matter [τὸ δὲ σαφὲς περὶ αὐτοῦ εἰσόμεθα] when, before asking in what way virtue comes to be in human beings, we attempt to search for what virtue is in itself [ἐπιχειρήσωμεν αὐτὸ καθ᾽ αὑτὸ ζητεῖν τί ποτ᾽ ἔστιν ἀρετή]" (100b4–6). The implication is clear: in concluding that virtue is divinely inspired, we ourselves have only an inspired belief (not clear knowledge) about what virtue is.

But then what exactly is required for a knowledge of virtue (and for virtue to be knowledge)? Socrates' closing remarks direct us back to a passage that has intentionally been skipped over (97d–98a). After Socrates suggests that true belief is as good as knowledge in guiding our actions, Meno asks why knowledge is then rated higher than belief.

Socrates replies that beliefs are like the statues of Daedalus: they wander about so much that one has a hard time keeping hold of them. Recall the wanderings of Socrates' own hypothetical arguments. The advantage of knowledge, however, is that it "ties down" (δῆσαι) these beliefs, with the result that they are no longer "beliefs." The means by which knowledge ties them down, Socrates tells us, is "a reasoning out of the cause" (αἰτίας λογισμός, 98a3–4). Many guesses have been made as to the meaning of this phrase.[81] However, the meaning is clear if the phrase is understood in the context of the distinction that has dominated the whole discussion: the distinction between what a thing *is* and how it is *qualified*. Socrates' view, as interpreted above, is that we cannot know the properties of a thing until we know what the thing itself is. This seems to assume that the nature of a thing (what it is) is the "cause" of its properties (precisely Socrates' view in the *Phaedo,* as will be seen in the next chapter). A thing has certain properties *because* of what it is and not vice versa; this is why we cannot know how the thing is qualified before we know what it is. To "reason out the cause," then, is simply to ask Socrates' What-is-x? question. It is one thing to have beliefs about the properties of virtue and another to ground these beliefs in an understanding of what virtue itself is. What is therefore contrasted here to true belief is not "knowledge" in a Cartesian sense (i.e., certainty that a given proposition is true), nor a comprehensive theory ("understanding" as characterized by some), but precisely that insight which the hypothetical method has proven incapable of providing. Required for such insight is not the certainty that some propositions *about* virtue are true, nor the systematization of such propositions, but rather "acquaintance" with what virtue *itself is,* an "acquaintance" acquired only through persistent inquiry in the face of virtue's "incommensurability."[82] The cause that is reasoned out here is simply the nature of virtue.[83]

Socrates in this passage also identifies "reasoning out the cause" with *recollection* (ἀνάμνησις). In inquiring into what a thing is (reasoning out the cause), we are recollecting what we already know. This is why the questioning and refutation of claims stating how a thing is qualified can be sufficient for leading us toward knowledge of what the thing is: what is implicit is only being made explicit. Socrates' mention of recollection here of course takes us back to the slave episode. It will be recalled that Socrates described the slave at the end of the inquiry as still in the dreamlike state of belief, but requiring only further questioning to be brought to knowledge. The goal was to lead the slave toward an understanding of what (the irrational number) he could not grasp in any formula or definition. It is precisely this recollection, this "reasoning out the cause," that Socrates recommends in stressing the importance of his What-is-x? question and that he sees as lying outside the bounds of the method of hypothesis. The cause can be reasoned out only by the kind of dialectic that we have seen employed in the aporetic dialogues. Note must also be made here of the reflexivity that was encountered in those dialogues and is found once again in this dialogue. We *are* virtuous in the very process of reasoning out the nature of virtue through recollection. The *knowledge* of virtue that Socrates describes here in terms of recollection is not distinct from *virtue itself.*

Recalling the slave episode makes possible another important observation. As seen above, the method of hypothesis need only be guided by "inspired" true belief. The drama of the dialogue, however, has shown that two significantly different kinds of inspiration are possible.[84] The first is what could be called *inspiration from within.* This is the kind of inspiration that gives rise to the slave's dreamlike true beliefs. Having a divine origin in the prenatal life of the soul, these beliefs are not acquired through our own mortal cleverness but lie dormant in us, only needing to be awakened. The important characteristic of this kind of inspiration is that it needs and fosters questioning. Rather than puffing him up with vain conceit, the slave's inspired true beliefs perplex him and force him to recognize his own ignorance. Because of its ambivalent and mysterious character, this inspiration does not harden into dogma. It is an inspiration that provides insight without "answers," understanding without "certainty." It is that philosophical inspiration described in chapter 5.

The second kind is quite different. It could be called *inspiration from without* and, as attributed elsewhere to the poets, is also described in chapter 5. Here it is attributed to statesmen as well as poets and is *exhibited* by Meno and Anytus. That Meno's "knowledge" is completely *borrowed* is made quite evident throughout the dialogue. None of the definitions of virtue he gives are his own. Meno is trying to walk on the road to virtue with the guidance of nothing but secondhand reports. All of the terms and concepts he uses have simply been taken from others (*not* understood). He seems utterly incapable of having an original insight, of discovering something for himself. His memory is full of answers, definitions, terms, and arguments that he has received (for a fee, of course) from the sophists.[85] In the way that the priestess at Delphi is simply a mouthpiece of the god, so is Meno simply a mouthpiece of the sophists. He has swallowed their teaching without really assimilating or understanding it; this teaching therefore simply speaks *through* him. This, then, is Meno's inspiration. Anytus, however, is also inspired, though in a different way. He hates the sophists, but this hatred is based on nothing but hearsay and public opinion, since he admits to having no personal *acquaintance* with them (92b). Because he thus claims knowledge without acquaintance, Socrates significantly calls him a "seer" (μάντις, 92c6). Anytus is therefore one of those possessed statesmen described at the end of the dialogue, though he is possessed not by a god, but by "the people." Anytus is the vox populi. Through him speak all the prejudices of his time. He does not respond to what Socrates says by trying to determine for himself whether it is right or wrong. All he can do is express the anger *of the people* at what Socrates says (94e–95a). He does not have his own mind; he is inspired from without.[86]

The main difference between the inspiration of Meno and Anytus and that of the slave is that the former, unlike the latter, does result in dogmatism and therefore is inimical to questioning. Meno and Anytus do not question their "knowledge" precisely because it is not their own. The external provenance of their opinions gives these opinions a certain "authority." There is also nothing ambivalent or mysterious about the inspiration of these two men: it provides them with clear-cut answers and opinions: "The sophists are bad and the statesmen are good"; "Virtue is teachable or it is not."

The existence of these two opposed kinds of inspiration creates a danger for the method of hypothesis. The method can be guided either by the dogmatic inspiration of a Meno or an Anytus or by an inspiration that provides genuine insight and is open to further inquiry. It can be based on a true belief that has degenerated into dogma or on a perplexed true belief that stimulates questioning. Before we can ensure that the method of hypothesis is based on the latter type of belief and not the former, we must recall what is responsible for this difference between the two types of belief. While the beliefs of Meno and Anytus are produced by sophistic teaching and popular opinion, the beliefs of the slave are awakened by *dialectic* (as understood in previous chapters). Therefore, the method of hypothesis needs to be led by this other method in order to avoid dogmatism. Beliefs that arise through dialectic are open to the "cause" (what a thing is) in a way that sophistic beliefs and the beliefs of everyday discourse are not.[87]

It is this kind of openness that the method of hypothesis needs in order to avoid degenerating into dogma, and it is this kind of openness that only dialectic can provide. If the method of hypothesis takes itself to be self-contained and its results to be final, then it is blind to that "whole" nature which must evade its grasp.[88] It will then please Meno, but not Socrates the philosopher. This, therefore, is the point behind Socrates' protest at the end of the dialogue. Even though the hypothetical method is distinct from dialectic, it needs to be guided by dialectic. The method in this case is still "hypothetical" (i.e., provisional, rooted in a specific context), but because it recognizes itself as such, it does not conceal the whole nature of a thing behind statements about the thing's properties. The contrast here is between clarity concerning what one cannot quite grasp and blind inspiration which thinks that it has grasped everything. The method of hypothesis is open to both possibilities, and its avoidance of blind inspiration depends on its subordination to dialectic. Dialectic provides the vision, and the method of hypothesis works around this vision.

7

A Second Sailing in the *Phaedo*

In the *Phaedo* Socrates once again employs the method of hypothesis. It here displays some of the same characteristics it was seen to have in the *Meno:* it is introduced to solve a specific problem, it is described as a "second-best" adopted only in default of direct inquiry into the nature of things, and its results are in need of reconsideration. There is, however, an important difference. In the *Meno* the method of hypothesis considers only the properties of a thing without addressing in any way the thing's actual nature or "form" (*eidos*, what it is). In the *Phaedo*, however, the method deals hypothetically with the "forms" themselves: the claim that a thing has a "form" irreducible to its properties is itself made a hypothesis. Here the hypothetical method seems to be encroaching upon what has so far been considered the domain of a distinct dialectic. The goal of the present chapter is therefore to explain why the method of hypothesis is introduced in the *Phaedo*, what it is contrasted to, and what it is supposed to accomplish.

The method is introduced in the course of Socrates' account of his search for the right kind of explanation. Having proven, by means of the theory of recollection and to the satisfaction of his interlocutors, that the soul existed prior to this life, Socrates is asked to show by means of another argument that the soul will continue to exist after death (since the recollection argument is not by itself sufficient to show that the soul is *immortal*). When Socrates produces his argument (which is based on the soul's affinity to the immutable forms), it meets with the objections of Simmias and Cebes. Simmias objects that the soul, though invisible and ruling the body, could still be like an "attunement" that can perish before the materials attuned and never survive them (85e–86d). Cebes objects that, even if one can show that the soul will survive many bodies, as the weaver outlives many cloaks throughout his lifetime, the soul could still, like the weaver, eventually cease to exist: in short, the soul can be *long-lasting* without being *immortal* (87a–88b). These objections result in the major crisis of the dialogue: seeing Socrates' argument thus defeated, the interlocutors, and even Echecrates, to whom Phaedo is narrating the discussion, are in danger of losing their trust in *all* arguments (88c–d). In a "digression," which is really the literal and symbolic center of the dialogue, Socrates warns his companions against this danger, which he calls "misology." Socrates does not consider this a minor danger to be dealt with quickly on the way to more important issues but asserts that "there is *no greater evil* one can suffer than to hate reasonable discourse [*logos*]" (89d2–3). This means, presumably, that misology is an even greater evil than the death that awaits Socrates: more important than the personal survival of Socrates is the survival of the argument. This is why Socrates first addresses the crisis by telling the young Phaedo not to cut his beautiful hair in mourning for Socrates' death, but to cut it only if the argument dies (89a–c). But how is this terrible danger of misology to be overcome, how is the argument to be kept alive? Socrates makes the important observation that misology, like misanthropy, has its origin in *excessive trust*, a trust which, given the imperfect natures of both human beings and arguments, will invariably be disappointed and thereby become its opposite: absolute distrust (89d–90c). This observation defines Socrates' very difficult project for the rest of the dialogue: he must show that there is some reliability in arguments while at the same time drawing attention to their necessary limitations. Only by thus steering a course between excessive trust and complete mistrust can this new Theseus save his companions from the Minotaur of misology.

Socrates disarms Simmias's objection by showing why the analogy between the soul and an attunement cannot hold (91e–95a). Cebes' objection, however, proves much more formidable. After spending some time in reflection, Socrates replies that to answer Cebes' objection is no light task: a thorough examination of the causes of generation and destruction is required (95e–96a). It is on Socrates' ensuing account of causation,[1] as well as on the role that the hypothetical method plays within it, that we must now focus.

Socrates begins by describing the extraordinary passion he had in his youth for natural science (96a6–7). He puzzled over questions such as whether or not the blood is the seat of thought and whether or not living creatures come to be through some sort of fermentation. Eventually, however, he was so blinded (ἐτυφλώθην, 96c6) by this sort of speculation that he unlearned everything he had previously thought he knew. He ceased to believe that one can explain human growth in terms of the intake of food and drink through which flesh is added to flesh and bone to bone. Such addition of physical parts cannot explain the growth of *one* whole human being. Similarly, he ceased to believe that one man is taller than another simply "by a head" and that ten is greater than eight simply through the addition of two units. The general problem Socrates encountered appears to be the reductionism inherent in natural science (and perhaps in mathematics as well): a whole is reduced to its parts and then explained in terms of these parts. Socrates' most revealing example of this problem is the difficulty of understanding how the mere addition of two units can form the number two. "I find it incredible that, although when separate each was one and they were not two, having now come together the cause of their becoming two is simply the union brought about by their juxtaposition" (97a2–6). Socrates is not denying here that we do add one and one together and see them as making two. The question is whether or not there is more involved in this addition than the units added. Can we, in other words, explain the number two completely in terms of the properties of its units, that is, in terms of their "coming together" or being "near" each other? Consider the following two points: " . . " What enables us to see them as *two* rather than simply as "one, one"? Is it their physical proximity that causes us to recognize them as *one* number? This, as Socrates says, seems highly implausible. Why should the fact that the two points are a fraction of an inch apart, rather than two, three, or four inches apart, make them any more *one* number? Clearly, our recognition of the two points as *two* (and thus as *one* number) requires a principle of unity distinct from the two points and their properties. This principle of unity, however, cannot be simply another unit of the same order, for then we would have the number *three*. Furthermore, in making the two points *one* number, this principle cannot make them one to such an extent that they cease to be *two*. The plurality must be preserved in the unity.

Therefore, the other explanation Socrates considers, though opposed to the first, is equally defective. This explanation reduces the number two to a unity and then tries to explain its origin from this unity by appealing to *division*. Take one unit, divide it, and you have two. Again, Socrates' dissatisfaction with this explanation does not deny that we can in fact divide something and subsequently recognize it to be two. The question is whether or not this division in itself can explain why the divided parts are *two*, rather than simply one unit here and one completely separate unit there. Socrates' answer is that division cannot in itself explain "duality." As he also points out, that the number two comes to be through *both* addition *and* division shows that neither process can be *the* cause of something being two.

The number two is both a unity (as *one* number) and a plurality (as *two*). The problem with the first explanation Socrates considers is that it reduces the unity to a plurality and then tries to regain it through mere juxtaposition. The problem with the second explanation is that it reduces the plurality to a unity and then tries to regain it, *while preserving the unity*, through mere division. The result in both cases is that the nature of "duality" is "broken up" into units in terms of which it then cannot be explained for what it is. Whether the growth of an organism is reduced to the addition of bone and flesh or the relation of tallness is reduced to the addition of "a head" or the number two is reduced to the juxtaposition of units, the principle is the same. What seems required in contrast is an explanation that would relate a thing's unity to its plurality in such a way as to avoid reducing the one to the other.

But what is the nature of the unity Socrates seeks if not merely the addition of parts or elements? Having deciding to reject altogether his previous method, Socrates says that he has haphazardly thrown together (εἰκῇ φύρω, 97b6) a method of his own. Before proceeding to describe this method, however, Socrates relates how his last hope to find the kind of cause he desires was dashed. Having heard someone read from a book by Anaxagoras, Socrates thought that this philosopher had made *mind* the fundamental principle of his cosmology. Mind, one would expect, acts according to what is *good*. And in that good Socrates recognized the kind of explanation he had been looking for: "Whoever wishes to discover the cause of each thing, that is, why it comes to be, ceases to be and *is*, must discover how it is best for this thing either to be or to do and suffer anything. According to this account, then, a human being should examine, concerning himself and everything else, nothing but the best and the highest good [τὸ ἄριστον καὶ τὸ βέλτιστον]" (97c6–d4). But why does Socrates think that the good is *the* cause of each thing? And how would explanation in terms of such a cause be any better than the kind of explanation that led Socrates so far astray?

The good seems to be precisely that source of unity missing in Socrates' earlier method of explanation. As directed toward the fulfilment of one end, all of a thing's elements are unified. If, for example, one wants to know what makes all these bones, blood, and flesh one living organism, one must inquire into the specific good to which these physical elements are meant to contribute. Knowledge of the proper good of an organism tells one what this organism *is* in a way that knowledge of its physical parts does not. Furthermore, the good of a thing clearly cannot be reduced to its elements. The good of an organism is clearly not its flesh or its bones, but rather that function which these are only meant to serve. Here, then, unity is preserved in multiplicity. The good in providing a thing with its purpose (its reason to be) *unifies* this thing's plurality of elements while not being reducible to this plurality. A thing's proper good is its proper unity, but it is not simply one of the thing's parts or even the addition of these parts. A thing's good is not a constituent of it, but is in a very important sense what the thing *is*.

Yet Socrates in the passage cited above describes the good as explaining *everything*, including, presumably, why two things are *two*. Though Socrates does not indicate in what sense it would be *best* for one and one to make two, he apparently considers this to be the only real explanation that could avoid the reductionism criticized above. An understanding of how the good might be the cause of a mathematical truth must wait until the discussion of the *Republic* in the next chapter.

When Socrates reads Anaxagoras's book, his hopes of learning more about his favored kind of cause are disappointed. After introducing mind to get the world started, Anaxagoras makes no more use of it, instead explaining everything in terms of physical causes. These kinds of causes, in Socrates' view, are only *necessary conditions,* that is, *that without which* the real cause could not function. Thus we have another way of characterizing a thing's elements or parts: they are only conditions of a thing being what it is, but not the real cause. The number two, for example, could not be what it is without the unit, but the unit is not the explanation of its being the number two (for reasons seen above). Socrates could not sit in prison without bones and muscles, but these are not the cause of his being there; the cause is instead his decision that it is *best* for him to obey the laws of Athens. However, though Socrates recognizes in the good the kind of cause he seeks, he does not quite understand its nature or how exactly it might work as a cause. This is what he had hoped to learn from Anaxagoras, but the natural philosopher had nothing to say: "I for my part would be glad to learn from anyone the nature of such a cause, but since I have been deprived of such knowledge and have not been able either to discover it for myself or to learn it from another, I will demonstrate, if you so wish, Cebes, how I have worked out a second-best method [δεύτερος πλοῦς] of searching for the cause" (99c6–d2). Judging from the context, Socrates' new approach is "second best" because it follows upon a failure to inquire into the nature of the good. The Greek expression *deuteros plous,* "second sailing," apparently refers to the act of resorting to oars when the sails of a ship are not picking up enough wind.[2] The "wind" that should be driving the present inquiry is the good; in its absence, however, Socrates has to resort to something else, and what that is he proceeds to tell us.[3]

The passage in which Socrates begins to describe his new method is very obscure and has accordingly occasioned a good deal of debate. I will present what I believe to be the most plausible interpretation by translating and commenting on the text line by line (99d–100a).

> After this, said Socrates, when I had worn myself out in examining beings [τὰ ὄντα].... (99d4–5)

The referent of "beings" has been much debated. Does the word refer to physical things? Or to the good? Or to forms in general? At this point it need not be confined to one of these meanings but can refer to those things which Socrates has just described himself as having examined, that is, *both* physical things *and* the good:[4]

> After this, said Socrates, when I had worn myself out in examining beings, it seemed to me that I should be careful not to suffer what is suffered by those who look at and contemplate the sun in eclipse. For some of them ruin their eyes if they do not look at a mere image [εἰκών] of the eclipsed sun in water or some other such medium. (99d4–e1)

The general meaning is clear enough. Two questions, however, must be answered: What corresponds to the eclipsed sun in Socrates' case? What does Socrates fear blinding? With regard to the first, Socrates has tried to look at both physical things and the good. Which one, then, threatens to blind him?

> I imagined, then, this kind of thing happening to me and feared that I might blind my soul completely in looking at things [πράγματα] with my eyes and trying with each of my senses to lay hold of them. (99de1–4)

In response to the second question, what Socrates fears is the blinding *of his soul*. However, what threatens to cause this blinding is the perception of physical objects. We have already seen how this might happen: Socrates' attempt to explain things in terms of their physical parts deprived him of all understanding of these things. It seems odd, however, that the good is not mentioned here at all, especially since the present method was necessitated by a failure to understand the good.

> It seemed to me necessary to take refuge in propositions [λόγοι] and examine in them the truth of beings [ἐν ἐκείνοις σκοπεῖν τῶν ὄντων τὴν ἀλήθειαν]. (99e4–6)

In terms of Socrates' analogy, the *logoi* here are clearly understood as reflecting the physical objects mentioned in the previous sentence in the way that water reflects the eclipsed sun. Fearing to perceive physical objects directly, Socrates has decided to examine them indirectly as reflected in propositions. It is hard, however, to see the point. If no more is reflected in the propositions than what is found in the physical objects themselves (in the way that no more is reflected in the water than is to be seen directly in the eclipsed sun), then there seems to be no advantage to taking refuge in such propositions. Talking exclusively about physical causes blinds the soul no less than perceiving such causes. But then is it really the case that the propositions reflect only the *pragmata* mentioned in the previous sentence? What Socrates claims to examine in propositions is "the truth of beings." But is the "truth of beings" here synonymous with "physical things"? This would seem incredibly restrictive. Socrates has just claimed that the good is *the* cause of a thing's being what it is. From this claim one does not have to go far to conclude that the good is the truth of beings, that is, that which makes them what they truly are.[5] If this interpretation of the "truth of beings" is accepted, then the problem raised above is solved: the propositions in which Socrates takes refuge reflect the good itself. This solution, however, faces another problem: it renders Socrates' analogy completely disanalogous. Socrates has clearly identified the eclipsed sun with physical objects. In the present interpretation, however, propositions, rather than reflecting these objects as water reflects the eclipsed sun, reflect something totally different: the good or "the truth of beings." This objection, however, is not fatal, since Socrates proceeds to admit:

> But perhaps my analogy is in a way not quite accurate, for I do not at all agree that someone who examines beings in propositions is examining them in images any more than someone who examines them in things [ἔργα]. (99e6–100a3)[6]

The general point here seems to be that physical things are no less images than are propositions. But then *of what* are physical things images? Since both they and propositions are equally images, we can suspect that they are images of the same thing, that is, "the truth of beings." If the "truth of beings" is identical to the ultimate cause that Socrates has identified as the good, then both propositions and physical things are images of the good. I do not see what else physical things could be images of in the present context.[7] Furthermore, if this interpretation is accepted, the disanalogy disappears. Because physical things are themselves images of the good, propositions that reflect these things will also be images of the good. A proposition, then, will reflect the truth of beings reflected in things. One question, however, remains: if both propositions and physical things are equally images, why does Socrates prefer the former to the latter and find them less "blinding"? The answer seems to be that in appealing to the senses, physical things conceal that of which they are images. Precisely because of their concreteness and their "brightness," physical things are not transparent to the truth of beings. If this is the case, we see why Socrates speaks of an "eclipsed sun": he wants us to see that the good, while reflected in physical things, is also "eclipsed" by them.[8] Perception of a thing reveals only its physical parts; in this way, however, perception blinds us to the good that defines the thing and gives it its unity. This is exactly what Socrates suffered in his pursuit of natural science. By now taking refuge in propositions, Socrates will avoid being blinded by the senses and thus will be better able to see the good that is eclipsed in physical objects.

It remains the case, however, that in confining himself to propositions Socrates is taking refuge not only from perceiving physical objects, but also from inquiring directly into the nature of the good. What can be accomplished by this confinement to propositions remains to be seen. Socrates' initial description of his method is very brief (100a3–7). In each case, he tells us, whether inquiring into causes or into anything else,[9] he first hypothesizes that account (λόγος) which appears to him the "strongest" (ἐρρωμενέστατον) and then sets down as true whatever agrees with it (συμφωνεῖν) and as false whatever disagrees. This brief description already reveals the consequences of Socrates' confinement to propositions. In the present method, what a statement must agree with in order to be accepted is not the "truth of beings" or the physical things from which Socrates has turned his eyes, but rather *another statement* judged to be "strongest" (the hypothesis). In other words, the truth of a proposition is here decided by another proposition. There is no direct access to that of which the propositions are images and by which they would therefore ideally be judged. As far as the hypothesis itself is concerned, the word "strongest" is indeed ambiguous but, given the context, must mean strongest *within discourse* and not strongest in relation to something outside discourse.[10] What makes the hypothesis strongest is not that it correctly represents the truth (i.e., good) of a thing, but rather that it has escaped refutation (though its irrefutability within discourse can of course be related to its expression of a truth that lies outside discourse). Thus what Socrates says here was anticipated by an earlier observation of Simmias that in the absence of an ability to learn the truth from others or discover it for ourselves (ἢ μάθειν . . . ἢ εὑρεῖν, just as Socrates was unable οὔτ'εὑρεῖν οὔτε . . . μάθειν [99c8–9] the nature of the good), we should sail through life on the least refutable (δυσεξελεγκτότατον) account we can find (85c7–d4).

Once such a hypothesis is found, another proposition will be either true or false depending on whether it agrees or disagrees with it. Here "agreement" (συμφωνεῖν) and "disagreement" (διαφωνεῖν) seem to mean simply consistency and inconsistency. Richard Robinson's objection to this interpretation is not decisive: he claims that it would be preposterous to think that a proposition is to be assumed true if it is simply *consistent* with the hypothesis.[11] This would indeed be preposterous if Socrates were speaking of just any propositions whatsoever: in this case, for example, we could assume that the proposition "the moon is made out of cheese" is true because it is consistent with the hypothesis "virtue is good." However, Socrates is clearly speaking here only about propositions pertinent to whatever is being examined in a particular case.[12] If, for example, he were hypothesizing that virtue is good, he would assume as true other relevant propositions about virtue that are consistent with this hypothesis and reject those that are inconsistent. But would he not still end up postulating as true all kinds of absurd claims about virtue, for instance, that virtue is blue, just because they are consistent with the hypothesis? This objection reads more into the text than is necessary or warranted: nothing Socrates says commits him to accepting as true a manifestly absurd proposition *just because* it "agrees" with the hypothesis. In other words, what Socrates says at 100a5, while clearly implying that "agreement" with the hypothesis is a *necessary* condition for truth, does not necessarily imply that it is a *sufficient* condition. Only propositions with a certain intuitive plausiblity will even recommend themselves for comparison with the hypothesis. The error of Robinson and others is to assume that the method described here is a completely self-contained, vacuum-tight logical system. This hypothetical method, like its counterpart in the *Meno,* depends in large part on intuition, where this intuition is expressed in certain background assumptions shared by the interlocutors. Finally, the reading of "agreement" here as "consistency" is compatible with granting inferential relations an important role in the method.[13] Some of the propostions will need to be in such relations, since we obviously cannot get very far with consistency alone. The point is that consistency is all we need to augment our one hypothesis into several hypotheses from which we can then proceed to draw inferences. Robinson's own forced interpretation of agreement as "entailment" is therefore unnecessary.

Socrates' description of his method so far seems to suggest that the initial hypothesis, once posited as the strongest, cannot itself be further questioned or examined, since other propositions are to be judged in terms of their consistency or inconsistency with it, not vice versa. That this is not the case, however, is shown by Socrates' later description of another part of the method:

If someone took hold [ἔχοιτο] of the hypothesis itself, you would let him be and not answer until you had examined what propositions follow from it [τὰ ἐπ' ἐκείνης ὁρμηθέντα] in order to see whether they appear to you to agree or disagree among themselves. When he required you to give an explanation [διδόναι λόγον] of the hypothesis itself, you would give it in this way, hypothesizing another hypothesis which seemed to you to be best from those above [τῶν ἄνωθεν], until you arrived at something sufficient [τι ἱκανόν]. (101d3–8)

What is apparently envisioned here is a case in which someone wants to discuss the hypothesis posited as "strongest," perhaps, though not necessarily, in order to refute it.[14] In such a case, Socrates says, one should not answer right away. Socrates is contrasting his method here to eristic (101e1–102a1). As the *Euthydemus* clearly shows, a characteristic of eristic is its total disregard of *context*. It depends on the ambiguity of a proposition for its success in refuting it; this ambiguity inherent in propositions, however, is partly remedied by the context of the discussion (why the proposition is made, how it relates to other propositions, what it seeks to accomplish, and so on). For this reason, eristic must at all cost ignore context; it must seize upon the proposition and insist on dealing with nothing but it. The opposed method Socrates recommends involves the following two steps:

1. You should first resist having the hypothesis considered in isolation by situating it within the context of the account (of causes or of anything else) to which it has given rise. The hypothesis is the first step of one's reasoning on the basis of which one accepts other propositions consistent with it and then proceeds to draw specific conclusions concerning the matter at hand. What must therefore be examined is whether or not there is any inconsistency within the resulting account as a whole, that is, either between those claims that have been individually postulated as consistent with the hypothesis or between the conclusions that have been inferred from the hypothesis in conjunction with the postulated claims and certain assumed beliefs.[15] Thus the phrase "τὰ ἐπ' ἐκείνης ὁρμηθέντα" covers a variety of propositions related to the hypothesis in different ways: some have simply been postulated as consistent with it, others have been inferred from its conjunction with other propositions either explicitly postulated or tacitly assumed. The "consequences" can even be different "applications" of the hypothesis, for example, applications of a general theory to different specific cases.[16] There is no warrant for restricting the phrase to propositions that have been strictly deduced from the initial hypothesis: what we have here is a complex process that

can only be vaguely described as involving the postulation of a hypothesis that seems strongest to the interlocutors and the consequent acceptance of certain other propositions on its basis. The process is so fluid that it could conceivably lead to the acceptance of mutually contradictory propositions. If such an inconsistency turns up, this shows that one's overall account has yet to be made coherent and not necessarily (though possibly) that the hypothesis is inadequate. Socrates' point is that until one's overall account is rendered consistent there is no point in discussing the hypothesis.

2. Once one has tested the account arising from the hypothesis for overall consistency, one can then proceed to justify and explain the hypothesis itself. This can presumably take different forms: if inadequacies in the hypothesis have been revealed either by the discovery of an inconsistency in one's overall theory or by the objections of one's interlocutor, then it will need to be significantly revised, if not entirely replaced by a better one; if, on the other hand, one's theory has proven consistent and the objections of one's interlocutor are simply the result of misunderstanding or doubt, then what is needed is a better explanation of the hypothesis, that is, one that would bring out more clearly its meaning as well as the presuppositions upon which it is based. Thus there is no reason for restricting the phrase τῶν ἄνωθεν ("the things above") to propositions from which the initial hypothesis could be strictly *deduced*.[17] Deduction is clearly *one* way in which you could relieve the doubts of you interlocutor: you could, for example, deduce the hypothesis in question from another hypothesis whose truth he accepts. Yet there are clearly other ways of accounting for the hypothesis: it could be made clearer by being reformulated, its presuppositions could be made explicit, or it could be shown to be equivalent to something that the interlocutor already accepts. A "higher" hypothesis need not be a hypothesis that is higher in a chain of deduction, but could simply be a *better* hypothesis, that is, better either in the sense of remedying the inadequacies of the initial hypothesis or in the sense of offering a better explanation of what was already stated in the initial hypothesis. Completely unwarranted is the attempt to read into the phrase τῶν ἄνωθεν an entire ontological hierarchy, where what is stated in the initial hypothesis is deduced from ever higher ontological principles until the ultimate principle of all reality is reached, which would no longer be a "hypothesis."[18] Such an interpretation, while of course not directly contradicted by the text, is such a blatant example of interpretative "overkill" that we must avoid it unless very strong reasons compel us to adopt it. It is clear from the context that when Socrates speaks of reaching "something sufficient," he is not talking about obtaining knowledge of the first principle of reality, but simply about reaching

some explanation that will finally satisfy one's interlocutor, that is, that will remove any major doubts and clear up any misunderstanding. There is also no reason to think that the discovery of "something sufficient" will involve an exhaustive explanation and justification of all the beliefs and propositions either contained in the account or presupposed by it. The "sufficient" hypothesis will be "sufficient" only because the interlocutor accepts its presuppositions and considers it self-evident enough not to require further explanation. The account as a whole will presumably contain ambiguous terms and implications whose significance has not been fully examined. It is not an airtight, deductive, and axiomatic system.

The above interpretation is the most natural. The procedure described by the passage is *not* one of testing the hypothesis by seeing if inconsistent conclusions can be deduced from it[19] and then deducing the hypothesis itself from some higher principle. Instead, it appears to be much more a matter of showing the coherency of the overall account to which the hypothesis gives rise and then revising, explaining, and justifying the hypothesis. This passage, therefore, like the previous one, shows us just how confined to propositions the method of hypothesis is. The hypothesis produces an account of the subject under discussion by being related to other propositions (those consistent with it or following from its conjunction with other propositions) and is itself accounted for in terms of other propositions. Nevertheless, the method clearly depends on something other than propositions, namely, the "truth of beings" reflected in them. In other words, intuition plays an indispensable role in the method, both in recommending propositions for consideration and in revealing the meanings of their terms. Such intuition is assumed in the concrete context of the discussion.

Apart from the greater detail, Socrates' general description of the hypothetical method in the *Phaedo* accords perfectly with his description of the method in the *Meno*. In both cases, the method turns away from direct inquiry into the nature of a thing (there virtue, here the good) and is confined to looking solely at propositions. In both cases, it is not self-contained and self-sufficing but must be guided by some sort of intuition. What must be considered next is the specific use which Socrates makes of the method in the *Phaedo*.

Socrates believes that his method can be applied to the problem of causation. He begins by hypothesizing what he claims to be nothing new: namely, that there is a good in itself, a beauty in itself, a large in itself, and all other such forms (100b4–7). Socrates is constantly speaking of these forms and has already referred to them in the present discussion. What he is doing now is making their existence an explicit *hypothesis* so that they can serve as a step in a specific argument. More exactly, the existence of the forms (and presumably what has been assumed earlier concerning their relation to sensible particulars) is chosen by Socrates as that "strongest" hypothesis in terms of which all other propositions in the inquiry are to be judged. Socrates does not here seek to know the nature of any one of the forms; he does not seek to know what the good is or what beauty is. He simply hypothesizes their existence to answer another question. Just how Socrates deals with the forms in his "second-best" inquiry will become clearer in what follows.

Having found the strongest hypothesis, Socrates now assumes to be true those explanations that "agree" with it and rejects his earlier explanations because they "disagree" with it.[20] The new type of explanation is as follows: any beautiful thing besides beauty itself is beautiful *because it participates in beauty itself* (διότι μετέχει ἐκείνου τοῦ καλοῦ, 100c4–6). Participation in its corresponding form is the sole cause of a thing's being what it is. There is therefore no need to look for any other more "sophisticated" causes (τὰς ἄλλας αἰτίας τὰς σοφάς, 100c9–10). In explaining why a certain thing is beautiful, Socrates will not cite its beautiful color or its shape or anything else of the kind; instead, dismissing these kinds of explanations, he will give the simple (ἁπλῶς), artless (ἀτέχνως), and naive (εὐήθως) answer that the thing is beautiful through the presence (παρουσία) or communion—or however else the relation is to be described—of beauty: he explicitly declines to commit himself to the exact nature of the relation (100c10–d8).[21] Socrates recommends his answer as the "safest" (ἀσφαλέστατον, 100d8), the one that will prevent you from being tripped up in an argument.

Socrates proceeds to employ his new type of explanation to answer the questions that had earlier so perplexed him. He will no longer cite "a head" as the cause of a person's tallness or shortness, since this explanation is vulnerable to the objection that it uses the same cause to explain two opposite relations. The safer answer Socrates will now give is that large things are large *through largeness* (μεγέθει) and small things are small *through smallness* (σμικρότητι, 100e–101b). Similarly, he will no longer say that division or addition are what make things *two;* instead he will offer the safe explanation that they are two through their participation in duality (101b–c). All other more sophisticated answers must be left alone.

The virtue of the kind of explanation Socrates advocates here is its avoidance of reductionism. The explanation of a thing's beauty in terms of its possession of a certain shape or color reduces beauty to something that at best only contributes to it. Such an explanation can therefore be easily refuted by citing something that either has a completely different shape or color and is equally beautiful, or has the same shape or color and is not beautiful. The "safe" explanation would avoid such refutation by saying that beauty and nothing else is the reason why a thing is beautiful. Likewise, instead of reducing the number two to the unit and then attempting to explain it by means of addition or division, Socrates can now simply say that duality is the cause of two things being two. In this way a thing's nature is, in the words of the *Meno,* kept whole.

It is precisely in thus preserving unity and avoiding reductionism that the present account "mirrors" the nature of the good. As has been seen, the good appealed to Socrates as a cause because it seemed capable of explaining the nature of a thing without reducing this nature to the plurality of the thing's material components. By explaining a thing in terms of what is *best* for it to be, that is, in terms of its one end or purpose, we are able to preserve its unity. Socrates' present account of causation therefore imitates the causality of the good in refusing to reduce beauty to what only contributes to it. The insight that a thing is beautiful solely because this is what is *best* for it to be is reflected in the proposition that a thing is beautiful for no other reason than beauty itself. By avoiding reductionism, Socrates' "haphazard" and "second-best" account of causation remains true to at least one aspect of the original insight.

However, it is not hard to see that this reflection in *logoi* captures only the surface of the original "truth of beings." As Socrates himself observes, his explanation is naive and simple-minded. To see why, we need only consider how unsatisfactory such an explanation would be in the dialectic of the aporetic dialogues. Imagine, for example, Laches responding in the following way to Socrates' request for the one thing that makes many different kinds of actions courageous: "Well, Socrates, what makes remaining at one's post and other acts *courageous* is simply their participation in courage; do not ask me to analyze courage in terms of anything else because I know nothing about such 'sophisticated' explanations." Such an answer would profit us not at all in our inquiry into the nature of courage. There can be no doubt, however, that this answer would be safer than the definitions proposed and refuted in the *Laches.* On the other hand, I argued in the second chapter that despite the failure of these definitions to express the whole truth about courage, the very process of examining and refuting them provides insight into the nature of courage. Such insight is exactly what is not provided by Socrates' "safer method."[22] The method is right in claiming that beauty is beauty and should not be reduced to anything else. This claim is empty, however, unless accompanied by insight into what beauty is.

Here we see most clearly the limits of the hypothetical method. The proposition that beauty is what makes a thing beautiful is true and "sufficient" for Socrates' purpose of proving the soul's immortality. What recommends it is its "safe" avoidance of reductionism. Yet this hypothesizing of the forms as causes is not at all the *aitias logismos* desired in the *Meno*.[23] The latter clearly involves insight into what a form is and not simply the safe tautology that it is itself. As the interpretation of the *Laches* in chapter 2 has shown, dialectic is inseparable from danger; its relation to the truth is precarious because it does not fool itself into thinking that it can anticipate or grasp this truth in any propositions. The method of hypothesis, on the other hand, is defined by its "safety"; by confining itself to propositions (thereby excluding any insight that might transcend these propositions), it hides from danger.

It is true that besides mirroring the function of the good in his account of causation, Socrates explicitly introduces the good as part of his hypothesis (100b6). However, this hypothetical way of dealing with the good differs significantly from the abandoned attempt to inquire directly into its nature. Before devising his safe method, Socrates wanted to know how the good might serve as the cause of a thing being what it is. He believed that if he knew a thing's proper good, he would thereby also know its essential nature. He therefore would not have been satisfied with the explanation that a beautiful thing is beautiful because it participates in beauty. He would have wanted to know just what beauty itself is, and this knowledge would apparently have been grounded in a knowledge of the good. Again, what exactly this knowledge of the good would have involved is not specified, but this is clearly the direction in which Socrates was heading, and this is clearly his preferred method. Now in the second-best method the good appears again, but only as hypothesized along with other forms. Rather than grounding all of our knowledge of the natures of things, it is now simply one cause among others. Furthermore, rather than providing us with any insight into a thing's being, the good as a "hypothetical" cause enables us to say only that a thing is good through its participation in the good.[24] This almost vacuous proposition falls far short not only of Socrates' preferred method, but also of the kind of knowledge of the good gained in dialogues such as the *Laches* and the *Charmides*. Here we see most clearly why the hypothetical method, despite addressing the forms in the present dialogue, must still be considered, as it is in the *Meno*, a second-best.[25]

These observations must lead one to agree at least partially with Vlastos's well-known argument (1971) that the forms are used in this section of the *Phaedo* as purely logical explanations rather than as real causes. What Vlastos fails to see, however, is that this is due solely to the limitations of the "second-best" hypothetical method and the forms here do not even provide good logical explanations. Concerning the first point, it is clear from what he says throughout the dialogue that Socrates considers the forms to be real entities, not logical classes, and that he believes sensible objects to be ontologically dependent on these forms both for their existence and their properties:[26] in short, that he sees the forms as *real causes* and not simply as "logical *aitiai* of classification and entailment" (166). The problem, however, is that Socrates cannot explain *how* they are real causes. He would have liked to explain their causality in terms of the good, but insight into the nature of the good proved beyond him. As a result he must have recourse to propositions and restrict himself to a purely logical explanation that, while true, reveals nothing about the essence of the form and its relation to sensible particulars. This observation takes us to the second point and the major problem with Vlastos's interpretation: Vlastos assumes throughout his paper that the logical *aitia* Socrates introduces is a *definition or account of the essence* of a form.[27] In this case the new method of explanation Socrates introduces would be neither tautologous nor simple nor unenlightening. However, Vlastos's assumption receives no confirmation from the text. Socrates never says, nor even implies, that his method is to explain why a thing is beautiful by first defining beauty itself and then showing that the beautiful thing conforms to this definition (hardly a "simple-minded" or "naive" explanation!). Instead, the example he himself gives, one which he never suggests is incomplete, is that a thing is beautiful because it "participates" in beauty: that is all. Similarly, the reason why a thing is good is that it "participates" in the good: that this explanation does not involve a definition of the essence of the good is clear, since such a definition would enable us to avoid the second-best method altogether. Furthermore, even the "more sophisticated" explanation Socrates offers later involves knowing only that two forms always accompany each other, not what each one in essence is. Not a single form is defined in this entire discussion, a peculiar fact indeed if Vlastos is correct. Vlastos, then, is clearly not correct: what we have in Socrates' second-best method are logical explanations that yet do not reveal anything either about a form's essence or about the real causality it exercises on those things which participate in it.

The remainder of Socrates' account can be briefly summarized. The major point he makes in further explanation of his hypothesis is that forms do not admit their opposites: largeness cannot be small, and smallness cannot be large (102d–103a). This point applies not only to the forms of largeness and smallness, but also to the largeness and smallness *in us* (τὸ ἐν ἡμῖν μέγεθος, 102d78). A person can of course be both small and large either at different times or in relation to different people. What Socrates claims to be impossible, however, is that the smallness in us should itself become large. If we change from being small to being large, one of two things must be the case: either the smallness in us has fled (it is hard to see what this means in this example), or it has been destroyed. Because largeness and smallness are opposites, the one cannot become the other.

At this point, however, an unnamed speaker objects (103a) that, though supposed to be an account of generation and destruction, Socrates' hypothesis (as now expanded) is not consistent with the fact pointed out earlier (70d ff.) that opposites come to be from, and are destroyed into, opposites. This kind of objection to the hypothesis is just what Socrates had anticipated in his general account of the method, and he answers it just as he had said it should be answered: he explains the hypothesis by explaining one of its presuppositions, namely, the distinction between forms and their instantiations. An opposite *thing* can come to be from an opposite *thing* (for example, a large thing can come to be from a small thing), Socrates explains, but the opposite itself (the form largeness) cannot come to be from its opposite (the form smallness) because they simply exclude one another. As long as one recognizes a distinction between a form and its instantiations, there is no problem. Socrates' response to the objection thus employs the method he had described earlier.

It is important to note, however, that this response is not entirely satisfying. That a large thing should come to be from a small thing seems to be rendered purely accidental by Socrates' explanation: because largeness itself does not come to be from smallness itself, there is apparently no necessity in a large thing coming to be from a small thing; it might equally have come to be from a red thing. In the passage to which the objector refers, however, Socrates was maintaining precisely such a necessity: a thing characterized by one form *must* come to be from a thing characterized by the opposite form. Therefore, the sharp distinction between form and particular presupposed by Socrates' theory of causation does indeed appear inconsistent with this theory's profession to explain generation and destruction. Though the theory can explain why a sensible thing *is* large, it does not seem capable of explaining how the thing *comes to be* large from being small. This is why the objection troubles Socrates, despite the ease with which he answers it: "At the same time he looked at Cebes and said, 'Were not you too, Cebes, troubled by something in what he said?' " (103c2–4).

Thus an objection that at first appeared naive leads Socrates to the recognition that he must take into account the generation and destruction of a form's instantiations if he is to say anything about the actual immortality of the soul. He therefore introduces another hypothesis that is simply a further refinement and development of the intitial hypothesis, now treated by Socrates as including the "safe" explanation (103c ff.):[28] anything that is always characterized by one form will not admit the opposite form without ceasing to be; fire, for example, cannot cease to be hot without ceasing to be fire (103d). A thing thus incapable of admitting a form (quality) opposed to the one it has can serve as the cause of other things having that form. Fire, rather than simply heat, can therefore be cited as the cause of something being hot (105b–c). This does not "disagree" with the initial hypothesis, since the same type of explanation is still ultimately at work: fire is itself hot only because it participates in heat. The recognition, however, that fire as long as it is fire *always* participates in heat allows the existence of an intermediary cause that introduces the causality of the form into the world of generation and destruction. The kind of explanation thereby made possible ("fire is the cause of something being hot"), though still "safe," is more "sophisticated" (κομψοτέραν, 105c2) than the previous one, apparently in the sense that it is more informative (though not necessarily more insightful).[29] This is clearly an example of what Socrates earlier described as going from the initial hypothesis to a "higher" hypothesis:[30] the new account of causation is "higher" in the sense of being better suited to the purpose at hand. Its "height" has nothing to do with ontological priority, since, by returning to things generable and destructible, it is ontologically "lower" than the initial form-hypothesis. Socrates is here turning his eyes back toward the natural world, and yet the greater sophistication thereby attained does not make his method any less of a "second-best." Indeed, this greater sophistication, by focusing one's attention back on particulars, leads the method further than ever from an understanding of the forms and the good. We are still postulating between forms and particulars a relation that we do not understand, and we are still speaking of forms without knowledge, but in now using particulars as causes we are less aware than ever of this ignorance.

The point of these remarks is not to argue that Socrates' proof for the immortality of the soul is worthless, but rather to show the limitations of the method that makes this proof possible. Because of the hypothetical method's positive results, one can easily overlook the cost at which those results are bought. As long as this cost is recognized, however, one can accept the positive results as such. Socrates' final proof of the soul's immortality is well known (105c–107a): the soul,, as what causes things to live, necessarily participates in life, just as fire, as what causes things to be hot, necessarily participates in heat; therefore, the soul can no more receive death while remaining the soul than fire can receive cold while remaining fire; therefore, the soul is deathless. But cannot the soul simply *cease to be* upon the approach of death in the way that fire can simply cease to be upon the approach of cold? Socrates dismisses this possibility by claiming that it makes no sense to say that the soul can *cease to be* if we have agreed that it is incapable of *dying* (106d).[31]

This proof seems fairly convincing, but the problems it leaves unconsidered are obvious. Though the soul participates in the form of life, it does not appear to be identical with this form. Can the soul then really be as eternal and deathless as the form itself? What exactly is the nature of the relation between a form and the particular always characterized by it? What is the "form of life" and how does it differ from the life of this or that organism? What is the relation between the forms and the cause that Socrates sought to know before turning to the present second-best method, that is, the good? Other such questions could be asked, but, as has been suggested, they lie beyond the scope of the present method and what it can tell us about causality.

Socrates displays confidence in his proof, though he applauds Simmias's observation that, due to the magnitude of the question and the weakness of human nature, one cannot help having some doubts. What Socrates then proceeds to say has been sometimes misinterpreted:

> You are right, Simmias, and, what is more, even if the first hypotheses appear to you convincing, nevertheless you should examine them more clearly [σαφέστερον]. And if you go through them sufficiently [ἱκανῶς], I believe that you will follow the account [ἀκολουθήσετε τῷ λόγῳ] as much as it is humanly possible to follow it. When you are sure that you have done this,[32] then will you seek no further [οὐδὲν ζητήσετε περαιτέρω]. (107b4–9)

It is sometimes assumed that Socrates is here speaking of attaining a certainty that would render the hypothetical method no longer "hypothetical."[33] In other words, it is thought that Socrates is here foreseeing the possibility of a proof that would overcome all the shortcomings of the method as it has been described so far. This interpretation seems confirmed by Socrates' description of a state in which one would *seek no further*. Yet when Socrates speaks of pursuing the present account as much as is "humanly possible," he is not talking about attaining certainty, but only about attaining *as much clarity as the present subject matter and the present method allow*. This passage must be understood in the context of Socrates' overall project in this second half of the dialogue: to counter the danger of misology which faced the interlocutors after the failure of the more dogmatic and presuming arguments of the first half. Misology was seen to have its origin precisely in that *excessive confidence* in arguments that some want to read into the present passage. Socrates therefore seeks to cure this greatest of evils, not through the pretense of attainable certainty, a pretense that would promote misology, but rather by "haphazardly throwing together" (97b6) a method than can achieve positive results while at the same time not hiding its serious limitations. There is no indication in the present passage that this method will ever overcome these limitations and become any less hypothetical and any more capable of providing the kind of knowledge attainable only through Socrates' preferred method, that is, the inquiry into the nature of the good. Even this preferred method is subject to human limits: in the present dialogue, Socrates confesses to having proved unable to understand the good; his elenchus in other dialogues, while providing nonpropositional insight into the natures of the different virtues well beyond what the hypothetical method can provide, cannot by means of this insight end the inquiry or offer propositional results. What Socrates is saying here is that we may come to know *as much as we need to know* to be as certain *as our nature allows us to be* of the immortality of the soul.

Thus when he speaks of "searching no further," he is not referring to the end of dialectic as such,[34] but rather to the end of an inquiry into a specific problem, where this inquiry is understood to be from start to finish "hypothetical" in the sense defined above, that is, in the sense that, confined to propositions, it cannot provide us with any real insight into the natures of which it speaks (which does not detract from its ability to provide a convincing solution to a specific problem). This limited sense of "searching no further" is found again in the *Timaeus*:

> Do not be surprised, Socrates, if, with regard to a great many subjects, including the gods and the generation of the universe, we are unable to offer each other accounts which are completely and in every way consistent and clear [ἀπηκριβωμένους], but if they fall short of no other accounts in likelihood [εἰκότας], be content with that, remembering that I the speaker and you the judges are only human, so that, having accepted the probable story [τὸν εἰκότα μῦθον] concerning these matters, it is right that *we should search no further* [μηδὲν ἔτι πέρα ζητεῖν]. (29c4–d3)

Here the reason for searching no further is clearly not that we have attained absolute certainty, but that we have attained as much clarity as the method (a μῦθος) and the subject allow. This is the kind of "clarity" of which Socrates speaks in the *Phaedo*. Precisely due to its limitations, the hypothetical method can achieve results and thus come to an end.

We must suspect, however, that these results and this end are thereby themselves limited.

In the *Phaedo,* the hypothetical inquiry into the immortality of the soul comes to end as Socrates drinks his hemlock. One can be assured, however, that Socratic questioning is meant to continue.

8

Idealization and the Destruction of Hypotheses in the *Republic*

What is implied in the *Phaedo* and can be inferred from what Socrates says there is made explicit in the *Republic*. The priority of dialectic as an inquiry into the nature of the good over the method of hypothesis, and thereby the inability of the latter to replace the former, receives expression in Socrates' simile of the Divided Line. The aim of the present chapter is therefore to develop further the main themes of the two preceding chapters through an interpretation of this simile. A related objective is to show to be mistaken a common interpretation of the Divided Line according to which *dialectic is simply an extension of, and therefore continuous with, the hypothetical method*. Since this interpretation usually coincides with the view that the hypotheses stand in some inferential or analytic/synthetic relation with the first principle, a major focus of this chapter will be the exact nature of the upward and downward movement between the top two sections of the Line.

Before turning to the Divided Line, it is necessary to examine carefully the context in which it is presented. The *Phaedo* has already suggested that the best method of inquiry would be one that in some way dealt directly with the good. Now in the *Republic* this view receives its most detailed presentation. After Socrates in book 6 has identified as philosophers the rulers of the ideal city he has been painting in words, he finds it necessary to examine their education again as if from the beginning (502e). After summarizing the account of this education given in previous books, Socrates claims that the rulers must now also be exercised in the greatest studies (μαθήματα μέγιστα, 503e4). Socrates reminds Adeimantus that while the definitions of justice, temperance, courage, and wisdom given earlier were considered sufficient for the discussion at hand, a longer way (μακροτέρα περίοδος) was said to be needed for a more perfect discernment (435d). This longer way is what Socrates is referring to now. A study greater than that of the virtues must be pursued by the philosopher-kings. Adeimantus at this point asks if anything could possibly be greater than justice and the other virtues. Socrates replies affirmatively and adds that even of the virtues only a sketch (ὑπογραφή) has been given so far (504d6–7). The greatest study (μέγιστον μάθημα), which has yet to be discussed and which would presumably "fill in" the "sketch" of the virtues, is *the idea of the good* (ἡ τοῦ ἀγαθοῦ ἰδέα, 505a2).

Socrates emphasizes the importance of this idea by claiming that it is what renders everything else beneficial, so that if we were to know everything *except* the good our knowledge would in no way benefit us. This point, it will be recalled, was already made in the *Charmides,* and here as there the problem is how we are to know this good upon which the usefulness of all our other knowledge depends. Socrates here asserts abruptly that we do not sufficiently know the good (αὐτὴν οὐχ ἱκανῶς ἴσμεν, 505a5–6). He then defends this assertion by showing that the good is neither of the two things with which it is normally identified, that is, it is neither *pleasure* nor *knowledge.* Those who identify the good with pleasure are eventually forced to admit that some pleasures are bad (505c–d). Those, on the other hand, who identify the good with knowledge, when asked *of what* it is knowledge, claim it to be knowledge of the good. This definition is obviously circular and leaves unexplained what it is supposed to explain (505b–c). This difficulty in understanding the relation between the knowledge of the good and the good itself is a central theme of the *Euthydemus* and the *Charmides*. The discussion in these two dialogues, however, was seen to suggest that the good, though not identical with knowledge, is nevertheless not external to it in the way that the other objects of knowledge are. Whether or not this is also thought to be the case in the present dialogue will be seen in what follows. In either case, Socrates is clearly right in maintaining that one does not know the good in simply identifying it with knowledge.

Yet Socrates' claim that we do not know the good seems odd. Does he mean that we do not know the good in any sense whatsoever, that we have no notion of what it is? Would not the very inquiry into the natures of the different virtues have been impossible if we did not have *some* awareness of what the good is? Would not our ordinary lives be rendered incoherent without such an awareness? Clearly many of our actions are purposive and benefit us: does this not show that we must have some inkling of the good? Socrates explains that every soul (ἅπασα ψυχή), though in *aporia* and incapable of fully grasping what the good is (οὐκ ἔχουσα λαβεῖν ἱκανῶς τί ποτ' ἐστίν), nevertheless has some *inspired intuition* of it (ἀπομαντευομένη, 505d11–e2). Faintly perceiving the good, the soul pursues it and does everything for its sake. What Socrates describes here is very much like the inspiration discussed in the *Meno*. Just as in our ordinary lives we act virtuously by being inspired with some awareness of what virtue is, so is our pursuit of the good guided by a similar inspiration. The existence of this kind of inspiration grounds the theory of education which Socrates will later defend while developing the Cave analogy (518b–d): education does not, as some people (presumably, the sophists) arrogantly profess, introduce knowledge into the mind as sight into blind eyes but rather turns in the right direction a mind already in possession of latent knowledge (ὡς ἔχοντι μεν αὐτό [τὸ ὡρᾶν, which is the metaphor here for ἐπιστήμη], 518d5–6), just as an eye already in possession of sight needs only to be turned away from the darkness and toward the light in order to see. Since what Socrates criticizes is the view of those who believe *that knowledge is not already in the soul* and therefore needs to be introduced by them (518b8–c1), what he in contrast sees the soul as already possessing must be *knowledge*, and not simply the *capacity* to know. Though perhaps the two cited passages do not require the full-blown "theory" of recollection, clearly something like it must be assumed here.[1] Socrates is maintaining that we already have some implicit awareness of the good which we seek and that we therefore cannot be "taught" the good in the ordinary sense of that word: but this is, after all, the kernel of the theory of recollection when stripped of its mythological and poetical dress. It is important, then, to keep in mind throughout the following discussion that Socrates is not speaking of coming to know something previously completely unknown.

When Socrates is asked by Glaucon to state his own view concerning the nature of the good, he professes ignorance: he does not have *knowledge* of the good but only *belief without understanding* (ἄνευ νοῦ, 506c8).[2] Thus Socrates does not claim much more for himself than the kind of "inspiration" he has just described; even the importance of the good is something he claims only to "divine" (μαντεύομαι, 506a6). Therefore, given the connection noted in the fifth chapter between inspiration and the use of images, it is not surprising that Socrates should agree to discuss the good only indirectly by means of an image. As an image of the good he chooses its "offspring" (ἔκγονος, 506e3): *the sun*.

First, however, Socrates desires Glaucon's agreement concerning something they have already discussed many times and on many occasions (507a–c). They have spoken of a plurality of beautiful things and a plurality of good things, where each good or beautiful thing is said *to be* and is distinguished in discourse from the others. However, they have also spoken of one idea that unifies each plurality of like things and signifies what each thing really is, for example, the good itself or the beautiful itself. They have also said that the particular good things or the particular beautiful things are perceived, while the ideas cannot be perceived, but only known. Once Socrates has again obtained Glaucon's agreement that there are such objects of knowledge, he can proceed to draw his analogy between the good and the sun (507c–509c). Vision, Socrates tells us, requires the medium of light in order to occur. Without light, the eye cannot see and the visible object cannot be seen. This light, in turn, has its source in the sun. The sun, therefore, is ultimately the cause of seeing and being seen, that is, of vision. But the sun as such a cause is not identical with vision nor, therefore, with the eye that sees or the object seen. Now Socrates proceeds to show how the good plays the same role in the intelligible realm. Just as the sun is the cause of seeing and being seen, so is the good the cause of knowing and being known. This means that our knowledge of beauty itself depends on the illumination of the good in the way that our vision of beautiful sensible objects depends on the illumination of the sun. Just as the sun is the source of the light that brings together that which sees and that which is seen, so is the good the source of the truth that "yokes" together the mind that knows and the forms that are known. The good is therefore the cause of both knowledge and truth (508e3–4). Consequently, as in the case of the sun, the good is identical with neither knowledge nor truth. However, just as vision and light could properly be described as "sunlike," so can knowledge and truth be described as "goodlike" (ἀγαθοειδής, 508e6–509a5). Socrates caps off his analogy with a yet greater proof of the good's supereminence. The sun is the cause not only of seeing and being seen, but also of the *being* of the thing that sees and of the thing that is seen (since it is thought that generation and growth depend on the sun). Likewise, Socrates maintains, the good is not only the cause of knowledge, but is also the cause of the being of the objects known. As the cause of being, however, the good cannot itself be being, but must be beyond being (509b6–10). This, then, is the extent of the good's transcendence.

The analogy is thereby stated, but not explained. Socrates makes perfectly perspicuous the correspondences between the sun and the good. He also explains in detail one side of the analogy by telling us just what role the sun plays in seeing and being seen. However, he offers no explanation of the other side of the analogy: that *the good* is the cause of all knowledge and truth is by no means as evident as that the sun is the cause of vision and light. Why should *the good* in particular be identified with such a cause? One might perhaps understand the role the good plays in moral truths, though even then it seems odd to say that the good is the cause of our *knowing* these truths. But what, for example, has the good to do with my knowledge that a triangle has angles totaling 180 degrees? This problem was already encountered in the *Phaedo,* where Socrates implies that the best explanation he could give of why one and one make two is that it is *best* for them to make two. There as here, however, this kind of explanation seems neither intelligible nor helpful. Explaining knowledge in terms of the good is like explaining sound in terms of color: there just seems to be no relation. What, then, can Socrates mean?[3]

Wolfgang Wieland, on the one hand, and Rafael Ferber and Theodor Ebert, on the other, have offered two different suggestions, both of which I find correct and illuminating. Wieland's main point is that the good is not an object of theoretical, propositional knowledge but is rather what governs our *use* of whatever knowledge of objects we do have. "The Idea of the Good marks instead the point from which must be regulated our dealings with all knowledge that can be formulated, if this knowledge is not to remain useless for the knower and lacking any goal or context."[4] As enabling us to use beneficially all other forms of knowledge, the knowledge of the good is what Wieland calls a *Gebrauchswissen.* This characterization cannot be reasonably rejected. First, as we have seen in the *Cratylus,* the *Euthydemus,* and *Republic* 10, *user's* knowledge is for Plato paradigmatic of the philosopher's or dialectician's knowledge. Second, we have the passage in the present book of the *Republic* in which Socrates claims that none of our possessions will be useful or beneficial without knowledge of the good (505a-b). Knowledge of the good is the *practical* knowledge we need to put to correct use everything else that we know.

However, even if knowledge of the good is more like practical than theoretical knowledge,[5] it seems wrong to deny it *any* theoretical content. In the first place, the good is for Plato not simply a practical principle existing in our minds, but rather an "objective" reality. We can therefore still inquire into its exact nature. Second, Wieland's view does not explain how the good, besides guiding the *use* we make of our knowledge, can also cause this knowledge itself. The Sun analogy clearly implies that in the absence of any understanding of the good, we would have no knowledge at all, whereas, on Wieland's view, we appprently would still have knowledge, though it would be useless. Third, the claim that the good is what regulates our use of everything else that we know seems rather empty. This "use" has to be given some content. For example, how exactly would a knowledge of the good enable us to use correctly the hypotheses of mathematics? Indeed, Wieland's characterization of the good, though correct as far as it goes, does not seem sufficient.[6]

Ferber's suggestion can remedy this insufficiency. His interpretation places the emphasis on the nature of the good and the forms, rather than on the character of our knowledge of them (his remarks on the latter issue—see, e.g., 1989, 59–60—are not as satisfying as Wieland's). His claim is that the forms are *ideals,* that is, not only things that *are* but things that *should be;* they are, in short, *norms.* "But the paradigmatic character of the Platonic Ideas means more: they are not only *Ideas* in the traditional ontic sense, but also *Ideals,* not just *onta,* but also *deonta,* in short, not just that which *is,* but also that which *should be:* they are in themselves *norms.*"[7] In characterizing the forms as norms and ideals Ferber is not implying that they are not objective realities. As he points out, to understand Plato's idea of the good we must abstract from the modern opposition between "being" and "value" (1989, 33). A form *is* in its very nature what *should be.* Once the forms are characterized in this way, it is not hard to see why the cause of both their being and their intelligibility should be the *good.* In order for a form to be an ideal or norm, it must be *good.* If the forms are different norms, then the good is that idea which makes possible the very existence and intelligibility of a norm.[8]

The significance of identifying the forms with "norms" and the good with the principle of such norms is made particularly clear in the observations of Theodor Ebert on the logic of the word "good" (1974, 143–46). Ebert points out that the word "good," like the word "real," does not have as its function the attribution of certain properties shared by the things of which it is predicated.[9] Therefore, it can never be a "class concept" or "genus." Instead it is what Ebert calls an *Ausschlussbegriff,* that is, it excludes, rather than assigns, certain characteristics. Since what the concept of the good excludes are imperfections or bad characteristics, Ebert goes on to claim that the idea of the good is responsible for revealing and making possible all those concepts that function as *norms* (146–51). Norms are not universal or class concepts that simply abstract from a plurality of things certain characteristics that are common to all of them. Normative concepts instead serve to order individuals in a hierarchy of greater or lesser approximation to some limiting case (Ebert therefore calls them *Grenzbegriffe*). Rather than abstracting a property from its instances, these concepts imagine it in a state of perfection, that is, they idealize it (Ebert therefore also calls them *ideative Begriffe*). The very existence of such ideal concepts, Ebert goes on to claim, clearly depends on the idea of the good (see also 171–72).

The observations of Ferber and Ebert are certainly correct and must be taken into account by any interpretation of what Socrates says in the *Republic.* There is no warrant for characterizing any Platonic form, including the good, as a genus or class derived through the abstraction of certain characteristics from a plurality of particulars. The form of beauty is not simply a collection of properties common to all things we call "beautiful"; it is rather an ideal that all things called "beautiful" merely approximate. This is not to say that the form of beauty does not *in any way* function as a general concept. To the extent that all beautiful things approximate the form (or "share in" it, as Plato would say), they are "covered" by it and "included" under it. However, the form of beauty is related to its instantiations as much through *exclusion* as through inclusion:[10] it is what its instantiations *should* be, but *fail* to be. To this extent the form functions not as a general concept, but as what we would call a "norm" (the term is anachronistic only insofar as it presupposes a being/value distinction foreign to Plato's thought). As such norms, the forms cannot be known through abstraction, and any talk of "genus," "species," or "class" cannot apply to them. When it is further seen that the idea of the good itself does not function as a general concept (what would be the content of such a concept?) and seems presupposed by any understanding of a norm *as such,* it becomes clear that it functions not only as a norm, but as some kind of metanorm.

This understanding of the good is clearly compatible with Wieland's characterization of the way in which we know the good.[11] If the good is the "norm of norms" or "ideal of ideals," then it seems only natural that our knowledge of the good should have the practical function of determining how we deal with and use everything else. After all, to call the forms "deonta" and "norms" is to make them in some sense practical. The suggestions of Wieland, Ferber, and Ebert can therefore be joined in the claim that the practical knowledge which regulates the use of all we possess is a knowledge *of* forms as ideals or norms, as well as *of* the principle that makes possible the existence and intelligibility of such ideals or norms.

In order to develop this interpretation further, let us consider the following mathematical truth: "A triangle has angles totaling 180 degrees." How do we know that this is true? The mathematician would say that it is self-evident or that it follows from premises that are self-evident. But what does "self-evident" mean here? Certainly no triangular object perceived through the senses has angles totaling 180 degrees. If, on the other hand, this truth has nothing to do with the senses, then how is it known? The explanation that it is known through the "mind's eye" does not seem plausible. Even an imagined triangle is a particular, imperfect one derived from the senses and as such can no more ground the above universal claim than can a perceived triangle. One remaining alternative is to say that the triangle is simply a "concept" we have. Unless, however, one is willing to admit that this concept is purely conventional (which Plato would not be), one must still explain how its *truth* is recognized.

This takes us back to our original question: how do we *know* that a triangle *truly* has angles totaling 180 degrees?

If we proceed along this line of thought, we come to see that a knowledge of this truth depends on an understanding of the good. The reason is as follows: knowledge of this truth depends on the realization that it is *the essence* of a triangle to have angles totaling 180 degrees, where this means that this is the proper *good* and *perfection* of a triangle.[12] The mathematical truth depends on the ability to distinguish the perfect triangle (what it really is to be a triangle) from its imperfect instantiations. *This idealization*[13] *itself, however, depends on an understanding of the good.* To know what a triangle *is*, we must know that it is *better* than any triangle we have perceived or imagined. Now we can extend this point beyond the present example and claim that *the ideas as ideas depend on the good because the good is the principle behind all idealization.* We can know what virtue *is* without reducing it to its imperfect and contingent instances only because our understanding of the good allows us to idealize virtue. With regard to a problem raised in the *Meno* and the *Phaedo*, we can also say that this idealization is what allows us to preserve the unity of virtue in the multiplicity of its properties and instances. We recognize that there is *more* to virtue than this multiplicity, but the transcendence implied in the word "more" depends on an understanding of the good.

To say that the good is a cause of our knowledge is to say that reality is not known by being *given* to us either in sense experience or in our "concepts." To know the nature of a thing, the mind must *project beyond* what is given. Knowledge is not of what things are, but rather of what they *should be.* To know a thing is not to know how it de facto exists, but what it *according to its nature* should be. This "should," is of course not a moral "should," and accordingly "good" is not for Plato an exclusively moral term. In short, the reason why the good is the cause of our knowledge is that all knowledge is a form of idealization. It is precisely through such idealization that we can know a thing as *more* than the multiplicity of its properties and thus know what it itself is in its unity.

From these observations we can also gather how the good is a cause of being. Before drawing his analogy between the sun and the good, Socrates took time to point out that the objects of knowledge are the forms or ideas. But what is a "form" or "idea"? What is "beauty itself" as opposed to this or that beautiful thing? This question cannot be answered without reference to the good. A form is to be understood as the proper good of those things which instantiate it, the good toward which they strive, but which they fall short of attaining.[14] To ask what it is *best* for a beautiful thing to be, as opposed to asking what shape or color it has, is to ask for *the form of beauty itself.* The form is nothing but this "best."[15]

Without the good, therefore, there would be no forms. There would be things characterized by certain properties of which we could give either accurate or inaccurate descriptions based on our perception of them; there would be nothing, however, in terms of which we could *judge* them and thereby *know* them. The form necessarily transcends what is merely "the case," but this is precisely why it depends for its being on the principle of this transcendence: the good.

But even if we now understand the role the good plays in knowledge, we face another problem: how can we come to know the good? Socrates insists on the importance of grasping sufficiently what the good itself is. This importance is now even more evident: since it is the cause of all our knowledge, we must know the good if we are really to know anything at all. Yet there is a serious difficulty in understanding how a knowledge of the good is possible: *if the good is presupposed by every act of knowing, how can it be itself an object of knowledge?* The paradox is that the good is so essential to our knowledge that it does not seem to be itself knowable. In speaking of a "knowledge of the good" we make the good an *object* of knowledge, and yet it has been seen to be the *cause* of all knowledge. Could it in some sense be both? But then in knowing the good we would be knowing that which makes possible our knowing the good (or anything else). Would not such a circle involve us in absurdity?[16]

This circle has been encountered in previous chapters, most explicitly in the discussions of the *Charmides* and the *Euthydemus*. Both dialogues confronted us with the difficulty of understanding the possibility of a knowledge that has only itself as its object, as well as the further difficulty of giving this "knowledge of knowledge" some *content*. More specifically, they set us the task of explaining how this "knowledge of knowledge" could be a knowledge of the good, since both dialogues seem to require us to identify the two. Now Socrates' description of the good in the *Republic* presents us with the same problems. Because the good is the cause or fundamental presupposition of knowledge, and because to know such a presupposition or cause is clearly in some sense to know the nature of knowledge itself, a knowledge of the good must necessarily be a knowledge of knowledge. But how is such a knowledge of knowledge possible and what prevents it from being empty? From what Socrates says in the *Republic,* a knowledge of the good clearly cannot be an empty knowledge of knowledge, but it also cannot be knowledge of an object that is external to knowledge in the way a triangle is. But what then is it? This is the same difficulty encountered in the other dialogues.

The *Republic,* however, not only shares the difficulty but suggests a similar solution. This can be seen most clearly if we formulate the above problem as follows: knowledge is not identical with the good, but neither can it have the good as a mere object external to itself. What exactly, then, is the nature of the relation between knowledge and the good in what is called "knowledge *of* the good"? Socrates provides a clear answer: the relation is best described by saying that knowledge is "goodlike" (ἀγαθοειδής, 509a3). The implications are clear: because knowledge is "*good*like," in knowing the good we will also know knowledge; because, however, knowledge is only "good*like,*" in knowing the good we will also know something more than knowledge. This solution, however, requires that we understand just what it means to say that knowledge is "goodlike." Because we know the forms through some sort of "idealization" (rather than "abstraction") and because the good is the principle that makes such idealization posssible, the good must be somehow manifest in the very activity of knowing (in the way that the light of the sun is manifest in the activity of seeing), rather than simply as an object or end result of knowing. This is exactly what the *Laches,* the *Charmides,* and the *Euthydemus* were seen to suggest: we become aware of the good in the very way in which we inquire. To this extent, Wieland's characterization of the knowledge of the good as a practical "user's knowledge" (*Gebrauchswissen*) is justified. There is still circularity here, but it is not vicious: it is simply the reflexivity involved in knowing the good when knowledge is itself "goodlike."[17] This reflexivity is most apparent in the *Laches* and the *Charmides* where the virtue sought is revealed in the very process of searching for it; all of the other dialogues considered, however, have shed light on what is involved in this reflexivity. Now all of this is summed up in the characterization of knowledge as "goodlike."

These observations imply that if we had to give a name to the kind of knowledge involved in knowing the good, we could do no better than call it "dialectical." In the dialogues examined in previous chapters, dialectic shows itself to have the reflexive character just described: what is sought is revealed not in any "results," but rather in the very search. Dialectic as practiced in these dialogues can therefore be said to be *the* way in which the good is known.

But how is dialectic described in the *Republic* itself? To answer this question we must finally turn to Socrates' simile of the Divided Line. This simile is meant to be a further explanation or illustration of the Sun analogy. Glaucon demands this explanation after Socrates confesses to having left out a great deal (συχνά γε ἀπολείπω, 509c7) in the analogy. However, Socrates points out that even in what follows he will need to leave out "much" (πολύ, 509c9). In the previous analogy Socrates distinguished between the visible realm ruled by the sun and the intelligible realm ruled by the good. Now Socrates asks us to imagine a Line divided into two unequal sections to represent these two realms.[18]

IDEALIZATION AND THE DESTRUCTION OF HYPOTHESES IN THE *REPUBLIC*

Each of these sections is in turn divided into two sections according to the same proportion. The first section of the visible realm represents *eikasia,* which has as its objects "images" (*eikones*), that is, shadows, reflections on bright surfaces, and other such things. Though Socrates has little to say here about this first section, it needs to be noted both that the Sun analogy and the Divided Line are themselves *eikones* (the former is explicitly called that at 509a9) and that Socrates in book 10 will criticize the poets for *their* use of images (or imitation). This section is therefore much more complex and problematic than it is here acknowledged to be: chapter 5 is devoted to the issues it raises. The second section represents belief (*pistis*), which has as its objects that *of which* the images in the first section are images, that is, plants, animals, and all manmade objects. Now Socrates proceeds to explain the division of the intelligible realm in a passage of extreme importance for the question at hand:

> In one section of it [the intelligible realm], the soul is compelled to investigate starting from hypotheses, while using as images those things [the concrete objects] imitated before [εἰκόσι χρωμένη ψυχὴ ζητεῖν ἀναγκάζεται ἐξ ὑποθέσεων], not proceeding to a first principle, but rather to a conclusion; in the other section, however, the soul proceeds from the hypotheses [ἐξ ὑποθέσεως] to an unhypothesized principle [ἐπ' ἀρχὴν ἀνυπόθετον] and does not use the images employed by the former section but conducts its search with forms and through forms. (510b4–9)

The first section, later identified as *dianoia,* appears to describe the hypothetical method as characterized in the previous two chapters. This method begins with hypotheses and remains confined to them; rather than in some way proceeding beyond the hypotheses, it simply works down from them to some conclusion. This is what was seen to take place in the discussion of virtue in the *Meno* and in the discussion of the soul's immortality in the *Phaedo*. The role assigned to images in the method is also relevant to these discussions. In the *Meno* Socrates had to employ the lack of teachers as a sign that virtue cannot be taught, and in the *Phaedo* he had to draw an analogy between the soul and things such as fire and snow. The first section therefore tells us nothing new, though one question about it has generated a great deal of controversy:[19] if the objects of the section below it are sensible things and the objects of the section above it are the intelligible forms, then the objects of the present section must be something *in between* sensible objects and the forms. But what could this be? Given the original/image relation that governs the Divided Line, the objects of *dianoia* must be the originals of which sensible objects are the images, while at the same time being themselves images of the forms. What objects, then, would meet these qualifications? If we anticipate what Socrates will proceed to say about mathematics and if we relate what is said here to the hypothetical method as practiced in other dialogues, the answer is not hard to find. The objects of *dianoia* are propositions that mirror the forms in abstract (i.e., not fully explicated or understood) concepts, which, as such, acquire content only when illustrated by sensible objects. Thus, while the specific objects of this section are propositions, these propositions point in the two opposed directions just mentioned: while mirroring in a one-sided, deficient way the forms to which their terms refer, they state universal (though abstract) truths that are mirrored by a plurality of sensible objects. But this is simply a description of the defect and virtue of the propositions to which we have seen the hypothetical method confined in the *Meno* and the *Phaedo*. This section of the Line therefore summarizes what these other dialogues have already shown us.

The second section, however (later identified as *noēsis*), is another matter. Here the soul is said to proceed beyond the hypotheses to a first principle that is itself not a hypothesis. Since the Divided Line is meant to be a further elucidation of the Sun analogy, we must suppose that this "unhypothesized" principle is the form of the good.[20] It is inconceivable that, while meant to serve this explanatory purpose, the Divided Line should not refer to the good at all, but should instead introduce an altogether different principle as the highest object of knowledge. Therefore, what Socrates attempts to explain in the Divided Line is precisely what remains unexplained in the Sun analogy, that is, how we can come to know the good. This knowledge requires an ascent beyond hypotheses. But what is the nature of this ascent? Elsewhere Socrates identifies the method of the ascent with *dialectic* (511b4). Yet this identification does not explain how dialectic can "ascend" to a knowledge of the good.

R. Robinson (1953) reviews the major interpretations of the ascent that had been offered up to that time and then offers his own. The theories he considers, along with his main criticisms and mine, are as follows:

1. *The Synthesis Theory*. The ascent involves proceeding up to a highest genus that encompasses everything else as its species. Here the ascent and the descent (to be discussed below) parallel "collection" and "division" in the later dialogues. Robinson, however, objects: (1) "it seems rather doubtful whether Plato would think of the Idea of the Good as being the *summum genus*, which he would have to do on this intrepretation" (163); (2) it is hard to see what the talk of "hypotheses" and the "unhypothesized" could possibly mean in this case (163); and (3) the parallel does not really hold, that is, the Divided Line makes

IDEALIZATION AND THE DESTRUCTION OF HYPOTHESES IN THE *REPUBLIC*

no mention of synthesis or division or definition (163–65). To the first objection can be added the arguments presented above against seeing the good as any kind of genus.

2. *The Analysis Theory.* Analysis shows the hypotheses to entail the good, which is already recognized to be true (ascent), and then synthesis deduces the hypotheses from the good (descent). Robinson's objection is that "the Idea of the Good is not antecedently known to be true; it is just the task of the upward path to lead us to our first knowledge of the Good" (166). Thus this description of the ascent does not seem compatible with Socrates' characterization of it as a method of *discovery*. However, there is a greater problem: in order for the first principle to be strictly entailed by the hypotheses that are in turn deduced from it, it and the hypotheses would need to be *convertible propositions* (as is the case in geometrical analysis).[21] Yet no one has succeeded in showing how the hypotheses of mathematics could possibly be convertible with some statement about the good. Finally, this interpretation collapses the distinction between the methods of mathematics and dialectic, and thus between *dianoia* and *noēsis,* in blatant contradiction to the text (more on this below).

3. *Axiomatization Theory.* The ascent is the search for a system in which everything is deduced from the fewest number of principles possible. Robinson is sympathetic with this view, but objects that Plato, due to his lack of "logical rigor," believes that one principle (rather than several axioms) is sufficient for his system (168), and that Plato did not want simply a self-contained system, but rather a guarantee of certainty (169). Because I will argue below that the ascent has nothing to do with "certainty," I have to reject the second of Robinson's objections. However, Robinson's claim that there is only one principle is correct, and nobody has shown, or ever will show, how Plato could have strictly deduced all of our knowledge from some statement about the good (and as I argue below, this was not Plato's aim). Another problem with the "axiomatization" view is that it does not really describe an "ascent" but only a "descent," that is, how we might go about systematizing our knowledge *after* we have attained knowledge of the first principle. This part of the theory I refute below by showing that the "descent" is not any process of "deduction."

4. Phaedo *Theory.*[22] The ascent involves the hypothetical method as Robinson sees it described in the *Phaedo,* that is, the examination of consequences through elenchus and the taking of hypotheses back to yet higher hypotheses. The argument is essentially as follows: if the *Phaedo* describes the means for arriving at better and better hypotheses, why not see these same means as involved in the ascent to the best possible hypothesis, that is, the first principle described in the Divided Line?

Robinson accepts this theory but does not consider it sufficient to explain the certainty at which, in his view, the ascent aims (172). Therefore he introduces the following, fifth theory.

5. *The Intuition Theory.* "I believe that Plato in the *Republic* claims the possibility of certainty for the dialectician without having any more method at his command than the *Phaedo* gave him. He merely claims that the man who completely and conscientiously practises this hypothetical and elenctic procedure will, or may, one day find himself in the possession of an unhypothetical certainty" (172–73). The certainty that a repeatedly examined hypothesis is true is provided, not by a new method, but by some kind of supervening "intuition."[23] This intuition is the ascent described in the Line.

A telling feature of Robinson's account,[24] and one of the serious objections against it, is that it collapses the *methodological* distinction between the two upper sections of the Line (as the "Analysis Theory" was seen to do). As Robinson himself appears to recognize, he leaves no essential distinction between the *method* of *dianoia* and the *method* of *noēsis:* the latter is only graced with a sudden "intuition of certainty" *not* arrived at through any method.[25] The method must simply await this intuition and accept it without question or argument when it comes.[26]

Another problem is precisely the assumption that what the ascent aims at is *certainty*. There is no word for "certainty" in the text.[27] Only a prior commitment to Robinson's interpretation could require one to understand the word "unhypothesized" to mean "certain." Why then accept this interpretation? What reason is there for believing that Socrates' project, like the Cartesian one, is to eliminate all doubt?[28] Robinson's interpretation depends on his understanding of Socrates' criticism of what takes place in the other section of the Line in which the soul proceeds from hypotheses down to conclusions. What is wrong with this procedure, in Robinson's view, is that it leaves these hypotheses uncertain or doubtful. The goal in going beyond these hypotheses is therefore to arrive at the certainty which they themselves lack. Presumably, this is accomplished by arriving at a principle from which the hypotheses can be *deduced* and which thus provides *knowledge* that the hypotheses are true. The characterization of knowledge as "certainty" is thus connected with a deduction model of knowledge.

But is "certainty" really what Socrates finds lacking in the method that does not go beyond hypotheses? The example Socrates gives of such a method is mathematics. Students of geometry, Socrates tells us, begin by "hypothesizing" the odd and the even, the different figures, the three kinds of angles, and other such things (510c3–5). They then proceed as if they knew these things, making them hypotheses and giving no account of them either to themselves or to others, but taking them to be evident to all (c6–d1). These students of geometry also use and talk about sensible things, even though they are *thinking* about intelligible realities (510d5–511a1). There is thus a lack of correspondence between the objects of their thought and the objects which they actually address in their discourse. They are incapable of addressing the square as such and therefore must resort to speaking of sensible squares.

What, then, is wanting in the method just described? Is it certainty? Socrates complains that the students of geometry act as if they *know* their hypotheses when presumably in Socrates' view they don't. Robinson would clearly take this to mean that the students of geometry are not *certain* that their hypotheses are true.[29] There is a far-reaching assumption here, namely, that "knowledge" for Plato, as for Descartes, is always "certainty that such and such is the case." What has been said above already implies that the knowledge of the good cannot have this character. Previous chapters have also shown that Plato recognizes a model of knowledge very different from the Cartesian one (see discussions of the "knowledge of knowledge" in the *Charmides* and the *Euthydemus*). But is Robinson's interpretation nevertheless *necessary* (as he clearly thinks it is)? Can Socrates in saying that the students of geometry do not know their hypotheses mean anything other than that they are not certain of the truth of these hypotheses?

Socrates' clearest description of what the mathematicians lack is the following:

> Concerning the rest, which we say touch upon a part of being, namely, geometry and those other sciences following upon it, we see that, while they dream about being [ὀνειρώττουσι μὲν περὶ τὸ ὄν], it is impossible for them to have a waking vision of reality as long as they leave unmoved [ἀκινήτους] the hypotheses which they employ, unable to give an account of them [λόγον διδόναι]. For when the first principle is unknown and the conclusion as well as everything in between remains "a tissue of things not really known,"[30] how is it possible that such agreement should ever become knowledge [τίς μηχανὴ τὴν τοιαύτην ὁμολογίαν ποτὲ ἐπιστήμην γενέσθαι]? (533b6–c5)

A reading of this passage committed to the deduction interpretation would have it say that what geometers need to awaken from their dream-like state is a *proof* of their hypotheses. Yet the only thing in the text that might support this reading is the implied request that geometers give an account (*logon didonai*) of their hypotheses. But the translation of "logon didonai" here as "to give a proof" is unwarranted.[31] Frequently coupled with *logon dexasthai* (to *receive* a *logos*), "giving a *logos*" is part of the process of mutual *clarification and explanation* that constitutes a dialectical discussion. Thus in the *Protagoras*, knowing how to give and receive a *logos* [ἐπίστασθαι λόγον τε δοῦναι καὶ δέξασθαι] is identified with the ability to engage in dialectic [οἷός τ'εἶναι διαλέγεσθαι, 336b9–c1]. Dialectic is here contrasted with Protagoras's practice of giving long speeches with no concern for whether or not his listeners are following what he says. In the *Republic* itself, Socrates asks Glaucon: "Do you think that those who are not able to give and receive a *logos* would ever know any of those things which we say must be known?" (531e4–5). Here knowledge is associated with the *ability* to engage in that reciprocal interchange known as a dialectical discussion. Similarly, shortly after describing the dialectician as someone who is able to give a *logos* of the *ousia* of a thing (534b3–6), Socrates proceeds to characterize dialectic as that study which enables people to ask and answer questions in the most knowledgeable manner (534d8–10). Dialectic is here a practical know-how.[32] When this context is returned to the activity of giving a *logos*, the absurdity of identifying this activity with "proving" becomes evident. Participants in a dialectical discussion do not take turns giving deductive proofs: instead they exhibit their knowledge of the subject matter in the very way in which they participate in the discussion, that is, in the extent to which they are able to explain themselves in different ways to different people, are able to respond to specific questions and meet unanticipated objections, can revise their statements as the truth demands, and so on. For example, in the *Protagoras* Socrates exhibits a knowledge of the subject matter through his very ability to conduct a dialectical discussion, while Protagoras's inability to do the same exposes his sham wisdom for what it is: this contrast obtains even though Socrates does not, any more than Protagoras, conclude the discussion with a "definition" or a satisfactory "proof."

One thing that has led scholars to give the phrase *logon didonai* a much stronger sense than is warranted by the text is the mistaken view that "giving a *logos*" is for Plato *identical* with having knowledge, rather than being simply a way in which knowledge can be exhibited. They interpret *logon didonai* as meaning the possession of a proof or definition that in their view first guarantees and constitutes knowledge. Yet Plato *nowhere* writes that knowledge is the *result* of giving a *logos* or that one must ever in fact give a *logos* in order to have knowledge.[33] He writes only that if one has knowledge, one will be *able* to give a *logos*.

Once *logon didonai* is understood as a process of explanation and clarification within a dialectical discussion, we can see that the passage cited above criticizes only the mathematician's inability to participate successfully in a dialectical discussion,[34] where this participation requires an understanding of the subject matter that goes beyond any of the particular hypotheses they might formulate about it. Whatever knowledge mathematicians have is confined to their abstract statements, which they therefore can only assert without explaining. What they lack is the discernment or insight that would render these hypotheses intelligible and give them content. This interpretation fits the dream metaphor much better: what is seen in a dream has a shadowy existence lacking substance. This is exactly the kind of existence which a form has when made a mere hypothesis. Unaccompanied by real insight into the form's nature, the hypothesis presents us with only a shadowy outline (like Socrates' own "sketch" of the virtues). The hypothesis is therefore far removed from the flood of light that characterizes insight into the good. Socrates' point in the above passage is therefore that a system of such shadowy outlines cannot, despite its consistency, provide us with any real understanding of the truth. This understanding is not gained by simply adding another premise to the system. Instead, it is gained when "the texture of things unknown" is rendered transparent in its intelligibility; and this involves seeing *beyond* the system. Knowledge is here a matter of *depth*.

The comparison of the mathematician's awareness of being with a state of dreaming recalls the distinction made at the end of book 5 between *doxa* and *epistēmē* (475d–480a). There this distinction is described precisely as one between dreaming and waking (476c–d), thus further recalling the parallel drawn between dreaming and true belief in the *Meno* (85c). However, what has always posed a problem for attempts to understand the passage in the *Republic* and to reconcile it with the characterization of belief in the *Meno*[35] is Socrates' claim that *doxa* and *epistēmē* have different objects, that is, sensible and intelligible objects respectively.[36] If *epistēmē* is understood as "justified true belief" or belief that is "proven" or "certain," this claim is simply nonsense. Surely we can have the different cognitive states of "true belief" and "justified true belief" in relation to the same objects. I can have the true belief that it is raining outside (while I am sitting indoors and away from any window) and then come to *know* this same fact by obtaining evidence that justifies my belief (I walk outside). But to avoid making Socrates' claim thus blatantly false we need simply recognize that the *epistēmē* which he opposes to true belief is best translated as "understanding." While we can have justified true belief about sensible objects, it is hard to see what it would mean to *understand* sensible objects. What we *understand* are the forms common to a plurality of sensible objects. In the case of virtue, for example, the distinction between *doxa* and *epistēmē* can be made as follows: we can truly believe and even "know" (in the modern sense) that a particular action is virtuous, but what we *understand* (*epistasthai*) is the nature of virtue itself (the intelligible form).[37] The distinction here is between, on the one hand, the shadowy awareness of virtue (belief) that is entirely focused on its sensible instantiations and that often enables us to make correct judgments about these instantiations and, on the other, a fuller understanding of virtue capable of seeing beyond these instantiations. This interpretation provides a reason *why* belief must be restricted to sensible objects: the awareness of a form provided by belief is limited to how this form is reflected in its sensible instantiations (which in the *Republic* are seen as *imitating* the form) and is therefore dependent on these instantiations. The lovers of sights and sounds are not blind to beauty, but their awareness of it is limited to the beautiful objects that dazzle their senses: as in a dream, they are unable to distinguish the original from the likenesses, the reality from the appearances (476c). The mathematician's dreaming must be understood in a similar way;[38] what compels him to use sensible diagrams is not the lack of "justified true belief," but the lack of an ability to *understand*, in separation from their reflections in sensible objects, the natures of the forms with which he deals. This understanding, of course, is not something that can be "deduced."[39]

This interpretation also allows us to reconcile what is said in the *Republic* with what is said in the *Meno*. The supposed contradiction between the two accounts is often stated as follows: while the *Meno* assigns to *doxa* and *epistēmē* the same objects and therefore describes the former as capable of being transformed into the latter (through an *aitias logismos*), the *Republic* assigns to them completely different objects, with the result that *doxa* about an object could never through any means become *epistēmē* of the same object.[40] This characterization of the account in the *Republic*, however, is extraordinarily crude. Given Socrates' description of sensible objects as likenesses of which the forms are the originals,[41] and given his description of *doxa* as a dreamlike inability to distinguish the original from the likenesses (476c), is it not clear that in one sense *doxa* and *epistēmē do* have the same object? The latter has the form itself as its object, while the former has the likeness of this form as its object: it is thus true *both* that they have different objects (the form itself versus its sensible instantiations) *and* that they have the same object (the form, in one case understood in itself, in the other case intuited only confusedly and indistinctly in its likenesses).[42] There is in this case no difficulty in explaining the transformation of *doxa* into *epistēmē*: the former is already an awareness of the form, though restricted to the recognition of its instantiations, and can therefore gradually become more distinct and explicit ("awake") until it is able to distinguish the form from its instantiations and *understand* it in itself. This is the process found in the

Symposium when the lover is described as advancing from a recognition of beauty only in bodies to the vision of beauty in and by itself. It is also the process described in *Republic* 7 through the analogy of the Cave: the ascent out of the Cave and the gradual adjusting of the eyes to the different kinds of objects outside are at each stage a movement from reflections or shadows to the originals that cast them.

Of course, all of this tells us very little about *the exact way* in which *doxa* can be converted into *epistēmē:* this must await an account of the ascent. It is already clear, however, that this conversion does *not* take place through proving, justifying, or rendering certain our beliefs. This view makes nonsense of what is said in *Republic* 5. Indeed, the reason why this part of the dialogue has presented interpreters with such great difficulties is that they have assumed an understanding of *doxa* and *epistēmē* incompatible with what is said there. If *doxa* is belief *that* sensible objects are such and such while *epistēmē* is knowledge *that* a form is such and such, then the view of *Republic* 5 not only severs any connection between the two, in contradiction to what is said in the *Meno,* but also appears indefensible and incoherent.[43] I already argued in chapter 6, however, that *doxa* is not "belief that," but a form of awareness, and that *epistēmē* is not "knowledge that," but nonpropositional insight: their description in *Republic* 5 only confirms this.

To return to the hypotheses of the mathematicians, there is a difference between being certain of the truth of these hypotheses and *understanding* them. Indeed, certainty and understanding are apparently independent of one another: not only can one understand something about whose truth one is not certain, but one can also be certain about the truth of something one does not really understand. For example, I can be certain that "2 + 2 = 4" without really understanding what this statement means, since I may not know, among other things, whether it is synthetic or analytic. I can also be certain that "virtue is good" (i.e., I can see no way of doubting this without the greatest absurdity) without necessarily understanding what virtue itself is or how it is related to the good. I can even be certain, with Descartes, that "I think, therefore I am," while remaining very confused as to what it means to think, to exist, and to be an "I." But clearing up this confusion would be as desirable as, perhaps even more desirable than, the certainty Descartes so values. One might object that what is being opposed to certainty here is simply a matter of clarifying concepts and does not therefore deserve the name of "knowledge." Yet Plato would certainly not see only "concepts" here. Even once we are certain, that is, cannot doubt, that virtue is good, there still remains a great deal to be known for Plato, namely, what virtue and the good themselves in essence *are.*

Is it, then, more plausible that what is lacking in mathematics and other hypothetical inquiries is *understanding* of the hypotheses, rather than certainty?[44] The first indication that this is the better explanation is the description of the students of mathematics as postulating (ὑποθέμενοι, 510c3), not statements that could be true or false, but *things*.[45] the odd and the even; squares, circles, and other figures; different kinds of angles *and other things akin to these*. They, of course, have as their objects those propositions which they formulate, but what they are seen as postulating are not these propositions themselves, but rather the notions employed in them. Proponents of the "certainty" interpretation have much difficulty explaining the claim that mathematicians are not certain of the truth of the odd and the even which they postulate. On the other hand, this passage makes perfect sense on the interpretation suggested above: the mathematicians do not really understand the natures of the things they postulate in their statements.[46] They talk about the odd and the even as if it were clear to everyone what they mean. However, as Socrates' difficulties in the *Phaedo* concerning the nature of number show, these notions are by no means perspicuous. The same is true of the different figures: we know what it means to call a sensible thing "triangular," but to understand what is meant by a purely intelligible triangle and how such a thing is even possible is another matter. Therefore, when Socrates criticizes the mathematicians for failing to give *an account* of the numbers and figures they postulate, what he is criticizing is not their failure to *prove* these things, but their inability to *explain* them in the give and take of dialectical discussion.

The other important indication that this is the correct interpretation is the description of mathematicians as compelled to employ sensible images (figures drawn in sand, for example) in their studies. Proponents of the "certainty" interpretation again have much difficulty explaining what the mathematician's use of sensible images could possibly have to do with the lack of certainty in his hypotheses.[47] This difficulty disappears on the present interpretation since, as shown especially by the characterization of the *doxa/epistēmē* distinction in *Republic* 5, there is an obvious connection between the mathematician's failure to understand the intelligible forms which he postulates and his having to resort to sensible images of these forms. Listen carefully to what Socrates says: "they use sensible images and address *them*, though they are not *thinking* of them, but rather of those things [the intelligible forms] which they resemble." Why is there this lack of correspondence between discourse and thought? The answer must be that the mathematicians do not sufficiently understand the intelligible forms they are thinking of to be able to deal with them and address them directly. Though they know that the triangle drawn in the sand before them is not what they really have in mind, this is the only kind of triangle which they really understand. The idea of a triangle remains empty for them unless it is given some sensible content. This means, of course, that they are incapable of giving the idea a purely intelligible content. Thus the necessity of resorting to sensible images is simply the flip side of their inability to explain and understand the things they postulate for what they *are*.

These observations should suffice to lay to rest the specter of Cartesian certainty that continues to haunt interpretations of the Divided Line. Not only is there no support for the view that what the hypothetical method lacks, and the ascent to a first principle achieves, is certainty, but another interpretation is available that makes much better sense of the text. In further articulating this interpretation, we must turn to two other theories of the Divided Line that also reject Robinson's epistemological assumptions.

6. *The Coherence Theory*. This theory has been defended specifically as an interpretation of the Divided Line by Fine (1990, 105–15),[48] Sayre (1995, 177–81), and Annas (1981),[49] and more generally as a characterization of Plato's epistemology by Nehamas (1989, 1992) and Burnyeat (1980, 1990, especially 216–17). What the ascent aims at, according to this view, is not some ultimate axiom from which the rest of our knowledge is to be deduced, but rather a greater degree of coherence and explanatory power in the knowledge we already have. The mathematicians at the level of *dianoia* have a coherent system of mutually explaining and supporting propositions; the ascent to a higher level of knowledge involves nothing more than expanding this system to include more explanatory accounts and further articulating the interrelations within the system. The movement is therefore not from uncertainty to certainty, but from lesser to greater coherence and thoroughness in the whole complex of explanatory accounts within a given field. The conception of knowledge this view attributes to Plato is described well by Fine (1990, 114) as one according to which "one knows more to the extent that one can explain more; knowledge requires, not a vision, and not some special sort of certainty or infallibility, but sufficiently rich, mutually supporting explanatory accounts. Knowledge, for Plato, does not proceed piecemeal; to know, one must master a whole field, by interrelating and explaining its diverse elements." In short, what is opposed here to Robinson's deductive model of knowledge is an "interrelational model of *epistēmē*."[50] There are some differences among the proponents of this theory. For example, whereas it leads Nehamas and Burnyeat to translate *epistēmē* as "understanding," Fine rejects this translation because she sees explanation as closely related to deduction and justification (1990, 107; 1992, 218–19 n19). However,

all of them reject Robinson's "foundationalist" account of knowledge, and most of them (the only exception being Sayre)[51] reject any identification of *epistēmē* with nonpropositional knowledge or "acquaintance." Even the "understanding" characterized by Nehamas and Burnyeat is achieved through the systematic completeness and interconnectedness of the propositions one knows.[52]

Although this theory avoids Robinson's deductive model of knowledge and places the emphasis, as I have above, on understanding or explanation, it is vulnerable to a number of serious objections. (1) One objection made against Robinson's theory, namely, that it collapses the distinction between *dianoia* and *noēsis,* is even more devastating for the present theory. This theory leaves no essential difference between the two top sections of the Divided Line, but *only one of degree:* lesser versus greater coherence.[53] There is not even a supervening intuition here, as there is in Robinson's theory, to help distinguish *noēsis* from *dianoia.* But how is the view that there is only a difference of degree here compatible with the sharp distinction Socrates makes between these two sections of the Line and the importance he gives it? How is it compatible with his making the distinction at all? Someone who simply does very well what the mathematician already does cannot be said to have a completely different kind of knowledge and to merit a completely different name (that of "dialectician"). In short, this theory eliminates any knowledge distinct in kind from *dianoia* and only allows for greater or lesser degrees of *dianoia* itself. (2) How are we on this theory to explain Socrates' claim that *dianoia* must refer to and employ sensible objects in a way that *noēsis* does not? (3) Like Robinson's, this theory finds no support in the text, but appears instead to derive its inspiration from a current trend in contemporary philosophy.[54] Nowhere does Socrates say that *epistēmē* consists of mutually explaining and supporting propositions. Instead, in the only passage in which he seems to speak of coherence among our propositions, *he denies that such coherence could ever provide knowledge.* This is the passage at 533b6–c5 discussed above. There agreement (*homologia*) is said to provide us with nothing but a "tissue of things not really known." One could of course try to make a distinction for Plato between "agreement' and "coherence," but I see no way of doing so without begging the question (and what other Greek word could Plato use for "coherence"?)[55] (4) This passage describes the major limitation that the hypothetical method was shown to have in the *Meno* and the *Phaedo,* and the characterization of knowledge behind the Coherence Theory was already shown in chapter 6 to suffer from this same limitation. Two objections against this theory that will be defended below are (5) that it makes no sense of the description of the ascent as "destroying the hypotheses" and (6) that it does not explain the descent. In the end, this theory will be shown to be untenable, if it has not been already.

7. *The Abstraction Theory.*[56] This theory, advanced by, among others, those who attribute to Plato "unwritten teachings," maintains that because the good is presupposed by, and in some sense "contained in," the hypotheses, the ascent involves simply *abstracting* the good from these hypotheses. The way in which the good is supposed to be "contained" in the hypotheses is as an *element* and/or *genus*. This is explained by an identification of the good with unity (the One). A definition of triangle (and this theory normally takes the hypotheses to be *definitions*) will implicitly contain and presuppose the good = one as an element and/or genus of triangle. The ascent, therefore, involves abstracting a definition of the good = one from these other defintions which presuppose it. This theory might seem supported by Socrates' description of the dialectician as "separating off" (ἀφελών) the good from everthing else (534b9–c1).[57] It might also appear to offer a distinctive characterization of the ascent that, unlike Robinson's Intuition Theory and the Coherence Theory, can keep distinct the top two sections of the Line. When examined more closely, however, this theory reveals itself to be implausible. Its proponents must assume that the good is *both* a genus *and* an element in order for the ascent to work:[58] this contradictory characterization of the good is hardly a recommendation. Furthermore, what is called "abstraction" here thus becomes really two methods: *analysis*, when the first principle is understood as an *element*, and *collection*, when it is understood as a *genus*. Not only is the interpretation thereby threatened with incoherence, but it also becomes vulnerable to the objections Robinson made against the Analysis and Synthesis Theories individually. Most important, the Abstraction Theory, like the Analysis Theory, does not do justice to the fact that the ascent is supposed to provide us with a knowledge of the first principle that we did not already have; instead, it appears to make the ascent *assume* knowledge of the first principle. Furthermore, to the extent that the abstraction involves analysis, it is only an extension of what is already done in mathematics and therefore does not in the end enable us to distinguish clearly between *dianoia* and *noēsis*.[59]

Another objection is that this interpretation assumes knowledge of the first principle to be propositional or, more specifically, knowledge of a *definition* of the good.[60] This assumption, however, is common to all of the theories discussed above and is widely held (the exception again being Sayre).[61] It is therefore one that should now be critically examined.

It first needs to be noted that this assumption is not supported by any textual evidence.[62] The only approximations to such evidence are the claims that the dialectician is able to give a *logos* of the *ousia* of a thing (534b3–4) and that he can "separate" the good from all else by distinguishing it in discourse (διορίσασθαι τῷ λόγῳ, 534b8–c1).[63] However, as was shown above, the former claim does not require the interpretation that the dialectician's knowledge consists in knowing a *definition* of a thing's essence. The latter claim as well will be shown below to be perfectly compatible with the view that the dialectician's knowledge of the good is nonpropositional. In addition to the lack of persuasive textual evidence, there appears to be no satisfactory explanation of what exactly propositional knowledge of the good would involve. Would it be simply a matter of knowing that "the good exists"? This statement appears too empty to do the kind of work that Robinson and others want the first principle to do. Is the propositional content of this knowledge therefore a definition? According to the interpretation of the Sun analogy defended above, the good cannot be a genus or class concept, that is, a set of properties shared by those things that fall under it. How, then, could it be defined? If, on the other hand, it is the ultimate "element" of all things, as the "abstractionists" believe, then it is absolutely simple and therefore indefinable.[64] Is the good, then, to be defined in terms of its effects? But Socrates has already told us its effects without thereby suggesting that he has provided us with knowledge of it. A view that would avoid these objections is that knowledge of the good is to be identified not with knowledge of the definition of some entity, but rather with knowledge of the whole set of interrelated propositions within a teleological system. In this case knowledge of the good would still be propositional. But is this identification justified? Or is it not the case, as the text appears to suggest, that knowledge of any "teleological structure" within which these propositions could be interrelated depends on a prior and distinct knowledge of what the good itself is? In other words, this interpretation appears to identify knowing the good with knowing propositions about what things are good and how they are good. The text (especially 505a–506a), however, does not support such an identification but suggests instead that the latter kind of knowledge depends on the former and is distinct from it. Furthermore, this interpretation depends on the *Coherence Theory* and therefore is subject to the objections presented above.

Finally, if previous chapters have succeeded in showing that knowledge of virtue is nonpropositional, we would expect knowledge of the good to be itself nonpropositional, especially if, as suggested above, it shares the "reflexive" character of the former. The good is not known as an object completely external to knowledge, but rather as the *cause* of all knowledge. More specifically, knowledge of the good is that *ability* to *idealize* that lies at the basis of all knowledge. Such idealization appears to have nothing to do with knowing propositions. Given what Socrates says about the good in the Sun analogy, clearly the best way to know it would not be to defend propositions about it, but to see it reflected in the activity of knowing. In other words, the idealization central to this activity, as presupposing the "light" of the good, would best reveal the good. Propositions are well suited to expressing knowledge of objects or facts; they can no more express knowledge of the good, however, than they can express knowledge-how or self-knowledge, both of which are involved in knowing the good.[65]

With the results gained from the above criticism of different theories of the ascent, it is now possible to sketch an alternative interpretation, one consistent with what was learned from the Sun analogy. The question that analogy provoked was, How does our knowledge of a triangle depend on the good? The suggested answer was that this knowledge depends on our ability to idealize the triangle, that is, to distinguish what it is in essence from its imperfect instantiations in both sense perception and the imagination. This idealization is itself impossible, however, without an understanding of the good. Therefore, knowledge of the true nature of the triangle or of any other form is inseparable from knowledge of the good. The good, however, is not known simply as an object besides the triangle, but rather as the very cause of our knowing the triangle. Now it is possible to see why the mathematician fails to understand those numbers and figures which he postulates. When a mathematician defines the properties of a triangle, he is not thinking of any specific triangle he has seen or imagined, but rather of what a triangle ideally is, what it *should be*. Because, however, he does not inquire into the nature of the good presupposed in this "should," he cannot sufficiently idealize the triangle and therefore cannot sufficiently know it. The fact that he is compelled to address and use sensible images shows the mathematician's failure at idealization, which in turn shows his failure to understand the good. When, therefore, Socrates says that the mathematician fails to rise above his hypotheses, what he means is that he lacks that insight into the nature of the good which would enable him to understand his objects no longer as *hypotheses*, but as what they in essence *are*. Here, as in the *Meno* and the *Phaedo*, to make something a "hypothesis" does not mean to render it doubtful or in need of proof but to present it only as it is *qualified* and thus to conceal and impede access to what it in essence is. The mathematician can talk very learnedly about those things which he hypothesizes; the fact, however, that these things must be illustrated with sensible objects shows that in these hypotheses they are known only as what they are like (*poion*) and not as what they are (*ti*). The "ascent" beyond hypotheses, then, is the attainment of that insight into the good that makes possible the kind of idealization needed in order for the odd and the even, the square and the circle, to be known as more than "hypotheses."

But it must not be forgotten that mathematics is only an example;[66] the above applies to any hypothetical inquiry, that is, any inquiry that hypothesizes certain forms or natures in order to arrive at specific conclusions about these natures (this is, of course, the kind of inquiry carried out in the *Meno* and the *Phaedo*).[67] If we were to ask what is needed to make the inquiry of the *Republic* itself more than "hypothetical," the answer would be the same: the attainment of that insight into the good that makes possible the kind of idealization needed in order for justice, courage, and temperance to be known as more than "hypotheses" (and thus as more than how they are qualified).

The assumption of this last claim needs some explanation and justification: Is it true that the *Republic* itself is only a hypothetical inquiry, like those of the *Meno* and the *Phaedo,* and therefore suffers from the same defects Socrates diagnoses in mathematics? Is the *Republic* itself incapable of providing that knowledge of the good that is the goal of dialectic? The aim of the following observations is to show that this is indeed the case and also in the process to illuminate further the meaning and significance of Socrates' distinction between the two top portions of the Line.

In the *Meno* the distinction between genuine dialectic and the hypothetical method is spelled out in terms of a distinction between what a thing *is* (*ti esti*) and what *kind* of a thing it is or how it is *qualified* (*poion ti*). At the end of book 1 of the *Republic,* Socrates reiterates this distinction. How, he asks, can we possibly know something *about* justice (περὶ αὐτοῦ, that is, whether it is knowledge or a virtue or good)[68] if we do not first know what it *is* (ὅ τί ποτ' ἐστίν)? Our interpretation of both the *Phaedo* and the present dialogue has indicated what role the good might play in this distinction: to know what virtue *itself is,* as opposed to knowing simply its properties, is to know what it is *best* for virtue to be. But on which side of this distinction should we situate the inquiry subsequent to book 1? Does the definition of justice finally provided in book 4 succeed in telling us what justice *is,* or can it still only tell us how justice is *qualified?* If the latter is the case, then it can be concluded that the inquiry carried out in the *Republic* is "hypothetical" in the sense which this word has been given in both this and previous chapters.[69]

The following points show that the definitions of justice and the other virtues provided in the *Republic* indeed tell us only how they are *qualified* and are therefore to be understood as "hypothetical" results.

1. What Socrates and his interlocutors seek to know in the *Republic* is how justice occurs in states and, by analogy, how it occurs in the human soul. This, however, seems quite different from knowing *what justice itself*

IDEALIZATION AND THE DESTRUCTION OF HYPOTHESES IN THE *REPUBLIC*

is in the sense of Socrates' What-is-x? question.[70] Indeed, the way in which Socrates sets up the inquiry here differs greatly from his procedure in the aporetic dialogues: he tells his interlocutors that they must first seek to know what kind of a thing justice is in cities (ἐν ταῖς πόλεσι ζητήσωμεν ποῖόν τί ἐστιν, 368e8–369a1) in order then to examine its likeness (ὁμοιότητα, a2) in the individual. The limitations and qualifications introduced here would not be tolerated in the aporetic dialogues. In the *Laches* Socrates does not simply want to know how courage occurs in the individual or how it occurs in cities: he wants to know what courage *is*, without qualification. Whether or not there is any point in asking such an unconditional question (I have argued that there is), this is clearly not the kind of question which Socrates undertakes to answer in the *Republic*. Instead, the language used in the passage cited above suggests that the question Socrates is addressing is the kind characteristic of the hypothetical method: "What kind of a thing is x?" or "What can be said *about* x?" or "What are some of the properties of x?" And it must be kept in mind that this question is itself subordinated to the guiding question of the *Republic:* is the just life the best life?

2. Socrates does not hide the limitations of the definitions he offers. One limitation is to be understood in terms of Socrates' distinction between philosophical virtue and "civic virtue," or the virtue of the ordinary citizen.[71] In one passage Socrates describes the philosopher as stamping onto human nature all the civic virtues (ξυμπάσης τῆς δημοτικῆς ἀρετῆς), using as his model the eternal ideas of which presumably only he has knowledge (500d). In another passage from the concluding myth, we have the description of a man who, having ascended to heaven after leading a virtuous life on earth, unthinkingly chooses as his next lot the life of a tyrant. After perceiving more clearly how horrible a life this will be, his despair is immeasurable. The fatal error is explained by the observation that this man was virtuous according to habit, not according to philosophy (619c–d). Given this distinction, do Socrates' definitions succeed in defining distinctly "philosophical" virtue, thereby providing us with philosophical knowledge of virtue? Or do they define only what Socrates would call "civic" virtue? We do not have to guess at the answer. When Glaucon agrees to accept Socrates' definition of courage, Socrates replies: "Do so and you will be right in accepting it, with the reservation [γε] that it is the courage of a citizen [πολιτικήν] [which is being defined]. Some other time, if you wish, we will have a more proper discussion about courage [ἔτι κάλλιον δίιμεν]" (430c3–5). Socrates does not repeat this reservation when he defines the other virtues, but I see no reason why it would not apply to these other definitions as well: Socrates gives us no indication that they are supposed to be markedly superior to

the definition of courage. Indeed, his definition of justice itself is hardly meant to inspire great confidence: "This doing one's own work, then, *when it occurs in a certain way,* is *probably* [κινδυνεύει] justice" (433b3–4).[72] The conclusion seems inevitable, therefore, that Socrates does not see these definitions as providing what he would call a distinctly philosophical understanding of virtue.

3. In book 6 Socrates tells us that his account of the virtues in book 4 is only a sketch or outline (ὑπογραφή, 504d6). The context shows that what is needed to "fill in" this sketch is a knowledge of the good. One can assume that this knowledge is also what is needed to turn civic virtue into philosophical virtue. The absence of a knowledge of the good in Socrates' account of the virtues is sufficient cause to see this account as hypothetical. Socrates' definitions tell us what the different virtues are *like,* they provide a *sketch* or *description* of these virtues, but they do not tell us what each virtue in essence *is:* this is something that could be known only through a knowledge of the good.[73]

4. The knowledge of the good that is missing from the account of the virtues in book 4 is not provided by the middle books of the *Republic.* Though the ascent to such knowledge is described by Socrates via a series of similes, the discussion itself clearly does not make this ascent.[74] The middle books serve the purpose of showing us the limitations of the inquiry carried out in the *Republic* and thus the need for such an ascent, but they remain no more than signposts pointing in the right direction. These books are indeed a *détour essentiel,*[75] but they do not themselves provide the knowledge required to make the *Republic* more than an elaborate "sketch."

The above points suggest, then, that Socrates in the *Republic* does not tell us what virtue *is,* but only how it is *qualified.* Indeed, any definition, if incapable of expressing that good which is the source of all our knowledge (as argued above), must be equally incapable of expressing the essence of virtue. Socrates' inquiry in this dialogue is therefore as "hypothetical" as mathematics, with the important difference that Socrates is not blind to the limitations of this method.[76] The Divided Line shows us what is needed to "fill in" Socrates' "sketch" of the virtues: not more propositions, but rather that understanding of the nature of the good acquired through the "ascent" beyond propositional hypotheses, an understanding that is itself nonpropositional.

On the suggested interpretation, the first principle or the good is "unhypothesized" in the sense that, rather than being postulated as a starting point of the inquiry, it is *already there before the inquiry* as the ground of its possibility, even if only as an "inspiration." The insight gained into this principle is insight gained in the "circle" that has been seen to characterize dialectic as practiced in dialogues such as the *Laches* and the *Charmides*. Dialectic, as defined in previous chapters, is the method of the ascent.

A major strength of this interpretation is that it does not require reading into the text "proofs," "absolutely certain propositions," or "coherent systems." Before this interpretation can be complete, however, another passage remains to be considered in which Socrates describes not only an ascent *to* the first principle, but also a descent *from* it. An explanation of this passage will clarify the exact method of the upward path (i.e., how exactly dialectic rises above the hypotheses to attain insight into the good) as well as take into account the downward path. The passage is as follows:

> Understand that by the other section of the intelligible I mean that which reason itself [αὐτὸς ὁ λόγος] lays hold of through the power of dialectic [τῇ τοῦ διαλέγεσθαι δυνάμει],[77] making the hypotheses [ὑποθέσεις] not first principles but truly *hypotheses*, like footings and springboards, until, going as far as the unhypothesized in reaching the first principle of all, it lays hold of it, then turning back, by depending on those hypotheses that depend on the principle[78] [ἐχόμενος τῶν ἐκείνης (τῆς ἀρχῆς) ἐχομένων], comes to a conclusion, making no use whatsoever of any sensible object, but proceeding with forms, through forms, towards forms, and ending with forms. (511b3–c2)

Two new elements of the highest section of the Divided Line are introduced by this passage: the positive role that the hypotheses can play in the ascent to a first principle by being "footings or springboards" (ἐπιβάσεις τε καὶ ὁρμάς) and the need for a descent from the first principle back to the hypotheses. These two elements of Socrates' simile must now be discussed and brought into harmony with the interpretation presented above.

It is first necessary to examine the exact role that hypotheses play in the ascent to the first principle. Are hypotheses *as hypotheses* indispensable? This question is in fact two questions: Could we ever come to attain knowledge without using hypotheses? Could we ever reach a state in which hypotheses *as hypotheses* are no longer needed (i.e., have simply been *replaced* by knowledge)? The first question is to be answered negatively on almost any interpretation of the Line. Clearly we cannot simply leap toward knowledge; the mediation of hypotheses is required to lead us gradually there. To understand virtue or a triangle it is not sufficient merely to hypothesize them; however, *at least* such hypothesization is required if we are to address them at all. We must be capable of describing how virtue is qualified in propositions before we can make any attempt to transcend these propositions in an understanding of what virtue itself in essence is. There must be a "footing" from which the insight is gained, and this footing is the hypothesis.

Though hypotheses are the necessary starting point of any inquiry, there are two directions an inquiry can take. It can let be the hypotheses as parts of a self-contained system, concerning itself only with achieving consistency within this system: this is the "coherentist" hypothetical method. Or the inquiry can make these hypotheses open to that which transcends them by, as Socrates puts it elsewhere, *destroying* them (τὰς ὑποθέσεις ἀναιροῦσα, 533c8): this is dialectic. Those who defend an interpretation of the Line like Robinson's cannot help but be puzzled by Socrates' claim that dialectic *destroys* the hypotheses, since on their view what dialectic does is *prove* the hypotheses (i.e., deduce them from the first principle). This talk of destruction is even more incomprehensible on the "coherentist" interpretation: how could rendering hypotheses mutually supporting and systematically interconnected be equated with "destroying" them? Robinson's commonly accepted subterfuge is not convincing: he claims that what Socrates means in saying that the hypotheses are destroyed is simply that *their hypothetical character* is destroyed.[79] As Ferber (1989, 105) has rightly pointed out, the main problem with this view is that for the mathematicians the "hypotheses" do not have hypothetical character but are first principles. Their hypothetical character is first recognized, rather than destroyed, through the ascent.[80] Therefore, "destroying the hypotheses" on Robinson's interpretation could *at most* be identified with the *descent* from the first principle, but the passage at 533c unmistakably identifies it with the ascent. Robinson's interpretation is therefore untenable. In addition, it should be noted that Socrates, in speaking of either the ascent or descent, always refers to the "hypotheses" as ὑποθέσεις and never suggests that they are transformed into anything else.

Socrates' claim that dialectic destroys the hypotheses is comprehensible if, rather than introducing a process of deduction foreign to the text, we simply relate this claim to dialectic as Socrates actually practices it in dialogues such as the *Laches* and the *Charmides*.[81] There Socrates is presented with different hypotheses as to what courage is or what temperance is, and each hypothesis is in a limited sense *true*. However, instead of accepting these hypotheses for whatever truth they are capable of expressing, Socrates proceeds to refute and thereby *destroy* every one of them. But why does he do this? Is not such a procedure rather extreme? Can he not be content with whatever truth there is in the hypotheses and simply make the needed qualifications? Why is he not willing to accept anything less than the unqualified and the unconditional? The reading of the *Laches* and the *Charmides* in chapter 2 has shown that Socrates there has a double purpose: one is to show that none of the proposed definitions can be substituted for a genuine knowledge of virtue, and the other is to communicate this knowledge in the very process of refuting the definitions (since an implicit knowledge of virtue is presupposed by this process). This seems to be exactly what Socrates describes at 533c. The dialectician destroys the hypotheses, first to show that they cannot express the good that alone would make their objects more than hypotheses, and second to rise to a knowledge of the good through this very activity of inquiry that presupposes it. In the very process of destroying the hypotheses one gains insight into the truth that lies beyond the hypotheses:[82]

Thus in book 7 Socrates describes as follows what the dialectician must be capable of doing:

> Whoever is unable to distinguish the form of the good in discourse, separating it from all other things, and cannot proceed with unfailing reason through a battle of refutations, striving to refute in accordance with true being [κατ'οὐσίαν] and not mere seeming [κατὰ δόξαν]—such a person, you should say, knows neither the good itself nor any other good thing, but if he lays hold of some image of it, this contact [ἐφάπτεσθαι] will come about through belief [δόξῃ], not knowledge: dreaming and sleeping through this present life, before waking up here he will arrive in Hades to fall asleep forever. (534b8–d1)

Because this passage is a description of what is involved in attaining knowledge of the good, it can also be seen as a more detailed description of the ascent to an unhypothesized principle represented by the fourth section of the Divided Line.[83] The first clause, often quoted in isolation from the rest of the sentence (especially by proponents of the Abstraction Theory described above), should be seen as further elaborated and illustrated by what follows. The dialectician must be able to separate the form of the good from all those things that presuppose it as the principle of their existence and intelligibility. But how? By submitting hypotheses to untiring refutations that will not rest at how things appear (how they are *qualified*), but will seek to uncover what they in truth *are*. With respect to the imperfect instantiations addressed in hypotheses, the "idealization" described above is also a process of *negation*. As seen in the *Charmides* and the *Laches,* by refuting one-sided and ambiguous hypotheses the dialectican can gain insight into what the form in question really is. Since the form is what it is *best* for a thing to be, this process of refutation or "purification" will ultimately lead to an understanding of the *good* itself. Thus in the *Charmides,* by proceeding through the refutations and persisting in the inquiry with unfailing reason, Socrates *reveals* the good, separating it off from the appearances of the good in Charmides and Critias. Of course, the *Charmides* is only an example here, and philosophical inquiry is not limited to what occurs in that dialogue: however, we see there the general process of making the ascent beyond hypotheses which can express only how a thing appears or is qualified and cannot provide understanding of its true nature (its *good*). We can proceed beyond the hypotheses only by destroying them through refutation. Again it needs to be emphasized that what makes a hypothesis "destructible" is *not* its lack of certainty, but rather its ambiguity, that is, its inability to express what it intends and presupposes. Socrates, for example, might refute the mathematician's claim that a triangle has angles totaling 180 degrees, not because this claim is uncertain, but because the mathematician cannot really explain what triangle he has in mind. His attempt at explanation would necessarily resort to sensible images and thus be vulnerable to refutation. A particularly good example of this vulnerability is the objection that Protagoras is said to have made against the geometers: the circle in fact touches the line not at a point, but along a small length.[84] What could the geometers have said in reply?

The other question asked above remains to be answered: once the hypotheses are "destroyed," can we simply dispense with them? The interpretation I propose must answer negatively. Even once we have gained insight into a truth that transcends the hypotheses, we must nevertheless return to them in our discourse and in our further inquiry. We must still talk about how a thing is qualified, even though we now have insight into what the thing in essence is. We must avoid the mistake of thinking that the insight we have gained is capable of making the propositions with which we started any more than "hypotheses" (Robinson's mistake, not Socrates'). This insight into something propositions cannot express does not make them any more capable of expressing it. Our propositions will still express only how a given form is qualified and therefore will still be "hypotheses," but we ourselves will now understand more *by them* than we did before. In short, the understanding gained through the medium of hypotheses does not remove the limitations of this medium itself.[85]

This interpretation appears to suggest that the *descent* from the first principle is simply a *return* to the hypothetical method. In order, however, to see the extent to which this is or is not true, we must turn to the description of this "descent" at 511b3–c2. The Coherence Theory discussed above appears not to offer any clear account of the descent, which is not surprising, given its inability to explain a true *ascent* from which this descent would return. More important, it appears to rule out any need for a descent: if the ascent involves comprehensive mastery

IDEALIZATION AND THE DESTRUCTION OF HYPOTHESES IN THE *REPUBLIC*

of a certain subject matter, what would be left for the descent?[86] The Abstraction Theory characterizes the descent as (at least in part) a process of "division" (*diairesis*). This characterization suffers from the same problems that were seen to plague the theory as a whole. More specifically, it requires that the good be seen as a divisible genus or class, something that proponents of this theory do not succeed in making very meaningful or even comprehensible.[87] The clearest and most widely accepted interpretation of the descent, on the other hand, is succinctly stated by Robinson (1953, 164): "Plato surely conceives of the downward path as a proof, a deduction, a demonstration, in which conclusions are drawn from the anhypoteton as from an axiom."[88] According to this view, then, the hypotheses cease to be *hypotheses* (their "hypothetical character" is "destroyed") by becoming conclusions deduced from some axiom. Here again any distinction between the methods of mathematics and dialectic is collapsed: both descend from their principles through deduction, the only difference being that the conclusions of dialectic are certain because deduced from a certain principle, while both the principles and conclusions of mathematics are uncertain.[89] The deductive model has already been seriously brought into question. Here, however, it must be challenged specifically as an account of the descent.[90]

Again a central problem is that the text does not easily admit the interpretation that has been imposed on it. What has been called the "downward path" is described by Socrates in the following words: "πάλιν αὖ ἐχόμενος τῶν ἐκείνης [τῆς ἀρχῆς] ἐχομένων οὕτως ἐπὶ τελευτὴν καταβαίνῃ" (511b7–8). The common translation, and thus the one used to support the common view that what is described here is deduction, takes the word "ἐχόμενος" to have completely opposed meanings in its two occurrences. Witness Shorey's translation: "again *taking hold* of the first *dependencies* from it, so to proceed downward to the conclusion."[91] That a word should thus change meaning in so short a space is highly implausible. Yet even if the clause were translated in this implausible way, it still would not describe the soul as deducing the hypotheses from the first principle, but only as "taking hold" of them and *then* deducing *from them* the conclusion. This is a very odd way of saying that the conclusion is ultimately deduced from the first principle itself.

If, on the other hand, the word "ἐχόμενος" is more plausibly given the same meaning in *both* of its occurrences, then the deduction interpretation is truly in desparate straits. An example of such a translation is the following: "so again clinging to the things that cling to that [the first principle], it proceeds downward to a conclusion."[92] Why would Socrates describe the descent from the first principle to the hypotheses as a matter of *clinging to* the hypotheses, when what he means is that the hypotheses are *deduced* from the first principle? In conclusion, whether the passage is translated plausibly or implausibly, the verdict on the deduction interpretation is the same.[93]

On the other hand, the text makes perfect sense on the interpretation suggested above. Socrates' point is that even after we have "touched upon" the ultimate principle presupposed by the very intelligibility of the hypotheses, even after we have "destroyed" the hypotheses by showing their limitations with respect to this principle, *we still depend on the hypotheses in reaching positive conclusions.* Here, then, we have the contrast made throughout this and preceeding chapters between: dialectic as a search for the unconditional that must "destroy" all hypotheses and therefore cannot of itself yield propositional results, and the hypothetical method, which can yield propositional results only by depending on hypotheses that as such are recognized to be only limited and conditional expressions of the truth. This interpretation still allows a place for deduction in the descent, but with the qualification that this deduction takes place *only from the hypotheses* and *not from the first principle.* Yet this is exactly what the text appears to say and why it proves so resistant to attempts to make it mean deduction from the first principle. Depending on the hypotheses, we hang onto them in drawing a conclusion, while recognizing that they themselves depend on the unhypothesized principle for their meaning and intelligibility (*not* for their "certainty").

On this interpretation, the good remains outside of any deductive system of knowledge. This is precisely the explanation of the sharp distinction between *dianoia* and *noēsis* explicit in the text, but unexplained by either Robinson or the Coherence Theory. Essential to understanding the superiority of dialectic over mathematics is the recognition that the good, as the fundamental presupposition of any systematic body of knowledge, as the "limit of the intelligible" (532b2), cannot itself be made a part of any system. Instead of completing the system, dialectic undermines it, "destroys" it, in order to expose the principle of intelligibility presupposed and yet not expressed by it. Dialectic is therefore opposed to the dogmatism of mathematics and *dianoia*,[94] where dogmatism means the conviction that the truth can be captured in a proposition or system of propositions.[95]

But this gap between the hypothetical method and dialectic makes it seem that the latter has no effect on the former. Thus we return to the important question raised above. After the ascent the soul still depends on the hypotheses as hypotheses in order to reach a conclusion. Does this then mean that the downward path is simply a return to the hypothetical method? In other words, has nothing been gained in the ascent? As the present discussion has tried to show, what is gained in the

IDEALIZATION AND THE DESTRUCTION OF HYPOTHESES IN THE *REPUBLIC*

ascent is not a new premise from which the hypotheses are to be deduced, but rather insight into the natures which these hypotheses are trying to express and therefore *understanding* of these hypotheses.[96] Consequently, in the downward path we do return to the hypothetical method, but now with a better understanding of the hypotheses, which means, *with better recognition of their limitations*. This understanding does not make the method and the system it produces any more self-sufficient or any less hypothetical.[97] On the contrary, the limitations of the hypothetical method are recognized only after and not before the ascent. Though the hypothetical method is the same in both cases, the way in which it is understood is entirely different: before the ascent it is practiced dogmatically, while after it is recognized to be truly hypothetical.

We return from the ascent with another important gain: because of the insight we now have into those natures that give content to the hypotheses, our discourse is no longer forced to address sensible objects. We saw that the mathematician must resort to sensible objects only because he lacks understanding of the true nature of the things his hypotheses are about. Now Socrates describes the downward path as proceeding only with, through, and toward forms (511c1–2). This independence from sensible objects is an important characteristic of Socrates' dialectic. For example, while Laches can understand courage only as instantiated in the specific action of remaining at one's post, Socrates can take the discussion beyond any examples of courage: he can deal with the "form" itself in its relation to other forms (such as virtue, knowledge, and the good). The cited passage need not be understood, however, as contradicting Socrates' frequent use of sensible images in both this dialogue and others (what, after all, are the similes themselves?). As was argued in chapter 5, Socrates' use of images is peculiar in that it exposes their limitations and destroys the pretense to truth they have in poetry. What dialectic enables us to abandon is the *reliance on sensible images* for understanding. Whereas the mathematician is forced to use sensible objects as surrogates for the forms he does not understand, the dialectician can treat them as purely negative provocations to the pursuit of a truth they fail to realize. Socrates indeed uses sensible images, but he does so in a way that continually demonstrates their uselessness. This is because he has glimpsed, if only very confusedly, what is truly useful: the good.

We must in conclusion recall not only Socrates' professed ignorance of the good, but also what he asserts to be *our* ignorance of the good. Even in the best of circumstances, the good is seen *just barely* (μόγις, 517c1). This of course is not to say that such a vision is unavailable to us. We all "divine" the good in our daily actions and pursuits, and dialectic, by "destroying" the different claims that we make about the good, can transform this obscure "divination" into genuine philosophical insight.[98] However, to the extent that we remain dependent on hypotheses, the ascent must be conquered again and again. It is not a one-time occurrence, as it must be on the deduction interpretation. We must repeatedly seek to gain insight into that which transcends the hypotheses. Because this insight cannot be captured once and for all in propositions, we can never be done with it.[99]

The *Meno*, the *Phaedo*, and the *Republic* show what a wealth of results are attainable through the hypothetical method. In all three dialogues, however, it is subordinated to dialectic as characterized in previous chapters. This subordination does not "belittle" the method or deny the value of its results. On the contrary, a failure to recognize the method's second-best status can lead one to sacrifice its limited results to the demand for an unconditional truth that it cannot possibly provide: this is what Socrates calls "misology." Socrates is equally careful, however, to guard against the opposite danger: dogmatism. Clearly a definition of courage as "preserving one's belief about what is to be feared and what is not" can be helpful and informative: the danger comes in thinking that the possession of such a definition provides *knowledge* of what courage *is*. No propositions (even if systematically interconnected in a theory) can substitute for the kind of knowledge gained through the process of an inquiry such as that carried out in the *Laches*. To think that such a substitution is possible is to elevate the hypothetical method to a position where it becomes more harmful than helpful, more concealing than revealing. This is why the method's propositional results, though capable of reflecting from different angles the insight gained through dialectic, must never be allowed to take its place. To avoid being deceptive, a proposition must reveal its limitations or "cracks" through which we might then be able to see what it cannot directly express. The proposition can serve such a function of disclosing, however, not by being made part of a self-contained system (no matter how "certain" or "coherent"), but by being continually "destroyed" in the ongoing process of dialectic.

9

Conclusion: Dialectic in the *Seventh Letter*

Introduction

Previous chapters have attributed to dialectic the aim of overcoming the limitations of the means it employs. Chapter 3 located the specific weakness of words in their conventionality and consequent opaqueness to a thing's true nature. It also showed that these weaknesses in one sense can and in another sense cannot be overcome: they cannot be eliminated through the construction of an "ideal language," but the dialectician can use words in a way that reveals the objective natures presupposed by their actual function of referring. Chapter 4 showed that the ambiguity of propositions, the inability of arguments as such to guarantee perception of the truth, and the consequent vulnerability to refutation, are the flaws that enable eristics such as Euthydemus and Dionysodorus to be always victorious. Again Socrates did not presume to be capable of eliminating these flaws, but instead showed how ambiguity, refutation, and even logical fallacy can be made to serve the protreptic function of turning a person toward philosophy and virtue. Chapter 5 demonstrated the unsuitableness of a sensible image for expressing an intelligible truth. It also showed that this unsuitableness cannot be overcome by making the sensible image as like the original as possible (this is the deception practiced by the poets); what is needed instead is a recognition of the profound *dissimilarity* between image and original, a recognition by which the nature of the latter can be revealed. In all three cases, the dialectician exposes the weaknesses of names, propositions, and images in order then to overcome these limitations in the actual process of dialectic. The result is an insight that transcends the weaknesses of the means used to attain it, but that for this very reason cannot be expressed by these means.

The last three chapters, however, introduced a method that allows us to remain satisfied with the limitations exposed in our means of attaining knowledge if our goal is to arrive at specific, conditional answers to specific, conditional questions. These chapters also provided a comprehensive way of understanding these limitations, namely, the view that our discourse can succeed in expressing only how a thing is *qualified,* or what kind of a thing it is, and not what it in essence *is.* Once again, however, we saw that these limitations can be overcome in a process described in the *Republic* as "destroying the hypotheses."

These conclusions have been inferred from what we are shown in specific dialogues. But does Plato anywhere explicitly state the views that my interpretation of these dialogues has attributed to him? Does he anywhere assert that names, propositions, and images are necessarily defective? Does he anywhere maintain that their defects can be overcome only through a specific way of dealing with them? Does he anywhere assert that propositions *necessarily* express only how a thing is *qualified,* when what we seek to know is what the thing in essence *is?* If Plato is the author of the *Seventh Letter,* then the answer to each of these questions is affirmative.

The authenticity of the *Seventh Letter* has been frequently questioned and is still debated. Recent scholarship seems to have tipped the scale in favor of authenticity, but there are still many dissenters. It is not the primary purpose of the present chapter to enter this debate. I believe that my conclusions have received sufficient support in previous chapters and that they therefore in no way depend on the testimony of the *Seventh Letter.* My reason for concluding with an interpretation of this text is that it provides an insightful and correct interpretation of dialectic as described and practiced in the dialogues examined by this study. If the letter was written by a forger, it is my view that this forger had a better understanding of Plato than many other scholars, both ancient and contemporary. For the purposes of this concluding chapter, therefore, it is sufficient if the letter is nothing but an excellent secondary source that brings together in a succinct exposition those aspects of dialectic that have been brought out in previous chapters through detailed interpretations of specific dialogues.

This is not to say that the present chapter has no bearing on the question of authenticity. Since arguments based on historical content or on style have proven inconclusive,[1] probably the strongest possible argument against the letter's authenticity is that the content of the so-called "philosophical digression" contradicts Plato's understanding of philosophy in the dialogues.[2] In showing that there is no such contradiction, the present chapter will deprive the opponents of authenticity of one of their key arguments (I say "one," because other kinds of arguments are conceivable).[3] In this way, this chapter will add some support to the case in favor of the letter's authenticity.[4] It is unlikely, however, that anything even approaching certainty on this issue will ever be attained.[5]

There is also a problem of chronology here. The internal evidence shows that the letter, if genuine, was written very late in Plato's career and therefore, assuming the commonly accepted chronology, later than the dialogues discussed in the preceding chapters.[6] Here as elsewhere, however, I want to avoid presuppositions concerning Plato's "development." My analysis of the content of the letter will show that the process of acquiring knowledge that it describes is essentially the same as the dialectic practiced in the *Laches* and the *Charmides*. How this parallel will affect our overall account of Plato's development is a question beyond the scope of the present inquiry and unimportant for its purposes.

There is no need here to discuss in detail the autobiographical content of the letter. It is addressed to the companions of Dion, a close friend of Plato who was murdered for his efforts to establish a constitutional government in Sicily. The core of the letter consists of Plato's description of his three trips to Sicily and of the role he played in political events there. Having been told that the tyrant of Syracuse, Dionysius II, had an interest in philosophy, "Plato" felt that he might be able to make the tyrant change his ways and become something approximating a "philosopher-king." This hope was dashed. After "testing" Dionysius by telling him of the great toil and sacrifice demanded by the genuine pursuit of philosophy, "Plato" soon saw that Dionysius desired no more than a superficial acquaintance with philosophy that could be acquired effortlessly and bring him glory. "Plato" did no more than begin to describe the difficult path leading toward philosophy when Dionysius claimed to have already acquired a complete mastery of the subject through what he had heard from others. Dionysius thus proved to be the kind of "polymath" and *doxosophos* derided in the *Phaedrus* (275b): he believed that certain doctrines picked up here and there had brought him into the possession of true wisdom. Dionysius' presumption went so far that he wrote a treatise in which he expounded these borrowed opinions as if they were his own. This is the point at which the so-called "philosophical digression" can be said to begin. Because this is such an important text and because it will be the focus of the rest of the chapter, I translate it here in full.[7]

Translation, 341b–344d

[341b] I even hear that he later wrote about the things of which I had spoken to him, compiling all that he had heard in a treatise presented as his own work [συνθέντα ὡς αὑτοῦ τέχνην] and not acknowledging his source. But of this I have no direct knowledge. I do indeed know that others have written about these same subjects, but who they are they themselves do not know. This much at least I can say concerning all past [c] or future writers who claim to have knowledge about those things I seriously study,[8] either as having heard about them from myself or others or as having discovered them for themselves: in my opinion it is not possible for them to have any knowledge of these matters. Indeed, there neither is now nor ever will be a written work [σύγγραμμα] by me on [what I seriously study]. The reason is that this subject matter cannot at all be expressed in words as other studies can,[9] but instead, from living with the subject itself in frequent dialogue [ἐκ πολλῆς συνουσίας γιγνομένης περὶ τὸ πρᾶγμα αὐτὸ καὶ τοῦ συζῆν], suddenly [ἐξαίφνης], as [d] a light kindled from a leaping flame, [knowledge] comes to be in the soul where it presently nourishes itself [αὐτὸ ἑαυτὸ ἤδη τρέφει].

Yet this much I know: that if these things [could be] expressed in speech or writing, I would be the person best qualified to do so. Indeed, I would not be the one least harmed if they were written about badly. If it seemed to me possible to write or speak about these things adequately before the public, what more noble deed could I have done in my life than write about something that would be of such benefit to my fellow human beings, bringing to light the nature of things [τὴν φύσιν] [e] for all [to see]? But I do not think that any so-called "essay"[10] on these matters would prove beneficial to others, with perhaps the exception of a few who can discover these things for themselves with minimal guidance.[11] As for the others, however, it would wrongly fill some with an improper and ugly contempt and others with a lofty and empty hope, as if [342a] they had learned something high and mighty.

I have in mind yet more that I would like to say and perhaps what I am presently talking about will become clearer when these other things are said. For there is a true argument that contradicts the person who dares to write anything about these matters and that, though spoken by me many times before, must apparently be repeated now.

CONCLUSION: DIALECTIC IN THE *SEVENTH LETTER*

In relation to each being there are three things that are the necessary means of attaining knowledge, and this knowledge must itself be placed beside them as a fourth thing: the first is the name [ὄνομα], the second is the definition [λόγος], the third is the image [εἴδωλον], and the fourth is knowledge [ἐπιστήμη]. To these we should add as a fifth thing [b] the being that is known and that is truly being.[12] If you want to understand what I have said, consider this example and then think of all other things in the same way. There is something called a circle, and its name is precisely this which we have just uttered. The definition of it is a second thing consisting of both names and predicates.[13] "That which is everywhere equidistant from the extremities to the center" would be the definition of that thing which is called "round," "spherical" [c], and "circle." A third thing would be the circle that is drawn and erased, that is turned on a lathe and destroyed; none of this is suffered by the circle itself to which all the [three] things [I have mentioned] are related, but from all of which it is distinct. A fourth thing is knowledge [ἐπιστήμη], insight [νοῦς], and true belief [ἀληθὴς δόξα] concerning the [first three];[14] these are to be set down as one [class[15] in so far as all of them] exist neither in articulate voice [as do words and statements] nor in the shapes of physical objects [as do images], but rather in [our] souls, thus being distinct both from the circle itself that exists in reality[16] and [d] from the three things just mentioned. Of these things[17] insight [νοῦς] is the nearest to the fifth in similarity and kinship, while the others [i.e., true belief and the knowledge confined to the first three] are further removed from it.

The same is true of the following: the straight and the round, and color; the beautiful, the good, and the just; all bodies whether manmade or natural, such as fire, water, and other things of this kind; all living things; all dispositions in the soul and all actions and passions. For if with respect to these things [e] one does not in some way lay hold of the four, one will never fully partake[18] of knowledge of the fifth. Furthermore, the four make manifest no less how a thing is *qualified* [τὸ ποῖόν τι] [343a] than what it *is* [τὸ ὄν], due to the weakness of language [τὸ τῶν λόγων ἀσθενές]. For this reason, no one with insight would dare fix his thoughts in [language], especially if [this language is] unalterable, as is the case with written words.

But again it is necessary to understand [more fully] what has been said. Each of the circles that is either drawn or turned on a lathe is full of what is opposite to the fifth, since it everywhere touches upon a straight line. We say, however, that the circle itself has neither a large nor a small share of the opposite nature. We also say that the name we attribute to any one of these [sensible circles] [b] has no stability [βέβαιον], for nothing prevents things presently called "round" from being called "straight" and things called "straight" from being called "round": names will be no less stable for those who thus switch them around and use them in the opposite way. Since a proposition is made up of names and predicates, the same can be said of it: it has no sufficiently unshakable stability.

Many more reasons can be given to show how each of the four is unclear [ἀσαφές], but the greatest is the one we mentioned a little before: given that the being of an object and its quality are two different things and that [c] what the soul seeks to know is not the quality, but the being [δυοῖν ὄντοιν, τοῦ τε ὄντος καὶ τοῦ ποιοῦ τινός, οὐ τὸ ποιόν τι, τὸ δὲ τί ζητούσης εἰδέναι τῆς ψυχῆς], each of the four offers the soul, both in words and in deeds, what it does not seek, so that what is said or shown by each is easily refuted by the senses. As a result they fill practically everyone with perplexity [ἀπορία] and confusion.

In cases where we are not accustomed to search for the truth due to bad training and where therefore whatever image we are offered suffices, those of us who are questioned are not made ridiculous by [d] those of us who ask the questions and are capable [δυναμένων] of refuting and upsetting the four.[19] In cases, however, where we are required to reveal as our answer the fifth [i.e., the true being of a thing], any one of those who are skilled at confutation wins the argument and makes the person who was first to speak or write or answer appear to many of the listeners to know nothing about what he attempted to express in speech or writing. The listeners do not understand that it is not the soul of the speaker or writer that is being refuted [ἐλέγχεται], but the defective nature of each of the four [πεφυκυῖα φαύλως].

[e] Yet the process of dealing with all four, moving up and down to each one, barely gives birth to knowledge of the ideal nature [what a thing truly is] in someone with an ideal nature [εὖ πεφυκότος εὖ πεφυκότι].[20] If, however, a person's nature is defective, as for most people the state of the soul with regard to learning and so-called morals is naturally defective (though in some cases this happens through corruption), not even a Lynceus could make people in such a state see. In short, someone who has no affinity with the subject matter will not be made [to see] by memory

or an ability to learn, for the principle or source [of knowledge] is not to be found in alien dispositions [τὴν ἀρχὴν γὰρ ἐν ἀλλοτρίαις ἕξεσιν οὐκ ἐγγίγνεται]. Therefore, those who are not naturally inclined and akin to justice and other goods, but can quickly learn and retain lesser matters, as well as those who have such an affinity, but are forgetful and find difficulty in learning, will never know as much as is possible the truth of virtue [b] and vice.

For these two must be learned together and along with them the truth and falsehood concerning the whole of being, something that requires much toil and time, as I said at the beginning. Only barely [μόγις], when the [three], that is, names, propositions, as well as appearances and perceptions, are rubbed against each other [τριβόμενα πρὸς ἄλληλα], each of them being refuted through well-meaning [nonadversarial] refutations [ἐν εὐμενέσιν ἐλέγχοις ἐλεγχόμενα] in a process of questioning and answering without envy, will wisdom [φρόνησις] along with insight [νοῦς] commence to cast its light in an effort [c] at the very limits of human possibility. For this reason, every serious person will refrain from writing about the things that are to be taken seriously, [not wishing to] expose them to the envy and perplexity of men.

In conclusion, when one sees a written work on law by a lawgiver or on any other subject by someone else, one must recognize that this work is not what the writer takes seriously, if he is a serious person, but that the truly serious things are laid away in the most noble part of him. If, on the other hand, he takes seriously what he has expressed in writing, [d] then it is not the gods but mortals themselves who have destroyed his understanding.

Interpretation of the "Philosophical Digression"

The first sentence of this digression might give the impression that what "Plato" finds objectionable is simply Dionysius's presumption in presenting as his own the thoughts of others. However, what "Plato" proceeds to say (341b5–342a6) makes clear that the target of his criticism is *any* attempt to express the principles in writing. Thus he asserts categorically that *anyone* who writes about these principles has no knowledge of them. "Plato" himself, in fact, has never written about these matters and never will. But why not? The esotericists find the answer to this question in "Plato's" claim that such a written work would be of no benefit to the majority of people but would instead inspire them with either arrogant contempt or empty confidence.[21] This answer, however, seems insufficient because it does not explain *why* such a work would not be beneficial. Why would it fill people with only the presumption of wisdom, rather than the real thing? "Plato's" answer to this question is clear: true wisdom cannot be expressed in writing. But why, then, is *this* true? Because the subject of this wisdom simply *cannot be expressed in words*. Here the criticism ceases to be confined to writing and extends to all forms of verbal expression. The target therefore includes the spoken word; writing is only a special case (though it has its own peculiar defect, as will be seen below).[22]

But what does it mean to say that the things to be taken seriously cannot be expressed in words? Can we not talk about them at all? Can we not even refer to or name the first principles? That this is not the meaning is shown by "Plato's" anger at Dionysius precisely for writing about the first principles.[23] The point is instead that neither written nor spoken words can express the principles *as what they are*. What is inexpressible is therefore *knowledge* of the principles. There are many parallels in ordinary discourse to this use of the word "inexpressible." When we say, for example, that we cannot express or describe our love for someone dear to us, we do not mean that we cannot talk about this love; we could do so ad nauseam. We mean instead that none of our words can do justice to the meaning of the experience itself. To *understand* this love, one must experience it *for oneself*. We likewise claim to be unable to describe the beauty of Olympia or the sublimity of Delphi. Here again words are available, but they cannot express the true character of either place, which is known only to the person who has actually been there. In the case of "Plato's" principles, as in the case of these examples, *there is no contradiction between being able to talk and write about them and being unable to express their true natures in words*. "Plato" *could* write about the principles (and no one would be better qualified than he to do so),[24] but he realizes that he could not thereby communicate *knowledge* of these principles. Of what benefit, then, would such a written work be? In the case of those few capable of discovering the truth on their own, it might serve as a helpful reminder. In the case of the majority, however, it would provide only words without any real insight and thus only the pretense of wisdom without the reality. This is precisely the pretense "Plato" criticizes in Dionysius. If the truth concerning the principles were expressible in words, Dionysius would be truly wise in his extensive knowledge of philosophical doctrines; however, the truth is *not* thus expressible.

But does not the existence of Plato's own dialogues contradict the claim that he has never written about the first principles? Scholars have attempted to solve this problem in various ways,[25] but the above observations point toward a simple solution. Though the good is indeed

CONCLUSION: DIALECTIC IN THE *SEVENTH LETTER*

mentioned and discussed in the *Republic*, it hardly seems right to say that this dialogue attempts to express the nature of the good in writing. On the contrary, Socrates avoids any direct description of the good and instead tries to communicate it indirectly by means of the similes. Furthermore, to the extent that knowledge of the other forms depends on knowledge of the good, Plato has not attempted to express even their natures in writing.[26] Plato indeed writes *about* justice and courage, but without attempting to express in words the essence of each one.

Yet if knowledge of the principles cannot be expressed in words, then how *can* it be acquired? "Plato" describes the alternative in the following words: "but instead, from living with the subject itself in frequent dialogue, suddenly, as a light kindled from a leaping flame, [knowledge] comes to be in the soul where it presently nourishes itself" (341c6–d2). The use of a metaphor is significant. "Plato" has just asserted that the knowledge in question cannot be expressed in words; therefore, if he is to talk about it at all, he must do so indirectly through an image. This indirect description suggests three important characteristics of this knowledge: (1) it is the result of living with *the thing itself* in conversation with others, as opposed to a solitary and purely theoretical grasp of propositions or doctrines, (2) it is nonpropositional, and (3) it is capable of sustaining itself. The first characteristic presupposes both that we have access to the thing itself and that this access occurs through dialogue. The second characteristic simply points out that inexpressible knowledge must be the kind of insight that "Plato" describes in terms of light and illumination and that we would call "nonpropositional."[27] The third characteristic provides the sharpest contrast to the pseudo-wisdom that depends on the written word: knowledge in the soul that depends on nothing but itself.

At this point, however, the letter leaves open many questions. What is the nature of the "dialogue" of which "Plato" speaks, and how can this dialogue provide us with any access to the thing itself? In what sense can knowledge be said to "nourish" itself? Yet there is an even more important question. Even if we understand the claim that the principles cannot be expressed in words, *why* should we believe that this claim is true? This is precisely the question "Plato" proceeds to answer in the second part of the digression (342a7–343a4), which is introduced as an argument that will refute anyone who dares to write about the things he takes seriously, that is, anyone who dares to think that these things can be expressed in words.

"Plato" begins by distinguishing between five things that must be involved in any process of coming to know something: the three means by which knowledge is attained, that is, names (*onoma*), propositions/

definitions (*logos*), and images (*eidolon*), the knowledge itself (*epistēmē*), and the entity known.[28] "Plato" then illustrates this classification with the example of knowing a circle. The name in this case is the word "circle," the definition is "That which is everywhere equidistant from the extremities to the center," and the image is the circle we draw in the sand or shape out of a certain material. The object that is known, on the other hand, is distinct from this image: "Plato" describes it as that which "truly is being." In this case, then, the object would be "the circle which truly is," as opposed to this or that sensible circle. The object of knowledge is therefore what is elsewhere called the "form."[29] Finally, in addition to the name, definition, and image of the circle as well as the "circle itself," we have our actual knowledge of the circle. An ambiguity, however, arises with regard to this knowledge. The text suggests that it is knowledge of the name, definition, and image of the circle, while the text also suggests that it is knowledge of none of these, but rather of the "circle itself." That there should be this ambiguity is understandable. Because knowledge is the "link" between names, definitions, and images, on the one hand, and the thing itself, on the other, it will sometimes be associated more with the former and sometimes more with the latter. This ambiguity and tension become particularly noticeable in what immediately follows.

Having used the example of the circle to explain his distinction between the five elements involved in the process of attaining knowledge, "Plato" proceeds to claim that this distinction applies to all kinds of objects.[30] The evidence is that unless one somehow (ἀμῶς γέ πως) lays hold of four of the elements, one will never fully (τελέως) partake of knowledge of the fifth.[31] This means that unless one makes use of names, definitions, images, and knowledge itself, one will never know what a thing truly is (its "form"). Here the ambiguity of the word "knowledge" is most apparent. Knowledge is here simply one of the four means required for the attainment of knowledge of what a thing truly is (the "fifth"). Clearly, knowledge as a means and knowledge as the end toward which the means are directed cannot be the same thing.[32] What, then, is the difference? Before we can answer this question, we must consider more closely what characterizes as a whole the three elements with which knowledge is associated and from which it is also sharply distinguished.

This common trait is precisely what "Plato" proceeds to describe: all four elements (thus including "knowledge") make manifest no less how a thing is *qualified* (*to poion ti*) than what it *is* (*to on;* 342e2–343a1). The weakness of language is then cited as responsible for this defect. Chapters 6 and 8 have shown the importance in Plato's thought of the distinction between what a thing *is* and how it is *qualified*. There it was argued that this distinction explains the other one between the method of hypothesis and dialectic. Here, however, "Plato" asserts unambiguously what could only be inferred from the dialogues: it is not an accidental and remediable defect that definitions or propositions in general express more how a thing is *qualified* than what it *is;* this is instead a weakness inherent in the very nature of language (τὸ τῶν λόγων ἀσθενές).[33] It is true that "Plato" here claims only that the four elements express a thing's quality *no less than* its being but, as some commentators have noted[34] and as a later passage will confirm, this is an understatement. The weakness inherent in language is that it expresses *more* how a thing is qualified than what it is. The reference to *to on* is clearly a reference to the "fifth" element, that is, that which "truly is being." Therefore, the defect of all four elements is that, rather than express "the fifth," they express more the quality of a thing.

Why, however, should this weakness be called a weakness *of language* when it is supposed to be a defect of names, images, and knowledge as well as of propositions?[35] The answer seems to be that though *logos* is only one of the four elements in the process of attaining knowledge, it is the central one that defines the role of the rest. That names serve as means in the attainment of knowledge only within the context of a proposition is clear enough. Yet it is harder to see the connection between the defect of a proposition and the defect of an *image*. This difficulty disappears, however, if we recall the connection the *Republic* makes between a geometer's use of hypotheses and his use of images. The geometer must resort to sensible images only because his definitions are incapable of expressing the true natures of the intelligible objects with which he deals. That the definition of a circle needs to be supplemented by the image of a circle drawn in sand shows that the definition is itself incapable of expressing what the circle truly *is*. In the present case, what is responsible for our having to resort to an image in seeking to know the true being of a thing is the defect inherent in propositions.[36]

What, then, is to be said of the connection between knowledge (as the fourth element) and the weakness of language? The very question indicates that the knowledge characterized here as defective is *propositional*. It would make no sense to characterize the defect of knowledge as due to a weakness inherent in language, if the kind of knowledge meant were not confined to propositions and therefore also to names and images. It is on account of such a confinement that it suffers from the defect of these three. Yet, as has been seen, the other form of knowledge to which names, propositions, images, and this defective knowledge itself are all subordinated is quite different: as a flash of insight that nourishes itself in the soul, it seems to be nonpropositional, and as knowledge of what is "truly being" (the "fifth"), it can hardly be confined to images and names.

A distinction is emerging here between a defective propositional knowledge and the nondefective, nonpropositional knowledge to which it is subordinated as means to end.[37] Because knowledge is the link between names, propositions, and images, on the one hand, and the thing itself, on the other, it exists in this tension between being defined in terms of the first three and somehow transcending them in knowledge of the "fifth." Thus the ambiguity of the word "knowledge" in the letter can be clarified in terms of a distinction between propositional knowledge, which suffers from the weakness inherent in language, and nonpropositional knowledge, which somehow and to some degree escapes this weakness.[38]

Though this distinction is required by the text, it is important to recognize that there *is* a *tension* here. What allows "Plato" to use the same word for both types of knowledge is that they are in some sense a unity. As will be seen below, nonpropositional knowledge of the fifth can be attained only through the mediation of our defective propositional knowledge (the fourth), and even then *just barely* (μόγις). This is nothing new. Previous chapters have already shown that the nonpropositional knowledge which is the goal of dialectic cannot be attained apart from and outside of a dialectical process that is itself clearly confined to dealing with propositions. It is this tension at the very heart of philosophical knowledge, this constant struggle of philosophical discourse to overcome itself, that is the lifeblood of dialectic as practiced in the dialogues and that will turn out to be the most important message of this philosophical digression of the *Seventh Letter*.

As has been noted, the whole point of "Plato's" argument here is to defend the claim that knowledge of the first principles cannot be expressed in words. Therefore, he concludes this part of the digression by citing the weakness inherent in language as the reason why "no one with intelligence would dare to fix his thoughts in [language], especially if [this language is] unalterable as is the case with written words" (343a1–4). In this way "Plato" has fulfilled his promise to present an argument that will refute anyone who dares to write about those things which he takes seriously. Given the weakness inherent in the very nature of language, it would be sheer folly to attempt to express the truth of the first principles in words, especially written words. Spoken words can be explained, modified, or retracted, whereas none of this is possible with the words frozen in writing. Yet an attempt to confine "Plato's" critique to writing would blatantly contradict the text: it applies *especially, but not only,* to the written word.

This part of the digression clearly presents only a sketch or outline. In distinguishing between the five elements, "Plato" has not described the peculiar defect of each of the first four, nor has he really explained the

CONCLUSION: DIALECTIC IN THE *SEVENTH LETTER*

general defect stemming from the distinction between a thing's being and its quality. This is what he proceeds to do in the third part of the digression (343a4–343c5), which is therefore introduced with the words "it is necessary to understand [more fully] what has been said."

The peculiar defect of an image is that, though an image of a specific nature (the fifth), it is full of that which is opposite to this nature. For example, it is essential to the nature of a circle that no part of its circumference be a straight line. This is clearly not true of the image of a circle as drawn in the sand. While there is a perceptible difference between a drawn octagon and a drawn circle possessing the same area, there may be no perceptible difference between this circle and a chiliagon, even though their intelligible natures are entirely different. The circle as drawn or turned on a lathe must everywhere, as "Plato" says, touch upon a straight line: this, however, makes it the opposite of that of which it is supposed to be the image.

In characterizing the defect of images in this way, the *Seventh Letter* is only stating one of the aspects of Plato's theory and use of images in the dialogues. As chapter 5 showed, while the image is like the original, it is also radically *unlike* it. Two equal sticks, for example, will also be unequal; in imitating the nature of equality, they also instantiate its opposite. The point of the critique of the imitative artists in *Republic* 10 is that, in confining themselves to the reproduction of images thus defective, they are as far removed as possible from reality. Yet what is most objectionable is their belief that they can eliminate the defect by making the image as "realistic" and "perfect" as possible. Every image necessarily contains the opposite of that of which it is the image, and therefore every image is in essence a "contradiction." As a result, an image that conceals its inferiority to the original and thus its essential defect is precisely for this reason the most deceptive kind of image. This is why Plato directs his harshest criticism against the most skilled image-makers, that is, the great poets. The characterization of images found in the dialogues and discussed in chapter 5 is precisely the one stated here in the *Seventh Letter*.

Next to be considered is the defect peculiar to *names*. "Plato" identifies this defect with a lack of "stability" (*bebaion*). He explains by saying that nothing prevents things presently called "round" from being called "straight" and vice versa. If the names attributed to things were the opposite of the ones now customary, they would not for this reason be any less stable. Here we have one of the conclusions of the *Cratylus* as interpreted in chapter 3. In that dialogue, the attempt is made to discover a natural correspondence between a name as a physical thing (i.e., as a collection of syllables or sounds) and the nature to which it refers and thus to find in names the "stability" of which "Plato" speaks in the present letter. This attempt proves an absurd failure. In looking for the natures of things in words, Socrates finds only other words (etymology) equally in need of being shown to be "natural" and "stable." In the end, Socrates accepts the conventionality of names and asserts that reality must be known in some way other than simply *in names*. What the *Cratylus* thus shows to be absurd is the very idea of an "ideal language," that is, a language that would eliminate the instability that is a necessary defect of words. This idea is as absurd, and as dangerous, as that of a "perfect image." Just as the poet thinks that the image can replace the reality if only it is made sufficiently elaborate and vivid, so does the etymologist think that the word can replace the reality by being shown to contain other words. What is said in the *Seventh Letter* thus only confirms the conclusion of the *Cratylus*. The defect of words is precisely the lack of a natural correspondence between themselves and things. An "ideal language" is impossible because there simply can be no such stability in words.

Of propositions "Plato" says only that they suffer from the same defect found in the words of which they are composed. But how exactly does this defect show itself in propositions? If there is no natural correspondence between words and the things to which they refer, the propositions composed of these words will be *ambiguous*. If the meaning of a word could be read in its physical makeup, there would be no ambiguity. Because this is not the case, however, a proposition will necessarily lack complete clarity. The discussion of the *Euthydemus* in chapter 4 showed that this lack of clarity is exactly what enables eristics to win every argument. Therefore, the *Seventh Letter* sees as a sign of the defect of propositions their *refutability*. This is a *necessary*, not accidental, defect. One cannot avoid refutation by making certain that the form of one's argument is valid or that one's propositions are as unambiguous as possible. Before looking at what exactly makes this refutation possible, however, we need to reconsider the general defect of all four means.

The specific defect of the fourth means still remains to be considered. However, after having described the specific defects of words, propositions, and images "Plato" skips over knowledge and concludes: "Many more reasons can be given to show how each of the four is unclear" (343b6–7). "Plato" thus writes as if he had discussed all four. The omission only confirms what has already been suspected, namely, that the "knowledge" included in the four is so confined to words, propositions, and images, that once these have been dealt with, there is no need to deal in addition with "knowledge" itself. Here again it is clear that this defective knowledge differs sharply from knowledge of a thing's true being (the "fifth").

CONCLUSION: DIALECTIC IN THE SEVENTH LETTER

After having described the specific defects of the four means, "Plato" proceeds to describe the general defect from which they all suffer and which he here calls the "greatest" reason for their unclarity: "given that the being of an object and its quality are two different things and that what the soul seeks to know is not the quality, but the being, each of the four offers the soul, both in words and in deeds, what it does not seek" (343b8–c3). In the sketchier presentation of the second part of the digression, the four were simply said to make manifest *no less* the quality of a thing than its being. The present passage, however, makes clear that *all* or *most* of what they make manifest is a thing's quality.[39] What the soul seeks is what has been identified as the fifth element, that is, the true being of a thing; what each of the four offers the soul, however, is a mere quality or likeness. In this way, this passage explains why all attempts in the dialogues to define the true being or essence of a thing end in *aporia*.[40] In the *Meno*, as well as in the aporetic dialogues, Socrates seeks to know the true being of a certain nature, whether it be temperance or courage or virtue in general. In each case, his attempt to find a definition that expresses this nature, and not merely some aspect or quality of it, ends in failure. Now we see the reason why: in seeking to know what a thing truly *is*, any proposition we may formulate will necessarily not give us what we want but will instead express the thing's *qualities*.

I have already argued in chapter 6 that the similar distinction in the *Meno* between *what* a thing *is* (*ti esti*) and how it is *qualified* (*poion ti*) cannot be understood as a distinction between essential and accidental properties. The same is true here: understanding the distinction in this way would make nonsense of the teaching of the *Seventh Letter*.[41] Since nothing would prevent a proposition from listing only a thing's essential properties, there is no reason why, on this interpretation, a proposition should not express *ti esti*. The distinction here, as in the *Meno*, must instead be understood as one between *all* of a thing's properties, on the one hand, and the thing itself in its unity, on the other. The presupposition of this distinction is that what a thing *is* cannot be reduced to a multiplicity of properties or qualities. This presupposition, though difficult in its implications, is intelligible. A proposition can never express more than a multiplicity of properties; if, therefore, knowledge of this multiplicity is not equivalent to knowledge of a thing's true nature, then the latter kind of knowledge is not to be sought in a proposition.

The consequence is that, as chapter 6 already suggested, Socrates' What-is-x? question is unanswerable.[42] Any suggested proposition, for example, will necessarily fail to answer the question "What is virtue?" by expressing only a quality of virtue. Therefore, if one examines various definitions for their ability to express the true nature of virtue, one will find oneself refuting all of them. "Plato" therefore goes on to say that as a result of this defect in the four elements, "what is said or shown by each [of the four] is easily refuted by the senses" (343c3–4). This claim recalls the use of examples in the *Charmides* and the *Laches* to refute suggested definitions. What makes the definitions vulnerable to counterexamples is their inability to express more than one aspect or quality of the nature in question. The present passage thus provides an explanation of what occurs in the aporetic dialogues. It is as a result of the inability to express a thing's being rather than its quality that the four "fill practically everyone with perplexity (*aporia*) and confusion" (343c4–5).

The *Seventh Letter* does not explain *why* names, propositions, and images must offer the soul the quality of a thing rather than its being, but a reason was already suggested in chapter 6. A proposition, as well as the names of which it is composed and the images to which it must refer, present us with a multiplicity where what is sought is a unity. The nature is *one* thing, but a definition of this nature necessarily breaks it up into a multiplicity of components or aspects. The result is that we are presented with different ways in which the thing is qualified rather than with a knowledge of the thing itself. The unity of a thing's being, though presupposed by the definition, must always escape being expressed by it. Furthermore, chapters 7 and 8 suggested that a thing's unity is to be found precisely in its *good*. Yet chapter 8 in particular showed that the good cannot be known in a definition, but only indirectly as a source of illumination for a purifying and idealizing elenchus.

Having described the specific and general defects of names, propositions, images, and "knowledge," "Plato" in the fourth and last part of the digression (343c5–344d2) proceeds to describe the practical consequences of what he has said. So far, the prospect for attaining knowledge of the true nature of a thing looks very bleak. Each of our means of attaining knowledge is essentially defective, and there is no way of remedying this defect. Instead, we must apparently suffer the fate of being refuted every time we open our mouths. "Plato," however, does describe one way of escaping refutation: "In cases where we are not accustomed to search for the truth due to bad training and where therefore whatever image we are offered suffices, those of us who are questioned are not made ridiculous by those of us who ask the questions and are capable of refuting and upsetting the four" (343c5–d2). Note that what enables us to escape refutation is not the strength of our argument (since the weakness of the four cannot be escaped), but rather the *limitation* of its scope. This is why this irrefutability is attributed not to great argumentative skill, but rather to "bad training." This bad training is apparently betrayed by an unwillingness to inquire further or ask for more. But what exactly is the

CONCLUSION: DIALECTIC IN THE *SEVENTH LETTER*

limitation here? As the sentence makes clear, we escape refutation by contenting ourselves with the image ("likeness") that each of the four means of knowledge can offer. We are satisfied with that knowledge of a thing's quality which is all that the weakness of language can provide.[43] What makes us vulnerable to refutation is precisely the search for the true being of a thing through means incapable of expressing it. If, consequently, we abandon this search for the truth, we cease to be vulnerable. We demand of the four means no more than they can offer.

What is described here is strikingly similar to Socrates' "safe" method of hypothesis. In chapter 6, this method was seen to be defined by its surrender of the search for what a thing *is* and its willingness to confine itself to propositions and what they can offer. It was also seen to be restricted to the question of how a thing is *qualified* and to save its results from refutation by means of such a restriction. On these points, the parallel is perfect. Although the letter's reference to "bad training" might seem too negative a description of the hypothetical method, it is not much more negative than the *Phaedo*'s characterization of the method's results as simple-minded and naive or the *Meno*'s implicit association of the method with mental laziness. What is clear is that the image offered by the four means "suffices" for the hypothetical method in the same way that it suffices for the people described in this passage.

Given this parallel, the *Seventh Letter* confirms what was argued in previous chapters, namely, that *there is no such thing as a nonhypothetical proposition,* since there is no such thing as a proposition that can express a thing's being rather than its quality. The "weakness of language" destroys the hope of ever reaching something nonhypothetical within propositional knowledge. But here, as in the dialogues, we can confine ourselves to what can be gained from propositions and thus to the level of hypothesis.[44]

This interpretation of the passage also further clarifies the ambiguity present in the word "knowledge." The defective knowledge confined to words, images, and propositions can now be identified with the knowledge produced by the hypothetical method. In the *Meno* and the *Phaedo*, this "knowledge" is perhaps more appropriately called "true belief," and even here in the *Seventh Letter* this identification is implied.[45] In the *Republic*, it is called *dianoia*. The important point, however, is that this defective "knowledge," which has seemed out of place in a discussion focused on knowledge of what is "truly being," can now be located by reference to the hypothetical method described in the dialogues. This "knowledge," because confined to names, propositions, and images, will suffer from their defects; for the purposes of the hypothetical method, however, such "knowledge" suffices.[46]

In the sentence immediately following the one cited and discussed above, "Plato" describes what happens when this knowledge does *not* suffice, that is, when we are looking for the true being of a thing (the "fifth") and not merely its quality: "In cases, however, where we are required to reveal as our answer the fifth, any one of those who are skilled at confutation wins the argument and makes the person who was first to speak or write or answer *appear* to many of the listeners to know nothing about what he attempted to express in speech or writing" (343d2–6). Yet this appearance is erroneous. "Plato" is claiming not that only those who are ignorant and incorrectly describe the fifth will be refuted, but that *any* attempt to describe the fifth will suffer this.[47] Here again the *aporia* of the aporetic dialogues proves *necessary*. Any answer someone might give to a Socratic What-is-x? question can be refuted.[48] But why is this the case? "Plato" tells us: "it is not the soul of the speaker or writer that is being refuted, but the defective nature of each of the four [πεφυκυῖα φαύλως]" (343d7–e1). The vulnerability to refutation has therefore nothing to do with a lack of knowledge in the speaker or writer. Instead, any attempt to express the true nature of a thing is open to refutation for the sole reason that words, images, and propositions express how a thing is *qualified*. In attempting to say what virtue is, we can succeed only in asserting certain properties *of* virtue. It is this discrepancy between what is sought from the four means and what they can offer that makes refutation unavoidable. What is defective is not the insight that nourishes itself in a person's soul, but rather the knowledge that is confined to words, images, and propositions.[49]

This "epistemology" seems incredibly pessimistic. It appears that either we must confine ourselves to knowing the mere likenesses and qualities of things or, if we seek more than this, we must resign ourselves to being continually refuted by any Euthydemus or Dionysodorus who happens to come our way. The problem is even more serious than the above passage suggests. This passage appears to confine the problem to the *communication* of knowledge one already has. The speaker or writer has a knowledge of the "fifth" safely locked away in his or her soul; the difficulty is simply in communicating this knowledge to others by means of words, images, and propositions. However, what is said elsewhere in the letter makes clear that these three things are not simply our only means of *communicating* knowledge of a thing's being, but also our only means of *attaining* this knowledge. As "Plato" unambiguously states, "if in respect to these things [i.e., the different objects of inquiry] one does not in some way lay hold of the four, one will never fully partake of knowledge of the fifth" (342d8–e2). The dilemma faced by any inquirer is therefore not hard to see: our only means of attaining knowledge of the true nature of a thing have the defect of being unable to express this nature.[50]

There may seem to be a way out of this dilemma: "Plato" never actually asserts that words, images, and propositions express *only* a thing's quality and *not at all* its being. As has been seen, in one passage he says only that they express a thing's quality *no less than* its being. In another passage, however, "Plato" was seen to say that they do not offer the soul the being which it seeks, but rather the quality. This claim is clearly incompatible with the view that the four offer the soul equally a thing's quality *and* its being. Furthermore, it is hard to see why the four on this view would be refutable. On the other hand, the word "virtue," the proposition "virtue is good," and an image or example of virtue, such as remaining at one's post, must all make some reference to the nature of virtue and must therefore presuppose some awareness, however obscure, of this nature.[51] After all, the soul can *seek* to understand what virtue is only because it already "divines" this in the words, propositions, and images with which it deals. While the four means cannot express the true being of a thing, they nevertheless must presuppose some intuition of this true being if they are not to be arbitrary and meaningless. In other words, even the expression of the qualities of a thing requires that this thing be itself somehow *in view*. The problem, however, is that the four means *hide* the true being they *presuppose* behind the qualities they *express*. As previous chapters have shown in detail, words, propositions, and images, while pointing to a being that transcends them, have the inherent tendency to substitute themselves and what they express for this being. Therefore, the dilemma persists: we can attain knowledge of what a thing is only by means of names, images, and propositions, but each of these means conceals a thing's true being in expressing only how it is qualified.

It is important to see that this dilemma is not peculiar to the *Seventh Letter*. The *Cratylus* presents the dilemma of how we can come to know a thing's nature or form if, while confined to words in our search, we cannot find this nature revealed *in words*. The *Euthydemus* presents the dilemma of how we can discover the truth if the rational argumentation on which we must rely seems as capable of leading us away from it as toward it. *Republic* 10 presents the dilemma of how we can gain access to reality through images that are radically unlike it. Finally, the texts discussed in chapters 2, 6, 7, and 8 present the problem of how we can attain insight that transcends the limitations of the propositions we must employ. In each case there is a tension between the means and the goal of philosophical inquiry.

Previous chapters suggested a solution to each of these specific dilemmas. Does "Plato" suggest a solution here? He does. Immediately after pointing out that what is refuted in any attempt to answer a question asking for the "fifth" is the defective nature of the four means of attaining knowledge, "Plato" adds: "*Yet* (δέ) the process of dealing with all four, moving up and down to each one, barely gives birth to knowledge of the ideal nature [what a thing truly is] in someone with an ideal nature" (343e1–3). The correspondence asserted here between the nature of what is known and the nature of the knower will be dealt with below. What demands immediate attention is the following: though "Plato" has asserted that due to their defective natures words, images, and propositions (and thus the defective knowledge confined to them) cannot *of themselves* provide us with knowledge of "the fifth" he here asserts that a certain way of *dealing* with them *can* provide this knowledge. The suggestion is that, while recognizing the necessary defects of these instruments, we can yet use them in such a way as to overcome these defects.

But what exactly does this use involve? What is the nature of the *diagōgē* which "Plato" believes can lead us through words, images, and propositions to knowledge of "the fifth"? This procedure is here described in very vague terms: it is said to involve "moving up and down" to each of the four. The nature of this movement must be something like the following: first, we have a name such as "virtue," then we give a definition of this name, and finally we test this definition by applying it to specific images of virtue (specific virtuous actions, for example). Given what we have already been told, however, either the reference to experience or certain other propositions will refute the definition, and we will need to start the process all over again. In this movement from name to definition to image and then back to the name and another definition, we clearly have the upward and downward movement "Plato" describes. The difficulty is in seeing how this process could ever provide us with knowledge of "the fifth." Though it may supply increasingly better definitions, none of them, for the reasons stated above, will succeed in expressing "the fifth," and thus each one will necessarily be refutable. It seems that the most this movement between names, images, and propositions could provide is the defective knowledge included here as one of the "four." In confining ourselves to movement between defective means, we can hardly attain knowledge that is not itself defective. Thus the upward and downward movement described here seems to be no more than the hypothetical method discussed in the previous three chapters. But then it is just as unable to provide knowledge of the true being of a thing.

It therefore seems that more must be involved in this movement if "Plato" really considers it capable of providing us with knowledge of "the fifth." It cannot be *confined* to words, images, and propositions if it is supposed to provide knowledge that transcends their defects. But how is this possible? More generally, how can any way of dealing with words, images, and propositions transcend their defects?[52] Fortunately, "Plato" offers a second, more detailed description of this process: "Only barely, when the [three], i.e., names, propositions, as well as appearances and perceptions, are rubbed against each other, each of them being refuted through well-meaning [nonadversarial] refutations in a process of questioning and answering without envy, will wisdom along with insight commence to cast its light in an effort at the very limits of human possibility" (344b3–c1). In place of the upward and downward movement of the earlier passage, we now have a "rubbing together" (*tribein*) of names, propositions, and images. But what does this metaphor mean? Basing themselves on the use of the word *tribein* in a passage from the *Republic* (435a1), some commentators have seen this "rubbing" as a metaphor for some kind of "comparison." However, that more is involved in the present passage is shown by what is apparently "Plato's" own explanation of the metaphor: the "rubbing together" of names, propositions, and images refers to the process of *refutation* that "Plato" immediately proceeds to describe. The word *tribein* is well suited to describing such a process, since it has the sense of a *vigorous* rubbing that wears things down.

But what exactly is the nature of this process? In calling the refutation "well-meaning," "Plato" clearly intends to distinguish it from that skill in confutation described earlier as making someone who has knowledge appear foolish before the public. However, there is nevertherless an important similarity between the present passage and the earlier one: in both cases, words, propositions, and images are *refuted* (*elenchein*). The refutation described here may be more "well-meaning" than eristic, but the results appear the same: on account of their defective natures, the three means of attaining knowledge are refuted in being opposed to ("rubbed against") one another. The process envisaged here is therefore something like the following: in answering a question asking for the true being of a thing (the fifth), one advances a definition that can express only a quality or likeness of the thing; this definition is then refuted by either an attack on the ambiguity of its terms or an appeal to specific examples (images) not covered by it or other propositions that themselves express only qualities of the thing, but qualities not captured by the proposed definition. In short, because a definition will never be able to express the true nature of a thing, it will always betray its weakness when "rubbed against" other means. This seems to be the process described here, a process that therefore does not essentially differ from eristic, however more "well-meaning" it may be.

In this case, however, the present description of how we attain knowledge must appear even more problematic than the earlier one. *For how can it be the case that, by exposing in the process of refutation the weaknesses of names, propositions, and images, we will come to have knowledge of the true being of a thing?* On the contrary, it seems that such a process of refutation would make us despair of any possibility of attaining knowledge. The present passage does solve *one* problem: it was argued above that no knowledge of the "fifth" can be attained as long as we remain *confined to* names, propositions, and images; the process described in the present passage frees us from this confinement by simply refuting these three means. However, this does not seem to be much of a liberation. We have come to recognize that our only means of attaining knowledge are necessarily defective, and such a recognition does indeed liberate us from blind subservience to them; yet it does not seem to bring us any closer to the *attainment* of the knowledge we seek. The difficulty, in short, is that the process described in the present passage seems much too negative to lead to so positive a result as philosophical knowledge.

It is incredible that practically all commentators[53] have glossed over this difficulty by eliminating the negative character of the process "Plato" describes through translations that are justifiable neither in terms of the Greek text nor in terms of the overall content of the *Seventh Letter*. The crucial phrase in the text is "ἐν εὐμενέσιν ἐλέγχοις ἐλεγχόμενα" (344b5). One strategy is to translate this phrase so vaguely that it becomes essentially meaningless. Thus Souilhé undertranslates: "lorsqu'on a discuté dans des discussions bienveillantes." Another strategy is to give the text a specific meaning it cannot plausibly have. Thus Bury: "proving them by kindly proofs" (I assume that Bury uses the word "proving" in what is today the rather obsolete sense of "testing"), Harward: "scrutiny and kindly testing," and Morrow: "testing" (for the whole phrase!). Two criticisms can be made. First, in every other case in the letter where names, propositions, and images are the objects of an *elenchos* (343c3, 343d1–2, 343d7–8), the meaning can only be that they are "refuted." How, then, can the meaning in the present passage be the entirely different one of "testing"? The second and more important point, however, is that these positive or quasi-positive translations are shown to be impossible by the *content* of the letter. Given "Plato's" belief in the "weakness of language," he cannot possibly be saying in the present passage that our propositions are simply "tested," with the implication that one of them could be found nondefective and irrefutable; he makes it perfectly clear that *no* proposition will succeed in expressing a thing's true being. The process described here must be the same as that for which the same word is used in other passages: names, propositions, and images are being *refuted*.[54]

CONCLUSION: DIALECTIC IN THE *SEVENTH LETTER*

The difficulty cannot be avoided: "Plato" is claiming that a process of refutation similar to eristic can lead to knowledge. Yet perhaps the characterization of this process as "well-meaning" does point to a solution after all. It is precisely in terms of such a characteristic that Socrates in the *Meno* (75d) distinguishes the dialectic he practices from eristic. Even though it too involves refutation, Socrates tells Meno that dialectic is "gentler" than eristic. We also know from elsewhere that Socrates' intention is not to make his interlocutors look foolish, but to get at the truth. Furthermore, the broader context of the present passage provides a perfect description of dialectic as practiced by Socrates in the *Laches* and the *Charmides:* there, definitions of, as well as statements about, temperance and courage are "rubbed against" each other and refuted in a process of questioning and answering that is clearly free of the adversity and enmity that characterize eristic.

Most commentators, however, have avoided making this obvious connection due to its implication that the kind of dialectic practiced in the *Laches* and the *Charmides* can lead to knowledge, something which they think cannot possibly be the case. Yet the interpretation offered in chapter 2 has removed this difficulty by showing that the dialectic practiced in these dialogues is indeed capable of providing knowledge. This dialectic is negative only in showing that no propositions can capture the specific nature in question; it is positive, however, insofar as the very process of examining and refuting suggested definitions can provide insight into what this nature is. Thus it was seen that a knowledge of temperance or courage is gained not in any propositional result, but rather in the very process of dialectic depicted in the dialogues. But this is exactly what the present passage describes: in the very process of refuting words, propositions, and images for their inability to express the nature in question (the "fifth"), insight is barely gained into what this nature is.[55] The qualification "barely" (μόγις) is important, because it shows that this insight, here as in the dialogues, is not the kind of knowledge that will put an end to all inquiry or that can be "grasped" once and for all.[56]

The description of dialectic in the present passage also parallels its description in the *Republic* as "destroying the hypotheses." A parallel has already been noted between the defective knowledge for which "the image suffices" described in the *Seventh Letter* and the method of hypothesis presented in the *Meno,* the *Phaedo,* and the *Republic.* Now "Plato's" claim in the letter that genuine knowledge is to be attained only through a refutation of this defective knowledge can be seen to parallel the description in the *Republic* of an ascent along which hypotheses are destroyed in the attainment of something nonhypothetical. It is true that the knowledge described in the letter is not explicitly identified with knowledge of the good, but the good is included in the list of "forms" to be classified as the "fifth" (342d4). There is even an indication in the letter (for which see below) of the good's preeminence among the forms.[57]

What characterizes the dialectical process as described both here in the *Seventh Letter* and in the *Republic,* and as seen at work in the *Laches* and the *Charmides,* is the view that while knowledge of the true being of a thing cannot be found in names, propositions, and images but transcends them (i.e., cannot be expressed by them), it is nevertheless possible for this knowledge to be gained through a certain way of using these means. As noted above, even though names, images, and propositions do not succeed in expressing or "offering" the true nature of a thing, they must nevertheless, in expressing this thing's qualities, refer to or presuppose its nature. This is what makes possible a particular way of dealing with these means that, by exposing them in refutation, opens them to the nature which they presuppose but conceal. Chapters 3 through 5 in particular illustrated this point. The discussion of the *Cratylus* showed that while the nature of a thing is not revealed in its name (as Cratylus would have it), it is revealed in the particular *use* which the dialectician makes of the name. The discussion of the *Euthydemus* showed that while arguments cannot in themselves guarantee the truth, they can nevertheless be used in such a way (protreptic) as to lead to recognition of the truth. The discussion of *Republic* 10 and related texts showed that although images are in themselves completely opaque to the real natures of which they are images, they can nevertheless be used in such a way as to reveal these natures. In each case, the use that enables the three means to awaken in us an awareness of that which they cannot themselves express is dialectic as described here and elsewhere: the process of question and answer in which we *expose* the weaknesses of the words, propositions, and images we use and thereby just barely glimpse through their cracks the true being which they all attempt but fail to express.

In retrospect, the other two, less-detailed descriptions in the *Seventh Letter* of the process through which knowledge is attained become much clearer. The *diagōgē* in which one moves up and down between words, propositions, and images need no longer be seen as confined to these; instead, as a process of refutation, this way of dealing with the three means can just barely provide us with a knowledge that transcends them. Likewise, the *sunousia* and *suzēn* of the first description can be seen to refer to Socratic conversation as we know it from the dialogues. Socrates inquires into a certain issue with interlocutors already in some way acquainted with it. As the second chapter showed, temperance and courage are not simply objects of discussion, but rather matters with which Socrates and his interlocutors have lived and which they *enact* in the very

CONCLUSION: DIALECTIC IN THE *SEVENTH LETTER*

inquiry. The description in the *Seventh Letter* is therefore more than apt as a description of this kind of conversation in which one really *lives* what is under discussion.[58]

This characteristic of dialectic is related to another that has yet to be examined: the second description cited above describes dialectic as giving rise to "knowledge of the ideal nature in someone with an ideal nature" (343e2–3). "Plato" proceeds to explain this claim by asserting that where there is no affinity between the subject and the object there can be no knowledge. The possession of a great memory or a facility for learning cannot take the place of such affinity and therefore without it count for nothing in the quest for knowledge. What this affinity involves is a correspondence between the goodness of one's soul and the goodness of the object known. If the state of one's soul is defective, either by nature or through corruption, one cannot have knowledge of the ideal nature of a thing, that is, the true being that entirely lacks the defects of any of its images. This characterization of the object of knowledge as ideal or *good* (εὖ) appears to imply its dependence on the form of the good, as this dependence is described in the *Republic* and discussed at length in chapter 8: a thing's true nature is what it is *best* for it to be, what it is seen to be by an idealization that transcends the defects of its expression in words, propositions, and images. The phrase "εὖ πεφυκότος εὖ πεφυκότι" (343e2–3), applied to the subject and object of knowledge, indeed stands in contrast to the phrase "πεφυκυῖα φαύλως" (343d8–e1), applied to the four means. A corrupt soul clearly can still have "knowledge" of words, propositions, and images about an ideal or good nature; what is ruled out is genuine knowledge of the ideal or good nature itself. The second and sixth chapters provided two examples of defective souls confined to defective knowledge: Critias, Nicias, and Meno. The "knowledge" of these interlocutors was seen not to go beyond words and definitions, and this defect was itself attributed to a lack of correspondence between their own natures and the virtue in question.

What is described by the phrase "εὖ πεφυκότος εὖ πεφυκότι" is precisely the reflexivity that has been encountered repeatedly in our examination of dialectic. In the *Laches,* the *Charmides,* the *Euthydemus,* and the *Meno,* Socrates exhibits, respectively, the courage, temperance, wisdom, or virtue he seeks to define. In the *Charmides* and the *Euthydemus,* this reflexivity is made thematic in the identification of dialectic with "knowledge of knowledge." In the *Republic,* the close affinity between the good and knowledge (the latter is caused by the former and instantiates it by being "goodlike") appears to make knowledge of the good inseparable from knowledge of knowledge. In each case the kind of affinity between subject and object described in the *Seventh Letter* is shown to be essential to dialectic. In the passage of the *Seventh Letter* where "Plato" explains the necessity of such affinity, we learn why knowledge of the true being of a thing must in a sense be self-knowledge: "the principle or source [of knowledge] is not to be found in alien dispositions" (344a4). The suggestion here is that if knowledge is to be gained at all through dialectic, its source must be found in one's own nature or disposition. But what exactly does this mean? The soul for Plato is not a clean slate which receives its knowledge "from outside"; it contains the principle of such knowledge within itself. As already noted above, the soul could not even *seek* the true nature of virtue if it did not already "divine" this nature in its defective instantiations. In the *Phaedrus* (249e) we are told that "every human soul has by nature seen all beings," though in varying degrees. A soul, therefore, whose nature neither is defective nor has been corrupted will have within itself a knowledge of what is and will thereby be akin to what is. All knowledge of what a thing is will therefore be inseparable from self-knowledge; without this kind of affinity between subject and object there simply can be no knowledge.[59] As "Plato" suggests at the very beginning of the digression, those who have attempted to write about the things he takes seriously not only do not know these things, but also do not know themselves (341b5–7).

The reflexivity expressed in the phrase "εὖ πεφυκότος εὖ πεφυκότι" is essential to the success of dialectic as it has been described so far. The process of exposing in refutation the weaknesses of words, propositions, and images cannot possibly spark within the soul knowledge of the true being of a thing unless the principle of such knowledge is already in the soul. In the *Meno*, the *Phaedo*, and the *Phaedrus*, Plato uses the word "recollection" to describe this aspect of the dialectical process. Whatever word one uses, however, it is clear that knowledge of the "ideal natures" must already be latent in the soul if the process described above is to succeed in "kindling" it. Once insight is gained, it will, in the letter's words, "nourish itself." By this "Plato" apparently means that it will not, like the defective "knowledge" described above, depend on what can be said or written. Instead, even though all the means by which it might attempt to express itself will be refuted, this knowledge, as something inexpressible, will itself remain irrefutable.[60]

In the last few sentences of the philosophical digression "Plato" returns to the claim with which the digression began: anyone with understanding will refrain from writing about serious matters. He now sees his characterization of the dialectical process as having demonstrated this claim. Clearly, if knowledge of the first principles is a nonpropositional insight gained through a process that exposes the weaknesses of names and propositions, it would be sheer folly to attempt to express this knowledge in writing. The focus on writing here is explained by the specific context (i.e., the criticism of the written works of Dionysius and others) and is not evidence that "Plato's" critique does not also apply to oral expression. Genuine knowledge is to be found in the soul (our "most noble part") and not in words of any kind.

The philosophical digression of the *Seventh Letter* thus presents a coherent and tight argument that confirms at every point the conclusions of the preceding chapters. What the letter offers is an outline of the main presuppositions and features of the dialectic practiced and discussed in the dialogues we have examined. Those who still insist on denying Plato's authorship must at least grant that the forger's understanding of Plato's dialectic is impeccable.

Conclusion

From this examination of the *Seventh Letter*, as well as from the interpretation of specific dialogues in previous chapters, it can be concluded that dialectic as Plato understands it in these works is guided by the following three presuppositions:

1. Names, propositions, and images are incapable of expressing what a thing truly is (*ti esti*) and consequently are always open to refutation.
2. Names, propositions, and images are nevertheless indispensable as means of attaining knowledge of what a thing truly is.
3. One can use these three means in such a way as to obtain an insight that transcends them, that is, an insight into that nature which they themselves presuppose but cannot express.

The first presupposition explains why dialectic does not attempt to distance itself from everyday experience. The conventionality of the symbols used in ordinary language, the ambiguities of propositions used in ordinary discourse, and the deceptiveness of the concrete images that guide our daily *praxis* are the results of a weakness inherent in our means of relating to the truth. The dialectician, therefore, does not fool himself into thinking that the flaws of ordinary experience can be overcome through the construction of an ideal language or the systematization of a formal logic. In our everyday use of words, propositions, and images, the true natures of things already stand revealed to us, however darkly (*doxa*). The task of the dialectician is not to abstract these three means from the concrete context that alone gives them meaning, but rather to use them to bring out the truth that already lies within this context. Because of their necessary weaknesses, words, propositions, and images cannot in themselves tell us anything about a thing's true nature; dialectic must therefore avoid opposing them to experience by abstracting and systematizing them.

The second presupposition is important in showing that, while the ultimate goal of dialectic is nonpropositional insight, the only means of attaining (and I would add, *sustaining*) this insight is a form of *discursive* reasoning. A criticism sometimes leveled against the *Seventh Letter* is that its negative characterization of discursive thought shows it to be the work of a mystic and mystagogue.[61] Edelstein (1966, 106) explains and defends this criticism as follows: "For if anything has been characteristic of mysticism in all ages and among all people, it is 'the temporary shattering of our ordinary spatial and temporal consciousness and of discursive intellect,' the extinction of thought, the renunciation of the word." Yet, while the letter describes the attainment of knowledge as involving refutation of the means of discursive thought, it does not advocate abandoning these means. In dealing dialectically with words, propositions, and images, we *just barely* (μόγις) get beyond them; even once we have attained some knowlege, we still remain vulnerable to their weaknesses.[62] The insight that transcends words cannot be attained except by means of words; what cannot be spoken becomes manifest in the very process of speaking.[63] Thus what we have in dialectic as Plato understands it is the wedding of discursive and nondiscursive thought.[64] Only through the process of examining and refuting propositions—a thoroughly discursive process—can we just barely obtain knowledge that is nonpropositional. It is precisely because dialectic has this character that it is so closely related to the method that confines itself to discursive thought, that is, the method of hypothesis. The difference is nevertheless unbridgeable: the knowledge obtained through dialectic is superior, and totally unlike (nonpropositional versus propositional), the kind of understanding obtained through the method of hypothesis. Yet it is also the case that what dialectic *uses* in awakening nonpropositional insight into a thing's nature is precisely the discursive reasoning cultivated by the hypothetical method.

And so it is the third presupposition, the uniting of our defective tools of expression with knowledge that transcends them, which is the heart and core of dialectic.[65] Such a union or mediation can take place only in the actual process of using these tools. Only in use can the defects of words, propositions, and images be just barely overcome. Thus in previous chapters, the notion of "use" (χρῆσις) has shown itself again and again to be central to dialectic. Dialectic, the primary object of which is the good, is essentially a "know-how." It is this identification of dialectic with *knowledge of use* that prevents it from being *solely* "knowledge by acquaintance" (direct, unmediated intuition) or *solely* propositional knowledge and makes it instead that process in which insight and discourse are reconciled.

What previous chapters have revealed about the nature of this use that defines dialectic can be outlined schematically, and therefore inadequately, as follows. It is a use of names, propositions, and images that exposes their limitations in elenchus and *thereby* reveals the truth. That the negative process of refutation should have this positive outcome is made possible by the fact that the truth, rather than being merely external to this process, is instantiated by it. In other words, the use that characterizes dialectic itself instantiates what it brings us to understand, so that this understanding is always *self-understanding* (in the sense of a "knowledge of knowledge"). This is why this use presupposes an affinity between the subject and the object. One must have and thus be acquainted with virtue and the good, even though only implicitly and confusedly, in order to inquire into them. The inquiry is only the realization and exercise of this affinity. As a user's knowledge, knowledge of virtue and the good is acquired and exhibited in the very practice of inquiry, rather than in any propositional results abstracted from this practice.

This characterization of dialectic has important implications for the interpretation of Plato's works. Though the *Seventh Letter* provides us with a schema of this method, as a "knowledge of use" dialectic must ultimately be seen *at work* in the dialogues. Thus there is a need for detailed interpretations of specific dialogues (such as those attempted in the preceding chapters) that avoid the error dialectic is meant to avoid, namely, the error of abstracting arguments and statements from their concrete context so as to elevate them to the status of "doctrines."

We are thus led back to the issues of interpretation discussed in the first chapter. If the characterization of dialectic resulting from the present study is correct, then philosophical knowledge for Plato does not consist of philosophical doctrines nor of a philosophical system. As the *Seventh Letter* explicitly argues, any "doctrines," whether formulated in writing or orally, would more distort than reveal the truth. Dialectic, therefore, cannot be seen as simply a "tool," or a "method" in the current sense of the word, for arriving at propositional conclusions. Instead, what reveals the truth, though without ever arriving at a "final result," is the process of dialectic itself, the discursive activity of "rubbing together" our defective means of inquiry with the goal of sparking an insight that barely transcends them. Because both the "developmentalist" and "esotericist" interpretations were seen to presuppose that knowledge for

Plato is (either entirely or in most cases) propositional and that dialectic is simply a means of arriving at knowledge that is itself "nondialectical" (i.e., constitutes a *system*), they must both be judged misguided. Both come to the dialogues with a conception of philosophy that is not Plato's own. Given what both the *Seventh Letter* and the dialogues have been shown to tell us, we cannot expect that Plato sought, either in writing or orally, to expound and defend specific doctrines. What he sought instead was to re-create that dialectical process which alone can reveal the truth, and he chose the dialogue form over the treatise for its ability, within the limitations of its medium, to do this.[66] On the other hand, the present characterization of dialectic has shown the "nondoctrinal" interpretation, in its purely skeptical form, to be equally misguided. Though there is no philosophical system in the dialogues, though the dialogues are notoriously unsuccesful in clearly presenting and defending specific doctrines (witness the so-called "Theory of Forms"), it is still the case that a great deal of philosophical knowledge is to be gained from them. The one requirement is that we do not approach them with our own preconception of what philosophical knowledge ought to be.

Indeed, what is probably most responsible for having led much Platonic scholarship astray is an unwillingness to share, even for interpretative purposes, a fundamental presupposition of Plato's dialectic: that words, propositions, and images should never be allowed to take the place of truth.

Notes

Chapter 1

1. This is not an infringement on Plato's "anonymity." By "Plato's answer" I mean the answer Plato's dialogues give us when interpreted as dramatic and argumentative wholes.

2. In thus seeing one group of dialogues as significantly different from another, I am not commiting myself to any chronology, much less to any developmental hypothesis. Despite the general complacency with which most scholars use the labels "early," "middle," and "late," I believe that a number of important recent studies have seriously brought into question the orthodox chronology and, in some cases, the very project of establishing a chronology: see Thesleff (1982, 1989), Howland (1991), Nails (1992, 1993, 1994, 1995, chs. 4–7). Nails even denies that there is any orthodoxy here: she shows that the apparent "early middle late consensus" to which many scholars appeal is *only apparent* (1995, 53–68). Ledger's recent stylometric study (1989) draws our attention to the circularity of previous stylometric studies. However, that Ledger's analysis does not itself fully avoid circularity is shown by Howland (1991, 210) and T. M. Robinson (1992, 378–79). For other problems with Ledger's analysis and with stylometry in general see Young (1994). Though the present study will not take any stand on the question of what, if any, chronology can be established through the study of Plato's style, its conclusions will eliminate the principal *philosophical reasons* that have been adduced for judging dialogues such as the *Laches* and the *Charmides* to be earlier than the *Meno* or the *Republic*.

3. Another book on this topic has appeared fairly recently in German: Stemmer (1992). Although in some respects I prefer this account to Robinson's, my many disagreements with it will be indicated throughout this study.

4. I agree with Seeskin's claim, apparently made in criticism of Robinson, that "If an account of method is supposed to be a series of procedures which can be taken up by any intelligent person and followed to a successful conclusion, then, I submit Socrates was opposed to method" (1987, 41). This is why the present study seeks, not to define dialectic as a logical method, but rather to describe its practice in the dialogues. On the other hand, I give more importance to Socrates' explicit accounts of dialectic, and see them as more closely related to Socrates' practice, than does Seeskin (see 38–41).

5. Robinson is therefore at a complete loss to explain why Plato so greatly valued the dialectical method. He can only suggest the rather ludicrous historical

explanation that Plato preferred dialectic over any other method "due in general to the fondness of the ancient Athenians for discussion" (1953, 83). For an excellent critique of Robinson on this point, see Stephens (1993). Stephens briefly defends two important claims that will receive detailed confirmation from the present study: elenchus not only serves to convert one to philosophy but is needed at every stage of philosophical inquiry to overcome the ever-present temptation to think that we know what we do not know (469–71), and the elenchus does not simply remove impediments to knowledge (so that, as Robinson assumes, another method would be needed to provide knowledge) but rather itself leads to knowledge in the form of some sort of vision (471–72).

6. "Upon the whole, the hypothetical method recommended in the middle dialogues is little exemplified there or elsewhere in Plato" (Robinson 1953, 204). Of course, Robinson does see that dialectic *as elenchus* is used in the early dialogues. Yet even here, he does not situate the method in its dramatic context, something that the second chapter of this book will show to be essential.

7. For this discussion of Schleiermacherianism I am partially indebted to Krämer's long and masterly account (1990a, 3–64). Krämer's discussion of the philosophical presuppositions of Schleiermacher's interpretative method is extremely valuable and enlightening. Krämer's agenda, however, is to defend his own "esotericist" interpretation by discrediting what I in the main text identify as the first presuppostion of Schleiermacher's approach.

8. Schleiermacher criticizes those who are content with a systematic presentation of Plato's individual doctrines (which he yet sees as possible and useful) and do not supplement this with a careful reading of the dialogues: "So also will those spectators of the analysis fail altogether to attain to a knowledge of the Philosophy of Plato, for in that, if in any thing, form and subject are inseparable, and no proposition is to be rightly understood, except in its own place, and with the combinations and limitations which Plato has assigned to it" ([1836] 1973, 14).

9. See Schleiermacher (1839, 98). In this work Schleiermacher, in addition to describing Plato as the first systematic philosopher, outlines a completely systematic exposition of Plato's philosophy (there is *no* reference here to the dramatic or artistic form of the dialogues). Even Schleiermacher's grouping of the dialogues in his famous introduction treats those in the last group (*Republic, Timaeus, Critias,* and *Laws*) as systematic treatises and subordinates to them all the others, which he characterizes as preliminary, introductory, or tentative. Therefore, like the developmentalists and esotericists, Schleiermacher sees little positive content in the "aporetic," Socratic dialogues. These dialogues merely point forward to the truly expository works and therefore seem, taken in themselves, imperfect and objectless (Schleiermacher [1836] 1973, 42). The attribution of a "system" to Plato is of course not new with Schleiermacher but goes back as far as Plato's successors in the Old Academy and was perpetuated by the Neoplatonists. For a brief history, see my introduction to Gonzalez (1995a, 2–5).

10. Karl Friedrich Hermann can be said to be the "father" of the modern "developmentalist" approach (though it can be said to have been initiated some-

what earlier by Friedrich Ast), and the combination of the notions of "evolution" and "system" which characterize this approach can be seen in the title of his unfinished magnum opus: *Geschichte und System der Platonischen Philosophie.* Hermann vehemently rejected Schleiermacher's view that the dialogues are to be seen as the gradual exposition of a system which was already complete in its essentials during the earliest period of Plato's writing career (see [1839] 1976, 347–57). He claimed that this view was incompatible with the obvious contradictions existing between the philosophical teachings of different dialogues ([1886] 1968, 352, 369; for examples of such contradictions see 371). He also made the "argument," often heard today, that it is inconceivable how a thinker could accept essentially the same philosophy throughout an active career of over fifty years and while subject during this time to the most diverse and numerous psychological, historical, and philosophical influences (355–56). What must be noted, however, is that Hermann not only accepts Schleiermacher's thesis concerning the unity of form and content in Plato's philosophy (345), *but actually grounds his own developmentalist thesis upon this unity* (370–71). For Hermann, the artistic form of a dialogue, rather than being determined by extrinsic pedagogical interests (which is Schleiermacher's view), is, like the content itself, an expression of Plato's "spirit," that is, what he thought and felt at the time he wrote the dialogue. Thus the unity of form and content for Hermann lies in the fact that both are simply the expression of Plato's *Geist.* This "romanticism" is essential to the developmentalist thesis: only when both the form and content of a dialogue are thought to reveal Plato's mind at the time of composition can the differences between two dialogues be seen as representing different stages in Plato's development: "je mehr wir seine Schriften als den treuen Abdruck seines Geistes betrachten, desto mehr nötigt uns ihre Verschiedenheit, gewisse Stadien in seinem eigenen Entwickelungsprozesse anzunehmen" (352). For an example of this romanticism in a modern developmentalist, see Vlastos's interpretation of the *Parmenides* as a record of Plato's honest perplexity (1965a, especially 254–55).

Hermann also shared Schleiermacher's other presupposition, that is, that Plato's philosophy is "systematic." After stating how essential the mythic and poetic elements of the dialogues are to their content, he insists that this content can nevertheless be stripped of these elements and given a systematic presentation (347). Hermann therefore shares Schleiermacher's low estimation of the aporetic dialogues (387) and, with some exceptions, his ordering of the dialogues from less to more "constructive" ones. Though modern "developmentalists" would not accept Hermann's specific account of Plato's evolution, they are still guided by his general principles and presuppositions.

11. Though Hermann considers the artistic form of the dialogues to be essential to their content, he is forced to distinguish sharply between this artistic form and the *dialogue* form itself, which he considers to be simply "eine beliebte und hergebrachte Einkleidungsweise" ([1839] 1976, 354–55). As pointed out above, Hermann sees the artistic form of Plato's writings as simply an expression of Plato's *Geist.* "Dialogue" clearly is not suited to expressing one person's psychic state, and therefore Hermann must make the highly implausible claim that

dialogue as such is not essential to the artistic form of Plato's writings. For a recent example of a developmentalist's failure to do justice to the dialogue form, see the following critiques of Terence Irwin: Roochnik (1988) and Tejera (1978).

12. Schleiermacher ([1836] 1973, 14).

13. This "nondoctrinal" approach to Plato's dialogues can hardly be called a uniform movement. There are great differences in the ways in which individual scholars actually carry out this kind of reading of the dialogues. Yet what unifies this movement is a professed rejection of attempts to find a system of doctrines in Plato's works. For a survey of different exponents of this approach and a brief history of its historical antecedents, see Gonzalez (1995a, 2–4, 8–11).

14. These questions are dealt with in a preliminary way by some of the essays collected in Griswold (1988) and Gonzalez (1995a).

15. Tigerstedt (1977, 103). This danger is faced by any approach which overemphasizes the dramatic and artistic qualities of Plato's dialogues at the cost of their philosophical content. One example of this weakness, to choose only one, is Arieti (1991). This book is full of titillating suggestions and rich insights concerning how individual dialogues work as plays. But Arieti nowhere makes clear how they are works of *philosophy*. He concludes that "insofar as the Platonic dialogues are art—and even the most hard-nosed critic admits their artistic qualities—*they aim at an emotional reaction* and not at discursive learning" (247–48, my emphasis). Arieti would admit that the dialogues are *more* than art, but he does not explain what this "more" is. Instead, when he does speak of Plato's philosophy, he places it, following Gaiser and Krämer, *outside* of the dialogues and in the Academy, so that the dialogues become *advertisements* for the Academy (13 n9; Arieti nevertheless sees himself as disagreeing with the position of the Tübingen School insofar as he does not deny that the dialogues have some didactic point; yet this is not a real disagreement, since Gaiser and Krämer nowhere deny that the dialogues teach us *some* things). In the end, the book leaves the crucial questions unanswered. Do the dialogues contain Plato's philosophy or not? If they do, in exactly what way are they works of *philosophy* (as distinct, for example, from a Sophoclean play)? What specifically is the nature of their philosophical content, and why can this content be communicated only in dialogue form? In my view, to answer these questions one must reject Arieti's dichotomy between "emotional reaction" and "discursive learning." These are not the only alternatives.

16. The classic presentation of this interpretation is to be found in Krämer (1959) and Gaiser (1968). The Tübingen position has been adopted and further developed in Reale (1989). Now we also have a very thorough explanation and defense of this position in English: Krämer (1990a).

17. For a thorough defense of the claim that what is said about dialectic and the good in the middle books of the *Republic* can be understood and explained only in light of the "unwritten doctrines," see Krämer (1966) and Reale (1989, 293–333).

18. For other objections against the developmentalist approach, see Reale (1990, 28–29).

NOTES TO PAGES 5-7

19. Krämer accuses Wolfgang Wieland of an *Entmetaphysizierung* and *Resokratisierung* of Plato (Krämer 1982, 580), as if this were the greatest of evils. The strategy of Krämer's polemic against this interpretation is to restrict the debate to a dichotomy between systematic metaphysics, on the one hand, and an endless, aimless and pointless philosophizing, on the other (as if there were no third option!). He characterizes the latter as follows: "Mit dem infinitischen Philosophiebegriff sind ferner wesentlich gebunden eine letzte Agnostik—und in ihren Konsequenz auch eine Inkommunikabilität des 'Unsagbaren'—sowie die Vorstellung von der Asystematizität einer nicht fixierbaren Denkbewegung" (Krämer 1990b, 85–86). Though the nondoctrinal interpretation is always in danger of collapsing Plato's philosophy into an empty and endless process of questioning, what Krämer says here distorts the more sophisticated positions he is criticizing: cf. Wieland (1976, 32). Gaiser (1987) indulges in the same misrepresentation of the opposition. See also Krämer (1988), which, while rightly critical of interpretations such as Schlegel's that anachronistically read back into Plato the radical subjectivism of modern philosophy, appears to recognize no alternative between this approach and the—in my view—equally anachronistic characterization of Plato as a systematic metaphysician. As Ferber points out, Plato "ist aber weder Finitist noch Infinitist, weder Dogmatiker noch Skeptiker hinsichtlich von deren [Ideen und Prinzipien] Erkenntnis" (1993, 50). The last chapter, however, will reveal important differences between my own characterization of this "neither/nor" and Ferber's.

20. This is acknowledged by Gaiser himself. In speaking of the debate between the esotericists and the anti-esotericists he writes: "In questa polemica svolgono un ruolo importante, da tutte e due le parti, anche se insapevolmente, le imagini personali, e moderne, di quel que dovrebbe essere una filosofia esemplare" (1980b, 53). For an excellent account of the philosophical agenda behind the esotericist interpretation (i.e., the attempt to depict Platonism as a continuous metaphysical tradition finding its culmination in Christianity), see Berti (1989, 289–300). Krämer (1988, 617) rejects "affinity" as a principle of interpretation, but, as I seek to show below, this principle is very much at work in his own interpretation.

21. Krämer (1990a, 65) quotes with full approval the following words of G. W. Leibniz: "Si quelcun reduisoit Platon en système, il rendroit un grand service au genre humain." The same quote stands as the motto to Reale (1989).

22. One of the esotericists, Thomas A. Szlezák (1978, 35), succinctly states the problem as follows: "Nun war zwar Schleiermacher selbst kein Gegner systematischer Platonauslegung, diese kam aber zweifellos mit der Verbreitung seiner Interpretationsprinzipien zum Erliegen." The solution for the esotericists is simply to reject these interpretative principles.

23. For an excellent discussion of the meaning of "system," see Heidegger (1988). Heidegger claims that neither Plato nor even Aristotle have a philosophical "system" (1988, 47; see also Heidegger 1952, 93). He does not mean that there is no unity in the thought of these two thinkers. Plato's thought is "systematic" in one sense, namely, it is "geleitet und getragen von einer ganz bestimmten inneren

Fügung und Ordnung des Fragens" (1988, 47). Yet this unity of questioning is not a "philosophical system" in the modern sense of the word. As Heidegger shows (1988, 52), a modern system depends on a characterization of knowledge as *demonstrative* in the manner of *mathematics* (e.g., Spinoza's "more geometrico demonstrata"). This kind of system, which Heidegger denies Plato has, is precisely the kind attributed to Plato by Gaiser and Krämer: Krämer explicitly associates Plato's position with the "Systembegriff der Neuzeit" (1994, 13; see also 14, 16, 20). See below, however, for the way in which both of them sometimes inconsistently retreat to using the word "system" in Heidegger's sense of "unity of questioning."

24. Gilbert Ryle (1949, 25–61) is primarily responsible for introducing the distinction between "knowledge that" and "knowledge how" into contemporary philosophical discourse.

25. This is of course a point that Wittgenstein makes in the *Tractatus Logico-Philosophicus* (1922) with regard to all those things which he calls "objects." An object is simple (2.02) and can only be named (3.221). What is said or asserted in a proposition, however, is a "state of affairs" (*Tatsache*), which is complex.

26. Lloyd appears to have this kind of nonpropositional thought in mind when he writes (1969–70, 261): "Roughly speaking, it would be a case of thinking, or thinking of, say beauty, without thinking something about beauty, say that beauty is truth." The view that all knowledge of objects is propositional is therefore the view that, in the words of Fine (1979, 366–67), "a sentence of the form '*a* knows *x*' can always be transformed into a sentence of the form '*a* knows what *x* is'; and the latter, in turn, is readily transformed into '*a* knows that *x* is *F*.'" I will argue that this is precisely the view that *cannot* be ascribed to Plato.

27. Compare this distinction to the following claim made by Wittgenstein in the *Tractatus:* "Ein Satz kann nur sagen, *wie* ein Ding ist, nicht *was* es ist" (3.221).

28. Though to my knowledge this possibility has hardly been explored, Lloyd (1969–70, 263), in discussing Plotinus, states the following condition of nonpropositional thought: "This kind of thinking involves no distinction between the thinker or the thinking on one side and the object of his thinking or the thought on the other side." The point seems to be that to distinguish the object from the subject is already to introduce complexity into the thinking, a complexity opposed to the simplicity of nonpropositional thought.

29. In distinguishing between the "manifest" and the "describable," I am arguing against precisely the view, most clearly articulated by Fine (1979, 366–67), that "Knowledge of things, for Plato, is description-dependent, not description independent."

30. For example, it will be argued that *virtue* is undefinable because it cannot be identified with a set of properties that would define it. It will also be argued that virtue is inseparable from the knowing subject and can therefore be known only through *self*-knowledge. Finally, the knowledge of virtue will be shown to be in large part a practical know-how. In all of these ways, the knowledge of virtue will prove to be nonpropositional. For an argument against the increasingly common view that Plato takes philosophical knowledge to be propositional, see Gonzalez (1998).

NOTES TO PAGES 9-10

31. This is the phrase used by both Gaiser (1968, 9; 1980b, 49) and Krämer (1994, 7) to avoid the charge that they are making Plato's philosophy rigid and dogmatic. Yet it is one thing to use this phrase and another to mean something specific by it. Gaiser explains that the philosopher, according to Plato, can attain only "eine vorläufige Annäherung" to the ultimate principles. This approximation consists of "Analogien, Aspekten, hypothetischen Entwürfen" (1968, 10). Plato's system seeks to represent reality "in modo sempre e solamente ipotetico e dialettico" (1980b, 49). But then is there any point in calling this kind of approximation a "system"? Krämer, on the other hand, explains that Plato's system is only a "project" and an "outline" (cited in Reale 1990, 24). But is it a project that can be completed? Is it an outline that can be filled in? If not, then why not? What is necessarily left out? Gaiser and Krämer are frustratingly unclear on these points. For further discussion of this issue, see below.

32. 1983a, revised as 1994a. Brickhouse and Smith (1994, 10–29) also defend a "constructivist" account of the elenchus; however, they reject Vlastos's attribution of constructive results to *individual* elenctic arguments, arguing that only *repeated* elenctic examinations can provide such results (1994, 12 n18, 18–21). Brickhouse and Smith also deny that this is the *sole* function of the elenchus. Irwin (1995, 17–30) sees the elenchus as giving support to moral convinctions *without* providing knowledge. Gentzler (1996, 260–67) also defends a "constructivist" account.

33. For versions of the "nonconstructivist" thesis, see Grote (1888, especially 1:420–21), R. Robinson (1953, 7–19); Vlastos (1956), Benson (1987, 1989, 1990a, 1990b, 1995), Kraut (1984, 249–62), Stemmer (1992, especially 142–43). Yet one of the most extreme versions of this position is that of Kierkegaard, who characterizes the elenchus as a "dialectical vacuum pump" (1965, 203) and claims that Socrates "was not only devoid of any positive system, but devoid of any positivity whatsoever" (238). Another is that of Ryle, who sees in the early dialogues nothing but eristic (1966, 120, 205), speaks of "the purely gymnastic and cathartic tasks of the Socratic Method" (134), and only grudgingly acknowledges Plato's desire to distinguish between "prize-fighting eristic" and "pedagogically serious eristic" (203; in contrast, Benson believes that his "nonconstructivist" interpretation can preserve the distinction between elenchus and eristic: see 1989, 593–97).

34. R. Robinson (1953), Elias (1968), Vlastos (1991, 107–31).

35. Most notably, Stemmer (1992). For an excellent critique of Vlastos's view, see Seeskin (1993).

36. Thus Stemmer (1992, 61) describes as follows Plato's method: "Die Suche nach einer Methode, ethische Sätze so zu sichern, dass sie ein hinreichendes Fundament für eine auf Vernunft gegründete Lebensführung abgeben, ist Anlass und Inhalt seiner philosophischen Arbeit."

37. See, for example, Krämer (1990a, 57) and Gaiser (1980a, 30 n31).

38. Gaiser and Krämer seem to be in disagreement about this point (though I am unaware of their having acknowledged this). What Gaiser says about the ineffability of the principles clearly seems to contradict Krämer's claim that

reality for Plato is "completely knowable and available" (see passage cited below), and one does not find Krämer making any concession to the nonpropositional character of philosophical knowledge for Plato.

39. "Das System bleibt vielmehr für Platon abbildhafter Ausdruck der Wahrheit, logische Vergegenwärtigung des *an sich nicht Sagbaren,* ein Entwurf, der in seiner Weise notwending, streng folgerichtig und verbindlich war (nicht etwa nur ein beliebiger Versuch neben anderen), aber schon allein wegen der *unausdenkbaren Gegensätzlichkeit der Prinzipien* nicht als geschlossen, sondern als über sich hinausweisend verstanden werden muss" (Gaiser 1968, 336; my emphasis).

40. See also Gaiser's claim that the oral teaching about the principles "keine perfekte Welterklärung bietet, sondern *systematisch zu einer einzigen, alles einbeziehenden Paradoxie* hinführt" (1968, 201). For the exact nature of the paradox and contradiction here, see note 48 below.

41. "So sind besonders auch alle begriffliche Bennenungen der Prinzipien—etwa als 'Einheit' und 'Vielheit'—abbildhaft und an sich 'nichtssagend'" (Gaiser 1968, 10).

42. "Es handelt sich hier um die Methode, nicht um das Wesen der platonischen Philosophie selbst" (Krämer 1969, 227).

43. The following remarks of Tigerstedt are therefore fully justified: "For the Socratic ignorance and the Socratic irony Krämer—like the Neoplatonists—has no use. That holds generally true of the Esotericists. Their Platonism is a Platonism without Socrates—a Hamlet without the Prince of Denmark. It is impossible not to feel that this amounts to a disastrous mutilation of Plato's thought" (1977, 86). This is one mistake that Schleiermacher did not make: "But in every way, not accidentally only, or from practice and tradition, but necessarily and naturally Plato's was a Socratic method" ([1836] 1973, 16).

44. Likewise, Gaiser claims that the dialogues, by allowing us to participate as much as possible in that living *dialegesthai* which Plato considers the essential condition for discovering the truth, first provide the "skeleton" (*Skelet*) of the systematic theory of principles with its "living form" (*sein lebensvolle Gestalt;* Gaiser 1968, 586). But then with what are we primarily to identify Plato's philosophy, with the *Skelet* or with the *lebensvolle Gestalt*? If the esotericists accept the latter alternative, then their position is greatly weakened. While the theory of principles may supplement the dialogues, it is empty without them.

45. The esotericists tend most often to explain the "oral" character of Plato's philosophy in terms of pedagogical and sociological factors. Witness Reale (1990, 15): "In sum, the prohibitions of Plato on writing about certain doctrines were not of a purely theoretical character, but were rooted in a conviction that was *chiefly* ethical, educative, and pedagogical, and assimilated from the example of Socrates." According to Reale, Plato feared that if he were to write down his teaching it would be misunderstood by those without sufficient philosophical preparation. Plato also existed in the rift between the oral tradition and the increasing spread of writing and therefore could not entirely abandon the earlier tradition. Yet when we turn to the *Seventh Letter* we see that Plato's reasons for the prohibition of writing are almost entirely theoretical. The esotericists, however,

consistently avoid reading beyond 341e and therefore make no real attempt to come to terms with the highly theoretical proof of the inexpressibility of the first principles which Plato gives starting at 342a. (See my account of this part of the letter in the final chapter.) Furthermore, the sociological and pedagogical factors which the esotericists cite can hardly explain why Plato would rule out writing in principle. Could he not have written his system down for the use of those students who *did* have sufficient philosophical preparation? It is due to difficulties such as this one that the esotericists are also inclined to see Plato's teaching as *essentially*, and not just accidentally, oral. For the confusion in which this results, see Gaiser (1980b, 48): the theory of principles "per la sua stessa essenza non doveva essere esposta per iscritto, e ciò per il motivo che Platone non voleva che lettori impreparati e inadatti fossero indotti in equivoci." There are *two* explanations here: the theory was not expressed in writing "per la sua stessa essenza" and also "per il motivo."

46. This weakness of the esotericist position is particularly evident in Szlezák (1989). According to Szlezák, a Platonic dialogue exhibits a succession of progressively higher levels of inquiry. The discussion begins at one level, runs into an impasse, and then is transposed by Socrates to a higher level through the introduction of new concepts and principles. Essential to Szlezák's esotericist thesis, however, is the claim that in the dialogues this succession of progressively higher levels of inquiry must always stop short of the highest level, i.e., that of the first principles: "die letzte, entscheidende 'Hilfe' oder Verteidigung ausserhalb der Schrift bleibt" (346). Yet the article provides no explanation of why this must be the case. If the reason is that Plato feared being misunderstood, then he should have left *all* levels of inquiry except the most basic outside of the written dialogues.

47. We can accept Aristotle as an authority for *what* Plato said while at the same time suspecting his ability and willingness to remain faithful to the *spirit* and *context* in which Plato said it. "Nicht die einzelnen Lehrstücke, aber die Beleuchtung des Ganzen stammt von Aristoteles" (Kuhn 1968, 156).

48. Gaiser (1987, 92) and Krämer (1990a, 81–82; 1994, 6) of course provide Plato with an explanation, or rather *two*. According to one, the lower or derivative parts of reality are related to the higher principles as composites to their *elements*. Here analysis/synthesis is the operative method. According to the other, the lower parts are related to the higher as particulars or species to *genera*. But a Platonic Form is not a genus under which sensible objects are classified, nor is it an element out of which sensible objects are constituted. Furthermore, the two explanations are not strengthened by being combined, since they are clearly incompatible. Gaiser recognizes a difficulty here, but asserts that the dialectician *must* be able to see the agreement and convergence of the two methods (1987, 92). Krämer speaks of "methodological pluralism" (and even compares this to the pluralism of perspectives in the dialogues!) without explaining how such pluralism is compatible with the unity that a philosophical "system" must by definition have (1990a, 82). The related comments made in Gaiser (1980b) are even stranger. After calling Plato's theory of the principles "dialectical," Gaiser explains that this

theory does not admit any one-sided or unilateral characterization: for example, it can be called both "monism" and "dualism" or neither. He then justifies this claim by saying that the theory is not subject to the principle of noncontradiction!

49. That accepting the evidence of the indirect tradition need not commit one to Krämer's conception of Plato's philosophy as an axiomatic-deductive system has been shown by Ferber (1991, 1993). Ferber accepts the existence of unwritten teachings but argues that they were only *opinions* and that Plato's philosophy is essentially "aporetic."

50. These are the words Gaiser uses (1968, 8) to distinguish the unwritten teaching from that of the dialogues. Yet elsewhere Gaiser's characterization of Plato as a "systematic" thinker appears to mean little more than that his philosophy is not a collection of disconnected, ad hoc insights and suggestions: see Gaiser (1968, 336; 1980b, 48). The meaning of the word "system" thereby becomes so weak that I do not see how it can support the esotericists' stronger claims.

51. I am here in agreement with R. Robinson (1953, 52): "The great theory of dialectic is the theory of the method of discovering essence." As Robinson also points out, however, "The What-is-X? question therefore owes its prominence in the early dialogues not to spatial predominance but to the emphasis which Socrates puts upon it" (49).

52. Vlastos (1983b, 74 n8), was forced to admit that his conclusions, in applying mainly to the *Gorgias*, tell us little about elenchus as practiced in the "aporetic" dialogues. For others who have commented on this limitation, see Benson (1995, 101), and Gentzler (1996, 269). As far as I can see, Vlastos has subsequently done little to remedy this defect. In an appendix to the revised version of his article on the elenchus (1994a, 33–36), Vlastos argues that while what he has identified as the presuppositions of the elenctic method are explicitly stated only in the *Gorgias*, they can also be read back into other Socratic dialogues. Elsewhere he explains: "Scrutiny of any of the aporetic dialogues should satsify anyone that en route to the eventual *aporia* Socrates produces elenctic justification of important theses whose truth is unaffected by the eventual failure to find the answer to the 'What is the F?' question" (1994b, 58 n44). Apart from the fact that such "elenctic justification" is the exception, rather than the norm, in the "aporetic dialogues," it is a strange account of a method which focuses on what the method accomplishes incidentally, outside of its principle aim (cf. Polansky 1985, 258). Of course, the reason why Vlastos focuses so exclusively on the *Gorgias* is that Socrates in this dialogue is advancing and defending *propositions*. It is possible here to identify "Socratic doctrines" which, given Vlastos's acceptance of the two assumptions discussed above, are the only positive results the Socratic method could have. I would claim, however, that Socrates' need to defend doctrines in the *Gorgias* shows the *limitations* of what he is doing there.

53. "First and foremost elenchus is *search*" (1994a, 4).

Chapter 2

1. Other dialogues that also focus on the What-is-x? question are *Euthyphro, Lysis, Hippias Major* (if it is authentic, which I doubt), and *Theaetetus* (which is

considered "late"). For how the first two fit the pattern I will uncover in the *Laches* and the *Charmides*, see note 88 below. Except for its "hypothetical" ending, the *Meno* too can be put in this group. Dialogues that do not address the What-is-x? question, but which I would call "aporetic," are the *Cratylus*, the *Euthydemus*, and the *Protagoras*. In this chapter I focus on the *Charmides* and the *Laches* because it is in these dialogues that the double-edged contrast I want to make between dialectic, on the one hand, and everyday discourse and sophistic discourse, on the other, is brought out most clearly.

2. Nehamas (1975) has argued against the common view that Socrates' interlocutors frequently misunderstand his What-is-x? question as asking for examples. He points out that even Laches' definition of courage as "remaining at one's post" does not refer to a specific action, but rather to a general kind of action and thus a universal (295–96). Benson (1992) agrees with Nehamas's conclusion but seeks to explain why Socrates in this case often objects that his interlocutor's answers are not only materially, but also *formally*, incorrect. His solution is that the interlocutors' answers, while universal, satisfy neither the requirement of being one (i.e., they simply state that virtue is this *and* this *and* this) nor the requirement of being complete (i.e., their definitions leave out certain kinds of actions that should be included). I would add the explanation that the interlocutor's vision is focused on ordinary experience in which the virtue under examination is neither one nor complete.

3. R. Robinson writes of the What-is-x? question: "it is, perhaps, when unsupported by a context, the vaguest of all forms of question except an inarticulate grunt" (1953, 59).

4. The historian/rhetor Theopompos of Chios apparently criticized Plato himself for doing what we see Socrates doing in the dialogues, i.e., asking others to define the good and the just, *as if people in daily speaking of these things did not already know what they are* (Jacoby 1929, 595).

5. For the application of the word *adoleschēs* to Socrates and the sophists in the comic poets, see Aristophanes' *Tagenistai* (fr. 490 Kock) and *Clouds* (1485), and Eupolis (fr. 352 Kock). For allusions in the dialogues to the common characterization of Socrates as *adoleschēs*, see *Phaedo* 70b10-c1, *Republic* 488e3–489a2, *Theaetetus* 195b10, *Phaedrus* 270a1, *Sophist* 225d10–11, and *Statesman* 299b7–8.

6. Woodruff makes this criticism: "Not surprisingly, Socrates found no one whose knowledge satisfied such a criterion, and all his attempts to define the virtues were frustrated" (1978, 464). Then in a note: "It is not surprising, I think, because Aristotle and the sophists are right. The best one can do with the virtues is to become expert in the many uses of the virtue words, and so to come to command a multiplicity of conflicting standards latent in ordinary language" (464 n28).

7. "Die Dialoge gehen also immer wieder aus einer faktischen Unwissenheit, erheben sich zu einem Wissensideal, erreichen es nicht und sinken damit wieder in die Ungewissenheit zurück" (Waldenfels 1961, 40–41).

8. Cf. Seeskin (1987, 45).

9. Cf. Taylor (1959, 47). Taylor, however, believes that the answer to this criticism is that definitions are required for true knowledge: "Failure in finding

the definition means that we really do not know what we admire, and so long as we do not know this, our moral life is at the mercy of sentimental half-thinking" (47). But then does Socrates' own failure to find irrefutable definitions prove him incapable of anything but "sentimental half-thinking"?

10. As noted in chapter 1, Ryle's "nonconstructivist" interpretation does not stop short of identifying the Socratic elenchus with eristic (1966, 120, 205), while that of Benson still wishes to preserve a distinction. The difference for Benson (1989) is that while eristic is concerned only with *verbal* consistency or inconsistency, the elenchus is concerned with consistency or inconsistency in the *beliefs* that an interlocutor truly holds. According to Benson, however, the elenchus will give the interlocutor no reason for favoring one belief over the other. But then the elenchus will leave the interlocutor with nothing more than the intuitions of ordinary experience for deciding between his inconsistent beliefs. Indeed, if the interlocutor is equally attached to all of his beliefs, he will be inclined to assume that what Socrates has uncovered is a purely verbal inconsistency. As for Socrates himself, Benson cannot deny that he has moral beliefs but argues that these beliefs are not based on elenctic arguments. But then does Socrates, like his interlocutors, base his beliefs on nothing more than ordinary experience and intution? Is he, in other words, as dogmatic as they are? Benson attempts to avoid this consequence by suggesting two possibilities: Socrates arrived at his beliefs through some other method (1995, 109–10), or Socrates believed that *repeated* elenctic examinations could produce doctrinal results (110–1). The first appears highly implausible: if Socrates had another method for arriving at the truth, why did he make the elenchus his preferred method? The second is the view of Brickhouse and Smith (1994, 10–29), but Benson neither does nor can explain its possibility. If each elenctic argument can establish *only* inconsistency or consistency, how could the mere multiplication of such arguments suddenly establish *truth*?

11. E.g., Goldschmidt (1947, 74–75): "Et, de toute manière, ces dialogues 'aporétiques' contiennent, pour peu qu' on y réfléchisse, une claire doctrine." The same view is expressed by Guthrie: "Although the search for a definition of courage ostensibly ends in failure, the positive conclusions are so evident, in the light of our general acquaintance with Socrates, that they can scarcely be called masked" (1962–78, 4:132). A variant of this interpretation is the view of the "esotericists" that a relatively stable system of doctrines is to be found "behind" the dialogues, both early and late. For a systematic application of this approach to the early dialogues, see Erler (1987).

12. A possible alternative to both the "constructivist" and the "nonconstructivist" interpretations is the characterization of the elenchus as having a positive *protreptic* function: the classic exposition of this view is Gaiser (1959), but see also Tarán (1985, 89). Because Tarán subscribes to the view that the aporetic dialogues do not provide us with positive knowledge (92–93), his view is still essentially "nonconstructivist." On the other hand, Gaiser's major, and surprisingly often ignored, thesis is that the protreptic of Socratic elenchus is not simply "preliminary" to some teaching but already in some sense provides the

knowledge toward which it turns one (1959, 5, 18, 28, 106, 110, 120, 131, 163–65, 168, 183, 186–87, 221). If protreptic is understood in this way, then I agree that the elenchus is essentially protreptic: but then it remains to determine what kind of knowledge protreptic provides and how. In my reading of the *Euthydemus* (chapter 4), I defend a thesis similar to Gaiser's.

13. Kahn (1986) sees this fact as supporting his thesis that the *Laches* was written as an introduction to a whole series of dialogues: the *Charmides, Euthyphro, Protagoras, Meno, Lysis,* and *Euthydemus*. However, the need for the long prologue can be explained in terms of what takes place in the *Laches* itself.

14. A major exception is Schmid (1992), almost half of which is devoted to the "prologue." Stefanini (1932, 1:43) also recognizes its importance.

15. Schmid (1992, 6–15) provides the best account available of the historical Laches and Nicias, one that demonstrates the striking parallels between their historical actions and what the dialogue reveals about their characters.

16. Schmid, unlike too many other scholars (such as Irwin, on whom see below), recognizes that these questions remain *open* at this point in the dialogue: he rightly points out that Socrates' "discussions of the so-called art of teaching virtue are everywhere so laden with irony that beyond the matter of refuting the claim of others to the art, it is difficult to say whether Socrates even believes such an art to be possible, much less whether Plato portrays Socrates as indeed possessing it" (1992, 80).

17. Cf. Schmid's claim (1992, 66–71) that Nicias represents Athenian Enlightenment while Laches represents distinctly Spartan virtues.

18. Cf. Schmid (1992, 86–87).

19. This is recognized by Griswold (1986, 185–86) and Arieti (1991, 59), but not by Roochnik (1996). For a critique of the latter's characterization of Laches, see note 42 below.

20. All translations in this book are my own, unless otherwise specified.

21. This is normally referred to as the "Socratic fallacy." W. D. Ross (1951, 16), Gully (1962, 3) and R. Robinson (1953, 53) all believe that Socrates is committed to the principle that we cannot recognize instances of x to be x unless we have a definition of x. In an influential article, Geach (1966) characterized this view as a hopeless fallacy. Beversluis (1974) has shown the disastrous results of this principle for Socrates' own method of inquiry, a method that involves testing proposed definitions of x against recognized instances of x, thus doing what this principle claims is impossible. In the very large body of literature on the subject, scholars have thrown Socrates a number of different lifesavers. One is what Vlastos has called the "sufficiency of true belief" interpretation, according to which Socrates' meaning is the following: though we cannot *know* instances of x to be x without a definition of x, we do not need a definition in order to have the *true belief* that they are instances of x, and this true belief provides a sufficient foundation and starting point for inquiry. For further consideration of this view and a critique of its "propositional" versions, see note 23 below and chapter 6, note 42. An alternative to qualifying the principle in this way is simply to deny that Socrates subscribes to it. This denial is reconciled with the texts in which

Socrates clearly maintains the priority of knowing what x is to knowing instances or properties of x by pointing out that these texts commit Socrates only to the view that the former knowledge is a *sufficient,* not a *necessary,* condition for the latter. According to this view, these texts leave open the possibility that there are *other ways* of knowing instances or properties of x besides knowing what x is. There are already suggestions of this interpretation in Santas (1972, especially 136–37). However, it has been most explicitly and thoroughly defended by Beversluis (1992, especially 111), and Vlastos (1994c, especially 76). Both Beversluis (1992, 120 n4) and Vlastos (1994c, 71, 85–86) nevertheless believe that the "Socratic fallacy" *is* committed in the *Lysis, Hippias Major, Meno,* and the *Republic.* Yet they lump these dialogues together in a "post-elenctic" period and in this way keep the fallacy that infects them from contaminating the "earlier" elenctic dialogues such as the *Euthyphro, Protagoras, Laches,* and *Charmides.* Vlastos thus finds the historical Socrates, whom he sees represented in the "early" elenctic dialogues, innocent of the fallacy, while making the guilt all Plato's, for whom "Socrates" in later dialogues is supposed to be a mere mask. Benson has made two decisive points against this interpretation. First, the "transitional" or "post-elenctic" dialogues cannot be so easily dismissed as evidence for Socrates' commitment to the fallacy in the "early" dialogues (Benson 1990b, 23–28). Second, while Beversluis and Vlastos are right in claiming that the "early" dialogues do not commit Socrates to the principle that knowledge of what x is is a *necessary* condition for knowing instances or properties of x, these texts do commit Socrates to other views best explained by this principle (Benson 1990b, 42–43; for a similar criticism of Santas's version of this interpretation, see Burnyeat 1977, 386 n9). Why, for example, does Socrates consider the What-is-x? question to be of such central importance if he believes, as Vlastos and Beversluis maintain, that there are other ways of knowing instances and properties of x? (Benson 1990b, 29–30). Benson claims that while the present passage of the *Laches* does not explicitly commit Socrates to the "fallacy," no other explanation of what Socrates says appears to be available (1990b, 37). For Benson's view that he can attribute the "fallacy" to Socrates and still avoid the difficulties pointed out in Beversluis (1974), see the following note. While I agree with most of Benson's arguments, I cannot, for reasons presented below, accept the assumption he shares with rival interpretations: that the knowledge Socrates seeks is definitional.

22. That this is a necessary consequence has been denied by Benson (1990b, 45–64). He first claims that Socrates' immediate aim in the elenctic dialogues, and the only aim achieved in them, is the testing of the interlocutor's knowledge (48–57). He then claims that in order to show that his interlocutors lack a knowledge of F-ness, Socrates only needs to show that their beliefs concerning F-ness are inconsistent: but showing such inconsistency does not require any knowledge that the alleged examples and properties of F-ness in fact are such (57–60). However, this characterization of Socrates' aim is incorrect, as I hope my interpretations of the *Laches* and the *Charmides* show. Furthermore, Benson's interpretation requires us to believe that Socrates really thought that he and Laches have no ability whatsoever to recognize examples and properties of courage and that whatever shared opinions they have are completely accidental.

NOTES TO PAGE 27

23. See Burnyeat (1977, 386–87), Irwin (1977, 40–41; 1995, 28–29), Fine (1992, 209). In Irwin's words, Socrates "can insist that without knowledge of what virtue is we cannot have fully justified beliefs about virtue, and still allow us true beliefs to recognize examples of virtue" (1977, 41). This view has come under criticism, especially by Beversluis and Vlastos. Vlastos objects: (1) In the *Hippias Major*, Socrates suggests that without a definition of beauty we are completely unable to recognize what is beautiful and what is not; (2) three passages from the *Gorgias* (505e4–5, 472c6–d1, 486e5–6) make clear that Socrates' aim is knowledge (Vlastos 1994c, 73). Contra (2): even if Socrates' aim is knowledge, he can still rely on true beliefs in his pursuit of this aim. Contra (1): the passage in question is heavily ironic. Beversluis objects: (3) in the early dialogues, Socrates appears interested only in the distinction between those who know and those who do not (Beversluis 1992, 115); (4) the later view that true belief is good enough for virtue is not one held by the Socrates of the early dialogues (Beversluis 1992, 116); (5) in the early dialogues there is no distinction between objects of belief and objects of knowledge (Beversluis 1992, 116). Contra (5): true belief and knowledge need not be assigned different objects in order to be distinguished. Contra (4): there is no need to take at face value Socrates' claim at the end of the *Meno* that only true belief is required to be virtuous. Contra (3): Socrates' "all or nothing" approach in the elenctic dialogues may simply be due to his desire to make his interlocutors see the importance of searching for knowledge and by no means commits him to rejecting the existence of that partial or confused awareness which he elsewhere calls "belief." Recently Brickhouse and Smith (1994, 46–55) have proposed an interpretation that resembles the "sufficiency of true belief" interpretation: they take Socrates to mean only that "without knowledge of the definition of F-ness, one's judgment of F things is subject to error" (46). However, there is an important difference: for Brickhouse and Smith, Socrates' principle does not rule out the possibility of having *knowledge* (in the sense of a completely justified true judgment) of some F things without a definition of F-ness; they take his claim to be only that without such a definition one cannot have knowledge of *all* F things. In other words, the consequence of not having a definition, on this interpretation, is not that all of one's judgments are subject to error (as the "sufficiency of true belief" interpretation maintains) but rather that not all of one's judgments are free from error. But why is it that some F things can be known without a definition while others cannot? Brickhouse and Smith must distinguish between difficult cases, where a definition would be needed to decide, e.g., whether or not a certain action is virtuous, and easy or straightforward cases, where an action could be recognized as virtuous without any such definition (see 54). An obvious problem with this interpretation is that Socrates apparently gives no hint of such a distinction between different kinds of instances. Furthermore, Brickhouse and Smith assume (though with some qualifications: see below) that what Socrates truly seeks is a definition.

24. "The knowledge Socrates seeks and evidently does not have would be based on knowledge of definitions" (Woodruff 1986, 30). "He [Socrates] believes, of course, that if one is to be morally virtuous, one must know what virtue is, and that if one truly knows what virtue is, one can correctly express its definition"

(Brickhouse and Smith 1994, 21). Unlike many others, however, Brickhouse and Smith are aware "of how inappropriate it is to attempt to understand Socrates' epistemology in terms of the conception of knowledge which has received the most philosophical attention in modern times: 'propositional knowledge,' or knowledge *that* such and such is the case" (1994, 44; see also 61). They emphasize the extent to which the knowledge Socrates seeks is knowledge *how* (44; see also 63–64). But then why do they hold on to the view that "knowledge of moral definitions is necessary for wisdom" (63)? Apparently, they consider Socrates' commitment to this view "obvious" and therefore indisputable, but, as I show below, it is no such thing. Even Seeskin, who also makes claims that one would expect to lead him away from this view, still accepts it (1987, 9).

25. "If failure in an elenchos is Socrates' evidence of other people's lack of knowledge, then he must take ability to give a definition to be necessary for knowledge" (Irwin 1995, 27).

26. "Socrates' aims were *anti*-Cognitivist, for his project of spurring the citizens of Athens to moral excellence depended on showing them that explicit verbal definitions stating necessary and sufficient conditions for the applicability of moral terms are *impossible,* and that if people believed their moral knowledge to consist in rules, then they did not know what they supposed they knew" (Matson and Leite 1991, 146).

27. Griswold documents the discussion's reliance on opinion and correctly points out that the opinions must be somehow grounded in truth if this reliance is to result in education, rather than dogma (1986, 191–93). He even mentions "recollection" in this context and suggests that "The nature of courage, among other things, is partially present to the soul in a prediscursive way, and this is the basis of the soul's ability to articulate something true about it" (192). I see such a prediscursive awareness, whether or not it is made the basis of an explicit "doctrine of recollection," as presupposed by Socrates' method of inquiry. I will deal with this issue in more detail in chapter 6 in the context of a discussion of recollection in the *Meno.*

28. Schmid cites a number of sources, especially poems by Tyrtaeus and Theognis, to show that Laches' definition "represents nothing less than the basic, traditional Greek conception of patriotic or political courage" (1992, 101).

29. Whether or not Socrates widens the scope of courage *too much* is disputed. This criticism has been made by, among others, Santas (1969, 441–42). Penner (1992c, 16–17) sees Socrates as hinting here that courage is not, counter to the original admission, only a *part* of virtue. Schmid, however, provides a great deal of textual evidence and argumentation (1992, 106–10) to show that Socrates is neither widening the concept of courage beyond the traditional Greek conception nor collapsing the distinction between courage and moderation by finding courage in the resistance of pleasures, as Santas and Penner maintain.

30. Schmid makes the very interesting suggestion that Socrates' choice of this example is not accidental since the connotations of the word "quickness" point to what is lacking in Laches' definition of courage as a passive endurance: "quickness is associated with boldness and decisiveness, the ability or inclination

to seize an opportunity, to wade in and attack, if sometimes rashly" (1992, 111–12; Schmid sees a similar point in Socrates' choice of the cavalry as a counterexample to Laches' first definition, 104).

31. "*Techne* is a deliberate application of human intelligence to some part of the world, yielding some control over *tuche;* it is concerned with the management of need and with prediction and control concerning future contingencies" (Nussbaum 1986, 95).

32. Because the *Laches* makes clear that courage is not to be identified with any kind of technical knowledge, Devereux has concluded that the point of the dialogue is to show us the untenability of the Socratic thesis that virtue is a kind of knowledge (1977, 129). A similar interpretation was defended much earlier by Stefanini (1932, 1:39–47). But what the dialogue questions is not *whether* courage is knowledge but rather *what kind of a knowledge* it could possibly be; cf. Griswold (1986, 187).

33. This is the notorious Socratic paradox: all moral error is due to ignorance and is therefore involuntary, because in knowing what is good we necessarily do what is good (cf. *Gorgias* 468, 509e; *Protagoras* 345d sq., 352c sq., 355). As Irwin notes (1977, 5), Plato "has no distinction between meta-ethics and normative ethics, or between the method of philosophical argument and the method of moral deliberation."

34. The circularity is even more striking if Schmid is correct in claiming that "This last phrase, *'autē hē karterēsis estin andreia'* may also be translated: 'this very endurance [i.e., the endurance needed in inquiry] is courage' " (1992, 128).

35. For another interpretation that takes into account the self-referential character of the *Laches,* see Griswold (1986). Griswold focuses on the relation between courage as an object of philosophical inquiry and courage as a characteristic of philosophical inquiry itself (see especially 178). This self-referential character of the dialogue is also noted and briefly commented on by Gaiser (1959, 163).

36. Schmid, like others, has seen a reference here to the historical Nicias's disastrous reliance on seers during the Sicilian expedition. Perhaps this allusion is meant to suggest that someone who, like Nicias, places such absolute confidence in human reason, considering it divinely infallible, will be the first to turn to superstition when this confidence is undermined (Schmid 1992, 135–37, 168). What is common to both Nicias's rationalism and his superstition is a desire to evade "freedom, risk and responsibility" (158, 170).

37. Surprisingly, Socrates in this debate sides with Laches against Nicias. However, Schmid has correctly explained what is going on here: Socrates is not objecting to Nicias's verbal distinction per se but rather to the motivation behind the distinction, i.e., Nicias's denigration of anything that is not technical, scientific knowledge to the level of the bestial and childish (149). Of course, Socrates himself is often considered to be the arch-Intellectualist, but this passage should show otherwise.

38. *Protagoras* 360d, *Republic* 429c, 442c. In the *Memorabilia,* Xenophon attributes to Socrates the following definition of courage: "knowing how to deal

well with terrors and dangers" (IV.vi.11). On the other hand, Socrates is also reported to have said that, while courage may be increased through learning and practice, it yet to some extent comes by nature; some souls are just naturally braver than others (III.ix.1–3).

39. *Gorgias* 511b–513c. This distinction between the specific arts and a knowledge of the good is also implied at *Republic* 332d–e and *Charmides* 164b–c.

40. Irwin (1977, 86, 302 n62; 1995, 42–44) and Penner (1992b, 175–76; 1992c) argue that the dialogue as a whole suggests that Socrates is more committed to the unity of virtue than to the view that courage is a "part" of virtue. For a critique of this interpretation, see Vlastos (1994d, 121–24) and Benson (1995, 84). While I am in general agreement with this interpretation, I believe that Irwin and Penner fail to answer, or even address, the crucial question: why does Socrates *reject* Nicias's definition for entailing the unity thesis? We must, in other words, explain why the dialogue does *not* end with a conclusion. After all, Socrates at the end could easily enough have encouraged Nicias to abandon the view that courage is only a part of virtue, especially since Nicias nowhere expresses any strong commitment to this view: as Vlastos rightly points out (1994d, 122), it is introduced by *Socrates*. There is a plausible explanation: while Socrates may believe the virtues to be one, he also rejects misunderstandings or oversimplifications of this view and does not presume to *tell* us just what kind of a unity this is. The *aporia* with which the *Laches* ends is not "solved" by simply denying any distinction between courage and virtue as a whole. The thesis "courage = virtue = a knowledge of good and evil" tells us nothing. It can be either so vague as to be acceptable to everyone or so specific (if, for example, a "technical" knowledge is meant) as to be rejected by Socrates himself. The sense in which the virtues are one is revealed only by the kind of knowledge Socrates exhibits in the inquiry.

41. Penner (1992c, 20–22), in contrast, gives a very positive characterization of Nicias, for no more reason, apparently, than that Nicias defends the right doctrines, being mistaken only in the belief that courage is a part of virtue. Penner indeed claims that Nicias does not know what courage is and therefore cannot even know that the propositions he correctly affirms are true (23–25). However, since Penner identifies the knowledge of what courage is with the knowledge of *all* true propositions about courage (1992c, 24; 1992a, 144), Socrates no more possesses this knowledge than does Nicias. For a general critique of Penner's characterization of the knowledge Socrates seeks, see chapter 6.

42. For an excellent account of the contrast between Laches and Nicias and their respective deficiencies, see O'Brien (1971, 303–15). O'Brien also recognizes that "In Socrates the theoretical strands of the dialogue come together and find their practical solution" (312). See also Hoerber (1968, 100), Arieti (1991, 60), and Rutherford (1995, 84–87). A surprising defect of Schmid's book (1992) is that while it provides by far the most thorough and insightful account of the characters, roles, and limitations of Laches and Nicias, it has surprisingly little to say about Socrates. Indeed, it seems to make Socrates little more than a referee for the debate between the two generals. The same criticism can be made of Roochnik's account (1996, 90–107). According to Roochnik, Laches is the one who exhibits

"philosophical courage" by exemplifying the Doric harmony of words and deeds (106). The following points tell against this interpretation: (1) When it comes to the relation between words and deeds, Laches is no less one-sided than is Nicias: in his mouth the "Doric harmony" represents, not a profound philosophical insight, but another way of saying that "talk is cheap." *Socrates is the only one in the dialogue who is praised equally* (by Laches and Nicias themselves) for *both* his deeds *and* his words. (2) While Laches at 194a6 indeed expresses *willingness* to endure in the inquiry, he is *unable* to make any more progress (which is why Socrates calls in Nicias; Laches' contribution to the rest of the discussion is purely negative and critical). (3) Laches' self-professed motive for continuing the inquiry, i.e., *the love of victory (philonikia)*, is hardly *philosophical.* Indeed, the personal abuse with which Laches greets Nicias's attempt to define courage (and for which Socrates must scold him, 195a7) seems in part motivated by his own failure to provide a definition (as Nicias himself suggests, 195a8–b1).

43. Laches confesses this motivation at 194a7–8, but it seems to explain Nicias's behavior as well.

44. At one point Socrates proposes seeing whether Nicias is really saying something or is only speaking for the sake of speaking (λόγου ἕνεκα, 196c1–2) The result of the discussion clearly shows the latter to be the case.

45. Bonitz has rightly pointed out that this dramatic ending would be unwarranted if the dialogue were negative in outcome (1871, 434), though I do not agree with his way of finding a solution (see note 53 below).

46. Hyland makes a distinction between "the stance of mastery" and the "stance of submission" (1981, 3–17). The latter stance is characterized by "openness," "letting things be," submitting to experience as it presents itself. The former stance, on the other hand, is an attempt to take complete control over the world around us (which is at the "disposal" of our technology). Hyland finds both of these stances in modern culture and considers both of them, in their extreme forms, objectionable. In Socrates, however, he finds a stance that mediates between the other two and avoids their excesses: the "interrogative stance." Such a stance clearly involves openness *as well as* a certain mastery and control. Though Hyland prefaces these remarks to an interpretation of the *Charmides,* I think that they are especially suited to describe the situation in the *Laches.* Laches, in seeing courage as mere "endurance," clearly represents the "stance of submission," while Nicias, in identifying courage with a certain technical knowledge, represents the "stance of mastery." True courage is to be found only between these extremes in Socrates' "interrogative stance." That the observations Hyland makes concerning the *Charmides* should apply so well to the *Laches* is not surprising, given the strong similarities between both works noted in this chapter.

47. According to Irwin, Socrates "argues that virtue is simply craft-knowledge" (1977, 7). Irwin believes that, starting with the *Gorgias,* Plato begins to see weaknesses in this view. In fact, however, this view receives its most devastating critique already in the *Laches* and therefore is not a view that Plato or Socrates ever held. How Irwin could fail to see this is explained by one of his critics: "Irwin tends to abstract the arguments Socrates uses from the dramatic context

and to pass them off as Plato's moral theory" (Klosko 1981, 101; this article as a whole demonstrates the lack of evidence for Irwin's view). As for why Socrates uses the *technē* analogy if he does not consider virtue a *technē*, Roochnik has provided a satisfying explanation: "Armed with his analogy, Socrates exhorts those interlocutors who are not committed to the active search for knowledge, and refutes those who believe they have already found their answers" (1992, 193; see 191–93 for a defense of this explanation). Irwin's view appears unchanged in 1995 (see especially 68–70), though he now appears to concede that Socrates' commitment to the identification of virtue with a craft is not as explicit as he suggested in 1977. His response to critics such as Klosko and Roochnik is for the most part silence. Nussbaum (1986) also believes Socrates to be in search of a *technē* of virtue. (Her view partly depends on committing Socrates to his ad hominem description of a science of measuring moral values in the *Protagoras;* for a critique, see Gonzalez [forthcoming]). This view is part of her broader thesis that Plato inaugurated an antitragic rational optimism according to which reason is capable of ensuring that there are no irresolvable moral conflicts (though Nussbaum thinks that Plato comes to see the limits of this rational optimism in the *Phaedrus* and the *Symposium*). For a thorough refutation of this thesis, see Roochnik (1989, 1990). Both Irwin's and Nussbaum's interpretations of the *technē* analogy itself receive a thorough book-length critique in Roochnik (1996).

48. As is recognized, for example, by Griswold (1986, 183 and 187) and Roochnik (1996, 90–107).

49. Irwin asserts: "In the *Charmides* and the *Laches* he never suggests that the sort of knowledge (*epistēmē*) he has in mind belongs to anything except a craft (*technē*)" (1995, 68). In addition to the fact that Socrates also never says that this knowledge *is* a craft, an aim of the present chapter is to show that both the *Laches* and the *Charmides*, when interpreted in their dramatic and argumentative integrity (something Irwin does not do), do suggest very strongly that it is not.

50. "Of course the commander must endure in preventing the fear of defeat and the uncertainty of battle from dislodging his judgment, *but the thinking itself is not fearful*" (Schmid 1992, 129; my emphasis).

51. C. Gould considers Socrates' argument against Laches to be invalid because it rests on the following equivocation: "Socrates conflates the distinction between (i) the agent perseveres in φ-ing unwisely, and (ii) the agent unwisely perseveres in φ-ing. In (i) 'unwisely' modifies 'φ-ing' whereas in (ii) 'unwisely' modifies 'perseveres'" (1987, 272). Perhaps the reason why Socrates does not make this distinction is that he does not consider it relevant to the issue at hand. Gould, however, sees in it the solution to the dialogue. While courage is not to be found in wisely φ-ing, it is to be found in wisely persevering in φ-ing, where the wisdom involved in perseverance is a knowledge of moral good and evil (274). In this way Gould, like Vlastos, claims that while courage cannot be identified with a knowledge of lesser goods, it can be identified with knowledge of the greatest good, i.e., moral good. The main difference is that Gould places greater emphasis on the importance of perseverance as an essential component of courage (though I fail to see how she avoids reducing perseverance to knowledge in the end).

52. Against Irwin, who not only claims that virtue for Socrates is a *technē*, but also assumes that as a *technē* it must be productive knowledge, Roochnik has argued (and, I believe, shown conclusively) that the word *technē* in the dialogues refers as much to the theoretical sciences as to the productive skills (1992, 185–90; see also Nussbaum 1986, 74, and Roochnik 1996, 113 and 271–82). Therefore, Irwin's translation of *technē* as "craft-knowledge" is simply erroneous. In 1995 Irwin replies to this criticism as follows: "While it is true that Socrates does not require a *technē* to produce a physical object distinct from the exercise of the craft itself, this fact does not show that he does not regard *technē* as—in Aristotle's terms—productive; for a physical artifact is not necessary for production, as Aristotle conceives it" (364–65 n15). This response is not only beside the point—a distinction between physical and nonphysical artifacts is irrelevant to Roochnik's argument—but also conveniently ignores *Charmides* 165e5–166a7 where *arithmetic and geometry* are described as *technai* that have objects *but no products*. Obviously, Aristotle would not consider these sciences productive in any sense. It is therefore not surprising that Irwin's summary of this part of the *Charmides* (39) skips over the cited passage. When he does refer to this passage, it is only to misrepresent it: he tells us that at 166a3–7 Socrates insists that every science must have a product (71), when in fact this passage makes no mention of a product. This point is important for understanding the *Laches*. The arguments against identifying courage with "technical" knowledge are not restricted to the productive skills but would apply equally to a theoretical, scientific knowledge of good and evil. The problem is the same in both cases: the mastery of a certain subject matter and the elimination of risk. However, the *Charmides* will make the clearest case for distinguishing moral knowledge from both types of *technē*.

53. This is why I cannot accept the interpretation that finds the "solution" to the dialogue in a simple combination of Laches' final definition with Nicias's definition: courage is endurance accompanied by a knowledge of good and evil; see Hoerber (1968, 102) and Bonitz (1871, 434–35). Though I agree that Laches and Nicias represent different facets of courage which must be combined, the nature of this combination is revealed not by a definition that merely asserts it, but rather by Socrates' practice throughout the whole dialogue. The "solution," in short, is not propositional, though propositions can be and are used to hint at it. For different criticisms of the Bonitz/Hoerber interpretation, see Schmid (1992, 42–45).

54. See Rutherford (1995, 89).

55. Hyland (1981, 41–42).

56. Charmides has complained to his uncle about his headaches and has asked him for a cure. When he hears that Socrates has a cure, he is very happy and eagerly prepares to write down the recipe. If Charmides' headaches are caused by heavy drinking, he does not seem to see the connection. Can Charmides be *that* dumb?

57. "We should note also that, since Charmides failed to define temperance he did not, presumably, possess it in the first place" (Sprague 1973, 95 n83; see also 1976, 30–31). If this is true, then the relation between Charmides' temperance

and that of Socrates is no longer a problem: Charmides does not possess any temperance at all. This claim, however, is not supported by what we are actually shown in the dialogue, especially in the scene just described. More important, Sprague does not explain why what she says of Charmides does not apply to Socrates as well: in her view Socrates' failure to define temperance does not rule out his possession of temperance (1973, vii).

58. That none of the definitions examined in the dialogue is rejected as completely false is a point forcefully made by Kosman (1983, 207).

59. Cf. Taylor (1959, 50).

60. Santas has objected to Socrates' opposition of quickness to quietness: "And 'done quickly' does not entail 'done not-quietly' any more than 'done quietly' entails 'done slowly' " (1973b, 115). This objection appears to misunderstand Charmides' definition. When Charmides identifies temperance with ἡσυχιότης, this word clearly does not refer simply to speaking quietly, but also to not being overly eager or aggressive, acting slowly and with deliberation. Socrates' objection is that one's mastery of any skill, whether it be wrestling or writing or playing the lyre, is measured by one's ability to act quickly and without much deliberation.

61. Lutoslawski long ago saw in this passage the "paralogism" of "inferring from the beauty of both temperance and quickness that quickness is temperate (159d)" (1897, 203). Lutoslawski generally did not rate very highly "the stage of logical advance" attained by Plato when he wrote his "smaller works" (203).

62. Santas's description of Critias is right on the mark: "And when it comes to Socrates' objections, he is like a windmill that is not in gear: on meeting the least resistance, he changes direction. Within the space of three pages he changes his definition of temperance three times, the changes being always greater than those required by Socrates' objections. . . . Critias, it seems, will say *anything* to get out of trouble" (1973b, 108).

63. For good surveys of the divergent views concerning the move from self-knowledge to a knowledge of knowledge, see Tuckey (1968, 33–37), Guthrie (1962–78, 4:169–70), and Ebert (1974, 59–61). This is an important question because if the transition from self-knowledge to a knowledge of knowledge is unwarranted, then the difficulties found in the latter notion will not necessarily be difficulties for the former. Tuckey himself does not see the transition as *clearly* illegitimate, since he believes that Plato is struggling here with real ambiguities and difficulties (Tuckey 1968, 110). Guthrie believes that the transition is explained by the context: it has been seen that in order to be temperate one must know not only how to do good things, but also *that one knows* how to do good things. My own interpretation seems to have been anticipated by Grube (1935, 218–19), and Ebert (1974, 65). Cf. Santas (1973b, 119), Morris (1989, 55), and Ketchum (1991, 81–84).

64. Thus at 169e4–5 Critias says, "Whenever one has knowledge that knows itself, one will then be knowing oneself." Socrates replies that he does not disagree.

65. Cf. Gaiser (1959, 165) and J. Klein (1965, 24).

66. "The echo of the *Apology* is unmistakable, and shows once again that whatever the fate of the discussion, the ideal of *sophrosyne* is for Plato embodied in

Socrates himself" (Guthrie 1962–78, 4:170). For a detailed account of the parallels between the *Apology* and the *Charmides*, see Sprague (1976, 36–38). McKim (1985) also recognizes these parallels *but draws the opposite conclusion:* that in identifying the knowledge of knowledge with Socrates' own method and then showing that this knowledge is neither possible nor beneficial and therefore not temperance, Plato aims to show that Socrates lacks temperance and that his elenctic method is incapable of providing any knowledge of virtue. While I agree with Mckim (63, 65) that we should not simply *assume* that Socrates is the ideal philosopher and that Plato completely identifies with him, I think that McKim has completely missed the point of the dialogue as whole. For criticism of his view, see note 74 below. This kind of interpretation of the *Charmides* as a critique of Socrates was defended much earlier by Stefanini (1932, 1:193–201).

67. Morris argues that this objection can be answered: one does not need a knowledge of medicine in order to find out if someone else knows medicine; it is enough to be able to spot contradictions in what this person says about medicine or between what he says and what he does (1989, 57–58). It does seem that even without a knowledge of medicine I would be able to discover that my doctor is a quack if he were one. But how? Presumably, by recognizing that the medicines he prescribes never work, that I only feel worse after every visit, etc. Yet could I be certain that this is the doctor's fault rather than the fault of a particularly virulent disease? Would I not have to go to another doctor to see if he or she could do better? And could I really get anywhere by *questioning* my doctor? Presumably a half-intelligent quack would not blatantly contradict himself. Morris himself admits that one would require "some degree of recognition of the things about which the doctor is talking and of the things which the doctor is manipulating" (1989, 58). But the doctor's frequent use of technical terms would make such recognition on the part of the layman often impossible. Furthermore, the *most* one could do by looking for contradictions is demonstrate the lack of medical knowledge; one could not show that a particular doctor *has* this knowledge. Mahoney, who defends a position similar to Morris's, recognizes this limitation (1996, 192–93, 195). It is worth noting that Benson's "nonconstructivist" account of the elenchus adopts a position similar to Morris's: according to Benson (1987; 1990b, 57–60), Socrates' elenchus does not presuppose a knowledge of the virtue under discussion and has the immediate aim of simply showing contradictions in the beliefs of the interlocutors (and *not* showing that these beliefs are true or false). This account therefore meets with the same difficulties discussed above. Particularly significant, however, is that in the *Charmides* we find Socrates arguing that the elenchus *as Benson characterizes it* (i.e., as a knowledge of knowledge divorced from a knowledge of good and evil) is neither possible nor beneficial.

68. The distinction Socrates suggests here between scientific knowledge and a knowledge of how to live well has been echoed recently by Richard Rorty: after the sciences have done their work "we ask such questions as 'What is the point?', 'What moral is to be drawn from our knowledge of how we, and the rest of nature work?' or 'What are we do to with ourselves now that we know the laws of our behaviour?' The primal error of systematic philosophy has always been

the notion that such questions are to be answered by some new ('metaphysical' or 'transcendental') descriptive or explanatory discourse (dealing with, e.g., 'man', 'spirit,' or 'language')" (1979, 382–83). Rorty, however, appears to assume that because questions about the good life cannot be answered by scientific or metaphysical knowledge, i.e., knowledge based on the correct description of objects, they demand *no knowledge at all,* but only "freedom" and choice (384). The mistaken assumption here is that philosophical knowledge must be scientific or no knowledge at all. In the *Charmides* and the *Laches,* on the other hand, Plato shows us both that there can be philosophical knowledge at the level of questions concerning the good life *and* that this knowledge does not consist of "descriptive or explanatory discourse." It is instead the dialectical knowledge that is revealed in the course of Socrates' inquiry and that I attempt to clarify in this and subsequent chapters.

69. Santas (1973b, 109–10). Santas arrives at this negative conclusion in large part because he sees the suggested definitions as disparate, unrelated, and therefore leading nowhere. The present interpretation, I hope, shows how mistaken this perception is.

70. Morris (1989) and Mahoney (1996). For a more specific criticism of Morris's argument than the one below, see note 67 above. Mahoney tries to show that the knowledge of knowledge, in the guise of elenchus, is beneficial (195–96). But because he believes that knowledge of the good is an *expertise* that the elenchus falls short of, he must conclude that there is no guarantee the elenchus will be beneficial (196).

71. Stefanini (1932, 1:193–201) and McKim (1985). According to McKim, Plato wants us to infer "that it is the knowledge of good and evil which must be *sōphrosunē,* not the knowledge of knowledge" (74). This interpretation appears to be assumed by Penner (1992b, 176–77) and Irwin (1995, 41–42). Ketchum (1991) defends the thesis that the arguments against the "knowledge of knowledge" are conclusive. His defense, however, depends on the unwarranted restriction of the "knowledge of knowledge" to "epistemology," i.e., knowledge of a definition of knowledge, and on reading 166e–172a completely out of the context of the dialogue as a whole, as if it were an independent treatise.

72. This is the interpretation suggested by Sprague (1976, 42), but without any explanation.

73. I find hardly convincing Morris's attempt to avoid the self-reflexivity problem by claiming that the knowledge of knowledge is a "body of propositions about how to conduct refutations," which can know itself by knowing these propositions (Morris 1989, 51–52). Is the knowledge of knowledge itself nothing more than these propositions at the time at which it is knowing these propositions? This view also seems to have the result of completely disassociating knowledge of knowledge from *self*-knowledge (or is the self simply a body of propositions too?).

74. This is a consequence McKim fully accepts. Apart from the criticisms in the main text, I find utterly implausible McKim's claim that Socrates is unaware that the self-knowledge under discussion is his own and that he believes his own self-knowledge to have a product and/or external object (McKim 1985, 66–67).

NOTES TO PAGES 55-56

75. As Roochnik has pointed out, the word *technē* is used in this passage to refer to *both* practical skills *and* theoretical sciences such as mathematics (1992, 187–89; see also 1996, 113, 271–82).

76. It is therefore no wonder that McKim (1985) does not consider this solution, since he assumes throughout his article that virtue is a *technē* with a product and/or object (note, for example, the strict analogy between virtue and medicine made on 75). Mahoney (1996) also assumes that virtue is "expert knowledge" of good and evil, though he sees Socrates' elenchus as only approximating such knowledge. That the dialogue is meant to show us that the knowledge of virtue is *not* a *technē* is recognized by Gaiser (1959, 121–23) and Roochnik (1996, 108–26).

77. Irwin maintains that the good = happiness *is* a "product" of which virtue is the *technē*. But for criticism of this view see note 52 above.

78. "Socratic knowledge, then, would seem to be in part a mode of being, and not, as contemporary epistemology seems to hold, a question of the correct formulation of propositions which are correctly verifiable" (Hyland 1981, 92).

79. Using the distinction of Gilbert Ryle (1949, 25–61) between knowing *how* and knowing *that*, J. Gould (1955) characterizes moral knowledge for Socrates in the following way: "In putting forward the thesis that ἀρετή is only to be attained by ἐπιστήμη, Socrates was *not* asserting that ἀρετή necessarily results from a personal apprehension of the nature of good and evil (still less, of Good and Evil), but that for the achievement of ἀρετή what is required is a form of moral *ability*, comparable in some respects to the creative or artistic ability of potters, shoemakers, and the like; that the ἐπιστήμη which Socrates envisaged was a form of knowing *how*, knowing, that is, *how to be moral*" (7). I believe that Gould is right in characterizing the *epistēmē* involved in *aretē* as a "knowing how." What Gould does not explain, however, is how the dialectical know-how of Socrates differs from the strictly practical know-how of Laches and Charmides. It seems to me that this difference can be maintained only if one claims, as I do here, that Socrates' know-how has theoretical content, both in the propositions it deals with (knowledge that) and in the nonpropositional insight that is gained through the process of inquiry. I therefore must disagree with Gould when he seems to deny such content to Socrates' knowledge in the early dialogues: "Socratic ἐπιστήμη was a simple, undifferentiated, indeed largely undefined, inward ability of the whole personality, an understanding of moral demands" (133). This could just as well be said of Charmides. For other criticisms of Gould's view by less sympathetic critics, see Vlastos (1957), Rist (1964), and Hintikka (1974b). Though all of them grant that Gould's thesis is justified to some degree, they also all claim that some form of "knowledge that" is more fundamental for Socrates than "knowledge how." As the present interpretation should make clear, this is a claim I join Gould in rejecting. For further discussion of Gould versus his critics, see Gonzalez (1995b, 183–84 n50).

80. I must here disagree with Tuckey's claim that unless the knowledge that is virtue has, like other sciences, some definite object, "we are at the mercy of sceptics who can prove the unreasonableness of all our laws and traditions and so leave us with no alternatives but to follow our own unguided inclinations" (Tuckey

1968, 100). Tuckey appears to make the mistaken assumption that virtue can be objective only in the way in which a *technē* such as geometry is objective. However, it is true that the unique character of the knowledge of virtue prevents Socrates from producing it in his interlocutors through any kind of positive instruction. He has no guarantee at the end of a discussion that his interlocutors will develop that self-knowledge which he has tried to awaken in them, as the case of Charmides and Critias shows.

81. Contra Findlay (1974, 84–85) who sees Socrates himself as striving for the empty, abstract "knowledge" that characterizes Critias.

82. Cf. Waldenfels (1961, 75): "Die doppelte Blickrichtung des Gespräches ergibt sich aus der Eigentumlichkeit der sokratischen Frage, in der *die Erkenntnis der Guten die Selbsterkenntnis in sich schliesst* und das Gute als das Ziel der Frage zugleich das 'Zugehörige' (οἰκεῖον) ist, in dem der Suchende sich selber findet."

83. I am here in agreement with Kosman's view that what is gained in the inquiry is not knowledge of a definition, but rather an understanding that emerges from "the confrontation between differing logoi" and is not embodied in any specific logos (Kosman 1983, 209, 211).

84. In the *Cratylus* (390c) and the *Euthydemus* (290c), the dialectician is characterized as someone who knows how to *use* things (words, in the first case, and kinds of knowledge, in the second). In the *Republic* (601c–602a) we are told that he who *uses* a thing, as opposed to *making* or *perceiving* it, is the one who really *knows* this thing (in the sense of knowing its proper good). (See my discussions of these passages in following chapters.) The best account available of the role which this *Gebrauchswissen* plays in Plato's philosophy is Wieland (1982).

85. Teloh (1986, 65) and Mahoney (1996) are therefore on the right track in looking for the solution to the *aporia* in the dialectic which Socrates himself practices. But Mahoney's commitment to the equation of virtue with expert knowledge prevents him from properly characterizing Socrates' dialectic and thus from truly solving the *aporia*.

86. Santas sees the absence of the definition of temperance as "self-control" or "moderation" as due to the characters of Charmides and Critias (1973b, 105–6).

87. Cf. the excellent accounts given by Griswold (1986, 192–93) and Schmid (1992, 179) of why Socrates is closer to Laches than he is to Nicias.

88. Though I have limited myself in this chapter to discussing the *Laches* and the *Charmides,* I believe that their characteristic of instantiating what they are about is shared by at least the *Euthyphro,* the *Lysis,* and the *Protagoras.* In the former dialogue Socrates sides with common-sense piety and against Euthyphro (who, we are told, is ridiculed by his fellow citizens for his unorthodox views). Socrates and the ordinary citizen express the same shock at Euthyphro's determination to take his own father to court. Just as he is unwilling to side with Critias and Nicias, even though the latter portray themselves as being in one way or another "Socratic," so is Socrates unwilling to side with Euthyphro's arrogant dismissal of common sense, even though Euthyphro insists that he and Socrates are fellow fighters against the stupidity of the herd. What is shown throughout the course

of the inquiry is that Socrates shares neither the naive, unquestioning attitude of the masses nor the unthinking dogmatism of Euthyphro. But for precisely this reason Socrates is the one who is shown in the dialogue to possess true piety: piety involves an openness to truth which is incompatible with the belief that one has understood all there is to know about the divine and our relation to it. In other words, what we are shown in the *Euthyphro* is that piety (just like temperance and courage) is impossible without Socrates' peculiar brand of ignorance. On the *Lysis* and the *Protagoras*, see Gonzalez (1995c, forthcoming, respectively). I am inclined to think that, to a greater or lesser degree, *all* of Plato's dialogues instantiate what they are about. Polansky (1992) has shown that this is true of an aporetic dialogue beyond the scope of the present study: the *Theaetetus* (see especially 245).

89. That the goal of the Socratic elenchus is self-knowledge has been argued recently by Rappe (1995). Rappe also appears to consider the knowledge of virtue, as self-knowledge, to be nonpropositional (see 13, 17). However, Rappe appears unable to give up the assumption that Socrates is searching for good definitions of moral terms (4). Seeskin recognizes to some extent the reflexivity of Socrates' elenchus: "Virtue is not only the object of the search but a determining factor in its success" (1987, 42; see also 84–92, 128, 144–45). Because, however, he assumes that the object of Socrates' search is a definition and a theory, he cannot do justice to this reflexivity: on his view, the virtue that is the object of the search and the virtue instantiated in the search must be two completely different things.

90. It should be noted that the knowledge described here cannot be identified with any one of the kinds of knowledge commonly recognized in contemporary philosophy (as they are distinguished, for example, in Price 1969, 42–71). As this and subsequent chapters show, Plato's conception of knowledge differs markedly from the ones current today. For a succinct account of the three mentioned characteristics of dialectical or philosophical knowledge in Plato and an attempt to show their relation to the dialogue form, see Gonzalez (1995b).

Chapter 3

1. If Socrates could in no way get beyond words, his method would be what Richard Robinson (1953, 54) describes it as being: "Thus, while, in the ordinary sense, he [Socrates] knows what the word X means (and what it means is surely the thing X), he nevertheless does not know what the thing X is. Yet he expects the answer to his question to be itself a set of words. It seems, therefore, that his procedure implies, though he was unaware of it, that there is a word or set of words which gives or enshrines a knowledge of the thing X in some way in which the word X does not enshrine a knowledge of the thing X even for those who understand it and use it correctly." As the present chapter demonstrates, however, what the *Cratylus* shows to be absurd is precisely this procedure of attempting to explain a word's meaning by abstracting it from its use and deriving it from other words that are supposed somehow to "enshrine" this meaning.

2. Both "name" and "word" are inadequate as translations of "ὄνομα." The translation "name" is too restrictive, since "ὄνομα" is used in the *Cratylus* to cover general terms (399b–c, 400b–c), adjectives (433e), and infinitives (414a–b), as well as proper names. On the other hand, the translation "word" obscures the primary importance that the dialogue gives to the activity of naming (see Palmer 1989, xiii). I therefore do not restrict myself to either translation, but let context decide in favor of one or the other.

3. As Baxter (1992, 18–19) notes, Hermogenes appears to waver between two different versions of conventionalism: the view that whatever several people (e.g., a particular society) agree to call x is the name of x, and the more extreme view that whatever an *individual* at any time decides to call x is the name of x. However, Baxter also suggests that there is no essential difference between the two versions: a name is equally arbitrary on both accounts, the only difference being the *number* of people who decide it. Sallis (1996, 193) sees *three* different versions here, since he distinguishes between the view that a name is posited by the agreement of several people and the view that it is posited by law and custom. As will be seen below, it is the latter version of conventionalism that Socrates will eventually adopt, though modified in such a way that it is rendered compatible with a version of "natural correctness." What is revealed here by the ambiguity between the different versions is what Sallis calls "a certain elusiveness of the positing activity" (193). The thesis of an original positer or legislator will prove so elusive by the end of the dialogue that it is dismissed as useless for an understanding of the nature of language; cf. Levin (1995, 103).

4. See Silverman (1992, 33) for a helpful discussion of this passage.

5. See Sallis (1996, 194).

6. Cf. Palmer (1989, 50).

7. The ambiguity is recognized by Ketchum (1979, 144), Kahn (1973, 165–67), and Palmer (1989, 28). On the other hand, R. Robinson (1969b) recognizes only one natural name theory in the dialogue, and that is the theory that a particular set of letters is assigned to a thing according to nature.

8. "This doctrine of what I may call the indifference of the syllables is disconcerting to me, and I imagine to most of my contemporaries. . . . It seems to make the name into a ghost that may take any form, which seems to entail that 'Socrates' can have no way of apprehending this ghost, or of distinguishing between correct and incorrect embodiments of it" (R. Robinson 1969a, 116; see also 1969b, 128).

9. Cf. Kretzmann (1971, 130). Kretzmann distinguishes between the Form of name and the model correct name because an incorrect name seems to participate in the Form of name as much as a correct one: "Thus what makes them correct in the sense that there ought to be just such a name in use cannot be explained by reference merely to the Form of name" (130–31). I see no textual support for this claim. Whether or not the legislator makes a correct name depends solely on his ability to embody in letters the Form of name. We are not told that besides this he must embody an ideal name distinct from this Form. As to what makes an incorrect name a name, Socrates appears willing to allow

convention to decide this. Nature is invoked only for correctness. For further criticism of Kretzmann's view, see Silverman (1992, 36 n22).

10. There is no justification for Baxter's claim (1992, 39–40) that what Socrates says here "seems" to require a stronger interpretation, namely, that the function of a name is to *describe* the thing to which it refers. For detailed criticism of this view, as held by Baxter and others, see below. Here it can be asked: if the "natural name" is distinct from the letters that compose the word, how can it be a description? What in the name would do the describing?

11. Thus a distinction is implied here, though not clearly stated in the text, between the "form of name" and the "natural name." The "form of name" is the general function itself of referring to some stable nature. There is only one such form. A "natural name," however, is the exemplification of this form with respect to one specific nature. Thus, there are as many "natural names" as there are different natures. This distinction, however, is a further refinement unnecessary for the argument. It should also be noted that Kretzmann's interpretation (discussed in note 9 above) appears to derive from a misconstrual of precisely this distinction.

12. Cf. Palmer (1989, 91). Kahn (1972, 569; 1973, 162–63, 173–76) identifies the "natural name" with "the sign-relation itself" but understands this relation in Fregean terms as involving the mediation of a sense = concept.

13. Palmer (1989, 88) characterizes the dialectician as one "who both knows the basic structure—the nature—of realities and who uses names in order to distinguish those realities." According to Kretzmann (1971, 132), what the dialectician provides is a "conceptual schema." Both of these interpretations, however, do not place sufficient emphasis on the fact that the dialectician is characterized here in terms not of what he knows, but *what he can do*. What places the dialectician above the name-maker or legislator is not the possession of some special intuitive, nonlinguistic knowledge, but rather the ability to use the names of a language in such a way that the natural names or functions they embody become manifest. This distinction between the legislator and the dialectician parallels that made in *Republic* 10 (601e7–602a1) between making, which requires only true belief, and using, which requires knowledge. The dialectician has knowledge, as opposed to true belief, precisely because he is a *user*, rather than a maker, of names.

14. See Ketchum (1979, 142): "The Proper Form of a name is the power a name has of revealing something."

15. "It is almost always the nature or being of a thing, not the thing named, that is said to be revealed or signified by the name" (Ketchum 1979, 142). Kahn similarly claims that what a name refers to is a Form (1973, 163). While Kahn sees Plato as assuming that names can refer to individuals, he finds no explanation in the *Cratylus* of how this is possible (170–71). The virtue of Silverman's interpretation, on the other hand, is that it provides such an explanation: his main thesis is that names "by nature" refer to Forms and "by convention" refer to sensible individuals (Silverman 1992, 27). Silverman's interpretation presupposes that names refer through descriptions. The description by which a name *naturally*

refers to a Form is a *definition* of the Form (28). When, therefore, the name is used to refer to things other than the Form, i.e., sensible individuals which participate in the Form, the name is referring by means of a description distinct from the definition (presumably a description of the sensible individuals; see Silverman, 42–43) and is referring *by convention* (29). The view that a name refers by description is one I criticize in detail below. Two other criticisms can be made here. First, Silverman provides no convincing textual evidence for the view that a name refers to individuals by convention. He finds an "indirect" indication of this view in Socrates' reintroduction of convention to refute Cratylus (54), but it is so indirect as to be nonexistent. On 63 he seems to make an attempt to derive his view from the text, but his argument makes so many leaps and is so convoluted that it leaves me more confused than enlightened. I also find unhelpful, as well as bizarre, Silverman's example on 66: he is apparently claiming that the name "black" names naturally the Form Blackness, names conventionally by likeness the property black (as a particular, I assume), and names conventionally by unlikeness horses and crows! Second, as Silverman himself notes, his view has the consequence that the two references of a name, Forms by nature and particulars by convention, "will be sharply segregated" (49). But such a segregation seems disastrous. If the word "virtue" refers to a particular virtuous act only by convention, then does this not mean that it could with equal warrant refer to an unvirtuous act? Clearly Plato would want to say that the word "virtue" refers "by nature" to virtuous actions and therefore, regardless of convention, cannot refer to vicious acts. Silverman seems to want to escape this consequence by claiming that the conventional reference of a name is based on its natural reference (69), but he does not explain how this is the case and how this is consistent with the "sharp segregation" his view maintains.

16. Schofield attributes to Socrates in this part of the dialogue the claim that "simply by considering the constitution of a name we should be able to tell what it is the name of" (1982, 61). Yet if we look at the passage Schofield cites for this view (386d–391a), we do not find Socrates making any such claim. On the contrary, Socrates asserts unambiguously that it is not the constituents of a name that reveal the nature of the thing referred to. This misreading leads astray the rest of Schofield's otherwise very helpful article. Schofield rightly concludes that Socrates at the end of the dialogue demonstrates the absurdity of any theory according to which names signify through a resemblance between their constituent letters and the things themselves. Schofield also recognizes that Socrates is therefore not allowing for the possibility of an "ideal language." Because, however, he does not see any difference between the theory that the constituents of a name are natural and Socrates' earlier theory that the *use* or *function* of a name is natural, Schofield must conclude that there is no sense in which names are natural for Socrates (and Plato). As a result, Socrates' position is rendered indistinguishable from Hermogenes'.

17. Cf. Sallis (1996, 215–16).

18. For a much more detailed account of the etymologies than can be offered here, see Baxter (1992, 86–163). Baxter draws our attention to the

NOTES TO PAGES 71–75

systematic character of the etymologies, which begin with the names of the gods (theology), proceed to the names of physical objects (natural philosophy), and then address the names of human virtues (ethics). He concludes that the whole series of etymologies forms "a general schematic view of Greek thought" (91–92) and attempts to show, with the help of detailed examination of the historical evidence, that the different etymological parodies target specific Greek thinkers and poets (94–163). According to Baxter, the target of Plato's critique, i.e., the view that words somehow contain the truth and that the truth can be derived from them (or in Cratylus's words, that to know the word is to know the thing itself) was widespread in ancient Greece (162). Plato is therefore not attacking a straw man, but rather a temptation to make language self-contained, to make it replace the things themselves, which was common during his own day and, I would add, is still widespread today. According to Levin (1995), Plato's main target is the literary tradition (see especially 94–99).

19. Sallis sees Socrates as referring here to the conversation of the *Euthyphro* (1996, 227). The connection according to Sallis is as follows (225–29): just as Euthyphro considers himself a seer (*mantis*) with knowledge of the gods, so both Cratylus's position and Socrates' parody of it claim to speak the speech of the gods, a speech that transcends mere mortal speech (at the beginning of the dialogue, Hermogenes describes Cratylus's position as "oracular" [384a5], and at 396d2–3 he describes Socrates as someone possessed and uttering oracles). Just as Socrates uses irony to undermine Euthyphro's claim to divine knowledge, so will he undermine Cratylus's pretension by parodying it in the etymologies. Sallis interestingly characterizes the etymologies as an attempt to find divine names embedded in human names, which in the end finds only more human names (232).

20. Cf. Baxter (1992, 109).

21. Sallis (1996) outlines three ways of interpreting the etymological section: (1) as serious scientific philology (233–34), (2) as comic parody, and (3) as serious comedy: the goal of this last interpretation is "to clarify what it is that the etymological investigations genuinely bring to light in connection with that which they are, in comic fashion, put forth *as* bringing to light" (234). This third option is the one chosen by Sallis as well as myself. The first option is, for example, assumed by Findlay (1974, 217), who appears to miss completely the irony of the etymological section, while the second option is adopted by Arieti (1991, 66–71) and, much earlier, Stallbaum (1835, 5:4), who claims that the etymologies are presented "ludibrii tantum et irrisionis gratia."

22. Baxter presents evidence (1992, 99–100) that some Greek thinkers did believe one could defend a certain conception of the soul with an etymology and claims they are Plato's targets. Sallis sees the etymologies of *psuchē* and *sōma* as bringing to light our own status as *namers*, i.e., our own confinement to spoken signs and the body and thus to *logos* (1996, 242–44).

23. Cf. Sallis (1996, 261, 308).

24. Baxter sees a distinction between the two methods and calls the first one "semantic" and the other "mimetic" (1992, 56–57). However, he later acknowl-

edges that they are really continuous (71, 73). As Sallis notes, in the etymologies, "the very discovery of the original names is based solely on the similarity of their sounds and syllables to those of the derivative names" (1996, 237). It is therefore no surprise that the meaning of a name should now be said to depend on these sounds and syllables themselves.

25. Baxter tries to avoid this contradiction between Socrates' original account of the nature of naming and the present mimetic theory, but see criticism in note 28 below.

26. Sallis characterizes in a related and illuminating way the failure of both models to do justice to a name's function of making manifest. He points out that because the *mimēsis* model characterizes names as *imitating* a reality that must therefore be already manifest, it attributes to language the function of *communicating* what is already manifest rather than *making manifest* (1996, 268; see also 281, 289–90). On the other hand, the tool model contradicts the manifesting function of language in the opposite way: by characterizing names as simply productive. To make manifest is *neither* to produce *nor* to imitate.

27. Cf. Sallis (1996, 273).

28. Baxter is so "inspired" by this view that he leaps, without argument or explanation, from Socrates' tool analogy to the mimetic account of letters and asserts dogmatically that the latter is meant to fill in the details of the former (Baxter 1992, 63–64). One looks in vain for any kind of defense of this position, finding instead only a series of dogmatic assertions. On 70–71 Baxter simply asserts that Plato approved of the mimetic account; on 77 he again simply asserts that the mimetic theory "*should* be seen as putting the abstract argument of the tool analogy passage into a more concrete form, thereby developing the prescriptive theory" (my emphasis); though Baxter sees the etymological section as a parody (109), on 79 he simply asserts that the mimetic theory *should* be exempted from this parody; finally, at the conclusion of the book (186) we are told that there is "no need to doubt" that Plato accepted the mimetic theory as a prescriptive ideal, though Baxter has considered none of the reasons other scholars have had for seriously doubting this nor has provided *any positive reason* for believing this. Besides the lack of any textual support, Baxter's thesis also faces a huge and, I would argue, insurmountable hurdle: the obvious contradiction between Socrates' tool analogy and the mimetic theory, namely, that the former does not consider a word's individual letters and syllables to be of any importance, while the latter considers them to be absolutely important. Baxter tries to evade this contradiction, but only by misrepresenting the text. For example, on 77 he admits that the mimetic theory puts "greater stress on what was before of little interest, the actual material of language." This is false: in Socrates' tool analogy particular letters are not of "little," but of *no* interest whatsoever. Baxter also tries to reconcile the mimetic theory with the tool analogy by qualifying it in a way that does not at all correspond to the text: "The mimetic values are not incorrigible but depend upon the decision of the namegiver, who could alter them; different namegivers could choose different values for particular sounds, thus allowing for a variety of languages. This means that there is no logical necessity to have just one true language, and that, in a sense, letters and syllables still do not have an

NOTES TO PAGES 77-81

intrinsic value: any values remain partially contingent upon the decision of the namegiver" (64–65). This not only does not correspond to Socrates' account of the mimetic function of letters but blatantly contradicts it: Socrates claims that the letter *r by nature* expresses motion, which is to say that its doing so does not *at all* depend on some namegiver. Note the unexplained qualifications: "in a sense" and "partially." I criticize Baxter's thesis in detail to show what violence interpreters are willing to do to the text for the sake of some a priori commitment to an "ideal language."

29. "The absurdity of the results should not blind us to the fact that this is the proper, technical way a namegiver should proceed, whether Greek has been so ordered or not" (Baxter 1992, 77).

30. This is an important disclaimer because it shows that Socrates is not providing a prescriptive ideal for a language which *we* are to create in the future. Here, as throughout the dialogue, he is talking about language as it actually exists. Of course, one could interpret Socrates' being "carried away" as an ironic hint that such a prescriptive ideal is what he in fact has in mind (even though "inspiration" has only led him astray so far in the dialogue), but such an interpretation would require further, independent evidence. For my view that such evidence is not to be found, see not only the main text, but also the criticism of Baxter's descriptive/prescriptive distinction in note 38 below.

31. Anagnostopoulos (1972, 729). The idea of such an ideal language has always, it seems, been very alluring. See Baxter's interesting discussion of the views of Leibniz (Baxter 1992, 67–68) and Commenius (68–72).

32. With the exception of Grote, who defends Plato's complete seriousness in the etymological section (Grote 1888, 3:302–12). Yet even he sees the detailed theory as involving "wonderful and violent transmutations of letters" and therefore places the emphasis on the general theory: "Plato held the general theory that names, in so far as they were framed with perfect rectitude, held embodied in words and syllables a likeness or imitation of the essence of things" (3:312).

33. Kretzmann (1971, 137). Baxter refers approvingly to Kretzmann's distinction (1992, 48 n78).

34. For a helpful discussion of the meaning of γλίσχρα ὁλκή, see Williams (1982, 93).

35. Kahn, who does not think Plato "was seriously tempted by the program of such an ideal language" (1973, 167), also makes this point: "One could not properly construct such a language unless one knew in detail *both* the elements of words and *also* the elements of things (424D1–4). Hence such a language might be used to express but could not possibly be used to *discover* the truth about the world" (167). Baxter also recognizes this problem (1992, 186) but nevertheless persists in his view that Plato is presenting a program for an ideal language.

36. Sallis rightly notes that at 388a–c the teaching function of naming is subordinated to the function of distinguishing beings; he sees in this subordination "Socrates' implicit *denial that the proper end of naming is communication*" (1996, 208). Sallis also recognizes that the later account of naming as imitation contradicts the earlier account by reducing the function of naming to communication (268).

37. "Thus Plato's ideal language would be unlike his dialogues, indeed

it would rule out 'dialogue' as nothing really needs to be discussed" (Baxter 1992, 54).

38. Baxter's interpretation of the *Cratylus* depends on a distinction between descriptive and prescriptive accounts of language. According to Baxter, the etymological section ridicules *only* the view that language *as it presently exists* already describes and imitates reality (96); the view that language *ought* to imitate reality is one that Plato accepts. Baxter also needs the descriptive/prescriptive distinction to explain away Socrates' critique of the mimetic theory: Socrates accepts the theory as an ideal but criticizes it as a description of how language currently functions (165). Given the importance of the distinction for Baxter's interpretation, one would expect him to present substantial evidence for finding it in the dialogue. This expectation is disappointed. Baxter appears to think (42–43) that the mention of a namegiver (388e7–389a3) itself shows that Plato is interested, not in language as it is, but in "the prescriptive ideal model of what a language should be" (43). Yet the namegiver is described as a mythic figure of the past, responsible for language as it presently is, not as a future creator of an ideal language. Baxter also thinks that the disappearance of the dialectician after the tool analogy "helps reinforce the point that the tool-analogy passage outlines a prescriptive ideal" (46). But this disappearance could be interpreted in many different ways, some incompatible with Baxter's interpretation. Baxter appears to think that these two meager pieces of "evidence" are enough, since on 49 he asserts categorically that "Socrates has put forward a highly abstract prescription for an ideal language." However, he has one more piece of evidence: he sees the distinction in Socrates' discussion of Homer between the names given by the gods and the names given by humans, as well as the distinction between the names given by men and the names given by women, as a distinction between the prescriptive ideal of language and the descriptive reality, respectively (50–51). Baxter conveniently ignores the heavy irony of this passage and deals with it in complete isolation from the etymological section.

39. See Palmer (1989, 104). Kahn nicely explains Cratylus's view by writing that it "identifies the sign relation with a positive truth-value for each application, and hence it makes falsehood impossible" (1973, 166).

40. There has been much discussion (for which see Baxter 1992, 32–37) of Socrates' view, first presented at 385b2–d1, that the truth or falsity of a statement presupposes that the words out of which it is composed are individually true or false. Baxter's own hesitant conclusion depends on his general interpretation of the dialogue which I criticize elsewhere. I believe Kahn's explanation of this claim to be generally correct: a statement about something is true if each of the names of which it is composed can be truly asserted of this thing (1973, 160; for specific variants of this view, see Baxter 1992, 34–35).

41. We thus see that a completely natural language is no language at all. This result is noted by Derbolav (1953, 41), who sees the dialogue as steering between a formal, arbitrary language and a language so concrete as to be identical with its object, and Weingartner (1970, 13): "a perfect representation of Cratylus in all his characteristics would not be a representation at all, but a second Cratylus. Hence

a completely natural language without any element of convention is logically impossible." Silverman, on the other hand, seems to miss the point of this criticism of Cratylus (1992, 52).

42. Silverman (1992, 60–62) rightly argues against the view that the role of convention is here limited to the "unlike" letters. Socrates himself claims (435a7–b3) that *both* like and unlike letters disclose their referent through convention. Silverman therefore concludes: "The key to understanding this passage is to recognize that Plato does not oppose *conventional unlikeness* to natural likeness. He opposes *convention* to natural likeness" (62).

43. Derbolav points out that in the return to convention at 435a ἔθος and συνθήκη do not have the same meaning they had at the beginning of the dialogue. They no longer refer to the arbitrary postulation of names but rather to the process of becoming part of a living tradition (1953, 47).

44. As Sallis nicely states the point, for Cratylus names are not *instruments* of teaching, as Socrates suggested earlier, but rather are themselves the teachers (1996, 291).

45. Cf. Sallis (1996, 276–77).

46. In this low estimation of words the *Cratylus* has arrived at a view found in other works by Plato. See *Theaetetus* 177e1–2, *Republic* 454a4–9, *Statesman* 261e5–7, and *Seventh Letter* 343a9–b3. R. Robinson is thus right in claiming that "The view that there are by nature correct names for things is never asserted in any work of Plato's except the *Cratylus*" (1969b, 120). For an excellent account of Plato's attitude toward language, see Stefanini (1932, 1:xxxv–xxxvii).

47. See Weingartner (1970, 9) and Sallis (1996, 297). Guthrie (1962–78, 5:30), on the other hand, unjustifiedly takes the conclusion of the dialogue to be that language is altogether dispensable for discovering the nature of things.

48. The point here is not simply to show the unreliability of etymologies in the narrow sense of the term, but more generally to show the limitations of any kind of conceptual analysis (which ultimately is an analysis of words). "When Socrates asked 'What is bravery?' and so forth, he did not want to know what the meaning of the word 'bravery' was. . . . His question . . . was not a request for a conceptual analysis (as usually conceived, the generating of a certain set of analytic truths about bravery)" (Penner 1992b, 164; see also 1992c, 11). Yet Penner goes too far in the opposite extreme by identifying the x in question with a "psychological state" (1992b, 165), thereby making Socrates' question no different from the general's. Vlastos (1981) rightly criticizes Penner's view, but only at the cost of falling back into the view that Socrates' question asks for nothing but conceptual analysis. The present interpretation distinguishes Socrates' question from both that of the analyst and that of the general.

49. For a thorough discussion of why Socrates speaks of a "dream" here, see Sallis (1996, 299–304).

50. The objection has often been made that all Socrates' argument requires is that these natures have some stability, not that they be *unchanging*: the objection is made by Kahn (1973, 171) and discussed at length by Baxter (1992, 176–83). Baxter characterizes the argument as ad hominem. Yet there is a better

solution. Although a beautiful painting requires only relative stability in order to be referred to as "beautiful," the possibility of this reference presupposes that "beauty itself" is completely unchanging. If "beauty itself" were to change at all, the meaning of the word "beautiful" would change. How in this case could we call things "beautiful" without equivocation? Change in beauty itself, not change in beautiful things, is what would undermine the possibility of meaningful discourse.

51. Some interpreters do not recognize the importance of the shuttle analogy and believe, in spite of the conclusions of the dialogue, that the *mimēsis* model is the one that for Plato most accurately characterizes the nature of language. The result is that the *use* of names (what the dialectician is said to be an expert in) is given no importance. See, e.g., Gaiser (1974, 126).

52. Derbolav wrongly believes that the importance of "use" in understanding the nature of language is seen by Plato in the *Seventh Letter*, but *not* in the *Cratylus,* and that a recognition of the role played by "use" in language excludes the possibility of any "natural correctness" (1953, 87).

53. Weingartner sees the possibility of dialectic as the unifying theme of the dialogue: "The *Cratylus,* in short, takes up the problem of naming, not simply for its own sake, but in relation to the Platonic conception of the method of philosophy" (1970, 6). He claims that Hermogenes' position makes dialectic impossible by denying that there is any stable relationship between names and the objects which they are meant to denote. Cratylus's view that *the very name of a thing reveals its nature,* on the other hand, also renders dialectic impossible. In the former case, a question such as "What is justice?" could not mean anything to us, while in the latter case, the question would already provide the answer in providing the name (11). In both cases there would be no incentive to dialectical inquiry.

54. R. Robinson fails to distinguish the dialectician's use of words from the everyday use when he writes: "The correct use of names, to take that first, consists almost entirely in using the customary name in a customary way" (1969b, 135). Derbolav also does not adequately explain the distinction when he describes what the dialectician can do as follows: "Das Best, was er tun kann, ist, bescheiden und seiner Grenzen wohl bewusst, in die Tiefe des geübten Sprachgebrauchs hinabzuhorchen, um in Übereinstimmung mit ihm, aber doch auf persönliche Weise, reden zu konnen" (1953, 49). Everything depends here on the meaning of "persönliche Weise."

55. For a clear statement of this distinction between dialectic (with the correctness of names it involves) and everyday discourse, see Gaiser (1974, 118). Yet Gaiser understands the relation between language and Ideas more in terms of the imitation model (the structure of language reflects the structure of reality) than in terms of the tool model.

56. R. Robinson (1969a, b), Kahn (1973), Kretzmann (1971), Palmer (1989), Fine (1977), Guthrie (1962–78, vol. 5), Lorenz and Mittelstrass (1967), Silverman (1992), and Baxter (1992). The view which they attribute to Plato apparently originates with Bertrand Russell: "Common words, even proper names, are usually really descriptions. That is to say, the thought in the mind of a person

NOTES TO PAGES 89-90

using a proper name correctly can generally only be expressed explicitly if one replaces the proper name by a description" (1963, 156). The assumption here is that the actual use of a name can be reduced to a thought in the mind of the person using it and that this thought can in turn be reduced to a description. This view that names function as descriptions goes hand in hand with the belief in the possibility of an ideal language. See, e.g., Commenius' outline of an ideal language in *Panglottia* (1660): "erit cuiuslibet rei appelatio . . . idem quod rei definitio; hoc est definitionibus nullis erit opus: ipsa cuiusque rei appelatio determinet quid res sit, genus suum, et differentiam suam secum ferens, ipsis compositurae suae partibus" (cited in Baxter 1992, 72).

57. Palmer (1989, 16) describing the thesis of Lorenz and Mittelstrass (1967).

58. There is an interesting similarity between the position of the *Cratylus* and Wittgenstein's claim in the *Tractatus* that names are "primitive signs" which do not admit of analysis or definition, but rather signify through their application: "Der Name ist durch keine Definition weiter zu zergliedern: er ist ein Urzeichen" (1922, 48; sec. 3.26). "Was in den Zeichen nicht zum Ausdruck kommt, das zeigt ihre Anwendung. Was die Zeichen verschluchen, das spricht ihre Anwendung aus" (50; sec. 3.262). However, when Wittgenstein denies (at least in the later *Philosophical Investigations*) that language presupposes the existence of stable, objective natures ("essences"), he sides with Hermogenes rather than with Socrates.

59. Even though this interpretation has already been criticized by others (see note 62 below), it is still often assumed without argument. Silverman's reading (1992) of the dialogue (on which see above) entirely depends on this assumption. Yet one looks in vain for any defense of it. On 38 he assumes that the dialectician can refer to a form only by means of a definition; on 43 he assumes that nondialectians can refer to sensible particulars only by means of a description. The same lack of any argumentation characterizes Baxter (1992), though Baxter tries to give the semblance of argumentation. In interpreting Socrates' tool analogy on 39–40, Baxter simply asserts that the attribution of "descriptive qualities" to names *seems* needed, without explaining why. On 40 we have another assertion that the "names-as-descriptions" view *seems* to be the claim that is being made. Suddenly on 44 this interpretation becomes more dogmatic (with no argument). On 47 Baxter again appears to assume without argument that names for Plato function as descriptions. The big leap, however, comes on 52. Baxter introduces Roy Harris's distinction between "surrogationalism" (the view that names are surrogates for things, depictions, or representations of things) and "instrumentalism" (the view that names are instruments serving various intentions where the intentions themselves provide the link between name and thing). He then assumes that the tool analogy commits Plato to the view that the function of names is to describe things and therefore to "surrogationalism." And what has led us to this conclusion is a series of completely unexplained "seem"s! The other possible interpretations of the tool analogy that Baxter mentions have by 52 conveniently and mysteriously disappeared from consideration.

60. In writing about the final argument of the *Cratylus,* Annas oddly claims

that "the only actual casualty of the argument is the particular *logos* of language put forward, namely that words function by revealing reality" (1982, 111). But what is criticized by the argument is only the view that words reveal reality in their specific constitutions. That a word's proper function is *somehow* to reveal reality is never questioned.

61. "It is not the job of a name to describe. The job of a name is to refer; and reference is not description, and does not usually describe. . . . The utterance of a thing's name does not tell a hearer what the thing is. It only refers him to the thing" (R. Robinson 1969b, 130). Robinson, however, says this in *criticism* of Plato, since he believes that Plato holds the position criticized. Robinson also fails to see that even reference to a thing involves some kind of manifestation of that thing.

62. The "names as descriptions" interpretation is also criticized by R. Levinson (1957, 37) and Richardson, who adds an important argument: "To say that Plato treats words as 'little statements' on the basis of the fact that he says that words can be true or false is to turn Plato's theory on its head, for when his Socrates is put on the spot by Cratylus and forced to defend his claim that sentences are true or false, he argues that sentences can be true or false because they are made up of words which are true or false, rather than vice versa" (1976, 143–44). The view that a name can be true or false rests on the fact that a name can make something manifest *prior* to being part of a sentence that describes this thing.

63. Palmer (1989, 61) claims that the reason why the positions of Hermogenes and Cratylus are really not opposed is that they are both forms of conventionalism. In response to Socrates' worry concerning the possibility of our being deceived by the first name-maker, Cratylus seems to believe that consistency is enough to ensure the correctness of names (436c). His position does not allow for the possibility of knowing reality independently of names and thus reveals itself to be a form of conventionalism. True naturalism, on the other hand, "places a premium on discovering what reality must be like independently of human perception and cognition." For a similar view, see Sallis (1996, 287–88). It should also be noted that the positions of Protagoras and Heraclitus, to which Hermogenes and Cratylus prove committed, respectively, are shown by Socrates in the *Theaetetus* to be the same.

64. Baxter rightly points out that the positions of both Cratylus and Hermogenes undermine dialectic (1992, 13, 21).

65. Cf. Derbolav (1953, 49). Derbolav, however, seems to go too far in the direction of conventionalism.

66. As Sallis states the point, what is "correct" for Socrates is not the name per se, but the *assignment* of the name (1996, 279–80).

67. As Derbolav aptly points out: "Sprache ist offenbar doch *mehr*, als sich mit sprachlichen Mitteln über sie ausmachen lässt" (1953, 46). See also Sallis on the "curious reflexive complication" involved in the very project of the dialogue (1996, 184, 191, 209, 218–19, 309–11).

68. I am indebted here to Sallis's excellent statement of this point (1996, 211).

Chapter 4

1. I am assuming here that the method practiced by Socrates in this dialogue is essentially the same as that practiced in the other aporetic dialogues. Vlastos, on the other hand, has maintained that in the *Euthydemus* the "elenchus" has been "jettisoned" (1991, 116–7; 1994a, 30). Vlastos's reasons appear to be the following: *R1:* Socrates' conversation with Cleinias is not adversative; *R2:* Cleinias is completely pliant ("he hangs on his [Socrates'] lips"; 1991, 116), so that the conversation is a virtual monologue; *R3:* the conversation begins with what is considered to be an indubitable truth. *R1* is clearly explained by the context: the two brothers deliver punch after punch to the bewildered Cleinias, and Socrates clearly wants to distinguish his own method as far as possible from their eristic. Furthermore, Vlastos's model for the "elenchus" appears to be, as usual, the *Gorgias:* he fails to consider that the *Laches* and the *Charmides* are much less "adversative." *R2* is exaggerated: even disregarding the questionable passage on "hunting arts" and dialectic, Cleinias disagrees with Socrates' suggestion that the art of making speeches is the art they are looking for and explains why (289c8–d7). If Cleinias does not disagree with anything before then, it is because he finds nothing to disagree with. Furthermore, disagreements with, or objections to, what Socrates says (not to mention "sustained resistance") are rare: the *Gorgias* and the *Protagoras* are not the norm. Finally, that Socrates here should sometimes develop his thought on his own is explained by the youth and inexperience of his interlocutor. Concerning *R3,* the views that "temperance is good" and "courage is good" are no less indubitable starting points in the *Charmides* and *Laches* than is here the claim that all men desire to be happy (and yet Socrates in *both* cases asks for his interlocutor's agreement). Furthermore, Socrates in the *Euthydemus* does not propound moral doctrine (in a "didactic style") but instead, as elsewhere, leads his interlocutor into *aporia.* As for why Socrates' discourse is specifically "protreptic" here, see below. A good antidote to Vlastos's view (written *before* Vlastos's defense of it), which pursues some of the points made above, is Hinrichs (1951). For a recent critique, see Gentzler (1996, 260–61 n16). Apart from these specific points, it should by now be clear that my general account of the "elenchus" completely differs from Vlastos's.

2. Though for a possible historical explanation of why the two brothers had to leave the colony, see Canto (1987, 105–6).

3. For some speculation on possible historical targets of Plato's criticism of eristic, see Hawtrey (1981, 23–30).

4. Therefore one can apply to the brothers Socrates' comparison in the *Republic* (537e–539a) of young dialecticians to orphans who, discovering late in life that their foster parents are not their true parents, are unable to discover who their true parents are. The young dialectician will undermine all beliefs he previously regarded as sacred (τιμία) and as his own (οἰκεῖα), without being able to replace them with the truth. Socrates identifies this dialectic *manquée* with eristic (ἀντιλογία, 539b4) and as such contrasts it to the genuine dialectic (539c–d) that can discover the truth and thus "find a home."

5. Cf. Sprague (1962, 2).

6. This claim is defended in Roochnik (1990b, see especially 214–15). See also Canto (1987, 116): "La *sophia* qui enseigne ce qui est partout le meilleur est tenue d'enseigner aussi que la meilleur chose à faire consiste à apprendre la *sophia*."

7. For a listing of these kinds questions in the *Euthydemus* and a discussion of the way in which they are employed, see Keulen (1971, 69 ff.).

8. Cf. Narcy (1984, 99). The brothers clearly play with ambiguity, but this does not mean that the ambiguity can be easily dissipated or that it is not inherent to the subject under discussion.

9. I doubt that Socrates himself finds his explanation entirely adequate. This is betrayed by his appeal to the authority of Prodicus (277e4). What Prodicus is most known for in the dialogues are his subtle verbal distinctions: see *Cratylus* 384b–c and *Protagoras* 358a. Euthydemus and his brother will be seen to differ about mere words. Socrates therefore seems to be pitting sophist against sophist.

10. Szlezák has argued (1980, 85–89) that the "seriousness" which the eristic lacks and the philosopher possesses is an esoteric theory of the ultimate principles. The dialogue as a whole, however, shows that this is *not* the difference between the philosopher and the eristic. Socrates proves as incapable as Euthydemus and his brother of defining and possessing in a theory that highest wisdom which will makes us happy. The all-important difference is in their *methods*. Preferable to Szlezák's view is therefore Canto's that the seriousness possessed by the philosopher and lacked by the eristic is "l'usage correct de l'entretien dialectique" (1987, 126).

11. In the *Republic* (487b–c) Socrates tells us that people make this same accusation against philosophy: the philosopher, like an expert draughts player, knows how to move around words in such a way as to trap the opponent in a contradiction, but such skill in no way affects the truth (487c3–4).

12. According to Stewart (1977, 29), a knowledge of ambiguity is for Plato "knowledge that of its nature has no serious use, because it cannot improve you and leaves you no wiser as to the nature of things." I do not, however, agree with Stewart's explanation that Plato lacked knowledge of most forms of ambiguity due to his lack of the "apparatus" for describing them (and to this extent I agree with the criticism of Stewart's view in Hawtrey 1981, 68–69). The reason why the *Euthydemus* is not a treatise on sophistic fallacies (like Aristotle's *De Sophisticis Elenchis;* see Chance 1992, 7–13) is that, as Stewart himself suggests, Plato does not think that such a treatise would help one know the true nature of things. Exposing and eliminating all ambiguity, even if possible, would not necessarily bring one any nearer the truth. Indeed, given the conclusions of chapter 2, the effect could conceivably be the opposite. In the *Laches* and the *Charmides,* each of the proposed definitions of courage or temperance, while not fully expressing the nature of the virtue, still sheds light on it and is qualifiedly true. If, therefore, we decided to eliminate ambiguity by confining the word "courage" or the word "temperance" to one of these definitions, we would cut off access to the true nature of the virtue, which always involves more than any one definition could

express. The best explanation of this point I have found is that of Watson (1995, 199–200), who contrasts dialectic to logic by pointing out that dialectic "depends on shifts in the meanings of terms that occur as we gain insight. It is when accepted meanings and beliefs become unsettled that new insights emerge."

13. This is precisely the way in which eristic is distinguished from dialectic in the *Republic*. Socrates is describing the danger of teaching the art of argumentation to those who are too young to make proper use of it. Young men misuse reasonings or arguments (*logoi*) for the purpose of contention (*antilogia*), thereby only "playing" with them (539b3–4). This *antilogia* is dangerous because it can lead to the conclusion that there is no true beauty or true justice. On the other hand, those who are older will use the art of argumentation correctly, i.e., dialectically (διαλέγεσθαι), to come within view of the truth (σκοπεῖν τἀληθές; 539c5–8).

14. The ambiguity here has its source in the phrase "eu prattein," which can mean both to act well and to be simply fortunate.

15. That fallacious reasoning is one of the main characteristics distinguishing eristic from dialectic is apparently the view of Stemmer: "Logische Scheinschlüsse und sprachliche Tricks sind die Mittel der Eristik" (1992, 107). This view apparently stems from Stemmer's belief that what Socrates' elenchus tests is a thesis, not the character of the interlocutor (112); how can dialectic and eristic in this case differ except in the ways in which they deduce and refute theses? On the other hand, Chance (1992, 67), Friedländer (1954–69, 2:181), and Sprague (1962, xiii) see that dialectic does not avoid fallacious reasoning and therefore can be distinguished from eristic only in terms of the purpose or intention with which it commits fallacies. For my disagreement with Sprague, see note 17 below.

16. Recognition of the role fallacy plays in Socrates' argumentation requires an appreciation of the dialogue form. Precisely because Socrates' arguments have at least in part the practical goal of converting rather than proving, they can be understood only in the context of a specific conversation. Certain arguments which in the artificially abstract context of a treatise are simply fallacious can be perfectly appropriate and revealing in the context of a dialogue. Because Socrates' argumentation is thus deeply rooted in the specific circumstances of the conversation and is adapted to the character of the interlocutor, Rossetti (1989, 1990) is right to insist that more attention be paid to Socrates' own use of those persuasive techniques normally identified with "rhetoric." If a Socratic argument were a purely formal deduction taking place in a vacuum, there would be an absolute difference between Socrates' dialectic and rhetoric. If the character of Socrates' argumentation is instead what I have described it as being, then the distinction between philosophy and rhetoric is much more problematic (see Roochnik 1995, 1996, 179–231). I believe, however, that the distinction can still be made if one recognizes that there is no contradiction in claiming that dialectic is both relative in form (i.e., relative to a particular situation and a particular interlocutor) *and* universal in content (i.e., can reveal a truth which transcends the particularity and contingency of the discussion). On this point see Watson (1995, 192–97).

17. Sprague (1962, 1–45, especially 44) has argued that Socrates uses fallacies *to show us something*. However, Sprague's view seems to be that what these fallacies show us is simply the distinctions that must be made in order to avoid them. Thus Socrates is here comparable to the teacher of an introductory logic course who writes a fallacious argument on the board so that his or her students may see for themselves what is wrong with it. Clearly, however, this does not explain the presence of fallacies in Socrates' protreptic argument: Cleinias does not learn anything from Socrates' equivocation between good fortune *secundum quid* and good fortune *simpliciter*. In my view, what Plato is showing us in the *Euthydemus* is not that logical fallacies can be "useful," but rather that they are *irrelevant* in certain philosophical contexts. That an argument is riddled with logical fallacies does not prevent it from showing us the truth of the matter under discussion.

18. Even when confronted with hostile, uncooperative interlocutors, as in the *Gorgias*, Socrates' aim is still not *to prove* that they are wrong in disagreeing with him, but *to show that they in fact agree with him*. Thus Socrates responds to the disagreement between himself and Polus as follows: "See whether or not you wish on your part to submit to the test by answering my questions. For I think that you and I and all other human beings believe that doing injustice is worse than suffering injustice and that avoiding punishment is worse than submitting to it" (474b1–5). If Polus did not in fact believe this, Socrates' dialectic could not accomplish anything.

19. As Roochnik points out, Socrates' argument would not convince someone who denies the existence of an objective good (1990b, 220–21). But, as Roochnik also appears to recognize, it does not need to.

20. By "fallacious reasoning" I mean informal as well as formal fallacies. Sprague makes the very interesting and, I believe, correct suggestion that the eristics are even *more* precise in their arguments than is Socrates: "Furthermore, since the victory aimed at is a *verbal* victory (the sophists are not exhorting Cleinias to choose anything except a form of words), the eristic arguments have to be phrased with much greater precision than the protreptic ones" (1977, 60). Because what the eristic practices is a wordplay without content, he depends, much more than does Socrates, on the *form* of his arguments. This is why the arguments of Euthydemus and Dionysodorus are very clear in structure and lend themselves much more easily to modern symbolic notation than do the arguments of Socrates. Ironically, this means that eristic, in its formality and precision, is much closer to modern logic than is dialectic. Cf. Chance (1992, 80).

21. Cf. Canto (1987, 136).

22. According to Bonitz, the basic presupposition of many of the eristic arguments is the identity of subject and predicate ([1886] 1968, 108). Bonitz's analysis of specific arguments, however, seems rather forced. What these arguments presuppose is not that the subject is identical with the predicate, but that one and the same subject cannot be assigned (verbally) contradictory predicates.

23. At one point (287a–b) Socrates asks how the brothers could claim earlier that they are capable of teaching virtue when they now claim that it is impossible to make mistakes. In reply Dionysodorus calls Socrates a "Cronos" for remembering

now what was said a long time ago rather than dealing with the present argument (287b2–5).

24. Canto claims, I believe rightly, that the two functions of producing and using are in fact identical in the case of the highest science (1987, 150). How this is possible will be made clear below.

25. Narcy suggests (1984, 143–44) that the word "λογοποιός" is used at 289d in a wide enough sense to include the argument-making skill of the two brothers. Chance even translates λογοποιίκη τέχνη as "art of logic production" (1992, 115–16), thereby making the reference to the brothers explicit. The suggestion of Narcy and Chance is attractive because it would make Socrates' criticism of the two brothers in this passage more direct. Szlezák (1980, 83) sees in the λογοποιίκη τέχνη a reference to dialectic itself, in particular to the ideal rhetoric of the *Phaedrus*, which *would* know how to use the *logoi* it produces. Canto (1987, 150–51) sees the passage as allowing for the possibility of a distinction between two different sciences of producing and using *logoi*, namely, rhetoric and dialectic. These suggestions are in agreement with the contrast between dialectic and eristic that will emerge from the discussion as a whole: a contrast between an art that knows how to use the arguments it produces and an art that does not.

26. Canto suggests that Socrates' abrupt introduction of the general's art as a candidate for *sophia* may be due to the fact that the brothers have practiced this art as well as the art of making speeches (1987, 152).

27. Hawtrey sees this passage as anticipating the system of education and the hierarchy of the sciences described in the *Republic* (1981, 127–29; 1978, 14–18). I agree, but do not accept Hawtrey's characterization of the hierarchy in the *Republic* as involving the deduction of hypotheses from first principles (1981, 128; nor do I think the reference is intended as a joke, as Hawtrey also suggests [129]). Canto appears nearer the mark in claiming that what the dialecticians do is provide the figures of the geometricians with true being by subjecting them to dialectic, as opposed, presumably, to allowing the figures to remain mere abstractions (1987, 154). See chapter 6 of the present work for my own interpretation of the relation between dialectic and mathematics. Szlezák also sees the present passage as anticipating the *Republic* (1980, 83).

28. Canto rightly sees here a missed opportunity (1987, 154–55).

29. This curious passage has predictably occasioned some disagreement. Szlezák claims that the words were spoken by Socrates, not Cleinias, and that the passsage is meant to show "der Wissensvorsprung" of Socrates (1980, 84). Chance believes Cleinias did speak the words and that this shows the truth to be latent in his soul (1992, 121–24). Hawtrey suspects that the speed with which Cleinias progresses may be a joke but acknowledges that it also may be intended as a serious demonstration of the success of Socrates' protreptic (1981, 130). Hawtrey also believes (1981, 131), as does Canto (1987, 160), that Critias understands the "higher being" to be Socrates himself. Vlastos simply assumes that the words are Socrates' own (1991, 117, 127). To a certain degree all of these interpretations are correct. The account of dialectic is an insight to which Cleinias could have been led through his very involvement with Socrates in a dialectical discussion, though

perhaps not as quickly as Socrates relates. We can also attribute this insight to Socrates himself, the foremost practitioner of dialectic. Most important, however, there is also a sense in which this insight is *beyond* both Cleinias and Socrates: as the concluding *aporia* shows, not even Socrates can grasp or define the nature of dialectic as that highest knowledge which will ensure our happiness. Therefore, whatever understanding of dialectic might emerge from the discussion must seem to come from a "higher power."

30. Wilamowitz-Moellendorf (1959, 240) suggests that the effect of having Socrates continue the discussion with Crito instead of Cleinias is that this part of the dialogue, through which we glimpse the inner connection between philosophy and politics, is given special prominence.

31. Canto sees Crito's interruption as causing Socrates to abandon the dialectical investigation, i.e., to give up his attempt to reproduce the dialectical process by showing all the details and steps of the argument (1987, 161–62). Canto sees the haphazard quality of the discussion between Socrates and Crito, as well as the lack of true engagement on the part of Crito, as showing that this discussion is not genuine dialectic. However, I find neither the haphazardness nor the lack of engagement which Canto finds.

32. Cf. Sprague (1976, 48–56).

33. Some scholars have asked how someone not already acquainted with Plato's conception of dialectic in the *Republic*, or with his theory of recollection, could understand the *Euthydemus:* see especially Hawtrey (1981, 129), Szlezák (1980, 85), and Kahn (1981, 317). The dialogue does appear to presuppose previous acquaintance with Plato's thought. However, it seems to me that a careful reader with no knowledge of the particular view of the *Republic*, or of any other specific theory, could be led by the discussion in the *Euthydemus* to see the necessity of identifying the political art with dialectic. That the account of dialectic is passed over without explanation after being attributed to a "higher power" is a very good hint that the nature of the political art which Socrates and his interlocutor have failed to define lies hidden in dialectic. The dramatic context of this dialogue has much to tell us, and we should therefore not abandon it too quickly in favor of supposed "doctrines" elsewhere.

34. Both Natorp (1921, 122) and Wilamowitz-Moellendorf (1959, 238) see the present passage as implying the identity of the political art and dialectic. But *why* is this identity left in the dark here? Wilamowitz-Moellendorf's answer is hardly satisfactory: "aber das kann Sokrates noch nicht sagen, oder, wenn Platon es ihn sagen lassen konnte, weil er es selber wusste, so passte es nicht hier in seinem spottenden Mund" (1959, 238). My own view is that the identity is not explicitly asserted here for the same reason that the identity between the "knowledge of knowledge" and the knowledge of the good is not asserted in the *Charmides:* such an assertion, besides being empty, would fool us into believing that the knowledge in question can be defined. By presenting us with a difficulty, rather than with an "answer," Plato hopes that we will gain real insight into the unique nature of this knowledge.

35. When in response to Socrates' questions Dionysodorus asserts further that there is no such thing as false belief and therefore no such thing as ignorance

(ἀμαθία), Socrates asks him whether he is arguing this simply for the sake of arguing or because he really believes it (286d11–13). We are left with no doubt as to what the answer is.

36. "Se Platone avesse voluto esaltare la 'luminosa' dialettica del maestro contro le degenerazioni eristiche, avrebbe dovuto esibire in nome di lui qualche cosa meno imperfetta di un circolo vizioso!" (Stefanini 1932, 1:192). Stefanini is thus led to the conclusion that the target of Plato's critique in the *Euthydemus* is not only eristic, but also Socrates.

37. Despite its apparent vagueness, the word "manifestation" means something very specific here. In both this and previous chapters, I have been arguing that there is a distinction, recognized by Plato, between *showing* and *describing*. The second chapter argues that though the *Laches* and the *Charmides* fail to describe courage and temperance in a proposition, they nevertheless show us what these two virtues are. The third chapter argues that though names are not descriptions of those natures they refer to, they can nevertheless reveal these natures in use. Likewise, "manifestation" here means a way of showing that transcends what can be described in a proposition. Though this is a negative definition, previous and succeeding chapters aim to show just what is involved in this "manifestation."

38. Thus the dialectician is characterized by Wieland as "der Inhaber eines Gebrauchswissens," a knowledge which cannot be objectified or communicated in propositions (1982, 299).

39. The view that dialectic is the one science that can be a hunting art *and* a productive art *and* a user's art, as well as an insightful explanation of how this is possible, can be found in Canto (1987, 154–55, 166–67).

40. Cf. Gaiser (1959, 138).

41. See Grote (1888, 2:198–99), Narcy (1984, 39), and Sprague (1962, 22). Yet Sprague makes it seem as if Socrates' dialectic does no more than prepare one for the reception of positive doctrines.

42. This distinction between dialectic and eristic as an "arguing for the sake of arguing" explains Stewart's observation that the eristics' arguments give "a greater impression of apriorism" than do Socrates' arguments (1977, 33).

43. As I hope to show in chapter 8, it is wrong to think, with Sprague (1976, 91–92), Hawtrey (1978, 16), Kahn (1988, 545), and Chance (1992, 127), that the *Republic* provides the "solution" to the *aporia* encountered in the *Euthydemus*: it only further illuminates this *aporia*. In general, Kahn's "proleptic" reading of the dialogues appears to find solutions where I see either different problems or the same problems formulated and approached in a new way. For a criticism of Kahn partly along these lines, see Griswold (1990, especially 254). For an excellent discussion of the *aporia* at the heart of the knowledge of the good, see Canto (1987, 164–65, 189–90).

44. If Plato were writing the *Euthydemus* as a logician who seeks to expose and remove all logical ambiguity, then he would discard the very notion of a "highest knowledge" as one that resists clear logical expression. That he does not do so is not a sign of the primitiveness of his thought, as Stewart appears to assume (1977, 25–26).

45. This reflexivity is recognized and clearly articulated by Chance (1992),

who comments that "the sought-after science is not just the end of the search, but also the very process or method of inquiry that seeks to discover itself; it is both the means and the end, the process and the result" (116; see also 129). Unfortunately, Chance does not pursue this suggestion with the thoroughness and consistency one could hope for.

46. My conclusion therefore agrees with Roochnik's that "If techne is the only form of knowledge, then there can be no knowledge of arete and Socratic protreptic cannot be distinguished from sophistry" (1990b, 227).

47. See Chance (1992, 154) and Szlezák (1980, 82).

48. Narcy describes the way in which other dialogues are echoed in what the two brothers say and concludes that this is what arouses Socrates' interest in them and also renders him rather vulnerable to their sophisms: in their mouths "le platonisme lui-même est rendu sophistique" (Narcy 1984, 82). Hawtrey considers these echoes to be at least in part jokes for Academic readers "in the know"! (1981, 21–22). Szlezák provides an especially thorough account of all the allusions to Platonic views (1980, 75–89) and claims that what is alluded to in each case is an "ausgearbeitete Theorie" (85) forming part of an "unwritten," "esoteric" "Prinzipienlehre" (85–86). But Szlezák does not in my view justify this claim. The "evidence" he provides is absurdly weak (for example, the ironic description of the two brothers as "gods" and the attribution of the account of dialectic to a "higher power" are taken as allusions to a theory of ultimate principles [85]). He also does not adequately answer the objection, which he himself raises (87), that the "theories" alluded to in the *Euthydemus* are found *written* in other dialogues.

49. Cf. Chance (1992, 154).

50. When Socrates is himself the questioner he often complains that his questions are not being answered. See *Protagoras* 336a.

51. For a remarkably clear and insightful articulation of this point, see Narcy (1984, 76). Very revealing is the exchange at 295b–c where Socrates insists that a word must have the *same* meaning for the questioner and the respondent, while Euthydemus replies that the respondent need only mean *something* by the word, even if this does not correspond to how the questioner understands it. Because the brothers' method has this character, Aristotle's exposé of sophistic fallacies would be an ineffectual weapon against them, as Hawtrey recognizes: "It is not what the respondent can do to defend himself; although Aristotle gives plenty of advice on the solution of fallacies, most of it would be ruled out of order by Euthydemus and Dionysodorus" (1981, 36).

52. "Alors qu'Aristote tient son succès de ce qu'il impose de conditions de validité du discours, pour Socrate la question demeure accessoire. Ce ne sont pas les mots qui importent, mais les choses ou, dirions-nous, les faits" (Narcy 1984, 176).

53. Canto rightly observes that the determination which the otherwise indeterminate and contradictory method of the brothers cannot escape is the determination of the good (1987, 186; see also 177–78). One should recall in this context Socrates' claim in the *Republic* (505d–e) that the good is the one thing concerning which no one prefers the appearance over the reality.

NOTES TO PAGES 120-21

54. Bonitz divides the sophisms of the dialogue into those that address matters of philosophical importance and those that address a great variety of philosophically irrelevant things. Bonitz rightly sees this diversity as showing that the subject matter is of complete indifference to the brothers ([1886] 1968, 114–5). Cf. Chance (1992, 103) and Canto (1987, 146). It must be added, however, that the subject matter of the eristic is not unimportant when it comes to maintaining the pretense that it is doing *more* than playing with words. The brothers' discussion of increasingly trivial and nonphilosophical topics coincides with Socrates' destruction of this pretense.

55. "Ἀλλὰ τίνα τρόπον, ἔφη, ἕτερον ἑτέρῳ παραγενομένου τὸ ἕτερον ἕτερον ἂν εἴη" (301a8–9). The Greek here is very ambiguous and has received many different translations. The problem is the meaning of the word "heteron" in each of its occurrences. Some translators opt for a literal rendering that leaves its referent completely unclear: "But in what way, he said, can the different be different just because the different is present with the different" (Sprague). This translation has the virtue of making the question vulnerable to Socrates' misinterpretation: as Hawtrey claims in support of Sprague, Dionysodorus's question cannot be too lucid (1981, 176–77). The translation's weakness, however, is that it makes indecipherable what Dionysodorus really intended to ask. Those translators, on the other hand, who attempt to make this clear fall into two camps: one takes Dionysodorus to be asking *how it is possible that, when one thing is present with another, the one should be different from the other:* "De quelle façon, cependant, reprit-il, une chose étant presente à une autre chose, l'une pourrait-elle être distincte de l'autre?" (Robin); "But how can it be, he said, that when a different thing is with a different thing, the different thing should be different?" (W. H. D. Rouse). The other camp, however, takes Dionysodorus to be asking *how it is possible that, when one thing is present with another, the one should be the other:* "But how, he said, by reason of one thing being present with another, will one thing be another?" (Jowett); "But just because something has turned up beside another entity, he said, how can that entity be the other" (Chance 1992, 179). Chance glosses the last phrase as, *"the one (different) entity to be the other (different entity)"* (179). Since Dionysodorus here is clearly speaking of the relation between beautiful things and beauty itself, the two questions he could be asking according to the above translations are, Q1: How can beauty be different from beautiful things if it is present with them? or Q2: How can beautiful things be beautiful by simply being present with beauty? Either question would serve Dionysodorus's purpose of refuting Socrates' notion of "presence" (or participation). Is a thing the same as or different from the thing in which it participates? Q2, however, fits in better with Dionysodorus's point that it is as silly to think that a beautiful thing becomes *kalon* through the presence of *to kalon* as it is to think that one becomes an ox through the presence of an ox. Furthermore, as Chance observes (1992, 271 n116), the Greek here is an idiomatic way of asking, "How can one thing be another?"

56. Contra Hawtrey (1981, 174–75).

57. "[I]n a plain, artless, and possibly simple-minded way, I hold this close

to myself: nothing else makes [a thing] beautiful except that beautiful itself (τὸ καλόν), whether by its presence or communion (παρουσία) or whatever the manner and nature of the relation may be; as I don't go so far as to affirm that, but only that it is by the beautiful that all beautiful things are beautiful" (*Phaedo* 100d3–8; Gallop trans.). Sprague has suggested that Socrates' "safe answer" in the *Phaedo* is safe because it avoids the objections of Euthydemus and others (1968, 632–35).

58. Cf. Narcy's defense of Dionysodorus against Bonitz's critique (1984, 87).

59. Hawtrey's discussion of this passage (1981, 178) apparently fails to notice that Socrates is here *intentionally* misinterpreting Dionysodorus's question.

60. Cf. Chance (1992, 192).

61. Szlezák in addition documents parallels between ten characteristics, distinct from the three discussed here, which Socrates attributes to the brothers throughout the dialogue and ten similar characteristics attributed to the philosopher elsewhere in Plato's writings (1980, 79–81). He in this way shows that Euthydemus and Dionysodorus are "das genaue Gegenbild des wahren Philosophen" (81). Recognizing that Socrates himself displays some of these characteristics in the dialogue, Szlezák also notes that Socrates' praise of the brothers really applies to himself (84).

62. Chance concludes, wrongly I think, that what Socrates says here does not refer to any passage of the dialogue (1992, 196).

63. That this is Dionysodorus's plan is also recognized by Hawtrey (1981, 174).

64. This also seems to be Diogenes Laertius's point when he accuses the brothers of γλισχρολογία (2.30).

65. Chance relates the mention of the speechwriter at the end of the dialogue to the claim in the second protreptic discourse that speechwriting cannot be that highest science which will make us happy (1992, 203). Concerning the identity of the speechwriter, Stefanini (1932, 1:190), Canto (1987, 225–26), and Rutherford (1995, 119–20), while like others seeing an allusion here to Isocrates, also rightly suggest that the criticism is directed more at a *type* of person than at a specific individual.

66. Cf. Chance (1992, 204–5).

67. For further, excellent discussion of the contrast in this dialogue between philosophy and the pretensions of *sophia*, see Canto (1987, 226–27).

68. Cf. Canto, who sees the dialogue as concluding that "il faut faire de la philosophie, avant de la définir, ou même de l'évaluer" (1987, 207). For an explanation of why this is the case, similar to the one I offer, see Canto (1987, 222, 240). Canto also rightly recognizes that no argument could demonstrate the necessity of practicing philosophy (241).

69. Cf. Narcy (1984, 39–40). Wilamowitz-Moellendorf is also uncomfortable with this (1959, 239–40). On the other hand, I find incredible Hawtrey's claim (1981, 32) that there is *no* irony in Socrates' closing conversation with Crito.

70. Misology is precisely the effect which Socrates describes eristic as having at *Phaedo* 89d–90d.

71. Canto suggests that what the speechwriter refuses to recognize is the connection between *sophia* and *dialegesthai*, a connection which is the source of the similarity between philosophy and eristic (1987, 203).

Chapter 5

1. Cf. Bloom's view that the dramatic details of the dialogues are "images of the problems" (1968, xvi).

2. For evidence that this was true of the historical Socrates, see Critias's criticism of Socrates as reported by Xenophon in *Memorabilia* I.ii.

3. "ὡς γλίσχρως εἰκάζω" (488a2). We have already encountered the word "γλίσχρος" in Diogenes Laertius's description of the argumentative method of Euthydemus and his brother as "γλισχρολογία" (2.30) and in Socrates' use of the phrase "γλίσχρα ὁλκή" in the *Cratylus* to describe the dragging in of imitation to explain the correctness of language. Related to the word for glue (γλία), the word "γλίσχρος" can mean "greedy," "stingy," and "niggardly" (it is used in this sense at *Republic* 553c3). The sense, then, is that Socrates desperately clings to images in the way that Euthydemus and his brother clung to arguments and Socrates himself and Cratylus clung to imitation as a means of explaining the truth of language.

4. Three further examples can be given of Socrates' use of images. In book 4 the education of the guardians is compared (ἐθέλω ἀπεικάσαι) to a permanent dye that will not fade (429d2). In book 7 what the Pythagoreans do to the strings of a musical instrument is compared to the torturing of a slave on a rack. The word used for this comparison is εἰκών (531b4). At another place in book 7 the abuser of dialectic is compared to an orphan. The word used is again εἰκών (538c5). On Socrates' use of poetic language and imagery in the *Republic*, see also Rutherford (1995, 235–36). For a good example of Socrates' use of images in other dialogues, see *Gorgias* 493d where he uses the image (εἰκών) of two jars, one sound and one with holes, to contrast the temperate and intemperate lives. Given all the evidence, there is no justification for Tecuşan's assertion that Socrates at *Republic* 489a is "forced" to use an image (1992, 76). For a good account of imagery (including analogy) in Plato, see R. Robinson (1953, 202–22). Robinson sees "an inconsistency between Plato's principles and his practice about images. According to what he says about them, he ought never to use them; yet his works are full of them" (220–21). Of the *Republic* in particular he writes: "a dialogue which emphatically condemns imitation . . . , and demands a form of cognition that uses no images at all . . . , is itself copiously splashed with elaborate images explicitly called 'images' by the speakers" (221). It is my hope that the present chapter will resolve this apparent contradiction.

5. In case it be objected here that an εἰκών is not a μίμημα, it should be pointed out that Socrates uses the word εἰκών in speaking of artistic imitation (401b2).

6. "Das in Bezug auf das Sein des Hervorgebrachten eingeschränkte Machen ist uneingeschränktes Machen in bezug auf seine Gegenstände" (Zimbrich 1984, 261).

7. This hierarchical way of thinking is introduced in book 9. The oligarch is three times removed from the king, and the tyrant is in turn three times removed from the oligarch (587c–d).

8. For a defense of the thesis that Socrates does not seek to banish the painters and that the sole target of his critique is poetry, see Nehamas (1982). Ferrari (1989, 109) makes the important observation that poetry is an especially dangerous form of imitation because in it "the image and that of which it is an image are not so clearly distinct from each other as in the visual arts."

9. "In holding that the Art of Painting imitates only τὰ τῶν δημιουργῶν ἔργα Plato degrades it to the level of photography, and the painter himself to a mere mechanical copyist whose intelligence does not rise above εἰκασία. . . . Yet the highest art has in every age claimed to portray, not the so-called actual, but the Ideal" (Adam 1963, 393). For a defense of Plato against this kind of criticism, see Verdenius (1949). For an attempt to resolve the apparent contradiction between Plato's critique of imitation and his decision to write imitative dialogues, see Laborderie (1978, 91–114). The present chapter will attempt to resolve it by means of an account of the philosopher's use of images.

10. The same point can be made with regard to Socrates' criticism of painting, since he compares himself to a painter several times throughout the *Republic* (414a, 488a, 501c, 548d; for comparisons involving statuary see 361d, 374a, 420c, 466a, 540c). Gallop (1965, 115) thinks there is an easy response to this criticism: "The answer is simple. Socrates is no ordinary painter, but a philosopher artist. As such, he depicts the Intelligible rather than the visible world, Reality rather than appearances, Forms rather than particulars. Hence his strictures upon the painter do not apply to himself." This answer is surely *too* simple. The only direct imitation of the forms that Socrates' hierarchical model recognizes is that of the craftsman (though even this is questioned by Socrates' revised model, as will be seen below). In comparison with the craftsman, the philosopher seems just as confined to appearance as the poet. If one maintains that nevertheless the philosopher in using the sensible images of the poet can reveal a reality to which the poet has no access, this is not a "simple answer," but rather a restatement of the problem. For further discussion of this point see note 19 below. Another simple solution that has been proposed is clearly untenable: according to Wiegmann (1990), *both* the philosopher and the poet imitate the Forms, differing only in the specific Forms they imitate (the poet imitates Beauty while the philosopher imitates the Good). For criticism of the view that Plato seeks to attribute to philosophy a kind of artistic imitation that imitates the forms directly, see Nehamas (1982, 58–60) and Ferrari (1989, 122).

11. This apparent flaw in Socrates' critique leads Rosen (1990) to question the difference between philosophy and poetry.

12. For more on the limitations of these definitions, see chapter 8.

13. Cf. Bloom's claim that "Book X begins with a criticism of Homeric poetry

and ends with an example of Socratic poetry" (1968, 427). MacIntyre (1988, 82) offers a very negative judgement on Socrates' myth: "That myth violates two of the educational prohibitions proposed in Book II: it includes direct speeches (615c–616a and 617d–e), and thus is an example of the mimesis which has just been condemned, and it speaks of the underworld in precisely the kind of way that was condemned earlier (compare 387b–d with 616a). Nothing could make it clearer that Socrates is disclaiming for himself the status of one who speaks from the standpoint of achieved *episteme:* he remains one who appeals to images and diagrams, and therefore who has not yet apprehended the forms." MacIntyre here appears to allow for no distinction at all between Socrates and the poets.

14. Referring to the passage in which Socrates describes the terrestrial rewards of the just man, Friedländer (1958–69, 3:131) writes: "This is a passage that could make one lose one's taste for all of Plato—if the passage had to be taken in complete seriousness." For a similarly negative assessment, see (Annas 1981, 348–50).

15. The detailed account of the argument of book 10 in Nehamas (1982) completely ignores the revised model and the user's art. Ferrari, on the other hand, recognizes the importance of this revised model (1989, 128–30): he sees that the user's art belongs to the philosopher (as does Bloom 1968, 431). However, what Ferrari does not recognize is that the philosopher's user's art is also confined to *images*. As a result, he attributes this art only to the *philosopher-king* and sees the fact that Socrates never wrote a law as representing a failure on his part (130). But Socrates' present legislation in speech must itself be based on a user's art that the poet does not possess.

16. The use of the word *doxa* here shows how Plato's understanding of "belief" differs from the one current in contemporary philosophy. In his thorough treatment of the subject, Price (1969, 72–79) has argued that the only kinds of belief and knowledge which can be contrasted are "belief that" and "knowledge that." The knowledge described in the present passage, however, is definitely not "knowledge that": it is instead knowledge of how to use something correctly. The contrast here therefore cannot be one between someone who knows, and someone who only believes, *that* such and such is the case. The contrast is more between firsthand acquaintance with a thing's use and an awareness of this use derived secondhand through verbal instructions. That this characterization of the knowledge/belief contrast is not an anomaly will be seen in chapter 8.

17. I see no justification for Annas's claim that the forms do not at all fit into this model (1981, 337). Her argument is that forms "are no objects of use" and that the user, the maker, and the imitator here relate to the same object: the concrete particular (337). Yet the point is that the person who knows how to *use* the flute knows in this use the form of the flute, i.e., what a flute is, while the person who makes the flute has only "true belief" about this form and the person who imitates the flute is completely ignorant of the form.

18. Adam (1963, 404) asserts that no metaphysical significance is to be given to the statement that the user has *knowledge*. He then qualifies this claim as follows: "There is no doubt a certain sense in which—if we have regard to *Crat.* 390B ff. and

Euthyd. 288E ff.—ὁ χρώμενος has not indeed scientific knowledge of the Idea, but something analogous thereto. Dialectic, which is the scientific knowledge of Ideas, is κατ' ἐξοχήν the χρωμένη ἐπιστήμη, the Science which alone knows in what respect each thing is good and *useful* and *uses* things accordingly (cf. *Euthyd.* 290C, *Crat.* 390C), proving itself thereby the royal or kingly science (VI 505A *n.*). . . . But if Plato had intended us to pursue this vein, he would, I think, have furnished us with some hints in the course of the argument itself." But the cited passages are among the very few in which we are told *anything* about the kind of knowledge involved in dialectic. Adam's view is shared by Murray (1996, 211–12). Hintikka (1974b, 41–43) assumes that the craftsman is paradigmatic for Plato's conception of knowledge. Because this assumption is contradicted by the distinction between maker's knowledge and user's knowledge and the priority Plato gives the latter, Hintikka implausibly dismisses this distinction as being sociological(!) rather than epistemological (47). Wieland's assessment (1982, 293) is more just: he sees user's knowledge in a craft as a paradigm meant by Plato to clarify the structure of *all* knowledge (not just knowledge of artifacts but even knowledge of the forms) and claims that this user's knowledge is knowledge in the strongest sense of the word, not something merely analogous thereto. Reeve (1988, 83) also takes seriously the implied identification of dialectic with a user's knowledge.

19. This account should be compared to Gallop's (1965). Focusing on Socrates' first model, Gallop understands the philosopher's superiority over the poet and the craftsman simply in terms of imitation: God makes the form of Bed, the philosopher directly imitates this form by making a word picture, the craftsman imitates the form by making a material bed, the artist imitates the material bed in words or paint. There are, however, serious problems with this schema: (1) according to it, both the philosopher and the craftsman imitate the form, though the first in words and the latter in concrete things. But why should this difference make the philosopher superior to the craftsman? (2) Since both the philosopher and the poet are simply makers of word pictures, the only difference for Gallop is in their objects: "Plato can thus be defended against the objection that mere word-painting, if it disqualifies the poet, should also disqualify the philosopher. Since the latter depicts Forms and not phenomena, the fact that he merely paints need not debar him from pronouncing upon morals and statecraft" (127). Gallop, however, does not explain how it is possible to imitate the forms directly. (For others who characterize philosophical imitation in this way, see note 25 below.) Socrates, just as much as the poets, imitates concrete actions and objects. He may indeed do so in such a way that the form is allowed to *appear through* this imitation, but then this is a specific *use* of a sensible image to reveal the form *indirectly*. (3) Gallop essentially ignores the "user's art." His schema uses only Socrates' first model and ignores the second, significantly revised model. He claims that his schema "can plausibly be related to the trio of user, maker, imitator" (124) but does not clearly explain *how*.

20. "Even if poetry depicted virtuous characters, it would do no more than to create a way in which someone who *seemed* virtuous, but who might in no way *be* virtuous, would act" (Nehamas 1982, 68). Cf. Tate (1928, 20).

21. It is true that according to 500d the philosopher is described as the producer (*dēmiourgos*) of all the virtues in the citizens. Yet because the citizens, and not the philosophers, are the ones implied to have only true opinion here, the analogue to the craftsman in Socrates' second hierarchical model is apparently not the philosopher who implants virtue as such in the characters of the citizens, but rather the citizen who "produces" specific instantiations of virtue (as the carpenter produces specific instantiations of "bedness"). It is nevertheless probable that in the *Republic*, as in the *Euthydemus*, the philosopher's "user's art" is seen as ultimately combined with a "productive art": the philosopher knows how to "use" the virtue which only he really knows how to "produce." Cf. Ferrari (1989, 129).

22. Cf. Bloom (1968, 431) and Reeve (1988, 86).

23. The same point is made in the *Euthydemus* (279b–281e) and the *Meno* (88b–d).

24. A question that cannot be addressed here without a reading of the *Republic* as a whole is whether or not the ideal republic with its philosopher-kings is recommended as a realizable goal. A negative answer is defended in Hyland (1995, ch. 3). As Hyland points out, Socrates' account of the philosopher in the *Republic* "suggests a man or woman (540c) who, by the standards of the other dialogues, is less a *lover* of wisdom, lacking and therefore striving after wisdom, than a *wise* person, with a comprehensive knowledge not only of the forms and their relation to phenomena, but even of the idea of the Good itself" (78), while, on the other hand, "the whole thrust of most other Platonic dialogues, and even of the discussion of the Good in the *Republic*, is that such a situation is humanly impossible" (79). For a similar point, see Sallis (1996, 371, 378). Yet it is also important to observe that the philosopher constructing the ideal republic in words, namely, Socrates, never claims wisdom in the dialogue, but repeatedly admits ignorance and expresses reservations and doubts. Noting this, Rutherford rightly concludes: "It seems that the exposition in the *Republic* is partial and tentative; the gap between what Socrates has achieved and what the poets can do is not so vast as we at first anticipated" (1995, 235).

25. Two other attempts to define a distinctly philosophical kind of imitation can be found in Tate (1928, 23) and Schaerer (1969, 163–64). However, both of them, like Gallop (see notes 10 and 19 above), characterize it as a direct imitation of the forms and therefore do not recognize the essential role played by the user's art. For a critique of Tate's distinction between two kinds of imitation, see Nehamas (1982, 48–50).

26. Cf. Verdenius (1949, 29) and Schaerer (1969, 164).

27. Cf. Moravcsik (1982, 40): "Only if these images are indeed viewed as mere images—that is, as leading us towards things that are on a higher ontological plain—can the artist's representations play a useful role."

28. Annas claims that book 10 banishes poetry entirely (1981, 341). She attempts to explain away the passage at 607a with the odd assertion that "Plato is enough of a creative artist himself to know that such productions are not real poetry" (344). Yet the language, specifically the phrase "ὅσον μόνον" (607a3), shows clearly enough that the hymns and eulogies are included in poetry and

therefore represent an *exception* to the general ban. Nehamas (1982, 48–54) also sees book 10 as banishing poetry entirely and therefore does not think that the apparent contradiction between this book and books 2–3 can ultimately be eliminated. He tries, however, to make the contradiction less serious by suggesting that while books 2–3 permit imitative poetry to play a role in the education of children, what book 10 prohibits is the exposure of *adults* to poetry. But Nehamas acknowledges that book 10 itself allows some poetry into the city (48–49), though he does not even attempt to explain *that* "contradiction." He instead simply asserts that the poetry admitted here "seems to me negligible and tailor-made for special occasions" (69); for the same view see Murray (1996, 228–29). Nevertheless, Nehamas is right in rejecting Tate's solution of distinguishing between two completely different kinds of imitation (48–50). Ferrari suggests the following solution: when Socrates in book 10 rejects such poetry as is "imitative," what he means is "prone to or valuing imitation." The Guardians in books 2–3 can imitate good characters without being "imitative" in this sense (1989, 124–25). This solution seems rather arbitrary.

29. Cf. Ferrari (1989, 134).

30. Friedländer (1958–69, 1:122) suggests that Plato's own dialogues are included in "hymns to the gods and the praises of good men."

31. After noting that "L'art ne trouve sa justification, chez Platon, que dans la dépréciation de soi-même," Schaerer points to some artistic imperfections of the Platonic dialogue and explains: "Les oeuvres douées d'une harmonie intérieure parfaite ne peuvent être philosophiques, car elles suscitent une satisfaction ennemie de l'amour" (1969, 168–69). For another defense of the same view, see Lasso de la Vega (1968, 328). If a Platonic dialogue satisfies as a work of art, it fails to serve its purpose. It must be understood as a fragment through whose cracks something else can be perceived. Gundert (1971, 10) states this best: "jeder Dialog ist ein Ganzes und zugleich Fragment, sofern er in einem wesentlichen Aspekt das Ganze im Auge hat, ohne es doch zu umfassen."

32. Even a bad person such as Thrasymachus, who not surprisingly is one of the most memorable characters in the dialogues, is portrayed, as Ferrari points out (1989, 119), more as a *caricature* than as a character, so that the reader will not identify with him.

33. McCabe argues that the myths or allegories in a dialogue are often in conflict with the arguments (1992, 61, 67).

34. "Los diálogos, en efeto, son también obras de arte. . . . Sólo que el diálogo difiere de una obra de pura literatura por la confesión que aquél si, y ésta no, hace de su insuficiencia. Al arte pretencioso, al vaniloquio infantil, se opone la ironia; a la seriedad ridicula, el juego muy serio" (Lasso de la Vega 1968, 369). Cf. Ferrari (1989, 144–48) on the merely "instrumental value" of the dialogues.

35. "Again and again Plato's written work is mimesis; but it struggles against being nothing but mimesis" (Friedländer 1958–69, 1:124).

36. "But the greatest poetry is that which threatens to become a value in its own right, and so an obstacle" (Ferrari 1989, 141).

37. R. Robinson (1953, 207) states this problem well with regard to analogies: "But it is a peculiar kind of intuition that analogy offers us, a sort of seing and

NOTES TO PAGES 146-48

not seeing at the same time. One case cannot really give us insight into another unless it gives us insight into the universal covering both; and yet analogy refuses to mention the universal. Thus it takes and does not take the universal."

38. Griswold (1981, 150). Griswold cites passages 499c1, 505e1, 506a6, 523a8, and concludes that "Philosophy, it seems, does not consist simply of 'logic,' 'mathematics,' or 'dialectic' understood in a technical, scientific sense."

39. Inspiration as such is not a target of Socrates' critique of the poets in the *Republic*. As Murray (1992, 39) observes, "It is striking that in the *Ion* and other dialogues in which poetic inspiration is discussed there is no mention of *mimēsis*. In the *Republic*, however, the opposite is the case: we have *mimēsis* but no inspiration." Yet Murray rightly concludes that inspiration is in a sense the same as *mimēsis* in both of the different meanings this term is given in books 3 and 10 of the *Republic* (46; see also 1996, 12). She supports her case by citing *Laws* 719c where the poet is characterized as both inspired and mimetic. See also Laborderie (1978, 75). I would add the explanation that since the goal of the *Republic* as a whole is to distinguish reality from appearance, Socrates in book 10 is more concerned with the poet's relation to this distinction than he is with the state of mind in which the poet composes his works.

40. Verdenius (1945, 146; see also 1949, 22) points out that the poet's inspired state is precisely what renders him incapable of seeing his work as παιδιά. In this context Verdenius cites Xenophon's characterization of an allegorical interpretation Socrates gave of a passage from Homer: τοιαῦτα μὲν περὶ τούτων ἔπαιζεν ἅμα σπουδάζων (*Memorabilia* I.iii.8). Socrates is "playing" in dealing with an imitation three times removed from the truth; yet he is "serious" in using this imitation to reveal the truth. Socrates plays with poetry in such a way as to go beyond it. In the *Phaedrus* (278b–c) Socrates claims that if a poet such as Homer composes his poetry with a knowledge of the truth, can subject his statements to refutation, and can himself show the inferiority of what he has written, then he deserves the name of philosopher. This means that poetry, when it recognizes its inferiority as play and subordinates itself to a higher knowledge, can become more than poetry, i.e., philosophy. This poetry which is yet more than poetry is precisely what I attempt to define in the present chapter. Cf. Woodruff's account of what "keeps poetic inspiration from being philosophy, or at least the beginning of philosophy" (1982, 138). Though my account differs from Woodruff's, I agree with his suggestion that it is the "self-containment" of poetry that prevents it from being "knowledge how" or "knowledge that" (146–47). Given the poet's failure to distinguish original from image, Woodruff is also right to characterize the poet's inspiration as "a case of recollection that has miscarried" (140).

41. This is why even in the *Phaedrus*, where he characterizes the poet as divinely inspired, Socrates ranks him and the "practitioner of some other form of imitative art" *sixth* in his hierarchy of lives, while the philosopher, though described as "a follower of the Muses," is ranked first (248d–e). Cf. Murray (1992, 44–45).

42. "La poésie est dangereuse si l'inspiration de la Muse n'est pas contrôllée par l'ἐπιστήμη" (Laborderie 1978, 114).

43. Moravcsik (1982, 30) characterizes the distinction between poet and

philosopher as one between artistic inspiration and noetic aspiration: "We saw already that for Plato the true 'erotic' person regards all stages of life as pointing toward the understanding of the Forms, with the accompanying freedom and self-determination. This erotic and noetic aspiration clashes with the inspiration of the artist. The inspired artist does not regard her work as pointing beyond itself, to higher levels of understanding. According to her, poetic inspiration and insight is the highest, or at least one of the highest levels of human attainment." This is correct, but it is important to note that the philosopher's noetic aspiration is itself in a sense "inspired."

44. The basic argument of Tecuşan (1992) is that images in Plato never have a heuristic value but are demanded only by the limitations and needs of the interlocutors. In other words, for every *eikōn* in the dialogues, there is an argument that could render it superfluous. Tecuşan recognizes that Socrates' use of images in the central books of the *Republic* appears to contradict this claim (79–82). I find Tecuşan's attempt to explain away this counterexample neither clear nor convincing. See my account of these images in chapter 8. In contrast, see Stefanini's excellent observations on the necessity in Plato's use of images or likenesses (1932, 1:xlvi–l).

Chapter 6

1. This is R. Robinson's view: "the *Meno*'s discussion of hypothetical method seems to have value as the symbol of a valuable change in Plato's writings. With the introduction of this method he is passing from destructive to constructive thinking, from elenchus and the refutation of other men's views to the elaboration of positive views of his own. The dialogue begins with refutations of Meno's definitions of virtue, and ends with attempts to say something positive about virtue, even if tentative and non-essential, by means of the hypothetical method. It is thus a microcosm of the whole series of Plato's dialogues; for on the whole those previous to the *Meno* are merely destructive and those after it are definitely constructive" (1953, 122). See also Elias (1968), who considers "deductive mathematics" to be the model for "Platonic dialectic" (209). Though for Vlastos the elenchus is constructive, he too believes that it was supplanted by the more demonstrative, scientific method of hypothesis. See the chapter "Elenchus and Mathematics" in Vlastos (1991, 107–31), where he tries to show how Plato, starting with the *Meno, Lysis,* and *Euthydemus,* abandons the elenchus in favor of the method proper to mathematics (see also 250 where he speaks of "the discarding of the elenchus as a method of philosophical investigation"). For an excellent critique of Vlastos's thesis, see Seeskin (1993). Sayre (1995, 135) goes so far as to claim that "cross examination of any sort—whether 'well-disposed' or otherwise—is not adequate by itself as a philosophic method. So Socratic elenchus by itself is not dialectic." His account of dialectic therefore discusses only the method of hypothesis, the method of collection and division in the "late" dialogues, and the method employed in the second half of the *Parmenides*. As I hope to show, the opposite is the truth: the elenchus remains for Plato in the "middle" dialogues the most genuine and fundamental sense of dialectic.

2. Later in the dialogue (91a) Socrates provides a context by telling Anytus that Meno longs to acquire virtue so as to be able to rule over the city, look after his parents, and entertain guests. The irony is that Meno nowhere expresses any such motivation. Therefore, I cannot agree with Seeskin (1987, 118): "There is, however, no reason to think that in asking how virtue is acquired, Meno is anything but sincere."

3. Cf. Arieti (1991, 202, 205; 1995, 126); and Sayre (1995, 56–57). Sternfeld and Zyskind (1978, 8) suggest another possibility: Meno is challenging Socrates to give the kind of display for which Gorgias is known.

4. There is disagreement on how to translate τὸ παράπαν. As an adverb, it clearly qualifies the verb "to know," but the focus can be on either the subject or the object of this verb. Understanding it in the first way, Nehamas (1992, 300) translates: knowing "*in any way at all.*" Understanding it in the second way, J. Klein (1965, 45) translates: knowing "what human excellence *all in all* is." Socrates' later insistence on knowing virtue "as a whole" without breaking it up into parts appears to lend support to Klein's translation. I choose the translation "altogether" because it in large part retains the ambiguity of the Greek ("altogether not knowing" and "not knowing what something altogether is") while also suggesting, without being restricted to, Klein's reading.

5. As does Fine (1992, 216 n6). For a general statement of the very common view that Plato identifies knowledge of what a thing is with knowledge of its essential properties, see Nehamas (1989, 269).

6. Fine argues that this view *is* defensible and finds such a defense in Aristotle's *Posterior Analytics* i.1–10 (1992, 203; 217 n13).

7. Fine (1992, 226 n42). Dimas (1996, 6) offers another objection: "For all we may know, he [Socrates] may think that there is a cluster of properties that are attributable uniquely to Meno and that to know Meno is to know that Meno is the possessor of these properties." This may be *logically possible* at this point, but *extremely unlikely*.

8. Among those who deny that Socrates is making any distinction between "knowledge by acquaintance" and propositional "knowledge by description" are Nehamas (1992, 300); Fine (1992, 225–26 n42); Dimas (1996, 5–7); and Sharples (1985, 125) (though Sharples claims only that this is "not clear"). See also the important debate between Cross (1954), who argues against finding "knowledge by acquaintance" in the dialogues, and Bluck (1956), who argues in favor. In my view, Bluck wins this debate, though it is important to note that his position is more subtle than normally recognized. Though he characterizes "knowledge by acquaintance" as being nonpropositional, he also sees it as involving the *ability* to give a *logos* or "explanatory account" (528). Furthermore, he identifies acquaintance not with the immediate intuition of some object, but with "an intuitively acquired teleological understanding" (528). Sternfeld and Zyskind appear to see the analogy as somehow identifying the knowledge of virtue with *both* knowledge of a definition *and* knowledge by acquaintance (1978, 23; see also 30–32, 36–37, 42).

9. This phrase is of course one used by Russell (1963), who defines it as follows: "I say that I am *acquainted* with an object when I have a direct cognitive

relation to that object, i.e., when I am directly aware of the object" (152). The *only* thing that the "knowledge by acquaintance" of which I speak here has in common with Russell's is that it is not reducible to a knowledge of propositions or "descriptions." I do not think that the direct, immediate intuition of some object has anything to do with a knowledge of virtue.

10. Ebert (1974, 43) distinguishes between two kinds of *Kennen:* one which admits degrees, "Eine Person kenne ich besser oder schlechter als eine andere, ebenso eine Stadt, eine Sprache, ein Wissensgebiet" (43), and one which does not admit degrees: I "kenne" a name or a melody or a picture, etc., either fully or not at all. Ebert then shows that *Kennen* understood in the second sense (which he explicitly identifies with Russell's "knowledge by acquaintance" [53 n25]) assumes a perceptual, object-oriented model of knowledge, in a way that the first sense apparently does not. Though this distinction between two senses of *Kennen* corresponds to my distinction between two forms of "acquaintance," Ebert unfortunately dismisses the first sense as being the least interesting of the two and understands *Kennen* in the second sense throughout the whole of his account of Plato's epistemology. Though one must agree with the negative thesis of Ebert's book, i.e., that Plato does not identify *epistēmē* with *Kennen* in the second sense, i.e., with "intellectual perception" of some "object," the book fails to do justice to how the word *epistēmē* is used in the dialogues as a result of not exploiting the analogy between knowledge and *Kennen* in the richer (and I would say much more interesting) first sense.

11. Fine argues that knowledge by acquaintance does not admit degrees and that therefore Plato's solution to Meno's eristic paradox, with its suggestion that there is something between total ignorance and knowledge, requires a *rejection* of the acquaintance model (1992, 220 n24; 222 n31). (Ebert [1974, 95–99] makes a similar argument.) Fine obviously understands "acquaintance" as something analogous to seeing a color: you either see it or you don't. But as I argue below, this is by no means the only legitimate sense of "acquaintance." Furthermore, Fine's argument can easily backfire. Smith (1979, 285) has convincingly argued that *propositional knowledge* also does not admit degrees: one either knows that p or one does not. Therefore, the "acquaintance" (in the narrow sense) and propositional models are in the same boat: neither by itself can make sense of Plato's solution of the paradox.

Smith (1979) tries to develop a third model: "knowledge what." He distinguishes this "knowledge what," which he sees as alone admitting degrees, from both propositional knowledge ("knowledge that") and "knowledge by acquaintance" (282–85). Since Plato describes *epistēmē* as both admitting degrees and having an intuitive element, Smith characterizes it as being "a blend of knowledge by acquaintance and knowledge what" (283). Unfortunately, Smith's attempt to provide a positive characterization of this "blend" is unsuccessful. Since in the end he is unable to distinguish "knowledge what" from propositional knowledge and "knowledge by acquaintance" from immediate intuition, the two elements in his description of *epistēmē* blend as well as oil and vinegar. He attempts to distinguish "knowledge what" from propositional knowledge as follows: "In this way, knowing what is much more like propositional knowledge, except that the truths for knowing what are essentially related to their subjects, while no such condition is required for propositional knowledge" (282). But knowledge of essential properties is just as propositional as knowledge of nonessential properties. The consequent impossibility of blending this "knowledge what" with "acquaintance" is evident in Smith's example of degrees of vision: "In one sense, T does not see the bird better than S, namely, in the sense in which both simply have visual perceptions of it. The reason we can say that T sees the bird better than S does is that T is able to see what the thing in the tree is" (286). But if the direct perceptions of the bird are identical, what is the knowledge that S lacks and T has except knowledge *that* the thing in the tree is a bird? Thus Smith's attempt to develop a third model fails: he ends up with simply a combination (rather than "blend") of knowledge by acquaintance and propositional knowledge. However, Smith's *project* is an extremely important one. I have pursued it in previous chapters by characterizing philosophical knowledge as *instantiating* its object (thus being neither a knowledge of propositions nor simply the "vision" of some object) and pursue it in the present chapter by showing at work in the *Meno* a kind of "knowledge by acquaintance" distinct from what is normally understood by this term.

Grene (1966) has more success in developing a third model. The knowledge of virtue as it is characterized in the *Meno* has much in common with the notion of "tacit personal knowledge" that Grene gets from Polanyi (for an excellent description, see 24–25). Oddly, however, she wrongly maintains, in obvious contradiction to the theory of recollection and to her own interpretation of the *Meno*, that for Plato all knowledge is explicit and impersonal (27). Also of importance is K. Ross (1987). Ross describes knowledge in Plato as "immediate," in the sense that it does not involve discursive thought (174), and also as "nonintuitive," in the sense that it is latent and never reaches fully explicit form (170–73). All of the mentioned studies are very suggestive, but clearly much more remains to be done.

12. This is therefore the kind of knowledge by acquaintance which Grene (1966, 21) finds in the *Meno* and describes as "transform[ing] the person himself who attains knowledge." This is certainly not true of Russellian "knowledge by acquaintance."

13. See W. Ross (1951, 16), R. Robinson (1953, 53), Gully (1962, 3), Geach (1966), Benson (1990b). Even the two scholars who have argued most thoroughly against attributing the fallacy to Socrates in the "early" dialogues have no doubt that he commits it in the *Meno*: Beversluis (1992, 120 n4) and Vlastos (1994c, 85) (Kraut [1984, 279] takes a similar view). Therefore, apparently the only scholars who can maintain *both* that what Socrates' *ti*-question seeks in the *Meno* is definitional knowledge *and* that Socrates does not commit the fallacy are (1) those who interpret Socrates' priority principle as allowing that we can have true beliefs about virtue before possessing a definition of virtue, though these beliefs cannot become *knowledge* without such a definition (for criticism of this view, see below); (2) Brickhouse and Smith (1994), who claim that knowledge of a definition of

virtue is necessary, not for knowledge of any specific true proposition about virtue, but only for knowledge of *all* true propositions about virtue (for discussion and criticism of this view see chapter 2, note 23); (3) Valditara (1991, 219), who distinguishes between two types of knowledge: the *recognition* with which the inquiry begins ("il senso riconoscitivo del *che cos'è*") and the knowledge of a definition with which it ends. As for this last view, there is no support in the text for this distinction between two radically different ways of knowing *"ti esti,"* though there is support for a distinction between different *degrees* of knowing *"ti esti"* (i.e., greater or lesser clarity of insight).

14. Cf. Desjardins (1985, 268) and Sallis (1996, 84).

15. Sallis makes the relation between wholes and parts central to his reading of the *Meno* (1996, 64–103).

16. Cf. Sharples (1985, 131–32) and S. Klein (1986, 361–62 n5). I do not find at all convincing Hoerber's suggestion that this definition provides the *"aitias logismos"* of shape ("figure" in his translation) because "color is the cause of our awareness of figure" (1960, 97).

17. See J. Klein's excellent remarks on this passage, which show how Socrates' second definition points ahead to the method of hypothesis and its defects (1965, 66). Cf. Seeskin (1987, 124; 1993, 41).

18. Vlastos is so excited by this second definition of shape (he considers it "evidence" for Plato's new interest in geometry) that he does not even acknowledge the existence of the first definition (1991, 120–22). He concludes: "With the geometrical definition . . . he [Socrates] has no fault to find. . . . Here again Plato is holding up geometry as a paradigmatic science" (122). Seeskin (1993, 40–42) adequately refutes this view by making some of the same points made here.

19. Interpreters disagree about which definition of shape Socrates is referring to when he says that the "other one" is better than the definition of color. While Guthrie (1962–78, 4:249 n1) believes that Socrates is referring to the *second* definition, J. Klein believes that he is referring to the *first* (1965, 70). I am inclined to agree with Klein's view. The virtue of the first definition is that it is concrete, intuitive, and nonreductive. The second definition's use of technical terms which Meno *thinks* he understands is a fault, rather than a virtue. For the present interpretation, however, nothing rests on this point. Tarrant (1993, 185–88) not only sees the reference as being to the first definition of shape, but argues that the second definition is out of place here and was probably inserted into the text by a later Platonist who found the first definition unworthy of Plato. He therefore recommends excising 75d7–76a7. I agree that the second definition adds nothing to the argument but still see it as serving a dramatic point.

20. This point is made by Seeskin (1993, 41). As Vlastos recognizes, Euclid defines shape (*schēma*) several books before he defines solid (*stereon*). However, Vlastos explains that this is "dictated by the architectonics of Euclid's treatise" (1991, 122). But the architectonic is itself clearly dictated by the need to explain the simpler notions of a science before the more complex. Hoerber spots another problem with the second definition of shape: it assumes "merely figures of three

dimensions, yet Plato makes it clear that many figures have only two dimensions" (1960, 96). This is an important point: are there not figures that are *not* the limits of a *solid*?

21. Kraut (1984, 280), in defending what is now a fairly popular view, argues that Socrates "can hardly be criticized for thinking that all he needs is one magical sentence about the virtues (or perhaps a separate one for each), and suddenly perfection will be achieved. Rather, he must believe that the search for a proper account of the virtues will require the discovery of a large series of moral truths, and that after we systematically explore these truths, we will be able to single out one statement about virtue (or perhaps one corresponding to each virtue) that will serve as our definition. That definition will form the most important part of our new theory, but it need not be understandable apart from its relation to all the rest." See also Seeskin (1987, 31–32, 44–45). What evidence is there for this interpretation? In this and other dialogues devoted to the What-is-x? question, Socrates is not seen exploring systematically a wide range of moral truths with the goal of constructing a comprehensive moral theory. On the contrary, he insists that his question be addressed in isolation from all other moral questions and dismisses as irrelevant any moral truths that do not directly answer it. For a similar objection to Kraut, see Brickhouse and Smith (1994, 62).

Though Penner (1992c) criticizes Kraut's identification of the knowledge of what virtue is with propositional knowledge (22–25), his own view is very similar to Kraut's, as he acknowledges elsewhere (1992a, 166 n72). Penner's basic argument is that knowledge of virtue is not for Socrates knowledge of some proposition about virtue, but rather knowledge of what this proposition *refers to* (1992a, 141). But for Penner, this latter knowledge is equivalent to knowing *all* true propositions about virtue; in other words, what *identifies* virtue is simply the sum total of all true propositions about it. Thus, Penner concludes: "To know anything at all about human goodness, one will have to know everything about it" (1992a, 142). Not only does this sound like Kraut's view, but Penner himself recognizes that his point does not really require nonpropositional knowledge (1992a, 143). The untenability of Penner's view is especially evident in its complete vulnerability to the "Socratic fallacy" (though Penner bizarrely sees himself as having solved it: 1992a, 168 n78). Witness the following passage: "to get anything right about the human good, you have to get everything right about it. Socrates still had lots of things to say more about, and to get right" (Penner, 1992a, 146). How on this view could Socrates get *anything* right in the first place? Kraut appears willing to live with the "fallacy" in the *Meno* (1984, 279), though he denies that this dialogue's priority principle is to be found in "earlier" dialogues.

Socrates sometimes does do something similar to what Kraut and Penner describe, namely, when he is pursuing the *method of hypothesis*. However, Socrates will be seen to recognize that no matter how well it may organize and systematize our beliefs, the hypothetical method will never provide us with knowledge of what virtue is.

22. Commenting on this part of the *Meno,* Sayre (1995, 50) observes: "Meaningful language thus appears to be held hostage between circularity and

regress, and with it the possibility of discursive knowledge that depends upon language for its acquisition." Thus the only way out of this dilemma is the recognition of some type of *nonpropositional* knowledge.

23. This mistaken inference mars the otherwise perceptive article by Dimas (1996, 8).

24. This aspect of the definition of color has been noted by J. Klein (1965, 68): "Socrates uses (with or without Empedocles' authority) the phrase *aporroē schēmatōn*. This latter phrase is significant because it implies the actual *identity* of color and bounded surface, which Socrates, as we have seen, did not assert."

25. Cf. Lafrance (1981, 85) and Irwin (1995, 131).

26. Nehamas notes in this connection that Meno at 80b4 and 80d5–6 uses the same word (τὸ παράπαν) that Socrates uses to emphasize his distinction between the *ti*-question and the *poion*-question and to maintain the absolute priority of the former (1992, 301). Nehamas rightly insists that this word is central to the paradox (303).

27. The view that learning is recollection is often thought to be new with the *Meno*. Yet, (1) Socrates could *assume* this view in other dialogues and simply have no occasion or need to defend it because no other interlocutor questions the very possibility of his inquiry. (2) Socrates' inquiry in the *Laches* and the *Charmides* was seen to presuppose that he and his interlocutors in some sense already have the knowledge they seek. The reflexivity noted in both dialogues itself suggests that learning is in fact some kind of "recollection." For defenses of the view that the Socratic elenchus depends on, or can be best explained by, the theory of recollection, see Seeskin (1987, 35–37) and Gentzler (1996). Seeskin even appears to claim that the goal of the *dialogue form* depends on the possibility of recollection in the reader (7, 17). (3) Even in the *Meno* Socrates does not commit himself to those aspects of the recollection theory that are clearly not to be found in "earlier" dialogues (e.g., the preexistence of the soul), but only to what in the theory explains and justifies the possibility of inquiry (86b–c). Of course, if knowledge of virtue were a *technē* that can be taught like other technical skills, then clearly it could not be said to be "recollected": "New in the *Meno* are the theory that what we call learning is really recollection, and a distinction between knowledge and true belief. A consequence of these developments is that the *techne*-model for knowledge is abandoned, for here Socrates considers a sort of knowledge that is always present in the knower, and so never taught" (Woodruff 1990, 81). When one recognizes, however, that Socrates does not subscribe to a "*techne*-model for knowledge" even in the aporetic dialogues (as I have argued in chapter 2), this reason for seeing the theory of recollection as something altogether "new" is no longer available.

28. Ebert (1974, 96) rightly claims that what afflicts Meno is not only ignorance of the nature of virtue but also ignorance of the nature of knowledge. It will become clear below that there is a necessary connection between these two kinds of ignorance.

29. "It is important to note the ostensible rationality of the boy's suggested solution" (Sternfeld and Zyskind 1978, 38).

30. Some scholars have asked whether or not the boy is already recollecting at this point. Nehamas (1992, 309) and Gentzler (1996, 278–79) deny that he is. Indeed, Nehamas is committed to the view that recollection does not take place *anywhere* in the slave episode, though he finds at the end something that is "deeply representative" of the process of recollection (309–10). Nehamas believes that the later description of recollection as an *aitias logismos* (98a3–5) is incompatible with the occurence of recollection during the slave episode. Below I argue that there is no incompatibility here. In addition, the text not only does not support but clearly contradicts Nehamas' interpretation. After the slave's initial answers have been refuted, Socrates asks: "Do you see, Meno, what point he has reached on the road of (*tou*) recollection?" (84a3–4). Nehamas attempts to disarm this text by translating: Do you see, Meno, "what point on the track *to* reminiscence he has reached?" (309). While this translation is possible, it seems strained. In any case, there is another passage that cannot even be forced to fit Nehamas's thesis. At 82e12–13, right *before* he begins his refutation of the boy's first answer, Socrates turns to Meno and says: "Watch him recollecting in order, as one should recollect." This request clearly rules out: (1) that recollection will not occur at all in what follows, and (2) that recollection will occur only in the last step of the discussion, as Gentzler appears to believe. (Recollecting "in order" clearly implies *several* steps).

On the other hand, the texts Nehamas cites in *support* of his thesis do not support it at all, e.g., the question at 85d6–7: "Isn't drawing out knowledge from within oneself recollection?" Nehamas infers that the boy does not recollect since what he draws out from within himself is only *true* opinion (309). But Nehamas is here interpreting 85d6–7 as an identity statement, which is not necessary. Furthermore, since knowledge results from questions that only further awaken (ἐπεγείρειν, 86a7) beliefs that have *already* been thus awoken (ἀνακεκίνηνται, 85c9), *both* true belief and knowledge must form stages of a single process of recollection. Finally, if knowledge is already "in us," it can already start to be recollected in the recognition that and why our beliefs are false. Cf. Vlastos (1965b, 154).

31. For other attempts to make sense of the fact that what Socrates asks for is an irrational number, see J. Klein (1965, 99–102, 185), Brown (1967, 77), Sternfeld and Zyskind (1978, 39–42), Lafrance (1981, 91 n51), Bedu-Addo (1983, 244–48), Narcy (1984, 136), Desjardins (1985, 271 n13, though she in fact makes little of it), Sharples (1985, 151), Seeskin (1987, 99), and Benson (1990a, 137). Brown recognizes that Socrates never receives an answer to his *ti*-question; what the slave comes to recognize answers only a different *poion*-question. Brown, however, makes this distinction one between arithmetic (where a number is sought) and bad geometry (where what is sought is a perception-dependent recognition of the side in question) (see also Vlastos 1991, 119). Brown unfortunately never states if and how Socrates' *ti*-question can be answered. For critiques of Brown's view, see Sharples (1985, 151), and Seeskin (1987, 113 n5). Sharples's own explanation is that Socrates needed a problem whose solution "would be obvious once stated, but difficult enough for the slave boy to go astray

at first" (151). Yet this purpose would clearly not be best served by giving the boy the *impossible* task of stating an irrational number. Bedu-Addo (1983), on the other hand, makes the important connection between the impossibility of giving "an absolutely accurate, arithmetically correct answer to the problem of doubling the square whose side is 2 feet" and the impossibility of "express[ing] the οὐσία of virtue in a definition." (246) It is hard to see, however, how this view is consistent with Bedu-Addo's suggestion that the αἰτίας λογισμός, which Socrates identifies with recollection, is *propositional knowledge* of the kind attained by the hypothetical method (247). The main source of unclarity in both Brown and Bedu-Addo is the failure to explain exactly what Socrates means when he distinguishes what a thing *is* from what *kind* of a thing it is.

32. I am not maintaining that the question is unanswerable for modern mathematics, but only for *Plato*. For a good account of the status of irrational numbers in mathematics at the time of the *Meno*'s composition, see Brown (1967, 77–93).

33. Socrates asks, "Ἀπὸ ποίας γραμμῆς," and the boy answers, "Ἀπὸ ταύτης" (85b1–2). It is true that the boy also learns the technical term "diagonal," but Socrates introduces the term only *after* the boy has recognized the right side. See Seeskin (1993, 43) and Sharples (1985, 154).

34. See Vlastos's critique of the view that the boy's knowledge is based solely on sense experience (1965b, 143–67). See also Sternfeld and Zyskind (1978, 39) and especially Blachowicz (1995, 418), who explicitly distinguishes between "*concrete* acquaintance" and empirical cognition.

35. Ebert rightly points out that the knowledge gained by the slave cannot be "acquaintance" in the sense of "Kenntnis" (i.e., direct perception of some object) because the slave had already seen the diagonal when Socrates drew the first diagram. However, Ebert is not right in claiming that the only knowledge the slave has gained is knowledge of the line "*als* die Grundseite des Quadrates von doppelter Grösse" (100). Ebert does not do justice to the *aporia* that still characterizes the boy's "true belief" and thus to its "intuitive," inexpressible side.

36. As Vlastos thinks (1991, 119). It is true that Socrates knows the answer to which he is leading the slave in a way not paralleled in the aporetic dialogues. Yet as Seeskin (1993, 43) and Dimas (1996, 23) correctly explain, for the purpose of demonstrating that knowledge can be recollected, Socrates "has to pick a problem whose answer he *and* Meno know in advance" (Seeskin 1993, 43; see also 1987, 102). Otherwise, how could Meno be sure that the slave had really arrived at the right result? Particularly significant, however, is Socrates' choice of a problem whose solution is *both* sufficiently known to meet this requirement *and yet* at the same time unknown in such a way as to make the point that virtue cannot be defined. Like Socrates' other examples in this dialogue, this one is very carefully chosen.

37. Cf. Sternfeld and Zyskind (1978, 41–42).

38. "The solution cannot be expressed numerically: the length of each of those lines is "unspeakable," is an *arrēton*. It can only be pointed at. But we comprehend, as the slave does, that this inexpressible length *is* the length of the sides of the double square" (J. Klein 1965, 185).

39. For a much more eloquent statement of the view I am defending here, see Narcy (1984, 136).

40. Sayre presents as evidence for his view that Plato did not place much confidence in the idea of recollection the fact that "no one in this dialogue (or in any other for that matter) is ever portrayed as reaching knowledge by way of recollection" (1995, 71). But as Sayre should know (see, e.g., his explanation of why knowledge is not satisfactorily defined in the *Theaetetus* [1995, 225–27]), there is a simple explanation for this: given that the knowledge in question is nonpropositional, written dialogues could not possibly portray its attainment. Though I argue in this chapter that even belief is not strictly speaking propositional, it still can be given some propositional content; the understanding that distinguishes knowledge from this belief, on the other hand, cannot be expressed in words.

41. Blachowicz (1995, 414–24), by characterizing the knowledge sought as mainly definitional, creates a greater discontinuity between belief and knowledge than is acknowledged by the text. Dimas (1996, 24–30) rightly argues, against Vlastos (1965b, 150), that the slave's "true belief" is not the result of an inference but is rather an immediate, intuitive grasp of the truth that can be *recognized as such* through the recollection of prior knowledge. However, Dimas assumes that the boy could arrive at knowledge only in an entirely different way, i.e., through some kind of *proof* (see 29). This assumption is contradicted not only by 85c, but also by Socrates' claim that *knowledge just as much as true belief* is *recollected*. Dimas makes the following objection to Vlastos's view: "if Plato wanted to make the point that the boy performed an inference of some sort in order to reach this belief, then surely inference of some form is what he would have called it and not recollection" (25). If "knowledge" is substituted for "this belief" and "will perform" for "performed," the same objection can be made to Dimas's view.

42. Fine (1992, 209) believes that Socrates' solution to Meno's eristic paradox is the following: "The slave can inquire, although he *entirely* lacks knowledge, because he has both true beliefs, and also the capacity for rational reflection and revision of his beliefs, and these are adequate for inquiry." Fine also considers this to be the solution to the "Socratic Fallacy": although Socrates does not know what virtue is, and therefore also does not know what *kind* of a thing it is, he can still inquire into virtue because he has true moral beliefs (1992, 209). This view is also defended by Irwin: "though the slave does not know, he has true beliefs about the questions discussed. . . . To inquire into x we need only enough true beliefs about x to fix the reference of the term 'x' so that when the inquiry is over, we can still refer to the same thing" (1977, 139; see also 1995, 132). Cf. Stemmer (1992, 46). Apart from the apparent absence of any textual support for this view, there are serious problems. (1) One criticism, made by Nehamas (1992, 307), is that in order for the slave's true beliefs "to fix the reference of the term 'x' " and thus make the inquiry possible, they would have to be actually *available* to him at the beginning of the inquiry. However, the true beliefs are described as initially only "in" the slave: they are not recovered until the *end* of the inquiry. Rather than starting with true beliefs, as Fine and Irwin claim, the inquiry ends with them. (To support her claim that the slave can inquire because he has true

beliefs, Fine refers to Socrates' attribution of true beliefs to the slave at the *end* of their inquiry [1992, 209]. Does Fine believe that the learning Socrates identifies with recollection does not at all take place *during* the slave episode, but only *after*? If this is her view, it clearly goes against the evidence of the text.) (2) Fine and Irwin ignore Socrates' explicit claim that what is present "in" the slave at the beginning of the inquiry is not only true belief, *but also knowledge* (85d3–4, 86a7–8). (3) As Fine admits, the true beliefs we, on her view, have at the beginning of an inquiry are not recognized by us *to be true* (212). But in this case it is hard to see how the existence of such beliefs solves Meno's paradox. Imagine looking for a squirrel with the following beliefs and no knowledge of which are true and which false: "squirrels eat acorns"; "squirrels have wings"; "squirrels have green scales"; "squirrels are rodents"; "squirrels make a chirping sound by rubbing their legs together"; "squirrels have bushy tails." Though there are some true beliefs here, is this set of beliefs as a whole going to help you find a squirrel or even recognize one once you have found it? Clearly, the Fine/Irwin solution is no solution at all. For a recent detailed critique of this "solution" in general agreement with the above, see Dimas (1996, 9–15). Fine does sometimes attribute to Socrates the view that in an inquiry we have *a tendency toward the truth,* but she is unable to explain this tendency: see note 75 below. Most recently, Fine (1996, 240) explores the possibility of substituting for this tendency toward the truth something else that might resolve the above problem: second-order beliefs, e.g., the belief that I should favor beliefs about principles and counterexamples over beliefs about definitions. Such a second-order belief would tell me which first-order beliefs to reject when presented with an inconsistency. This "solution," apart from being a deus ex machina, merely postpones the problem. If I am very attached to a particular definition, why would I accept a second-order belief that requires me to reject it in favor of some principle to which I am not very committed? Is there some third-order belief that second-order beliefs are to be favored over first-order beliefs?

43. Vlastos denies that in claiming that the knowledge of p is "within us" Plato means that it is *latent* knowledge (1965b, 153 n14). Instead, he believes Plato to mean either that p is *entailed* by known propositions that are themselves in us or that p is simply the clarification of the logical structure of familiar concepts we already have (159, 164). Vlastos recognizes that the answer to the question "What is virtue?" cannot be "in us" in the former sense, since Socrates denies that we can know anything about virtue before we know what virtue itself is (156 n26). Therefore, it must be "in us" in the sense that it involves simply the clarification of a concept of virtue we already possess. But how can we account for our "possession" of the concept without speaking of latent or implicit knowledge? Apparently, Vlastos must say that we possess this concept only in the sense that we already explicitly know certain things about it and can on the basis of this knowledge proceed to clarify it further. This option, however, is not available since, as Vlastos recognizes, Socrates maintains that we can know *nothing* about virtue until we know what it is. One way of avoiding this problem is to maintain that the concept of virtue we already "possess" consists only of *true beliefs*. But then how could the mere clarification of such beliefs, which are not *known* to be

true, ever yield *knowledge?* See the criticism of this view in the preceding note. In short, once we abandon any notion of latent or implicit knowledge, the theory of recollection can only mean that we begin an inquiry *either* with *explicit true beliefs or* with *explicit knowledge:* the problem is that neither interpretation can make sense of, or is even consistent with, what Socrates actually says. For a similar critique of Vlastos, see Blachowicz (1995, 425–26 nn11, 16). Morgan (1989, 177) and Sallis (1996, 91), in contrast, recognize that the solution of Meno's paradox requires the existence of truths in the soul that are not grasped or affirmed. Morgan's explanation, however, that for Plato at this time the Forms were only thoughts existing in the soul (178) is highly implausible and unnecessary. The possibility of knowledge that is not explicitly affirmed or grasped has been partly explained by Grene (1966), with the idea of "tacit, personal knowledge," and K. Ross (1987), with the idea of "non-intuitive immediate knowledge." See also note 75 below.

44. See Gaiser (1959, 183) and J. Klein (1965, 184). Andic (1971, 264) also suggests that "virtue for Socrates is the inquiry into what virtue is." However, because he fails to explain what this means and is unable to abandon the idea that virtue is some result distinct from the inquiry, he progressively weakens his position throughout the paper: compare with the above 304 and 310–12.

45. Cf. J. Klein (1965, 188–89).

46. Stemmer (1992, 240) points out that Socrates' demonstration of recollection does not really provide any practical help to someone who wishes to inquire. The conviction that you already implicitly know what you seek to know does not make it any *easier* for you to inquire. This is why Socrates' demonstration has not made the lazy Meno any more willing to inquire.

47. That all three answers which Meno considers exclusive alternatives are correct has been suggested by Hoerber (1960, 83–89), Andic (1971, 262, 304), Sallis (1996, 94), and Desjardins (1985, 273–78), who acknowledges *four* answers, since she includes "divine inspiration."

48. Socrates' elenchus therefore does not always succeed in making his interlocutors recollect. But this simply shows that the success of the elenchus depends on the nature of the interlocutor and not, as Sayre (1995, 72) assumes, that Plato had serious reservations about the whole theory of recollection. See Seeskin (1987, 128–29).

49. Cf. Gundert (1968, 31).

50. Even though Sternfeld and Zyskind (1978, 7–18) wish to characterize Meno as making some progress in the dialogue, they nevertheless must admit that "It is hard to imagine an interlocutor, fond of discourse and willing to talk, who would be more impervious to Socrates than is Meno" (18; see also 114). I see no reason to accept Seeskin's view that Meno undergoes a change in the second half of the dialogue to the point of acquiring "a thirst for inquiry" and embodying "the virtues which make conversation possible" (1987, 127).

51. Sternfeld and Zyskind (1977) interpret the problem as having to do with the inscribing of an equilateral triangle in a circle. Though they consider this problem perfectly solvable, they observe that it involves a reference to incommensurable lengths: the side of the inscribable triangle and the length of the radius. They recognize the significance of this for the rest of the dialogue: "For those who

believe the slave-boy episode is pushing the limits of Greek geometrical knowledge about incommensurable lines, this interpretation provides further grist" (210). Allen (1984, 145) disagrees with this general line of interpretation and describes the problem instead as follows: "The problem is in fact that of determining whether it is possible for a given circle to be equal in area to a given triangle. Since the area of any triangle is equal to that of some square, the problem is equivalent to that of squaring the circle, quadrature." Yet even on this interpretation Socrates would be introducing again the notion of incommensurability, since the problem would concern whether or not the areas of the triangle and the circle are commensurable. (For a similar view, see Desjardins 1985, 271–72 n13.) An important difference between the two interpretations, however, is that on Allen's "we deal here with a question which mathematics at the end of the fifth century B.C. was powerless to solve" (145). Thus Socrates could be emphasizing here, as in the slave episode, that the What-is-x? question which the hypothetical method fails to address is not one that could receive a definitive answer. Socrates may even be deliberately making the geometrical problem here as obscure as possible with precisely this intention. Vlastos's explanation of the obscurity, i.e., that "Plato is preening himself on his own expertise in geometry" (1991, 123), hardly merits comment. For the opposite view, i.e., that Plato is trying to show the *inadequacy* of geometry, see Seeskin (1993, 46).

52. This represents a problem for R. Robinson (1953, 118). His own solution is that Socrates' argument is hypothetical because it has the form of what Aristotle calls in the *Posterior Analytics* (50a16–28) a "hypothetical syllogism." Such a syllogism does not directly prove the conclusion (as would a regular syllogism) but instead hypothesizes that the conclusion follows from another proposition which it can directly prove. In the present case, for example, Socrates does not directly prove that virtue is teachable but instead hypothesizes that it will be teachable *if* it is knowledge and then proceeds to prove directly that it is knowledge. For why Robinson's account is inadequate, see Bluck (1961, 87–88). The main problem is that Robinson insists on locating the provisionality of the argument in the form of deduction involved, while Socrates clearly locates it elsewhere, namely, in a failure to examine the *meanings* of the terms used. What the method of hypothesis lacks is not logical rigor, but *understanding*. This is something which Bluck does not fail to note: "Thus our premiss 'ἀρετή is ἀγαθόν' is making an assumption about the meaning of the unknown quantity ἀρετή, inasmuch as it attributes to it a quality, or identifies it with a quality, which is not *known* to be contained in the meaning of ἀρετή. The result is that this premiss, and the argument as a whole, are, in the strict sense, hypothetical" (Bluck 1961, 88). Stemmer, on the other hand, like Robinson, assumes that what makes the argument "hypothetical" is that it contains premises that have not been proven, an assumption that entangles him in a number of unnecessary difficulties (1992, 251 ff.).

53. As Sternfeld and Zyskind observe, "hypothetical" arguments as understood here "are not grounded in the nature of things. The method is appropriate to the *poion* problem, for it organizes and systematizes our opinions in 'proof' form" (1978, 56; see also 63).

54. Referring to the role played by intuition in formulating a hypothesis, Bluck comments: "Now Plato would almost certainly have attributed our ability to carry out this sort of procedure to recollection, and if so the hypothetical method itself includes the use of recollection; though inasmuch as any hypothesis is only provisional, the recollection achieved will be only partial and incomplete: hence the use of the elenchus" (1961, 92).

55. Stemmer describes this "sense" well in writing that "Auch Sokrates und Menon kennen die Wörter 'Arete' und 'gut' und verfügen damit bereits über einen vorreflexiven und unthematischen Vorbegriff davon, was Arete ist, obwohl sie nicht sagen können, was sie ist" (1992, 247). However, Stemmer attributes this "Vorbegriff" to convention, *while clearly the point of the idea of recollection is to suggest that this implicit, inarticulate understanding has a deeper source than convention.* Many of our beliefs may indeed be purely conventional, but once these beliefs are removed through refutation, other beliefs can emerge, which as recollected have their source in the soul. S. Klein (1986, 360) sees Socrates as appealing to *endoxa*, but rightly emphasizes that these are not conventional opinions. However, Klein's claim that these *endoxa* are "regulative," while partially true, cannot be the whole picture.

56. See Schaerer on hypothesis and inspiration (1969, 311–19).

57. See Dorter (1982, 134).

58. The positive aspect of the hypothetical method is brought out well by Schaerer (1969, 313–14), who sees the hypothesis as playing a mediating role between our thought and the transcendent object of knowledge.

59. Moline (1981), Moravcsik (1979), Burnyeat (1980; 1990, 216–71; Burnyeat 1981, 1987 address a similar theme, but deal with Plato only in passing), Nehamas (1989, 1992).

60. The exceptions are Moline and Moravcsik. Moline translates *epistēmē* as "understanding" mainly to make the point that the Greek word for Plato has not simply cognitive but also *conative* connotations (see 1981, 12–31). Moravcsik means by "understanding" "insight + skill" (1979, 59) and "the proper intuitive grasp of key concepts" (64). These characterizations of *epistēmē* are much closer to my own than the one discussed below. That characterization can be attributed to both Burnyeat and Nehamas, though in defending his "interrelational model of *epistēmē*," Nehamas (1989, 275) criticizes Burnyeat for subscribing to the "additive model." This criticism to some extent seems verbal hair-splitting. I do not see that their two positions are that different: Burnyeat too rejects the view that beliefs are converted into *epistēmē* through the addition of some "justification"; he too emphasizes the "systematic" character of "understanding," identifying it with the synoptic grasp and total mastery of a certain domain through definition, analysis, and classification; he too plays down (especially in 1980) that element of "acquaintance" which, in my view, is part of Plato's characterization of *epistēmē*. Nehamas, however, does appear to go further in the direction I criticize. For example, the cases of knowing the road to Larissa (in the *Meno*) and being an eyewitness (in the *Theatetus*) are accepted as cases of *epistēmē* by Burnyeat, but are rejected by Nehamas because they do not involve "systematization, proof, explanation, or account" (1992, 312–13). Fine should also be included with

Burnyeat and Nehamas, even though she rejects the translation of *epistēmē* as "understanding" (1992, 218 n19), apparently because she does not think that *epistēmē* is based on explanation *instead of* justification, but maintains that both are equally important to it (see 1990, 107). However, Fine nevertheless subscribes to the "interrelational model" of *epistēmē:* see especially Fine (1979).

61. In glossing Socrates' description of beliefs being bound by a "logismos aitias," Nehamas describes them as becoming "properly organized and systematized" (1992, 307).

62. Nehamas's view agrees with that of Kraut and Penner (discussed in note 21 above) in maintaining that a definiton is not an isolated proposition but rather involves "the mastery of the whole field to which the object of definition belongs, and hence a science of the field in question" (1989, 284–85). Nehamas is referring specifically to the *Theaetetus* here, but his view on definition in the *Meno* does not appear much different.

63. Nehamas maintains that "beliefs which are candidates for knowledge are those which concern a thing's essence. In addition, we have seen, such beliefs concern interrelations of each thing with others belonging along with it to the same structured domain" (1989, 278). But the identification that Nehamas appears to be making here (at least on an epistemological level) between a thing's essence and its relations to other things in the same domain collapses the distinction between what a thing is (*ti esti*) and what *kind* of a thing it is (*poion ti esti*), a distinction whose importance Socrates affirms throughout the dialogue.

64. Contra Fine: "If the circle of our beliefs is sufficiently large, and the interconnections suitably comprehensive, the links in the circle are transformed from true beliefs into pieces of knowledge" (1979, 397).

65. There in fact appears to be a kind of nonpropositional component in Nehamas's concept of "understanding." In arguing that this "understanding," unlike knowledge, is nontransmissable, Nehamas explains that "it is precisely the mastering of these connections and relations that cannot be transmitted (cf. *Rep.* 518b6–7) because these connnections are methods and rules for proceeding in a properly justified manner, from one item of knowledge to another. And even if such rules and methods can be formulated, and in that sense, transmitted, what cannot be transmitted in the same manner is the ability to follow the methods and to apply the rules" (1992, 313). I too see understanding as a nontransmissable practical ability. The difference is that in my view understanding is not an ability to connect beliefs systematically but rather an ability to *inquire:* precisely that ability which Socrates demonstrates in the dialogues (I do not see Socrates in any dialogue doing what Nehamas describes), an ability which by itself provides an "acquaintance" with virtue.

66. Simply recognizing as such the relations into which virtue enters (if they are more than relations of logical consistency and inconsistency) presupposes an understanding of virtue "as a whole." The network of relations presupposes a unity (and the understanding of that unity) which cannot be reduced to the network itself. Therefore, far from providing us with an understanding of virtue, Nehamas's method depends upon such an understanding. Absorbed in

the activity of analyzing and classifying, the method is blind to what such activity presupposes. This is precisely the weakness Socrates sees in the hypothetical method. Cf. Rosen's brief critique of the "interrelational model" (1986, 297).

67. I do not think that it is illegitimate to speak of an "understanding" that is fundamentally inexpressible. As Roberts (1984, 229) points out, "'understanding' does not always carry the connotations of articulateness that it sometimes seems to when contrasted with knowledge. There is no outright contradiction in saying that one understands something, but cannot explain it."

68. Cf. Sternfeld and Zyskind 1978, (67–69).

69. Cf. Schaerer (1969, 318).

70. In criticizing Vlastos's view that the method of hypothesis aims at certainty, Seeskin (1993, 48–49) rightly points out that in this case Plato would not have illustrated the method by showing it to lead to contradictory results.

71. Burger (1981, 7) points out that this example appears to contradict the assumption that knowledge can be taught: no one can be taught knowledge of the road to Larissa, but only true belief; knowledge requires that one actually experience the road for oneself. She finds the solution to this apparent contradiction in an understanding of "teaching" in terms of recollection, rather than in terms of the transmission of information (8).

72. Nehamas argues that "knowing the road to Larissa" is not for Plato an actual case of knowledge but only an analogy (1992, 312–13). Sternfeld and Zyskind (1978, 95–98) take the opposite view, seeing Plato here as allowing for the knowledge of particular facts. Fine (1992, 218 n19) also apparently adopts this view, since she uses "knowing the road to Larissa" as a counterexample to Nehamas's view that *epistēmē* involves explanation, failing to recognize that Nehamas does not acknowledge it to be an example of knowledge. I agree with Nehamas that "knowing the road to Larissa" is only an analogy; after all, there appears to be no sense in which knowledge of this road could be said to be "in" us and learned through "recollection." (Sternfeld and Zyskind [1978, 96–97] are forced by their interpretation to claim that the recollection mentioned by Socrates in this later part of the dialogue differs from the recollection demonstrated with the slave.) However, Nehamas's characterization of *epistēmē* (discussed above) makes the example entirely *disanalogous*. *Epistēmē* on his interpretation would be comparable to accumulating and systematically organizing a great deal of information about the road to Larissa without actually traveling on it, precisely what Socrates in the example refuses to call *epistēmē*. Nehamas attempts to explain the analogy by claiming that the *ability* to carry out the activity he describes is nontransmissable and must in this sense, like knowledge of the road to Larissa, be acquired firsthand (1992, 313). But this is not enough: what must be known "firsthand" according to the analogy is the *object* of *epistēmē*, not simply some skill or ability.

73. I would suggest that the introduction of *doxa* in this dialogue is necessarily linked to the introduction of the hypothetical method. In his use of the latter method Socrates no longer seeks unconditional knowledge but settles for something which, though not knowledge, is yet also not ignorance. The need

therefore arises to account for this state between ignorance and knowledge. Conversely, such a need does not arise in the aporetic dialogues because the search for knowledge of *ti esti* has not there been abandoned in favor of a "second-best": what is wanted is knowledge or nothing. See Gundert (1971, 47).

74. One reason why Price does not contrast knowledge with any kind of belief except "belief that" (for example, he does not allow that there is a type of belief corresponding to knowledge by acquaintance) is that the verb "to believe" does not take a direct object except in cases where it simply means "believing what someone says" ("I believe him"; see Price 1969, 72–73). This, however, is not true of the Greek verb δοξάζειν. At *Theaetetus* 209b2–3, the phrase σὲ μᾶλλον ἐδόξαζον means "my belief was more about you," *not* "I believed you more." There is no indication in the text that Socrates' Greek is here unnatural or forced (see also 190d4, d7). But is this a rare usage? The answer depends on how one interprets δοξάζειν in the belief/knowledge distinction of *Republic* 5 (478c6), as well as in Socrates' identification of possessing the truth (ἀληθεύειν) with τὸ τὰ ὄντα δοξάζειν in book 3 (413a7–8). Though it is not impossible for this latter phrase to mean simply "believing propositions that are true," it is also possible that τὰ ὄντα is here an external object of δοξάζειν in the same way in which the pronoun σὲ is an external object of δοξάζειν in the *Theaetetus* passage. Cf. Benitez (1996, 538).

75. Those who do not acknowledge the existence of this kind of nonverbalized intuition are completely unable to explain Socrates' evident assumption that, as Fine puts it, "in inquiry, we tend to favor true over false beliefs" (1992, 213; see also 212, 214). However, Fine does not even attempt to explain this tendency toward the truth or why Socrates assumes its existence with such absolute confidence. This assumption has also given Vlastos a great deal of trouble. In his influential account of the elenchus, Vlastos originally ascribed to Socrates the assumption that whoever has a false moral belief will always have at the same time *true* moral beliefs that entail the negation of that false belief (1983a, 48–52). Critics quickly objected to the obvious circularity of including a distinction between true and false beliefs in an assumption that is meant to explain how Socrates determines which moral beliefs are true: see Kraut (1983, 68) and Brickhouse and Smith (1984, 188–90). In response Vlastos later scaled down the assumption by removing the word "true": see both (1985, 18–19 n44) and its later version (1994b, 56–57 n43). This "scaling down," however, appears disastrous. Polansky (1985, 254) does not think so: given that there will always be beliefs (true or false) which will contradict a false moral belief, the fact that Socrates (or anyone else) has consistent beliefs shows that he has no false moral belief. But if a "false moral belief" is simply "a belief contradicted by one's other beliefs," then the assumption is tautologous: whoever has a belief that is negated by his other beliefs will always have at the same time beliefs entailing the negation of that belief. All that could be concluded from such an assumption is that Socrates' beliefs are consistent and the interlocutor's are not: truth falls out of the picture altogether. This is perhaps why Vlastos oddly "scales up" the assumption again by reintroducing the reference to "*true* beliefs" (1991, 113–14; 1994a, 25). In the

latter, however, Vlastos provides a new explanation of why Socrates assumes that the beliefs he uses to refute others are *true:* "For he would have to fall back on nothing better than the pragmatic values of those beliefs: they articulate intuitions which prove practically viable in his own experience; they tell him who is happy and who isn't; he does what they tell him and he *is* happy" (1994a, 26). So Vlastos must in the last resort attribute to Socrates a pragmatist conception of truth! Even leaving aside the absurdity of the kind of practical test Vlastos describes (what criterion would Socrates have, independently of and prior to his moral beliefs, for determining whether or not he or anyone else is happy?), an explanation so far removed from the text betrays desperation. (A similar view, though less extreme, appears implied by the conclusion of Brickhouse and Smith [1994, 21] that "Socrates has good reason to think that propositions whose negations are continually defeated by the *elenchos* are moral propositions which everyone would be *better off believing*" [my emphasis]).

Both Fine (1992, 213) and Vlastos (1994a, 29) recognize that the explanation might lie in the theory of recollection. However, this theory can provide a solution only if it maintains that we already possess an awareness of the truth which, though "in us" and not explicit, is yet able to direct, in a way we cannot articulate or express, our actions and our inquiry. The mere possession of knowledge in a previous life does not explain the tendency toward the truth we have *now*. Stefanini (1932, 1:lv–lvi, 101–3), Seeskin (1987, 35–37), Blachowicz (1995, 413–16, 421), and Gentzler (1996) see the correct solution here. Gentzler explicitly proposes the theory of recollection as the solution to what Vlastos has called "the problem of the elenchus," i.e., the problem of how the elenchus can be truth-conducive. She also recognizes that the theory can provide such a solution only if it "explains how we have the propensity to form conscious beliefs about instances of moral and mathematical properties" (293). The explanation, as Gentzler rightly sees, is that from the very start of the inquiry our unconscious true beliefs about the natures of moral and mathematical properties "constrain the way in which we conceptualize the world" (294). Yet Gentzler does not make clear how exactly these beliefs constrain us: her characterization of them as both explicit and unconscious (281 n49) appears to render them incapable of influencing our judgments until they are fully recollected; I believe that they must instead be characterized as *implicit* and *conscious* in order to do what Gentzler requires of them. Gentzler also wrongly assumes that what recollection provides is an account or theory: for a critique of this aspect of her interpretation, see Cicovacki (1996, 301–8). For different accounts of latent or implicit knowledge, as well as a critique of Vlastos's attempt to deny its role in recollection, see note 43 above.

76. Cf. Viano (1952, 175). Sprute (1962, 113) rightly claims that *doxa* at *Phaedrus* 237d8 cannot be translated as "opinion" (*Meinung*) and commends Schleiermacher's translation of *Gesinnung*.

77. A central question concerning *doxa* in Plato's dialogues is whether it is (1) something analogous to perception (*Vorstellung, représentation*) or (2) a form of judgment (*Meinung*). For the debate, see Lafrance (1981, 12). Lafrance's argument against (1), i.e., that in this case *doxa* could be neither true nor

false, assumes what is in question, namely, that truth is simply a property of judgments (1981, 12). His further argument that (1) would reduce *doxa* to "une connaissance sensible" is also incorrect: to identify *doxa* with some sort of intuition is not necessarily to identify it with sensible intuition. However, Lafrance also shows problems with (2): how would this interpretation distinguish *doxa* from knowledge and how would it explain the claim in *Republic* 5 that *doxa* is confined to sensible objects? (1981, 12). Elsewhere, Lafrance appears to suggest that the distinction between (1) and (2) is not relevant, that both are correct (1982, 125–26). The above debate also leads to the question of whether *doxa* is propositional or nonpropositional. Gully (1962, 65) asserts emphatically that it is propositional. Bluck (1963, 259), on the other hand, asserts that "the Greek word δόξα is not necessarily to be associated with propositions. It may refer simply to what a thing 'seems like.' . . . There is no reason to suppose that at the time of the *Republic* Plato associated δόξα any more than ἐπιστήμη with propositions; and the indications are that even in the *Theaetetus* he is not introducing δόξα as something essentially propositional." Bluck proceeds to claim that Plato apparently sees *doxa* as a kind of "mental image" (260). The view I am defending is that of Bluck and interpretation (1) above. However, it is necessary to point out that the exact kind of "intuition" or "mental image" involved must be specified, something I can only partially do here, and that *doxa* still can be, and very often is, a propositional judgment. To this extent, both of the interpretations above are correct, as Lafrance suggests. However, they can both be correct only because propositional *doxa* presupposes nonpropositional *doxa* and is thus derivative.

78. As was noted in chapter 5, the craftsman's true belief as described in *Republic* 10, and as opposed there to the user's knowledge, cannot be reduced to "belief that" (601e–602a). What the *Meno* reveals about belief only confirms this.

79. This comparison shows that the inspiration spoken of here is not the distinctly philosophical inspiration discussed in chapter 5 (which was seen to be compatible with knowledge), but rather the kind of inspiration that is confined to images.

80. Cf. Waldenfels (1961, 36).

81. Lafrance (1981, 112–14) identifies two possible interpretations: the *aitia* is a form and the *logismos* is the movement of dialectic toward the form, and the *aitias logismos* is a process of deduction and systematization. The second is by far the more popular interpretation. It is defended by Lafrance himself (1981, 112; 1982, 128), Bluck (1961, 412–13), Vlastos (1965b, 154–55), and apparently Fine (1992, 218–19 n19).

There is, however, a third interpretation which, though similar to the second, is yet distinct: the *aitias logismos* is not any justification added to beliefs, but rather the comprehensive multiplication and systematic organization of such beliefs. This interpretation has been defended at greatest length by Nehamas (1992, 307, 309, 310), but also by Desjardins (1985, 269), who describes the *aitias logismos* as securing judgments "by deriving them within a theoretically coherent conceptual system."

My reasons for rejecting the last two interpretations are, first, they presuppose interpretations of "recollection" I argue against above; second, they (especially the second) depend on a much too narrow translation of *"logismos"* (see note 83 below); and finally, they both would require us to conclude that recollection does not even begin to take place in the slave episode, since an *aitias logismos* as they interpret it is nowhere to be found there: the boy does not even begin to construct a proof or develop a comprehensive theory of geometry (Nehamas accepts this consequence [1992, 309–10], but see my crticism above). The first interpretation is therefore the one I defend, though only in the specific way I characterize it. Hoerber (1960, 91) also appears to accept some version of this interpretation.

82. Burger (1981, 7), Hoerber (1960, 91), and Sprute (1962, 62) see a tension between the example of "knowing the road to Larissa" and the present passage. Though the three of them provide different characterizations of the *aitias logismos*, the problem is the same: they find it hard to reconcile the example's suggestion that knowledge involves "direct experience" with the claim that knowledge involves an *aitias logismos*. On my interpretation, the *aitias logismos* is itself a form of "acquaintance," and the problem disappears.

83. Several passages can be cited in which the word *logismos* is associated with knowledge of the forms. From the *Phaedo:* at 66a1 *logismos* is apparently the thought (διανοία) with which we attempt to grasp what each being is in its purity and "in itself"; at 79a3 we are said to lay hold of (ἐπιλάβειν) those things which are unchanging τῷ τῆς διανοίας λογισμῷ; at 84a8 the *logismos* is described as a means of *seeing* the truth and the divine. At *Sophist* 254a8 *logismos* is what brings the philosopher into contact with the idea of being, an idea that blinds him with its brightness (see also 248a11). At *Parmenides* 130a2 Socrates distinguishes the forms from sensible particulars by saying that they are known by means of *logismos*. At *Republic* 611c3–4 we are told that the true nature of the soul can be *seen* only by means of *logismos:* λογισμῷ διαθεατέον. These passsages should suffice to show that the common tendency (Sharples 1985, 184; Lafrance, 1982, 128; Bluck 1961, 412; Vlastos 1965b, 154) to restrict the meaning of *logismos* to "calculation" or "reckoning" is unjustified. This restriction is the result of unwarranted generalization from the frequent use of the word to mean arithmetic calculation (see, for example, *Republic* 522c ff.). The cited passages also show that *logismos* often means what I claim it means in the *Meno:* a reasoning process that results in knowledge ("vision") of a form (*ti esti*). The word *logismos* can therefore describe Socrates' dialectic. (It is even closely associated with νοῦς at *Republic* 586d2 and *Timaeus* 77b5.) However, the essential passage for understanding how this word is used in the *Meno* comes from the *Phaedrus*. After claiming that no soul that has not seen the truth will enter a human body, Socrates explains: "δεῖ γὰρ ἄνθρωπον συνιέναι κατ' εἶδος λεγόμενον, ἐκ πολλῶν ἰὸν αἰσθησέων εἰς ἓν λογισμῷ συναιρούμενον" (249b6–c1). Here *logismos* involves proceeding from a plurality of perceptions to a unity in which they are "comprehended." Since Socrates has just told us that the soul has already "seen" the form that provides this unity, all the *logismos* does is *uncover* the unity that the perceptions presuppose. We perceive a plurality of things as possessing the same form, but this perception itself presupposes an implicit knowledge of the form. The *logismos* recovers this knowlege and makes it explicit. Socrates therefore proceeds to

identify the process which he has just described with *recollection* (249c1–2). This passage from the *Phaedrus* thus confirms my interpretation of the *aitias logismos* in the *Meno* (also identified with recollection) as referring to the process of going beyond the plurality of instances and characteristics (*poion ti*) known through perception to a knowledge of the form (*ti*) that unifies this plurality.

84. Desjardins (1985, 276–77) also feels a need to distinguish between two kinds of inspiration, though she says very little about the distinction.

85. A major thesis of J. Klein (1965) is that Meno is nothing but "memory," where such memory is to be distinguished from the recollection which leads to knowledge (186).

86. The attempt of Sternfeld and Zyskind (1978; see 78–93, 103–4) to find a positive "operationist" and "realist" political theory in the last part of the dialogue overlooks the dogmatic, unquestioning, and therefore dangerous character of the "inspiration" which Socrates attributes to the statesmen.

87. Both Brown (1967, 64–65) and Bedu-Addo (1983, 237) see no difference between the kind of belief gained by Meno and the kind gained by the slave.

88. This is the mistake made in thinking that the *Meno*, in distinction from the aporetic dialogues, is "complete" and conclusive. At the deepest level, the *Meno* is no more conclusive than those other dialogues. See Stefanini (1932, 1:99) and Bluck (1961, 43).

Chapter 7

1. What Socrates is investigating throughout the following discussion are *aitiai*. Vlastos (1971) has argued that the word *aitia* is much broader in meaning than our word "cause." See also Rowe (1993a, 229) and Gallop (1975, 170). Though Vlastos is clearly right, the other available translations of *aitia*, namely, "explanation" and "reason," are not any better, and perhaps even worse, than "cause." The *aitiai* of which Socrates speaks are always real entities taken to be really responsible, in some way or another, for the way things are, whether these entities be sensible objects, the good, or the forms. To translate *aitia* as "reason" or "explanation" is to obscure completely this ontological dimension. To say that Socrates is searching for the "reasons for coming-to-be and destruction," that he expected to learn from Anaxagoras "the reason for things," that though he fails to discover the nature of the good he would like to learn about "a reason of that sort," that his "second voyage" is "in quest of the reason," and that Socrates' method is "both about a reason and about everything else" (all of these translations are taken from Gallop 1993), seems to me to be *at least as* misleading and unnatural as saying that the "cause" of a thing's being beautiful is its participation in beauty itself (though I do not in fact find the latter that misleading). Furthermore, our word "cause," though usually understood as "efficient cause," need not be so restricted. When the translation "cause" is used in what follows, it is to be understood in the most general sense possible: the "cause" of x is simply that which is really responsible for x being what it is. Socrates himself does not presume to

explain *the exact way* in which either the good or the forms are "causes." See below for further explanation of both my disagreement and agreement with Vlastos's interpretation.

2. Eustathius *in Od.* 1453, 20.

3. Cf. Rowe (1993a, 238–39) and Tait (1986, 457). Wiggins (1986) argues that Socrates is not turning away from the good at all, since he expects to find in his *deuteros plous* the same teleological explanation he vainly sought from Anaxagoras. I find this thesis extremely implausible. After this point in the text Socrates does not refer to teleological explanation again. Though the good is introduced as a form at 100b6 and is thereore one of Socrates' new *aitiai*, it is given no prominence over the other forms. See also the criticisms of Wiggins's interpretation in Rowe (1993b, 68–69).

4. On this point see Hackforth (1972, 136).

5. This identification is also made by Dorter (1982, 122).

6. I do not find Dorter's translation of ἔργα as "operations" at all helpful (1982, 121 ff.). As Burnet observes: "The word ἔργα is equivalent to ὄντα and πράγματα, and is used here because it is the standing opposite to λόγοι" (Burnet 1911, 109).

7. Of course, physical things are elsewhere understood to be images of the forms (see Rowe 1993a, 240), but since the good is the form that has been most recently mentioned and since it has been identified with the *aitia* of all things, it seems best in the present context to identify what is imitated with the good.

8. This interpretation of the "eclipsed sun" was offered in Archer-Hind ([1894], 1973, 160–61. More recently, it has been defended by Dorter (1982, 123).

9. It is sometimes thought that Socrates is here speaking of postulating a hypothesis that is the strongest *with regard to every inquiry*. "It would be natural to suppose that there can only be one hypothesis that is the 'strongest', i.e., stronger than all others, and if so it should apparently be that one which Socrates adopts on all occasions" (Bostock 1986, 163). I see no reason to suppose this. It is much more natural to think that what Socrates does is postulate *on each occasion* (ἑκάστοτε) that hypothesis which appears strongest *on that occasion, with those specific interlocutors* and *for the purposes of the specific question at hand*.

10. I see no justification for Tait's view that Socrates' judgment that a certain theory is "the strongest" can involve an appeal to sense experience (1986, 465). I agree with Tait (457–58) that the second-best method does not abandon sensible phenomena altogether, since its goal is the same as that of the best method: to explain why large things are large, why beautiful things are beautiful, etc. Yet the explanation provided by this method has nothing to do with any sensible properties: e.g., why an object is beautiful has nothing to do with its color or shape.

11. R. Robinson 1953, 126. Robinson maintains that "agreement" (*sumphōnein*) must mean "entailment" if any sense is to be made of Socrates' directive that we should assume to be true whatever "agrees" with the hypothesis (so also Tait 1986, 465). Yet Robinson recognizes that this interpretation would result in another absurdity: it would ascribe to Socrates the unjustifiable principle that

whatever is not entailed by the hypothesis should be assumed *false*. Robinson is therefore caught in a dilemma: he believes that "consistency" and "entailment" are the only two possible meanings of *sumphōnein* and sees major difficulties in both. Sayre pretends to solve Robinson's problem by arguing that *sumphōnein* means *mutual entailment of convertible propositions* (1983, 195; 1995, 138). As Sayre himself recognizes, however, there is no indication that Socrates' method, like geometrical analysis, deals exclusively with mutually convertible propositions. Sayre's attempt to put the blame for this difficulty on Plato's supposed inability to distinguish adequately between mathematics and philosophy is hardly convincing (1983, 196; see also 1995, 138, 140). Gentzler (1991) suggests, more promisingly, that *sumphōnein* refers to *coherence* understood as follows: "A proposition *P* coheres with *Q* if and only if *P* is consistent with *Q* and stands either in a suitable inductive or deductive inferential relation to *Q*" (268–69). The difference between this reading and Robinson's does not appear very great, since the reference to consistency here does not add anything: if *P* is in an inferential relation to *Q*, it will necessarily be consistent with *Q*. The reference to "induction" might represent an important departure from Robinson, but Gentzler does not explain this addition. The major advantage of Gentzler's interpretation, however, is her reading of *diaphōnein:* by claiming that it is only the *contrary,* rather than the *contradictory,* of *sumphōnein,* she can take it to refer *only* to *inconsistency* and thus avoid the absurdity in which Robinson gets caught (269–70). However, while I obviously agree with this reading of *diaphōnein,* I do not find Gentzler's reading of *sumphōnein* any more necessary or convincing than Robinson's. While Gentzler's interpretation would not, like Robinson's, require Socrates to say that two propositions "disagree" when, though consistent, they are not in an inferential relation, it *would* require Socrates to say that *they fail to sumphōnein.* Would not this latter claim too be strange and arbitrary? For other criticisms, see below.

12. Bostock (1986, 162–63) also fails to see this and accordingly considers the talk of "agreement" here "a slip on Socrates' part." Gentzler (1991, 271) recognizes that even on her interpretation the field of the propositions being considered needs to be restricted, but she oddly does not see that this is accomplished by the specific subject under discussion.

13. R. Robinson (1953, 128) objects against the "consistency" interpretation that "the mere activity of positing every propostion that was consistent with the hypothesis would not lead in any given direction. It would merely amass a heap of assertions." Gentzler (1991, 226) quotes this objection with approval. However, the postulating of propositions that "agree" with the hypothesis is only one part of the hypothetical method. Reading "consistency" here does not require one to restrict the whole method to consistency. Specifically, I take the phrase τὰ ἐπ' ἐκείνης ὁρμηθέντα at 101d4–5 to refer to more than propositions that "agree" with the initial hypothesis.

14. The word "ἔχοιτο" is ambiguous. At 101d2 the verb means "to hold on to," which should therefore also be the meaning at 101d4. As to whether the person holds on to the hypothesis in order to *attack and refute* it or simply to ask questions about it, the word itself gives us no clue. Rowe suggests a third

translation: "proposed firm acceptance of it [i.e., the hypothesis]" (1993b, 63; see also 1993a, 247). In this case Socrates' point would be that we should first look at the consequences of applying the hypothesis before accepting it. For a critique of Rowe's translation, as well as a defense of the translation "attack," see van Eck (1996, 221 n10); Rowe (1996, 240) responds that van Eck may be right, but does not think that much hangs on the point. Tait is at least consistent in translating "ἔχοιτο" as "questioned" in *both* of its occurences (1986, 475), but I do not see how this translation can make sense in the first occurence and Tait is obviously wrong in claiming that the translation "hung on to" does not make sense in the second. Again the looseness of the language should caution us against imposing too strict an interpretation on what Socrates says.

15. As pointed out above, the method is not pursued within a vacuum, but rather within the context of certain background assumptions shared by the interlocutors. Even R. Robinson (1953, 131–3), after some initial perplexity, recognizes that the hypothesis need not be an "atomic" proposition. See also Gentzler (1991, 273).

16. This is Rowe's suggestion (1993b, 61), but see my criticism below of one aspect of this view.

17. Sayre (1995, 139–40) appears to assume such a restriction.

18. R. Robinson (1953, 138) rightly denies that the *ti hikanon* of the *Phaedo* is the *archē anhypothetos* of the *Republic*. Both reviewers of the first edition of Robinson's book, Friedländer and Cherniss, strongly objected. Cherniss claimed that there was "every reason" to make the identification (1947, 141). Friedländer even went so far as to write: "There is hardly anyone, I venture to say, who has not identified the *hikanon* of the *Phaedo* with the *anhypotheton* of the *Republic* (511b)" (1945, 256). Friedländer's statement was not true even at the time at which he wrote it, since such an identification had already been denied by Archer-Hind ([1894], 1973, 103–4) and Stenzel (1940, 7–8). Today hardly anyone would accept the identification: see Hackforth (1972, 141), Dorter (1982, 133–34), Rowe (1993a, 247–48; 1993b, 58), Stemmer (1992, 265–67). An exception is Tait (1986, 476), who assumes the identification without argument. Gallop (1975, 191) does not seem to have made up his mind on the question.

19. R. Robinson (1953, 134) describes the whole method as follows: "The whole method as so far described comes to this: in order to reach a desired conclusion, (1) hypothesize whichever hypothesis seems strongest to you of those that seem likely to lead to the conclusion; (2) draw the consequences of this hypothesis; (3) see whether they give rise to any contradiction; if they do, begin from the beginning again with another hypothesis; but, so long as they do not, (4) posit as true that which the hypothesis entails, and as false that of which the hypothesis entails the contradictory." Thus Robinson assigns to step (4) what Socrates clearly describes as the second step. Bostock rightly protests against step (3): "One would suppose that a hypothesis which had inconsistent consequences would never have appealed to you as a 'strongest' hypothesis in the first place. Moreover, if this test is a serious one, then one would suppose that it should be carried out before the hypothesis is even proposed" (1986, 168). Bostock,

however, sees no plausible alternative to Robinson's interpretation and concludes that "we simply have to swallow the difficulties" (169).

20. Central to the recent debate between Rowe and van Eck is the question concerning the identity of the initial hypothesis: Rowe maintains that the hypothesis *includes* Socrates' specific theory of causality and that what is accepted as agreeing with the hypothesis are simply specific applications of this theory, while the "wise" *aitiai* are rejected as disagreeing with it (1993a, 242; 1993b, 52–53; 1996, 230–36); van Eck maintains that the hypothesis is *only* the existence of the forms (1994, 22, 29; 1996, 215–17) and that at this point nothing is accepted or rejected as agreeing or disagreeing with it: the method is applied only later in Socrates' account (1994, 29–33; 1996, 225). My own position is somewhere in the middle. With van Eck I agree (1) that what is hypothesized in this passage is simply the existence of the forms, and (2) that Rowe's view renders "agreement" and "disagreement" with the hypothesis trivial (see van Eck 1996, 218, and Rowe's reply, 1996, 229–30). On the other hand, I agree with Rowe on the following: (3) a sharp distinction such as van Eck's between the form hypothesis and the theory of causation leaves the status of the latter within the method entirely opaque. A solution, and the one I accept, is that Socrates' theory of causation is accepted and its rivals rejected on account of their agreement or disagreement with the form hypothesis. As Rowe points out (1996, 229–34), van Eck himself tends to characterize the relation between the form hypothesis and the causality theory in this way (see 1994, 31; 1996, 216, 220). But then he is wrong to insist that the test of agreement or disagreement is not applied until later in Socrates' account. To his argument that the "wise" *aitiai* are not rejected because they do not accord with the hypothesis but because they are confusing and unsafe (1994, 29; 1996, 217–18), Rowe gives a satisfactory reply (1996, 232 n17). (4) Rowe (1996, 234–36) cites one very strong piece of evidence in favor of his interpretation: 101d2 where Socrates refers to that "safe (part) of the hypothesis": since what has earlier been called "safe" is the account of causality, Socrates here clearly includes that account in the hypothesis. Is there any way of reconciling this description of the hypothesis at 101d2 with van Eck's reading of the hypothesis at 100b5–7? Rowe himself (1996, 236) suggests a way: once Socrates posits his account of causality as agreeing with the form hypothesis, he sees the agreement as so strong that for the purposes of the rest of the argument he can treat the two as an inseparable unity. In my account of Socrates' argument I assume this interpretation, combining aspects of van Eck's and Rowe's as outlined in the four points above, as the most plausible.

21. Stemmer (1992, 39) lists the variety of prepositions with which the dialogues describe the relation between the one form and the many things (*ta polla*) and concludes that the relation "nur vage bestimmt ist." This is an understatement.

22. Burnet (1911, 108–9) does not consider Socrates' method to be "second-best" at all, because he thinks that it *does* tell us what it means for a thing to be x. While the method indeed tells us that for a thing to *be* good means for it to *participate* in the good, clearly more than this is required for us to really know what it means for a thing to be good (or beautiful or two or large, etc.). Bostock

considers an interpretation like Burnet's according to which the *deuteros plous* involves an elucidation of concepts, but must in the end reject it: "This so-called explanation [that a thing is *P* because it participates in *P*] apparently offers us *no* elucidation or clarification of the concept of being *P,* just because you can say exactly the same of any concept whatever. . . . No one who had been subjected to Socratic questioning would think that this formula was going to get him anywhere" (1986, 150). See also my criticism of Vlastos's interpretation below.

23. *Pace* Hackforth (1972, 142).

24. This limitation of the hypothetical understanding of the forms is seen by Stenzel (1940, 11): "in Plato's opinion it is not the whole nature of Ideas to be hypotheses—they must also have some metaphysical significance. 'Hypothesis' is only one side of the meaning of the Idea, and to Plato not the more essential side; for it lacks the power to satisfy those demands for an End, of which he had given a clear formulation in the *Phaedo* and elsewhere before that." See also Kuhn (1968, 167).

25. R. Robinson puzzles over why the method of hypothesis is introduced where it is in the *Phaedo:* "What has the hypothetical method to do with the new kind of cause?" (1953, 143). What Robinson fails to see is that the transition Socrates describes is not from the search for the good as cause to the search for the forms as causes, as he assumes, but rather from the search for a knowledge of the good, *in which would be grounded an understanding of the nature of each of the other forms,* to the hypothesizing of forms as causes (*the good included*) with no attempt to understand their natures. This is why Socrates can describe the transition as one from direct vision to looking at things indirectly in propositions, a description that, as Robinson himself recognizes, makes no sense on his interpretation.

26. Vlastos acknowledges that the function of the forms as logical *aitiai* has a metaphysical foundation (1971, 148). However, he still insists that "Plato's Squareness has no more causal efficacy than has the nominalist's; it has no power to spawn earthly squares; if it did, so would the Form, Myriagon, and each of the countless others that have had no mundane progeny and never will" (148). If Vlastos is restricting "causal efficacy" to "efficient causality" (as his example suggests), then I agree: Vlastos rightly rejects Aristotle's notorious interpretation of this passage (144–46). In this case, however, Vlastos's point is trivial. On the other hand, if he is maintaining that the forms have no causal efficacy whatsoever, that there is no sense in which they bring about the being of the sensible objects that "participate" in them (as is suggested by his claim that they have *no more* causal efficacy than the nominalist's concepts), then I find his claim bizarre and manifestly false. In this case, the ontological link between forms and sensible particulars is lost. Vlastos appears to assume that because Socrates cannot explain the causal efficacy of the forms, he does not believe them to have any. Thus on 143–44 Vlastos apparently infers (invalidly) that the form for Socrates is not a "teleological cause" from Socrates' failure to discover how such a cause would work.

27. See especially Vlastos (1971, 16, 148, 154–56). On 146 Vlastos gives the following example of Socrates' *aitia:* "Why is this figure a square? *Because* it has

four equal sides and four equal angles." Yet this example does not correspond to *any* of the ones Socrates himself provides, all of which are of the form: Why is this figure a square? *Because* it participates in Squareness. Never does Socrates provide a definition of the term in question or even suggest that one is needed. Another example of reading too much into what Socrates says is Tait's view that the second-best method provides a theory of natural science and that "it is here . . . we first find expressed the idea of science organized as a deductive system in the sense of Euclid" (1986, 477). This is simply fanciful.

28. For a defense of this last point, see note 20 above.

29. "The 'more subtle' causes introduced in 103c10–105c8 are quite clearly *not* elucidations of the relevant concepts" (Bostock 1986, 150).

30. It may be objected that the initial hypothesis was the existence of forms and that the new kind of explanation does not seem to be in any sense "higher" than that. However, as Rowe recognizes (see note 20 above), Socrates does not make a sharp distinction between the theory of forms and the general theory of explanation but appears at 101d2 to treat both as the initial hypothesis. Furthermore, the "more sophisticated" explanation does introduce a new claim about the forms themselves: that some are necessarily associated with one another and that some necessarily exclude each other. Rowe's own suggestion is that the hypotheses "above" the initial hypothesis are simply different formulations of the form-particular relation or of "participation" (1993b, 55–58; 1993a, 246). According to this interpretation, Socrates hypothesizes on each occasion the formulation of the form-particular relation which appears strongest to him, until he finds one that is "adequate." Yet there are serious problems with this interpretation: (1) Socrates' method never provides *any* specific formulation of the relation between forms and particulars; Rowe must therefore claim, quite implausibly, that Socrates is not fully employing his method (1993b, 62). (2) Socrates' emphatic unwillingness at 100d4–6 to commit himself to any particular characterization of the form-particular relation hardly makes sense if "Socrates' 'second voyage' consists in positing whichever version of the Form-participation hypothesis seems to him 'strongest' . . . , and applying it to any problem that happens to be at hand" (1993b, 61–62). Rowe himself (1993a, 243) translates what Socrates says at 100d6 as "I no longer affirm this with confidence." Does this suggest that the goal of Socrates' method is to affirm this in the near future or *ever*? Van Eck has criticized Rowe for different reasons: he maintains (1) that the initial hypothesis is *only* the existence of the forms, not the account of causation (see note 20 above) and (2) that there are higher hypotheses by which the existence of the forms might be defended (1996, 222), for example, the distinction between true opinion and knowledge in the *Timaeus* 51d3–e2. (Van Eck thus also answers an objection in Tait 1986, 468). Rowe's reply to (1) has already been mentioned. In reply to (2) he grants that the "hypotheses above" may include hypotheses of the kind van Eck mentions, since he considers the two parts of the initial hypothesis to be for practical purposes inseparable. He wrongly continues to insist, however, that the different accounts of participation at 100d are the most obvious candidates (1996, 236–40). I find van Eck's suggestions plausible, but my

contention is that we have an example of a higher hypothesis in the *Phaedo* itself. As implausible as Rowe's suggestion, and for the same basic reasons, is Dorter's view that the initial hypothesis is a specific formulation of the theory of forms and that the "hypotheses above" are better formulations (1982, 132): Socrates does not commit himself to any specific formulation of the theory and shows no interest in doing so.

31. Cf. Bostock (1986, 191).

32. κἂν τοῦτο αὐτὸ σαφὲς γένηται; 107b8–9. The Greek is (ironically) unclear: my translation follows Burnet (1911, 124). Rowe (1993a, 265), on the other hand, suggests a completely different translation: "and if this very thing becomes clear." However, even if Rowe is right, the mentioned "clarity" must be understood to be qualified by the immediately preceding reference to what is humanly possible.

33. See, e.g., Hackforth (1972, 141).

34. For the view I am criticizing, see Hackforth (1972, 166).

Chapter 8

1. See Adam (1963, 2:98); Irwin (1995, 301–2, 316); and Rawson (1996, 109–10). Rawson also offers very helpful observations on the use of the verb *manteuesthai* and its cognates in Plato to refer to the state of mind of someone with true belief (110).

2. The esotericists like to point out that Socrates dismisses a discussion of the good itself *only for the time being* (506d8–e3), that he admits to be *passing over much* in what he says here (509c8–10), and that he would prefer to present the truth as it appears to him, rather than a mere image of it (533a2–4). These comments do indeed imply that Socrates, or rather Plato, has more to say about the nature of the good than what we are told in the *Republic*. Plato clearly wants us to go beyond the three images Socrates offers and hopes that they will provoke further inquiry. (I myself respond to this challenge below.) The crucial question, however, concerns the nature of what is being "held back." Is it a fully worked out, deductive system of principles, as the esotericists believe? The text does not support this thesis: (1) at 505a5–6 Socrates claims that "we" have no adequate knowledge of the good, and there is no reason to think that this "we" does not include Socrates and Plato; (2) at 505e1–2 *every* soul, therefore Socrates and Plato included, is described as *aporousa* (see Ferber 1991, 17); (3) the justification Socrates gives for his refusal to express his full opinion on the good is that it is just that: an *opinion* and not *knowledge* (506b-d; see Ferber 1989, 158–59; 1991, 16); (4) likewise at 533a2–5 what Socrates says is that for his part he would like to present no longer an image, but the truth "as it appears to me—though whether rightly or not I may not properly affirm." Krämer (1990b, 92–96) attempts to deal with these passages by suggesting that what Socrates means is simply the following: to *know* the truth of a proposition one must *deduce* it from higher propositions or principles; there are no principles higher than the good; therefore, the good strictly cannot be

known. This is such an utterly implausible interpretation of what Socrates says that it betrays desperation.

3. For a detailed catalog of the perplexity which Socrates' discussion of the good has occasioned among interpreters, see Krämer (1966, 43–46 n3). Krämer's own solution is to identify the good with "the one" and then define the first principle as follows: "Der Ursprung ist exaktestes, d.h., absolut teilloses Mass der ersten Vielheit und Zahl" (66–67). The same interpretation has been defended at length in Reale (1989, 293–333; the definition is stated on 333). For a defense of the identification of the good with unity that does not rely on an appeal to unwritten doctrines, but instead shows the role this identification plays in the *Republic* as a whole, see Hitchcock (1985), as well as the briefer discussion in Sallis (1996, 410–12). It cannot be denied that the good must in some sense be identified with unity. The reading of the *Meno* in chapter 6 shows that the What-is-x? question is fundamentally a search for unity. The reading of the *Phaedo* in chapter 7 shows that the good can apparently provide the unity which reductive, materialistic explanations of phenomena fail to provide (i.e., by an explanation of why a thing is *best*). Finally, the characterization of the good as a principle of "idealization" in the present chapter clearly makes it the unity behind the ideas in the way that each form is the unity behind the phenomena "sharing" in it. The disagreement is in our characterization of *how we know* the good/one. This disagreement is pursued below.

4. My translation. "Die Idee des Guten markiert vielmehr jenen Punkt, von dem aus auch der Umgang mit allem formulierbaren Wissen überhaupt reguliert werden muss, wenn dieses Wissen nicht ziel- und zusammenhanglos und für den Wissenden nutzlos bleiben soll" (Wieland 1976, 33; see also 1982, 159–85).

5. "Es handelt sich um eine Einsicht, die weniger dem Typus des theoretischen Wissens als dem Typus des praktischen Könnens zugehört" (Wieland 1976, 32).

6. This is in essence Gaiser's criticism of Wieland: "Alles Metaphysische wird eliminiert. Die höchste Erkenntnis wird zu einer Fähigkeit des 'know how' " (1987, 79). Gaiser wrongly believes, however, that one must therefore completely reject Wieland's claim that the knowledge of the good is not a "gegenständliches Tatsachenwissen."

7. My translation. "Doch meint der paradigmatische Charackter der platonischen Ideen mehr: Sie sind nicht nur *Ideen* im bisherigen ontischen Sinne, sondern auch *Ideale*, nicht nur *Onta*, sondern auch *Deonta*, kurz, nicht nur das, was *ist*, sondern auch das, was *sein soll:* Sie sind an sich gegebene *Normen*" (1989, 30).

8. I am here leaving out of consideration the main thesis of Ferber's book, i.e., that the Idea of the good functions to ground and explain a Parmenidean identity between thought and being by serving as a third item ("das Dritte") that unites ("yokes together") thought and being while transcending them (*epikeina tes ousias*). This is a provocative suggestion but cannot be dealt with here. Of particular interest is Ferber's discussion of how the Parmenidean identity persists in the philosophies of Kant, Wittgenstein, Fichte, and Heidegger, while only

the latter two deal directly with the "third item" that grounds and explains this identity.

9. The failure to recognize this point leads astray the otherwise similar interpretation in Santas (1983). Santas identifies the form of the good with attributes that all of the other forms have in common (see especially 240, 251–52). He must therefore make a sharp distinction between the proper attributes of a form (e.g., beauty is an attribute peculiar to the form of beauty) and "ideal attributes" shared by all of the forms (e.g., all forms are eternal, unchanging, the best of their kind). The form of the good, as common to all of the other forms, is defined by these ideal attributes: "The Ideal attributes of all the Forms other than the Form of the Good are proper attributes of the Form of the Good" (238). A problem recognized by Santas himself (249–51) and by Sayre's critique of Santas (1995, 184, 261 n41), is that Plato does not sharply distinguish between proper and ideal attributes. For example, the attributes of the form of beauty described in the *Symposium* appear to be both ideal and proper (or neither): "always being beautiful," "being beautiful in all respects," "being beautiful in comparison to no matter what," and "being beautiful to all who apprehend it." Of course, one might try to avoid this problem in the way Santas does by claiming that the ideal attributes here are simply "always being the same," "being the same in all respects," etc. But apart from the lack of evidence that *Plato* would have distinguished ideal from proper attributes in this way (indeed, his view that a thing is not truly beautiful unless it is eternally, constantly, and in all respects beautiful clearly rules out such a distinction), there are other problems with this interpretation recognized by Santas himself (248–49; though he tries to blame them on Plato). (1) It commits Plato to "self-predication": the form of beauty is simply a beautiful thing that happens also to be a form through the added attributes of being eternal, unchanging, etc. We can avoid this if we do not see the form as a thing that is beautiful *and* eternal, but instead identify it with the property of beauty, with *beauty itself,* which is *inherently* eternal, unchanging, and unlimited because it is not the beauty *of* this or that. The two options are the following: are eternality, sameness, ideality, etc., *added* to beauty as properties distinct from it (Santas's view), or is beauty inherently eternal, unchanging, ideal, etc., and limited only by those imperfections external to it in the sensible objects which only *have* beauty as one attribute among others? In the latter case, the function of the form of the good is not to provide beauty, justice, triangularity, and equality with common attributes (as if these attributes were extrinsic to them), but to *exclude* everything alien to the ideality *intrinsic* to each one. In this case the good functions as the kind of *Ausschlussbegriff* Ebert describes. (See note 15 below for more on self-predication.) (2) On Santas's interpretation, sensible objects in imitating the forms would actually be imitating two distinct sets of attributes: the proper and the ideal (248). Which is the most important criterion for judging the goodness of a sensible thing? Again, if Santas's distinction is rejected, the problem is avoided. To be truly beautiful is to be eternally beautiful. (3) Another problem is that a form such as justice seems to depend on the form of the good not only for its ideal attributes, but also for its proper attributes (248–49). The solution

is that *every* form depends on the form of the good for both types of attributes because there is no distinction between them. Equality cannot be *equality* without the ideality and the negation of imperfections that the good makes possible. In short, all of these problems can be avoided if, along with Ebert, we do not identify the form of the good (nor any other form, for that matter) with a set of common attributes.

10. Thus Socrates claims in book 5 that each of the sensible particulars *no more is than is not* that which we call it (479b).

11. Wieland seems to recognize in passing the possibility of an interpretation like Ferber's: "Das Gute ist—übrigens ganz in Übereinstimmung mit dem griechischen Sprachgebrauch—zwar im Bereich menschlichen Handelns und Verhaltens zentriert, jedoch keineswegs auf ihn beschränkt. Jede Prädikation, insbesondere jedes Singulärurteil enthält stets ein normatives Moment" (1982, 183). Then in a footnote he adds: "Von hier aus lässt sich verstehen, dass die Idee des Guten nicht nur Prinzip des Handelns, sondern auch des Seins und des Erkennens ist (Rep. 517b, vgl. 508af.)" (183 n66). Yet Wieland normally characterizes as norms only the moral forms (see 185–96), and when he turns to a detailed discussion (198–201) of the Sun analogy (508a ff.), he does not develop the footnote's suggestion.

12. Miller (1985) seems to be making a similar point by focusing on the notion of "perfection." He describes as follows the being of the forms: "To generalize from the geometrical cases, each form just *is* 'the perfect' with regard to—or the perfection of—some definite character" (180). Because the good is the cause of the being of the forms, Miller describes *its* nature as follows: "The nature of the Good, therefore, must be just this, perfection itself: the Good will be 'the perfect' *as such*" (182). A similar interpretation is found in Sprute (1962, 89), and is articulated with particular clarity in Hare (1965, 36): "If we wish to know what it is to be a circle (to know the Idea of circularity, or to know what the Circle is), we have to find out what it is to be a good or perfect circle. And this involves knowing the Idea of the Good, or what the Good is" (36). (See also Santas 1983, 240–41, on Plato's identification of reality with goodness.) Hare claims that this view has been proven false by Aristotle's demonstration that "there is no *single* quality of goodness which is possessed by all good things" (36). But I do not see why the view Hare describes must commit Plato to the belief that the goodness or perfection of a triangle is the same as the goodness or perfection of a circle. Hare wrongly assumes that the good functions as a common concept or genus defined by qualities shared by all good things. Sayre (1995, 185–88) characterizes the good as what guarantees an objective *"being right"* and in this way makes possible the existence and intelligibility of forms as objective norms or standards. I honestly find Sayre's account very unclear, in part due to the obscure status of this "objective being right" and "value," which he clearly distinguishes from the forms themselves. Perhaps for this reason his account does not appear to add much to the ones cited above.

13. Today "to idealize" often means "to falsify." But it is important to ask why this is so since, after all, idealizing something simply means imagining it in its

most perfect and excellent form. The answer is simple: an ideal is false because nothing like it is to be found in experience. But in contradiction to this kind of "positivism," Plato views idealization as a source of truth. We know the true nature of a triangle or of courage not by perceiving their imperfect instantiations in experience, but by projecting in our thought perfect triangularity or perfect courage. I use the word "idealization," therefore, partly *because of*, and not just *in spite of*, its current association with falsehood. This word emphasizes just how much Plato's thought goes against some of our own preconceptions.

14. Talk here of all things "striving" to attain the good is of course metaphorical. Attempts to characterize the Platonic good as an end of action in an Aristotelian sense clearly fail to do justice to everything that Plato says about the good. An example of such an attempt is Stemmer's identification of the form of the good with *happiness* (1992, see especially 158–67, 183–84). Stemmer himself recognizes the major difficulty with this view: if the form of the good is simply happiness, how is one to explain the three similes, especially the claim that the good is the cause of knowing and being known as well as of the being of what is known? Stemmer asserts that an explanation "scheint mir indes keineswegs aussichtslos zu sein" (184) but conveniently declines to provide one. Shorey (1980, 79) similarly attempts to give a purely "ethical," as opposed to "ontological," interpretation. Shorey at least tries to work out the details but can do so only by attributing the causality of the good to the "idea of what is best" *existing in the minds of the rulers* (67). This view is clearly incompatible with the text. Rawson (1996) sees the good as causing knowledge by being an object of desire. Rawson's emphasis on the role of desire draws attention to an aspect of dialectic that I must neglect here, though it should be understood that the "idealization" of which I speak is at its core desire or *erōs*. On Rawson's account, however, desire for the good appears to remain too external to the other functions of the good and therefore too strictly teleological. A similar interpretation is defended by Reeve (1988), who interprets the claim that the good itself causes us to know and knowable things to be known as meaning that we seek to know the good because this knowledge alone can give us the stable long-term happiness we desire (91); he even identifies the good itself (at least in part) with the *political* good or "what the blueprint of the Kallipolis picks out" (84). For an excellent general critique of "teleological" interpretations of the good, see Ebert (1974, 140–42).

15. I do not mean here that the idea of beauty is the best *instance* of beauty, unlike Santas who writes that "each Form is the best object of its kind there is or can be" (1983, 239) and sees Plato as thereby commited to the absurdities of self-predication (248). For a critique of Santas's interpretation, see note 9 above. Here I can add that the word "best," however misleading, need not commit one to self-predication. In speaking of the "best beauty," I could be referring to a thing that best instantiates the essence of beauty (what it is to be beautiful). However, I could also be referring to the essence of beauty itself, which is "best" not in the sense of being the best *instantiation* of beauty but, on the contrary, in the sense of *not being an instantiation at all*. The form of beauty is "more beautiful" than its instantiations *only* in the sense that it is not the beauty of this or that but

beauty itself. To state the point in a different way, the form of beauty is "best" in the sense that *it is what I mean by the word "best"* when I say that one beautiful thing is better than another. This is why I write that the form is "nothing but this 'best,' " rather than that it is the best *thing* of its class. The form is "best" because it is the normative standard, not because it is an "exemplar." These two things differ because it is only by means of a normative standard that I can judge whether or not a particular thing is to count as an exemplar (see Sayre, 185). As the *Parmenides* shows, there are difficulties with this view, but they arise mainly from the fact that, on the one hand, the forms cannot be understood as "things" or "objects" in the normal senses of these words (in which they refer to substances that only *have* properties with which they are not identical) while, on the other hand, it is hard, if not impossible, to talk about them without understanding them in this way. Two objections made by Sayre (1995) against Santas, but that might also seem to apply to my own interpretation, can be quickly dealt with here. First, Sayre asks how a form of the Good, as opposed to a form of the Best, can explain a form's being the *best* of its kind, as opposed to merely a *good* instance (183–84). This objection wrongly assumes that the good functions as a general class concept. Second, Sayre argues that the forms "receive from the Good . . . not their being itself, but rather their being objective norms" (186). Sayre here assumes, anachronistically, a sharp dichotomy between "being" and "value." My point is precisely that the *being* of the forms is nothing but their *being norms*.

16. The circularity is well expressed in the case of the sun being seen by what it causes: "αἴτιος δ' ὢν αὐτῆς ὁρᾶται ὑπ' αὐτῆς ταύτης" (508b9–10). Of course, the sun *cannot* be seen directly in the way that objects illuminated by the sun can. As Xenophon's Socrates observes, in comparing the sun to the god who puts the whole cosmos in order, but is manifest only in his works: "even the sun, which seems manifest to all, does not allow itself to be seen clearly [ἀκριβῶς] by human beings, but destroys the eyes of anyone reckless enough to attempt gazing upon it" (*Memorabilia* IV.iii.14). In a parallel way, Plato describes the good as *barely* (μόγις) being seen by the person who emerges from the Cave (517c1). See Stefanini (1932, 1:252) and Hyland (1995, 191–93). Sprague (1976, 92–93) comments briefly on the reflexivity of knowledge of the good but does not pursue it very far.

17. As was seen in chapter 2, this reflexivity also explains how in coming to know the good one becomes oneself good: "in the full act of knowledge the knower not only knows the goodness (i.e., the truth) of whatever it is he understands, but by that very fact he himself is good or, to put it more precisely, he is 'like the Good' " (Sinaiko 1965, 137–38).

18. For a review of different interpretations of the Divided Line, see Lafrance (1981, 167 ff.; especially 1986). Besides providing detailed summaries of 156 major works concerned with the Divided Line, Lafrance 1986 also offers a bibliography containing 741 items divided according to subject. Yet even in the "tour de Babel" (Lafrance's description: 13) presented by this book, all of the detailed interpretations of the ascent to, and descent from, the first principle seem to fall under one of the general interpretations I outline. In many cases,

however, scholars simply gloss over the difficulties of this section of the Divided Line without reaching any definite conclusions. This may in large part be due to the spread of a certain cynicism according to which Plato was just hopelessly muddled here: see Sayre (1969, 54) and Guthrie (1962–78, 4:512).

19. For a review and resolution of the controversy there is no better study than Boyle (1973). Boyle lists eight criteria that must be met by any account of the objects of *dianoia* (3) and then demonstrates that the major proposed solutions (including the postulation of "mathematical intermediates") fail to meet all eight criteria. (For another detailed critique of the "mathematical intermediates" interpretation, see Morgan 1983, 93–99). Boyle then proposes a solution which he believes meets all of the criteria: "The objects of *dianoia* are the mathematicians' *hypotheseis*, viz. assumed, unexamined propositions concerning mathematical forms, of which they are in Plato's view the intelligible images" (6). Boyle rightly cites *Phaedo* 99d–e as evidence that Plato could consider propositions to be images of the forms. Though I agree in essence with this solution, there are two problems with it as stated: its restriction of the objects of *dianoia* to *mathematical* propositions when mathematics is only a particularly good *example* of *dianoia* and its failure to mention the role that sensible objects play in this kind of knowledge. Though the primary objects of *dianoia* are propositions, it clearly also has as objects those sensible things which it uses to illustrate these propositions and to which it refers in discourse. The importance of sensible objects for this section of the Line is acknowledged by Bedu-Addo's proposal that "the hypotheses of διάνοια are statements or propositions *involving notions or conceptions* of Forms derived from sense-experience" (1978, 116), but to say that these conceptions are *derived* from sense-experience is going too far. Shorey maintains that both *dianoia* and *noēsis* are "equally conversant with ideas" (Shorey 1980, 74), but I fail to see how a significant distinction between the two could be maintained on this view.

20. This identification of the "unhypothesized" principle with the good is denied by Bedu-Addo (1978, 122–25) and Sayre (1995, 173–81). There is some truth in this denial: through dialectic we come to understand not only the good, but also *each one* of the forms. Since, as Bedu-Addo argues, there is no evidence in the text for the view that knowledge of the forms is *deduced* from knowledge of the good, each form, and not just the good, can be said to be an "unhypothesized principle." However, as I attempt to show, our knowledge of the forms *does* depend on knowledge of the good (though not through "deduction"). Therefore, though one cannot deny that all forms are in a sense "unhypothesized principles," it is yet possible to recognize the good as the *ultimate* principle. Sayre's main argument is that the good cannot play the epistemological role assigned to the nonhypothetical *archē* (174–75). By this Sayre apparently means that the good cannot be the basis for any kind of inferences. Yet this is an odd argument, given Sayre's own recognition that the word ἐχομένων at 511b8 need not refer to logical consequences (258 n15; though he still translates "implications," 174) and that the nonhypothetical *archē* is not a logical premise or "some kind of 'super proposition' " from which the truths of mathematics and other sciences are to be deduced (175–77).

21. Cornford (1965) is one of the proponents of the view that the ascent is to be identified with geometrical analysis. However, Conford does not see geometrical analysis as involving strict deduction by means of convertible propositions. Instead he sees it as involving an intuitive "leap" to the first principle (67, 76) or, as he also puts it, an "upward *spring* of thought" (72). But as R. Robinson points out (1953, 166), this is simply incorrect. For a more accurate account of geometrical analysis, see Lafrance (1980, 80–84). Lafrance's own interpretation of the dialectical ascent, though detailed and suggestive, is very unclear. He sees the ascent as involving no other method than geometrical analysis and synthesis (1980, 88; see also 77). But this view confronts him with the major problems I mention, the last of which he states with perfect clarity: "Abolir cette distinction entre la dianoia et la noêsis en réduisant la méthode dialectique à la méthode analytique et synthétique des géomètres grecs serait donc retirer tout son sens à la classification des savoirs dans notre texte de la *République*" (84). Lafrance therefore backs away from a strict identification of the ascent with geometrical analysis, asserts some kind of weak identification (86), and then in the end apparently accepts Robinson's intuition theory (with no significant alterations that I can see). If I do not misunderstand him, Lafrance seems to want to have it both ways: he wants to claim that the principle is deduced through analysis *and* that it can be known only through intuition. This attempt to make compatible two incompatible interpretations is betrayed by the following claim: "L'intuition dont il s'agit en *République*, 511b–c apparaît plutôt comme le résultat et le produit de la méthode déductive" (90; see also Lafrance 1994, 368–69). An "intuition" is not *deduced*, as Robinson recognizes (1953, 173).

22. This is the theory advocated by Shorey (1980), who denies that the unhypothesized principle is something "absolutely unconditioned" (73), sees it as simply the hypothesis with which the interlocutors in a specific ethical discussion all agree (72), and therefore considers it to be the "logical equivalent" of the *ti hikanon* of the *Phaedo* (73).

23. Likewise, Hare (1965) argues that while dialecticians could not produce an indestructible definition through elenchus alone, they could do so by seeing the object itself with "the mind's eyes" (35).

24. Robinson's account of the ascent appears to be accepted in toto by Cross and Woozley (1964, 249–54). Sayre (1969) can accept neither Robinson's own account nor any of the others which Robinson discusses; therefore, he simply gives up: "The answer, it seems to me, is that Plato himself was not clear about what was involved in this phase of the dialectician's procedure" (54). However, Sayre (1995) appears, like Robinson, to see no major difference between the hypothetical method of the *Phaedo* and the dialectical method of the *Republic* (144). Yet he distinguishes the *ti hikanon* from the unhypothetical principle and characterizes the latter in a way that appears to commit him to the Coherence Theory discussed below.

25. "[I]ntuition' means certain knowledge not reached by method" (1953, 173).

26. Lafrance (1980, 88–93) and Cornford (1965, 93–95) also find it necessary to supplement with some sort of "intuition" a dialectical method which

they otherwise see as mathematical, propositional, and deductive. See Annas's warranted criticisms of what she calls a "crazy method" (1981, 283).

27. The only word that could with any plausibility be taken to refer to "certainty" is *"to bebaion."* The corresponding verb is used in one passage of the *Republic* in connection with the first principle: at 533c3–d1 dialectic is said to move toward the first principle "ἵνα βεβαιώσηται." The question is whether or not this "stability" at which dialectic aims is to be interpreted as "propositional certainty." The present chapter provides what I think are convincing arguments against this view, but the following points show in addition that it does not receive any support from the verb "βεβαιοῦσθαι." (1) Plato does call a *logos bebaios* when it survives scrutiny and testing (*Phaedo* 85d3, 90c9), but this means simply that the *logos* is reliable, not that it is absolutely certain. This seems to be the kind of reliability J. Gould has in mind when he writes (1955, 23): "Philosophy is the achievement of certainty, and certainty, as Socrates meant it, is the inward agreement of one with another's views, only to be achieved in 'ad hominem' conversation, only to be expressed in action." (2) The *Timaeus* (37b–c) distinguishes between *doxai bebaioi* (which the modern reader might be tempted to translate as "justified true beliefs") and *epistēmē*: the soul possesses the former with regard to sensible objects and the latter with regard to intelligible objects. This passage thus rules out the possibility of turning beliefs into knowledge by simply making them *bebaioi*. (3) Knowledge of course involves its own type of *bebaiotēs*, but this stability is explained in terms of *its objects*, rather than in terms of the certainty of a proposition (*Philebus* 59b). (4) In a passage from the *Statesman*, the Stranger tells his interlocutor that they should carefully examine the remaining divisions ἵνα αὐτοὺς εἰδῶμεν βεβαιότερον (289d4). The word *"bebaion"* can thus be used of intellectual vision. This, I suggest, is how the word is to be understood in the *Republic*: the "stability" attained through the dialectical process is *the fixity of the mind's gaze* on its eternal, intelligible objects (the good, in particular). This interpretation accords quite well with the strict correspondence Plato maintains between the stability of knowledge and the stability of its objects. For more on this issue, see chapter 9, note 60.

28. Descartes's method is clearly in R. Robinson's mind as he interprets the Divided Line: "La raison pourquoi Platon regardait sa méthode d'hypothèses comme un pis-aller, n'est pas difficile à découvrir. C'est qu'il croyait, tout comme Descartes, que la possibilité existe d'atteindre à un savoir absolu et incorrigible" (1954, 257). In the same article Robinson explicitly credits Plato with inaugurating what John Dewey called the "quest for certainty" (266). Lafrance sees Plato as sharing with Aristotle and Descartes the belief that human beings can discover an absolute truth from which could be deduced infallible conclusions (1980, 92).

29. This is also a widespread interpretation: "It is the commonly accepted—and correct—view that Plato proposes to remedy the former defects of geometry by establishing a science, which he calls dialectic, which can somehow be used to establish the axioms which geometers have left unproved" (White 1976, 96).

30. I am borrowing the phrase in quotation marks from Shorey's translation in the Loeb edition.

31. The interpretation I am criticizing often relies on giving Greek words a

much narrower sense than they will plausibly allow. In discussion of *Phaedo* 101d, Gallop writes: "the most natural sense for [λόγον διδόναι] to bear here is 'give a proof,' i.e., support or justify the initial hypothesis" (1975, 190). The only other sense he considers is "give a definition" (132–33; this is the sense suggested by Hare 1965, 22). See also Stemmer (1992, 198–99 n30), for whom the only possible translations of "λόγον λαμβάνειν" are "Rechenschaft fordern," "eine Definition fordern," and "eine Definition erfassen." Proof and definition, however, are very narrow, specialized activities, and there is no warrant for restricting *logon didonai* in this way. To the passages cited in the main text can be added the following: in the *Phaedo*, a *logos* is given in the process of asking and answering questions (78d1–2). In the *Sophist*, we reach consensus by giving each other a *logos* (λόγον ἑαυτοῖς δόντες, 230a5). See also *Statesman* 286a4–5 and *Theaetetus* 202c2–5. Even in the couple of passages where the phrase comes close to meaning "to give a proof" (*Charmides* 165b3–4 and *Phaedo* 95d7–e1), what is meant is an argument which is convincing *within the present discussion:* "Nun kann man niemals in abstracto über etwas Rechenschaft geben, sondern immer nur gegenüber einem bestimmten Partner" (Wieland 1982, 298).

32. In reference to the passage at 534d, Stemmer rightly characterizes dialectic as a "knowing how" instead of a "knowing that" (1992, 195–96). He even grants that it is "dispositional" knowledge and to this extent nonpropositional (221 n116). However, he still insists that dialectic aims at propositional knowledge (196). His reason is that dialectic cannot be pursued for its own sake but must aim at some result external to itself. However, as seen in preceding chapters, especially in the discussion of the *Euthydemus*, this characterization of dialectic as having a product distinct from itself is erroneous.

33. This point is made by Cherniss (1983, 156) and Sayre (1988, 245; 1993a, 188; 1995, 195).

34. The mathematician Theodorus is an excellent example of this inability to engage in dialectic: see *Theaetetus* 146b3, 162a–b, 165a1–3, 177c, 183c.

35. For examples of the general tendency to view this characterization of belief and knowledge as incoherent or philosophically indefensible, see Cross and Woozley (1964), and Lafrance (1981, 132 ff.) (for a critique of their interpretations see note 43 below). Attempts to make sense of this part of *Republic* 5 have varied greatly and have not approached anything near consensus. Gully interprets the distinction between *doxa* and *epistēmē* as one between *two kinds of knowledge:* empirical versus a priori (1962, 62). Though there is some truth in this view, it is much too simplistic, not to say anachronistic. Hintikka (1974a, 9–10) has argued that Plato identifies the functions, aims, or results of knowledge and belief with their objects. This identification is what allows Plato to conclude that because belief and knowledge have different functions (as shown by the fallibility of one and the infallibility of the other) they must have different objects (12–13). Santas (1973a, 38–42), however, has presented textual evidence to show that Plato does not make such an identification. Santas argues that we need only attribute to Plato the assumption that there is a necessary relation between functions and objects. Knowledge can carry out its function of bringing about "cognitive states

that are always free from error and only states that are always free from error" (45–46) only in relation to objects that do not change (46). Belief can carry out its function of bringing about "cognitive states that are sometimes free from error and sometimes not" (47) only in relation to things that change (48–49). One problem with this solution is that it appears blatantly false. As Lafrance (1981, 135) argues, we can clearly make fallible judgments about unchanging objects and infallible judgments about changing objects. Furthermore, one can argue, as Morgan does, that Plato is not committed even to a necessary correspondence between function and object (1983, 97). Ebert (1974) finds the account of the distinction between belief and knowledge in *Republic* 5 so problematic that he is at great pains to show that it does not represent Plato's view. Instead, he attributes it to a misunderstanding on the part of Socrates' interlocutor, Glaucon (121).

36. The most radical solution to this problem is to *deny* that Socrates is in fact saying that belief and knowledge have different objects, as do Gosling (1968) and Fine (1978, 1990). This interpretation is accepted by Irwin (1995, 267). Annas advocates a qualified form of it by arguing that some sensible characteristics *can* be objects of knowledge. For my detailed critique of this interpretation, see Gonzalez (1996). For another, very different critique of Fine, see Benitez (1996). The major difference is Benitez's view that a rejection of Fine's "content analysis" requires a rejection of the "dialectical requirement" to which she appeals; I argue that the "dialectical requirement" is in fact not met by Fine's interpretation and is compatible with the "two-worlds theory" she rejects. For a shorter, but helpful critique, see Reeve (1988, 288–89 n13).

37. This interpretation of *Republic* 5 is suggested by Moravcsik (1979, 65): "regarding sensible things, all we can hope for is the reaching of some views or judgement; but with regard to the Forms understanding is possible." Burnyeat (1981) solves in a similar way a problem posed by Aristotle's claim in the *Posterior Analytics* (71b12, 15–16) that *epistēmē* is of what cannot be otherwise. If *epistēmē* is understood as "justified true belief," this claim is simply false: I can be completely justified in my belief that it is raining outside without it being true that the weather could not have been otherwise. If *epistēmē* is translated as "understanding," however, Aristotle is making the perfectly intelligible point "that understanding depends on explanation and what gets explained in the sciences . . . which produce that understanding . . . is *general* regularities and connections: lawlike regularities in the modern jargon, necessary connections in Aristotle's" (108–9). For more general defenses of the view that *epistēmē* should be translated as "understanding," see Moline (1981; for Moline's excellent account of the historical evidence see 12–31) and Burnyeat (1980, 1987). Though Annas does not suggest the translation, she repeatedly argues that what is central to Plato's conception of knowledge is not certainty, but understanding (see 1981, 193, 200, 212–13, 238–39). However, though I agree that *epistēmē* is more like "understanding" than like "knowledge" in our sense, I do not agree, as will be seen below, with some of the specific ways in which these scholars characterize this "understanding."

38. It is true that in book 6 the mathematician's awareness is *distinguished*

from *doxa* and identified with *dianoia*. The aim, however, is to show the ambivalence of mathematics (and the method of hypothesis generally) with regard to the distinction between belief and knowledge in book 5: because he refers to sensible objects at the same time that he is thinking of intelligible forms, the mathematician has, as it were, one foot in belief and one foot in knowledge. This means, however, that he still suffers from the defects of the former, the principle one of which is lack of insight into what each form is in itself. Therefore, Morgan (1983, 84) is justified in characterizing *dianoia* as a "kind of belief," even though it is classified under *epistēmē*. He characterizes *dianoia* more specifically as "Bi-Polar Belief," by which he means that it has in a sense two objects: sensible objects *about which* it speaks and forms *for the sake of which* it speaks (88). It thus serves as a bridge between belief and knowledge as described in book 5.

39. One should here recall the way in which *doxa* and *epistēmē* are distinguished in book 10. The craftsman in making a thing has true belief with regard to this thing's good and proper use, while the person who actually uses this thing has *knowledge* (601d–602a). Here too *epistēmē* cannot possibly be identified with "justified true belief" nor, accordingly, can the *doxa* contrasted to it be identified with belief *that* something is the case.

40. Practically all interpretations of *Republic* 5 have seen it as incompatible with the *Meno*: see, e.g., Lafrance (1981, 148–49), Morgan (1983, 72), and Bertozzi (1948, 40–41). Lafrance and Sprute make similar attempts to resolve the apparent contradiction. Lafrance (1982, 125–26) makes a distinction between an ontological object (which exists independently of our knowledge) and an epistemological object (which exists only in the knowing subject). He then claims that the discussion in the *Republic* concerns only the former, while that in the *Meno* concerns only the latter. The problem is that he does not explain how exactly epistemology and ontology are related for Plato (as they clearly are). Sprute's solution (1962, 123) is that while there is no essential difference between *doxa* and *epistēmē* as *processes* (which is what the *Meno* claims), there is yet an unbridgeable difference in their *content* (which is what the *Republic* claims). But this has the implausible result of making the content of each "process" completely external to it; indeed, in Sprute's view the only thing that distinguishes knowledge from belief is a sudden, "irrational" illumination (122–23). A common assumption made by those who see a contradiction or significant difference between the accounts of the *Meno* and of the *Republic* is that the *aitias logismos* mentioned in the former refers to some kind of justification (see Sprute 1962, 62; Lafrance 1981, 114; 1982, 128). But as I argue in chapter 6, this interpretation is unnecessary and incorrect.

41. See Stefanini (1932, 1:241) for documentation.

42. Sallis appears to be one of the few who have recognized this: the distinction between the knowable and the opinable "is a distinction between a showing in which an *eidos* shows itself as it itself is (as one) *and* a showing in which an *eidos* shows itself as it is not (as many). In both cases *what shows itself is the same thing* (the *eidos*)—which is to say that the knowable and the opinable are not two parallel regions of things" (1996, 394; see also 406–7).

43. Because Cross and Woozley (1964) assume that "belief" can only be

"belief that" (171–72) and that therefore the contrasting knowledge must be "knowledge that" (172–73), they must conclude that the thesis of *Republic* 5 is plain nonsense (173–75). Yet they betray their assumption when they confess that "there are times here too when he [Plato] seems to mean by belief some sort of immediate awareness, whereas he *also* uses it elsewhere to mean belief that" (176, my emphasis; see also 143–44). Similarly, Lafrance's objection that the fallibility or infallibility of a judgment has nothing to do with the nature of its object (1981, 135) rests on the assumption that both *doxa* and *epistēmē* are "judgments" *that* something is the case (127).

44. The view that what the mathematicians lack is *understanding* is defended by Annas (1981, 282) and Moravcsik (1979, 64). A similar view appears to be behind Hackforth's claim that the "Ideas" are "hypothetical" not because they are *assumed*, but because they need to be *explained* (1942, 8). Sayre likewise locates the deficiency of the mathematicians "in their mental grasp of the objects about which they reason" (1988, 100). Sayre is here retracting his earlier "discursive" interpretation of the Divided Line in 1969. As will be seen below (note 52), on the other hand, the "understanding" of which Annas speaks remains discursive and propositional.

45. Cf. Hare (1965, 22–23), Sayre (1995, 176), and Sallis (1996, 427). Especially suggestive is Hare's description of the hypotheses as "surrogate or suppositious Ideas" (24).

46. The problem is not that mathematicians fail to *define* their concepts since, as Santas (1983, 255) points out by citing Euclid's *Elements*, they clearly *did* define their concepts. Instead, the problem is that their definitions provide no real insight into the nature of their objects. I do not, however, agree with Santas that this lack can be remedied by a "theory of objects that mathematical hypotheses must be about if mathematics is to be knowledge" (256): what is needed, as I argue below, is not a "theory," but elenchus. Cf. Stemmer (1992, 203–6).

47. R. Robinson (1953, 154–56) suggests that the mathematician's use of sensible images is what prevents him from recognizing his hypotheses *as hypotheses*. But this interpretation has the undesirable consequence that the use of images would be the *only* shortcoming of the mathematician.

48. Irwin (1995, 272–80) appears to defend a similar interpretation. See also Fine (1979).

49. Neither Sayre nor Annas explicitly appeal to "coherentism" or to an "interrelational model of knowledge." Nevertheless, their interpretations are in important respects like Fine's. Annas claims that what distinguishes *noēsis* from *dianoia* is that it does not study the forms in isolation but "studies them for their own sake, and in systematic connection, as being dependent on the Form of the Good for their nature and intelligibility" (1981, 251). She also equates vision of the forms and of the form of the good with "the state of understanding that has come about by the time the person concerned has attained complete mastery of the subject matter and thorough familiarity with it and its structure and has insight into what was formerly seen to be true, but without understanding of its

significance" (283–84; see also 200, 243). Sayre identifies the nonhypothetical *archē* with "the interconnected field of eternal Forms—i.e., the totality of Forms in their natural relationships" (1995, 178). What makes the *archē nonhypothetical* in Sayre's view is "the unrestricted completeness of the field of view that the dialectician achieves when the *archē* is reached" (181). However, there is one major difference, discussed below, between Sayre's interpretation and the others I classify here: his characterization of the dialectician's knowledge as *nonpropositional*. Reeve (1988) could perhaps also be included in the Coherence Theory. He describes the upward path of dialectic as consisting in "developing the dialectically defensible unified theory of everything from the true theories of the visible world produced by the mathematical sciences" (77), calls this characterization of dialectical knowledge "epistemological holism" (79), and identifies the good itself with "a rational or intelligible structure of forms" (84).

50. This is the phrase used by both Nehamas (1989, 281) and Fine (1979, 397).

51. See Sayre (1995, 195). However, I must confess to not understanding why or how knowledge of "the interconnected field of eternal Forms" is for Sayre nonpropositional. Knowledge by collection and division, which appears to be the paradigm Sayre has in mind here and throughout the book (see 178–79), would seem to be thoroughly propositional. Sayre concludes his interpretation of the *Theaetetus* with the suggestion that "*logos* might itself constitute knowledge" and that the *Sophist* provides a characterization of just what sort of a *logos* this is (232). How is this characterization of knowledge compatible with Sayre's claim that it is inexpressible in either speech or writing?

52. Burnyeat (1980, 187) characterizes knowledge of the forms as being "definitional knowledge" and plays down those elements of direct vision and acquaintance that also characterize knowledge as Plato understands it (the jury members cannot *know* who committed the crime because they were not eyewitnesses; one must have traveled on the road to Larissa in other to *know* it; one must have met Meno in order to *know* him). Though Moravcsik (1979) characterizes "understanding" in Plato as consisting of "insight + skill" (59), he too appears to identify such insight with conceptual (and therefore definitional?) knowledge: "Understanding, according to Plato, involves insight, and this insight is the grasp of, or having an adequate concept of, special abstract entities, the Forms, which make up the domain that understanding is concerned with" (59–60). Though Annas rejects the crude view that the unhypothesized principle is a proposition (1981, 289), she sees Plato as recommending conceptual analysis and the search for a definition (287) and does not see him as making any strong distinction between concepts and propositions (290).

53. "[I]t is not coherence as such that makes L3 [*dianoia*] inferior to L4 [*noēsis*], but the degree and kind of coherence" (Fine 1990, 113). "L4 thus relies on coherence no less than does L3; but its coherentist explanations are fuller and richer, and that is why L4 counts as a better sort of knowledge" (114). Annas also appears to make the difference one of degree, claiming that "Philosophical understanding is, as it were, geometrical understanding writ large" (1981, 290).

Sayre's description of the dialectical method in the top portion of the Line does not appear to distinguish it from the hypothetical method of the *Phaedo* (1995, 144). This does not collapse the distinction between the two top sections for Sayre because he believes that the *dianoia* of mathematics cannot do one thing the hypothetical method in the *Phaedo* demands: i.e., give an account of its hypotheses in terms of "higher" hypotheses (142). However, the description of mathematics in the *Republic* does not deny the obvious fact that mathematicians can deduce some hypotheses from more basic hypotheses: the criticism is that they cannot go beyond *hypotheses as such*.

54. Fine is clearly encouraged by the fact that her interpretation makes Plato "surprisingly up to date" (1990, 115).

55. Fine (1990, 110) attempts to explain away 533c3–5 by claiming that, first, coherence involves more than the consistency or agreement which this passage claims to be insufficient for knowledge; coherence requires in addition that consistent beliefs "be mutually supporting and explanatory, and form a sufficiently large group," and second, "not even such coherence is sufficient for knowledge, but only for justification; knowledge also requires truth." The first point depends on an unjustfiedly narrow interpretation of *homologia* as mere logical consistency. In referring to a first principle, a conclusion, and "everything in between," Socrates is clearly referring to a set of propositions that are not simply logically consistent, but that in some way support and explain each other. In any case, Fine's interpretation refutes itself at this point: Socrates at 533b–c is describing what mathematicians do, and Fine attributes to mathematics and *dianoia* "coherence" in the strong sense of the word (109). Therefore, either Socrates at 533b–c is claiming that mathematics is characterized only by logical consistency and lacks "coherence" in the strong sense of the word, in contradiction to Fine's interpretation, or Socrates is claiming that mathematics posseses this "coherence," but that such coherence can never lead to knowledge, again in contradiction to Fine's interpretation. Fine's second point is baffling: if the only criterion of truth is coherence, truth cannot magically appear from somewhere else. Annas suggests that what is lacking in the consistent reasoning described at 533c is "insight" (1981, 284), but without explaining what this "insight" is and why the explanatory system of mathematics (which she claims to be Plato's model of knowledge, 243) is incapable by itself of providing it (see vague language on 284).

56. This interpretation is defended by Boyle (1974); the "esotericists," i.e., Krämer (1959, 1966, 1990a), Gaiser (1968, 1980b, 1987), and Reale (1989); and Ferber (1989, 101–7).

57. Yet there is no warrant, besides the demands of the interpretation itself, for taking the word "ἀφελών" here to mean "abstraction" in a technical, Aristotelian sense (see Reale 1989, 331–32).

58. Boyle (1974) must be commended for giving us a concrete example of how the ascent would work on his interpretation. He starts with a definition of a square (the "hypothesis") and "reduces" it (takes it back) to another definition, which is then "reduced" to yet another, etc., until a definition of the good is

reached ("the good is one," 12). This example, however, only exposes the problems. The definition of a square is "reduced" to the definition of a quadrilateral (which is clearly its genus), while the definition of a line is "reduced" to the definition of a point (which is clearly not its genus, but its "element"). Boyle recognizes this fundamental difference in the relations between different steps of the "reduction" but says that this "ought not to disturb us" (17 n35). But how could this *not* disturb us? Gaiser (1987, 92) and Krämer (1990a, 81–82) also recognize this problem, but they too can offer no solution, except to suggest that *somehow* the dialetician would be able to reconcile these two divergent procedures. Another problem is that one definition can be "reduced" to another only if we assume a causal connection between the two things they define. Boyle therefore has to introduce at each stage of the ascent what he calls "causal *logoi*," e.g., "it is by reason of the quadrilateral itself that the square itself exists" (the esotericists do not seem to recoginze the need for such causal *logoi*). But how do we come to know the truth of these causal statements? Are they not just arbitrary assumptions here? At this point, Boyle's account exhibits the general flaw of the Abstraction Theory: it requires that we know before making the ascent everything that we are supposed to discover through the ascent.

59. The assimilation of dialectic to mathematics and its methods is most evident in the "esotericist" interpretation. Gaiser states a basic principle of this interpretation when he asserts that "Die mathematischen Wissenschaften werden hier as Modellbereich dargestellt, an dem sich die Dialektik orientiert" (1968, 94). Thus, Gaiser's reading of the Divided Line makes mathematics the model for dialectic rather than vice versa. He appears to recognize no significant difference between the methods of the two disciplines (see, e.g., 92) and ignores the many harsh criticisms of mathematics found in the *Republic*. This assimilation of dialectic to mathematics explains the insistence of Gaiser and the other esotericists that Plato's philosophy is a *system*. As Heidegger has correctly pointed out (1988, 52), the development of the notion of a philosophical system in modern philosophy coincided with the use of mathematics as the model for philosophical knowledge (this is most evident, of course, in the work of Spinoza). Socrates indeed assigns mathematics an important role in leading one to knowledge of the good, but the reason has been best explained by Ebert (1974, 208): the existence of objective norms or ideals (what he calls "ideative Begriffe") is more evident in the field of mathematics than it is in the field of morality.

60. Ferber himself recognizes that the first principle cannot be a definition of the good, since the good is "das Undefinierbare" (1989, 106). Ferber even admits that the first principle is not a statement (*Satz*) about the good (107). How can Ferber make these admissions and still defend the Abstraction Theory? What remains at the end of the process of abstraction if not a definition or proposition? Just a name?

61. White (1976, 99–100) claims that the unhypothesized beginning "will have to do with the Form of the Good and will presumably be a proposition or set of propositions about the Form." Sayre, on the other hand, claims (against his view in 1969) that the first principle is nonpropositional (1988, 100; 1995, 175–77).

NOTES TO PAGES 231–34

62. One could see as textual evidence *against* this assumption the description of the first principle as something that is "seen" or "touched"; see 511b7, 516b6, 517c1, 532b1, and 540a8. On 511b, see Wieland (1982, 216). However, as Stemmer points out (1992, 76–78), this is very weak evidence, since we ourselves speak of "seeing" the truth of a proposition and "grasping" a proposition.

63. One begs the question if one identifies the "distinguishing in discourse" named by "διορίσασθαι τῷ λόγῳ" with *defining*. That Socrates himself does not identify the two things is made clear in the following passage: "We say that there are many beautiful things and many good things, and so on, and we distinguish them in discourse (διορίζομεν τῷ λόγῳ)" (507b2–3). The meaning here is clearly *not* that we "define" the particular good things. This passage also shows that Socrates' frequent use of visual language with regard to the good is perfectly compatible with the word "διορίζειν." We can "see" the good as distinct from the other forms without having to define it in a proposition. See also 346b3 and 477c8. The phrase "διορίζειν τῷ λόγῳ" therefore cannot be used as evidence that knowledge of the good for Plato is propositional, as it is by Sorabji (1982, 300) when he translates "to define with an account" and then concludes: "The thinking described here seems propositional. For the questions, answers and refutations all bear on propositions and what is being sought is definitions." Reale translates "definire con il ragionamento" (1989, 331), and all of the other esotericists take for granted that what the dialectician seeks is to define the good, even while admitting, as do Ferber and even Krämer (see following notes), that this is impossible! Hackforth's remarks on this passage are much more reasonable: he denies that τῷ λόγῳ can mean "in a formula" and writes: "He cannot mean that any *form of words* can express it; still less that it can be defined *per genus et differentiam*" (1942, 7 n1).

64. Krämer argues against the view that the good can be defined in terms of genus or species (1966, 44–45), but also recognizes that his identification of the good with the one does not solve the problem, since the one, as what is both most universal and simplest, cannot itself be defined: we can only say what it is *not* or, more postively, what it is related to ("worauf hin es ist," 62). Krämer adopts the latter, more positive, approach. However, he soon seems to lose sight of the fact that he has not thereby defined the essence of the good, and his description of Plato's "axiomatic system" betrays no hint of the *aporia* and ineffability hidden at its core.

65. For an excellent statement of the contradictions faced by any attempt to express the nature of the good, see Ferber (1989, 149–51).

66. This is forgotten too often (for example, Annas [1981, 250] assumes that *dianoia* "is confined to mathematical thinking"), and so the following comments of Sinaiko deserve quotation: "According to this formulation almost every human conversation involves some activity proper to the third segment [of the Line]. Whenever general terms are introduced in a discussion and are used to explain or interpret the particular things being discussed, the conversation is at least momentarily above the level of mere sensible objects and in the realm of the intelligible. The gap separating such conversations from the rigorous, disciplined demonstrations of a mathematician is purely one of degree—the scientist is as

ignorant of the true nature of his unquestioned assumptions as the ordinary citizen discussing politics is of his" (1965, 160). It was in part a failure to see this that led Cornford to the conclusion "that dialectical procedure is not the same in the mathematical as in the moral field, though the exercise of intuition and deductive reasoning is common to both" (1965, 92; see also note 83 below). Hackforth (1942) rejects this distinction between two kinds of dialectic (5–7) and throughout his article points out that mathematics is an *illustration* (see especially 2–3). See also Wieland (1982, 209) and Fine (1990, 105). It is important to keep in mind that Socrates focuses on mathematics because it is an example which his interlocutor, Glaucon, can be expected to understand (510b–c).

67. Lafrance's objection (1994, 366) that the hypotheses of the *Meno* are not, like those of mathematics in the *Republic,* considered "evident to all" is not decisive: it is quite likely that Socrates considers the hypotheses "virtue is good" and "If virtue is knowledge, it is teachable" to be as evident as any of the hypotheses of mathematics.

68. It may seem odd that the good is mentioned here as something only said *about* justice. A characteristic of the hypothetical method, however, is that, confined to the level of *poion ti*, it can do no more than predicate of a thing as a property what is in fact the thing's essence. With regard to this method in the *Meno*, Goldschmidt (1947, 125) writes: "La science a été attribué à la vertu comme une qualité, alors qu'il fallait comprendre qu'on tenait l'essence, que dire vertu, c'était dire science." Gundert (1971, 50) makes a similar point.

69. I do not wish to deny here something often noted, i.e., that the very structure of the *Republic* mirrors dialectic as it is described in the Divided Line. For example, there is clearly an "ascent" from the first books to the middle books and a corresponding "descent" from the middle books to the last book. More specific parallels between dialectic and the discussion carried out in the dialogue have been well mapped out in Brumbaugh (1989, 29–37) and Sallis (1996, 313–20, 450–54). Yet such parallels exist because the dialogue is an *imitation* of dialectic, not because it is dialectic itself. The *Republic* as a whole is like one of those visible diagrams used by geometers to illustrate something invisible. It is precisely as an imitation of the ascent to the good that the dialogue is "hypothetical." Yet it must have been Plato's hope that we the readers would use the dialogue as a "springboard" and "footing" from which to engage in dialectic itself.

70. "Socrates offers a definition of the just city and the just man; he never even asks for a definition of Justice itself. Can Plato have abandoned the view that to know the meaning of 'justice' is to know the Form of Justice? Or does he have a motive for leaving this doctrine more or less in the background?" (Kahn 1972, 570).

71. This distinction is also made at *Phaedo* 82a–b.

72. Cf. Sallis (1996, 365–66).

73. According to Stemmer, when Socrates claims that the definitions of book 4 are only a sketch, what he means is that they do not show that it is good to have these virtues (1992, 175). Yet Stemmer's view that book 4 only answers the question "What is justice?" and not the question "Is justice good?" seems untenable. Socrates agrees with Glaucon's claim that it is absurd to question

the goodness of justice after it has been defined in the way it has (445a–b). The problem, and what makes Socrates continue, is that this definition does not provide knowledge of what justice *is* (as opposed to what it is *like*) and *therefore* does not provide knowledge of its goodness. The sharp distinction present throughout Stemmer's book between the "descriptive content" and the "evaluative content" of a word such as "justice" is as anachronistic as the fact/value distinction. Stemmer defends this distinction by claiming (16–25) that Thrasymachus leaves unquestioned the descriptive content of the word "justice" (being just involves obeying the laws and having an equal share) but completely alters its evaluative content (so that he considers just actions bad and foolish, unjust actions good and wise). Yet clearly Plato would not say that Thrasymachus knows what justice is and only fails to value it. Thrasymachus does not consider justice good because he has no real understanding of *what* it *is* (the definition Stemmer cites is simply a conventional opinion). If knowledge of virtue were in fact knowledge of a description or definition, as Stemmer assumes, then such knowledge would be distinct from knowing the *value* of the virtue described or defined. But the fact that Plato does not make this kind of distinction is precisely one of the reasons why, as earlier chapters have shown, knowledge of virtue for him is *not* knowledge of a definition.

74. See Fine (1990, 105–6), Irwin (1995, 279), and Sallis (1996, 440–41).

75. This is the expression used by Goldschmidt to refer to a common structural feature of what he calls the "achieved" dialogues (i.e., dialogues which attain positive propositional results): namely, a digression in which the interlocutors deal with substantive issues indispensable to an understanding of the specific conclusions of the main inquiry. Such is the "detour" on being and nonbeing in the *Sophist* and the "detour" on the good in the *Republic*. Goldschmidt, however, recognizes that even these "detours" cannot of themselves provide "l'événement pur de la vision de l'Essence" (1947, 160).

76. Goldschmidt describes the definitions in the *Republic* and other "achieved" dialogues "comme une solution vraie, mais comme une solution de facilité" (1947, 203).

77. As noted by Lafrance's comment on this passage (1994, 364), Robin translates "τῇ τοῦ διαλέγεσθαι δυνάμει" as "par la vertu du dialogue," and R. Robinson (1953, 170) also sees the phrase as referring to dialogue carried out by means of question and answer and elenchus. Robinson even translates the subject of the sentence as "pure discussion." Though I have chosen a more abstract translation to avoid begging the question, my interpretation, in showing that there is no essential difference between the dialectic described in the Line and Socratic elenctic dialogue, will confirm these translations of Robin and Robinson. Lafrance's objection that dialogue plays no role in what the Line describes (1994, 362–65, 380) itself begs the question.

78. For an explanation of this translation, see below.

79. This explanation has been widely accepted: see, e.g., Cross and Woozley (1964, 248), Boyle (1974, 15 n5), Bedu-Addo (1978, 124), Annas (1981, 287), Hitchcock (1985, 74, 90 n59), and Reeve (1988, 77).

80. Probably because he is aware of this difficulty, Boyle (1974, 15 n5)

prefers to emend the text to read ἀναίρουσα ("taking one's *hypothesis* right up to the *archē*") instead of ἀναιροῦσα. Such a reading, however, is rendered unnecessary by an adequate interpretation of the ascent.

81. Adam (1963, 2:176–77) and Stemmer (1992, 191–225, especially 199, 213) also equate the dialectical method of the ascent with the elenctic method of the aporetic dialogues.

82. This positive aspect of Socrates' elenchus is recognized by Furley (1989, 45) when he claims that truth for both Parmenides and Plato is simply "what survives the elenchos." This truth is *not a true proposition*, as Furley appears to recognize: "The Forms are not propositions, nor definitions, nor are they just universal concepts or predicates" (45).

83. Because Cornford interprets the highest section of the Divided Line in terms of geometrical analysis and deduction, he cannot reconcile the Divided Line with Socrates' description of dialectic at 534b–c (1965, 86). He therefore is forced to distinguish between two kinds of dialectic: mathematical and moral, a distinction without any textual support.

84. Aristotle, *Metaphysics* 998a3.

85. For an excellent description of both the limitations and the indispensability of the hypotheses, see Goldschmidt (1970, 32–33).

86. Annas recognizes this problem (1981, 291). The only possible solution she sees is to characterize the descent as simply "a way of presenting and expounding" the understanding that has already been achieved (291). Yet, as Annas herself recognizes, understanding for Plato is clearly not something that is handed over to another by being "expounded" (292–93).

87. If the first principle is, as Ferber (1989) maintains, neither a definition of the good nor even a proposition (106), it is hard to see how one could derive anything from it through *diairesis* (107). What Ferber seems to have in mind is something like the following: the good is a genus; the form of temperance and the form of triangularity are both *eternal* and thereby *good;* these forms are therefore both species of the good. Yet both this characterization of the good as an "Oberklasse" and the resulting derivation seem rather trivial.

88. See also Cornford (1965, 85). A fundamental presupposition of the "esotericists" and of many "developmentalists," one for which there is no evidence, either written or "unwritten," is clearly stated by Krämer (1990b, 93): "Wissen liegt für Platon stricto sensu nur dort vor, wo eine Ableitung aus übergeordneten Sätzen und Prinzipien möglich ist."

89. For Sayre (1969, 43), the only difference between the "downward movement" in dialectic and in mathematics is the certainty of the principles. For a similar collapse of the methodological distinction, see Nuño Montes (1962, 63–64). In Sayre (1995) there is, from what I can see, no clear account of the descent.

90. For other criticisms of the deduction interpretation, see Ferber (1989, 107) and Santas (1983, 253–54).

91. Similarly Cornford: "holding to that which depends on it" (1965, 73).

92. R. Robinson himself translates the clause as "clinging to the things that cling to that" (1953, 149) but unfortunately offers no explanation. Lafrance

(1994, 360) translates "suivant," but even this (in my view) less accurate translation does not support the deduction interpretation: why say simply that we "follow" the hypotheses if what is meant is that we *deduce* them? Surprisingly, Lafrance's otherwise thorough commentary on the text neither defends his translation nor acknowledges other divergent translations.

93. It is incredible that Boyle (1974, 8) not only *assumes* that Plato in the Divided Line is speaking of a deductive system but actually uses this assumption to argue that the first principle must be a proposition.

94. Those who support the deduction interpretation must conclude that, despite the claims in the text to the contrary, dialectic is just as dogmatic as mathematics: "The peculiarity of the Line is that, while Plato is trying to get away from the dogmatism of mathematics, he himself hopes to arrive at a dogma, namely the anhypotheton" (R. Robinson, 1953, 157). White (1976, 96) asks: "Because they both seem to contain unproved assumptions, why should the unproved assumptions of geometry be any worse, for being unproved, than the unproved assumptions of dialectic?"

95. "Dogmatism as a way of thinking, whether in ordinary knowledge or in the study of philosophy, is nothing else but the view that truth consists in a proposition, which is a fixed and final result, or again which is directly known. To questions like, 'When was Caesar born?,' 'How many feet make a furlong?,' etc., a straight answer ought to be given; just as it is absolutely true that the square of the hypotenuse is equal to the sum of the squares of the other two sides of a right-angled triangle. But the nature of a so-called truth of that sort is different from the nature of philosophical truth" (Hegel 1967, 99–100).

96. At 511d1–2 we are told that the mathematicians lack *nous* concerning the things they hypothesize, even though these things "are intelligible in conjunction with the first principle" (νοητῶν ὄντων μετὰ ἀρχῆς). It is therefore this intelligibility that the ascent presumably provides. Those who have been outside the Cave and have returned are said to have gained, not proofs or an axiomatic system, but infinitely greater understanding (vision) of the things within the Cave (520c3–6).

97. Hare (1965) considers two possibilities: either Plato believed that mathematics *could* stop "dreaming" and become genuine knowledge, or he believed that it is inherently and irremediably defective (30). Hare chooses the first option, arguing that mathematics could be connected with the form of the good and thereby become knowledge and that mathematics, though incapable of dispensing with all diagrams whatsoever, could abandon sensible ones in favor of "imagined ones" (30–31). But if Hare is right, is it not extremely surprising that there is no indication in the text that mathematics could ever dispense with sensible diagrams or that it could ever cease to be "hypothetical"? Even the mathematics that book 7 makes central to the educational curriculum of the philosopher-kings still only "dreams" about being. The textual evidence clearly supports the second option.

98. The conclusions of this chapter agree with Hyland's excellent account of the nature of *noēsis* and its incompleteness (1995, 179–95). Especially helpful

are his distinction between "archaic" *noēsis* and "telic" *noēsis* and his argument that neither is reducible to "dianoetic speech" (182).

99. Contra R. Robinson: "Now the Line certainly suggests that dialectic is tentative and approximative as mathematics is not. But that is only half of what it suggests; and the other is that through this provisionality dialectic finally reaches a certainty that is real and not, like that of mathematics, illusory" (1953, 158). Schaerer, on the other hand, defends a view similar to that defended here (1969, 295).

Chapter 9

1. The charge that the letter is historically inaccurate has been answered in detail by Morrow (1962, 17–43). As for the style of the letter, Morrow himself reports that "with striking unanimity the philological researches of the last forty years have confirmed the claims to genuineness of at least the *Seventh* and *Eighth Epistles*" (11), but he is referring here to the turn of the century. Since then there has been further debate. Levinson, Morton, and Winspear (1968) rejected the letter on the basis of computer-based studies. But for the rebuttal see Deane (1973). More recently, Ledger's computer analyses (1989) have shown the *Seventh Letter* to be so close in style to the "late" dialogues (the *Laws* in particular) that he takes its authenticity to be virtually proven (148–50, 199). Given the thoroughness of Ledger's investigation ("a far more comprehensive survey of the entire corpus of Platonic dialogues than has ever been attempted before," 226), the stylometric evidence can at present be said to be on the side of authenticity, though it is doubtful that such evidence could ever amount to anything near a proof. For a recent review and rebuttal of the arguments against authenticity, see Sayre (1995, xviii–xxiii).

2. This is the thesis of Müller (1986) and Edelstein (1966). Müller's arguments are refuted with great skill by von Fritz (1971). See Solmsen (1969) for a very critical review of Edelstein's book. See below for my own criticisms.

3. Tarrant (1983) has presented a novel argument: though the rest of the letter was very well known to the early Middle Platonists, they make no use of the "philosophical digression" where one would expect them to; therefore, this digression was not written until the late first century B.C. to early first century A.D. and not widely circulated until even later. Tarrant mentions Thrasyllus as the possible author and in 1993 (108–47) presents evidence of a relation between the digression and Thrasyllan epistemology. I believe that Tarrant's case is weakened if the digression is as in line with Plato's thought in the dialogues as I argue it to be and if it thus lacks the foreign accretions that Tarrant seems to find (see, e.g., 1983, 84–85 on the "Fifth," 88 on the *poion ti/ti* distinction, 91 on location of the Ideas in the divine mind, and 101–2 n78 on the presence of Academic Skepticism in the letter), and that one would expect to find if it had been written at such a late date.

4. Specifically, this chapter will support the conclusion reached by von Fritz (1971, 425): that the author of the philosophical digression "is not only an

outstanding Platonist, but an extremely good philosopher, a philosopher, I am inclined to say, as distinguished as Plato himself. Since this, after all, is something very rare and since nothing remarkable is otherwise known about the author of the *Seventh Letter,* if he is not Plato, this seems to me to argue very strongly in favour of identifying the author with Plato." Stefanini (1932, 1:xxix n2) claims that the philosophical digression is so faithful and clear an exposition of Plato's thought that it suffices by itself to prove the authenticity of the entire letter.

5. I do not understand Edelstein's claim that "the burden of proof lies with those who consider the letter genuine" (1966, 2). Contra, see Sayre (1995, xix–xx) and Tarrant (1983, 75), who also reasonably rejects the opposite claim, i.e., that the letter must be accepted as genuine until proven spurious. Ancient letters are generally suspect, but as Sayre (1995, xx) points out, the *Seventh Letter* goes far beyond the average letter, both in length and in range of content.

6. Since the letter must have been written shortly after Dion's death in 354 B.C., Plato was at the time of its composition approximately six years away from his own death in 347 and seventy-five years old.

7. In working on this translation I have consulted the following editions, translations, and discussions: Bury (1929), Novotný (1930), Harward (1932), Bluck (1947), Souilhé (1960), Morrow (1962), Gundert (1977, 99–119), Guthrie (1962–78, 5:402–17), Tulli (1989). The Greek text I use is that of Burnet. I will by default refer to the author as "Plato."

8. περὶ ὧν ἐγὼ σπουδάζω. These things are clearly the περὶ φύσεως ἄκρα καὶ πρῶτα mentioned at 344d4–5. Tulli (1989, 18–19) may be right in suggesting that "Plato" intends a contrast here between the verbs σπουδάζω and εἰδέναι: while others claim to *know* the subject matter of philosophy, "Plato" takes this subject matter seriously enough not to presume such knowledge. Ferber (1991, 34) likewise argues that σπουδάζω rules out possession and therefore knowledge. I will find occasion below, however, to disagree with Ferber's general thesis that "Plato" denies any knowledge of the ultimate principles.

9. ῥητὸν γὰρ οὐδαμῶς ὡς ἄλλα μαθήματα. Sometimes the attempt is made to translate this passage in such a way that the negation expressed by οὐδαμῶς is only relative: "this subject-matter cannot be expressed in words *in the same way as* other studies can." This translation implies, of course, that this subject matter *can* be expressed in words. It is therefore the translation needed by the esotericists, who claim that the ultimate principles were expressed by Plato orally within the academy: see Gaiser (1980a, 30 n31) and Krämer (1959, 401, 465–66). However, as Gundert (1977, 106) argues, this is not a plausible translation of the Greek, since it is contradicted by "der Charakter ausschliesslicher Verneinung der in οὐδ' ἁμῶς (auch nicht auf irgendeine Weise) immer zu liegen scheint" and is also without parallel. Furthermore, the philosophical reasons behind this translation are misguided, as will be argued below.

10. ἐπιχείρησιν. It is hard to know how to translate this word here. The qualification λεγομένην (which I have translated as "so-called") seems to indicate that the word is being used in a special sense. Suggested translations differ markedly: "thesis" (Bluck), "argumenter" (Souilhé), "disquisition" (Harward),

"examination" (Morrow), "expositio" (Novotný), "disquisire" (Tulli). Bury reads (with Bonitz) γενομένην for λεγομένην and translates: "undertaking this task." My gloss on my own translation (which plays on both senses of the word "essay") is that "Plato" is speaking here of an attempt to grasp and express the principles directly that thus differs from the indirect approach he recommends.

11. σμικρᾶς ἐνδείξεως. Bluck rightly contrasts this with the πολλὴ συνουσία mentioned above and writes: "Much help of a 'maieutic' kind—πολλὴ συνουσία—is required in dialectic; but very little *direction* (ἔνδειξις) towards truth is possible" (1947, 121).

12. ἀληθῶς ἐστιν ὄν. Some manuscripts have ἀληθές ἐστιν ὦν, and this is the reading given by Bury in the Loeb edition.

13. ἐξ ὀνομάτων καὶ ῥημάτων. The intended distinction here is unclear, but Bluck seems to be on the right track: "As ὄνομα here includes both nouns and adjectives . . . —anything that an object may be *called*—it is probable that ῥήματα is used widely to mean 'predicates' " (1947, 124).

14. Περὶ ταῦτ'. As Bluck recognizes (1947, 124), this phrase must refer to the three means of attaining knowledge just mentioned. Morrow's translation ignores the phrase altogether (1962, 238), while Harward and Souilhé translate it vaguely as "about these things" (1932, 136) and "relatives à ces objets" (1960, 52). The phrase clearly *cannot* mean: "concerning that which truly is (such as the circle in itself)." Therefore, at least one of the three kinds of cognition listed here cannot be the same as that knowledge of "the fifth" which crowns the dialectical process. It is not clear, however, whether the phrase Περὶ ταῦτ' qualifies the whole sentence or only ἀληθὴς δόξα.

15. Nothing "Plato" says here commits him to the view that "knowledge," "insight," and "true belief" are synonymous. What they have in common is that they all exist in the soul, but in the very next sentence "Plato" will point out a major difference, namely, that "insight" is the most akin to the fifth.

16. ἕτερόν τε ὂν αὐτοῦ τοῦ κύκλου τῆς φύσεως. This phrase is more commonly translated: "other than the nature of the circle itself." However, because the text does not read τῆς αὐτοῦ τοῦ κύκλου φύσεως and because τῆς φύσεως seems to stand in contrast to ἐν ψύχαις ἐνόν, I am inclined to take the genitive not with ἕτερον ον, but with the circle itself: "the circle itself of nature or reality, i.e., existing in nature or reality" (this is also apparently how Novotný takes it [1930, 218], as well as Tulli, who translates: "quello vero"). I recognize that elsewhere in Plato only the dative ἐν φύσει, and not the genitive, has this meaning. On either translation, however, the general sense is clear: while knowledge exists in the soul, the circle itself is an objective nature existing outside of the soul.

17. τούτων. This word is sometimes taken to refer to all four means of attaining knowledge (it is thus understood by Bury [1929, 535] and Souilhé [1960, 52]). In this case, "Plato" is saying simply that *nous* is more akin to the fifth than are names, definitions, and images. However, Novotný (1930, 222), Harward (1932, 215), Morrow (1962, 239), Gundert (1977, 108), and Guthrie (1962–78, 5:406) take the passage to mean that *of the three states of mind* that have been classed together as things found only in the soul, "insight" is the one

most akin to the fifth. Both interpretations are acceptable: *nous* is here being distinguished *both* from names, definitions, and images, on the one hand, *and* from that form of "knowledge" (true belief) restricted to them. For more on the latter distinction, see below.

18. μέτοχος. As Ferber (1991, 42) argues, fully *partaking* of knowledge is not the same as fully *possessing* knowledge. This observation is essential to reconciling the present passage with the claim made later in the letter that we can only *barely* attain knowledge of the "fifth."

19. Bury, Morrow, and Souilhé take the subject of "δυναμένων" to be those who are questioned rather than the questioners. Though the text does not rule out this translation, I fail to see how it can make any sense of the passage.

20. Bluck believes that εὖ πεφυκότος refers not to the subject matter, but to the nature of the teacher (1947, 131). I find this highly implausible, since the affinity discussed in the immediately succeeding sentences is between the nature of the student and the nature of the object. For a better explanation of the passage, see Tulli (1989, 34).

21. Gaiser thus explains that Plato did not write down his theory of the principles "per il motivo che Platone non voleva che lettori impreparati e inadatti fossero indotti in equivoci" (1980b, 48).

22. For detailed rebuttal of the esotericists' view that oral discourse is somehow exempted from the letter's critique, see Tulli (1989, especially 48) and Sayre (1988a, 95–97; 1993a, 180–81; 1993b, 172–76; 1995, 11–12).

23. Szlezák (1985, 398) argues that because "Plato" blames Dionysius for having written about the principles, he must allow that they can be expressed in words, but only not *in the same way* as other studies can (for other proponents of this translation of the Greek and my critique, see note 9 above). Ferber (1991, 35–36) also defends this view, and for the same reasons. Yet there is clearly a difference between writing about the principles and expressing the truth of the principles in writing. As Wieland (1991, 35) has noted, while there is no object of knowledge concerning which one could not make an analyzable assertion, it does not follow that all objects of knowledge themselves have propositional structure and therefore can be truly expressed in propositions. Ferber himself attributes to "Plato" the view that words cannot express the natures or essences of the things philosophy is concerned with (1991, 36, 74 n86). But then it would be reasonable for "Plato" to say that what he takes seriously, i.e., what these things truly and in essence are, cannot be expressed in words *at all*. See Graeser (1989, 38) and Sayre (1993a, 184–85; 1995, 11–12, 89–90).

24. See the rhetorical question von Fritz (1971, 437) addresses to the esotericists: "But if a young German philologist is able to transmit an adequate insight into Plato's 'highest subjects' by means of the written word, should we not suppose that Plato himself must have been able to do the same?"

25. One common solution is to claim that Plato's dialogues are not *sungrammata*. Thus Guthrie (1962–78, 5:411): "The *Republic* is no ordinary written work (σύγγραμμα, *Ep.* 7, 341c5)." Szlezák, however, has shown that there is no warrant for restricting the meaning of *sungramma* to exclude dialogues (1985, 376–85).

Ferber agrees (1991, 34–35). Yet the line of interpretation pursued by Tulli (1989, 16–17) offers another possibility: *sungramma* can be taken to refer back to the word *technē,* whose meaning does seem restricted to treatises or technical manuals. As Tulli shows (19), the word *sungramma can* be given a narrow sense by the context. Perhaps, then, the reference to Dionysius's *technē* provides this context.

26. Cf. Ferber (1991, 35) and Graeser (1989, 39).

27. As Graeser (1989, 33) points out, the knowledge which no intelligent person would commit to words cannot be propositional "knowledge that," since such knowledge could always be fully articulated in words.

28. As Thurnher observes (1975, 74), the three means of which "Plato" speaks here are nothing mysterious, but are simply our ordinary, and indispensable, means of coming into contact with things in everyday experience.

29. The words *eidos* and *idea* do not occur in the philosophical digression, but I do not see any major significance in their absence. The self-same, incorruptible natures appear to be the same here and in the dialogues, whatever words might be used in either case to refer to them.

30. For an excellent explanation of why the catalog of objects at 342d contains the items it does and of how colors, passions, and actions can be regarded there as objects of *knowledge,* see Isnardi-Parente (1964, 257–69).

31. "Hier ist zunächst auffällig, dass die unvollkommene Erfassung der niederen Stufen Voraussetzung für die vollkommene der höheren sein soll, und wir müssen das, da es nirgends aufgeklärt werden wird, zunächst als eine stilistische Ungeschichlichkeit buchen" (Müller 1986, 149). But given what is said later, the contrast between ἀμῶς γέ πως and τελέως seems to mean the following: partaking fully of knowledge of the fifth (which need not mean fully *possessing* this knowledge) does not correspond to, and does not require, a perfect grasp of propositions or images.

32. Cf. Graeser (1989, 9–10). Graeser even goes on to distinguish between *three* kinds of knowledge in the letter (30–31), but this seems unnecessary.

33. There is absolutely no warrant in the text for taking the "weakness of language" to be a temporary defect or one afflicting only "ordinary language." Some commentators, e.g., Findlay (1974, 300), nevertheless insist on misunderstanding the passage in this way. See also note 47 below.

34. See Guthrie (1962–78, 5:408 n2) and Gundert (1977, 109 n22).

35. An inability to solve this problem leads Graeser (1989, 15–16) to suggest that the meaning of the text would be better served if the reference to "the weakness of language" were struck out.

36. Bluck thus points out that "εἴδωλα would not be used for reference at all if it were not for the weakness of language" (1947, 127). Thurnher (1975, 76) correctly relates what is said in the *Seventh Letter* about images to the way in which Socrates' interlocutors in the aporetic dialogues must resort to images in their failure to express the true nature of a thing.

37. Isnardi-Parente (1964, 279) likewise claims that the *Seventh Letter* distinguishes *noēsis,* as immediate intuition of an intelligible object, from both true opinion, which is based on sensation, and *epistēmē,* understood as discursive

knowledge. However, for the problem with making the distinction too sharply, see the criticism of White in the following note.

38. I believe that this is the solution to the debate between White (1988) and Gadamer (1988). White rightly points out that the *Seventh Letter* requires us to make a distinction between defective and nondefective types of knowledge (253–54). However, he seems to take this distinction to mean that the nondefective type can altogether dispense with the words, propositions, and images to which the defective type is completely confined (something explicitly denied at 342d8–e2). Gadamer rightly criticizes White for this mistake, but in doing so makes the opposite mistake of denying the distinction altogether (261). The solution is to recognize that it is the tension of the dialectical process itself (involving, as it does, the negative movement of refutation) that mediates between the four defective means and the knowledge that transcends them. (In 1976, White makes no mention of the passage at 344b in which this dialectical process of refutation is described). Ferber (1991, 41–45) allows that the word *epistēmē* has both a broader and a narrower meaning in the *Seventh Letter* but insists that in both cases what is referred to is *defective* knowledge. Thus he, like Gadamer, rejects White's claim that the letter recognizes a "nondefective sort of cognition" (1991, 76 n101; 1993, 45–49). For criticism of the skeptical conclusion to which Ferber is thereby led, see below.

39. For a discussion of the differences between the two formulations of this principle, as well as for the suggestion that the first formulation is to be interpreted in the light of the second and not vice versa, see Graeser (1989, 12–16, 37) and Ferber (1993, 46–49).

40. Contra Graeser (1989, 21–22), who, because he mistakenly believes that according to the dialogues the What-is-x? question can be answered with a definition, sees what the *Seventh Letter* says here as contradicting them.

41. Müller takes the distinction between *ti* and *poion ti* to be one between *essential and accidental properties:* "Das ποῖον bezeichnet also ganz simpel die nicht konstitutiven Eigenschaften" (1986, 151). It is this mistaken interpretation that leads him to conclude that the doctrine of the *Seventh Letter* is absurd. Both Graeser (1989, 17) and Isnardi-Parente (1964, 281–82) rightly reject this interpretation. Graeser unfortunately believes that the *Meno* is committed to the view that *what* a thing *is* (*ti esti*) is definable (18) and therefore must deny the parallel between the distinction in the letter and the distinction in the *Meno*. Isnardi-Parente in the end seems to identify the *poion ti* with accidental properties understood as *sensible* properties (286). Sayre appears to adopt a similar view: (1993a, 182; 1995, 14–15). Yet this interpretation is ruled out by the text: even though the kind of knowledge which the letter calls the "fourth" is said to exist only "in the soul" and not in "articulate voice" nor in "the shapes of physical bodies" (342c4–d1), it is nevertheless described as suffering from the weakness of expressing *to poion ti* rather than *to ti* (342e2–343a1).

42. See Ferber (1991, 47), as well as Sprute (1962, 127), who observes that for Plato knowing beauty is not equivalent to knowing "*that* beauty is such and such" and sees in this a reason for the aporetic endings of so many dialogues.

43. "The weakness of language is such that names and definitions, even when illustrated by the use of εἴδωλα, provide us with an ἐπιστήμη that is no more than knowledge of τὸ ποῖόν τι" (Bluck 1947, 127).

44. That according to the *Seventh Letter* all propositions must be in some sense "hypotheses" is also noted by Derbolav (1953, 75).

45. At 342c4–5 "Plato" classifies under "knowledge" *epistēmē, nous,* and *alēthēs doxa*. However, in referring to the knowledge of "the fifth" gained through the dialectical process (343e2, 344b7), "Plato" uses only the words *epistēmē* and *nous*. The implication is that *alēthēs doxa* refers only to that defective knowledge afflicted with the weakness of language.

46. The connection between the method of hypothesis and the defective knowledge described in the *Seventh Letter* is recognized by Gundert (1977, 115–16).

47. It is sometimes thought, particularly by those who support the esotericist thesis, that what "Plato" calls the "weakness of language" applies only to a certain kind of language. This view, however, receives absolutely no support from the text. On the contrary, "Plato" makes quite clear that *any* form of verbal expression is incapable of expressing "the fifth" and is therefore refutable. Findlay is therefore choosing to ignore the text when he writes: "It will be noted that Plato in these passages does not hold philosophical insight to be ineffable and private, only that it cannot be shared *while words are used in a routine manner* based on examples culled from the commerce of the senses" (1974, 301; my emphasis).

48. It is important to note that what is said here applies only to propositions that attempt to state the "fifth" and therefore not necessarily to propositions of the kind Socrates defends in the *Gorgias:* "It is better to suffer injustice than to do it" and "Once having done injustice it is better to suffer than to escape punishment." Neither of these propositions attempts to say what justice itself is and therefore may not be refutable in the way described here.

49. Von Fritz's claims that the refutation described in this passage is only *apparent:* "Thus the deficiencies of the first four stages of the approach to knowledge or insight are *shown up* by pointing out that it is these deficiencies that make it possible to raise false objections leading to *apparent but false* refutations" (1971, 423). It is true that, as "Plato" tells us, the knowledge existing in the soul is not refuted. Yet the point of the passage is that this knowledge *cannot be expressed* in answer to the question asking for the fifth and that it is for this reason that the answer is *really,* and not just apparently, refuted.

50. Cf. Gundert (1977, 17).

51. I owe much of what I say here to the excellent account in Ferber (1993, 48).

52. "Wie in aller Welt soll das Eidos von der gutbeschaffenen Seele erkannt werden durch Auf- und Absteigen in der Stufenordnung brüchiger Erkenntnismittel?" (Müller 1986, 153).

53. Of all the commentators I have consulted, the only exceptions are Bluck and Tulli. Bluck translates "ἐλέγχοις" as "refutations," while Tulli translates "confutazioni" (though for some reason he translates ἐλεγχόμενα simply

as "discusso"). Bluck's note on the passage is on the mark: "In dialectic . . . the ἡγέμων or questioner asks for a λόγος of some Form, and refutes the respondent's ὑπόθεσις by showing him its inadequacy. New attempts are made, and the procedure should end with a sudden flash of understanding, a vision of the Form concerned, in the mind of the respondent" (1947, 133).

54. Another example of a misinterpretation is that of W. Ross (1951). Ignoring the phrase "ἐν εὐμενέσιν ἐλέγχοις ἐλεγχόμενα," as well as everything said in the letter about the necessary defect of words and propositions, Ross (141) identifies the insight attained at the end of the dialectical process with a "precise definition"!

55. Gundert (1977, 97) recognizes that the "weakness of language" discussed in the *Seventh Letter* has as a consequence that the "divine" cannot be grasped in a single communicable proposition, but only in a movement through propositions.

56. Ferber, I believe, goes too far in reaching the purely skeptical conclusion that the subject matter of philosophy, i.e., the "fifth," cannot be known (see especially 1991, 41–45, 51; also 1993, 44–49). Ferber is apparently led to this conclusion by his conviction that knowledge must be propositional (see 1991, 47–48, 80 n139, and Ferber's rejection of Sayre's interpretation, 76 n103), coupled with the fact that propositional knowledge does not admit degrees. This conviction, however, prevents Ferber from making sense of important passages of the text. For example, in interpreting the claim at 342d8–e2 that we can "partake" of knowledge of the "fifth" only after grasping the four means, a claim that appears to contradict his thesis that we can have no knowledge of the "fifth," Ferber insists, rightly, that "partaking" is to be distinguished from full possession (1991, 42). Yet he never explains this distinction. Instead, his final conclusion that the "fifth" cannot be known seems to leave this passage out of account. Likewise, in interpreting the "rubbing together" passage at 344b3–c1, another one that appears to contradict his skeptical thesis, Ferber argues that the knowledge gained is not one which *adequately* but only *most adequately* expresses the "fifth"; that the knowledge is not *objective*, but only *most objective* (1991, 55). Again Ferber's conclusion drops this talk of "approximation." Though this talk is demanded by the text, Ferber neither does nor apparently *can* explain it: given the sharp distinction between *ti esti* and *poion esti*, if knowledge of the former is impossible, how can any knowledge of *poion esti* more adequately or more objectively express *ti esti* than any other? In (1993, 51–52), Ferber explicitly characterizes "Plato's" position in the letter as an *Approximativismus*, according to which all that is possible is an *Annäherung an die Wahrheit*. Again, this claim is exactly right, but again Ferber does not appear to explain it. The solution, it seems to me, is to drop Ferber's presupposition: we must recognize in the text a distinctive form of nonpropositional knowledge which, unlike strictly propositional knowledge, can vary in degrees, providing clearer or dimmer glimpses beyond what propositions can express, but never fully freeing itself from propositions and their weakness (on this last point Ferber and I are in agreement). For further discussion of Ferber (1991), see Gonzalez (1994).

57. Cf. Ferber (1991, 34).

58. This identity between the *sunousia* described in the *Seventh Letter* and that depicted in the dialogues is noted and excellently explained by Niewöhner (1971, 231). Sayre, in contrast, asserts that the *elenchus* to which Socrates subjects his interlocutors "by itself cannot be the 'well-disposed' elenchus of which Plato speaks in the Seventh Letter, if for no other reason than most of Socrates' respondents in the early dialogues were not capable of the kind of understanding for which this elenchus was an early stage of preparation" (1995, 61). But what happens in the dialogues only shows what the letter itself should lead us to expect: that the "well-disposed" elenchus will fail when the interlocutors lack the suitable nature or affinity with the subject. It is indeed striking that Plato so often depicts the Socratic elenchus as failing. But there are two possible reasons for this: first, the *success* of the elenchus, because it is defined by the attainment of nonpropositional understanding, is not something that could be depicted in writing; but second, we the readers can nevertheless gain the understanding at which the elenchus aims precisely by seeing how and why the elenchus fails with this particular interlocutor.

59. Edelstein claims that because the *Seventh Letter* speaks only of the kindling of an "inner light" (ἑαυτὸ τρέφει), does not mention a "beyond," describes knowledge as being closer to the fifth than the other three elements (Edelstein fails to distinguish between two kinds of knowledge here), and requires of the learner a "special nature," the author of the letter must hold that the Ideas are thoughts existing only in the soul. The author, therefore, cannot be Plato (1966, 96–101). This non sequitur is unfortunately typical of Edelstein's arguments against the letter's authenticity. What makes this argument especially unfortunate is that it is easily refuted by the text: knowledge, insight, and true belief "exist neither in articulate voice nor in shapes of physical objects but rather in [our] souls, thus being distinct from the circle itself which exists in reality as well as from the three things just mentioned." Even if one does not accept my translation of τῆς φύσεως here, the sense of the passage is nevertheless clear: the circle itself is distinct from knowledge in that it *does not* exist in the soul, but is an objective nature (see note 16). Yet Edelstein conveniently leaves τῆς φύσεως untranslated (97). Tarrant rejects Edelstein's interpretation for similar reasons, but his own attempt to find in the letter the view that the Ideas exist in the Divine Mind is not much less fanciful (1983, 90–92).

60. Thus a kind of "certainty" is attained here, but as I suggest in my discussion of the word *bebaion* in chapter 8, the "certainty" that characterizes knowledge for Plato is nonpropositional: it is simply the fixity and inalienability of insight. Thus Gundert (1968, 15) describes as a "paradox" the fact that the clarity and fixity which Plato requires of knowledge are to be found in the *movement* of dialectic, rather than in any fixity of propositions (which, after all, have very little stability according to Plato).

61. This criticism goes back at least as far as Immanuel Kant. After giving a brief description of the epistemology of the letter, Kant describes its author (whom he did not believe to be Plato) as a pretentious mystagogue: "Wer sieht

NOTES TO PAGES 272-74

hier nicht den Mystagogen, der nicht bloss für sich schwärmt, sondern zugleich Klubbist ist und, indem er zu seinen Adepten im Gegensatz von dem Volke (worunter alle Uneingeweihte verstanden werden) spricht, mit seiner vorgeblichen Philosophie vornehm thut!" (1912, 398). For a criticism of the "mystical" interpretation, and of Kant in particular, see Ferber (1991, 37-40).

62. As Stenzel observes (1956, 168), what distinguishes "Plato" from the mystics is his recognition of our dependence on the four means of knowledge: "Wenn Platon glaubte, dass jenes Fünfte sich absolut, losgelöst von jenen vier Stufen, erfassen liesse, so wäre er Mystiker." See also Stefanini (1932, 1:xxxiii).

63. "Although knowledge worthy of philosophy cannot be expressed discursively, it does not follow that language has no role to play in the philosopher's quest for understanding. Skillfully conducted conversation can be *next to* indispensable in preparing the mind for that intellectual grasp of reality that constitutes philosophic knowledge" (Sayre 1988, 108; my italics). I would drop the italicized qualification. See also Sayre (1995, 90-91, 159, 195).

64. In this way a reconciliation is achieved between the two models of knowledge Teloh (1981, 6-7) has found at odds with each other in the dialogues: one discursive and one "visual."

65. If this account is correct, one of the major defects of the account of dialectic in Stemmer (1992) is the failure to recognize the possibility expressed by this third presupposition (see 151). Stemmer maintains that Plato's recognition of the defective character *and* the necessity of the elenctic method is incompatible with a belief in the possibility of nonpropositional knowledge. His argument is that, if we could know the forms as simply and as immediately as we know that a table has a certain color, the defective elenctic method would be completely dispensable. Unfortunately, this characterization of nonpropositional knowledge as knowledge that requires no preparation, is complete and absolute the moment it occurs, and can dispense once and for all with discourse is a *caricature*. On the other hand, Stefanini's characterization of Plato's thought as "constructive *skepsis*" is one of the few to do justice to the three presuppositions of dialectic I outline: "un'intuizione che instantaneamente e prodigiosamente si eleva in alto, e una dialettica faticosa che non riesce mai a imprigionare la subitanea rivelazione e pur è necessario presupposto e conseguenza di questa: ecco l'atteggiamento essenziale del pensiero platonico" (1932, 1:xxxiii; see also xxxii-xxxiv). Stefanini's characterization of the process by which knowledge is partially and imperfectly attained, as well as of this knowledge itself, differs from my own in important respects, some noted in previous chapters. Nevertheless, I still believe that much remains to be learned from Stefanini's extraordinary book. For another characterization of dialectic as both positive and negative, neither skeptical nor dogmatic, see Watson (1995, 197-200).

66. To this extent I agree with Sayre's characterization of the dialogues as surrogates for dialectical conversations (1995, 21-27). However, as notes to preceding chapters have documented, my own account of dialectic differs radically from Sayre's. For my more detailed account of the relation between Plato's conception of philosophy and the dialogue form, see Gonzalez (1995b).

Works Cited

Adam, James. 1963. *The Republic of Plato*. 2d ed. 2 vols. Cambridge: Cambridge University Press.

Allen, R. E. 1984. *The Dialogues of Plato*. Vol. 1. New Haven: Yale University Press.

Anagnostopoulos, Georgios. 1972. "Plato's *Cratylus:* Two Theories of the Correctness of Names." *Review of Metaphysics* 25(4):691–736.

Andic, Martin. 1971. "Inquiry and Virtue in the *Meno*." In *Plato's Meno*, ed. Malcolm Brown, 262–314. Indianapolis: Bobbs-Merrill.

Annas, Julia. 1981. *An Introduction to Plato's Republic*. Oxford: Clarendon Press.

———. 1982. "Knowledge and Language in the *Theaetetus* and the *Cratylus*." In *Language and Logos*, ed. Malcolm Schofield and Martha Craven Nussbaum, 95–114. Cambridge: Cambridge University Press.

Archer-Hind, R. D. [1894] 1973. *The Phaedo of Plato*. 2d ed. London: Macmillan. Reprint, New York: Arno Press.

Arieti, James. 1991. *Interpreting Plato: The Dialogues as Drama*. Lanham, Md.: Rowman & Littlefield Publishers.

———. 1995. "How to Read a Platonic Dialogue." In *The Third Way: New Directions in Platonic Studies*, ed. Francisco J. Gonzalez, 119–32. Lanham, Md.: Rowman & Littlefield.

Baxter, Timothy M. S. 1992. *The Cratylus: Plato's Critique of Naming*. Leiden: E. J. Brill.

Bedu-Addo, J. T. 1978. "Mathematics, Dialectic and the Good in the Republic VI–VII." *Platon* 30:111–27.

———. 1983. "Sense Experience and Recollection in Plato's *Meno*." *American Journal of Philology* 104:228–48.

Benitez, Eugenio. 1996. "*Republic* 476d6–e2: Plato's Dialectical Requirement." *Review of Metaphysics* 49:515–46.

Benson, Hugh. 1987. "The Problem of the Elenchus Reconsidered." *Ancient Philosophy* 7:67–85.

———. 1989. "A Note on Eristic and the Socratic Elenchus." *Journal of the History of Philosophy* 27:591–99.

———. 1990a. "Meno, the Slave Boy and the Elenchos." *Phronesis* 35(2):128–58.

———. 1990b. "The Priority of Definition and the Socratic Elenchus." *Oxford Studies in Ancient Philosophy* 8:19–65.

———. 1992. "Misunderstanding the 'What is F-ness?' Question." In *Essays on the Philosophy of Socrates,* ed. Hugh H. Benson, 123–36. New York: Oxford University Press.

———. 1995. "The Dissolution of the Problem of the *Elenchus.*" *Oxford Studies in Ancient Philosophy* 13:45–112.
Berti, Enrico. 1989. "Strategie di interpretazione dei filosofi antichi: Platone et Aristotele." *Elenchos* 10:289–315.
Bertozzi, A. 1948. "Il termine doxa nei dialoghi di Platone." *Giornale di Metafisica* 3:37–43.
Beversluis, John. 1974. "Socratic Definition." *American Philosophical Quarterly* 11:331–36.
———. 1992. "Does Socrates Commit the Socratic Fallacy?" In *Essays on the Philosophy of Socrates,* ed. Hugh H. Benson, 107–22. Oxford: Oxford University Press.
Blachowicz, James. 1995. "Platonic 'True Belief' and the Paradox of Inquiry." *Southern Journal of Philosophy* 33:403–29.
Bloom, Allan. 1968. *Plato's Republic.* New York: Basic Books.
Bluck, R. S. 1947. *Plato's Seventh and Eighth Letters.* Cambridge: Cambridge University Press.
———. 1956. "Logos and Forms in Plato: A Reply to Professor Cross." *Mind* 65:522–29.
———. 1961. *Plato's Meno.* Cambridge: Cambridge University Press.
———. 1963. "Knowledge by Acquaintance in Plato's *Theaetetus.*" *Mind* 72:259–63.
Bonitz, Hermann. 1871. "Zur Erklärung platonischer Dialoge." *Hermes* 5:413–42.
———. [1886] 1968. *Platonische Studien.* Reprint, Hildesheim: Georg Olms.
Bostock, David. 1986. *Plato's Phaedo.* Oxford: Clarendon Press.
Boyle, A. J. 1973. "Plato's Divided Line. Essay I: The Problem of *dianoia.*" *Apeiron* 7:1–11.
———. 1974. "Plato's Divided Line. Essay II: Mathematics and Dialectic." *Apeiron* 8:7–21.
Brickhouse, T., and N. D. Smith. 1984. "Vlastos on the Elenchus." *Oxford Studies in Ancient Philosophy* 2:185–96.
———. 1994. *Plato's Socrates.* New York: Oxford University Press.
Brown, M. S. 1967. "Plato Disapproves of the Slaveboy's Answers." *Review of Metaphysics* 21(1):57–93.
Brumbaugh, Robert S. 1989. *Platonic Studies of Greek Philosophy: Form, Arts, Gadgets, and Hemlock.* Albany: State University of New York Press.
Burger, R. 1981. "Belief, Knowledge, and Socratic Knowledge of Ignorance." *Tulane Studies in Philosophy* 30:1–23.
Burnet, John. 1911. *Plato's Phaedo.* Oxford: Oxford University Press.
Burnyeat, M. F. 1977. "Examples in Epistemology: Socrates, Theaetetus and G. E. Moore." *Philosophy* 52:381–98.
———. 1980. "Socrates and the Jury: Paradoxes in Plato's Distinction between Knowledge and True Belief." *Proceedings of the Aristotelian Society,* Suppl. 54:173–91.
———. 1981. "Aristotle on Understanding Knowledge." In *Aristotle on Science: The "Posterior Analytics,"* ed. Enrico Berti, 97–139. Padua: Editrice Antenore.

WORKS CITED

———. 1987. "Wittgenstein and Augustine *De Magistro*." *Proceedings of the Aristotelian Society*, Suppl. 61:1–24.
———. 1990. *The Theaetetus of Plato*. Indianapolis: Hackett, 1990.
Bury, R. G., trans. 1929. *Plato*. Loeb Classical Library, vol. 9. Cambridge, Mass.: Harvard University Press.
Canto, Monique. 1987. *L'intrigue philosophique: essai sur l'Euthydème de Platon*. Paris: J. Vrin.
Chance, Thomas. 1992. *Plato's Euthydemus: Analysis of What Is and Is Not Philosophy*. Berkeley: University of California Press.
Cherniss, Harold. 1947. Review of *Plato's Earlier Dialectic*, by Richard Robinson. *American Journal of Philology* 68:133–46.
———. 1983. "Lafrance on Doxa." *Dialogue* 22:137–62.
Cicovacki, Predrag. 1996. "Commentary on Gentzler." In *Proceedings of the Boston Area Colloquium in Ancient Philosophy (1994)*, ed. John J. Cleary and William Wians, 10:296–308. Lanham, Md.: University Press of America.
Cornford, F. M. 1965. "Mathematics and Dialectic in the 'Republic' VI–VII." In *Studies in Plato's Metaphysics*, ed. R. E. Allen, 61–95. London: Routledge & Kegan Paul.
Cross, R. C. 1954. "Logos and Forms in Plato." *Mind* 63:433–50.
Cross, R. C., and A. D. Woozley. 1964. *Plato's Republic: A Philosophical Commentary*. London: Macmillan.
Deane, P. 1973. "Stylometrics Do Not Exclude the Seventh Letter." *Mind* 82:113–17.
Derbolav, Joseph. 1953. *Der Dialog Kratylos*. Saarbrucken: West-Ost Verlag.
Desjardins, R. 1985. "Knowledge and Virtue: Paradox in Plato's *Meno*." *Review of Metaphysics* 39:261–81.
Devereux, Daniel T. 1977. "Courage and Wisdom in Plato's *Laches*." *Journal of the History of Philosophy* 15:129–41.
Dimas, Panagiotis. 1996. "True Belief in the *Meno*." *Oxford Studies in Ancient Philosophy* 14:5–32.
Dorter, Kenneth. 1982. *Plato's Phaedo: An Interpretation*. Toronto: University of Toronto Press.
Ebert, Theodor. 1974. *Meinung und Wissen in der Philosophie Platons*. Berlin: Walter de Gruyter.
Eck, Job van. 1994. "Σκοπεῖν ἐν λόγοις: On *Phaedo* 99d–103c." *Ancient Philosophy* 14:21–40.
———. 1996. "Resailing Socrates' Δεύτερος Πλοῦς: A Criticism of Rowe's 'Explanation in *Phaedo* 99c6–102a8.'" *Oxford Studies in Ancient Philosophy* 14:211–26.
Edelstein, Ludwig. 1966. *Plato's Seventh Letter*. Leiden: E. J. Brill.
Elias, Julias A. 1968. "'Socratic' vs. 'Platonic' Dialectic." *Journal of the History of Philosophy* 6:205–16.
Erler, M. 1987. *Der Sinn der Aporien in den Dialogen Platons: Übungsstücke zur Anleitung im philosophischen Denken*. Berlin: Walter de Gruyter.
Ferber, Rafael. 1989. *Platos Idee des Guten*. 2d ed. Sankt Augustin: Academia Verlag Richarz.

WORKS CITED

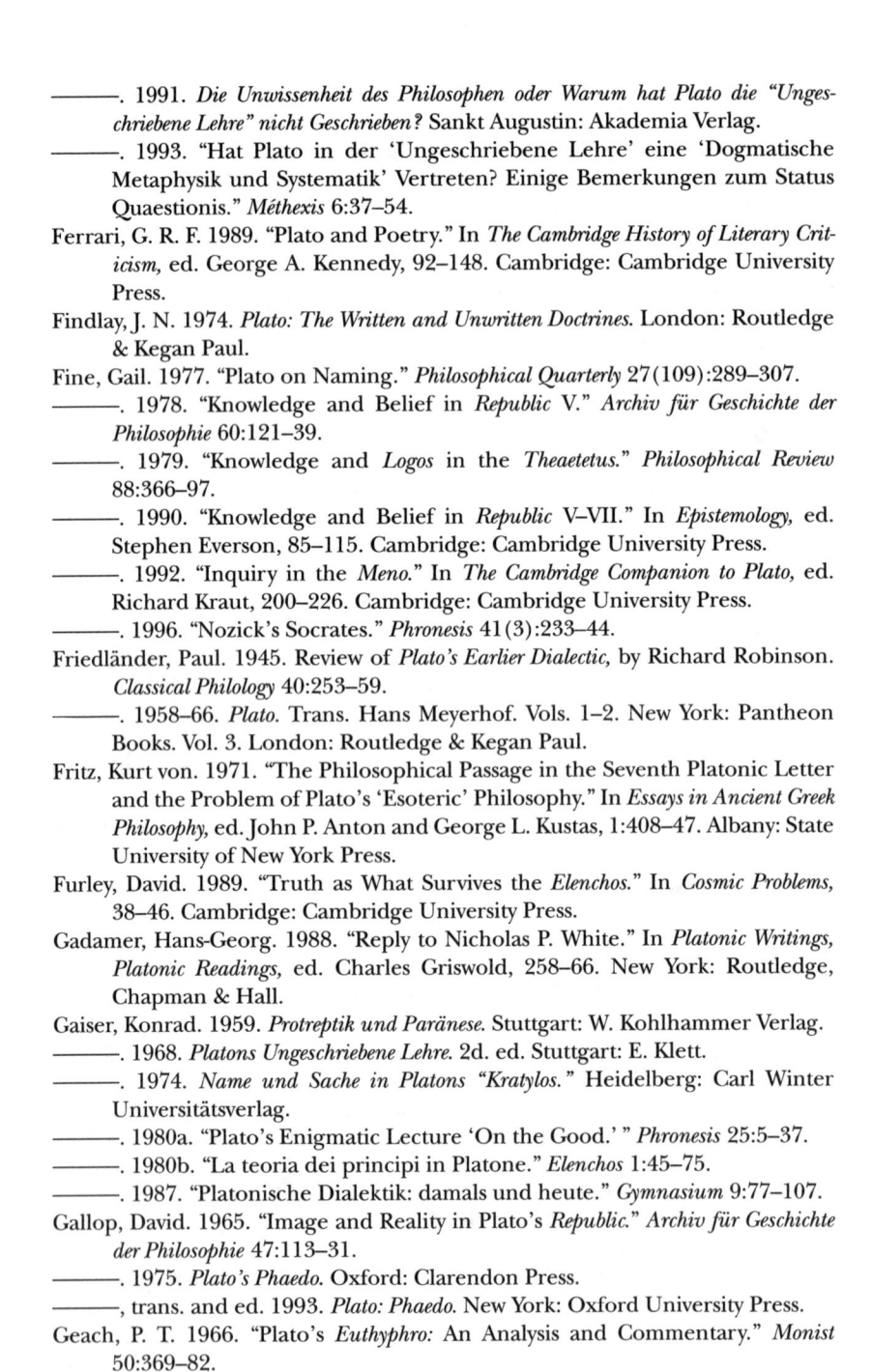

———. 1991. *Die Unwissenheit des Philosophen oder Warum hat Plato die "Ungeschriebene Lehre" nicht Geschrieben?* Sankt Augustin: Akademia Verlag.

———. 1993. "Hat Plato in der 'Ungeschriebene Lehre' eine 'Dogmatische Metaphysik und Systematik' Vertreten? Einige Bemerkungen zum Status Quaestionis." *Méthexis* 6:37–54.

Ferrari, G. R. F. 1989. "Plato and Poetry." In *The Cambridge History of Literary Criticism*, ed. George A. Kennedy, 92–148. Cambridge: Cambridge University Press.

Findlay, J. N. 1974. *Plato: The Written and Unwritten Doctrines.* London: Routledge & Kegan Paul.

Fine, Gail. 1977. "Plato on Naming." *Philosophical Quarterly* 27(109):289–307.

———. 1978. "Knowledge and Belief in *Republic* V." *Archiv für Geschichte der Philosophie* 60:121–39.

———. 1979. "Knowledge and *Logos* in the *Theaetetus*." *Philosophical Review* 88:366–97.

———. 1990. "Knowledge and Belief in *Republic* V–VII." In *Epistemology*, ed. Stephen Everson, 85–115. Cambridge: Cambridge University Press.

———. 1992. "Inquiry in the *Meno*." In *The Cambridge Companion to Plato*, ed. Richard Kraut, 200–226. Cambridge: Cambridge University Press.

———. 1996. "Nozick's Socrates." *Phronesis* 41(3):233–44.

Friedländer, Paul. 1945. Review of *Plato's Earlier Dialectic*, by Richard Robinson. *Classical Philology* 40:253–59.

———. 1958–66. *Plato*. Trans. Hans Meyerhof. Vols. 1–2. New York: Pantheon Books. Vol. 3. London: Routledge & Kegan Paul.

Fritz, Kurt von. 1971. "The Philosophical Passage in the Seventh Platonic Letter and the Problem of Plato's 'Esoteric' Philosophy." In *Essays in Ancient Greek Philosophy*, ed. John P. Anton and George L. Kustas, 1:408–47. Albany: State University of New York Press.

Furley, David. 1989. "Truth as What Survives the *Elenchos*." In *Cosmic Problems*, 38–46. Cambridge: Cambridge University Press.

Gadamer, Hans-Georg. 1988. "Reply to Nicholas P. White." In *Platonic Writings, Platonic Readings*, ed. Charles Griswold, 258–66. New York: Routledge, Chapman & Hall.

Gaiser, Konrad. 1959. *Protreptik und Paränese*. Stuttgart: W. Kohlhammer Verlag.

———. 1968. *Platons Ungeschriebene Lehre*. 2d. ed. Stuttgart: E. Klett.

———. 1974. *Name und Sache in Platons "Kratylos."* Heidelberg: Carl Winter Universitätsverlag.

———. 1980a. "Plato's Enigmatic Lecture 'On the Good.'" *Phronesis* 25:5–37.

———. 1980b. "La teoria dei principi in Platone." *Elenchos* 1:45–75.

———. 1987. "Platonische Dialektik: damals und heute." *Gymnasium* 9:77–107.

Gallop, David. 1965. "Image and Reality in Plato's *Republic*." *Archiv für Geschichte der Philosophie* 47:113–31.

———. 1975. *Plato's Phaedo*. Oxford: Clarendon Press.

———, trans. and ed. 1993. *Plato: Phaedo*. New York: Oxford University Press.

Geach, P. T. 1966. "Plato's *Euthyphro*: An Analysis and Commentary." *Monist* 50:369–82.

WORKS CITED

Gentzler, Jyl. 1991. "'συμφωνεῖν' in Plato's *Phaedo.*" *Phronesis* 36(3):265–76.
———. 1996. "Recollection and 'The Problem of the Socratic Elenchus.'" In *Proceedings of the Boston Area Colloquium in Ancient Philosophy (1994),* ed. John J. Cleary and William Wians, 10:257–95. Lanham, Md.: University Press of America.
Goldschmidt, Victor. 1947. *Les dialogues de Platon: structure et méthode dialectique.* Paris: Presses Universitaires de France.
———. 1970. *Questions Platoniciennes.* Paris: Librairie Philosophique J. Vrin.
Gonzalez, Francisco J. 1994. Review of *Die Unwissenheit des Philosophen oder Warum hat Plato die "Ungeschriebene Lehre" Geschrieben,* by Rafael Ferber. *Journal of the History of Philosophy* 32(3):483–44.
———, ed. 1995a. *The Third Way: New Directions in Platonic Studies.* Lanham, Md.: Rowman & Littlefield.
———. 1995b. "Self-Knowledge, Practical Knowledge and Insight: Plato's Dialectic and the Dialogue Form." In *The Third Way: New Directions in Platonic Studies,* 155–87.
———. 1995c. "Plato's *Lysis:* An Enactment of Philosophical Kinship." *Ancient Philosophy* 15:69–90.
———. 1996. "Propositions or Objects? Gail Fine on Knowledge and Belief in *Republic* V." *Phronesis* 41(3):245–75.
———. 1998. "Nonpropositional Knowledge in Plato." *Apeitron,* forthcoming.
———. Forthcoming. "Giving Thought to the Good Together: Virtue in Plato's *Protagoras.*" In *Retracing the Platonic Text,* ed. John Sallis and John Russon, chap. 9. Evanston, Ill.: Northwestern University Press.
Gosling, J. C. 1968. "*Doxa* and *Dunamis* in Plato's *Republic.*" *Phronesis* 13:119–30.
Gould, Carol S. 1987. "Socratic Intellectualism and the Problem of Courage: An Interpretation of Plato's *Laches.*" *History of Philosophy Quarterly* 4:265–79.
Gould, John. 1955. *The Development of Plato's Ethics.* New York: Russell & Russell.
Graeser, Andreas. 1989. *Philosophische Erkenntnis und begriffliche Darstellung: Bemerkungen zum erkenntnistheoretischen Exkurs des VII. Briefs.* Mainz: Akademie der Wissenschaften und der Literatur.
Grene, Marjorie. 1966. "The Legacy of the *Meno.*" In *The Knower and the Known,* 18–35. London: Faber & Faber.
Griswold, Charles. 1981. "The Ideas and the Criticism of Poetry in Plato's *Republic,* Book 10." *Journal of the History of Philosophy* 19:135–50.
———. 1986. "Philosophy, Education, and Courage in Plato's *Laches.*" *Interpretation* 14:177–93.
———. 1990. "Unifying Plato: Charles Kahn on Platonic *Prolepsis.*" *Ancient Philosophy* 10(2):243–62.
———, ed. 1988. *Platonic Readings, Platonic Writings.* New York: Routledge, Chapman & Hall.
Grote, G. 1888. *Plato and the Other Companions of Socrates.* New ed. 4 vols. London: J. Murray.
Grube, G. M. A. 1935. *Plato's Thought.* London: Methuen.
Gully, Norman. 1962. *Plato's Theory of Knowledge.* London: Methuen.

WORKS CITED

Gundert, Hermann. 1968. *Der platonische Dialog.* Heidelberg: Carl Winter Universitätsverlag.
———. 1971. *Dialog und Dialektik.* Amsterdam: Verlag B. R. Grüner.
———. 1977. *Platonische Studien.* Amsterdam: Verlag B. R. Grüner.
Guthrie, W. K. C. 1962–78. *A History of Greek Philosophy.* 5 vols. Cambridge: Cambridge University Press.
Hackforth, R. 1942. "Plato's Divided Line and Dialectic." *Classical Quarterly* 36:1–9.
———. 1972. *Plato's Phaedo.* Cambridge: Cambridge University Press.
Hare, R. M. 1965. "Plato and the Mathematicians." In *New Essays on Plato and Aristotle,* ed. Renford Bambrough, 21–38. London: Routledge & Kegan Paul.
Harward, J. 1932. *The Platonic Epistles.* Cambridge: Cambridge University Press.
Hawtrey, R. S. W. 1978. "How Do Dialecticians Use Diagrams—Plato, *Euthydemus* 290b–c." *Apeiron* 12:14–18.
———. 1981. *Commentary on Plato's Euthydemus.* Philadelphia: American Philosophical Society.
Hegel, G. W. F. 1967. *The Phenomenology of Mind.* Trans. J. B. Baillie. New York: Harper & Row.
Heidegger, Martin. 1952. "Die Zeit des Weltbildes." In *Holzwege,* 69–104. Frankfurt am Main: Vittorio Klostermann, 1963.
———. 1988. *Schelling: Vom Wesen der Menschlichen Freiheit (1809).* In *Gesamtausgabe* 42. Frankfurt am Main: Vittorio Klostermann.
Hermann, Karl Friedrich. [1839] 1976. *Geschichte und System der Philosophie.* Heidelberg. Reprint, New York: Arno Press.
Hinrichs, Gerard. 1951. "The *Euthydemus* as a Locus of the Socratic Elenchus." *New Scholasticism* 25:178–83.
Hintikka, J. 1974a. "Knowledge and Its Objects in Plato." In *Knowledge and the Known: Historical Perspectives in Epistemology,* 1–30. Dordrecht: Reidel.
———. 1974b. "Plato on Knowing How, Knowing That, and Knowing What." In *Knowledge and the Known: Historical Perspectives in Epistemology,* 31–49. Dordrecht: Reidel.
Hitchcock, David. 1985. "The Good in Plato's *Republic.*" *Apeiron* 19:65–92.
Hoerber, R. G. 1960. "Plato's *Meno.*" *Phronesis* 5:78–102.
———. 1968. "Plato's *Laches.*" *Classical Philology* 63:95–105.
Howland, Jacob. 1991. "Re-reading Plato: The Problem of Platonic Chronology Reconsidered." *Phoenix* 45:189–214.
Hyland, Drew A. 1981. *The Virtue of Philosophy: An Interpretation of Plato's Charmides.* Athens: Ohio University Press.
———. 1995. *Finitude and Transcendence in the Platonic Dialogues.* Albany: SUNY Press.
Irwin, Terence. 1977. *Plato's Moral Theory.* Oxford: Clarendon Press.
———. 1995. *Plato's Ethics.* New York: Oxford University Press.
Isnardi-Parente, Margherita. 1964. "Per l'interpretazione dell' excursus filosofico della VII Epistola Platonica." *Parola del Passato* 19:241–90.

WORKS CITED

Jacoby, Felix. 1929. *Die Fragmente der griechischen Historiker.* 2d. part. Berlin: Weidmannsche Buchhandlung.
Kahn, Charles. 1972. "The Meaning of 'Justice' and the Theory of Forms." *Journal of Philosophy* 69(18):567–79.
———. 1973. "Language and Ontology in the *Cratylus.*" In *Exegesis and Argument: Studies in Greek Philosophy Presented to Gregory Vlastos,* ed. E. N. Lee, A. P. D. Mourelatos, and R. M. Rorty, 152–76. Phronesis Supplementary Vol. 1. Amsterdam: Assen.
———. 1981. "Did Plato Write Socratic Dialogues?" *Classical Quarterly* 31:305–20.
———. 1986. "Plato's Methodology in the *Laches.*" *Revue Internationale de Philosophie* 40:7–21.
———. 1988. "Plato's *Charmides* and the Proleptic Reading of Socratic Dialogues." *Journal of Philosophy* 85:541–51.
Kant, Immanuel. 1912. *Von einem neuerdings erhobenen Ton in der Philosophie.* In *Gesammelte Schriften,* ed. Königlich Preussischen Akademie der Wissenschaften, 8:387–406. Berlin: Georg Reimer.
Ketchum, Richard. 1979. "Names, Forms and Conventionalism: *Cratylus,* 383–95." *Phronesis* 24(2):133–47.
———. 1991. "Plato on the Uselessness of Epistemology: *Charmides* 166e–172a." *Apeiron* 24:81–98.
Keulen, Hermann. 1971. *Untersuchungen zu Platons Euthydem.* Wiesbaden: Otto Harrassowitz.
Kierkegaard, Søren. 1965. *The Concept of Irony: With Constant Reference to Socrates.* Trans. Lee M. Chapel. New York: Harper & Row.
Klein, Jacob. 1965. *A Commentary on Plato's Meno.* Chapel Hill: University of North Carolina Press.
Klein, Sherwin. 1986. "Socratic Dialectic in the *Meno.*" *Southern Journal of Philosophy* 24:351–63.
Klosko, George. 1981. "The Technical Conception of Virtue." *Journal of the History of Philosophy* 19:95–102.
Kosman, L. A. 1983. "*Charmides*' First Definition: Sophrosyne as Quietness." In *Essays in Ancient Greek Philosophy,* vol. 2, ed. John P. Anton and Anthony Preus, 203–16. Albany: State University of New York Press.
Krämer, H. J. 1959. *Arete bei Platon und Aristoteles: zum Wesen und zur Geschichte der platonischen Ontologie.* Heidelberg: C. Winter.
———. 1966. "Über den Zusammenhang von Principienlehre und Dialektik bei Platon; zur Definition des Dialektikers Politeia 534B–C." *Philologus* 110:35–70.
———. 1969. "Die platonische Akademie und das Problem einer systematischen Interpretation der Philosophie Platons." In *Das Platonbild: Zehn Beiträge zum Platonverständnis,* ed. K. Gaiser, 198–230. Hildesheim: G. Olms.
———. 1982. "Kritische Bemerkungen zu den jüngsten Äusserungen von W. Wieland und G. Patzig über Platons Ungeschriebene Lehre." *Revista di Filosofia Neoscolastica* 74(4):579–92.
———. 1988. "Fichte, Schlegel und der Infinitismus in der Platondeutung."

Deutsche Vierteljahrsschrift für Literaturwissenschaft und Geistesgeschichte 4:583–621.

———. 1990a. *Plato and the Foundations of Metaphysics*. Trans. John R. Catan. Albany: State University of New York Press.

———. 1990b "Zur Aktuellen Diskussion um den Philosophiebegriff Platons." *Perspektiven der Philosophie* 19:85–107.

———. 1994. "Das neue Platonbild." *Zeitschrift für philosophische Forschung* 48:1–20.

Kraut, Richard. 1983. "Comments on Gregory Vlastos' 'The Socratic Elenchus.'" *Oxford Studies in Ancient Philosophy* 1:59–70.

———. 1984. *Socrates and the State*. Princeton: Princeton University Press.

Kretzmann, Norman. 1971. "Plato on the Correctness of Names." *American Philosophical Quarterly* 8:126–38.

Kuhn, Helmut. 1968. "Plato und die Grenze philosophischer Mitteilung." In *Idee und Zahl: Studien zur platonischen Philosophie*, ed. H. G. Gadamer and W. Schadewaldt, 151–73. Heidelberg: C. Winter.

Laborderie, Jean. 1978. *Le dialogue Platonicien de la maturité*. Paris: Société d'édition 'Les Belles Lettres.'

Lafrance, Yvon. 1980. "Platon et la géométrie: la méthode dialectique en République 509d-511e." *Dialogue* 19:46–93.

———. 1981. *La theorie Platonicienne de la doxa*. Montreal: Bellarmin, Paris: Les Belles Lettres.

———. 1982. "Les fonctions de la doxa-épistèmè dans les dialogues de Platon." *Laval Théologique et Philosophique* 38:115–35.

———. 1986. *Pour interpréter Platon: la ligne en République VI 509d–511e. Bilan analytique des études (1804–1984)*. Montreal: Editions Bellarmin.

———. 1994. *Pour interpréter Platon: la ligne en République VI, 509d–511e. Le texte et son histoire*. Vol. 2. Montreal: Editions Bellarmin.

Lasso de la Vega, J. S. 1968. "El diálogo y la filosofia Platónica." *Estudios Classicos* 54:311–74.

Ledger, Gerard R. 1989. *Re-counting Plato: A Computer Analysis of Plato's Style*. Oxford: Clarendon Press.

Levin, Susan B. 1995. "What's in a Name? A Reconsideration of the *Cratylus*' Historical Sources and Topics." *Ancient Philosophy* 15:91–115.

Levinson, M., A. Q. Morton and A. D. Windspear. 1968. "The Seventh Letter of Plato." *Mind* 77:309–25.

Levinson, Ronald B. 1957. "Language and the *Cratylus:* Four Questions." *Review of Metaphysics* 11(1):28–41.

Lloyd, A. C. 1969–70. "Non-discursive Thought: An Enigma of Greek Philosophy." *Aristotelian Society Proceedings* 70:261–74.

Lorenz, Kuno, and Jürgen Mittelstrass. 1967. "On Rational Philosophy of Language: The Programme of Plato's *Cratylus* Reconsidered." *Psychology and Philosophy* 76(301):1–20.

Lutoslawski, Wincenty. 1897. *The Origin and Growth of Plato's Logic*. London: Longmans, Green.

MacIntyre, Alasdair. 1988. *Whose Justice? Which Rationality?* Notre Dame, Ind.: University of Notre Dame Press.

WORKS CITED

Mahoney, Timothy A. 1996. "The *Charmides:* Socratic *Sōphrosunē,* Human *Sōphrosunē.*" *Southern Journal of Philosophy* 34:183–99.
Matson, Wallace I., and Adam Leite. 1991. "Socrates' Critique of Cognitivism." *Philosophy* 66:145–67.
McCabe, Mary Margaret. 1992. "Myth, Allegory and Argument in Plato." *Apeiron* 25(4):47–67.
McKim, Richard. 1985. "Socratic Self-knowledge and 'Knowledge of Knowledge' in Plato's *Charmides.*" *Transactions of the American Philological Association* 115:59–77.
Miller, Mitchell. 1985. "Platonic Provocations: Reflections on the Soul and the Good in the *Republic.*" In *Platonic Investigations,* ed. Dominic J. O'Meara, 163–93. Washington, D.C.: Catholic University of America Press.
Moline, Jon. 1981. *Plato's Theory of Understanding.* Madison: University of Wisconsin Press.
Moravcsik, Julius M. E. 1979. "Understanding and Knowledge in Plato's Philosophy." *Neue Hefte für Philosophie* 15/16:53–69.
———. 1982. "Noetic Aspiration and Artistic Inspiration." In *Plato on Beauty, Wisdom and the Arts,* ed. Julius Moravcsik and Philip Tempo, 29–46. Totowa, N.J.: Rowman and Littlefield.
Morgan, Michael L. 1983. "Belief, Knowledge, and Learning in Plato's Middle Dialogues." *Canadian Journal of Philosophy,* Supp. 9:63–100.
———. 1989. "How does Plato Solve the Paradox of Inquiry in the *Meno?* " In *Essays in Ancient Greek Philosophy 3: Plato,* ed. J. P. Anton and A. Preus, 169–82. Albany: SUNY Press.
Morris, T. F. 1989. "Knowledge of Knowledge and of the Lack of Knowledge in the *Charmides.*" *International Studies in Philosophy* 21:49–61.
Morrow, Glenn R. 1962. *Plato's Epistles.* Indianapolis: Bobbs-Merrill.
Müller, Gerhard. 1986. "Die Philosophie im pseudoplatonischen Brief." In *Platonische Studien,* ed. Andreas Graeser and Dieter Maue, 146–71. Heidelberg: Carl Winter Universitätsverlag.
Murray, Penelope. 1992. "Inspiration and *Mimēsis* in Plato." *Apeiron* 25(4):27–46.
———. 1996. *Plato on Poetry.* Cambridge: Cambridge University Press.
Nails, Debra. 1992. "Platonic Chronology Reconsidered." *Bryn Mawr Classical Review* 3:314–27.
———. 1993. "Problems with Vlastos' Platonic Developmentalism." *Ancient Philosophy* 13:273–91.
———. 1994. "Plato's Middle Cluster." *Phoenix* 48:62–67.
———. 1995. *Agora, Academy, and the Conduct of Philosophy.* Dordrecht: Kluwer.
Narcy, Michel. 1984. *Le Philosophe et son double: un commentaire de l'Euthydeme de Platon.* Paris: J. Vrin.
Natorp, Paul. 1921. *Platos Ideenlehre.* 2d ed. Leipzig: F. Meiner.
Nehamas, Alexander. 1975. "Confusing Universals and Particulars in Plato's Early Dialogues." *Review of Metaphysics* 29:287–306.
———. 1982. "Plato on Imitation and Poetry in *Republic* 10." In *Plato on Beauty, Wisdom and the Arts,* ed. Julius Moravcsik and Philip Tempo, 47–78. Totowa, N.J.: Rowman and Littlefield.

———. 1989. "*Epistēmē* and *Logos* in Plato's Later Thought." In *Essays in Ancient Greek Philosophy: Plato*, vol. 3, ed. John P. Anton and Anthony Preus, 267–92. Albany: State University of New York Press.

———. 1992. "Meno's Paradox and Socrates as a Teacher." *Essays on the Philosophy of Socrates*, ed. Hugh H. Benson, 298–316. New York: Oxford University Press.

Niewöhner, Friedrich Wilhelm. 1971. *Dialog und Dialektik in Platon's "Parmenides."* Meisenheim am Glan: A. Hain.

Novotný, Frantisek. 1930. *Platonis epistulae commentariis illustratae.* Brno: Vydava Filosoficka Fakulta.

Nuño Montes, Juan A. 1962. *La dialectica Platonica.* Caracas: Universidad Central de Venezuela.

Nussbaum, Martha. 1986. *The Fragility of Goodness.* Cambridge: Cambridge University Press.

O'Brien, Michael. 1971. "The Unity of the Laches." In *Essays in Ancient Greek Philosophy*, ed. John P. Anton and Anthony P. Preus, 1:303–15. Albany: State University of New York Press.

Palmer, Michael D. 1989. *Names, Reference and Correctness in Plato's Cratylus.* New York: Peter Lang.

Penner, Terry. 1992a. "Socrates and the Early Dialogues." In *The Cambridge Companion to Plato*, ed. Richard Kraut, 121–69. Cambridge: Cambridge University Press.

———. 1992b. "The Unity of Virtue." In *Essays on the Philosophy of Socrates*, ed. Hugh Benson, 162–84. New York: Oxford University Press. First published in *Philosophical Review* 82 (1973): 35–68.

———. 1992c. "What Laches and Nicias Miss—And Whether Socrates Thinks Courage Merely a Part of Virtue." *Ancient Philosophy* 12:1–27.

Polansky, Ronald. 1985. "Professor Vlastos' Analysis of Socratic Elenchus." *Oxford Studies in Ancient Philosophy* 3:247–60.

———. 1992. *Philosophy and Knowledge.* London and Toronto: Associated University Presses.

Price, H. H. 1969. *Belief.* London: George Allen & Unwin.

Rappe, Sara L. 1995. "Socrates and Self-Knowledge." *Apeiron* 28:1–24.

Rawson, Glenn. 1996. "Knowledge and Desire of the Good in Plato's *Republic*." *Southwest Philosophy Review* 12:103–15.

Reale, G. 1989. *Per una nuova interpretatione di Platone: relettura della metafisica dei grandi dialoghi alla luce delle "Dottrine non scritte."* 6th ed. Milan: Università Cattolica del Sacro Cuore.

———. 1990. *Plato and Aristotle: A History of Ancient Philosophy.* Ed. and trans. John R. Catan. Albany: State University of New York Press.

Reeve, C. D. C. 1988. *Philosopher-Kings: The Argument of Plato's* Republic. Princeton: Princeton University Press.

Richardson, Mary. 1976. "True and False Names in the *Cratylus*." *Phronesis* 21:135–45.

Rist, John. 1964. "Knowing How and Knowing That." In *Eros and Psyche: Studies in Plato, Plotinus and Origen*, 115–41. Toronto: University of Toronto Press.

Roberts, Jean. 1984. "Knowing about Understanding: A Discussion of J. Moline's *Plato's Theory of Understanding.*" *Oxford Studies in Ancient Philosophy* 2:223–35.
Robinson, Richard. 1953. *Plato's Earlier Dialectic.* 2d ed., Oxford: Clarendon Press. 1st ed., Ithaca, N.Y.: Cornell University Press, 1941.
———. 1954. "L'emploi des hypothèses selon Platon." *Revue de Métaphysique et de Morale* 59:253–68.
———. 1969a. "The Theory of Names in Plato's *Cratylus.*" In *Essays in Greek Philosophy,* 100–17. Oxford: Clarendon Press.
———. 1969b. "A Criticism of Plato's *Cratylus.*" In *Essays in Greek Philosophy,* 118–38. Oxford: Clarendon Press.
Robinson, T. M. 1992. "Plato and the Computer." *Ancient Philosophy* 12:375–82.
Roochnik, David. 1988. "Terence Irwin's Reading of Plato." In *Platonic Writings, Platonic Readings,* ed. Charles Griswold, 183–93. New York: Routledge, Chapmann & Hall.
———. 1989. "The Tragic Philosopher: A Critique of Martha Nussbaum." *Ancient Philosophy* 8:285–99.
———. 1990. *The Tragedy of Reason: Toward a Platonic Conception of Logos.* New York: Routledge.
———. 1990b. "The Serious Play of Plato's *Euthydemus.*" *Interpretation* 18:211–33.
———. 1992. "Socrates' Use of the Techne Analogy." In *Essays on the Philosophy of Socrates,* ed. Hugh Benson, 185–97. New York: Oxford University Press. First published in *Journal of the History of Philosophy* 24 (1986): 295–310.
———. 1995. "Socrates' Rhetorical Attack on Rhetoric." In *The Third Way: New Directions in Platonic Studies,* ed. Francisco J. Gonzalez, 81–94. Lanham, Md.: Rowman & Littlefield.
———. 1996. *Of Art and Wisdom: Plato's Understanding of Techne.* University Park: Pennsylvania State University Press.
Rorty, Richard. 1979. *Philosophy and the Mirror of Nature.* Princeton: Princeton University Press.
Rosen, Stanley. 1986. "Platonic Hermeneutics: On the Interpretation of a Platonic Dialogue. Reply to Cynthia Freeland." In *Proceedings of the Boston Area Colloquium in Ancient Philosophy,* ed. John Cleary, 1:296–97. New York: University Press of America.
———. 1990. "La querelle entre la philosophie et la poésie." In *La naissance de la raison en Grèce,* ed. Jean-Francois Mattéi, 325–31. Paris: Presse Universitaires de France.
Ross, Kelley L. 1987. "Non-intuitive Immediate Knowledge." *Ratio* 29:163–79.
Ross, W. D. 1951. *Plato's Theory of Ideas.* Oxford: Clarendon Press.
Rossetti, Livio. 1989. "The Rhetoric of Socrates." *Philosophy and Rhetoric* 22:225–38
———. 1990. "Sulla dimensione retorica del dialogare socratico." *Méthexis* 3:15–32.
Rowe, Christopher J. 1993a. *Plato: Phaedo.* Cambridge: Cambridge University Press.
———. 1993b. "Explanation in *Phaedo* 99C6–102A8." *Oxford Studies in Ancient Philosophy* 11:49–69.
———. 1996. "A Reply to van Eck." *Oxford Studies in Ancient Philosophy* 14:227–40.

Russell, Bertrand. 1963. "Knowledge by Acquaintance and Knowledge by Description." In *Mysticism and Logic,* 152–67. London: Unwin Books.
Rutherford, R. B. 1995. *The Art of Plato.* Cambridge, Mass.: Harvard University Press.
Ryle, Gilbert. 1949. *The Concept of Mind.* London: Hutchinson.
———. 1966. *Plato's Progress.* Cambridge: Cambridge University Press.
Sallis, John. 1996. *Being and Logos: Reading the Platonic Dialogues.* 3d ed. Indianapolis: Indiana University Press.
Santas, Gerasimos Xenophon. 1969. "Socrates at Work on Virtue and Knowledge in Plato's *Laches.*" *Review of Metaphysics* 22:433–60.
———. 1972. "The Socratic Fallacy." *Journal of the History of Philosophy* 10:127–41.
———. 1973a. "Hintikka on Knowledge and Its Objects in Plato." In *Patterns in Plato's Thought,* ed. J. M. E. Moravcsik, 31–51. Dordecht: Reidel.
———. 1973b. "Socrates at Work on Virtue and Knowledge in Plato's *Charmides.*" In *Exegesis and Argument: Studies in Greek Philosophy Presented to Gregory Vlastos,* ed. E. N. Lee, A. P. D. Mourelatos, and R. M. Rorty, 105–32. Phronesis Supplementary Vol. 1. Amsterdam: Assen.
———. 1983. "The Form of the Good in Plato's *Republic.*" In *Essays in Ancient Greek Philosophy,* ed. John P. Anton and Anthony Preus, 2:232–63. Albany: State University of New York Press.
Sayre, Kenneth. 1969. *Plato's Analytic Method.* Chicago: University of Chicago Press.
———. 1983. *Plato's Late Ontology.* Princeton: Princeton University Press.
———. 1988a. "Plato's Dialogues in the Light of the *Seventh Letter.*" In *Platonic Readings, Platonic Writings,* ed. Charles Griswold, 93–109. New York: Routledge, Chapman & Hall.
———. 1988b. "Reply to Jon Moline." In *Platonic Readings, Platonic Writings,* ed. Charles Griswold, 240–46. New York: Routledge, Chapman & Hall.
———. 1993a. "Why Plato Never Had a Theory of Forms." In *Proceedings of the Boston Area Colloquium in Ancient Philosophy,* ed. John J. Clearly and William Wians, 9:167–99. Lanham, Md.: University Press of America.
———. 1993b. Review of *Plato and the Foundations of Metaphysics,* by H. J. Krämer. *Ancient Philosophy* 13:167–84.
———. 1995. *Plato's Literary Garden: How to Read a Platonic Dialogue.* Notre Dame, Ind.: University of Notre Dame Press.
Schaerer, René. 1969. *La questionne Platonicienne.* 2d. ed., Neuchatel: Secretariat de l'Université.
Schleiermacher, F. E. D. 1839. *Geschichte der Philosophie: Aus Schleiermachers handschriftlichen Nachlasse.* Ed. H. Ritter. In *Sämmtliche Werke III,* 4, 1. Berlin: G. Reimer.
———. 1857. *Platons Werke.* 3d ed. Berlin: Georg Reimer.
———. [1836] 1973. *Introductions to the Dialogues of Plato.* Trans. William Dobson. Reprint, New York: Arno Press.
Schmid, Walter T. 1992. *On Manly Courage: A Study of Plato's Laches.* Carbondale: Southern Illinois University Press.
Schofield, Malcolm. 1982. "The Dénouement of the *Cratylus.*" In *Language and*

Logos, ed. Malcolm Schofield and Martha Craven Nussbaum, 61–81. Cambridge: Cambridge University Press.

Seeskin, Kenneth. 1987. *Dialogue and Discovery: A Study in Socratic Method.* Albany: State University of New York Press.

———. 1993. "Vlastos on Elenchus and Mathematics." *Ancient Philosophy* 13:37–53.

Sharples, R. W. 1985. *Plato's Meno.* Chicago: Bolchazy-Carducci.

Shorey, Paul. 1980. "The Idea of the Good in Plato's *Republic:* A Study in the Logic of Speculative Ethics." In *Selected Papers,* 2:28–79. New York: Garland.

Silverman, Allan. 1992. "Plato's *Cratylus:* The Naming of Nature and the Nature of Naming." *Oxford Studies in Ancient Philosophy* 10:25–71.

Sinaiko, H. L. 1965. *Love, Knowledge, and Discourse in Plato: Dialogue and Dialectic in Phaedrus, Republic, Parmenides.* Chicago: University of Chicago Press.

Smith, N. D. 1979. "Knowledge by Acquaintance and 'Knowing What' in Plato's *Republic.*" *Dialogue* 18:281–88.

Solmsen, F. 1969. Review of *Plato's Seventh Letter* by Ludwig Edelstein. *Gnomon* 41:29–34.

Sorabji, Richard. 1982. "Myths about Non-propositional Thought." In *Language and Logos,* ed. Malcom Schofield and Martha Craven Nussbaum, 295–314. Cambridge: Cambridge University Press.

Souilhé, Joseph. 1960. *Lettres.* Vol. 13, 1st part of *Platon: oeuvres complètes* (Budé edition). Paris: Société d'Edition 'Les Belles Lettres.'

Sprague, Rosamond Kent. 1962. *Plato's Use of Fallacy: A Study of the Euthydemus and Some Other Dialogues.* London: Routledge & Kegan Paul.

———. 1968. "Socrates' Safest Answer: *Phaedo* 100D." *Hermes* 96:632–35.

———, ed. and trans. 1973. *Laches and Charmides.* Indianapolis: Bobbs-Merrill.

———. 1976. *Plato's Philosopher-King: A Study of the Theoretical Background.* Columbia: University of South Carolina Press.

———. 1977. "Plato's Sophistry." *Proceedings of the Aristotelian Society,* Suppl. 51:45–61.

Sprute, J. 1962. *Der Begriff der Doxa in der platonischen Philosophie.* Göttingen: Vandenhoeck & Ruprecht.

Stallbaum, Godofredus. 1835–36. *Platonis Opera Omnia.* Vols. 5–6. Gotha and Erfurt, Germany: G. Hennings.

Stefanini, Luigi. 1932. *Platone.* 2 vols. Padova: CEDAM.

Stemmer, Peter. 1992. *Platons Dialektik: Die früheren und mittleren Dialoge.* Berlin: Walter de Gruyter.

Stenzel, Julius. 1940. *Plato's Method of Dialectic.* Trans. and ed. D. J. Allan. Oxford: Clarendon Press.

———. 1956. "Der Begriff der Erleuchtung bei Platon." In *Kleine Schriften zur griechischen Philosophie,* 151–70. Darmstadt: Wissenschaftliche Buchgesellschaft.

Stephens, James. 1993. "Plato on Dialectic and Dialogue." *Journal of Value Inquiry* 27:465–73.

Sternfeld, Robert, and Harold Zyskind. 1977. "Plato's *Meno:* 86E–87A: The Geometrical Illustration of the Argument by Hypothesis." *Phronesis* 22(3):206–11.

———. 1978. *Plato's Meno: A Philosophy of Man as Acquisitive*. Carbondale: Southern Illinois University Press.

Stewart, M. A. 1977. "Plato's Sophistry." *Proceedings of the Aristotelian Society*, Suppl. 51:20–44.

Szlezák, Thomas Alexander. 1978. "Probleme der Platoninterpretation." *Göttingische Gelehrte Anzeigen* 230:1–37.

———. 1980. "Sokrates Spott über Geheimhaltung: zum Bild des φιλόσοφος in Platons *Euthydemus*." *Antike und Abendland* 26:75–89.

———. 1985. *Platon und die Schriftlichkeit der Philosophie*. Berlin: Walter de Gruyter.

———. 1989. "Platon und die neuzeitliche Theorie des platonischen Dialogs." *Elenchos* 10:337–57.

Tarán, Leonardo. 1985. "Platonism and Socratic Ignorance." In *Platonic Investigations*, ed. Dominic J. O'Meara, 85–110. Washington, D.C.: Catholic University of America Press.

Tait, W. W. 1986. "Plato's Second Best Method." *Review of Metaphysics* 39:455–82.

Tarrant, Harrold. 1983. "Middle Platonism and the Seventh Letter." *Phronesis* 28:75–103.

———. 1993. *Thrasyllan Platonism*. Ithaca: Cornell University Press.

Tate, J. 1928. "'Imitation' in Plato's *Republic*." *Classical Quarterly* 22:16–23.

Taylor, A. E. 1959. *Plato*. New York: Meridan Books.

Tecuşan, Manuela. 1992. "Speaking about the Unspeakable: Plato's Use of Imagery." *Apeiron* 25(4):69–87.

Tejera, Victorino. 1978. "Methodology of a Misreading: A Critical Note on T. Irwin's 'Plato's Moral Theory.'" *International Studies in Philosophy* 10:131–36.

Teloh, Henry. 1981. *The Development of Plato's Metaphysics*. University Park: Pennsylvania State University Press.

———. 1986. *Socratic Education in Plato's Early Dialogues*. Notre Dame, Ind.: University of Notre Dame Press.

Thesleff, Holger. 1982. *Studies in Platonic Chronology*. Helsinki: Societas Scientiarum Fennica.

———. 1989. "Platonic Chronology." *Phronesis* 34:1–26.

Thurnher, Rainer. 1975. *Der Siebte Platonbrief*. Meisenheim am Glan: Verlag Anton Hain.

Tigerstedt, E. N. 1977. *Interpreting Plato*. Stockholm: Almquist & Wiksell.

Tuckey, T. G. 1968. *Plato's Charmides*. Amsterdam: Adolf M. Hakkert.

Tulli, Mauro. 1989. *Dialettica e scrittura nella VII Lettera di Platone*. Pisa: Giardini.

Valditara, Linda M. Napolitano. 1991. "ΤΙ ΕΣΤΙ—ΠΟΙΟΝ ΕΣΤΙ: Un aspetto dell'argomentatività dialettica del *Menone*." *Elenchos* 12:197–220.

Verdenius, Wilhelm Jacob. 1945. "Platon et la poesie." *Mnemosyne* 12:118–50.

———. 1949. *Mimesis: Plato's Doctrine of Artistic Imitation and Its Meaning to Us*. Leiden: E. J. Brill.

Viano, C. A. 1952. "Il Significato della 'doxa' nella filosofia di Platone." *Rivista di Filosofia* 43:167–85.

WORKS CITED

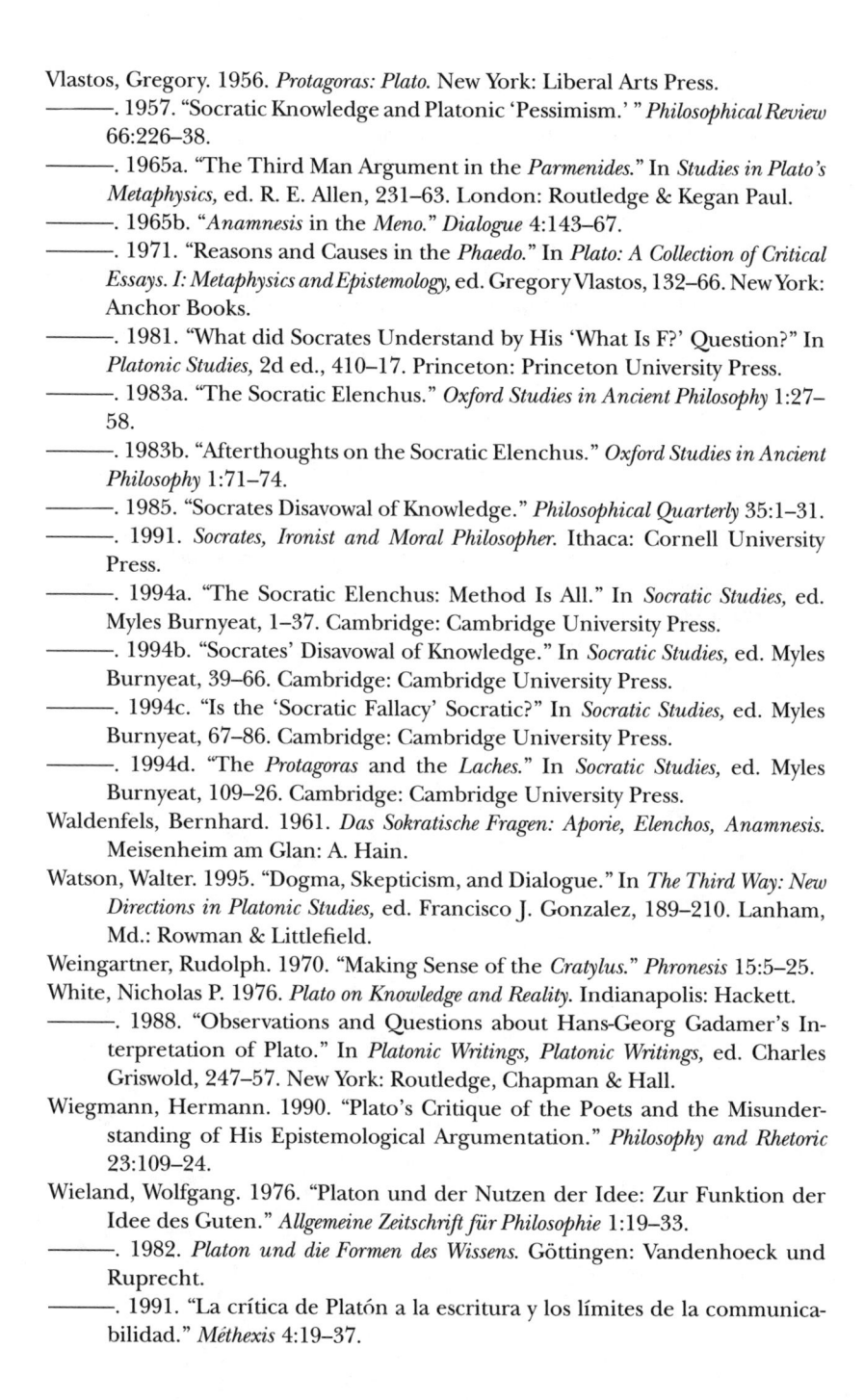

Vlastos, Gregory. 1956. *Protagoras: Plato.* New York: Liberal Arts Press.
———. 1957. "Socratic Knowledge and Platonic 'Pessimism.'" *Philosophical Review* 66:226–38.
———. 1965a. "The Third Man Argument in the *Parmenides*." In *Studies in Plato's Metaphysics,* ed. R. E. Allen, 231–63. London: Routledge & Kegan Paul.
———. 1965b. "*Anamnesis* in the *Meno*." *Dialogue* 4:143–67.
———. 1971. "Reasons and Causes in the *Phaedo*." In *Plato: A Collection of Critical Essays. I: Metaphysics and Epistemology,* ed. Gregory Vlastos, 132–66. New York: Anchor Books.
———. 1981. "What did Socrates Understand by His 'What Is F?' Question?" In *Platonic Studies,* 2d ed., 410–17. Princeton: Princeton University Press.
———. 1983a. "The Socratic Elenchus." *Oxford Studies in Ancient Philosophy* 1:27–58.
———. 1983b. "Afterthoughts on the Socratic Elenchus." *Oxford Studies in Ancient Philosophy* 1:71–74.
———. 1985. "Socrates Disavowal of Knowledge." *Philosophical Quarterly* 35:1–31.
———. 1991. *Socrates, Ironist and Moral Philosopher.* Ithaca: Cornell University Press.
———. 1994a. "The Socratic Elenchus: Method Is All." In *Socratic Studies,* ed. Myles Burnyeat, 1–37. Cambridge: Cambridge University Press.
———. 1994b. "Socrates' Disavowal of Knowledge." In *Socratic Studies,* ed. Myles Burnyeat, 39–66. Cambridge: Cambridge University Press.
———. 1994c. "Is the 'Socratic Fallacy' Socratic?" In *Socratic Studies,* ed. Myles Burnyeat, 67–86. Cambridge: Cambridge University Press.
———. 1994d. "The *Protagoras* and the *Laches*." In *Socratic Studies,* ed. Myles Burnyeat, 109–26. Cambridge: Cambridge University Press.
Waldenfels, Bernhard. 1961. *Das Sokratische Fragen: Aporie, Elenchos, Anamnesis.* Meisenheim am Glan: A. Hain.
Watson, Walter. 1995. "Dogma, Skepticism, and Dialogue." In *The Third Way: New Directions in Platonic Studies,* ed. Francisco J. Gonzalez, 189–210. Lanham, Md.: Rowman & Littlefield.
Weingartner, Rudolph. 1970. "Making Sense of the *Cratylus*." *Phronesis* 15:5–25.
White, Nicholas P. 1976. *Plato on Knowledge and Reality.* Indianapolis: Hackett.
———. 1988. "Observations and Questions about Hans-Georg Gadamer's Interpretation of Plato." In *Platonic Writings, Platonic Writings,* ed. Charles Griswold, 247–57. New York: Routledge, Chapman & Hall.
Wiegmann, Hermann. 1990. "Plato's Critique of the Poets and the Misunderstanding of His Epistemological Argumentation." *Philosophy and Rhetoric* 23:109–24.
Wieland, Wolfgang. 1976. "Platon und der Nutzen der Idee: Zur Funktion der Idee des Guten." *Allgemeine Zeitschrift für Philosophie* 1:19–33.
———. 1982. *Platon und die Formen des Wissens.* Göttingen: Vandenhoeck und Ruprecht.
———. 1991. "La crítica de Platón a la escritura y los límites de la communicabilidad." *Méthexis* 4:19–37.

Wiggins, David. 1986. "Teleology and the Good in Plato's *Phaedo.*" *Oxford Studies in Ancient Philosophy* 4:1–18.
Wilamowitz-Moellendorf, Ulrich von. 1959. *Platon: Sein Leben und Seine Werke.* 5th ed. Berlin: Weidmannsche Verlagsbuchhandlung.
Williams, Bernard. 1982. "Cratylus' Theory of Names and Its Refutation." In *Language and Logos,* ed. Malcolm Schofield and Martha Craven Nussbaum, 83–93. Cambridge: Cambridge University Press.
Wittgenstein, Ludwig. 1922. *Tractatus-Logico Philosophicus.* Trans. C. K. Ogden with parallel German text. London: Routledge & Kegan Paul.
Woodruff, Paul. 1978. "The Socratic Approach to Semantic Incompleteness." *Philosophy and Phenomenological Research* 38:453–68.
———. 1982. "Why Plato's Poets Fail." In *Plato on Beauty, Wisdom and the Arts,* ed. Julius Moravcsik and Philip Tempo, 137–50. Totowa, N.J.: Rowman and Littlefield.
———. 1986. "The Skeptical Side of Plato's Method." *Revue Internationale de Philosophie* 40:22–37.
———. 1990. "Plato's Early Theory of Knowledge." In *Epistemology,* ed. Stephen Everson, 60–84. Cambridge: Cambridge University Press.
Young, Charles M. 1994. "Plato and Computer Dating." *Oxford Studies in Ancient Philosophy* 12:227–50.
Zimbrich, Ulrike. 1984. *Mimesis bei Platon.* Frankfurt am Main: Peter Lang.

Name Index

Adam, James, 324n. 9, 325–26n. 18, 357n. 1, 376n. 81
Allen, R. E., 342n. 51
Anagnostopoulos, Georgios, 307n. 31
Andic, Martin, 341nn. 44, 47
Annas, Julia, 229, 311n. 60, 325n. 17, 327n. 28, 365n. 26, 367nn. 36–37, 369nn. 44, 49, 370nn. 52–53, 371n. 55, 375n. 79, 376n. 86
Archer-Hind, R. D., 351n. 8, 353n. 18
Arieti, James, 145, 278n. 15, 287n. 19, 292n. 42, 305n. 21, 331n. 3
Aristotle, 6, 12, 106, 116, 283n. 47, 314n. 12, 320n. 51, 331n. 6, 342n. 52, 355n. 26, 360n. 12, 367n. 37
Ast, F., 1, 277n. 10

Baxter, Timothy M. S., 302n. 3, 303n. 10, 304–5n. 18, 305nn. 20, 22, 24, 306nn. 25, 28, 307nn. 29, 31, 33, 35, 308nn. 37–38, 40, 309n. 50, 310n. 56, 311nn. 56, 59, 312n. 64
Bedu-Addo, J. T., 337n. 31, 350n. 87, 363nn. 19–20, 375n. 79
Benitez, Eugenio, 346n. 74, 367n. 36
Benson, Hugh, 281n. 33, 284n. 52, 285n. 2, 286n. 10, 288nn. 21–22, 292n. 40, 297n. 67, 333n. 13, 337n. 31
Berti, Enrico, 279n. 20
Bertozzi, A., 368n. 40
Beversluis, John, 287–88n. 21, 289n. 23, 333n. 13
Blachowicz, James, 338n. 34, 339n. 41, 341n. 43, 347n. 75
Bloom, Allan, 323n. 1, 324n. 13, 325n. 15, 327n. 22
Bluck, R. S., 331n. 8, 342n. 52, 343n. 54, 348nn. 77, 81, 349n. 83, 350n. 88, 379nn. 7, 10, 380nn. 11, 13–14, 381n. 20, 382n. 36, 384n. 43, 384–85n. 53
Bonitz, Hermann, 293n.45, 295n. 53, 316n. 22, 321n. 54, 322n. 58
Bostock, David, 351n. 9, 352n. 12, 353–54n. 19, 354–55n. 22, 356n. 29, 357n. 31
Boyle, A. J., 363n. 19, 371n. 56, 371–72n. 58, 375n. 79, 375–76n. 80, 377n. 93
Brickhouse, T., 281n. 32, 286n. 10, 289n. 23, 290n. 24, 335n. 21, 346–47n. 75
Brown, M. S., 337n. 31, 350n. 87
Brumbaugh, Robert S., 374n. 69
Burger, R., 345n. 71, 349n. 82
Burnet, John, 351n. 6, 354n. 22, 357n. 32
Burnyeat, M. F., 229–30, 288n. 21, 289n. 23, 343n. 59, 343–44n. 60, 367n. 37, 370n. 52
Bury, R. G., 266, 379n. 7, 380nn. 10, 17, 381n. 19

Canto, Monique, 102, 313n. 2, 314nn. 6, 10, 317nn. 24–29, 318n. 31, 319nn. 39, 43, 320n. 53, 321n. 54, 322nn. 65, 67–68, 323n. 71
Chance, Thomas, 314n. 12, 315n. 15, 316n. 20, 317nn. 25, 28, 319nn. 43, 45, 320nn. 47, 49, 321nn. 54–55, 322nn. 60, 62, 65–66
Cherniss, Harold, 353n. 18, 366n. 33
Cicovacki, Predrag, 347n. 75
Commenius, 307n. 31, 311n. 56
Cornford, F. M., 364nn. 21, 26, 374n. 66, 376nn. 83, 88, 91
Cross, R. C., 331n. 8, 364n. 24, 366n. 35, 368–69n. 43, 375n. 79

Deane, P., 378n. 1

405

NAME INDEX

Derbolav, Joseph, 308n. 41, 309n. 43, 310nn. 52, 54, 312nn. 65, 67, 384n. 44
Descartes, René, 365n. 28
Desjardins, R., 334n. 14, 337n. 31, 341n. 47, 342n. 51, 348n. 81, 350n. 84
Devereux, Daniel T., 291n. 32
Dewey, John, 365n. 28
Dimas, Panagiotis, 331nn. 7–8, 336n. 23, 338n. 36, 339n. 41, 340n. 42
Diogenes Laertius, 322n. 64, 323n. 3
Dorter, Kenneth, 343n. 57, 351nn. 5–6, 8, 353n. 18

Ebert, Theodor, 213–15, 296n. 63, 332nn. 10–11, 336n. 28, 338n. 35, 359–60n. 9, 361n. 14, 367n. 35, 372n. 59
Eck, Job van, 353n. 14, 354n. 20, 356–57n. 30
Edelstein, Ludwig, 272, 378n. 2, 379n. 5, 386n. 59
Elias, Julias A., 281n. 34, 330n. 1
Erler, M., 286n. 11
Eustathius, 351n. 2

Ferber, Rafael, 213–15, 238, 279n. 19, 284n. 49, 357n. 2, 358–59n. 8, 360n. 11, 371n. 56, 372n. 60, 373n. 65, 376nn. 87, 90, 379n. 8, 381nn. 18, 23, 382nn. 25–26, 383nn. 38–39, 42, 384n. 51, 385n. 56, 386n. 57, 387n. 61
Ferrari, G. R. F., 324nn. 8, 10, 325n. 15, 327n. 21, 328nn. 28–29, 32, 34, 36
Findlay, J. N., 5–6, 300n. 81, 305n. 21, 382n. 33, 384n. 47
Fine, Gail, 89, 156, 229, 280nn. 26, 29, 289n. 23, 310n. 56, 331nn. 5–8, 332n. 11, 339–40n. 42, 343–44n. 60, 344n. 64, 346–47n. 75, 348n. 81, 367n. 36, 369n. 48, 370nn. 50, 53, 371nn. 54–55, 374n. 66, 375n. 74
Friedländer, Paul, 315n. 15, 325n. 14, 328nn. 30, 35, 353n. 18
Fritz, Kurt von, 378n. 2, 378–79n. 4, 381n. 24, 384n. 49
Furley, David, 376n. 82

Gadamer, Hans-Georg, 383n. 38
Gaiser, Konrad, 5, 10, 278nn. 15–16, 279nn. 19–20, 280n. 23, 281nn. 31, 37–38, 282nn. 39–41, 44, 283nn. 45, 48, 284n. 50, 286–87n. 12, 291n. 35, 296n. 65, 299n. 76, 310nn. 51, 55, 319n. 40, 341n. 44, 358n. 6, 371n. 56, 372n. 58, 379n. 9, 381n. 21
Gallop, David, 324n. 10, 326n. 19, 350n. 1, 353n. 18, 366n. 31
Geach, P. T., 287n. 21, 333n. 13
Gentzler, Jyl, 281n. 32, 284n. 52, 313n. 1, 336n. 27, 337n. 30, 347n. 75, 352nn. 11–13, 353n. 15
Goldschimdt, Victor, 286n. 11, 374n. 68, 375nn. 75–76, 376n. 85
Gonzalez, Francisco J., 276n. 9, 278nn. 13–14, 280n. 30, 294n. 47, 299n. 79, 301nn. 88, 90, 367n. 36, 385n. 55, 387n. 66
Gosling, J. C., 367n. 36
Gould, Carol S., 39–40, 294n. 51
Gould, John, 299n. 79, 365n. 27
Graeser, Andreas, 381n. 23, 382nn. 26–27, 32, 35, 383nn. 39–41
Grene, Marjorie, 333nn. 11–12, 341n. 43
Griswold, Charles, 278n. 14, 287n. 19, 290n. 27, 291nn. 32, 35, 294n. 48, 300n. 87, 319n. 43, 329n. 38
Grote, G., 78, 281n. 33, 307n. 32, 319n. 41
Grube, G. M. A., 296n. 63
Gully, Norman, 287n. 21, 333n. 13, 348n. 77, 366n. 35
Gundert, Hermann, 328n. 31, 341n. 49, 346n. 73, 374n. 68, 379nn. 7, 9, 380n. 17, 382n. 34, 384nn. 46, 50, 385n. 55, 386n. 60
Guthrie, W. K. C., 296n. 63, 297n. 66, 309n. 47, 310n. 56, 334n. 19, 363n. 18, 379n. 7, 380n. 17, 381n. 25, 382n. 34

Hackforth, R., 351n. 4, 353n. 18, 355n. 23, 357nn. 33–34, 369n. 44, 373n. 63, 374n. 66
Hare, R. M., 360n. 12, 364n. 23, 366n. 31, 369n. 45, 377n. 97
Harris, Roy, 311n. 59
Harward, J., 266, 379nn. 7, 10, 380nn. 14, 17
Hawtrey, R. S. W., 99, 313n. 3, 314n. 12, 317nn. 27, 29, 318n. 33, 319n. 43, 320n. 51, 321nn. 55–56, 322nn. 59, 63, 69
Hegel, G. W. F., 377n. 95
Heidegger, Martin, 279–80n. 23, 372n. 59

NAME INDEX

Hermann, Karl Friedrich, 276–78nn.10–11
Hinrichs, Gerard, 313n. 1
Hintikka, J., 299n. 79, 326n. 18, 366n. 35
Hitchcock, David, 358n. 3, 375n. 79
Hoerber, R. G., 292n. 42, 295n. 53, 334n. 16, 334–35n. 20, 341n. 47, 349nn. 81, 82
Howland, Jacob, 275n. 2
Hyland, Drew A., 293n. 45, 299n. 78, 327n. 24, 362n. 16, 377–78n. 98

Irwin, Terence, 278n. 11, 281n. 32, 289n. 23, 290n. 25, 291n. 33, 292n. 40, 293n. 46, 295n. 52, 298n. 71, 299n. 77, 336n. 25, 339–40n. 42, 357n. 1, 367n. 36, 369n. 48, 375n. 74
Isnardi-Parente, Margherita, 382n. 30, 382–83n. 37, 383n. 41
Isocrates, 322n. 65

Jacoby, Felix, 285n. 4

Kahn, Charles, 287n. 13, 302n. 7, 303nn. 12, 15, 307n. 35, 308nn. 39–40, 309n. 50, 310n. 56, 318n. 33, 319n. 43, 374n. 70
Kant, Immanuel, 386–87n. 61
Ketchum, Richard, 296n. 63, 298n. 71, 302n. 7, 303nn. 14–15
Keulen, Hermann, 314n. 7
Kierkegaard, Søren, 281n. 33
Klein, Jacob, 296n. 65, 331n. 4, 334nn. 17, 19, 336n. 24, 337n. 31, 338n. 38, 341nn. 44–45, 350n. 85
Klein, Sherwin, 334n. 16, 343n. 55
Klosko, George, 293–94n. 47
Kosman, L. A., 296n. 58, 300n. 83
Krämer, H. J., 5, 10–11, 13, 276n. 7, 278nn. 15–17, 279nn. 19–21, 280n. 23, 281nn. 31, 37–8, 282nn. 42–43, 283n. 48, 284n. 49, 357–58n. 2, 358n. 3, 371n. 56, 372n. 58, 373n. 64, 376n. 88, 379n. 9
Kraut, Richard, 281n. 33, 333n. 13, 335n. 21, 346n. 75
Kretzmann, Norman, 78, 302n. 9, 303nn. 11, 13, 310n. 56
Kuhn, Helmut, 283n. 47, 355n. 24

Laborderie, Jean, 324n. 9, 329n. 42

Lafrance, Yvon, 336n. 25, 337n. 31, 347–48n. 77, 348n. 81, 349n. 83, 362n. 18, 364nn. 21, 26, 365n. 28, 366n. 35, 367n. 35, 368n. 40, 369n. 43, 374n. 67, 375n. 77, 377n. 92
Lasso de la Vega, J. S., 328nn. 31, 34
Ledger, Gerard R., 378n. 1
Leibniz, G. W., 279n. 21, 307n. 31
Leite, Adam, 290n. 26
Levin, Susan B., 302n. 3, 305n. 18
Levinson, M., 378n. 1
Levinson, Ronald B., 312n. 62
Lloyd, A. C., 280nn. 26, 28
Lorenz, Kuno, 310n. 56, 311n. 57
Lutoslawski, Wincenty, 296n. 61

McCabe, Mary Margaret, 328n. 33
MacIntyre, Alasdair, 325n. 13
Mahoney, Timothy A., 297n. 67, 298n. 70, 299n. 76, 300n. 85
McKim, Richard, 297n. 66, 298nn. 71, 74, 299n. 76
Matson, Wallace I., 290n. 26
Miller, Mitchell, 360n. 12
Mittelstrass, Jürgen, 310n. 56, 311n. 57
Moline, Jon, 343nn. 59–60, 367n. 37
Moravcsik, Julius M. E., 327n. 27, 329–30n. 43, 343nn. 59–60, 367n. 37, 369n. 44, 370n. 52
Morgan, Michael L., 341n. 43, 363n. 19, 367n. 35, 368nn. 38, 40
Morris, T. F. 296n. 63, 297n. 67, 298nn. 70, 73
Morrow, Glenn R., 266, 378n. 1, 379n. 7, 380nn. 10, 14, 17, 381n. 19
Morton, A. Q., 378n. 1
Müller, Gerhard, 378n. 2, 383n. 41, 384n. 52
Murray, Penelope, 326n. 18, 328n. 28, 329nn. 39, 41

Nails, Debra, 275n. 2
Narcy, Michel, 314n. 8, 317n. 25, 319n. 41, 320nn. 48, 51–52, 322nn. 58, 69, 337n. 31, 339n. 39
Natorp, Paul, 318n. 34
Nehamas, Alexander, 178, 229–30, 285n. 2, 324nn. 8, 10, 325n. 15, 326n. 20, 327n. 25, 328n. 28, 331nn. 4–5, 8, 336n. 26, 337n. 30, 339n. 42, 343n. 59,

NAME INDEX

343–44n. 60, 344nn. 61–63, 65, 345n. 72, 348–49n. 81, 370n. 50
Niewöhner, Friedrich Wilhelm, 386n. 58
Novotny, Frantisek, 379n. 7, 380nn. 10, 16–17
Nuño Montes, Juan A., 376n. 89
Nussbaum, Martha, 291n. 31, 294n. 47, 295n. 52

O'Brien, Michael, 292n.42

Palmer, Michael D., 90, 302nn. 2, 6–7, 303nn. 12–13, 308n. 39, 310n. 56, 311n. 57, 312n. 63
Penner, Terry, 290n. 29, 292nn. 40–41, 298n. 71, 309n. 48, 335n. 21
Polansky, Ronald, 284n. 52, 301n. 88, 346n. 75
Price, H. H., 181, 301n. 90, 325n. 16, 346n. 74

Rappe, Sara L., 301n. 89
Rawson, Glenn, 357n. 1, 361n. 14
Reale, G., 278nn. 16–18, 279n. 21, 281n. 31, 282n. 45, 358n. 3, 371nn. 56–57, 373n. 63
Reeve, C. D. C., 326n. 18, 327n. 22, 361n. 14, 367n. 36, 370n. 49, 375n. 79
Richardson, Mary, 312n. 62
Rist, John, 299n. 79
Roberts, Jean, 345n. 67
Robinson, Richard, 2–3, 177, 196, 220–23, 229–31, 238, 240–42, 275–76nn. 3–6, 281nn. 33–34, 284n. 51, 285n. 3, 287n. 21, 301n. 1, 302nn. 7–8, 309n. 46, 310nn. 54, 56, 312n. 61, 323n. 4, 328–29n. 37, 330n. 1, 333n. 13, 342n. 52, 351–52n. 11, 352n. 13, 353nn. 15, 18–19, 355n. 25, 364nn. 21, 24, 365n. 28, 369n. 47, 375n. 77, 376–77n. 92, 377n. 94, 378n. 99
Robinson, T. M., 275n. 2
Roochnik, David, 278n. 11, 287n. 19, 292–93n. 42, 293–94n. 47–48, 295n. 52, 299nn. 75–76, 314n. 6, 316n. 19, 320n. 46
Rorty, Richard, 297–98n. 68
Rosen, Stanley, 324n. 11, 345n. 66
Ross, Kelley L., 333n. 11, 341n. 43
Ross, W. D., 287n. 21, 333nn. 11, 13, 333n. 13, 385n. 54

Rossetti, Livio, 315n. 16
Rowe, Christopher J., 350n. 1, 351nn. 3, 7, 352–53n. 14, 353nn. 16, 18, 354n. 20, 356–57n. 30
Russell, Bertrand, 310n. 56, 331–32n. 9, 333n. 12
Rutherford, R. B., 292n.42, 295n. 54, 322n. 65, 323n. 4, 327n. 24
Ryle, Gilbert, 280n. 24, 281n. 33, 286n. 10, 299n. 79

Sallis, John, 302nn. 3, 5, 304n. 17, 305nn. 19, 21–23, 306nn. 24, 26–27, 307n. 36, 309nn. 44–45, 47, 49, 312n. 63, 312nn. 66–68, 327n. 24, 334nn. 14–15, 341nn. 43, 47, 358n. 3, 368n. 42, 369n. 45, 374nn. 69, 72, 375n. 74
Santas, Gerasimos Xenophon, 39–40, 288n. 21, 290n. 29, 296nn. 60, 62–63, 298n. 69, 300n. 86, 359–60n. 9, 360n. 12, 361–62n. 15, 366–67n. 35, 369n. 46, 369–70n. 49, 376n. 90
Sayre, Kenneth, 229–31, 330n. 1, 331n. 3, 335–36n. 22, 339n. 40, 352n. 11, 353n. 17, 359n. 9, 360n. 12, 362n. 15, 363nn. 18, 20, 364n. 24, 366n. 33, 369nn. 44–45, 49, 370n. 51, 371n. 53, 372n. 61, 376n. 89, 378n. 1, 379n. 5, 381nn. 22–23, 383n. 41, 387nn. 63, 66
Schaerer, René, 327nn. 25–26, 328n. 31, 343nn. 56, 58, 345n. 69, 378n. 99
Schleiermacher, F. E. D., 3–6, 13, 78, 276–77nn. 7–10, 282n. 43
Schmid, Walter T., 287nn. 14–18, 290nn. 28–30, 291nn. 34–37, 292n.42, 294n. 50, 295n. 53, 300n. 87
Schofield, Malcolm, 304n. 16
Seeskin, Kenneth, 275n. 4, 281n. 35, 285n. 8, 290n. 24, 301n. 89, 330n. 1, 331n. 2, 334nn. 17–18, 20, 335n. 21, 336n. 27, 337n. 31, 338nn. 33, 36, 341nn. 48, 50, 342n. 51, 345n. 70, 347n. 75
Sharples, R. W., 331n. 8, 334n. 16, 337–38n. 31, 338n. 33, 349n. 83
Shorey, Paul, 361n. 14, 363n. 19, 364n. 22
Silverman, Allan, 302n. 4, 303n. 9, 303–4n. 15, 309nn. 41–42, 311n. 59
Sinaiko, H. L., 362n. 17, 373–74n. 66
Smith, N. D., 281n. 32, 286n. 10, 289n.

NAME INDEX

23, 290n. 24, 332–33n. 11, 335n. 21, 346–47n. 75
Solmsen, F., 378n. 2
Sorabji, Richard, 373n. 63
Souilhé, Joseph, 266, 379nn. 7, 10, 380nn. 14, 17, 381n. 19
Sprague, Rosamond Kent, 295–96n. 57, 297n. 66, 298n. 72, 314n. 5, 315n. 15, 316nn. 17, 20, 318n. 32, 319nn. 41, 43, 321n. 55, 322n. 57, 362n. 16
Sprute, J., 347n. 76, 349n. 82, 360n. 12, 368n. 40, 383n. 42
Stallbaum, Godofredus, 305n. 21
Stefanini, Luigi, 287n. 14, 291n. 32, 297n. 66, 298n. 71, 309n. 46, 319n. 36, 322n. 65, 330n. 44, 347n. 75, 350n. 88, 362n. 16, 368n. 41, 379n. 4, 387nn. 62, 65
Stemmer, Peter, 275n. 3, 281nn. 33, 35–36, 315n. 15, 339n. 42, 341n. 46, 343n. 55, 353n. 18, 361n. 14, 366nn. 31–32, 369n. 46, 373n. 62, 3747–5n. 73, 376n. 81, 387n. 65
Stenzel, Julius, 353n. 18, 355n. 24, 387n. 62
Stephens, James, 276n. 5
Sternfeld, Robert, 331nn. 3, 8, 336n. 29, 337n. 31, 338nn. 34, 37, 341n. 50, 341–42n. 51, 342n. 53, 345nn. 68, 72, 350n. 86
Stewart, M. A., 314n. 12, 319n. 42, 354n. 21
Szlezák, Thomas Alexander, 279n. 22, 283n. 46, 314n. 10, 317nn. 25, 27, 29, 318n. 33, 320nn. 47–48, 322n. 61, 381nn. 23, 25

Tait, W. W., 351nn. 3, 10–11, 353nn. 14, 18, 356nn. 27, 30
Tarán, Leonardo, 286–87n. 12
Tarrant, Harrold, 334n. 19, 378n. 3, 378n. 5, 386n. 59
Tate, J., 326n. 20, 327n. 25
Taylor, A. E., 285–86n. 9, 296n. 59
Tecuşan, Manuela, 323n. 4, 330n. 44
Tejera, Victorino, 278n. 11
Teloh, Henry, 300n. 85, 387n. 64
Theopompos of Chios, 285n. 4
Thesleff, Holger, 275n. 2
Thurnher, Rainer, 382nn. 28, 36
Tigerstedt, E. N., 278n. 15, 282n. 43

Tuckey, T. G., 296n. 63, 299–300n. 80
Tulli, Mauro, 379nn. 7–8, 380nn. 10, 16, 381nn. 20, 22, 382n. 25, 384n. 53

Valditara, Linda M. Napolitano, 334n. 13
Verdenius, Wilhelm Jacob, 324n. 9, 327n. 26, 329n. 40
Viano, C. A., 347n. 76
Vlastos, Gregory, 15, 21, 39–40, 202–3, 277n. 10, 281nn. 33–35, 284n. 52, 288n. 21, 292n. 40, 299n. 79, 309n. 48, 313n. 1, 317n. 29, 330n. 1, 333n. 13, 337nn. 30–31, 338nn. 34, 36, 339n. 41, 340n. 43, 345n. 70, 346–47n. 75, 348n. 81, 349n. 83, 350–51n. 1, 355n. 26, 355–56n. 27

Waldenfels, Bernhard, 285n. 7, 300n. 82, 348n. 80
Watson, Walter, 315nn. 12, 16, 387n. 65
Weingartner, Rudolph, 78–79, 308n. 41, 309n. 47, 310n. 53
White, Nicholas P., 365n. 29, 372n. 61, 377n. 94, 383n. 38
Wiegmann, Hermann, 324n. 10
Wieland, Wolfgang, 213–15, 218, 279n. 19, 300n. 84, 319n. 38, 326n. 18, 360n. 11, 366n. 31, 373n. 62, 374n. 66, 381n. 23
Wiggins, David, 351n. 3
Wilamovitz-Moellendorf, Ulrich von, 318nn. 30, 34, 322n. 69
Williams, Bernard, 307n. 34
Windspear, A. D., 378n. 1
Wittgenstein, Ludwig, 280nn. 25, 27, 311n. 58
Woodruff, Paul, 285n. 6, 289n. 24, 329n. 40, 336n. 27
Woozley, A. D., 364n. 24, 366n. 35, 368–69n. 43, 375n. 79

Xenophon, 291–92n. 38, 323n. 2, 329n. 40, 362n. 16

Young, Charles M., 275n. 2

Zimbrich, Ulrike, 423n. 6
Zyskind, Harold, 331nn. 3, 8, 336n. 29, 337n. 31, 338nn. 34, 37, 341n. 50, 341–42n. 51, 342n. 53, 345nn. 68, 72, 350n. 86

Subject Index

acquaintance, knowledge by, 168, 185–86, 331n. 8
  admits degrees, 157, 171
  and *aitias logismos*, 349n. 82
  both practical and theoretical, 158
  dialectic not solely, 273
  versus justified true belief, 177
  knowledge of virtue as, 156–58, 172, 184, 344n. 65
  ordinary meaning versus philosophical (Russellian) meaning of, 157, 178, 331–32nn. 9–10
  See also nonpropositional knowledge
aitia (cause)
  meaning of, in the *Phaedo*, 202–3, 350–51n. 1
  versus necessary conditions, 192
aitias logismos. *See under logos*
anonymity, Plato's, 275n. 1
Anytus, 179, 185–86
Apology, 51, 57
aporia
  essential component of virtue, 173 (*see also* virtue, inquiry [ignorance] essential part of)
  necessity of, 41, 58, 61, 112, 116, 259–60, 262
  as positive result, 59, 116, 169–70

bebaios, meaning of, 365n. 27. *See also* certainty
belief (*doxa*)
  cannot solve paradox of inquiry, 339–40n. 42
  δοξάζειν capable of taking direct object, 346n. 74
  as dreamlike state, 170–71, 181–82, 225–27
  whether form of judgment or something analogous to perception, 347–48n. 77
  as good a practical guide as knowledge, 180
  as inspiration, intuition, or state of awareness, 176, 181, 211, 271, 325n. 16
  versus knowledge, 140, 171, 180, 181–84, 225–27, 325n. 16, 365n. 27, 368n. 39
  meaning of *doxa* in Plato, 181–82
  not necessarily "belief that" or propositional, 171–72, 181–82, 227, 348nn. 77–78, 368n. 39, 368–69n. 43
  in the *Seventh Letter*, 261, 384n. 45
  sufficiency of, for recognizing examples of x (or as solution to "Socratic fallacy"), 287n. 21, 289n. 23, 339n. 42
  why aporetic dialogues do not acknowledge, 345–46n. 73

cause: see *aitia* (cause)
Cave, analogy of, 131–32, 149, 211, 227, 362n. 16, 377n. 96
certainty
  versus fixity of intellectual intuition, 365n. 27, 386n. 60
  not achievable by the hypothetical method, 206–8
  not the aim of dialectic in the Divided Line, 222–29
  pretense of, promotes misology, 207
  versus understanding, 227
Charmides
  exhibits degree of self-knowledge, 43–45

SUBJECT INDEX

lacks self-control, 60
temperance of, 42–43, 46
chreia, meaning of, in Plato, 141–42. See also user's art
chronology, of Plato's dialogues, 247, 275n. 2
conjecture. See *eikasia*. (conjecture)
courage (*andreia*)
  as characteristic of inquiry, 32, 172
  versus daring, 33
  neither foolish nor wise endurance, 29–30
  found not only in war, 29
  incompatible with moral science, 38–40
  incompatible with *technē*, 23, 30–31, 33, 38
  knowledge of, not definitional, 41
  as knowledge of what inspires fear and confidence, 32–35
  as pursuit of wisdom in the face of ignorance, 37–38
  See also good, the; virtue
Critias
  intemperance of, 47–48, 57
  lacks self-control, 60
  lacks self-knowledge, 48–51
Crito, 122

definitional knowledge, Socrates not committed to. See What-is-x? question
definitions
  essential, necessarily reductionistic, 160, 164, 259
  limitations of, 161–63, 234–36
  presuppose rather than provide knowledge, 163
  purpose of, 164, 169
  See also *logos*; propositions
developmentalist interpretation, 3–4, 9–10, 273–74, 275n. 2, 276–77n. 10, 278n. 18, 376n. 88
dialectic
  versus eristic, 94, 105, 113–16, 121, 123–25, 265, 267, 313n. 4, 315n. 13, 316n. 20 (see also eristic)
  versus etymology, 88–89
  versus hypothetical method, 153, 186–88, 201–2, 238–40, 242–44, 267–68 (see also elenchus, versus hypothetical method)
  immune to charge of fallacy, 104–5

incompatible with ideal language, 81
as know-how, 61, 224, 272–73, 366n. 32 (see also knowledge-how)
as knowledge of knowledge, 57–59, 114–15, 217–18 (see also knowledge, [*epistēmē*], of knowledge)
learned quickly, 123, 125
versus logic, 2, 118, 314–15n. 12
not tool or method, 9, 11, 97, 273, 275n. 4
between ordinary and sophistic discourse, 19–22, 35–36, 47, 58, 60–61, 88–89, 126–28, 179, 186, 271–72
as political art, 112–13, 126
reflexivity of, 61, 97, 114–15, 126, 172, 185, 217–18, 236–37, 268–70
three presuppositions of, 271–73
as user's art, 14, 67–68, 87–89, 110, 114–15, 141, 213, 268, 272–73, 303n. 13, 325n. 15 (see also user's art)
as well-meaning refutation, 265, 267
See also elenchus; philosophy, conception of; *and under* nonpropositional knowledge; words (names)
dialogues, Plato's
  as imitation, 145, 374n. 69
  as leaving ultimate truths unexpressed, 252–53
  and logical fallacies, 315n. 16 (see also fallacy, Socrates' use of)
  reflexivity of, 31–32, 45–46, 48, 57–58, 61, 116, 183, 291n. 35, 300–1n. 88
  relation of form to philosophical content in, 3–6, 13, 277–78n. 11, 278n. 15
  versus treatises, 4, 274
dianoia
  and belief, 367–68n. 38
  objects of, 219–20, 363n. 19
  not restricted to mathematics, 234, 363n. 19
  in the *Seventh Letter*, 261
  See also hypothetical method
διαφωνεῖν. See συμφωνεῖν
Divided Line, different interpretations of
  Abstraction Theory, 231, 241
  Analysis Theory, 22, 231

SUBJECT INDEX

as ascent to understanding of the good through idealization and refutation, 228–29, 233–34, 238–40, 242–43
Axiomatization Theory, 221
Coherence Theory, 229–31, 238, 240–42
Intuition/Deduction Theory, 222–29, 231, 238, 241–42
Phaedo Theory, 221–22
Synthesis Theory, 220–21, 231
See also good, the, as unhypothesized principle of the Divided Line
doxa. See belief

ἔχεσθαι, meaning of
in the *Phaedo*, 352–53n. 14
in the *Republic*, 241–42, 363n. 20
eikasia (conjecture), 146, 219. See also images (*eikones*)
elenchus
aims at self-knowledge, 301n. 89 (*see also* dialectic, as knowledge of knowledge; dialectic, reflexivity of; self-knowledge, as characteristic of dialectical knowledge)
as ascent to the good, 239–40, 375n. 77
cannot teach a *technē*, 28
capable of providing knowledge, 37–38, 58–59, 168, 265–68, 273, 276n. 5
constructivist versus nonconstructivist interpretations of, 9, 21, 37, 281nn. 32–33, 286n. 10, 297n. 67
in the *Euthydemus*, 313n. 1
frequent failure of, 60, 341n. 48, 386n. 58
versus hypothetical method, 9, 153, 201, 207, 330n. 1 (*see also* dialectic)
versus mathematics, 330n. 1
meaning of *elenchein* in the *Seventh Letter*, 266
presupposes implicit knowledge, 28, 31, 43
as protreptic, 286–87n. 12 (*see also* protreptic, philosophy as)
and recollection, 290n. 27, 336n. 27, 341n. 48, 347n. 75
as truth-conducive, 346–47n. 75
See also dialectic; What-is-x? question
epistēmē

interrelational model of, 178, 229, 344–45n. 66
translation of, as "understanding," 177–78, 184, 225–26, 229, 367n. 37 (*see also under* nonpropositional knowledge)
See also knowledge (*epistēmē*)
eristic
as arguing for the sake of arguing, 113
attitude of, toward logical fallacies, 104
characteristics of, ironically praised by Socrates, 121–25
defeatable only through assimilation, 118–20, 127–28
and etymology, 106–7
features of eristic arguments, 97–100, 107–8, 197
as a game lacking seriousness, 99, 107–8, 119–20
incompatible with protreptic, 108
as misuse of arguments, 94, 101, 115, 119, 317n. 25
parasitic on dialectic, 119
and the principle of noncontradiction, 106
rootlessness of, 95
as self-refuting, 108–9, 120, 124
See also sophists; *and under* dialectic; good, the
esotericist interpretation, 286n. 11, 371n. 56
agenda of, 279n. 20
as assimilating dialectic to mathematics, 372n. 59
assumptions of, 10–13, 273–74, 282n. 43, 283n. 46, 376n. 88
as critique of other interpretations, 5–6
on the *Republic*, 357–58n. 2, 373n. 63
on the *Seventh Letter*, 251, 379n. 9, 381nn. 22, 24, 384n. 47
See also unwritten doctrines, Plato's
etymologies. See *under* dialectic; words (names)
Euthyphro, 300–1n. 88

fact/value distinction, 39, 214–15, 375n. 73
fallacy, Socrates' use of, 102–5
Form of the Good. *See* good, the; Sun analogy, of the good
forms (Ideas), 199, 212

SUBJECT INDEX

as causes, 200, 202–3
not exemplars, 362n. 15
neither genus nor element, 214–15, 283n. 48
images mediate knowledge of, 149, 243
imitated by the craftsman, 132–33
known by the user, 140 (*see also* user's art)
as necessary presuppositions of discourse, 86–87, 124–25
as norms, 214–17
relation of, to sensible particulars, 5, 12, 120–21, 124–25, 146, 200, 204–6, 226, 354n. 21, 355n. 26, 356n. 30
in the *Seventh Letter*, 254, 382n. 29
self-predication of, 359n. 9, 361–62n. 15
theory of, 274

γλίσχρος, meaning of, 323n. 3
good, the
as cause of being, 212, 216–17
as cause of knowing and being known, 212–16
as cause of unity, 191–92, 201, 216, 358n. 3
indefinable, 232
knowledge of, a reflexive knowledge of knowledge, 55–59, 115, 217–18, 232–33, 269
knowledge of, a type of know-how, 56, 213, 215, 233
knowledge of, not propositional, 231–33, 236
known through process of refutation, 239–40 (*see also* elenchus)
neither object nor product of knowledge, 55–56, 217–18, 232
not general class concept, 215, 232, 241, 359–60n. 9, 360n. 12
as principle of idealization, 214–17, 269, 360–61n. 13
protreptic central to knowledge of, 115–16 (*see also* protreptic, philosophy as)
reality of, preferred over the semblance, 137
relation between eristic and, 119
relation between knowledge and, 116, 210, 217–18

revealed only in use, 58–59, 114–15, 213, 218
in the *Seventh Letter*, 267–69
Socrates ignorant of, 192, 207, 211, 243, 327n. 24
teleological interpretation of, 361n. 14
as unhypothesized principle of the Divided Line, 220 (*see also under* hypothesis)
we do not sufficiently know, but have inspired intuition of, 210–11, 236, 243–44
See also forms (Ideas); virtue
Gorgias, 15, 45, 284n. 52, 316n. 18, 384n. 48

Homer, 70, 131, 133–35, 138
hypothesis
agreement versus disagreement with (*see* συμφωνεῖν)
destroyed by dialectic, 238–40
"higher," 198–99, 205
meaning of, 174–75, 233, 240
as necessary starting point of inquiry, 237–38
"strongest," 195
"sufficient" (*hikanon*), 198–99
"unhypothesized," meaning of, 222, 236, 370n. 49
hypothetical method
advantages of, 177, 242
based on kind of inspiration or intuition, 176, 183, 196, 199
confined to propositions, 195, 199, 220, 244, 261, 272 (*see also under* propositions)
defects or limitations of, 176–77, 180, 186, 201–2, 207–8, 220, 225, 234, 335n. 21, 344–45n. 66
dependent on distinct form of dialectic, 186–87, 244
dependent on theory of recollection, 176
incapable of attaining certainty, 206–8
and interrelational model of knowledge, 178 (*see also under epistēmē*)
procedure of, 197–99, 204–5
relation of, to belief (*doxa*), 180–81, 345–46n. 73
the *Republic* as practice of, 234–36

restricted to how a thing is *qualified*,
174, 261, 374n. 68 (*see also under*
poion ti versus *ti* distinction)
as "safe," 202
as second-best, 192, 202
in the *Seventh Letter*, 261, 264, 267
See also dianoia and *under* dialectic;
elenchus

ideal language. *See under* language
Ideas. *See* forms (Ideas)
images (*eikones*)
as concealing, 263
defect of, 143–46, 257
present at three different levels in the
dialogues, 129–30
Socrates' frequent use of, 131–32, 219,
243, 323n. 4
See also eikasia; imitation (*mimēsis*);
poetry; *and under logos*;
mathematics; nonpropositional
knowledge
imitation (*mimēsis*)
cannot be perfect, 82, 258
danger of, 130–31, 136–38, 257
as form of sophistry, 133
language as, 75–76, 80, 82–83
nature of, 132–33, 144–45
philosophical use of, 142–43, 145–46,
148–49, 243, 253, 268
Plato's dialogues as, 145
See also eikasia; images (*eikones*);
inspiration; poetry
inquiry, paradox of
implicit, prepropositional knowledge
required for solution of, 170–72
knowledge capable of admitting
degrees required for solution of,
332n. 11
not solved by appeal to true beliefs,
339–40n. 42
poses serious problem for priority of
What-is-x? question, 165
See also recollection, learning as;
"Socratic fallacy"; What-is-x?
question
inspiration
danger of, 72, 74–75, 81, 87, 148
and imitation, 329n. 39
philosophical, 146–47

philosophical versus nonphilosophical
(including poetic), 147–48,
185–86
presupposed by the means of attaining
knowledge, 263, 270
pursuit of the good guided by, 211, 236,
243–44
true belief as form of, 176
See also imitation (*mimēsis*); poetry; *and
under* belief (*doxa*); good, the;
hypothetical method
Ion, 130, 147–48
irony, Socratic, 69, 95, 123, 127, 282n. 43

knowledge (*epistēmē*)
barely (μόγις) attainable, 243, 267, 272,
362n. 16, 381n. 18, 385n. 56
versus belief, 140, 171, 180, 181–84,
225–27, 325n. 16, 365n. 27, 368n.
39
versus coherence, 229–30 (*see also
epistēmē*, interrelational model of;
system)
not certainty for Plato, 223–29 (*see also*
certainty)
defective versus nondefective, 254–56,
258, 261–62, 383n. 38
not descriptive or explanatory
discourse, 297–98n. 68, 375n. 73
entails *ability* to give *logos*, but not *result*
of giving *logos*, 224 (*see also logos*,
logon didonai)
as idealization, 216
ignorance compatible with, 22, 37–38,
40, 267
implicit or tacit, 340–41n. 43, 347n. 75
of knowledge, 49–59, 112–15, 217
means by which attained, 253–54
more than systematization and
organization of our beliefs, 178
(*see also* system)
not justified true belief for Plato,
225–26, 368n. 39
neither propositional nor simple
intuition of objects, 332–33n. 11
See also acquaintance, knowledge
by; *epistēmē*; knowledge-how;
nonpropositional knowledge;
self-knowledge; *technē*
knowledge-how
dialectical versus practical, 299n. 79

SUBJECT INDEX

versus knowledge-that, 280n. 24, 290n. 24, 299n. 79, 366n. 32
as nonpropositional, 8, 233, 366n.32
See also user's art; *and under* dialectic; good, the; virtue

Laches
  disassociates virtue from knowledge, 23, 33
  endures in inquiry but lacks courage to move forward, 32, 34, 36, 293n. 42
  motivated by contentiousness, rather than truth, 36, 293n. 42
  values deeds above words, 25, 293n. 42
language
  as brute fact, 89–90, 92–93
  descriptive versus prescriptive accounts of, 308n. 38
  ideal, 77–81, 90, 245, 258, 271, 304n. 16, 311n. 56
  as imitation, 75–76, 80, 82–83
  presupposes distinction between universals and particulars, 124 (*see also* forms [Ideas], as necessary presuppositions of discourse)
  two models of, 65–66, 68–69, 76, 93, 306n. 26
  See also ὄνομα; propositions; words (names)
legislator of names. *See under* words (names)
logos
  aitias logismos, 184, 202, 348–50nn. 81–83
  logon didonai, 223–24, 365–66n. 31
  relation between deeds (*ergon*) and, 25, 134–36, 194–95, 293–94n. 42
  τῷ λόγῳ διορίσασθαι, 373n. 63
  relation of, to sensible images, 255
  weakness of, 255, 258–59
  See also definitions; language; propositions
Lysis, 145

manifestation, versus description, 8, 90–91, 280n. 29, 319n. 37. *See also* nonpropositional knowledge
mathematics
  as failing at idealization, 233
  irremediably defective, 377n. 97
  as lacking understanding of its objects, 228–29 (*see also epistēmē*, translation of, as "understanding")
  not Plato's model for philosophy, 9–10, 372n. 59
  subordinate to dialectic, 110, 233–34, 240, 242
  uses images, 223, 228–29, 240, 243
  See also dianoia; hypothetical method
Meno
  lacks virtue, 173
  memory of, incapable of genuine recollection, 159, 161, 166, 350n. 85
  motives of, 154, 173, 331n. 2
  not stimulated to inquire by *aporia*, 165, 173
  opinions of, borrowed from the sophists, 185
  pretends to wisdom, 163, 186
misology, 25, 127, 189, 206–7, 244

names. *See* words (names)
Nicias
  motivated by contentiousness rather than truth, 36
  sees knowledge as playing central role in virtue, 23, 33–34
  superstitious, 291n. 36
  uncourageous in tenaciously clinging to secondhand, empty opinions, 34–36
  as unsocratic Socratic, 35
  values words above deeds, 24–25
nondoctrinal interpretation, 4–7, 274, 278n. 13
nonpropositional knowledge
  circularity or regress of definitions escaped only by, 336n. 22 (*see also* definitions)
  as giving content to propositions, 170
  images transcended by, 149
  inexpressible and expressible, 7, 10, 252–53, 381n. 23
  versus interrelational model of knowledge, 178, 229–30 (*see also* system)
  versus knowledge by collection and division, 370n. 51
  nature of, 7–10

neglect of, in contemporary scholarship, 290n. 24, 335n. 21
not mystical, 153, 272
as positive outcome of the aporetic dialogues, 21–22, 58–59, 61, 168, 295n. 53
types of, 8, 280n. 30
as "understanding," 177–78, 230, 345n. 67 (*see also under epistēmē*)
wedded to propositional knowledge in dialectic, 272–73
See also acquaintance, knowledge by; *epistēmē*; good, the; knowledge (*epistēmē*); knowledge-how; self-knowledge; virtue; What-is-x? question, does not commit Socrates to definitional knowledge

ὄνομα, meaning of, 302n. 2. *See also* words (names)
opinion. *See* belief (*doxa*).
oral versus written discourse in Plato, 11–12, 252, 256, 282–83n. 45

Parmenides, 349n. 83
Phaedrus, 130, 146–48, 247, 270, 329nn. 40–41, 349–50n. 83
philosophy, conception of
 need for new, 151–56
 in the *Republic* versus other dialogues, 327n. 24
 as source of greatest discord in the interpretation of Plato, 1–2
See also dialectic
Platonism, 15–16, 279n. 20
poetry
 critique of, 134, 136–37
 extent to which banished from the *Republic*, 143–44, 327–28n. 28
 and philosophy, 138–43, 148
See also imitation (*mimēsis*); inspiration
poion ti versus *ti* distinction, 154–56, 344n. 63
 as expressing limitation of definitions, 169, 234–36, 254–55, 262–63
 and hypothetical method, 174, 233, 246, 261
 meaning of, 155–56
 and nonpropositional knowledge, 8

not distinction between accidental and essential properties, 155–56, 259
not distinction between sensible and nonsensible properties, 383n. 41
and "reasoning out the cause," 184
See also What-is-x? question
political art, incapable of producing good distinct from itself, 111–12. *See also* dialectic
propositions
 always hypothetical, 261
 ambiguous, 97–98, 177, 197, 245, 258, 314–15n. 12
 cannot provide knowledge, 244
 as having a tendency to conceal, 244, 263
 as images, 135–36, 193–94, 220
 nature of, 7–8
 presuppose intuition they cannot express, 263
 vulnerable to refutation, 258, 384n. 48
See also definitions; *logos*
Protagoras, 63–66, 92, 240
Protagoras, 15, 154, 224
protreptic, philosophy as, 96–97, 104–5, 115–16, 126, 172, 245, 268, 286–87n. 12

"reasoning out the cause." *See logos, aitias logismos*
recollection, learning as, 117–18, 188, 333n. 11, 339n. 40, 343n. 55, 349–50n. 83
 in the aporetic dialogues, 336n. 27
 demonstration of, in the *Meno*, 166–67, 170–72, 337n. 30
 as presupposed by hypothetical method, 176
 as presupposing existence of implicit, tacit knowledge, 339–41nn. 42–43, 347n. 75
 as "reasoning out the cause," 184
 and reflexivity, 336n. 27
 in the *Republic*, 211
 role of images in, 143, 146–47
 in the *Seventh Letter*, 270
 versus teaching, 166, 180 (*see also* virtue, unteachable in a sense)
See also elenchus, and recollection; inquiry, paradox of

SUBJECT INDEX

reductionism, problem of, 75, 77, 83, 160, 164, 169, 171, 177, 190–91, 200–201, 259, 260
rhetoric, versus philosophy, 315n. 16, 317n. 25

self-knowledge
   as characteristic of dialectical knowledge, 61, 270, 273
   inseparable from knowledge of the good, 56–57, 233
   as knowledge of knowledge, 50, 296n. 63, 298n. 73
   nonpropositional, 8, 233, 298n. 73
   and shame, 45
   and temperance, 48–57
   See also knowledge (*epistēmē*), of knowledge
self-predication of the forms. *See under* forms (Ideas)
Seventh Letter, authenticity of, 246–47
Socrates
   as *adoleschēs*, 285n. 5
   courage of, 37–38
   elitist and egalitarian, 122–23
   exhibits harmony between words and deeds, 25 (*see also logos*, relation between deeds [*ergon*] and)
   ignorance of, 19, 22, 24, 36–38, 40, 43, 63, 69, 132, 282n. 43 (*see also* knowledge [*epistēmē*], ignorance compatible with)
   moral theory not sought by, 163, 335n. 21
   as poet, 138–39
   as practicing knowledge of knowledge, 57–58
   as stingray, 122, 124–25, 165
   temperance of, 42, 50–51, 54, 59
   virtue of, 172
"Socratic fallacy," 26, 159, 287–88n. 21, 289n. 23, 333–34n. 13, 335n. 21, 339n. 42. *See also* What-is-x? question, priority of
Socratic paradoxes, 291nn. 32–33. *See also* virtue, as knowledge; virtue, unity of
Sophist, 133, 349n. 83
sophists
   cannot teach virtue, 179–80
   characterized by peculiar confinement to words, 62
   as imitators, 133
   profess expertise on the soul, 24
   teach correctness of names, 69–70
   See also eristic
Statesman, 365n. 27
συμφωνεῖν and διαφωνεῖν ("agreement" and "disagreement"), meaning of in the *Phaedo*, 195–96. *See also* hypothetical method, procedure of
Sun analogy, of the good, 212–18, 233. *See also* good, the
Symposium, 25, 45, 141
system
   meaning of, 279–80n. 23
   traditional characterization of Plato's philosophy as, 3–6, 276n. 9, 277n. 10
   why Plato's philosophy is not, 1, 7, 9, 11–13, 225, 242, 244, 272–74, 284n. 49
   See also knowledge (*epistēmē*), versus coherence; knowledge (*epistēmē*), more than systematization and organization of our beliefs; nonpropositional knowledge, versus interrelational model of knowledge

technē (technical knowledge)
   as analogy, 294n. 47
   danger of relying on, 23
   does not make us good or happy, 33, 35, 52–53, 55
   nature of, 30, 55
   versus philosophical knowledge, 28, 31, 38, 114–15, 294n. 49
   theoretical or practical, 55, 110, 295n. 52, 299n. 75
   versus virtue, 30–31, 33, 38–39, 55–56, 299n. 76
   See also knowledge (*epistēmē*)
temperance (*sōphrosunē*)
   as characteristic of inquiry, 57–58
   as doing one's own business, 47
   as doing what is good, 48
   knowledge of, nondefinitional and open, 58–59
   as knowledge of both knowledge and the good, 53–58
   as knowledge of good and evil, 53
   as quickness, 44

SUBJECT INDEX

as quietness or stillness, 43–44
as self-control, 60
as self-knowledge or knowledge of knowledge, 48–53
as shame, 45
See also good, the; virtue
Theaetetus, 117
Timaeus, 207, 365n. 27
ti-question. *See* What-is-x? question
tribein, 265
truth, tendency of Socratic inquiry toward, 340n. 42, 346–47n. 75. *See also* inquiry, paradox of

understanding. *See epistēmē*
unhypothesized principle. *See under* hypothesis
unwritten doctrines, Plato's, 6, 11–12, 278n. 17, 320n. 48. *See also* esotericist interpretation
user's art , 94, 100–1, 140–42, 144
knowledge of the good as, 218
ranked higher than productive art, 140
reveals original of an image, 140–41
united in dialectic with discovery and production, 114–15
See also chreia; meaning of, in Plato's dialogues; dialectic, as user's art; knowledge-how

virtue
acquired how, 173
civic versus philosophical, 142, 235–36
good only when guided by wisdom, 101, 142, 174
indefinable, 157, 168, 170, 236
inquiry (ignorance) essential part of, 163, 169, 172
as know-how, 299n. 79
as knowledge, 185
known by type of acquaintance (*see under* acquaintance, knowledge by)
nature of, 172–73
unity of, 35, 41, 292n. 40
unteachable in a sense, 96, 173, 179, 182, 300n. 80
See also courage (*andreia*); good, the; temperance (*sōphrosunē*)

What-is-x? question
considered easy to answer by Socrates' interlocutors, 27–29
does not commit Socrates to definitional knowledge, 27–28, 163–64, 170, 383nn. 40–41 (*see also* definitions)
goals of, 27–28, 163, 239
Gorgias and *Protagoras* do not pursue, 15
versus ordinary experience, 19–21, 26, 67–68
presupposes distinction between manifestation and description, 91
priority of, 26–28, 154–59, 165, 167–70 (*see also* "Socratic fallacy")
as "reasoning out the cause," 184–85
Republic does not ask, 235
seeks more than verbal analysis, 62, 73–74, 92–93, 309n. 48
type of answer demanded by, 29–30, 159–60, 162, 285n. 2
unanswerable, 158, 164–65, 169, 259, 262 (*see also* nonpropositional knowledge)
See also dialectic; elenchus; inquiry, paradox of; *poion ti* versus *ti* distinction
words (names)
can be false or true, 81–83, 308n. 40
as concealing, 263
conventionality and unreliability of, 83–86, 92, 257–58
dialectic's use of, 67–68, 87–89, 268
etymologies distort nature of, 71–75, 87
form of, 65–66, 89
function of, to make manifest, 66, 75–76, 81, 84
legislator of, 65, 67, 76, 84–86, 302n. 3, 303 n. 13
nature of, manifest in use, 67–70
not descriptions, 89–90, 303n. 10
presuppose existence of stable natures, 87 (*see also* forms [Ideas], as necessary presuppositions of discourse)
two possible ways of being natural, 64–66, 70–71, 92
See also language; ὄνομα, meaning of

The word most commonly used in Plato's dialogues to name philosophical inquiry and distinguish it from other types of activity is "dialectic." *Dialectic and Dialogue* seeks to define the method and the aims of Plato's dialectic in both the "inconclusive" dialogues and the dialogues that describe and practice a method of hypothesis.

Gonzalez not only discusses Plato's few explicit descriptions of the dialectical method but also relates these descriptions to how the method is actually practiced, examining the contrast between dialectic and the opposite poles of ordinary discourse and sophistic discourse.

In a radical departure from most other treatments of Plato, Gonzalez argues that the philosophical knowledge at which dialectic aims is nonpropositional, practical, and reflexive. The result is a radical reassessment of how Plato understood the nature of philosophy, one that is highly relevant to our contemporary struggles with the nature, purpose, and value of the philosophical enterprise.

SPEP Studies in Historical Philosophy

John McCumber and David Kolb,
General Editors

Francisco J. Gonzalez is associate professor of philosophy at Skidmore College. He is the editor of *The Third Way: New Directions in Platonic Studies* (Rowman & Littlefield, 1995).

ISBN 0-8101-1530-1